ANNUAL REVIEW OF SOCIOLOGY

EDITORIAL COMMITTEE (1987)

ANNUAL REVIEW OF SOCIOLOGY

VOLUME 13, 1987

W. RICHARD SCOTT, *Editor*

Stanford University

JAMES F. SHORT, JR., *Associate Editor*

Washington State University

ANNUAL REVIEWS INC.   4139 EL CAMINO WAY   P.O. BOX 10139   PALO ALTO, CALIFORNIA 94303-0899

ANNUAL REVIEWS INC.
Palo Alto, California, USA

International Standard Serial Number: 0360-0572
International Standard Book Number: 0-8243-2213-4
Library of Congress Catalog Card Number: 75-648500

Annual Review and publication titles are registered trademarks of Annual Reviews Inc.

Annual Reviews Inc. and the Editors of its publications assume no responsibility for the statements expressed by the contributors to this *Review*.

Typesetting by Kachina Typesetting Inc., Tempe, Arizona; John Olson, President
Typesetting coordinator, Janis Hoffman

PRINTED AND BOUND IN THE UNITED STATES OF AMERICA

PREFACE

The opening chapter of this volume continues a feature initiated in Volume 12. For this year, the Editorial Committee asked Robert K. Merton to contribute an essay on a topic of his choice. The resulting article, "Three Fragments from a Sociologist's Notebooks," is both a stimulating collection of insights into the sociology of science and a delight to read. The appetite is sharpened by the "menu" of 46 topics (listed in an appendix) of which these "fragments" are a sample. We are confident that more nuggets from these notebooks will soon appear in other forums.

The Editorial Committee expects to feature a prefatory essay by a distinguished sociologist in each volume. We hope that this tradition not only will give special recognition to some of our most illustrious colleagues but also will constitute an important resource for historians of the discipline.

The primary purpose of the *Annual Review of Sociology* continues to be to provide authoritative surveys of recent important sociological theory and research in specialized fields (or of recent literature from other disciplines that is important for the development of a speciality within sociology). Authors are asked to provide not annotated bibliographies but critical assessments of current work in the field surveyed. The most useful chapters both summarize past contributions and identify future directions that appear promising.

We continue our practice of identifying 12 broad categories that provide a general framework within which the review chapters can be housed. These categories serve as a heuristic device rather than a rigid structure; some topics fit into more than one category. Within this loose framework, the specific topics for review change each year.

The essays contributed to this volume strongly reflect three important features of contemporary sociology. First, our discipline is increasingly international in membership composition. Current contributors are drawn not only from the United States but from Canada, England, Hungary, Italy, and West Germany. Second, sociology is increasingly interdependent with other disciplines. Contributors include not only sociologists but historians, social workers, and social scientists working in schools of management and business administration. Third, our approach to issues and problem areas is increasingly comparative. Whether the topic is strategic decision-making, mobility, industrialization, or the use of time budgets, analysts are able to draw upon data sources that range over broad periods of time and/or across ethnic and societal boundaries. We celebrate these trends as evidence of the increasing maturation of our discipline.

This volume also signals the end of an era. It is the last that will benefit from the thoughtful and insightful editorial influence of Ralph H. Turner. Professor Turner was a founding member of the Editorial Committee (which first met in 1973 to plan the initial volume, which appeared in 1975). He continued to serve on the Committee every year up to 1986. He was Acting Editor for volume 4 and Associate Editor for volumes 5 and 6. In 1981, Professor Turner assumed the Editorship and subsequently presided over the organization of volumes 7 through 12.

We will miss his steady hand and wise judgment. We will also do our utmost to continue to maintain the high editorial standards which he helped to establish.

Annual Review of Sociology
Volume 13, 1987

CONTENTS

(Continued)

RELATED ARTICLES FROM OTHER ANNUAL REVIEWS

From the *Annual Review of Anthropology,* Volume 16 (1987)

Trends in the Study of Later European Prehistory, *S. J. Shennan*
The Relation Between Written and Spoken Language, *Wallace Chafe and Deborah Tannen*
Cross-Cultural Surveys Today, *Michael L. Burton and Douglas R. White*
Economic and Ecological Approaches to Land Fragmentation: In Defense of a Much-Maligned Phenomenon, *Jeffery W. Bentley*
The Cross-Cultural Study of Human Sexuality, *D. L. Davis and R. G. Whitten*

From the *Annual Review of Psychology,* Volume 38 (1987)

Developmental Psychobiology: Prenatal, Perinatal, and Early Postnatal Aspects of Behavioral Development, *W. G. Hall and R. W. Oppenheim*
Adult Development and Aging, *Nancy Datan, Dean Rodeheaver, and Fergus Hughes*
Concept, Knowledge, and Thought, *Gregg C. Oden*
The Dynamic Self-Concept: A Social Psychological Perspective, *Hazel Markus and Elissa Wurf*
Organizational Change and Development, *Michael Beer and Anna Elise Walton*
Social Cognition and Social Perception, *E. Tory Higgins and John A. Bargh*
Social and Community Interventions, *Ellis L. Gesten and Leonard A. Jason*
Social Motivation, *Thane S. Pittman and Jack F. Heller*
Attitudes and Attitude Change, *Shelly Chaiken and Charles Stangor*

From the *Annual Review of Public Health,* Volume 8 (1987)

The Use of Large Data Bases in Health Care Studies, *Frederick A. Connell, Paula Diehr, and L. Gary Hart*
Social/Economic Status and Disease, *M. G. Marmot, M. Kogevinas, and M. A. Elston*
Health Status Measures: An Overview and Guide for Selection, *Marilyn Bergner and Margaret L. Rothman*
Trends in the Health of the Elderly Population, *Jacob A. Brody, Dwight B. Brock, and T. Franklin Williams*
Women, Work, and Health, *Glorian Sorensen and Lois M. Verbrugge*

For the convenience of readers, a detachable order form/envelope is bound into the back of this volume.

Ann. Rev. Sociol. 1987. 13:1–28

THREE FRAGMENTS FROM A SOCIOLOGIST'S NOTEBOOKS:
Establishing the Phenomenon, Specified Ignorance, and Strategic Research Materials

Robert K. Merton

University Professor Emeritus, Columbia University, New York, New York 10027, and Russell Sage Foundation, 112 East 64 Street, New York, New York 10021

Abstract

This occasionally biographical paper deals with three cognitive and social patterns in the practice of science (not '*the* scientific method'). The first, "establishing the phenomenon," involves the doctrine (universally accepted in the abstract) that phenomena should of course be shown to exist or to occur before one explains why they exist or how they come to be; sources of departure in practice from this seemingly self-evident principle are examined. One parochial case of such a departure is considered in detail. The second pattern is the particular form of ignorance described as "specified ignorance": the express recognition of what is not yet known but needs to be known in order to lay the foundation for still more knowledge. The substantial role of this practice in the sciences is identified and the case of successive specification of ignorance in the evolving sociological theory of deviant behavior by four thought-collectives is sketched out. Reference is made to the virtual institutionalization of specified ignorance in some sciences and the question is raised whether scientific disciplines differ in the extent of routinely specifying ignorance and how this affects the growth of knowledge. The two patterns of scientific practice are linked to a third: the use of "strategic research materials (SRMs)" i.e. strategic research sites, objects, or events that exhibit the phenomena to be explained or interpreted to such advantage and in such accessible form that they enable the fruitful investigation of previously stub-

0360-0572/87/0815-0001$02.00

born problems and the discovery of new problems for further inquiry. The development of biology is taken as a self-exemplifying case since it provides innumerable SRMs for the sociological study of the selection and consequences of SRMs in science. The differing role of SRMs in the natural sciences and in the *Geisteswissenschaften* is identified and several cases of strategic research sites and events in sociology, explored.

INTRODUCTION

In his youthful journal, the exacting and agonistic literary scholar, C. S. Lewis (1975:76), makes benign reference to "the inexhaustible loquacity of educated age." Plainly alert to that capability, the Editors of *Annual Review of Sociology* wisely limit the space allotted prefatory chapters. In my own case, it was understood further that, unlike the prototypes that have long appeared in *Annual Reviews* of many other disciplines, this chapter would be neither a capsule intellectual autobiography nor an overview of the field. Instead, I tell only sporadically of biographical moments; for the rest, the asked-for personal aspect comes from my drawing upon fragments from notebooks assembled over the years and upon pieces published in obscure or improbable places. It was soon obvious that space would allow only for limited reflections on just 3 of the menu of 45 subjects I had itemized for the Editors—see Appendix, "The Menu"—the three being cognitive and social patterns in the practice of science that have long interested me. The patterns—"establishing the phenomenon," "specified ignorance" and "strategic research material"— have to do, not with scientific methods, let alone with "*the* scientific method," but with scientific practices (although there is, of course, much method in those practices).

ESTABLISHING THE PHENOMENON

In the abstract, it need hardly be said that before one proceeds to explain or to interpret a phenomenon, it is advisable to establish that the phenomenon actually exists, that it is enough of a regularity to require and to allow explanation. Yet, sometimes in science as often in everyday life, explanations are provided of matters that are not and never were. We need not reach back only to ancient days for such episodes as the younger Seneca explaining why some waters are so dense that no object, however heavy, will sink in them or explaining why lightning freezes wine. Our own century provides ample instances. There is René Blondlot's report of having discovered a "new species of invisible radiation," dubbed N rays. These were later "observed" by a dozen or so other investigators in France, but there were no comparable replications in England, Germany, or the United States. Intensive further inquiry, by French scientists as well as others, established the fact that the phenomenon was not one of N rays but rather of wishful perception and self-fulfilling prophecy. After that, N rays were no longer observed (Rostand 1960:12–29, Price 1961:85–90). Or again, there is Boris Deryagin's "discovery" of polywater in the 1960s, later found to be wholly artifactual (Franks 1981). Such episodes return us to Claude Bernard's observation that "if the facts used as a basis for reasoning are ill-established or erroneous, everything will crumble or be falsified; and it is thus that errors in scientific theories most often originate in errors of fact" (Bernard [1865] 1949:13).

No small part of sociological inquiry is given over to the establishing of social facts before proceeding to explain how they come to be. Often enough, the empirical data run contrary to widespread beliefs. Thus, it would seem premature to ask why "urbanization is accompanied by destruction of the social and moral order" inasmuch as evidence accumulates (Fischer 1977) to suggest that the connection is rather more an assumption than a repeatedly demonstrated fact.

In sociology as in other disciplines [see Leontief (1971) on economics], efforts to establish recurring social patterns are often described—sometimes of course with justice—as simply "fact-finding" or "fact-mongering" by those preferring swift explanation. Yet years ago, at the turn of the century, the exemplary scientist-philosopher C. S. Peirce was reminding us of the analytic function of fact-finding in what he described as the salient process of abduction (in turn related to processes of deduction and induction):

> Accepting the conclusion that an explanation is needed when facts contrary to what we should expect emerge, it follows that the explanation must be such a proposition as would lead to prediction of the observed facts, either as necessary consequences or at least as very probable under the circumstances. A hypothesis, then, has to be adopted, which is likely in itself, and renders the facts likely. This step of adopting a hypothesis *as being suggested by the facts,* is what I call *abduction* (Peirce 1958:VII 121–22; emphasis supplied).

The ex post facto phase of an empirical inquiry—or as some prefer; the post factum or post festem phase—has us introduce a hypothesis adopted, of course, only "on probation," while the ex ante phase draws out necessary and probable experiential consequences which can be put to falsifying or confirming test. Practiced investigators take it as a matter of course that, along with the free play of imagination drawing upon explicit and tacit knowledge, factual evidence often brings fruitful ideas to mind. To recognize this is not to engage in enumerative induction, pure and excessively simple. (I tried to elucidate these notions in "The bearing of empirical research upon the development of social theory," Merton 1948).

As I have noted, the basic role of empirical research designed to "establish the phenomenon" is at times downgraded as "mere empiricism." Yet we know that "pseudo-facts have a way of inducing pseudo-problems, which cannot be solved because matters are not as they purport to be" (Merton 1959:xv). Social scientists of diverse theoretical and value orientations have found it useful to address this matter of pseudo-facts; as examples, see Zeitlin (1974:1074–75) on the separation of ownership and control in large corporations, Gutman (1976:462–63) on the black family, and Sowell (1981:59) on ethnic education. To repeat myself: "only when tedious recitations of unrelated fact [and fact-claims] are substituted for fact-related ideas does inquiry decline into 'mere fact-finding.' " Otherwise, of course, it is a crucial element in scientific inquiry.

As Neil Smelser reminded me upon reading this piece, establishing the phenomenon has its political dimension as well. In the cognitive domain as in others, there is competition among groups or collectivities "to capture what Heidegger ([1927]1962) called the 'public interpretation of reality.' With varying degrees of intent, groups in conflict want to make their interpretation the prevailing one of how things were and are and will be" (Merton 1973:110–11). In significant degree, that "interpretation of reality" involves establishing the phenomena that are an integral part of it.

The governing question in establishing the phenomenon—"Is it really so?"—holds as much for historical particularities as for sociological generalizations. Strongly held theoretical expectations or ideologically induced expectations can lead to perceptions of historical and social "facts" even when these are readily refutable by strong evidence close at hand. This is not so much wishful thinking as expectational thinking.

In the mode of collective biography called for by *Annual Review,* I turn for a parochial instance to the Department of Sociology at Columbia. In his widely read *The Coming Crisis of Western Sociology,* Alvin Gouldner (1970), himself a much-esteemed onetime student at Columbia (Merton 1982) observed that "C. Wright Mills never became a full professor" there. Having presented this as historical fact, he went on to draw its sociological and moral implications: Mills's " 'failure' may remind us that the serious players [in sociological criticism] are always those who have an ability to pay costs" (Gouldner 1970:15). Despite what I have reason to know was Alvin Gouldner's commitment to scholarship, it appears that an overriding sense of the fitness of things and the expectation linked with it helped to create this pseudo-fact although evidence to the contrary was a matter of public record set down in easily accessible documents (such as the University bulletins with their rosters of faculty members). The evidentiary fact that Wright Mills, in a later academic cohort, had become a full professor at a younger age than the quintessential Establishment figure in sociology, Talcott Parsons, would scarcely have served to illustrate the premise or to reach the conclusion. In effect, Gouldner had tried to transform a historical event that never was into a social phenomenon that sometimes is.

The process of hagiographic creation of pseudo-facts did not stop there. Once set down in scholarly print as facts, pseudo-facts have a way of diffusing and becoming amplified (in the fashion long since established experimentally in the study of rumor). The same politically turbulent year of 1970 which saw the publication of Gouldner's book saw the translation into German of the book by Hans Gerth and C. Wright Mills, *Character and Social Structure* (for which I had happily written the foreword when it was first published in 1953). The German publishers went on to specify the pseudo-fact by declaring that Mills had "lost his professorship during the McCarthy period" ("verlor wahrend der McCarthy-Zeit seinen Lehrstuhl"). Not long afterward, an article in the Yugoslavian journal *Praxis,* also ignoring the biographical entry in the widely available *International Encyclopedia of the Social Sciences* which begins "C. Wright Mills (1916–62) was at his death professor of sociology at Columbia University" (Wallerstein 1968: Vol. 10, p. 362), explained the now elaborated nonfact to the contrary in these decisive terms: "C. Wright Mills was dismissed from Columbia University in USA because of his Marxist orientation" (Golubović 1973:363, noted by Oromaner 1974:7).

It is symbolically apt that a shared interest in the then nascent field of the sociology of knowledge had led Alvin Gouldner to adopt me as mentor when he arrived at Columbia in 1943—the story is told in Merton (1982)—just as a few years before, a similar interest had led Wright Mills, then still a graduate student at the University of Wisconsin, to have me vet his manuscripts in that field. So it was that, 30 years after our first meeting, when Alvin and I were reviewing this episode of the unwittingly fabricated 'fact,' he soon subordinated scholarly chagrin to shared intellectual pleasure in the episode as he agreed that it provided a sociological and methodological parable: Take care to establish a phenomenon (or a historical event) before proceeding to interpret or explain it.[1] As for the Wright Mills I knew, since the time in 1939 when he first sent me those manuscripts—he would probably have hooted at the ideological pieties that invited first the invention and then the successive explanations of these nonevents. Or perhaps Wright's ironic self might have argued for the symbolic if not the historical truth of that evolving myth of his never having become a full professor at Columbia, with all its seeming

---

[1]After our talk, Alvin Gouldner took quick action to erase that pseudo-fact, noting that "shortly after the publication of the *Crisis* I discovered (from Robert Merton) that my assertion that C. Wright Mills had never been made a Professor at Columbia was in error. Having discovered this, I immediately had this statement removed from the Avon paperback edition of the *Crisis,* which was then in production" (Gouldner 1973:130–131). The import of the episode apparently stayed with Alvin, for years later, and in quite a different context, he took care to observe: "Whether anything *might be* or even *should* have been is one thing; whether it was in fact, is quite another" (Gouldner 1980:281).

implications, and of his ideologically motivated dismissal from that professorship he had never held.[2]

The manifest advisability of establishing the phenomenon before undertaking to explain it has long been recognized in principle if not always observed in practice. They understood this abundantly well, for example, in seventeenth-century England (as I found during my years-long stay in that time and place). Consider only this reminder as set forth by the jurist and orientalist, John Selden, in his widely-read *Table Talk* ([1689]1890:139): "The Reason of a Thing is not to be enquired after, till you are sure the Thing itself be so. We commonly are at *What's the Reason of it?* before we are sure of the Thing." So, too, Bernard Fontenelle, the polymath destined to become a centenarian and the almost but not quite literally *secrétaire perpétuel* of the French Academy of Sciences—he served for only 42 years—was observing in his *Histoire des oracles* ([1686]1908:33): "I am convinced that our ignorance consists not so much in failing to explain what is as in explaining what is not. In other words, we not only lack principles that lead to the true but hold others that readily lead to the false." What Fontenelle did not take occasion to observe, however, is that a certain kind of ignorance advances scientific knowledge.

SPECIFIED IGNORANCE

It was Francis Bacon who made "the advancement of learning" a watchword in the culture of science emerging in the seventeenth century. From then till now, efforts to understand how science develops have largely centered on the modes of replacing ignorance by knowledge, with little attention to the formation of a useful kind of ignorance, as distinct from the manifestly

---

[2]That some (unknown number of) academic careers have been curbed or halted by political or ideological commitments is, of course, a matter of historical record (Lazarsfeld & Thielens 1958, Schrecker 1986). But it was Bernhard J. Stern, not Mills, who, an announced Marxist and cofounder of the Marxist journal *Science and Society,* never advanced beyond a lectureship in the Columbia Department of Sociology, despite departmental recommendations for promotion. Just as again, it was Bernhard J. Stern, not C. Wright Mills, who was attacked by Joe McCarthy as an alleged Communist only to have the University respond by continuing Stern in his marginal post as Lecturer. During the McCarthy period, actual events often transcended social categories such as Establishment and self-declared anti-Establishment figures. Thus, when McCarthy's associate, the then vice-presidential candidate, Richard Nixon, was charged by some Columbia professors with having "violated an elementary rule of public morality" by the way he had accumulated campaign funds, he responded by ransacking the files of the House Committee on UnAmerican Activities and then catapulting nine of those professors onto banner headlines in the New York Daily News and the Chicago Tribune as alleged subversives; the infamous nine included the literary critic Mark van Doren, the philosopher Irwin Edman, the historian Henry Steele Commager, and the sociologists, Robert M. MacIver, Paul F. Lazarsfeld, and Robert K. Merton—but not, as he himself ironically noted, C. Wright Mills.

dysfunctional kind. Karl Popper provides the monumental contemporary exception that illuminates the rule, most powerfully in his analytical essay "On the sources of knowledge and of ignorance" ([1960]1962). The general inattention to the formation of useful ignorance has long obtained as well in the sociology of scientific knowledge [but now see Smithson (1985) along with the early collateral paper on the functions of ignorance in social life by Moore & Tumin (1949)].

These retrospective notes focus on the dynamic cognitive role played by the particular form of ignorance I describe as "specified ignorance": "the express recognition of what is not yet known but needs to be known in order to lay the foundation for still more knowledge" (Merton 1971:191). "As the history of thought, both great and small, attests, *specified* ignorance is often a first step toward supplanting that ignorance with knowledge" (Merton 1957:417).

The concept of *specified* ignorance hints at various other kinds and shades of acknowledged ignorance in science. The familiar kind of a general, rote, and vague admission of ultimate ignorance serves little direct cognitive purpose though it may have symbolic significance in reminding us of our limitations. This kind, however, does not issue in definite questions. And vague questions evoke dusty answers. After all, it takes no great courage, or skill, in the domain of science to acknowledge a general want of knowledge. It is not merely that Socrates set an ancient pattern of announcing one's ignorance. Beyond that, the values of modern science have long put a premium on the public admission of one's limitations or the expression of humility in the face of the vast unknown. Scientists of epic stature have variously insisted on how little they have come to know and to understand in the course of their lives. We remember Galileo teaching himself and his pupils to reiterate: "I do not know." And then, inevitably, one recalls the "memorable sentiment" reportedly uttered by Newton "a short time before his death":

> I do not know what I may appear to the world, but to myself I seem to have been only like a boy playing on the seashore, and diverting myself in now and then finding a smoother pebble or prettier shell than ordinary, whilst the great ocean of truth lay all undiscovered before me (Brewster 1855: II, 407).

Or again, Laplace—the French Newton—is said to have put much the same sentiment in a typically Gallic epigram: "What we know is not much; what we do not know is immense" (Bell 1937:172). What the mathematician Bell (1931:204) describes elsewhere as "a common and engaging trait of the truly eminent scientist [found] in his frequent confession of how little he knows" can be identified sociologically as the living up to a normative expectation of ultimate humility in a community of sometimes egocentric scientists. It is not simply that a goodly number of scientists happen to express these self-belittling sentiments; they are applauded for doing so.

But of course these paradigmatic figures in science do not confine themselves to such generic confessions of ignorance as may reinforce the norm of a decent humility without directly shaping the growth of scientific knowledge. They repeatedly adopt the cognitively consequential practice of specifying this or that piece of ignorance derived from having acquired the added degree of knowledge that made it possible to identify definite portions of the still unknown. In workaday science, it is not enough to confess one's ignorance; the point is to specify it. That, of course, amounts to instituting, or finding, a new, worthy, and soluble scientific problem.

Thus, as I have had occasion to propose, the process of successive specification of our ignorance in light of newfound knowledge provides a recurrent sociocognitive pattern:

> As particular theoretical orientations come to be at the focus of a sufficient number of workers in the field to constitute a thought collective, interactively engaged in developing a distinctive thought style (Fleck [1935] 1979), they give rise to a variety of key questions requiring investigation. As the theoretical orientation is put to increasing use, further implications become identifiable. In anything but a paradoxical sense, newly acquired knowledge produces newly acquired ignorance. For the growth of knowledge and understanding within a field of inquiry brings with it the growth of *specifiable and specified ignorance:* a new awareness of what is not yet known or understood and a rationale for its being worth the knowing. To the extent that current theoretical frameworks prove unequal to the task of dealing with some of the newly emerging key questions, there develops a composite social-and-cognitive pressure within the discipline for new or revised frameworks. But typically, the new does not wholly crowd out the old, as [long as] earlier theoretical perspectives remain capable of dealing with problems distinctive to them (Merton 1981:v–vi).

It requires a newly informed theoretical eye to detect long obscured pockets of ignorance as a prelude to newly focussed inquiry. Each theoretical orientation or paradigm has its own problematics, its own sets of specified questions. As these questions about selected aspects of complex phenomena are provisionally answered, the new knowledge leads some scientists both within and without the given thought collective to become aware of other, newly identified aspects of the phenomena. There then develops a succession of specified ignorance.

As a case in point, consider the sociological theory of deviant behavior as it was developed in four thought collectives. (I draw upon the summary in Merton 1976.) Initiated in the 1920s, E. H. Sutherland's ([1925–1951] 1956) theory of differential association centered on the problem of the *social transmission* of deviant behavior. Its key question therefore inquired into the modes of socialization through which patterns of deviant behavior are learned from others. But as the brilliant philosopher of literature, Kenneth Burke, has reminded us: "A way of seeing is also a way of not seeing—a focus upon object A involves a neglect of object B" (Burke 1935:70). In this case, Sutherland's focus on the acquisition of these deviant patterns left largely untouched specifiable ignorance about the ways in which the patterns emerged in the first place.

Upon identifying that pocket of theoretical neglect, Merton (1938a) proposed the theory of anomie-and-opportunity-structures, that rates of various types of deviant behavior tend to be high among people so located in the social structure as to have little access to socially legitimate pathways for achieving culturally induced personal goals. The Sutherland and Merton theories were consolidated and extended by Cohen (1955) who proposed that delinquency subcultures arise as adaptations to this disjunction between culturally induced goals and the legitimate opportunity-structure and by Cloward & Ohlin (1960) who proposed that the social structure also provides differential access to *illegitimate* opportunities. Since that composite of theories centered on socially structured *sources* of deviant behavior, it had next to nothing to say about how these patterns of misbehavior are transmitted or about how these initial departures from the social rules sometimes crystallize into deviant careers, yet another sphere of specifiable ignorance.

That part of the evolving problematics was taken up in labeling (or societal reaction) theory as initiated by Lemert (1951) and Becker ([1963] 1973) and advanced by Erikson (1964), Cicourel (1968), and Kitsuse (1964). It centered on the processes through which some people are assigned a social identity by being labeled as "delinquents," "criminals," "psychotics," and the like and how, by responding to such stigmatization, they enter upon careers as deviants. In Becker's words: "Treating a person as though he were generally rather than specifically deviant produces a self-fulfilling prophecy. It sets in motion several mechanisms which conspire to shape the person in the image people have of him" (Becker [1963] 1973:34). With this problem as its focus, labeling theory has little to say about the sources of primary deviance or the making of societal rules defining deviance. As Lemert (1973:462) specified this ignorance: "When attention is turned to the rise and fall of moral ideas and the transformation of definitions of deviance, labeling theory and ethnomethodology do little to enlighten the process."

It is precisely this problem that the conflict theory of deviance took as central. Its main thrust, as variously set forth by Turk (1969) and Quinney (1970), for example, holds that a more or less homogeneous power elite incorporates its interests in the making and imposing of legal rules. It thus addresses questions neglected by the earlier theories: How do legal rules get formulated, how does this process affect their substance, and how are they differentially administered?

The case of deviance theory indicates how a dimly felt sense of sociological ignorance was successively specified for one class of social phenomena. But it is not yet known whether scientific disciplines differ in the practice of specifying ignorance—in the extent to which their practitioners state what it is about an established phenomenon that is not yet known and *why it matters* for generic knowledge that it become known.[3] Such specified ignorance is at a far remove from that familiar rote sentence which concludes not a few scientific papers to the effect that "more research is needed." Serendipity aside, questions not asked are questions seldom answered. The specification of ignorance amounts to problem-finding as a prelude to problem-solving.

It is being proposed that the socially defined role of the scientist calls for both the augmenting of knowledge and the specifying of ignorance. Just as yesterday's uncommon knowledge becomes today's common knowledge, so yesterday's unrecognized ignorance becomes today's specified ignorance (Merton 1957:417, Popper [1960] 1962, Sztompka 1986:97–98). As new contributions to knowledge bring about a new awareness of something else not yet known, the sum of manifest human ignorance increases along with the sum of manifest human knowledge.

STRATEGIC RESEARCH MATERIALS (SRMs)

Establishing the phenomenon and specifying ignorance link up with a third pattern of scientific practice that has long been of interest to me. This is the ongoing search, variously evident in the various sciences, for "strategic research material" (a cumbrous nine-syllable phrase better shortened to SRM). By SRM is meant the empirical material that exhibits the phenomena to be explained or interpreted to such advantage and in such accessible form that it enables the fruitful investigation of previously stubborn problems and

---

[3]Mathematics, of course, has a long tradition of publishing fundamental problems (long ago, in the form of challenges). Upon reading this portion of the chapter, my colleagues, Joshua Lederberg and Eugene Garfield, informed me of their episodic interest in institutionalizing what amounts to the specification of ignorance. For one expression of that interest in print, see Garfield's (1974) "The Unanswered Questions of Science." Lederberg has made me the beneficiary of his 1974 permuterm bibliography entitled "Unsolved Problems" in the various sciences and has referred me to a specimen volume entitled *100 Problems in Environmental Health* (McKee et al 1961). My attention was also redirected to that superb and lively anthology I had misplaced, *The Scientist Speculates: An Anthology of Partly Baked Ideas* (Good et al 1962), which is designed "to raise more questions than it answers." Of particular interest is the piece in the anthology happily entitled "Ignoratica" by one Félix Serratosa who ascribes the essential idea of a "science of unknowns" to the explosive imagination of that prolific and often paradoxical Florentine critic, novelist, poet, and journalist Giovanni Papini. However that may all be, it can be said in self-exemplifying style: That the specification of ignorance is indispensable to the advancement of knowledge, I do not doubt; whether disciplines do differ notably in the practice of such specification, I do not know. Since the phenomenon is not yet established, I do not undertake to explain such possible variation. But one can still speculate . . .

the discovery of new problems for further inquiry (Merton [1963a]1973:371–82). SRMs take differing forms in the various disciplines: among them, the (location) strategic research site (SRS) and the (temporal) strategic research event (SRE). Differing in operative detail, these forms have much the same functions. Just as the invention of new technologies for scientific investigation can facilitate the advance of scientific knowledge, so with the finding or creating of SRMs.

The concept of SRM provides a guide to the understanding of certain turning points in the sciences. Problems that have long remained intransigent become amenable as investigators identify new kinds of empirical materials that effectively exhibit the structure and workings of the phenomena to be understood. An inventory of SRMs in the history of the various sciences would, of course, run to unconscionable, not to say unmanageable, length, but even this capsule account has room for a conspicuous few, drawn from various times, places, and disciplines.

At times, scientists create an SRM or select one by design; at other times, they come upon such material serendipitously, recognizing its strategic character for the study of a particular problem only afterward. The seventeenth-century father of embryology, Marcello Malpighi, provides an SRS of the first kind: He elected to examine the lungs of frogs microscopically because of their great "simplicity and transparency" and thus observed for the first time so fine a feature as the capillary, not otherwise observable through microscopes of the time. It was this SRS—a "microscope of Nature" as the metaphor has it—that enabled Malpighi to see the blood move through the capillaries and thus helped him to round out Harvey's understanding of the greater circulation of the blood (Wilson 1960:165; Adelmann 1966).

A truly classic case of the second, serendipitous, kind of SRS was inadvertently provided by the Canadian trapper, Alexis St. Martin, when he suffered a gunshot wound that opened a large and permanent fistula into his stomach. This enabled his physician-and-friend, the early nineteenth-century physiologist, William Beaumont, to "look directly into the cavity of the Stomach, and almost see the process of digestion," as he put it in his notebook upon going on to his long series of pioneering experiments. The successful use of this serendipitous SRS in turn led the French chemist, Nicolas Blondlot (father of the hapless René), to create SRSs systematically by introducing similar fistulas in animals. But it was Beaumont's ingenious use of the singular fortituous SRS that deeply impressed the incomparable physician-humanist, William Osler, who held that it had led this "backwood physiologist" to the most consequential contributions to the physiology of digestion made in the nineteenth century. So impressed was Osler that, upon St. Martin's death—57 years after his scientifically fruitful accident (and his subsequent fathering of 20 children)—he wanted to conduct a postmortem examination and to deposit that strategic stomach, hole and all, in an appropriate museum. To round out the episode, I should report that intent was not translated into event: Osler refrained, upon receiving a warning telegram from St. Martin's French-Canadian community that read "Don't come for autopsy; will be killed" (Osler 1908:159–88, Cushing 1925: I, 177–79).

The early geneticists and especially the more recent molecular biologists hit upon a multitudinous variety of materials that strategically exhibit processes of reproduction and replication and lend themselves to the requisite research. In touching upon these, I surely indict myself as one of those benighted characters who insist on carrying coals to Newcastle, faggots into the wood, owls to Athens, and the concept of SRM to biology. I can only plead that biology is a self-exemplifying case: the history of biology itself provides strategic research materials for the study of the selection and consequences of strategic research materials.

Some time ago, there were, of course, Mendel's pea plants and then, de Vries' "pure species" of evening primrose with the ensuing complex story of his discovery of "mutation" (Mayr 1982:742–44). Harriet Zuckerman's unpublished inventory [1964] of research materials utilized in Nobel prize-winning work is fairly saturated with SRMs that gave rise to new lines of genetic inquiry and discovery. Among the many, I note only Morgan's choice of the fruit fly, so " 'easily and cheaply bred in the laboratory' " (Morgan in Allen 1975:331); Beadle & Tatum's "daring and astute selection of experimental material," the red bread mold *Neurospora crassa,* enabling them to advance biochemical genetics; Tatum & Lederberg's choice of *E. coli K-12* leading to the discovery of genetic recombination in bacteria and laying a "foundation of bacterial genetics and what has flowed from it" (Zuckerman & Lederberg 1986; Lederberg 1951, 1986); and to go no further, "that material of great convenience for studying many aspects of virus behavior," the filtrable virus bacteriophage (fondly shortened to phage) which, after their first collaboration in 1940, Delbrück and Luria converted into the SRM of that thought collective known as "the Phage group" that has contributed so much to the rise of molecular biology (Cairns et al 1966).

The recurrent pattern is one of identifying lineaments of materials that make them strategic for investigating a range of otherwise inaccessible scientific problems. Outside the sphere of genetics, Szent-Györgi's Hungarian paprika provided a rich source of ascorbic acid, enabling him to discover the role of Vitamin C in biological combustion, just as the newly available germanium and silicon crystals enabled Shockley, Bardeen, and Brattain to discover the transistor effect. Understandably, research workers become devoted to—not to say, captivated by—their fruitful SRMs. Hodgkin pays tribute to the nerve fiber of his giant squids as "an absolute gold mine," opening up all sorts of possibilities for study of physiological mechanisms in the transmission of messages.

My colleague, the neurobiologist, Eric Kandel, has also been known to wax eloquent about his prime SRM, the sea snail *Aplysia californica,* with its large and accessible nerve cells allowing investigation in molecular terms of such complex processes as learning and memory. Looking back on an earlier "encounter between neurobiology and molecular biology," he observes:

> These intellectual precursors shared an experimental approach that depended on model building and therefore on a willingness to study preparations that best exemplified the phenomena of interest. This led to a search for conveniently simple systems that provided abundant material. Thus, geneticists interested in inheritance in higher organisms first studied *Drosophila* and *Escherichia coli;* crystallographers first analyzed keratin and hemoglobin; and molecular biologists interested in replication of DNA studied bacterial viruses. Although the impetus was to understand complex phenomena, study was governed by optimization of simple experimental systems and by the presumed universality of the phenomena chosen for study (Kandel 1983:891).

Quite evidently, then, the biological sciences have long involved the search for SRMs and their sustained intensive investigation. That experimental tradition is at a considerable remove from the largely nonexperimental work in the social and behavioral sciences. Nevertheless, in those disciplines also we observe a hunt for empirical materials, research sites, and events that are judged strategic for investigating a generic scientific problem and for identifying new problems. Still, there is at times a profound difference in the orientations of biological scientists and social scientists toward the phenomena they establish and investigate. To a degree, that difference relates to the well-known distinction proposed by the philosopher Wilhelm Windelband (1884) and substantially developed by his student, Heinrich Rickert ([1902] 1921). That is the distinction between the *Naturwissenschaften* (readily translated as "the natural sciences") and the *Geisteswissenschaften* (not as readily and variously translated as "the human sciences," "the social sciences," or perhaps as "the sociocultural sciences"). Associated as he was with Rickert in several respects, Max Weber (1922) nevertheless transcended the Windelband-Rickert distinction between the natural sciences as adopting methods exclusively designed for nomothetic or generalizing objectives and the social sciences as exclusively adopting quite different methods for understanding the idiographic or individual character of a sociocultural reality.

For in place of this drastic, all-or-none choice between the two methodological orientations, one may choose the composite of intrinsic interest in understanding the particular "historical individuals"—for example, the capitalistic society of nineteenth-century England or the French Revolution or, for that matter, the Great Depression of the 1930s—*and* of an instrumental interest in those sociocultural phenomena as instructive specimens leading to discovery of general regularities which can then be drawn upon to understand other historical individuals. Thus, Sorokin (1925) examines a variety of revolutions over the centuries—from ancient Rome to our own time—to arrive at his nomothetic or generalizing work, *The Sociology of Revolution,* and to reach an understanding of the Russian Revolution he experienced at first hand. Or again, Thomas & Znaniecki (1918–1920) examine the historical case of *The Polish Peasant in Europe and America* both for its distinctive ("unique") characteristics and for its presumably generic patterns of social and personality change.

In short, it is being proposed that the history of sociological inquiry has its own complement of researches which relate variously to the use of strategic research sites and events: In one type, the empirical case is selected wholly because of intrinsic interest in it as a historical individual on grounds of its relevance to values *(Wertbeziehung),* which Rickert held to be distinctive of the *Geisteswissenschaften.* In another type, the empirical case is regarded wholly as an SRS or SRE leading to provisional generalizations. And in what I take to be the most felicitous mode, the concrete materials hold both intrinsic interest as involving human values and instrumental interest as an SRS or SRE that may advance our general sociological knowledge.

Karl Marx provides us with a prime early instance of this last type. In the preface to the first German edition of *Capital,* he begins with a not uninteresting allusion to the logic of inquiry adopted by physicists and then goes on to the rationale for adopting a particular site for his own inquiry:

> The physicist either observes physical phenomena where they occur in their most typical form and most free from disturbing influence or, wherever possible, he makes experiments under conditions that assure the occurrence of the phenomenon in its normality. In this work I have to examine the capitalist mode of production, and the conditions of production and exchange corresponding to that mode. Up to the present time, their classic ground is England. That is the reason why England is used as the chief illustration in the development of my theoretical ideas (Marx [1867] 1906:12–13).

Marx goes on to elucidate the choice of England as an SRS(ite) by maintaining that the country which is "more developed industrially only shows, to the less developed, the image of its own future." And then, almost in the manner of an early biologist assaying a potential SRS, Marx assesses the research value of his elected case by noting that "The social statistics of Germany and the rest of Continental Western Europe are, in comparison of those of England, wretchedly compiled." Although this SRS scarcely has the same quality of exhibiting closely reproducible regularities on demand as SRMs in the physics to which Marx refers, it does not seem too much to suggest that Marx's choice of his SRS has had its own array of notable consequences, cognitive as well as social.

The sociological literature is chockfull of work that combines intrinsic interest in the particular sociocultural case with instrumental interest in it as leading to provisional general conclusions. Here, it is enough to instance Max Weber's monumental volumes (1910–1921) in the sociology of religion, with their intensive sociological analyses of Protestantism, Confucianism and Taoism, Hinduism and Buddhism, and ancient Judaism. The idiographic analyses of these historical materials which hold great intrinsic interest for many of us are powerfully joined with their instrumental use as SRSs leading to nomothetic hypotheses about such abstract sociological problems as the relations between institutionalized ideas and social organization as well as the modes and dynamics of structural interdependence of seemingly unconnected social institutions—all this best exemplified by the interplay between religious ideas and economic developments, not least in the prototypal case of ascetic Protestantism and the emergence of modern capitalism.

Other founders of modern sociology worked with a variety of strategic research sites and events. Durkheim, of course, notably so in his analyses of the division of labor, suicide, religious ceremony and ritual, and moral education, among others. As Hanan Selvin pointed out to me in correspondence (1976) on the evolving concept of SRS, Durkheim's first empirical study of suicide in 1888, antedating his famous monograph by a decade, rested on the strategic selection of "European nations as the units of recording and analysis. The availability of suicide rates as [assumed] indicators of national unhappiness was surely what led him to make this choice." Elsewhere, Selvin (1976) notes how Durkheim adopted a more fine-grained SRS to analyze—as it happens, erroneously—relationships between the proportions of German-speaking people and the suicide rate in 15 provinces of Austro-Hungary, this in an effort to identify the effects of German culture on the suicide rate while presumably neutralizing the effects of possible genetic dispositions to suicide. It is in this context, after the manner of one subjecting natural history to systematic analysis, that Durkheim (1888) emitted the metaphor: "Austria offers us the complete natural laboratory"—a kind of metaphor often echoed by Park, Burgess and others of that remarkable group of sociologists that made the city of Chicago a sociological "laboratory."

Familiar empirical materials were put to unfamiliar theoretical use. Thus, Durkheim (1899–1900) and, in kindred fashion, George H. Mead (1918) elected to tackle the problem of the social bases of moral indignation, integral to an understanding of mechanisms of social control, by turning to situations in which people react strongly to violations of social norms *even though they are not directly injured by them.* Systems of punishment and behavioral responses to violations of deep-seated rules provided an SRS not so much for the then-and-since traditional problem of the deterrent effects of punishment in curbing crime as for the problem of their other societal functions; in Mead's language, the "uniting all members of the community in the emotional solidarity of aggression." In an Excursus of the kind to which he was much given, to the lasting benefit of the rest of us, Simmel ([1908] 1950:402–408) focused on "the phenomenon of the stranger" in order to analyze how "the unity of nearness and remoteness in every human relation is organized" just as, in direct theoretical continuity, Park (1928) focused on the behavior of immigrants as providing strategic materials for coming to understand the structural bases of "the marginal man"—the men and women who, living in disparate social worlds, do not feel at home or fully accepted in any of them.

Following upon these and many another early prototype, the exponentially growing numbers of sociologists have adopted a numerous variety of strategic research sites and events. But of all these, nothing more can be said here. Instead, I obey the injunction of the Editors of *Annual Review* to make this prefatory piece as personal as I can bring myself to do and close out these capsule notes on the concept of SRM in two steps. First, I want to examine a turning point in the history of psychoanalysis that I have often singled out as a classic instance of an acute theoretical sensibility—to wit, Freud himself— transmuting seemingly trivial phenomena into strategic research material (however different present-day appraisals of that material may be). This invites attention to the apparently paradoxical theme of the occasional, per- haps frequent, importance in science and scholarship of what appear to be humanly insignificant phenomena. From that historic episode I move to three distinctly minor efforts on my own part to set forth an explicit rationale for adopting various kinds of sociological SRMs.

The "Trivial" as Strategic Research Material

It was back in the 1940s that I first found myself focussing on Freud's analytic decision to study seemingly trivial mistakes in everyday life as "strategic" in the sense being developed here:

> . . . in noting that the unexpected fact must be 'strategic,' *i.e.* that it must permit implications which bear upon generalized theory, we are, of course, referring rather to what the observer brings to the datum than to the datum itself. For it obviously requires a theoretically sensitive observer to detect the universal in the particular. After all, men had for centuries noticed such 'trivial' occurrences as slips of the tongue, slips of the pen, typographical errors, and lapses of memory, but it required the theoretic sensitivity of a Freud to see these as strategic data through which he could extend his theory of repression and symptomatic acts (Merton 1948:507).

Freud had signalled his intention of transmuting these seemingly trivial matters into basic theoretical matters by the emphasis given them in the title of the book where he first dealt systematically with them: *The Psychopathology of Everyday Life: Forgetting, Slips of the Tongue, Bungled Actions, Superstition and Errors* (Freud [1901] 1960). He proceeded to group these varied mishaps in the coined word-and-concept, *Fehlleistungen* (a psychological oxymoron translated in *The Standard Edition . . . of Freud* by the made-up Greek-like word, "parapraxes"[4] but as Bettleheim has tellingly noted, best rendered as "faulty achievements." Returning intensively to these same matters 15 years later in his *Introductory Lectures on Psycho-Analysis,* Freud forcefully states the case for his focussing on these "apparent trivialities":

> It is to these phenomena, then, that I now propose to draw your attention. But you will protest with some annoyance: 'There are so many vast problems in the [wide] universe, as well as within the narrower confines of our minds, . . . that it does really seem gratuitous to waste labour and interest on such trivialities. . . .'
>
> I should reply: Patience, Ladies and Gentlemen! I think your criticism has gone astray. It is true that psycho-analysis cannot boast that it has never concerned itself with trivialities. On the contrary, the material for its observations is usually provided by the inconsiderable events which have been put aside by the other sciences as being too unimportant—the dregs, one might say, of the world of phenomena. But are you not making a confusion in your criticism between the vastness of the problems and the consciousness of what points to them? Are there not very important things which can only reveal themselves, under certain conditions and at certain times, by quite feeble indications? (Freud [1916] 1961:26–27).

Freud is telling his audience that the seeming insignificance of these "phenomena" for everyday life says nothing about their significance for psychological science. That observation on the strategic theoretical value of such slips and errors holds quite apart from their evidentiary value for Freud's own theory that they result from repression [as is clear from the thoroughgoing analysis of Freud's "flawed reasoning" and from the review of alternative explanations of these phenomena by the philosopher of science, A. Grünbaum (1984:190–21)].

I cannot dwell on the enduring theme of the potential importance of the seemingly trivial in science and scholarship as it has appeared over the centuries—the seventeenth, for example, was chockfull of this theme, both as understood and as misunderstood. A few archetypal observations to this effect in our own century must serve. Having been taxed from time to time for

---

[4]As others have held and as Bettleheim has emphatically observed, this awkward term is a misleading translation of a central concept. Unable to improve upon Bettleheim's analysis, I do service by transmitting it here: "Freud coined *Fehlleistung* to signify a phenomenon that he had recognized—one that is common to the various ways in which our unconscious manages to prevail over our conscious intentions in everyday occurrences. The term combines two common, strangely opposite nouns, with which everybody has immediate and significant association. *Leistung* has the basic meaning of accomplishment, achievement, performance, which is qualified by the *Fehl* to indicate an achievement that somehow failed—was off the mark, in error. What happens in *Fehlleistung* is simultaneously—albeit on different levels of consciousness—a real achievement and a howling mistake. Normally, when we think of a mistake we feel that something has gone wrong, and when we refer to an accomplishment we approve of it. In *Fehlleistung,* the two responses become somehow merged: we both approve and disapprove, admire and disdain". (Bettelheim 1983:86–87).

attending to the apparently insignificant, Veblen (1932:42) took one occasion to observe that "All this may seem to be taking pains about trivialities. But the data with which any scientific inquiry has to do are trivialities in some other bearing than that one in which they are of account." And inevitably, in these reminiscent pages, I am put in mind of how this matter was being reiterated by teachers at Harvard during my time as a student and instructor there. Here is the biochemist and self-taught social scientist, L. J. Henderson, typically diluting his cogent observations by his passionate Paretan insistence that social scientists really must learn to quell their passions:

> This illustration has been chosen because, among other reasons, it is a simple case that is likely to seem trivial. Note well, however, that nothing is trivial, but thinking (or feeling) makes it so, and that we must ever guard against coloring facts with our prejudices. There was a time not so very long ago when electro-magnetic interactions, mosquitoes, and microorganisms seemed trivial. It is when we study the social sciences that the risk of mixing our prejudices and passions with the facts, and thus spoiling our analysis, is most likely to prevail (Henderson [1941] 1970:19; see also Bernard Barber's comment introducing this passage in Henderson's oral publication which Barber arranged to have put into print).

Whether Henderson alerted Talcott Parsons to this theme of the possible scientific importance of otherwise trivial phenomena, I cannot say. He may have done so during his close editing of Parsons' masterwork, *The Structure of Social Action* (1937), for, as the Preface gratefully states and as we young colleagues of them both knew, Henderson had "subjected the manuscript to important revision at many points, particularly in relation to general scientific methodology. . . ." In any case, Parsons picks up and develops the theme in the important section entitled "Theory and Empirical Fact," which virtually opens his immensely consequential treatise:

> A scientifically unimportant discovery is one which, however true and however interesting for other reasons, has no consequences for a system of theory with which scientists in that field are concerned. Conversely, even the most trivial observation from any other point of view—a very small deviation of the observed from the calculated position of a star, for instance—may be not only important but of revolutionary importance, if its logical consequences for the structure of theory are far-reaching (Parsons 1937:7-8).

In summary, then, it has long been recognized in a variety of disciplines that there is no necessary relation between the socially ascribed importance of the empirical materials under study and their importance for the better understanding of how nature or society works. The scientific and the human significance of those materials can be, although most emphatically they need not be, poles apart. This is often lost to view when a charge of triviality rests wholly on a commonsense appraisal of the subject-matter alone, as it often is, for example, by satirizing members of Congress. In gauging the human significance of the sociological *problem* rather than the empirical materials, many of us have argued, we sociologists have found no better general criterion than that advanced by Max Weber in the concept of *Wertbeziehung* (value relevance). Their values may lead scientists to refuse to work on certain scientific problems—for example, research that will lead to still more catastrophic weapon systems—or may lead them to focus on other scientific problems—for example, research on cancer or on the social mechanisms that perpetuate racial discrimination. There still remains the question of identifying the research materials that enable one to investigate these humanly important problems most effectively, the question of hitting upon strategic research sites or events.

In saying all this, I prefer not to be misunderstood. It is surely not the case that SRMs for investigating a particular scientific problem must be humanly trivial. Nor is it being said in the mood defensive that there is no authentically trivial work in today's sociology any more than it can be said that there was no trivial work in, for instance, the physical science of the seventeenth century. Our journals of sociology may have as impressive a complement of authentic trivia as the *Transactions* of the Royal Society had during its first century or so. But these are trivia in the strict rather than the unthinking rhetorical sense: They are inconsequential, both intellectually and humanly. The central point is only this: The social and the scientific significance of a concrete subject can be—although, of course, they need not be—of quite different magnitudes.

Some Personal Choices of SRMs

Responding again to the Editors' amiable reminder that these prefatory essays generally call for personal moments, I sketch out three abbreviated rationales, early and late, for my selecting or adopting certain empirical materials that seemed strategic for studying particular problems in sociology and social psychology.

I think back to the ancient days of 1943 and my interest, largely stimulated by my newfound collaborator, Paul F. Lazarsfeld, in understanding the workings and consequences of mass propaganda. "The radio marathon," then a wholly new historical phenomenon, promised to provide a strategic case for investigating the collective behavior of mass persuasion. In the course of 18 consecutive hours on the air, the pop singer Kate Smith, widely identified as the sincere patriot incarnate, spoke a series of prepared texts on 65 occasions, and elicited the then unprecedented sum of $39,000,000 in war bond pledges (Merton et al 1946). From the start, the concrete idiosyncratic and behavioral materials were delimited from their potential scientific interest: "Although her name inevitably recurs time and again throughout the book, this is *not* a study of Kate Smith." Rather, the collective bond-drive would "provide a peculiarly instructive case for research into the social psychology of mass persuasion."

Severely condensed, the stated attributes of this assumed strategic research event were these: First, it was a "real-life" situation, not an isolated, recognizably contrived situation of the kind that limits the transferability of laboratory findings in social psychology to the world outside. Second, the bond purchases provided a behavioral index of effective persuasion which, however crude, was far better than the hypothetical pencil-and-paper responses common in the laboratory research of the time. Third, there was reason to suppose that the event would be emotionally freighted in varying degree for listeners, both those who pledged bond purchases and those who did not. Fourth, unlike field studies of other collective behavior, such as race riots, we would have full and sustained access to parts of the developing collective situation in the form of content analyses of the recorded broadcasts. Fifth, the self-selected individuals and groups engaging in this behavior would come from widely differing social strata rather than being drawn, after the fashion of the time (and, often enough, today) from the dependent, rather homogenous aggregates of college students dragooned as "subjects" by their instructors. Finally, it was assumed that this attempt at truly mass persuasion would link up with identifiable sociocultural contexts.

In the course of the study, we did find such social phenomena, among them, the operation of "pseudo-Gemeinschaft" (the feigning of common values and primary concern with the other as a means of advancing one's own interests); processes in the formation of what we described by the new concept of "public image"; and a pervasive public distrust. Not least, in unanticipated and self-exemplifying fashion, the study reactivated a sense of the moral implications of the framing of scientific problems in one or another fashion, leading to a specific elucidation of the Rickert-Weber idea of *Wertbeziehung* that questioned a naive form of positivistic orientation common at the time:

> [The] social scientist investigating mass opinion may adopt the standpoint of the positivist, proclaim the ethical neutrality of science, insist upon his exclusive concern with the advancement of knowledge, explain that science deals only with the discovery of uniformities and not with ends and assert that in his role as a detached and dispassionate scientist, he has no traffic with values. He may, in short, affirm an occupational philosophy which appears to absolve him of any responsibility for the use to which his discoveries in methods of mass persuasion may be put. With its specious and delusory distinction [in this context] between 'ends' and 'means' and its insistence that the intrusion of social values into the work of scientists makes for special pleading, this philosophy fails to note that the investigator's social values do influence his choice and definition of problems. The investigator may naively suppose that he is engaged in the value-free activity of research, whereas in fact he may simply have so defined his research problems that the results will be of use to one group in the society, and not to others. His very choice and definition of a problem reflects his tacit values (Merton et al 1946:187–88).

And so on in further specifying detail drawn from this study of a public event involving mass persuasion and the workings of what came to be described as "technicians in sentiment." The point of dwelling on these matters, I suppose, is simply to note, once again, that however focused an SRS is for the investigation of previously identified problems, it may lead to other, unanticipated, findings and problems.

By the way of necessarily quick conclusion, two contrasting episodes also involving my own work may illuminate a general point regarding SRMs in sociology: Studies of social institutions, social movements, and other macro-sociological inquiries require little explicit rationale, since their relation to values is taken as self-evident but the selection of seemingly peripheral, innocuous, or 'trivial' social data as strategic for investigating basic sociological problems, does, precisely because of the seeming distance of the data from prized values.

Back in the 1930s, when the sociology of science was far from having been legitimated as a scholarly field of inquiry, even the historians of science most critical of a study of the social and cultural contexts of the efflorescence of science in seventeenth-century England (Merton [1938] 1970) did not question its scholarly relevance. Some were even prepared to accept, on probation, its substantive hypotheses of linkages between Puritanism and the emergence of the new science as well as its hypotheses of the partial shaping of foci of scientific interest by economic and technological developments of the time. Some went on to take friendly note of the use in that study of the then newly developed procedures of prosopography (analysis of collective biography) (Stone 1971:50–51, Shapin & Thackray 1974:22) and the quantitative analysis of changing scientific foci through content-analysis of the new journal of the new science, *Philosophical Transactions. Wertbeziehung* gave immediate scholarly warrant to the "subjects" under study.

Not so, however, with another study of mine two decades later. In it I had elected to focus on a recurrent phenomenon in science over the centuries, though one which had been ignored for systematic study: priority-conflicts among scientists, including the greatest among them, who wanted to reap the glory of having been first to make a particular scientific discovery or scholarly contribution. This was paradoxically coupled with strong denials, by themselves and by disciples, of their ever having had such an "unworthy and puerile" motive for doing science.[5] The initial and subsequent response to that study is captured in a remarkably candid account by the historian of science and editor-in-chief of the 16-volume *Dictionary of Scientific Biography,*

---

[5]Those self-deprecatory words are Freud's. Still, his biographer and disciple, Ernest Jones (1957, III:105) writes that "Freud was never interested in questions of priority which he found merely boring," thus providing another case of fashioning a biographical pseudo-fact although abundant and accessible evidence testifies otherwise. Elinor Barber and I have identified some 150 occasions on which Freud exhibited an interest in priority. With typical self-awareness, he reports having even dreamt about priority and the credit normatively due scientists for their contributions (Merton [1963] 1973:385–91).

Charles C. Gillispie (1974:656–60). A colleague at a distance, he first responded with considerably less than enthusiasm. I can do no better than have him tell the telling story:

> Some years ago, probably in early 1958, Merton sent me an offprint of . . . his presidential address to the American Sociological Association on "Priorities in Scientific Discovery" [(1957) 1973:286–324]. It starts by noting (pp. 286–87) "the great frequency with which the history of science is punctuated by disputes, often by sordid disputes, over priority of discovery." As I read on, dismay overtook amusement at the parade of eminent scientists arguing and frequently quarreling with each other, not over what the truth was, but over who had it first, Newton or Leibniz, Newton or Hooke, Cavendish or Watt or Lavoisier, Adams or LeVerrier, Jenner or Pearson or Rabaut, Freud or Janet. Sometimes the great men themselves abstained from contending in the lists of professional recognition for title to their intellectual property only to have their claims championed by disciples or compatriots. All too clearly the particular instances that Merton adduced in a number of variations on the theme of intellectual possessiveness could have been multiplied almost indefinitely.
>
> In a note of acknowledgment to Merton, I wrote that, although it seemed surprising that the phenomenon was so nearly universal an accompaniment to scientific discovery, I did wonder whether the matter wasn't a bit trivial. I don't believe I also said "unworthy" but recollect that such a dark thought was in my mind (Gillispie 1974:656).

I do not recall Gillispie actually having said "unworthy." He did, however, signal his friendly concern over my having lavished so much attention on the distinctly minor "subject" of priority-conflicts. But a change in his own theoretical perspectives on the scope and character of the historiography of science evidently led to a changed perception. He no longer took the descriptive raw materials of priority-conflicts as the subject-matter in hand; rather, he came to see them for what they were being redesigned to be: as strategic research materials for identifying the reward system distinctive of the social institution of science, one in which peer recognition of original scientific work was the golden coinage of the scientific realm. Gillispie also came to see that the sociological analysis of priority-conflicts as SRMs led one to find a contradiction between that reward system and other parts of the social and normative structure of science, such as the system of free and open communication (at least, for scientists outside the world of industry).

Gillispie indicatively describes this shift in perception:

> Only a few years later, when I began to study and teach materials in the social and institutional as well as the more traditional internal and intellectual history of science, did I come to take the full thrust of what he had in fact said, and said clearly and convincingly. It was that such behavior occurs in service to social norms; that norms arise in the life of real communities governing the conduct of their members; that the phrase 'scientific community' is, therefore, no mere manner of speaking about some shared pleasure in the study of nature but refers to an effective social entity; and that, within its membership, which is bounded professionally and not geographically, two main sets of norms constrain behavior and do so in ways that conflict, the one enjoining selflessness in the advancement of knowledge, and the other ambition for professional reputation, which in science accrues from originality in discovery and from that alone. The analysis exhibits the scientific

community to be one wherein the dynamics derive from the competition for honor even as the dynamics of the classical economic community do from the competition for profit, and neither of those statements is in any way incompatible with agreeing that the competitors characteristically like their work and choose it for that reason (Gillispie 1974:656).

Gillispie goes on to report that the substance of James Watson's *The Double Helix* (1968) came as no surprise. After all, that confessional account of intense competition and marginal if not sharp practices in the author's quest for a Nobel variously exemplified what was set down in the sociological analysis of intellectual property and the race for priority in science which had appeared a decade before.

One further observation will round out this impromptu case study of a strategic research site in the sociology of science. Were Charles Gillispie reflecting on his shifting response to that early study of priority-conflicts today, after the quite recent spate of concern over the occurrence of fraud in science, he might have elucidated his account further. He might have gone on to observe that the study had proposed the strongly stated hypothesis that contradictions between the reward-system and the normative system of science made for such pathologies as the occasional felonies of plagiarism and the cooking of fraudulent data, the presumably more frequent misdemeanors of hoarding one's own data while making free use of others' data, and the breaching of the mores of science by failing to acknowledge the contributions of predecessors, the collective giant on whose shoulders one stood to see a bit or, rarely, a great deal farther. Gillispie might have noted that this 1957 paper was the first to set out a sociological analysis of fraud in science, a good many years before currently publicized cases of such scientific felonies had forced widespread attention, both scholarly and popular, to the phenomenon (Zuckerman 1977, Broad & Wade 1982). Now for me to visit this observation on Charles Gillispie might be taken as a self-exemplifying claim to priority (as no doubt it is). But the chief point is less a matter of priority than of attending to the sources of that early sociologically grounded focus on the phenomenon of fraud in science. That focus derived theoretically from anomie-and-opportunity-structure theory and empirically from the selection of priority-conflicts as a strategic research site. And this, in turn, suggests that once problems are theoretically identified, materials that were previously peripheral or of no interest at all become reassessed as, in effect, strategic research materials.

CODA

It is now plain why the preceding pages are described as fragments. Obviously, much more is needed to establish these three patterns of scientific practice as phenomena, to specify our current ignorance about each of them in the form of new feasible problems, and to propose a range of research materials strategic for their solution. To my way of thinking, that is work for the near future.

ACKNOWLEDGMENTS

I thank colleagues near and far for their thoughtful reading of early and late drafts of this paper; in the first instance, Joshua Lederberg, Robert C. Merton, and Harriet Zuckerman, and then, Orville G. Brim, Jr., Jonathan R. Cole, Cynthia F. Epstein, Jonathan Rieder, David L. Sills, D. K. Simonton, Neil J. Smelser, and Stephen M. Stigler. I acknowledge aid of another kind from the John D. & Catherine T. MacArthur Foundation and the Russell Sage Foundation.

APPENDIX: THE MENU

(On the suggestion of several readers by way of providing context, I append the list of subjects from which these three were drawn.)

I. Patterns of Scientific Practice

1. Establishing the Phenomenon
2. Specified Ignorance
3. Strategic Research Materials
4. Fact as Theory-Laden: A Periodic Rediscovery
5. Naive Falsificationism: When Trust Theory, When Trust Fact
6. Unanticipated Consequences of the Reward System in Science: A Model of the Sequencing of Problem-Choices (with R. C. Merton)
7. The Self-Fulfilling Prophecy in Scientific Work
8. Toward a Sociological Theory of Error:
    8a. Patterned Misunderstandings in Science and Learning
    8b. Fallacy of the Latest Word
    8c. The Phoenix Phenomenon
9. Disciplined Eclecticism
10. Confirmation and the Fallacy of Affirming the Consequent
11. A *Fortiori* Reasoning in the Design of Scientific Inquiry
12. Tacit Counterfactual History
13. The (William) James Distinction: Acquaintance With and Knowledge About
14. The (Kenneth) Burke Theorem: Seeing as a Way of Not-Seeing
15. The (L. J.) Henderson Maxim: It's a Good Thing to Know What You Are Doing

II. Patterns in Transmission, Change, and Growth of Scientific Knowledge

1. Selective Accumulation of Scientific Knowledge: Paradox of Progress
2. OBI: *O*bliteration (of Source of Ideas, Methods, or Findings) *by* *I*ncorporation (in Canonical Knowledge)
3. "Trained Incapacity": A Case of OBI
4. Cognitive Conduits for the Blurred Central Message
5. The Retroactive Effect in the Transmission and Growth of Knowledge
6. The Matthew Effect II: Accumulation of Advantage and the Symbolism of Intellectual Property
7. Oral Publication and Publication in Print
8. The Scientific Paper as Tacit Reconstruction of Knowledge
9. Insiders and Outsiders: Privileged Access to Knowledge
10. The Adumbrationist Credo: What's New is Not True; What's True is not New
11. The Symbolism of Eponyms in Science
12. Fathers and Mothers of the Sciences
13. Fraud and Other Deviant Behaviors in Science: A Case of Goal Displacement
14. Taboo Knowledge
15. Givens: The 'Of-Course Mood' in Scientific Discourse
16. Francis Bacon as Sociologist of Knowledge
17. Organized Skepticism: The Social Organization and Functions of Criticism in Science and Scholarship

III. Neologisms as Sociological Concepts: History and Analysis

1. On The Origin and Character of the Word *Scientist*
2. Self-Exemplifying Ideas: in the Sociology of Science and Elsewhere
3. Influentials: Evolution of a Concept
4. Institutionalized Evasions and Other Patterned Evasions
5. SED: Socially Expected Durations as a Temporal Dimension of Social Structure
6. Homophily and Heterophily: Types of Friendship Patterns
7. "Whatever Is, Is Possible": A Brief Biography of the Theorem
8. Opportunity Structures: A Brief Biography of the Concept
9. "Haunting Presence of the Functionally Irrelevant Status": The Structural Analysis of Status-Sets
10. "Phatic Communion": Malinowski's Need of a Cognitive Conduit
11. Comte's "Cerebral Hygiene" and the Presumed Dangers of Erudition for Originality

12. *Veritas Filia Temporis:* Temporal Contexts of Scientific Knowledge
13. *Pseudo-Gemeinschaft* and Public Distrust
14. The Travels and Adventures of Serendipity: A Study in Historical
    Semantics and the Sociology of Science (with Elinor Barber)

Literature Cited

Adelmann, H. B. 1966. *Marcello Malpighi and the Evolution of Embryology.* Ithaca, NY: Cornell Univ. Press

Allen, G. E. 1975. The introduction of *Drosophila* into the study of heredity and evolution: 1900–1910. *Isis* 66:322–33

Becker, H. S. [1963] 1973. *Outsiders.* New York: Free Press

Becker, H. S., ed. 1964. *The Other Side: Perspectives on Deviance.* New York: Free Press

Bell, E. T. 1931. Mathematics and speculation. *Sci. Mon.* 32:193–209

Bell, E. T. 1937. *Men of Mathematics.* New York: Simon & Schuster

Bernard, C. [1865] 1949. *An Introduction to the Study of Experimental Medicine.* New York: Henry Schuman

Bettelheim, B. 1983. *Freud and Man's Soul.* New York: Knopf

Broad, W., Wade, N. 1982. *Betrayers of the Truth: Fraud and Deceit in the Halls of Science.* New York: Simon & Schuster

Brewster, D. 1855. *Memoirs of the Life, Writings, and Discoveries of Sir Isaac Newton.* 2 vols. Edinburgh: Thomas Constable

Burke, K. 1935. *Permanence and Change.* New York: New Republic

Cairns, J., Stent, G. S., Watson, J. D. eds. 1966. *Phage and the Origins of Molecular Biology.* Cold Spring Harbor, Me: Cold Spring Harbor Lab. Quant. Biol.

Cicourel, A. 1968. *The Social Organization of Juvenile Justice.* New York: Wiley

Cloward, R. A., Ohlin, L. E. 1960. *Delinquency and Opportunity.* New York: Free Press

Cohen, A. K. 1955. *Delinquent Boys.* New York: Free Press

Cushing, H. 1925. *The Life of Sir William Osler.* 2 vol. Oxford: Clarendon

Durkheim, E. 1899–1900. Deux lois de l'evolution pénale. *L'Année sociologique* 4:55–95

Durkheim, E. 1888. Suicide et natalité: études de statistique morale. *Revue philosophique* 26:444–63

Erikson, K. T. 1964. Notes on the sociology of deviance. See Becker 1964:9–21

Fischer, C. S. 1977. *Networks and Places: Social Relations in the Urban Setting.* New York: Free Press

Fleck, L. [1935] 1979. *Genesis and Development of a Scientific Fact,* ed. T. J. Trenn, R. K. Merton. Chicago: Univ. Chicago Press

Fontenelle, B. [1686] 1908. *Histoire des oracles.* Paris: Hachette

Franks, F. 1981. *Polywater.* Cambridge: MIT Press

Freud, S. [1901] 1960. *The Psychopathology of Everyday Life.* Vol. 6 In *The Standard Edition of the Complete Psychological Works of Sigmund Freud,* ed. J. Strachey. London: Hogarth

Freud, S. [1916] 1961. *Introductory Lectures on Psychoanalysis.* Vol. 15 in *The Standard Edition of the Complete Psychological Works of Sigmund Freud,* ed. J. Strachey. London: Hogarth

Garfield, E. The unanswered questions of science. 1974. *Curr. Contents* June 5:5–6

Gerth, H. H., Mills, C. W. 1953. *Character and Social Structure.* New York: Harcourt Brace Jovanovich

Gillispie, C. C. 1974. Mertonian theses. *Science* 184:656–60

Golubović, Z. 1973. Why is functionalism more desirable in present-day Yugoslavia than marxism? *Praxis* 4:357–68

Gouldner, A. W. 1970. *The Coming Crisis of Western Sociology.* New York: Basic Books

Gouldner, A. W. 1973. *For Sociology.* New York: Basic Books

Gouldner, A. W. 1980. *The Two Marxisms.* New York: Seabury

Grünbaum, A. 1984. *The Foundations of Psychoanalysis: A Philosophical Critique.* Berkeley: Univ. Calif. Press

Gutman, H. G. 1976. *The Black Family in Slavery and Freedom: 1750–1925.* New York: Pantheon

Henderson, L. J. [1941] 1970. *On the Social System,* ed. B. Barber. Chicago: Univ. Chicago Press

Heidegger, M. [1927] 1962. *Being and Time.* New York: Harper

Jones, E. 1957. *Sigmund Freud: Life and Work.* 3 vols. London: Hogarth

Kandel, E. R. 1983. Neurobiology and molecular biology. *Cold Spring Harbor Symposia on Quantitative Biol.* 48:891–908

Kitsuse, J. I. 1964. Societal reaction to deviant behavior. See Becker 1964, pp. 87–102

Lazarsfeld, P. F., Thielens, W. Jr. 1958. *The Academic Mind.* New York: Free Press

Lederberg, J. 1951. Genetic studies with bacteria. In *Genetics in the 20th Century,* ed. L. C. Dunn, pp. 263–89. New York: Macmillan

Lederberg, J. 1986. Forty years of genetic recombination in bacteria. *Nature* 324 (6098):627–28

Lemert, E. M. 1951. *Social Pathology.* New York: McGraw-Hill

Lemert, E. M. 1973. Beyond Mead: The societal reaction to deviance. *Soc. Probl.* 21:457–68

Leontief, W. 1971. Theoretical assumptions and nonobserved facts. *Am. Econ. Rev.* 21:457–68

Lewis, C. S. 1975. *Letters of C. S. Lewis,* ed. W. H. Lewis. New York: Harcourt Brace Jovanovich

Marx, K. [1867] 1906. *Capital: A Critique of Political Economy,* Vol. 1, (Ed. F. Engels). Chicago: C. H. Kerr

Mayr, E. 1982. *The Growth of Biological Thought.* Cambridge: Harvard Univ. Press

McKee, J. E. 1961. *100 Problems in Environmental Health.* Washington, D.C.: Jones Composition

Mead, G. H. 1918. The psychology of punitive justice. *Am. J. Sociol.* 23:577–602

Merton, R. K. 1938a. Social structure and anomie. *Am. Sociol. Rev.* 3:672–82

Merton, R. K. [1938b] 1970. *Science, Technology and Society in 17th-Century England.* New York: Howard Fertig

Merton, R. K. 1948. The bearing of empirical research upon the development of sociological theory. *Am. Sociol. Rev.* 13:505–15

Merton, R. K. 1957. *Social Theory and Social Structure.* New York: Free Press

Merton, R. K. 1959. Notes on problemfinding in sociology. In *Sociology Today: Problems and Prospects,* ed. R. K. Merton, L. Broom, L. S. Cottrell. New York: Basic Books

Merton, R. K. [1963a] 1973. Multiple discoveries as strategic research site. See Merton 1973, pp. 371–82

Merton, R. K. [1963b] 1973. The ambivalence of scientists. See Merton 1973, pp. 383–412

Merton, R. K. 1971. The precarious foundations of detachment in sociology. In *The Phenomenon of Sociology,* ed. E. A. Tiryakian, pp. 188–99. New York: Appleton-Century-Crofts

Merton, R. K. 1973. *The Sociology of Science,* ed. N. W. Storer. Chicago: Univ. Chicago Press

Merton, R. K. 1976. The sociology of social problems. In *Contemporary Social Problems,* ed. R. K. Merton, R. A. Nisbet, pp. 3–43. New York: Harcourt Brace Jovanovich

Merton, R. K. 1981. Remarks on theoretical pluralism. In *Continuities in Structural Inquiry,* ed. P. M. Blau, R. K. Merton, pp. i–vii. London: Sage

Merton, R. K. 1982. Alvin W. Gouldner: Genesis and growth of a friendship. *Theory and Society* 11:915–38

Merton, R. K., Fiske, M., Curtis, A. [1946] 1971. *Mass Persuasion.* Westport, Conn: Greenwood

Moore, W. E., Tumin, M. M. 1949. Some social functions of ignorance. *Am. Sociol. Rev.* 14:787–95

Oromaner, M. August, 1974. Critical function of errors. *Am. Sociol. Assn. Footnotes* 2:7

Osler, W. 1908. *An Alabama Student, and Other Biographical Essays,* pp. 159–88. New York: Oxford Univ. Press

Park, R. E. 1928. Human migration and the marginal man. *Am. J. Sociol.* 33:881–93

Parsons, T. 1937. *The Structure of Social Action.* New York: McGraw-Hill

Peirce, C. S. [c. 1903] 1958. *Collected Papers,* Vol. 7:121–144. Cambridge: Harvard Univ. Press

Popper, K. [1960] 1962. *Conjectures and Refutations: The Growth of Scientific Knowledge.* London: Routledge & Kegan Paul

Price, D. J. deS. 1961. *Science Since Babylon.* New Haven: Yale Univ. Press

Quinney, R. 1970. *The Social Reality of Crime.* Boston: Little, Brown

Rickert, H. [1902] 1921. *Die Grenzen der naturwissenschaftlichen Begriffsbildung.* Tübingen: J. C. Mohr. 4th ed.

Rostand, J. 1960. *Error and Deception in Science.* London: Hutchinson

Schrecker, E. 1986. *No Ivory Tower: McCarthyism in the Universities.* New York: Oxford Univ. Press

Selden, J. [1689] 1890. *Table Talk.* London: Reeves & Turner

Selvin, H. C. 1976. Durkheim, Booth and Yule: non-diffusion of an intellectual innovation. *Archives Européenes de sociol.* 17:39–51

Serratosa, F. 1962. Ignoratica. In *The Scientist Speculates,* ed. I. J. Good, pp. 4–9. New York: Basic Books

Shapin, S., Thackray, A. 1974. Prosopography as a research tool in history of science: The British scientific community 1700–1900. *Hist. Sci.* 12:1–28

Simmel, G. [1908] 1950. *The Sociology of Georg Simmel,* ed. K. H. Wolff, pp. 402–8. New York: Free Press

Smithson, M. 1985. Toward a social theory of ignorance. *J. Theory Soc. Behav.* 15:149–70

Sorokin, P. A. 1925. *The Sociology of Revolutions.* Philadelphia, Pa: Lippincott

Sowell, T. 1981. Assumptions versus history in ethnic education. *Teachers College Record* 83:37–69

Stone, L. 1971. Prosopography. *Daedalus.* Winter: 46–79

Sutherland, E. H. [1925–1951] 1956. *The Sutherland Papers*, ed. A. K. Cohen et al. Bloomington: Indiana Univ. Press

Sztompka, P. 1986. *Robert K. Merton: An Intellectual Profile.* New York: St. Martin's Press

Thomas, W. I., Znaniecki, F. [1918–20] 1927. *The Polish Peasant in Europe and America.* 2 vols. New York: Knopf

Turk, A. 1969. *Criminality and the Legal Order.* Chicago: Rand McNally

Veblen, T. 1932. *The Place of Science in Modern Civilization.* New York: Viking

Wallerstein, I. 1968. C. Wright Mills. *International Encyclopedia of the Social Sciences,* ed. D. L. Sills. New York: Macmillan & The Free Press

Watson, J. D. 1968. *The Double Helix.* New York: Atheneum

Weber, M. 1920–1921 *Gesammelte Aufsätze zur Religionssoziologie.* 3 vols. Tübingen: J. C. B. Mohr

Weber, M. 1922. *Gesammelte Aufsätze zur Wissenschaftslehre.* Tübingen: J. C. B. Mohr

Wilson, L. G. 1960. The transformation of ancient concepts of respiration in the 17th century. *Isis* 51:161–72

Windelband, W. 1884. *Präludien: Aufsätze und Reden zur Einleitung in die Philosophie.* Freiburg

Zeitlin, M. 1974. Corporate ownership and control. *Am. J. Sociol.* 79:1073–1119

Zuckerman, H., Lederberg, J. 1986. Postmature scientific discovery. *Nature* 324 (6098):629–31

Zuckerman, H. 1977. Deviant behavior and social control in science. In *Deviance and Social Change,* ed. E. Sagarin, pp. 87–138. Beverly Hills, Calif: Sage

Ann. Rev. Sociol. 1987. 13:29–47

ON THE DEGRADATION OF SKILLS

William Form

Department of Sociology, Ohio State University, Columbus, Ohio 43210-1353

Abstract

Although social scientists have long believed that mechanization degrades skills, they disagree on the meaning and measurement of skills. A dominant view stresses that capitalists simplify skills to increase efficiency and profits; another, that managers deskill jobs to increase control over workers and work organization. Although case studies document the disappearance of many crafts during the industrial transformation of Britain and the United States, they do not show that skills as a whole declined. Recent historical studies reveal that industrialization may have created as many new skills as it destroyed, that early manufacturing used many traditional skills, and that new industrial skills were genuine. They also show that scientific management deskilled workers slightly and that management successfully wrested control of work organization from the traditional crafts. Twentieth-century census data reveal little aggregate compositional change in the skill distribution of major occupations. Short-term studies of individual occupational skills show little or no aggregate change. Finally, case studies of automation suggest that its deskilling effects vary greatly by occupation and industry. Firm conclusions about skill degradation must await time-series analysis of national surveys that measure components of occupational skills in different industries.

INTRODUCTION

For over two centuries social scientists believed that the mechanization of labor and the factory system speeded up the division of labor, diluted workers' skills, and increased their unhappiness. In 1776 Adam Smith described the stultifying effects of specialization in terms quite like those that Marx used in 1850 to condemn capitalism's mechanization of labor. And in 1893 Durkheim (1964:371) condemned as immoral the process whereby mechaniza-

29

0360-0572/87/0815-0029$02 00

tion was turning workers into appendages of machines. In his essays on workmanship, absentee ownership, and the engineers, Veblen (1914, 1921, 1923) traced the history of capitalism's avaricious drive to mechanize, to destroy workers' skill, and to subjugate science and government to its purposes. A generation later Mills (1951:Ch. 10) concisely elaborated Veblen's analysis. From Walker & Guest's *Man on the Assembly Line* (1952) to Aronowitz's (1973) *False Promises,* a steady stream of case studies documented Mills's scenario. Therefore, sociologists who knew this literature were surprised at the enthusiastic reception given to Braverman's (1974) thesis of the degradation of work in the twentieth century. But Braverman was riding a wave of concern about the crisis of work in America (see US HEW 1973), a crisis that empirical research failed to confirm (Form 1974, Hamilton & Wright 1986:68).

However, Braverman did make three contributions. By framing deskilling as an evidentiary debate between Marxists and non-Marxists, he opened a long-needed channel of communication between the two. He integrated scattered ideas on skill degradation into a coherent Marxist framework. He modernized Marxist thought by showing that monopoly capital was using automation to deskill blue- and white-collar jobs just as early capitalists used mechanization to deskill the proletariat. Thus, automation continues to enlarge the working class and the reserve army of labor by deskilling the jobs of clerical, technical, and professional workers.

This essay examines the widely-held historical proposition that most Marxists and non-Marxists share: that work under capitalism is deskilled. The validity of many related ideas (e.g. control of work or the labor process, growth of the proletariat) depends on the prior validity of the deskilling thesis. Yet three stubborn facts obstruct consensus about skill change. First, scholars disagree on the meaning and measurement of skill. Second, since researchers have not compared deskilling in capitalist and noncapitalist societies, they cannot conclude that whatever happened under capitalist industrialization was unique. Third, even the best historical data cannot provide definitive answers to questions about skill trends. Below the first and third problems are discussed in detail.

MEANING AND MEASUREMENT OF SKILL

All scholars ostensibly agree that skill refers to job complexity: the level, scope, and integration of mental, interpersonal, and manipulative tasks required in a job (Spenner 1979). Yet in their research scholars introduce four different conceptions of skill that obscure the centrality of job complexity (Steiger 1985). First, scholars in the idealistic tradition postulate that the fulfillment of human nature requires work that balances physical and mental skills. Human potential cannot be realized unless workers as total personalities engage in meaningfully skilled tasks, using their minds to conceive and plan while they use their hands and tools. Anything less damages the human spirit. Since this craft-artisan ideal requires a balanced integration of mental and physical skills, the labor of both the mathematician and the assembler are degraded because their work is unbalanced (Steiger 1985). Consequently, whatever empirical research discovers, idealists insist that most industrial occupations are degraded because they do not allow this balance of skills. In practice, the professions are not thought to be as degraded as manual labor even though professions do not require physical skills. Idealists also assume that most preindustrial workers were skilled (Form 1976) and therefore more fulfilled than today's employees. Finally, because idealists think of skills as being in the person rather than in the job, they conclude that most workers are deskilled because they have more skills than their jobs require.

Second, some scholars use a market or a human capital view of skill. They implicitly accept high market demand or individual capacity to perform complex tasks as measures of skill. Both the teamster of horses and the file clerk are unskilled because there is no demand for horse teamsters and almost all workers can file. Obviously, neither market demand nor individual capacities are necessarily related to skill requirements of jobs.

Third, degree of job skill is often confused with extent of specialization and routinization. The more divided and routine a job, the more unskilled it is and vice versa. This view equates task specialization and routineness with task simplicity. Obviously, specializations and routines may be simple or complex; they may require short or long preparation (Smith & Snow 1976). Brain surgeons are more specialized but not necessarily less skilled than general practitioners. Though both assembling and typing are routine jobs, illiterates can quickly learn assembly work but not typing.

Fourth, some scholars think that self-direction, autonomy, and task improvising (Kohn & Schooler 1983) or responsibility or control over people and resources (Spaeth 1985) necessarily make jobs more complex. Obviously, many exceptions exist. Janitors have high work autonomy and task variety, but all tasks may be simple. Also, supervisors' work is often less complex than that of their subordinates. Because most professionals and administrators receive higher incomes than subordinates, the former jobs are considered more skilled. Thus, a market view of skill adds on the autonomy-supervision criterion to justify income inequality (Johnson 1980).

Scholars who avoid the pitfalls of these four perspectives have concluded that skill is multidimensional and that it contains at least two primary dimensions: substantive complexity and autonomy. Though the two dimensions correlate quite highly (.50–.70), measures of complexity are superior to those of autonomy (Spenner 1986). In factor analysis, reliable indicators of each factor appear in the structure of the other (Miller et al 1980 : 180), suggesting interaction complexities. Since specific jobs contain different mixes of the two dimensions, using both dimensions complicates the comparison of overall job skills. Because the substantive complexity of jobs consistently correlates highly with all variables dealing with autonomy, supervision, task variety, control, and repetition (Spenner 1980), substantive complexity is a satisfactory general measure of skill. Though researchers are aware of shortcomings in the measure of substantive complexity (Miller et al 1980), they rely on the *Dictionary of Occupational Titles* (DOT) measure as the best available. When such a measure is unavailable, as in historical research, probably the best indicator is the total preparation time a job requires for an average worker to attain an average level performance. This should include years of general education, time for special vocational or professional training, and on-the-job experience. Yet, three major sources of error appear in this measure. First, though jobs are specific to specific organizations, researchers can only compare workers who share occupational titles. Since the fit between specific jobs and occupational titles varies widely by place and time, considerable variation enters the measure. Second, because informal agreements, labor union practices, and occupational licensing have built-in credentialism (Collins 1979), total preparation time for many occupations is inflated or unknown. Third, some jobs and their incumbents grow in skill over time (Spenner 1986).

Without a comprehensive measure of occupational skill, we cannot conclusively answer such basic questions as: How much skill do occupations require? How much do occupational skills change over time? What is the skill range in the labor force, and how much does it change over time? Although answers to these questions require representative samples of occupations and industries over extended periods, scholars do not hesitate to forge theories about societal trends based on a few cases that extend over short periods. This chapter reviews studies that attempt to measure skill changes in the West for three periods: the early era of industrial transformation, the era of mature industrialism, and the age of automation.

CRAFTS IN THE ERA OF INDUSTRIAL TRANSFORMATION

Efficiency and Power Theories on the Division of Labor

Both Adam Smith and Karl Marx thought that capitalists divided labor and deskilled workers to increase productivity and profits. Though Durkheim disagreed with this motivational theory of the division of labor, sociologists have generally ignored Durkheim and embraced the Smithian utilitarian position (Kemper 1972): Managers divide labor and introduce machinery to reduce labor costs and increase profits. This theory fits both classic economic and traditional materialist theories of capitalist development (Form 1980).

In 1971, Marglin proposed a power theory (see Krause 1982). In an attack on efficiency theory, he contended that at the onset of the industrial revolution, capitalists devised the factory system not to increase productivity and profits but to increase their control over workers. Since the technology, division of labor, and productivity of early textile factories were not superior to those of home production, capitalists must have corralled workers into factories not to increase profits but to deskill them, deprive them of control over production, and thereby end their monopoly of knowledge about production. Though capitalists could have introduced machines that preserved workers' skills and yet maintained profit margins, they chose the control option. In short, capitalists made a social or power choice rather than an efficiency one in deskilling labor and introducing new technology. Though Marglin reversed the causal direction between the forces and relations of production, the theory is still considered Marxist.

Two important ideas were added to Marglin's theory. First, owners continued to label some jobs as skilled in order to divide the working class and weaken its ability to fight management (Aronowitz 1973). Often with the collaboration of the "skilled," managers initiated training programs and awarded diplomas to maintain a facade of skill mobility. Second, Taylor's (1911) scientific management movement systemized the attack on workers' skills and their control of production. Scholars disagree about the historical evidence that supports each theory. Power theorists point to many case studies of management's successes (Zimbalist 1979), while efficiency theorists argue that the cases are not representative. Below I trace this controversy in the case studies.

Industrial transformation first occurred in England from roughly the late eighteenth to the late nineteenth centuries, from the first appearance of textile factories to the later consolidation of heavy industries. Though many scholars have studied this era, the picture of what happened to skills is still incomplete. Evidence has to be untangled from studies of other issues such as class conflict, proletarianization, resistance to mechanization, strikes, and technological change (see Tilly 1978).

Much of the research on the efficiency-power debate can be analyzed in terms of four propositions from power theory, taken from two critical studies: Marglin's (1974) research on the early British textile industry and Stone's (1974) study of the US steel industry in the late nineteenth century. The four propositions are: (a) capitalists devised the factory system and invented machines primarily to deskill workers and wrest from them control of production; (b) a system of internal factory subcontracting in which artisan masters actually controlled production slowed down deskilling and management control over production; (c) management later eliminated subcontracting and gained imperative control over production and the deskilling process; (d) management retained skills nominally as social constructions to split the working class.

Factory System and Deskilling

Evidence that the factory system existed well before the advent of the machine (Durkheim 1964) somewhat weakens Marglin's thesis that industrial capitalism initiated the destruction of craft communities. Dividing and deskilling labor were underway long before the industrial revolution. Darnton (1984) showed that preindustrial large-scale artisan production was not marked by harmony among masters, journeymen, apprentices, and day laborers, and Dobson's (1980) research on labor disputes in preindustrial England suggests that alienation, impersonality, work fragmentation, and work monotony were as widespread before as after the onset of the industrial revolution. No study could be located that both controlled technology and compared profits in the putting-out and factory systems when they existed side by side; such controls are needed to test Marglin's theory. If profits were the same or lower in the factory, the control argument could be supported. Of course, early factories could have increased both profits and controls.

Increasingly, historical evidence shows that many early factory workers remained skilled despite technological change. Mechanization most affected unskilled labor. The shift from artisan to machine production occurred slowly, especially in France (Hanagan 1977). The shift from worker to management control of production was also gradual and episodic. Freifeld's (1986) findings on deskilling in early British textile factories depart markedly from Marglin's. She found that through most of the nineteenth century, mule spinners remained skilled aristocrats of labor, retained their wage advantages over the less skilled, and continued to supervise production and monopolize knowledge about it. Though manufacturers of the self-acting spinning mules advertised that they would eliminate skilled labor, the machines had to be adjusted constantly in response to changing climatic and production conditions. In effect, spinners learned new skills in response to the new technology, while laborers remained unskilled.

Stone's (1974) study of the introduction of the blast furnace in US steel production in 1892 concluded that it led to a crucial strike; management finally deskilled craft workers and wrested from them control over production and exclusive knowledge of steel making. This deskilling of craft workers and the upgrading of unskilled labor to machine operatives equalized wages. Later, management introduced a finely scaled wage ladder to discourage working-class solidarity and militancy.

However, in reviewing steel production manuals from 1865–1940, Freifeld (1984) found that the introduction of blast furnaces did not eliminate the skills of melters, blowers, and rollers in steel-making because they continued until 1940 to make production decisions in the same pragmatic and judgment-based way. The new technology mechanized mainly the unskilled jobs of material handling, loading, and the moving of ore, molten metal, and finished products from one part of the plant to another. Craft workers did lose overall control of the daily management of the mills, including the training and control of helpers, but this did not affect their craft skills. Nor did management create new labor hierarchies because labor had always been hierarchical and highly inegalitarian. In this case the skilled maintained their skills while the unskilled were upgraded to semiskilled machine operators.

More (1980) studied the critical period of rapid industrialization (1870–1914) in Britain when the alleged homogenization of skills led to the formation of industrial unions. In analyzing 440 biographies of manual workers who started to work in the Edwardian era, he found that mechanization's impact on skills varied by industry. Although Marx's analysis of the textile industry was correct, the industry was not representative. Thus, skill requirements increased in metal manufacturing, chemicals, electricity, gas, and maintenance services. Here the labor aristocracy shifted its traditional skills to fit the new basic industries (Hobsbawm 1964). More (1980) further concluded that the rise of industrial unions resulted not so much from the erosion of craft skills but from upgrading the education and task requirements of unskilled labor.

Subcontracting and Retention of Skills

Clawson (1980) amplified Braverman's thesis that capitalism's drive to deskill workers was delayed by the practice of internal subcontracting that persisted up to the 1870s. In the early factories, artisan subcontractors, rather than management, controlled production and the use of technology. Subcontractors operated efficiently because they shared production knowledge with skilled workers. Capitalists later eliminated subcontracting, deskilled the workers, and changed the foreman's function from directing production to securing worker obedience. Owners' decisions were motivated by a desire not to increase plant efficiency but to establish class hegemony over knowledge and control of production.

Littler (1982a,b) examined subcontracting in more industries and countries and over longer periods. He concluded that Braverman's thesis is too simple, ethnocentric, and general. For example, owners as well as subcontractors controlled nineteenth-century shops. Indirect owner control took different forms in different industries. It was not a hindrance to capitalist industrial hegemony. Indeed, subcontractors themselves sometimes behaved like employers as well as employees. Braverman equated internal subcontracting and craft control. Yet work was subcontracted to families in textiles, to artisan masters in construction and metal working, and to gang bosses in mining and ship loading. Direct employer and foreman control typically prevailed in new industries such as brewing and government services. External subcontracting dominated sweated trades such as clothing and shoemaking. Subcontracting and craft control persisted in some industries much longer than heretofore assumed, perhaps up to World War I. Craft deskilling (and upgrading) occurred largely in a nonconfrontational framework—as in the redistribution of occupations in new industries—and as a response to new production processes (Littler 1982a: 144). Again, no study could be found that compared the efficiency of a shop before and after the termination of artisan subcontracting, so the motive for the change and its economic consequences remain speculative.

Craft Responses to Managerial Controls

By World War I, managers had drastically reduced subcontracting and centralized their control over production. Power theorists assert that management, by introducing new technology and organizational controls, successfully deskilled the crafts and gained control over the work process. Whatever their stance on the deskilling issue, most scholars do not accept the contention that management successfully overcame worker resistance. Unfortunately, the literature on this topic is troubled by inconsistent terminology: artisan, master, skilled worker, small entrepreneur, and craft worker can refer to the same or different occupations. Thus, Foner (1976) stated that 75% of artisans, petty tradesmen, skilled and unskilled workers in colonial New York were common laborers and seamen. Moreover, occupational designations (shoemakers) sometimes refer to a trade or an industry that contains several occupations (stitchers, cutters, finishers) of varying skills.

Although most studies of deskilling describe the situation in large factories, artisan industries probably employed a majority of production workers until 1900. Bauman's (1972) history of unskilled, semiskilled, and craft workers, and union officials in British industry from 1750 to 1924 revealed that working-class stratification persisted during the entire period. Artisan skills were needed in the early factories because the first primitive machines replaced mostly unskilled labor. Even later machines that did more complicated work did not eradicate all of the old skills; e.g. the linotype did not eliminate compositors (Wallace & Kalleberg 1982). Moreover, many new machines often required new skills and craft workers typically operated them. Since management still needed some of the old crafts, managers shifted some craft workers to the new machines. And skilled workers demanded to operate the machines to establish control over them.

Penn (1982) showed that skilled workers resisted deskilling in the cotton and engineering industries especially when their labor was scarce. In printing and construction (Jackson 1984) the crafts both protected and changed their skills in the face of new technology. The expansion of product markets sometimes did not reduce the number of skilled workers; instead it expanded unskilled and semiskilled jobs. In some instances craft unions (Jackson 1984) and unorganized craft workers who were socially cohesive (Calhoun 1982) (rather than management) aggressively shaped the work organization in response to new technology. In other situations some occupational skills were mechanized (making of windows, cabinets, and molding for carpenters) but not others (Calhoun 1982). Sadler (1970) showed that the skill requirements of new machines were often unknown, but their newness and prestige called for skilled operators who were later replaced by semiskilled workers. This often happened in newly industrializing societies (Form & Pampel 1978). On the other hand, new industries could be and were launched that used mostly unskilled and semiskilled labor. In short, the pattern of skill changes varied widely in response to many conditions (Hall and Miller 1975).

Social Construction of Skills

Finally, power theory holds that skills no longer exist among manual workers except as social constructions that capitalists impose to split the working class. Support for the thesis rests on five propositions: Skill is a status and not a functional designation (many "skills" take a short time to learn); job training is unrelated to skills used on the job; employers use degrees and certificates to eliminate "undesirable" applicants; most workers are overeducated for their jobs; and work performed by the "skilled" is eventually transferred to the less skilled (Sadler 1970). Though these propositions are backed by impressive case studies (Collins 1979), other studies challenge them as unrepresentative and inconclusive.

Hobsbawm's (1964) classic history of the labor aristocracy showed that it was formed from 1840 to 1890, the period when skilled workers shifted from traditional crafts to the new basic industries. During this era, the crafts resisted deskilling not only by restricting their own supply but also by inaugurating training programs to teach the new skills needed to operate the new machines (Penn 1984). More (1980) also examined the certification thesis in the Edwardian era (1870–1914) in England, when certification presumably began. Data from his 440 working-class biographies show that apprenticeship survived and grew, especially in the newly expanding mechanized industries. More argues that if skills were not needed, apprenticeship would have declined, but it did not. Moreover, strikes by skilled workers succeeded without the support of the nonskilled. This suggests that skills were difficult to replace and that craft workers did not need the help of the less skilled. The crafts did gradually lose control of the apprentice system and management began to train semiskilled workers to perform some skilled tasks.

Lindert & Williamson's (1977) US study of a century of skill wage differentials and Penn's (1985) study of a century of British differentials showed that they remained high from 1850 to 1950, hardly possible if skills were easy to acquire. Comparing the backgrounds of 40 contemporary US occupational groups, Bielby & Kalleberg (1977) found that craft workers were unique for their long and specific vocational training. In attacking the hierarchy fetishism thesis, Sabel (1982) explains that intermediate level workers steadily acquire skills especially when technology is changing. Once they acquire skills, workers regard them as valuable property to be protected. Finally, the need for skills in changing industries explains both the continuous training feature in the internal labor markets of large industries (Roomkin & Sommers 1974) and the high turnover of skilled workers in the turbulent labor markets of small innovative industries (Sabel 1982). In short, it appears that the least supported proposition in power theory is that hierarchy fetishism is a managerial innovation to split the working class. A wealth of studies show that skilled workers in both capitalist and socialist societies struggle to preserve wage differentials without help from management (Form 1986). Historically, managers try to reduce both wage differentials and their reliance on skilled workers.

These case histories are suggestive but not decisive on the extent and type of skill changes that occurred during the transition from handicraft to mechanical production, and least conclusive of all for clerical, professional, and managerial occupations. However, the cases do reveal a process much more complex than recognized heretofore. Mechanization undoubtedly had different effects on different occupations in different industries under different market conditions. The effect also varied with type of machines introduced, management policies, type of labor union, class organization, economic structure, and other factors. These contingencies impede the ability to generalize about trends over the past two centuries. Only one finding seems certain: craft workers lost control over the organization of production in the factories, if not control over their own work. Insofar as this loss diminished job complexity, craft workers lost some skill. Whether this was compensated by other skill gains is unknown.

SKILL CHANGES IN INDUSTRIAL SOCIETIES

The inconclusiveness of case studies forces researchers to examine skill changes in the occupational structure as a whole. This enterprise may be undertaken in three ways. First, on the assumption that occupational skills do not change, researchers may examine the changing number of workers in the occupations (graded by skill level) over a period of time to ascertain whether the aggregate changes point to increasing or decreasing skill. Second, researchers may consider individual occupations as units and examine skill changes in them over time. These changes are then aggregated to determine the direction of skill changes. Third, both methods can be combined; compositional changes in the occupations may be examined along with changes in the skills of the occupations. Though the third method is the best, all three methods are fraught with difficulties, not the least of which is that new occupations appear and old ones die. The second and third methods especially depend on the availability of reasonably accurate historical data on occupational complexity.

Unfortunately, adequate occupational census data are not available before 1900 and even current data leave much to be desired. Nonetheless, skill degradation theory holds that skills have declined steadily since the beginning of the industrial revolution. Mechanization, division of labor, and centralization of managerial authority were the devices that owners used to deskill workers until the twentieth century. At that time, the theory holds, scientific management turned ad hoc attacks on skills into a systematic drive. I examine below studies of skill changes in the occupational structure of mature industrial societies.

Skills in Early Industrial Cities

Many scholars assume that skills in early industries societies were higher than in mature industrialism. Although adequate data on the occupational composition of eighteenth and nineteenth century cities are not available, social historians have tried to reconstruct them for some cities. Rancière (1983) believes that historians have overestimated the skills of manual workers in these cities. I located fourteen studies that reconstructed the skills of manual workers in early US and European cities (Form 1980). Artisans and skilled workers comprised from 25% to 54% of the totals, while laborers, servants, and other unskilled workers ranged from 25% to 50%. All of the studies counted male household heads, the most likely to be skilled. But all studies omitted one or more categories in which workers were less likely to be skilled: single males, women in domestic and industrial employment, unpaid family workers, women and children who worked for their room and board, transients, vagabonds, and the unemployed (see Beier 1978, Brown 1977). I estimated that these studies omitted from 15% to 40% of the less skilled. These limited data suggest that manual skills in industrial cities before 1900 probably differed little from those today.

Scientific Management and Skills

According to skill degradation theory, Taylor's (1911) scientific management movement was the decisive social invention that deskilled workers and gave management imperative control over all work. Since the movement's high point coincided with business's largely successful drive to eliminate unions, some scholars claim that Taylorism was a rallying business ideology to justify management's industrial dictatorship in the name of efficiency (Burawoy 1978, Calhoun 1982:202) and to undermine public support for union goals (Montgomery 1976). However, Nelson's (1980) careful study of Taylor holds that workers occupied a small place in his total system. He devoted less attention to time and motion studies and wage systems than to reorganizing managerial planning, the tool room, purchasing and accounting methods, functional supervision, and plant organization. As a program for management centralization, Taylorism threatened the vested interests of lower and middle management more than it did those of labor. Similarly, Littler (1982a) suggests that in Britain workers resisted the Bedeaux system (a form of Taylorism) less than foremen who insisted on "guiding" its application in their departments.

The cumulated studies suggest that Taylorism was implemented in various degrees in different industries, but in no country did it become widespread. Edwards (1979:101) asserts that Taylorism failed to solve the crisis of work control in the United States because most big corporations did not implement it, and where they did, workers fought it to a standsill. In England, Littler (1982a) reports that Taylorism spread to only a few industries that had not been established on a craft basis: beverage, tobacco, chemical, and textile. Taylorism was most successful in nonunionized firms that used mostly low-skilled labor. There it did more to control the pace of work than to dilute workers' skills. In short, though the exact impact of Taylorism on skills is unknown, it probably had only a marginal impact on the substance of skills. More likely, it subjected both workers and middle management to more centralized control, an observation that fits the conclusion of many case studies. Insofar as loss of autonomy reduces overall skill, Taylorism, where applied, must have reduced skills to a degree.

Compositional Skill Changes in Occupations

Some theorists argue that long-term urban occupational trends reveal that industrialization has increased skills by reducing unskilled work and increasing semiskilled, skilled, clerical, technical, professional, and administrative work. Postindustrial theorists (Bell 1973) proclaim that unskilled labor may ultimately disappear and that technical and professional work will predominate. Power theorists reply that census trends are illusory, that the numbers of skilled farmers have declined, clerical workers have become the new unskilled proletariat, the growing service sector is mostly unskilled, professional work and administrative work are losing skill, and rising educational requirements represent blatant credentialism (Braverman 1974:440).

Since all observers face difficulties in interpreting the loss of skills due to the decline in farming, they focus on the urban labor force. Power theorists claim that manual workers were more skilled in 1900 than today and that census figures now contain an upward skill bias. However, prior to 1900 the US Census reported occupational data by trades (shoes, printing, backing) and not by skill level. In 1900, the census shifted to classifying specific occupations by skill level, with the result that numbers of skilled workers were reduced by one-half, from the 1890 to the 1900 census; (Form 1979), contrary to the charge that the Census inflated skills (Hirsch 1978).

Scholars have tried to make occupational censuses comparable since 1900 (US Bureau of the Census 1975). Compositional changes in occupational strata from 1900 to 1980 point to skill upgrading as the pattern. Among manual workers, the unskilled declined, the semiskilled increased substantially, and the skilled increased slightly. Among women, the distribution of manual skills remained almost constant, domestics declined, and service and white-collar workers increased. But female labor force participation grew enormously. If skills did not decline in any occupational strata, the expanding white-collar sector alone would account for skill upgrading in the labor force (Fritscher 1977). Moore (1970) holds that professional, managerial, and administrative work have all become more complex. If true, skill degradation as a trend would depend critically on skill changes in the burgeoning feminized clerical occupations. As with manual workers, case studies of clerical workers tend to point to deskilling (Glenn & Feldberg 1977). But other scholars claim that clerical workers have always done routine work: copying, adding figures, and storing paper. Unless they were family members, few nineteenth-century clerks became business owners and managers (Davies 1974).

Unfortunately, measures of skill change do not go back for more than a few years. On the assumption that occupations do not change in skill, Dubnoff (1978) examined compositional changes (number of workers in each occupation) in US censuses from 1900 to 1970, using 1960 DOT measures of occupational complexity as the base: complexity of handling data, people, and things; general educational demands (GED), and special vocational preparation (SVP). He applied 1960 DOT measures to the 295 most populous occupations of the 559 in each Census and aggregated the increases or decreases in the occupations to obtain an overall skill change index. Summarizing changes in the high and low skill scores in 1900 and 1970, Dubnoff found compositional downskilling, particularly for women in lower skilled clerical occupations that deal primarily with data and people. Slight downgrading also appeared in manual occupations that deal primarily with things. SVP went down while GED went up.

Observing that Dubnoff's conclusions were based on visual inspection of complex cross-classifications of data that are hard to trace, Spenner (1982) reanalyzed Dubnoff's data with log-linear strategy for each Census from 1900 to 1970. Analyzing each DOT skill indicator separately as a multicontingency table, the association by year, gender, occupational sector (manual vs non-manual), and skill, Spenner found that the dominant pattern of association was unrelated to compositional shifts by year. Rather, the association of skill level with gender and skill with occupational sector accounted for over 90% of the total skill association in all tables but one. Using five central indicators of skill level, he found no systematic evidence for a net compositional upgrading or downgrading for the United States for the period from 1900 to 1970. In short, apart from the dubious assumptions that occupations do not change in complexity and that 53% of the occupations represent the entire structure, Spenner demonstrated that we cannot accept any extant hypothesis about skill change.

Skill Changes in Individual Occupations

Spenner (1983) also completed the most comprehensive review of research on changes in the substantive complexity of the individual occupations in the US occupational structure. Eleven studies used direct measures of occupational skill. All together, the studies used 27 national data sets, including 16 census reports, 8 surveys, and 3 studies of the DOT. Seven studies used DOT skill measures that, despite imperfections, have sufficient construct validity to reflect skill changes (Parcel & Benefo 1987). Four investigations used self-reports of skill changes. Collectively, the studies covered a 40-year period, but the mode of the periods studied was about a decade. Six studies reported small occupational skill upgrading, four found mixed changes that cancelled each other, and one, which used percentage in supervisory occupations as a skill measure, found downgrading. The most careful of these studies (Spenner 1979) found that, even after all sources of error were considered, there was either no aggregate change or a slight upgrading of skills over a 12 year period.

The most comprehensive national survey (Mueller 1969) of individual self-reports of skill changes that occurred over a five-year period found skill upgrading both for workers who did not change jobs and workers who did. In short, despite Spenner's cautious conclusion that other dimensions of skill should also be investigated (especially autonomy), these studies of change in the complexity of all occupations cast serious doubt on the skill degradation hypothesis and any hypothesis of skill change.

SKILLS IN THE AGE OF AUTOMATION

While previous studies dealt with skill changes in the mechanization era, automation, a different form of technology, could affect skills differently.

Automation's distinctive feature is the use of electronic information feedback to operate equipment. When automation first appeared in the 1950s, many feared that it would cause even greater unemployment and deskilling than mechanization. Sustained prosperity temporarily allayed these fears; scores of studies reported skill upgrading effects (Wolfbein 1962). Changing economic conditions and further case studies spawned four theories on automation's effects. First, Blauner (1964) proposed a U theory: Mechanization caused deskilling whereas automation reverses that trend. Second, Braverman (1974) popularized Bright's (1966) "hump" theory: Automation first upgrades skills and then it accelerates the historic deskilling trend. Third, some writers (Danziger 1985) proposed a polarizing trend: Automation upgrades skilled jobs and downgrades the others. Fourth, Simpson (1985) summarized a contingency theory: Automation's effects are contingent on type of industry, occupation, market, and other factors. These four theories were also applied to automation's impact on worker autonomy.

Despite hundreds of automation studies, no one has tested all four hypotheses for major occupational and industrial groups. Unfortunately, one cannot aggregate the case studies to produce generalizations. For example, Bright's hump pattern seemed to apply to clerks: Most studies of early office automations found mildly positive effects (Hardin et al 1965, Shepard 1971), while recent studies found deskilling and proletarianization (Glenn & Feldberg 1977). But Attewell (1987) warned against premature conclusions: Most case studies have covered brief time periods, selected the most routine jobs for study, and ignored national surveys.

Perhaps because Braverman (1974) found that the application of numerical control (NC) technology to complex machining operations degraded machinists' skills, a stream of researchers have studied NC operations. Although Zicklin (1984) showed that Braverman systematically avoided contrary evidence, Noble's (1978) highly detailed case studies confirmed Braverman's contention that management makes a social and not an economic choice in designing NC systems in order to deskill machinists and break their monopoly of knowledge and control over production. But other case studies (Sabel 1982, Penn 1984) concluded that skill upgrading may be the norm. Jones' (1982) research convincingly supports contingency theory. In his study of several NC plants that varied in size, type of industry, innovation strategy, union and management structure, he concluded that though all these factors play a role, type of industry and type of production were critical. Deskilling occurred only in large-scale batch production industries. Nothing inherent about NC machines or the law of capitalistic exploitation forced a uniform response to automation.

Recently, researchers have studied "high tech" industries, where most employees work with automated equipment, to learn whether automation's effects are distinctive there. These industries vary so much in size, equipment, product or service, occupational structure, and internal organization that generalizing about them may be as dangerous as it is for mechanical industries. Patterns vary widely by industry. Thus, automation destroyed old skills in publishing without creating comparable new ones (Wallace & Kalleberg 1982). In an information processing enterprise that provided patent and chemical information to professional clients, automation produced a one-machine industry. All workers, from professional chemists to clerks, worked with virtually the same desktop computers. Their responses to it had almost nothing to do with the computer's capability as a machine; rather, workers differed in the complexity of instructions that they fed the computers that, in turn, depended heavily on their educational level. While the computer enabled more intensive monitoring of simple jobs, it had no effect on traditional professional autonomy. In high-risk automated industries like atomic power, Hirschhorn (1984) reported that skill enlargement (workers learn more overlapping jobs) had to occur for all workers in order to reduce accident risk. In a study of 22 high-tech firms, Hodson (1985) found that skill disruption rather than skill up- or downgrading was the norm. Automation required that workers abandon old skills and learn new ones. Despite painful crises in organizational and work commitment, workers experienced a heightened sense of craft in response to demands for high quality work. Finally, Sullivan & Cornfield's (1979) analysis of Census findings disputed the claim that high-tech industries polarize skills. The limited national evidence points to upgrading.

In short, current research shows a bewildering variety of skill changes in high-tech industries. The case studies of automation seem to have the same liabilities as those of mechanical industries: They cover short periods, and they are not representative of industries, their occupations, technology, economic situation, and other relevant variables. The findings are not additive because replications are infrequent and studies neglect variables that may affect skill changes.

CONCLUSION

Skill degradation theory found most support in early case studies of dying crafts. Later historical research into a wider set of occupations demonstrated that these early findings could not be generalized. Still later studies of all occupations in the labor force pointed to little or no aggregate skill change. Increasingly, research has shown that skill changes depend on type of technology, industrial organization, product and labor markets, labor union strength, business power, and many other factors. But a list of contingencies does not comprise a coherent theory. Social science research has made little progress beyond disproving that single factor explanations (technology, capitalist avarice, the free market) explain skill changes or beyond listing of possible factors that do. Clearly, no current theory can explain skill change in all stages of development in any industrial society. This suggests that for at least the present, our theories must be more historically specific and more sociological.

Because skills are embedded in a network of socially organized occupations, skill change should be studied as a result of on-going bargaining among occupations. Even in highly stratified work organizations, occupations struggle to divide skill, authority, earnings, work control, status, and privileges. It is naive to assume that all occupations place highest priority on preserving or increasing skills. Trade-offs among valued goods always occur. Therefore, research should examine how skill changes among interacting occupations accompany changes in the distribution of earnings, work control, profits, unemployment, and other valued goods. Perhaps the unit of observation should not be individual occupations but clusters of interdependent occupations that appear in different types of work organizations. Some labor union contracts, for example, contain data on the distribution of valued goods. An historical analysis of contracts might provide cues about how the distribution of skills and valued goods change in different industries and countries.

ACKNOWLEDGMENTS

I am grateful to Joan Huber for suggestions that improved the manuscript and to Michael Wallace, Toby Parcel, and Robert Kaufman for hearing me out and giving me sage advice, even though I did not always follow it.

Literature Cited

Aronowitz, S. 1973. *False Promises.* New York: McGraw-Hill
Attewell, P. 1987. The deskilling controversy. *Work Occup.* In press
Baron, N. J., Bielby, W. T. 1982. Workers and machines. *Am. Sociol. Rev.* 47:175–88
Bauman, Z. 1972. *Between Class and Elite.* Manchester: Manchester Univ. Press
Beier, A. L. 1978. Social problems in Elizabethan London. *J. Interdisciplinary Hist.* 9:203–21
Bell, D. 1973. *The Coming of Post-Industrial Society.* New York: Basic Books
Bielby, W. T., Kalleberg, A. L. 1977. *Structure of occupational inequality.* Unpubl. ms. Madison: Univ. Wisc.
Blauner, R. 1964. *Alienation and Freedom,* Chicago: Univ. Chicago Press
Braverman, H. 1974. *Labor and Monopoly Capital.* New York: Monthly Rev.
Bright, J. R. 1966. Increasing automation and skill requirements. *Technology and the American Economy.* Washington: USGPO
Brown, H. P. 1977. *Inequality of Pay.* Berkeley: Univ. Calif. Press

Burawoy, M. 1978. Toward a Marxist theory of the labor process: Braverman and beyond. *Polit. Soc.* 8:247–312
Calhoun, C. 1982. *The Question of Class Struggle.* Chicago: Univ. Chicago Press
Clawson, D. 1980. *Bureaucracy and the Labor Process.* New York: Monthly Rev.
Collins, R. 1979. *The Credential Society.* New York: Academic
Danziger, J. N. 1985. Social science and the impact of computer technology. *Soc. Sci. Q.* 66:3–21
Darnton, R. 1984. *The Great Cat Massacre.* New York: Basic Books
Davies, M. 1974. Women's place is at the typewriter. *Radical Am.* 8:1–28
Dobson, C. R. 1980. *Masters and Journeymen: A Prehistory of Industrial Relations: 1717–1800.* New York: Rowman & Littlefield
Dubnoff, S. 1978. *Inter-occupational shifts and changes in the American economy.* Unpubl. ms. Ann Arbor, Mich: Inst. Soc. Res.
Durkheim, E. 1964 (1893). *Division of Labor in Society.* Glencoe, Ill: Free Press

Edwards, R. 1979. *Contested Terrain.* New York: Basic Books

Foner, S. P. 1976. *Labor and the American Revolution.* Westport, Conn: Greenwood

Form, W. 1974. Review of *Work in America.* US HEW Task Force. In *Am. J. Sociol* 79:1550–2

Form, W. 1976. Conflict within the working class. In *Uses of Controversy in Sociology,* ed. L. A. Coser, O. N. Larson, pp. 51–73. New York: Free Press

Form, W. 1979. Comparative industrial sociology and the convergence hypothesis. *Ann. Rev. Sociol.* 5:1–25

Form, W. 1980. Resolving ideological issues on the division of labor. In *Sociological Theory and Research,* ed. H. M. Blalock. New York: Free Press

Form, W. 1986. *Divided We Stand.* Urbana, Ill: Univ. Ill. Press

Form, W., Pampel, F. C. 1978. Stratification and the development of urban labor markets. *Soc. Forc.* 57:119–35

Freifeld, M. 1984. *Corporate authority and artisan technology in the steel industry: Development of labor process and training, 1865–1940.* Unpublished ms. Univ. Calif., San Diego

Freifeld, M. 1986. Technological change and the 'self-acting' mule: A study of skill and sexual division of labor. *Soc. Hist.* 11:000

Fritschner, L. M. 1977. Women's work and women's education. *Work Occup.* 4:209–34

Glenn, E. N., Feldberg, R. L. 1977. Degraded and deskilled: The proletarianization of clerical work. *Soc. Probl.* 5:52–64

Hall, K., Miller, I. 1975. *Retraining and Tradition: The Skilled Worker in an Era of Change.* London: Allen & Unwin

Hamilton, R. F., Wright, J. D. 1986. *The State of the Masses.* New York: Aldine

Hanagan, M. P. 1977. The logic of solidarity. *J. Urban Hist.* 21:560–77

Hardin, E., Shepard, J. M., Spier, M. S. 1965. *Economic and Social Implications of Automation.* E. Lansing, Mich: Mich. State Univ. Press

Hirsch, S. E. 1978. *Roots of the American Working Class: Crafts in Newark, 1800–1860.* Philadelphia: Univ. Penn. Press

Hirschhorn, L. 1984. *Beyond Mechanization.* Cambridge, Mass: MIT Press

Hobsbawm, E. J. 1964. The labor aristocracy in the nineteenth century. In *Laboring Men,* ed. E. J. Hobsbawm, pp. 272–316. New York: Basic Books

Hodson, R. 1985. Working in high-tech. *Sociol. Q.* 26:351–64

Jackson, R. M. 1984. *The Formation of Crafts Markets.* New York: Academic Press

Johnson, T. 1980. Work and power. In *The Politics of Work and Occupations,* ed. G.

Esland, G. Salaman, pp. 335–71. Toronto: Univ. Toronto Press

Jones, B. 1982. Destruction or redistribution of engineering skills. In *The Degradation of Labor?,* ed. S. Wood, pp. 179–200. London: Hutchison

Kemper, T. 1972. The division of labor: a post-Durkheimian view. *Am. Sociol. Rev.* 37:739–53

Kohn, M. L., Schooler, C. 1983. *Work and Personality.* Norwood, NJ: Ablex

Krause, E. 1982. *Division of Labor.* Westport, Conn: Greenwood

Lindert, P. H., Williamson, J. C. 1977. Three centuries of American inequalitiy. In *Res. Econ. Hist.* 1:69–223

Littler, C. R. 1982a. Deskilling and changing structures of control. In *The Degradation of Labor?,* ed. S. Wood, pp. 122–45. London: Hutchison

Littler, C. R. 1982b. *The Development of the Labor Process in Capitalist Societies.* Exeter, NH: Heinemann

Marglin, S. 1974. What do bosses do? *Rev. Radical Econ.* 6:60–112

Miller, A. R., Treiman, D. J., Cain, P. S., Ross, A. 1980. *Work, Jobs, and Occupations.* Washington, DC: Natl. Acad.

Mills, C. W. 1951. *White Collar.* New York: Oxford

Montgomery, D. 1976. Worker's control of machine production in the nineteenth century. *Labor Hist.* 7:485–509

Moore, W. E. 1970. *The Professions.* New York: Russell Sage

More, C. 1980. *Skill and the English Working Class: 1870–1914.* London: Croom Helm

Mueller, E. 1969. *Technological Advance in an Expanding Economy.* Ann Arbor, Mich: Braun-Brumfield

Nelson, D. 1980. *Frederick W. Taylor and the Rise of Scientific Management.* Madison: Univ. Wisconsin Press

Noble, D. F. 1978. *Social Choice in Machine Design.* New York: Monthly Rev.

Parcel, T., Benefo, K. 1987. Temporal changes in occupational differentiation. *Work and Occup.* In print

Penn, R. 1982. Skilled manual workers in the labour process: 1856–1964. In *The Degradation of Labor?,* ed. S. Wood, pp. 90–108. London: Hutchison

Penn, R. 1984. *Technological Change, Skilled Manual Work, and the Division of Labor.* Lancaster: Lancaster Univ. Press

Penn, R. 1985. *Skilled Workers in the Class Structure.* Cambridge: Cambridge Univ. Press

Ranciere, J. 1983. The myth of the artisan. *Int. Labor Working Class Hist.* 24:1–16

Roomkin, M., Sommers, G. G. 1974. The wage benefits of alternative sources of skill development. *Ind. Labor Relat. Rev.* 27:228–41

Sabel, C. F. 1982. *Work and Politics.* Cambridge: Cambridge Univ. Press

Sadler, P. 1970. Sociological aspects of skill. *Br. J. Indust. Relat.* 8:22–31

Shepard, J. M. 1971. *Automation and Alienation.* Cambridge, Mass: MIT Press

Simpson, R. L. 1985. Social control of occupations and work. *Ann. Rev. Sociol.* 11:515–36

Smith, D. L., Snow, R. E. 1976. The division of labor: Conceptual and methological issues. *Soc. Forc.* 55:520–28

Spaeth, J. L. 1985. Job power and earnings. *Am. Sociol. Rev.* 50:603–17

Spenner, K. I. 1979. Temporal changes in work content. *Am. Sociol. Rev.* 44:968–75

Spenner, K. I. 1980. Occupational characteristics and classification systems of the DOT in research. *Sociol. Methods Res.* 9:239–64

Spenner, K. I. 1982. *Temporal changes in the skill levels of work: Method and comparison.* Unpubl. ms. Duke Univ., Durham, NC

Spenner, K. I. 1983. Deciphering Prometheus: Temporal changes in work. *Am. Sociol. Rev.* 48:824–37

Spenner, K. I. 1986. *Occupations, work settings and adult development.* Unpubl. ms. Duke Univ., Durham, NC

Steiger, T. L. 1985. *Ideologies of skill in the division of labor.* Unpubl. ms. Univ. Ill., Urbana, Ill.

Stone, K. 1974. The origin of job structures in the steel industry. *Rev. Radical Polit. Econ.* 6:113–73

Sullivan, T. A., Cornfield, D. B. 1979. Downgrading computer workers. *Work Occup.* 6:184–203

Taylor, F. W. 1911. *Principles of Scientific Management.* New York: Harper

Tilly, C. 1978. *From Mobilization to Revolution.* Reading, Mass: Addison-Wesley

US Bureau of the Census. 1975. *Historical Statistics of the U.S.: Colonial Times to 1970.* Washington, DC: USGPO

US HEW. 1973. *Work in America.* Cambridge, Mass: MIT Press

Veblen, T. 1914. *The Instinct of Workmanship.* New York: Viking

Veblen, T. 1921. *The Engineers and the Price System,* New York: Viking

Veblen, T. 1923. *Absentee Ownership.* New York: Huebsch

Walker, C. R., Guest, R. H. 1952. *Man on the Assembly Line.* Cambridge, Mass: Harvard Univ. Press

Wallace, M., Kalleberg, A. L. 1982. Industrial transformation and the decline of crafts. *Am. Sociol. Rev.* 47:307–24

Wolfbein, S. L. 1962. Automation and skill. *Ann. Am. Acad. Polit. Soc. Sci.* 340:53–9

Zicklin, G. 1984. *Braverman and deskilling: NC operators.* Unpubl. manuscript. Montclair State Coll., Montclair, NJ

Zimbalist, A., ed. 1979. *Case Studies on the Labor Process.* New York: Monthly Rev.

Ann. Rev. Sociol. 1987. 13:49–66

NETWORK APPROACHES TO SOCIAL EVALUATION

C. David Gartrell

Department of Sociology, University of Victoria, Victoria, British Columbia V8W 2Y2 Canada

Abstract

Social evaluation—the way that people learn about themselves by comparing themselves with others—is a prosaic, age-old process. Periodic efforts have been made to integrate theories and empirical studies of reference groups, social comparison, equity and justice, and relative deprivation (e.g. Pettigrew 1967). Despite these efforts, research has remained fragmented and continues to be dominated by psychologists. Network imagery, models, and findings run through this literature as far back as the last century and play a central role in contemporary applications of social evaluation to research on social support, class consciousness, and the diffusion of innovations. I argue that the network approach will help to resolve fundamental, unanswered questions about social evaluation first raised in 1950 by Merton and Rossi— specifically, the *origins* of comparative frameworks and the relation between individual and categorical or group reference points. Such an approach provides an integrative focus for sociological research in this area.

INTRODUCTION

The central tenets of "social evaluation"—that "human beings learn about themselves by comparing themselves to others . . . [and that] the process of social evaluation leads to positive, neutral, or negative self-ratings that are relative to the standards set by the individuals employed for comparison" (Pettigrew 1967:243)—are at least as old as written history (see, e.g. Matthew 20:1–24). The idea that networks of interpersonal relations shape social evaluation (SE hereafter) has sociological roots stretching back into the last century. For example, Marx (1963) and Mead (1934) each observed that SE

49

processes as diverse as the formation of class consciousness and the development of self-conception occur in the context of relationships within individuals' social circles. Over the past 40 years, network effects have peppered the various lines of research that make up the SE landscape, including reference groups, relative deprivation, equity, and social comparison. These subspecialties share a number of specific research questions, such as who are the people chosen as comparative reference points and on which attributes are they compared; how are evaluations made, given a comparative framework; and what outcomes follow such evaluation.

The network initiatives I review in the first section of this paper define the comparative framework within which SE occurs and suggest how network characteristics affect SE processes. In the second section, I examine application of these ideas in three diverse realms—class consciousness, social support, and the diffusion of innovations. In the last section I turn to the thorny problem of how networks contribute to explaining social evaluation processes, and I suggest some directions for future work in this area.

NETWORKS AND SOCIAL EVALUATION

As I use the term here, network analysis refers to a body of social science approaches that explain social behavior and patterns by analyzing *relations* among concrete social entities—e.g. persons, groups, and organizations (recent reviews include Wellman 1983, Marsden & Lauman 1984). As a matter of convenience my review of networks and SE proceeds through each SE subspecialty, although it becomes clear that there are many points of intersection and opportunities for integration. Attention is focused primarily on interpersonal and intergroup relations.

Reference Groups

Reviewing the preceding 25 years of empirical and theoretical work on reference groups Hyman & Singer note that "if the groups to which individuals refer themselves . . . are empirically determined, knowledge and prediction of attitude, self-evaluation, and conduct will be enhanced . . . Such is the hope of reference group theory and research and the basis of its attractiveness to social scientists" (1968:3–4).

Network imagery runs through many of the earliest studies of both the "normative" and "comparative" functions of reference groups (Kelley 1952; for a review, see Singer 1981:72–81). Hyman, who first coined the term "reference group," observed as early as 1942 that personal contacts provide more meaningful referents than broad social aggregates (1942:24; see also Stern & Keller 1953; Shibutani 1955). Perhaps the clearest statement of the significance of interpersonal networks as a source of reference-group standards comes from the pathbreaking analysis of Merton and Rossi (Merton & Kitt 1950) who point to the need for cumulative research on " . . . *the relative effectiveness of frames of reference yielded by associates and by more general status categories*" (1950:66).

More recent studies of reference groups have measured network characteristics more directly. For instance, Newcomb's (1943, 1967) studies of Bennington students suggest a developing awareness of the importance of reference-group theory and assess the role of friendship networks in promoting convergence of norms and attitudes. Studies drawing on longitudinal data have established that friendship both induces common norms and behaviors and is influenced in turn by selection on the basis of similarity of attitudes (Kandel 1978, Cohen 1977, Walsh et al 1976).

Two leading network researchers have examined the implications of formal models of network structure for reference group processes. Erickson suggests that "one can predict attitude agreement by predicting patterns of social comparison which in turn derive from patterns of social relationships" (1982:164). Clique models stress that interaction leads to comparison, influence, and similarity. For example, Festinger et al (1950) found that students occupying sets of dwellings grouped in a court who rated each other as friends were more likely to express similar attitudes than were those who belonged to courts where friendship networks were less dense (1950:91). Models of "structural equivalence" such as blockmodels add the possibility of considering reference points shared by actors who may otherwise not be in contact. Structurally equivalent actors have similar attitudes because they tend to interact with the same types of people in similar ways (Erickson 1983:21)[1]. Attitude similarity is further enhanced if ties connect structurally equivalent actors so that they come to agree on appropriate referents. Erickson calls for a comparison of these models' predictions, noting that such tests would be not only informative about which aspects of network structure affect attitudes but also suggestive of how social comparison works in real-life networks.

Burt (1982) provides such a test in a study of the orientations to professional journals of the elite among sociological methodologists. The data favor a structural equivalence or "positional" model, suggesting that scientists put themselves in the position of those of their colleagues within an invisible college whom they perceive to be structural peers. This helps them to imagine the evaluations of these colleagues (1982:226). This interpretation of normative reference group effects as imaginative "role taking" relates to the work of Mead (1934) and more recently, of Turner (1956).

---

[1]Discussions and applications of "structural equivalence" may be found in White et al (1976), Light & Mullins (1979), Burt (1982).

Relative Deprivation

Relative deprivation or gratification occurs "when an individual or class of individuals feels deprived in comparison to relevant reference groups and individuals. Thus, comparisons with a nondeprived referent lead to high expectations that if unfulfilled lead in turn to severe feelings of deprivation and unfairness" (Pettigrew 1978:32). Much of the impetus for contemporary developments came from *The American Soldier* by Stouffer et al (1949), who found relative deprivation among groups of US servicemen in World War II. Despite Merton and Rossi's clarion call for research on the comparative significance of networks and impersonal social categories, subsequent developments in this field have largely bypassed this distinction. In part this seems to be due to the fact that reference group theory became "well known by name if not by content" (Burt 1982:191). The *groups* and *categories* of *The American Soldier* (e.g. air corps–military police, married-unmarried, black-white) are remembered, not the interpersonal contacts from which they arose—the careful review of both types of reference points by Merton and Rossi notwithstanding. Research on relative deprivation proceeded on the basis of ready-made, categorical, comparative frameworks. For instance, Davis's (1959) formal theory of relative deprivation outlines a method of predicting proportions of persons in a system who will experience relative deprivation or gratification, on the assumption that the system is divided into deprived and nondeprived *groups*. Runciman observed that individual referents are embedded in social networks (1966:229), and he developed the egoistic-fraternalistic distinction. The research based on this distinction has removed the question of the relative salience of egoistic and fraternalistic comparisons from the network context in which it was first raised by Merton and Rossi. The spheres in which fraternal relative deprivation most successfully predicts social action—racial unrest, voting, and political protest— usually contain dichotomous, reciprocally paired social groupings in conflict that define comparative boundaries (Pettigrew 1978:36). How aggregate comparisons are related to primary social experiences is not considered.

On the other hand, theoretical developments in "egoistic" relative deprivation focus on intraindividual psychological conditions that precede the experience of relative deprivation in a way that extracts individuals from the moorings of ongoing social relationships (Crosby 1976, 1982). Sophisticated typologies of individual and aggregate comparisons have been devised (Walker & Pettigrew 1984), and theoretical progress has been made in defining the determinants of egoistic or fraternalistic relative deprivation, such as distributions of resources within and between groups (Martin 1981; Williams 1975:368). But the relevant individuals and groups are assumed already to populate the social landscape. To learn *how* they become salient—the issue raised by Merton and Rossi—requires, as I will argue in the concluding section, recognition that individuals associate in networks and that categorical imagery is generated in part as a result of these contacts.

Burt's application of his formal model of interests in network structures to relative deprivation phenomena is a significant departure from the tendency to uproot actors from social networks (1982: 191–98). The model can be applied to situations in which an actor experiences deprivation because a structurally equivalent alter increases his/her resource control, or it may be because the actor's position changes from one occupied by persons with lower resource control than the actor to one occupied by persons with greater resource control (1982: 194–5). Burt illustrates how the model explains empirical results from *The American Soldier,* and he argues that his formulation has the advantage of specifying a precise functional form for relative deprivation effects that links relative deprivation to a general perceptual model—Stevens' psychophysical laws—with wide application in such areas as the perception of prestige (1982: 175).

Equity and Distributive Justice

All of the major theoretical formulations of distributive justice emphasize that justice is evaluated relationally: people compare their own outcomes and inputs with those of other persons or groups (e.g. Adams 1965, Walster et al 1978, Berger et al 1972). Despite this relational property, empirical research has treated justice sentiments as individual attributes to be cumulated into distributions, whether in experimental studies or in surveys (for a review see Gartrell 1985). The sole formal treatment of collective justice sentiments is distributional rather than relational (Jasso 1980).

The relational nature of justice evaluations is important in internal labor market theory dealing with the treatment of wage determination (Gartrell 1979). Wage comparisons and justice evaluations among people in positions in a wage structure have been likened to a web of interdependence such that wage changes in one position may create ripple effects throughout the system (Doeringer & Piore 1971). Developing relational models to represent complex patterns of justice sentiments in wage structures and investigating the causes and consequences of these patterns are important for future network approaches in this area (Gartrell 1987).

Equity in networks raises the question of "generalized exchange" (Cook 1982, Kadushin 1981)—giving without expectation of direct return. Without abandoning the insights equity theory offers about dyadic exchange, Kadushin (1981) considers broader aspects of culture and social systems—especially trust—that must be present for such exchanges to work. Galaskiewicz's (1982) relational analysis of corporate philanthropy can be seen as an example of generalized exchange if one first accepts that corporations expect some indirect reciprocation in rewards other than money (e.g. prestige). Further development of this line of research within the "exchange-dependency" tradition seems promising since these researchers are able to manipulate directly key network properties such as size and visibility that in all likelihood affect trust (Cook 1982).

Social Comparison

Perhaps the best supported theory of comparison choices is Festinger's (1954) "social comparison" theory, although with a few notable exceptions (e.g. Martin 1981), tests of the theory have been restricted to laboratory settings (Latane 1966, Suls & Miller 1977). In his landmark review of SE research, Pettigrew observes that "work on the theory . . . has generally not considered the larger social context in which the social comparison process operates" (1967:248). In the same vein, Williams notes that "the experimental work . . . dealt with individuals—not with enduring collectivities, groups, or statuses" (1975:358). The same issues are raised in recent evaluations of social comparison theory by social psychologists (Suls & Miller 1977).

An ongoing program of research by Nosanchuk & Erickson takes the study of social comparison into the real world of a network of contract bridge players (1985). This research not only adds realism to the study of comparison processes but also addresses the question of how choices are made *given* the comparative framework of an established network of relations among actors.

APPLICATIONS

Subjective Social Class

As Wright has pointed out, Marx's theoretical expectation of class consciousness focused on the polarities of the bourgeoisie and proletariat, and it is complicated by his actual descriptions of a plethora of class fractions (Wright 1983:4). The nature of contemporary class structures continues to be a matter of debate among neo-Marxists and others (for reviews see Wright 1983, Jackman & Jackman 1983). This diverse array of class definitions is matched by an equally diverse and occasionally contradictory stream of literature on class consciousness. For instance, in a recent review Marshall (1983) identifies four distinct depictions of workers' conceptions of class, each with a substantial range of findings to support it.

Network effects emerge throughout this somewhat confusing and contradictory stream of literature. It has been widely conjectured that direct social relations with persons of diverse class, status, and power positions generate implicit models of social class (Bott 1957:165; Inkeles 1960–1961:2; Lockwood 1966:249). Yet evidence for this conjecture has been less than uniform. For instance, Wright's comparative cross-national study of class and class consciousness demonstrates that class locations based on exploitation relations and operationalized in part with ego-centered network data have corresponding class identifications and attitudes (Wright 1982a,b, 1983, 1984). On the other hand, Jackman & Jackman (1983:190) find little support, among a national probability sample of US adults, for the importance of network contacts in the formation of class identification.

Case studies of workers' consciousness in "occupational communities" further qualify the conjecture that everyday experiences of power and prestige in social networks are mapped directly into class imagery.[2] Occupational communities develop where workers in particular occupations are isolated physically or temporally by their work from the rest of society. Thus isolated, workers' workplace associations spill over into leisure time so that the occupational group "is the reference group; its standards of behavior, its system of status and rank, guide conduct" (Blauner 1960:351). While tightly knit social relations among workers might be expected to engender proletarian consciousness (Lockwood 1966), other characteristics of social networks in these communities shape the development of class consciousness so that an oppositional, "two-valued power model" often is not realized. For instance, friendship networks that encircle both workers and managers are characteristic of Canadian single-industry communities (Lucas 1971). These cross-class networks develop as managers who have been promoted from the rank-and-file remain friends with former workmates. Moreover, the geographical isolation of these communities limits the range of non-work foci for workers and managers alike: Thus, "it is pretty hard to be enemies with someone you fish with, golf with and go to church with" (Lucas 1971:141). Similarly, work organized on the basis of cooperative relations and interdependent outcomes appears to defuse an oppositional, "us-them" consciousness (Lummis 1977). Other social forces may divide one or another class against itself. For instance, apprenticeship and other social relations that tie British shipbuilding workers to particular occupational groups help to fragment proletarian consciousness along the lines of occupational interests and identities (Brown & Brannen 1970). These studies demonstrate that the form and content of social networks in the workplace have a substantial impact on workers' consciousness.

In addition to providing the primary experiences on which class imagery is based, network contacts also serve as channels for the diffusion of a wide range of customs, values, attitudes, standards, and the like. Occupational communities often are characterized by norms of "localism" that distinguish insiders—both workers and management—from outsiders (Lucas 1971, Lummis 1977, Brown & Brannen 1970, Walker 1950). Similarly, studies of

[2]This discussion draws heavily on a review of the literature on working class communities and consciousness by Tanner (1985).

"aristocratic" or "affluent" workers in the United States (Mackenzie 1973) and England (Goldthorpe et al 1969) illustrate the impact of workplace and community social networks on a wide range of reference group standards.

Yet such interpersonal processes may not elevate class consciousness beyond a parochial awareness of opposition or solidarity (Bott 1957, Parkin 1971, Westergaard 1975). Social institutions that promote class-based models of society have a significant impact on class awareness, in part by making available an acceptable language in which class interests can be articulated (Emmison 1985). Among such institutions, trade unions and political parties have notable effects (e.g. Johnston & Ornstein 1982, Lash 1984, Ogmundson & Ng 1982, Archer 1985, Wright 1984, Scase 1974). From a SE point of view one could argue that if trade unions and political parties constitute significant foci in people's lives (Feld 1981), their network affiliations become organized around them and other members become an important source of normative standards.

Social Support

It is generally accepted that reactions to stressors and corresponding health outcomes can be mediated by social relationships and that social comparisons with other persons in these networks are a central element of the support process (e.g. Gottlieb 1983a,b; Shumaker & Brownell 1984; Whittaker & Garbarino 1983; Thoits 1983, 1984, 1985; Hall & Wellman 1985; Pancoast et al 1983).

Comparisons with others in one's social network can have both beneficial and harmful effects. On the positive side, supportive peers who were also exposed to a similar stressor on previous occasions may convey reassurance "through a covert process of social comparison or through an overt discussion of the event's significance for personal well-being" (Gottlieb 1983c:281; see also Thoits 1985). Cognitively, actors avoid blaming themselves by seeking "consensus" information that others have reacted in similar ways to similar circumstances (Gottlieb 1983c, 1985b; Fiske & Taylor 1984). Such persons also provide the most effective models for "vicariously learning" how to respond to a stressor, a process that implicitly involves social comparison (Kunkel & Nagasawa 1973).

Community psychologists have applied these insights in efforts to *create* social networks that optimize the comparative process. Members of "self help" groups provide similar reference points and models and a shared "perspective" on a common problem, to use Shibutani's term (Richardson 1983:210, Deneke 1983:140, Bakker & Karel 1983:164). Yet exposure to others can be maladaptive, and this raises the general question of how to structure interpersonal contacts in lay helping networks to avoid dysfunctional comparisons (Gottlieb 1985a:27–30). Research on arthritis (Gross & Brandt

1981, Potts & Brandt 1982) and mastectomy patients (Taylor 1983) suggests the ways in which patients' self-enhancement and information-seeking motives direct their comparisons. Yet research on this issue is still in the formative stages (Gottlieb 1985a:30).

Most of the prevailing definitions of "social support" stress the supportive nature of *ongoing* transactions in social networks. For instance, Caplan's benchmark formulation defines support systems as " . . . continuing social aggregates that provide individuals with opportunities for feedback about themselves and for validations for their expectations about others . . ." (Caplan 1974:4). These social aggregates provide normative standards associated with reference groups (Caplan 1974:5–6). Thoits' work also underlines the supportive impact of evaluations generated in ongoing social interactions with others (1983, 1984, 1985). Typically the networks involved are organized around roles, and "identities are claimed and sustained in reciprocal role relationships" (1983:175).

Ongoing relationships in naturally occurring social networks can also produce dysfunctional comparison processes. Schizophrenia has been associated with a lack of consistent, socializing feedback from networks (Hammer et al 1978, D'Augelli 1983). Wilcox (1983) reports that among divorced women dense networks are maladaptive due to their high concentration of family members, who tend to be more judgmental than nonkin (1983:108). Hirsch (1983) reports similar findings among a sample of recent younger widows and mature women (over age 30) returning to college. These findings should reinforce the view that the terms "support" and "network" are not logically equivalent (Hall & Wellman 1985, D'Augelli 1983).

Social support often is defined in terms of exchanges marked by a concern for equity or "fair exchange" (Gottlieb 1983c, 1985b; Hooyman 1983; Shumaker & Brownell 1984; Tietjen 1985). On the other hand, studies of transactions in urban social networks (e.g. Wellman 1982) suggest that in general people tolerate substantial imbalance in helping relationships. Although some have conjectured that nonreciprocated, "generalized" exchange may be specific to relationships with close kin (Gottlieb 1985b, Shumaker & Brownell 1984), such exchanges appear to go considerably beyond the bounds of the family (Wellman 1982, Deutsch 1985). Future research could profitably link these issues with the emerging network interest in generalized exchange (e.g. Cook 1982, Kadushin 1981, Galaskiewicz 1982).

Diffusion of Innovations

Social comparison is at the heart of the innovation-decision process (Rogers 1983:166, 170). For instance, Coleman et al (1966) discovered that when doctors were confronted with making a decision about a new drug in an ambiguous situation, those who were in close interaction with their colleagues interpreted for one another the new stimulus and arrived at a shared way of looking at it (1966:118–19). The network context is important since its morphological and interactional characteristics determine the rate at which the innovation spreads (Rogers 1983:293).

Normative reference group processes influence the timing of innovation. Those who are well integrated into a social system's networks are early to adopt innovations that are normatively consistent and so become "opinion leaders"; those who are marginal or on the network's periphery are more likely to innovate with respect to nonnormative innovations (for reviews see Rogers 1983:ch. 8; Granovetter 1973:1366–68; Burt 1982:198–201). Presumably, opinion leaders care about others' evaluations of their attitudes and behavior while marginal individuals are less concerned about these reference standards. While weak ties play an important role in the diffusion of new ideas and behaviors across social structure (Granovetter 1973), the reference group processes that produce a common group attitude—interaction, social comparison, and influence (Erickson 1982)—more likely entail strong ties than weak (Burt 1982:201; Rogers 1983:299).

Burt has argued that innovation decisions can be conceptualized within his general model of interests in network structures (1982:205). This conceptualization explains why marginal actors are nonnormatively innovative (i.e. they are structurally unique and innovate for personal reasons). It also shows that since structural uniqueness may occur at points in a network other than on the periphery, *any* structurally unique actor is as likely to show the same lack of concern with norms as do those who occupy marginal positions (1982:205–10).

Although he is not identified with either tradition, Cancian's theory regarding rank and innovation has significant network and SE content (1979, 1981). The theory predicts that the relationship between status and innovation has the form of a cubic polynomial such that those of upper-middle class status are less likely to innovate early in the spread of an innovation than those of lower-middle status. Cancian's elaborations of the curvilinear hypothesis stress that the effects of rank occur within a "community of reference," an internally differentiated membership group that is crucial to the day-to-day self definitions of its members, and that is "in large part locally (spatially) defined and based heavily on face-to-face contacts" (1979:36). Curvilinearity results in part from the assumption that rank relative to others inhibits innovation so that specifying the relevant community of reference is important.

Cancian has not attempted to operationalize this relational conception of community of reference, due in part to limitations of survey data used to test his theory (instead he opts for an ingenious numerical "filter" to eliminate datasets that are likely to combine heterogeneous communities of reference). Future research could profitably consult actors directly about the nature of their status comparisons within the community of reference and the relevance of these comparisons to innovation decisions (Gartrell & Gartrell 1985).

DISCUSSION

It is one thing to say that networks have an effect on SE processes and quite another to say precisely what the effects are, how they are produced, and more generally, what networks add to the explanation of SE phenomena. This is a tall order, and I suggest some issues and directions without making any claims to have covered the waterfront.

Let us begin by considering the "Achilles heel" of SE theory: "the weak link . . . [remains] the failure to explain adequately *how the relevant comparisons are selected in the first place*" (Pettigrew 1978:36, emphasis added; see also Walker & Pettigrew 1984:308, Singer 1981:91, Gartrell 1982). This emphasis on *selection* or *choice* of referents assumes that actors already are aware of sets of referents from which choices are made. This distinction was noted early on by Merton and Rossi who suggest studying comparisons by offering respondents ordered arrays of comparative contexts that exhaust their potential reference points (Merton & Kitt 1950:69). This insight has remained blurred until the present (examples are discussed by Gartrell 1982:121), and most of the more recent models discussed in this review overlook it (a notable exception is Rogers 1983:307).

I believe that a resolution of this problem lies in distinguishing between the active seeking or choosing of referents and a more passive view of SE processes that sees comparison as a byproduct of interactions in social networks. Given the tendency toward homophily or similarity in friendship networks (Berscheid & Walster 1978), comparison information gained in this way is optimal since comparisons with similar others are more useful and precise (Goodman 1974, Cook 1975) and entail fewer costs (Gartrell 1982:138–39).

These insights dovetail with research in social cognition which suggests that stimuli that are concrete and proximate tend to be most vivid (Fiske & Taylor 1984: ch. 7). Social cognition also lends credence to the "cheap, easy and precise" advantages of SE within networks. People appear to be somewhat lazy information processors, preferring short-cuts and heuristics to complex analysis of information about the social world (Tversky & Kahneman 1974, Fiske & Taylor 1984:96; see also Berger & Luckmann 1966:22–23, 33).

Networks impose limits on SE in the sense that they constrain potential reference points. *Choices* are made from this set according to the various comparison motives studied in experimental studies of social comparison theory (Suls & Miller 1977, Nosanchuk & Erickson 1985). Thus, comparison choices could affect the very network structures that gave rise to awareness of a set of potential referents in the first place.

A second general issue concerns *the relationship between frames of reference yielded by contacts in social networks and those that consist of groups or broad status categories.* As does the distinction between awareness and choice of referents, this question dates to Merton and Rossi's analysis of reference groups: "The theory of reference group behavior must include in its fuller psychological elaboration some treatment of the dynamics of perception (of individuals, groups and norms) and in its sociological elaboration, some treatment of channels of communication through which this knowledge is gained" (Merton & Kitt 1950:67, see also Kelley 1952:413, Allcorn & Marsh 1975:215, Kuhn 1967:183). While theories of perception have been invoked in SE phenomena—e.g. Helson's (1964) concept of "adaptation level" in Brickman & Campbell (1971); Sherif & Hovland's (1961) "lattitudes of acceptance" in Pettigrew (1967); Stevens' psychophysical laws (1957, 1962) in Burt (1982)—to my knowledge none has directly addressed the question of the relationship between individual social contacts and social imagery based on groups and broad status categories[3].

If SE theory is to take seriously the network-categories distinction and the research agenda outlined by Merton and Rossi, two avenues of research seem promising. The first would consider how social cognition works in the context of network structures to generate categorical imagery. For instance, "schemas," defined as "cognitive structures that represent organized knowledge about a given concept or type of stimulus" (Fiske & Taylor 1984:140), are implicit theories that guide perception and memory about people and their characteristics (including oneself), sequences of events, and properties of roles. People appear to generalize schemas from experiences with particular instances of the category in question, and the abstractness of schemas increases with the frequency of these examples (Fiske & Taylor 1984:171–75). Thus, awareness of categories and their relationships—whether classes or other social groupings—emerges through a cumulation of interactions with others. Social cognition also points to distortions in social imagery that can result from such generalizations. For instance, people seem willing to gen-

---

[3]Despite Tajfel's emphasis on the importance of categorical social imagery in identity and its autonomy from interindividual relations (1981:chapter 11), he acknowledges the impact of everyday social experiences (ch. 7) in producing such imagery. He also implies that interpersonal relationships may play an important role in modifying preestablished categorical social imagery (1981:231).

eralize to categories on the basis of small, biased sets of concrete instances and experiences (Tversky & Kahneman 1974, Fiske & Taylor 1984:250–1); similarly, the "availability" heuristic slants estimates of the likelihood of events toward the direction of personal experience: "For example, if I am asked whether a lot of women my age are having babies now, I will likely think over the number of friends and acquaintances I know who have or are about to have babies . . ." (1984:270). These examples merely scratch the surface of the social cognition literature; organizing it to provide a general theory of the network origins of social imagery remains a fundamental task for future SE research.

A related tack has been suggested by symbolic interactionists. Fine & Kleinman (1983) argue that an interactionist approach to networks should study people's conceptions of networks as a whole or as meaningful segments, the fundamental question being "do these ties constitute a symbolic entity to some or all participants?" Moreover, like social cognition research in experimental social psychology, symbolic interactionism posits cognitive processes such as "typification" and "causality" (Hewitt 1984:ch. 5) that link general properties of actors' roles and events with concrete social interaction.

The "sociological" side of Merton and Rossi's proposed research agenda—a focus on how information about individuals, groups, and norms is communicated—raises other considerations. For instance, Tajfel (1981) has argued that social categories form an integral part of identity and that social comparisons proceed from this base. These designations begin in early childhood and develop across the life span (Tajfel 1981:134–36, 158–59). Along the way, "institutional definitions of the social structure . . . may focus the attention of members of a group or occupants of a social status upon certain *common* reference groups" (Merton & Kitt 1950:65). Yet categorical reference models are not only "injected" as a "received view" in socialization but are inferred from patterns of interaction defined by the relevant categories and statuses. A categorical focus thus becomes part of one's identity and a basis for comparing, to the degree that others act toward one in terms of the category (Kuhn 1967:183).

Future researchers who consider these and related questions should bear in mind two further themes that emerge from this stream of literature. First, there have been repeated calls for greater reliance on ethnographic approaches in the areas of class consciousness (Marshall 1983:288–90), equity and distributive justice (Gartrell 1982, 1985), social comparison (Austin 1977), and social support (Gottlieb 1985a). Despite the long history of SE theory and research, we are just beginning to study how SE works in the context of real-world social networks. The fine-grained insights of case studies in field settings will help to "generate" valid representations of these SE processes both in formal models (Fararo 1984) and in laboratory experiments. Secondly, given the many points of convergence among the approaches reviewed here, it should be clear that the boundaries between the various social evaluation theories are somewhat artificial. Despite periodic efforts to integrate them (e.g. Pettigrew 1967, Martin & Murray 1983), relatively little progress has been made on general questions they all share, such as those first raised by Merton and Rossi (Merton & Kitt 1950). The network approach may stimulate such progress. Indeed, network approaches to SE cut across sociological perspectives—consider e.g. symbolic interactionist concepts of "motive talk" and "role-taking" incorporated into, respectively, research on class consciousness (Emmison 1985) and mathematical network models (Burt 1982). Thus, work in this area appears to have general integrative potential.

ACKNOWLEDGMENTS

Preparation of this paper was supported in part by Social Sciences and Humanities Research Council of Canada Grant 494-84-0018 and by Faculty Research Grants from the University of Victoria. I am grateful to Scott Lewis and Pam Whitaker for help with the literature review and to Jim Anglin, Bill Carroll, Reed Early, Bonnie Erickson, Mark Granovetter, Bob Hagedorn, Rick Ogmundson, Anna Paletta, David Tindall, Rennie Warburton, Barry Wellman, and to the Editor and anonymous referees of the Review for helpful comments and advice that led to substantial improvements in the manuscript. The support and advice of Penny Hocking and Vicky Drader are also gratefully acknowledged. Earlier drafts were presented at the Annual Meetings of the Canadian Sociology and Anthropology Association, Montreal, May 28, 1985 and at the Annual Meetings of the Pacific Sociological Association, Denver, April 11, 1986.

Literature Cited

Adams, J. S. 1965. Inequity in social exchange. *Adv. Exp. Soc. Psychol.* 2:267–99

Allcorn, D. G., Marsh, C. M. 1975. Occupational communities—communities of what? In *Working Class Images of Society,* ed. M. Bulmer, pp. 206–18. London: Routledge & Kegan Paul

Archer, K. 1985. The failure of the New Democratic Party: unions, unionists, and politics in Canada. *Can. J. Polit. Sci.* 18:353–67

Austin, W. 1977. Equity theory and social comparison processes. See Suls & Miller 1977, pp. 279–305

Bakker, B., Karel M. 1983. Self-help: Wolf or lamb? See Pancoast et al 1983, pp. 159–82

Berger, J., Zelditch, M. Jr., Anderson, B., Cohen B. P. 1972. Structural aspects of distributive justice: a status value formulation. In *Sociological Theories in Progress,* ed. J. Berger, M. Zelditch Jr., B. Anderson, 2:119–46. Boston: Houghton-Mifflin

Berger, P. L., Luckmann, T. 1966. *The Social Construction of Reality: A Treatise in the Sociology of Knowledge.* Garden City: Doubleday

Berscheid, E., Walster, E. H. 1978. *Interpersonal Attraction.* Reading: Addison-Wesley

Blauner, R. 1960. Work satisfaction and industrial trends in modern society. In *Labor and Trade Unionism,* ed. W. Galenson, S. M. Lipset, pp. 339–60. New York: Wiley

Bott, E. 1957. *Family and Social Network.* London: Tavistock

Brickman, P., Campbell, D. T. 1971. Hedonic relativism and planning in the good society. In *Adaptation Level Theory: A Symposium,* ed. M. H. Appley, pp. 287–302. New York: Academic

Brown, R., Brannen, P. 1970. Social relations and social perspectives amongst shipbuilding workers: A preliminary statement. *Sociology* 4:71–84

Burt, R. S. 1982. *Toward a Structural Theory of Action.* New York: Academic

Cancian, F. 1979. *The Innovator's Situation: Upper-Middle-Class Conservatism in Agricultural Communities.* Stanford: Stanford Univ. Press

Cancian, F. 1981. Community of reference in rural stratification research. *Rural Sociol.* 46:626–45

Caplan, G. 1974. *Support Systems and Community Mental Health.* New York: Behavioral Publ.

Cohen, J. M. 1977. Sources of peer group homogeneity. *Sociol. Educ.* 50:227–41

Coleman, J. S., Katz, E., Menzel, H. 1966. *Medical Innovation: A Diffusion Study.* New York: Bobbs-Merrill

Cook, K. S. 1975. Expectations, evaluations and equity. *Am. Sociol. Rev.* 40:372–88

Cook, K. S. 1982. Network structures from an exchange perspective. In *Social Structure and Social Networks,* ed. P. V. Marsden, N. Lin, pp. 177–200. Beverly Hills: Sage

Crosby, F. 1976. A model of egoistical relative deprivation. *Psychol. Rev.* 83:85–113

Crosby, F. 1982. *Relative Deprivation and Working Women.* New Haven: Yale Univ. Press

D'Augelli, A. 1983. Social support networks in mental health. See Whittaker & Garabino 1983, pp. 71–106

Davis, J. A. 1959. A formal interpretation of the theory of relative deprivation. *Sociometry* 22:280–96

Deneke, C. 1983. How professionals view self-help. See Pancoast et al 1983, pp. 125–42

Deutsch, M. 1985. *Distributive Justice: A Social-Psychological Perspective.* New Haven: Yale Univ. Press

Doeringer, P. B., Piore, M. J. 1971. *Internal Labor Markets and Manpower Analysis.* Lexington, Mass: Heath

Emmison, M. 1985. Class images of 'the economy': Opposition and ideological incorporation within working class consciousness. *Sociology* 19:19–38

Erickson, B. H. 1982. Networks, ideologies, and belief systems. In *Social Structure and*

Network Analysis, ed. P. V. Marsden, N. Lin, pp. 159–72. Beverly Hills: Sage

Erickson, B. H. 1983. *The relational basis of attitudes. Univ. Toronto Struc. Anal. Prog. Working Paper No. 38*

Fararo, T. J. 1984. Neoclassical theorizing and formalization in sociology. *J. Math. Sociol.* 10:361–93

Feld, S. L. 1981. The focused organization of social ties. *Am. J. Sociol.* 86:1015–35

Festinger, L. 1954. A theory of social comparison processes. *Hum. Relat.* 7:117–40

Festinger, L., Schacter, S., Back, K. W. 1950. *Social Pressures in Informal Groups.* Stanford: Stanford Univ. Press

Fine, G. A., Kleinman, S. 1983. Network and meaning: An interactionist approach to structure. *Symb. Interaction* 6:97–110

Fiske, S. T., Taylor, S. E. 1984. *Social Cognition.* New York: Random

Galaskiewicz, J. 1982. Models of resource allocation: Corporate contributions to nonprofit organizations. In *Social Structure and Network Analysis,* ed. P. V. Marsden, N. Lin, pp. 235–54. Beverly Hills: Sage

Gartrell, C. D. 1979. *Interdependence and Inflation.* Ottawa: Supply and Services Canada

Gartrell, C. D. 1982. On the visibility of wage referents. *Can. J. Sociol.* 7:117–43

Gartrell, C. D. 1985. Relational and distributional models of collective justice sentiments. *Soc. Forc.* 64:64–83

Gartrell, C. D. 1987. Representing justice sentiments with blockmodels: Response to Markovsky and Ford. *Soc. Forc.* In press

Gartrell, C. D., Gartrell, J. W. 1985. Social status and agricultural innovation: A meta-analysis. *Rural Sociol.* 50:38–50

Goldthorpe, J. H., Lockwood, D., Bechhofer, F., Platt, J. 1969. *The Affluent Worker in the Class Structure.* Cambridge: Cambridge Univ. Press

Goodman, P. S. 1974. An examination of referents used in the evaluation of pay. *Organ. Behav. Hum. Perform.* 12:170–95

Gottlieb, B. H. 1983a. *Social Networks and Social Support.* Beverly Hills: Sage

Gottlieb, B. H. 1983b. *Social Support Strategies: Guidelines for Mental Health.* Beverly Hills: Sage

Gottlieb, B. H. 1983c. Social support as a focus for integrative research in psychology. *Am. Psychol.* 38:278–87

Gottlieb, B. H. 1985a. Marshaling and augmenting social support for medical patients and their families. Unpublished manuscript, Univ. Guelph, Ont., Can.

Gottlieb, B. H. 1985b. Social support and the study of personal relationships. *J. Soc. Personal Relat.* 2:351–75

Granovetter, M. S. 1973. The strength of weak ties. *Am. J. Sociol.* 78:1360–80

Gross, M., Brandt, K. 1981. Educational support groups for patients with ankylosing spondylitis: A preliminary report. *Patient Couns. Health Educ.* 3:6–12

Hall, A., Wellman, B. 1985. Social networks and social support. In *Social Support and Health*, ed. S. Cohen, S. L. Syme, pp. 23–41. Orlando: Academic Press

Hammer, M., Makiesky-Barrow, S., Gutwirth, L. 1978. Social networks and schizophrenia. *Schizophrenia Bull.* 4:522–45

Helson, H. 1964. *Adaptation-Level Theory*. New York: Harper & Row.

Hewitt, J. P. 1984. *Self and Society: A Symbolic Interactionist Social Psychology*. Boston: Allyn & Bacon

Hirsch, B. J. 1983. Social networks and the coping process: Creating personal communities. See Gottlieb 1983a, pp. 149–70

Hooyman, N. 1983. Social support networks in services to the elderly. See Whittaker & Garabino 1983, pp. 134–64

Hyman, H. H. 1942. The psychology of status. *Arch. Psychol.* 38(269)

Hyman, H. H., Singer, E. 1968. *Readings in Reference Group Theory and Research*. New York: Free Press

Inkeles, A. 1960–1961. Industrial man: The relation of status to experience, perception and values. *Am. J. Sociol.* 66:1–31

Jackman, M. R., Jackman, R. W. 1983. *Class Awareness in the United States*. Berkeley: Univ. Calif. Press

Jasso, G. 1980. A new theory of distributive justice. *Am. Sociol. Rev.* 45:3–32

Johnston, W., Ornstein, M. D. 1982. Class, work and politics. *Can. Rev. Sociol. & Anthropol.* 19:196–214

Kadushin, C. 1981. Notes on expectations of reward in N-person networks. In *Continuities in Structural Inquiry*, ed. P. M. Blau, R. K. Merton, pp. 235–54. Beverly Hills: Sage

Kandel, D. B. 1978. Homophily, selection, and socialization in adolescent friendships. *Am. J. Sociol.* 84:427–36

Kelley, H. H. 1952. Two functions of reference groups. In *Readings in Social Psychology*, ed. G. E. Swanson, T. M. Newcomb, E. L. Hartley, pp. 410–14. New York: Holt

Kuhn, M. H. 1967. The reference group reconsidered. In *Symbolic Interaction: A Reader in Social Psychology*, ed. J. G. Manis, B. N. Meltzer, pp. 171–84. Boston: Allyn & Bacon

Kunkel, J. H., Nagasawa, R. H. 1973. A behavioral model of man: Propositions and implications. *Am. Sociol. Rev.* 38:540–43

Lash, S. 1984. *The Militant Worker*. London: Heinemann

Latane, B. 1966. Studies in social comparison. *J. Exp. Soc. Psychol.* 2 (Suppl. 1):1–115

Light, J. M., Mullins, N. C. 1979. A primer on blockmodeling procedure. In *Perspectives on Social Network Research*, ed. P. W. Holland, S. Leinhardt, pp. 85–118. New York: Academic Press

Lockwood, D. 1966. Sources of variation in working class images of society. *Sociol. Rev.* 14:249–67

Lucas, R. A. 1971. *Minetown, Milltown, Railtown: Life in Canadian Communities of Single Industry*. Toronto: Univ. Toronto Press

Lummis, T. 1977. The occupational community of East Anglian fishermen. *Br. J. Sociol.* 28:51–73

Mackenzie, G. 1973. *The Aristocracy of Labor*. Cambridge: Cambridge Univ. Press

Marsden, P. V., Laumann, E. O. 1984. Mathematical ideas in social structural analysis. *J. Math. Sociol.* 10:271–94

Marshall, G. 1983. Some remarks on the study of working-class consciousness. *Polit. Soc.* 12:263–301

Martin, J. 1981. Relative deprivation: A theory of distributive injustice for an era of shrinking resources. In *Res. Organ. Behav.*, ed. L. L. Cummings, B. M. Staw, 3:53–107. Greenwich, Conn: JAI

Martin, J., Murray, A. 1983. Distributive justice and unfair exchange. In *Equity Theory: Psychological and Sociological Perspectives*, ed. D. M. Messick, K. S. Cook, pp. 169–206. New York: Praeger

Marx, K. [1852.] 1963. *The Eighteenth Brumaire of Louis Bonaparte*. New York: International

Mead, G. H. 1934. *Mind, Self, and Society*. Chicago: Univ. Chicago Press

Merton, R. K., Kitt, A. 1950. Contributions to the theory of reference group behavior. In *Continuities in Social Research: Studies in the Scope and Method of "The American Soldier,"* ed. R. K. Merton, P. F. Lazarsfeld, pp. 40–105. Glencoe: Free Press

Moore, R. S. 1975. Religion as a source of variation in working-class images of society. In *Working Class Images of Society*, ed. M. Bulmer, pp. 35–54. London: Routledge & Kegan Paul

Newcomb, T. M. 1943. *Personality and Social Change*. New York: Holt, Rinehart & Winston

Newcomb, T. M. 1967. *Persistence and Change: Bennington College and Its Students After Twenty-five Years*. New York: Wiley

Nosanchuk, T. A., Erickson, B. H. 1985. How high is up? Calibrating social comparison in the real world. *J. Pers. Soc. Psychol.* 48:624–34

Ogmundson, R., Ng, M. 1982. On the inference of voter motivation: A comparison of the subjective class vote in Canada and the United Kingdon. *Can. J. Sociol.* 7:41–59

Pancoast, D. L., Parker, P., Froland, C. 1983. *Rediscovering Self-Help.* Beverly Hills: Sage

Parkin, F. 1971. *Class Inequality and Political Order.* London: MacGibbon & Kee

Pettigrew, T. F. 1967. Social evaluation theory. In *Nebraska Symposium on Motivation,* ed. D. Levine, pp. 241–311. Lincoln: Univ. Nebraska Press

Pettigrew, T. F. 1978. Three issues in ethnicity: Boundaries, deprivations, and perceptions. In *Major Social Issues,* ed. J. M. Yinger, S. J. Cutler, pp. 25–49. New York: Free Press

Potts, M., Brandt, K. 1982. Analysis of education-support groups for patients with rheumatoid arthritis. *Patient Couns. Health Educ.* 4:161–66

Richardson, A. 1983. English self-help: Varied patterns and practices. See Pancoast et al 1983, pp. 203–24

Rogers, E. M. 1983. *Diffusion of Innovations.* New York: Free Press

Runciman, W. G. 1966. *Relative Deprivation and Social Justice.* London: Routledge & Kegan Paul

Scase, R., 1974. Conceptions of the class structure and political ideology: Some observations on attitudes in England and Sweden. In *The Social Analysis of Class Structure,* ed. F. Parkin, pp. 149–178. London: Tavistock

Sherif, M., Hovland, C. I. 1961. *Social Judgment.* New Haven: Yale Univ. Press

Shibutani, T. 1955. Reference groups as perspectives. *Am. J. Sociol.* 60:562–70

Shumaker, S. A., Brownell, A. 1984. Toward a theory of social support: Closing conceptual gaps. *J. Soc. Issues* 40:11–36

Singer, E. 1981. Reference groups and social evaluation. *Social Psychology: Sociological Perspectives,* ed. M. Rosenberg, R. H. Turner, pp. 66–93. New York: Basic Books

Stern, E., Keller, S. 1953. Spontaneous group reference in France. *Public Opin. Q.* 17:208–17

Stevens, S. S. 1957. On the psychophysical law. *Psychol. Rev.* 64:153–181

Stevens, S. S. 1962. The surprising simplicity of sensory metrics. *Am. Psychol.* 17:29–39

Stouffer, S. A., Suchman, E. A., DeVinney, L. C., Star, S. A., Williams, R. M. Jr. 1949. *The American Soldier. Vol I. Adjustment During Army Life.* Princeton: Princeton Univ. Press

Suls, J., Miller, R. 1977. *Social Comparison Processes.* Washington: Hemisphere

Tajfel, H. 1981. *Human Groups and Social Categories.* Cambridge: Cambridge Univ. Press

Tanner, J. 1985. Working class community, working class consciousness: A reexamination. Unpublished ms., Univ. Alberta, Edmonton

Taylor, S. E. 1983. Adjustment to threatening events: A theory of cognitive adaptation. *Am. Psychol.* 38:1161–73

Thoits, P. A. 1983. Multiple identities and psychological well-being: A reformulation and test of the social isolation hypothesis. *Am. Sociol. Rev.* 48:174–87

Thoits, P. A. 1984. Coping, Social support and psychological outcomes: The central role of emotion. In *Rev. Pers. Soc. Psychol.,* ed. P. Shaver, 5:219–38. Beverly Hills: Sage

Thoits, P. A. 1985. Social support and psychological well-being: Theoretical possibilities. In *Social Support: Theory, Research, and Applications,* ed. I. G. Sarason, B. R. Sarason, pp. 51–72. Dordrecht, The Netherlands: Martinus Nijhoff

Tietjen, A. M. 1985. The social networks and social support of married and single mothers in Sweden. *J. Marriage Fam.* 47:489–96

Turner, R. H. 1956. Role-taking, role standpoint, and reference group behavior. *Am. J. Sociol.* 61:316–28

Tversky, A., Kahneman, D. 1974. Judgment under uncertainty: Heuristics and biases. *Science* 185:1124–31

Walker, C. R. 1950. *Steeltown.* New York: Harper & Row

Walker, I., Pettigrew, T. F. 1984. Relative deprivation theory: An overview and conceptual critique. *Br. J. Soc. Psychol.* 23:301–10

Walsh, R. H., Ferrell, M. A., Tolone, W. L. 1976. Selection of reference group, perceived reference group permissiveness, and personal permissiveness attitudes and behavior: A study of two consecutive panels (1967–1971; 1970–1974). *J. Marriage Fam.* 38:495–507

Walster, E., Walster, G. W., Berscheid, E. 1978. *Equity: Theory and Research.* Boston: Allyn & Bacon

Wellman, B. 1982. Studying personal communities. In *Social Structure and Network Analysis,* ed. P. V. Marsden, N. Lin, pp. 61–80. Beverly Hills: Sage

Wellman, B. 1983. Network analysis: Some basic principles. In *Sociological Theory 1983,* ed. R. Collins, pp. 155–200. San Francisco: Jossey Bass

Westergaard, J. H. 1975. Radical class consciousness: A comment. In *Working Class Images of Society,* ed. M. Bulmer, pp. 251–6. London: Routledge & Kegan Paul

Whittaker, J. K., Garbarino, J. 1983. *Social Support Networks: Informal Helping in the Human Services*. New York: Aldine

White, H. C., Boorman, S. A., Breiger, R. L. 1976. Social structure from multiple networks I: Blockmodels of roles and positions. *Am. J. Sociol.* 81:730–80

Wilcox, B. L. 1983. Social support in adjusting to marital disruption: A network analysis. See Gottlieb 1983a, pp. 97–116

Williams, R. M. Jr. 1975. Relative deprivation. In *The Idea of Social Structure: Papers in Honor of Robert K. Merton*. New York: Harcourt Brace & Jovanovich

Wright, E. O. 1982a. *The comparative project on class structure and class consciousness: an overview. Comp. Proj. on Class Struct.* Class Consciousness Work. Pap. Ser. No. 1, Univ. Wisc., Madison

Wright, E. O. 1982b. *The questionnaire on class structure, class biography and class consciousness. Comp. Proj. on Class Struct. and Class Consciousness Work. Pap. Ser. No. 2*, Univ. Wisc., Madison

Wright, E. O. 1983. *What is neo and what is Marxist in neo-Marxist class analysis? Comp. Proj. on Class Struct. and Class Consciousness Work. Pap. Ser. No. 17*, Univ. Wisc., Madison

Wright, E. O. 1984. *Class structure and class consciousness in contemporary capitalism: A comparative analysis of Sweden and the United States. Comp. Proj. on Class Struct. and Class Consciousness Work. Pap. Ser. No. 19*, Univ. Wisc., Madison

Ann. Rev. Sociol. 1987. 13:67–88

A CRITICAL EXAMINATION OF MACRO PERSPECTIVES ON CRIME CONTROL

Allen E. Liska

Department of Sociology, State University of New York at Albany, Albany, NY 12222

Abstract

A large number of studies examine the causes and the consequences of crime control at both the micro and macro levels of analysis. This paper focuses on the macro studies. Most macro research on crime control is loosely organized and weakly linked to theoretical perspectives. Studies are reviewed that relate to one of two general sociological perspectives—structural functionalism and conflict; and these perspectives are contrasted with the economic perspective. Empirical studies are employed both to specify more clearly and to evaluate the causal structures and processes implied by the perspectives.

INTRODUCTION

Crime control refers to authorized activities intended to control crime by constraining people's behavior. Some activities—such as detaining, arresting, prosecuting, and executing offenders, directly constrain people's behavior and thus may well be described as forms of legal or quasi-legal punishment. Other activities, such as police and prison expenditures create or maintain the infrastructure necessary for supporting actions that directly constrain people's behavior.

Traditionally, most crime control research, stimulated by deterrence theory, has focused on the extent to which these activities actually control crime. More recently, inspired by various sociological perspectives, research has focused on crime control as a dependent variable. Most such studies use

67

0360-0572/87/0815-0067$02.00

the individual as the unit of analysis and examine how various crime control activities, like arresting, prosecuting, and sentencing, are affected by the legal, psychological, and social characteristics of people and their behavior. These microlevel studies are not discussed here.

Some studies use collectivities, e.g. police organizations and communities, as the unit of analysis and examine how crime control patterns are affected by social structures. Most of this research takes the form of historical case studies which illustrate rather than test sociological perspectives on crime control (Erikson 1966, Harring 1983). These studies provide significant theoretical insights and some empirical support for these perspectives. Yet, macro research need not be limited to historical case studies; certainly, nothing inherent in sociological perspectives prevents comparative research of both historical and contemporary cases. While such theory testing research has appeared, these studies are isolated from each other and do not constitute a recognized body of research, "a literature." Thus, their implications for these perspectives have not been fully exploited.

This paper organizes these studies into a literature that directly tests two general sociological perspectives on crime control: (a) structural functionalism and (b) conflict. It then uses the literature to evaluate and elaborate both perspectives.

ECONOMIC PERSPECTIVE

Before discussing these two sociological perspectives, consider briefly the economic perspective as an alternative point of departure. Within this perspective crime control research is generally macro, comparative, and theory testing; and it constitutes a recognized body of research that bears on general economic theory. Hence, it cannot and should not be ignored.

The perspective (Becker 1968, Ehrlich 1973, Schmidt & Witte 1984) assumes that people have relatively stable preferences or interests, that they weigh the benefits and costs of behavior alternatives and behave so as to maximize the ratio of benefits to costs. Within this perspective the study of crime control is always considered with regard to its impact on crime; that is, the perspective is oriented toward developing policies and programs to control crime. Crime control and crime are thus part of one general model, composed of three equations which predict: (a) criminal behavior (crime generation equation); (b) crime control activities, such as arrests and convictions, that affect the cost of criminal behavior (production function equation); and (c) crime control resources, such as capital and labor, that affect the production of crime control activities (demand equation). (See Figure 1A.)

Criminal behavior is thought to be just another behavior alternative. People engage in crime when the ratio of benefits to costs is higher for criminal behavior than for noncriminal alternatives. Effective crime control policies should decrease the benefits and increase the costs of crime, and/or increase the benefits and decrease the costs of alternatives to crime (Ehrlich 1973, Becker 1968). One major cost of crime is punishment. Crime rates (Equation 1) are thought to be a negative function of the level of punishment, especially the severity and certainty of punishment (Blumstein et al 1978, Cook 1977).

The level of crime control activity, e.g. the relative certainty of punishment, is conceptualized as a production function (Equation 2). Hence, it is assumed to be negatively affected by workload (crime rates) and positively affected by resources (capital and labor). That is, given constant resources, as the crime rate increases, the proportion of crimes cleared by arrests, prosecutions, or convictions, should decrease; and given a constant crime rate, as resources increase, the proportion of crimes cleared by arrests, prosecutions, and convictions should increase. Research (Phillips & Votey 1981, Liska et al 1985) examines the effect of capital investment (e.g. computer technologies), labor (e.g. police numbers and salaries), and the organization of labor (e.g. two officer patrols and high density patrolling) on crime control activities (e.g. the certainty of arrest).

Crime control resources (capital and labor) are viewed as a positive function of community fiscal capacity and workload, such as crime rates (Equation 3). Resources allocated to crime control are thought to be constrained by a community's fiscal capacity, in the sense that a rich community can afford more crime control per capita (as it can afford more social services in general) than can a poor community (Phillips & Votey 1981). Work in the 1950s and 1960s focused on the effect of a community's mean income, its tax rate, and the extent of intergovernmental transfers on crime control resources (Weicher 1970). By the 1970s, interest shifted to the effect of crime rates (workload) on resources. As crime increases, citizens are thought to demand more crime control services. They are willing to increase revenues for crime control and to support political candidates who advocate strong crime control (McPheters & Stronge 1974, Phillips & Votey 1981, Carr-Hill & Stern 1979). Indeed, much of the work during and after the 1970s has focused on estimating the reciprocal effects of crime rates and crime control resources (Greenwood & Wadycki 1973).

In sum, economists have approached crime control as part of a clearly specified model, linking crime rates and crime control, which can be derived from a general economic perspective on behavior. This has led to some very rigorous theory testing research which bears not only on the crime control model but on the economic perspective itself. Sociologists could learn much from the logical and empirical rigor of this work. Yet, the perspective—particularly the three equation model of crime and crime control—has been built on some very questionable assumptions (Loftin & McDowall 1982), which have directed research away from some fundamental questions.

Two assumptions, regarding interests and power, are particularly relevant to the study of crime control. First, crime is assumed to be more or less costly to all citizens, and thus all are assumed to be motivated toward or interested in controlling it. The power to influence crime control policy is equated with the vote, and elections are equated with a free market where people have information on candidates' crime control policies (Becker 1968, Ehrlich 1973, Phillips & Votey 1981). In effect, people are thought to have similar and enlightened self-interests regarding crime control and equal power to influence crime control policy. These assumptions depoliticize crime control, and direct attention to the aggregate demand for crime control and the objective social conditions that influence the aggregate demand, such as crime rates and community resources.

The two assumptions should be considered very carefully. Interests and motivations to control crime are not self-evident. Indeed, they seem to be quite variable—varying over time, among societies, and among social statuses within societies. For example, within a society such interests may vary with the rate of victimization experienced by members of each status group and by the needs of each status to protect itself and its property. Perhaps those who can afford to live in low crime neighborhoods and to insure their property against theft (the very rich), as well as those who have little to lose (the very poor), have a minimal interest in crime control, compared to those who have something to lose but cannot afford to protect themselves (the middle-class). While the right to vote is equally distributed, information on candidates' crime control policies and the resources to influence them are certainly not equally distributed. Economists appear to be generally unconcerned with

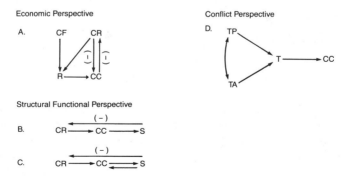

Figure 1 Causal structures underlying the three perspectives. CF, community fiscal capacity; R, resources; CR, crime rates; CC, crime control; S, solidarity; T, threat; TA, threatening acts; TP, threatening people.

explaining either the distribution of interests in crime control or the distribution of power to influence crime control policy, nor in taking these distributions into account in explaining variation in crime control between social units.

STRUCTURAL FUNCTIONAL PERSPECTIVE

The structural functional perspective traditionally conceives of society as integrated and orderly. It assumes that a general consensus exists on goals and values, that general needs for survival can be identified, that social structures (persistent patterns of behavior) function to maintain society's values, goals, and needs, and that social structures can be explained by these functions. Rapid change in the social structure is conceived as an extraordinary event, which is brought about by an equally extraordinary event in the external environment of the system.

While "modern or neo" structural functionalism may not make many of these assumptions, much contemporary crime control theory and research is guided by them. The structure of crime control, as of any other behavior, is thought to maintain society's values-goals-needs, particularly needs for social control, and it is thought to be explained by these functions. To the extent that structure of crime control is effective—functional—it is assumed to persist and remain stable, only changing in response to extraordinary events in the external environment.

This perspective has some general similarities to the economic perspective. Both assume that there is a consensus and stability of values and goals (in economic terms, preferences and interests) and that persistent patterns of crime control come into existence and are maintained because they contribute to society's values and goals. While economists explicate the underlying processes in terms of enlightened self interests and market mechanisms, structural functionalists talk more vaguely about social values and hidden feedback mechanisms, frequently couched in teleological and evolutionary terms.

From the general structural functional perspective three propositions can be identified regarding consequences, stability, and change in crime control.

Consequences

Durkheim (1938) noted various consequences of punishment as a form of crime control, including maintenance of social solidarity, a social identity, and social boundaries, as well as the control of crime. Social systems are assumed to sustain the level of punishment required to maintain necessary social states, such as social solidarity and social boundaries. Whether or not punishment controls crime is of secondary importance to its other functions.

Crime enters into the analysis not as a negative social state to be controlled but as a stimulant to crime control (punishment). Thus, crime is frequently thought of as making positive contributions to society.

The "consequences" proposition has generated a loosely organized body of research composed of historical (Erikson 1966, Currie 1968, Connor 1972, Ben-Yehuda 1980), field observational (Dentler & Erikson 1959, Scott 1976) and laboratory-experimental studies (Lauderdale 1976, Lauderdale et al 1984). The historical and field-observational studies tend to "illustrate" rather than to test the proposition. Case studies are selected that illustrate how crime control either functions to increase boundary maintenance and solidarity (Erikson 1966) or fails to do so (Ben-Yehuda 1980). For example, Erikson (1966) describes in fascinating detail three crises in Puritan society initiated by the immigration of culturally dissimilar groups. He argues that these crises (Quaker persecution, Antinomian controversy, and witchcraft hysteria) stimulated crime control, which in turn functioned to redefine moral boundaries and sustain social solidarity. Theory testing research is limited to a few laboratory and survey studies. For example, Lauderdale's (1976) experimental research shows that external threat increases both the rejection of deviants and the affirmation of social solidarity; but it does not show that the rejection of deviants mediates the effect of external threat on solidarity.

With the possible exception of Lauderdale's work, we have been unable to locate any strong evidence that crime control in the form of punishment or the general reaction to crime (or deviance) affects any social state—such as social solidarity, social boundaries, or cultural identities—thought to be important to group survival. Unless such effects are empirically established, it is premature to become embroiled in controversy over whether or not patterns of crime and crime control can be explained by their consequences.

Change in Punishment

Within the structural functional perspective on crime control, social change tends to be treated as an extraordinary event. Yet, from time to time social systems, even those that are predominantly stable, experience events, (e.g. political movements, immigration, economic inflation/depression, and war) that threaten the social order. According to the perspective, people respond to these threats with acts that reaffirm and strengthen their collective values and identity. In times of social stress, simple norm infractions are magnified and take on great symbolic significance, whereas in normal times they may just be ignored. Hence, during times of stress we might expect little tolerance and considerable punishment for norm violations.

Some support for this proposition can be found in historical studies, especially in studies on witchcraft. Erikson (1966), Currie (1968), and Ben-Yehuda (1980) interpret changes in the punishment of witchcraft as a response to boundary crises precipitated by socially disruptive events, such as an influx of culturally different people or a technological revolution. Yet, as previously indicated, most of these studies illustrate, rather than test, the theory. They are steeped in the contextual detail of a particular time and place, making comparisons across time and across studies difficult. Pivotal concepts, such as "boundary crisis," are not clearly defined so that they can be operationalized across historical contexts.

Inverarity (1976) attempts to test this general theory by examining the link between mechanical solidarity and repressive punishment. He examines a sample of parishes in post–Civil War Louisiana that are assumed to have undergone a boundary crisis precipitated by the Populist movement. Following Durkheim, he assumes that a social crisis precipitates an increase in punishment only in those parishes where mechanical solidarity is strong. Measuring mechanical solidarity as the proportion of the parish population that is black and the extent of urbanization and of religious homogeneity, and measuring repressive punishment as numbers of lynching, he reports support for the hypothesis: mechanical solidarity, coupled with a social crisis, increases repressive punishment. This work has been extensively criticized, perhaps because it claims to be one of the few rigorous tests of the functional thesis (Pope & Ragin 1977, Wasserman 1977, Bohrnstedt 1977, Bagozzi 1977, Berk 1977). For example, critics have questioned whether the post–Civil War Populist movement in Louisiana really constituted a boundary crisis and whether the above indicators constitute a valid operationalization of mechanical solidarity.

Stability of Punishment

Within the structural functional perspective, functional patterns of behavior are assumed to persist (remain stable); since punishment is assumed to be functional, it too is assumed to be stable. This reasoning leads to an interesting corollary. Assuming that the overall level of punishment is stable, then as the crime rate increases, only the most serious crimes can be punished and the less serious crimes must be ignored. Indeed, Durkheim (1938) argued that even the social definition of crime expands and contracts in relationship to the general volume of undesirable behavior. He described this in what has come to be known as the society of saints parable (1938:68–69):

> Imagine a society of saints, perfect cloister of exemplary individuals, crimes, properly so called, will there be unknown; but faults which appear venial to the layman will create there the same scandal that the ordinary offense does in ordinary consciousness. If, then, this society has the power to judge and punish, it will define these acts as criminal and treat them as such.

Considerable theory testing research, stimulated by the work of Blumstein and his colleagues, has addressed this issue. Their work has two interrelated thrusts: documenting the stability of punishment and identifying the causal processes that underlie it.

Blumstein and associates (Blumstein & Cohen 1973, Blumstein et al 1976, Blumstein & Moitra 1979) use time series techniques to examine the stability of imprisonment rates in the United States from 1926 to 1974, in Canada from 1880 to 1959 and in Norway from 1880 to 1964. They argue that imprisonment rates in these countries are generated by a stationary process, that is, the observed statistical variation in punishment over time can be modelled as statistical variation around a constant mean. In a reanalysis of these data, Rauma (1981a) argues that, while a stationary process may indeed generate these observations, there is just as much evidence that a nonstationary process generates them. Furthermore, he (1981b) argues that a univariate time series analysis can tell us very little about the causal processes, as specified by Durkheim and others, which underlie whatever level of stability is observed.

In a second related research thrust, Blumstein tries to show how stability in punishment is maintained by continual adjustments in the type of behavior punished. In one study Blumstein & Cohen (1973) examine the relationship between crime and arrest rates for serious and nonserious crimes in the United States. Their findings suggest that as the general crime rate increases, the arrest rate of nonserious crimes decreases, and as the crime rate decreases, the arrest rate of nonserious crimes increases, thereby maintaining a stable general arrest rate. In a second study, Blumstein et al (1976) analyze the flow rates between conformists, criminals, and prisoners in Canada. Making certain assumptions about the stability and state of the prison population, they deduce flow rates among these groups that generally approximate the observed rates.

In short, Blumstein and his associates have attempted to model the social process that underlies the stability of punishment. The model, however, is underidentified. They circumvent this problem by studying either the outcomes of the process (univariate times series) or by providing "guesstimates" of some of the parameters. Their work takes us further than we have been before and has stimulated considerable debate (Rauma 1981a). What is needed now is research measuring more of the model variables and empirically estimating more of the model parameters.

Continuing in the Blumstein tradition, Berk et al (1981) have also attempted to identify the equilibrium mechanism that underlies the stability of punishment. Assuming that the punishment rate varies somewhat around a specific level that is functional for a given society—the system target—then the growth rate of punishment is a simple function of the growth rate of the population. If for some reason punishment rates exceed the target, responding to changes in the external environment, future growth rates in punishment should decrease; and if rates fall below the target, future growth rates should increase. Growth rates of punishment are then the "mechanism" by which societies adjust the punishment rate to system targets. Berk et al (1981), using various time series of imprisonment rates in California from 1851 to 1970, find no empirical support for the equilibrium hypothesis.

Generally, research leaves considerable doubt that the punishment rate in social systems is stable over time and that this stability is sustained because it is somehow functional. Moreover, research suffers from theoretical ambiguity in conceptualizing the social process underlying stability—an ambiguity that can be traced to Durkheim. Theorists and researchers alike assume that societies have certain requisites for survival, such as solidarity and boundary maintenance, and that a level of punishment persists because it functions to maintain these needs; but neither Durkheim nor recent researchers such as Erikson, Blumstein, Rauma, or Berk clearly specify the social process by which that level of punishment persists to maintain a system's requisites for survival. Instead, research examines the logical consequences of the punishment stability assumption. Assuming that punishment is stable, Blumstein & Cohen (1973) suggest that if the crime rate is high, then only the most serious crimes can be punished; and Berk et al (1981) imply that, if the punishment rate is high, then the punishment growth rate will be low. These relationships are construed as the dynamic mechanism by which stability is sustained. This is correct, but only in a logical or definitional sense. If the relationship between the rate of punishment and the growth of that rate is negative, then, of course, the punishment rate will tend toward stability. Yet the study of such relationships does not shed light on the substantive causal processes by which this stability is sustained—that is, those causal processes by which the consequences of punishment, such as solidarity or boundary maintenance, influence punishment so as to sustain a stable level of punishment.

Some researchers (Erikson 1966, Berk et al 1983), and to a lesser extent even Blumstein & Cohen (1973), argue that the observed stability of punishment may simply reflect stability in the processing capacity of control systems. For example, stability in the prison population may simply reflect stability in prison size. In a recent paper Berk et al (1983) argue that the constraints of prison capacity operate through the many daily admission and release decisions of criminal justice administrators. This explanation should be regarded with some caution. Considerable research shows that the capacity of control systems is not necessarily stable; rather, it may expand and contract in response to social conditions (Currie 1968, Connor 1972). More importantly, this explanation of punishment stability is unrelated to the logic of structural functionalism. That is, if the capacity of a control system is stable, thereby limiting and stabilizing the level of punishment, then the postulation of unobservable goals, targets, and needs to explain stability is quite unnecessary. Blumstein et al (1976:319–20), apparently unsatisfied with an explanation in terms of system capacity, argue "that social forces accounting for stability include more than simple prison-cell capacity. . . . More fundamental considerations of social structure are probably at work. If too large a portion of society is declared deviant, then the fundamental stability of society will be disrupted. Likewise, if too few are punished, the identifying values of society will not be adequately articulated and reinforced, again leading to social instability."

It is interesting that Erikson, Blumstein, and Berk make references both to unobservable targets, goals, and needs, and to the capacity of the social control system, in order to explain the stability of punishment. Emphasis on the latter links their research to an explicit causal mechanism missing in the former, and emphasis on the former links their work to a general theoretical framework missing in the latter.

Feedback Loops and System Estimation

In contemporary economics and much sociology, the problem of identifying causal processes consistent with a traditional functional explanation has been dealt with by postulating causal feedback loops (Stinchcombe 1968). Consider just one possible consequence of punishment, "social solidarity." Based on the structural functional tradition, it is reasonable to assume that crime positively affects punishment which positively affects solidarity, which in turn negatively affects crime (see Figure 1B). Changes in any one of the variables, brought about by changes in various exogeneous variables, vibrate through the system and dampen over time; and because the causal loop consists of both positive and negative causal effects, the system tends toward long-term stability. For example, an increase in crime, brought about by an increase in unemployment, increases punishment, which increases solidarity, which in turn decreases crime. Alternatively, the emergence of an external threat, like a war, may increase solidarity, which decreases crime, which decreases punishment, which in turn decreases solidarity. In both cases the initial random shock to the system is counteracted by the feedback loop and dampened over time.

The system can be further complicated by postulating additional feedback loops (see Figure 1C). This system has two feedback loops, an internal and external loop. In addition to indirectly decreasing punishment through decreasing crime, solidarity may directly increase punishment. To put it simply, as solidarity increases, the resolve to control crime may increase. The inner loop amplifies the effect of an initial random shock to the system, and the outer loop controls it. The net effect depends on the relative strengths and time lags of the two loops.

While complex feedback loops make it difficult to see intuitively the outcome of random shocks to the causal system and make the parameters of the system difficult to estimate, explicit feedback loops with a control structure transform the traditional teleology of functionalism into a testable causal theory (Stinchcombe 1968). Assumptions about unobservable needs, goals, and targets are rendered unnecessary, and functional theories simply become special cases of causal theories.

Also, making explicit the causal logic underlying the assumed stability of punishment clarifies the interrelationships between the three propositions regarding consequences, change, and stability. Much of the theory and research on each proposition is not integrated with the work on the other propositions. Yet, these interrelationships are significant in estimating each proposition. Indeed, for models B and C in Figure 1, estimates of the specific causal paths will be biased without considering the model as a whole. For example, estimates of the effect of crime rates on crime control will be biased unless the indirect effect of crime control on crime rates is controlled.

This sensitizes us to the structure of random shocks. In the language of simultaneous equation modeling, random shocks constitute exogenous variables and can thus serve as instruments to identify the structural coefficients linking the endogenous variables. Identification of models 1B and 1C requires that some of the exogenous variables (random shocks) affect one but not the other endogenous variables. Hence, in studying feedback systems it is not only important that we study external variables which shock the system, but that we study those exogenous variables that shock only some endogenous variables in the system.

CONFLICT PERSPECTIVE

Similar to the economic perspective, the conflict perspective (Turk 1969, Quinney 1977, Spitzer 1975, Beirne 1979) assumes enlightened self-interests, especially on the part of economic elites; contrary to the economic perspective, however, the conflict perspective assumes an uneven distribution of self-interests in crime control and an uneven distribution of power to implement self-interests into social policy. Theory and research focus on how these distributions of interests and power come into being, persist, and influence crime control, i.e. law making and enforcement. Law making is assumed to reflect the interests of the powerful; those activities are criminalized that threaten their interests. Assuming that the violation of some laws is more threatening than the violation of others, the conflict perspective asserts that those laws that most protect the interests of the powerful will be most enforced. Assuming that law violations are more threatening when committed by some people than by others, the perspective asserts that laws are most enforced against those people who most threaten the interests of the powerful. Hence, the conflict perspective asserts that the greater the number of acts and people threatening to the interests of the powerful, the greater the level of crime control—the threat proposition. (See Figure 1D.)

Perhaps the major problem with this perspective is that of epistemic and theoretical linkages. Concerning the former, the major concepts, like interest and threat, are not clearly defined and are rarely measured. Instead, research examines the extent to which the level and distribution of acts (e.g. civil disorders) and people (e.g. percentage unemployed and percentage nonwhite) assumed to be threatening to the interests of the ruling class affect various forms of crime control. Yet it is not clear theoretically, how the level and distribution of these acts and people generate a threat to the interests of the ruling class and how that threat leads to specific forms of crime control.

Because the critical causal variables are not well defined, theoretically and operationally, and are not clearly linked to each other in the form of propositions or a causal model, the relevant research literature is also not well defined and integrated. Studies are categorized by the substantive forms of crime control (imprisonment, arrests, lynching, and police size), rather than by theoretical propositions. Researchers studying imprisonment are criminologists interested in prisons, and researchers studying lynching are specialists in race relations or collective behavior. Conflict theory is employed to guide research loosely and to interpret findings, and explanatory variables are selected because they are readily accessible and/or are generally amenable to a conflict interpretation.

We now briefly review these research areas to identify commonalities that can be used to elaborate theoretically the causal structure of the conflict perspective on crime control. These research areas are organized by the degree and mode of force into three categories (deadly force, physical restraint, and economic controls) ranging from the stick to the carrot. They are tied together by their focus on similar structural variables assumed to represent a threat to the interests of authorities. Some studies refer to the level and distribution of threatening people (percentage unemployed, percentage nonwhite, and degree of income inequality) and some refer to the level and distribution of threatening acts (crime and civil disorders).

Deadly Force

Deadly force refers to those forms of social control where the threatening population is controlled through homicide—the most extreme form of social control. This section examines two forms of deadly force: police homicide of citizens and lynchings.

Considerable research on homicide by police has been conducted (Fyfe 1982); however, we have been able to locate only a few macro studies that bear on the conflict perspective model in Figure 1D. The findings are mixed. Using states as the unit of analysis, Kania & Mackey (1977) report a substantial and statistically significant correlation between the rate of homicides by police and various measures of poverty, conceptualized as indicators of the presence of a threatening population. Yet, they also report a statistically insignificant correlation between such homicide and riots, a clear indicator of threatening acts. Sherman & Langworthy (1979), using cities, report a negative relationship between homicides by police and unemployment, also conceptualized as an indicator of threat. Perhaps the strongest support for the threat hypothesis comes from Jacobs & Britt (1979). Using states as the unit of analysis and controlling for various other variables, such as violent crime, they report that economic inequality, conceptualized as an indicator of threat, shows a statistically significant effect on homicides by police.

While lynching is certainly not an official form of control, the distinction between official and unofficial forms of control of the black population was not always clear in the South from the Civil War to World War I. Vigilante groups were common, and some were supported and linked with local crime control agents.

A few lynching studies have been stimulated by Blalock's hypothesis (1967) that links racial discrimination to the percentage of nonwhites. He argues that as the percentage of nonwhites increases, nonwhites constitute a growing economic and political threat to whites. Economically, nonwhites compete for jobs, and politically, they compete for power. Racial discrimination—economic and political—is conceptualized as an attempt by whites, the ruling racial group, to control a threatening nonwhite population. Lynching is simply part of this pattern.

A few studies (Reed 1972, Inverarity 1976, Corzine et al 1983) link the rate of lynching to the percentage of blacks in Southern counties. Corzine et al (1983) further report that the relationship is nonlinear with an increasing slope and that the relationship is strongest in the deep South particularly after the voter registration drives in the 1890s. They argue that these relationships support a threat hypothesis. Blacks, historically, have been perceived as more of a threat in the deep South than other regions, and racial conflict was accentuated in the voter registration drives of the late nineteenth century.

Physical Constraints

Physical constraints refer both to the activities of social control agents (arrests and imprisonment) and to the infrastructure of crime control bureaucracies (police size and prison size) which supports these activities. Most macro research on control activities is historical (Harring 1983) and emphasizes the role of economic forces in the development of crime control in the western world (Rusche & Kirchheimer 1939). For two crime control bureaucracies (police and prisons) this section examines the primary crime control activity (arrests and imprisonment) and their capacity to perform that activity (police and prison size).

PRISON   Conflict theorists explain the development of prisons during the seventeenth, eighteenth, and nineteenth centuries as a strategy of authorities to control the urban masses of immigrants and migrants and to manage the labor supply. A capitalistic system needs a ready supply of laborers who respect private property. Prison segregates those who do not respect property rights from the ranks of labor (a divide and conquer strategy) and instills moral (Ignatieff 1978) and work (Foucault 1978) discipline in the masses. Rusche & Kirchheimer (1939) argue that during times of economic depression prisons absorb the unemployed and during times of prosperity they provide a ready supply of labor. Developing this theme, contemporary conflict theorists emphasize the threat that unemployment poses to the social relationships of production.

While much debate has ensued over the explanation of this hypothesized relationship between unemployment and imprisonment, only a few studies have systematically examined it. Most of these, using time series analysis, yield consistent results but suffer methodological problems which leave the results inconclusive. For example, Yeager (1979) studies the relationship in the United States from 1952 to 1974; Greenberg (1977) studies it in Canada from 1950 to 1972; and Box & Hale (1982) study it in England and Wales from 1949 to 1979. All report a positive relationship between unemployment and imprisonment rates, controlling for crime rates. These studies share one major limitation: the time series from World War II to the mid 1970s (about 25 to 30 years) is a relatively short period in which to examine unemployment cycles and covers a peculiar period of time characterized by neither a major war nor an economic depression. Indeed, Jankovic (1977), using a series in the United States from 1929 to 1974, reports that the positive relationship between unemployment and imprisonment rates does not hold during the depression and war years. His analysis highlights the fact that prisons can only absorb a small proportion of the population. In "normal" times they can absorb a significant portion of the unemployed, but when the rate of unemployment reaches epidemic proportions, such as during a depression, they can absorb only an insignificant proportion of them. Berk et al (1982), studying a long California time series from 1851 to 1970 over four depressions, do observe a positive relationship between depressions and growth in imprisonment rates. Because they do not control for the crime rate, however, the underlying causal process remains unclear.

Additionally, it is not at all clear how unemployment explains the substantial growth in the rate of imprisonment in the United States since the early 1970s, during which time the unemployment rate has been variable. Using a cross section of states and controlling for crime rates, Galster & Scaturo

(1985) find little empirical support for a positive effect of unemployment on the imprisonment rate for any year from 1976 to 1981. Clearly, much more work remains to be done in documenting the relationship between unemployment and imprisonment rates before we can fine tune a conflict explanation of it.

POLICE   Four recent studies (Jacobs 1979, Jackson & Carroll 1981, Liska et al 1981, Greenberg et al 1985) examine police size in the United States from 1950 to 1980. These studies use civil disorders as an indicator of the presence of threatening acts and use the percentage of poor, percentage of nonwhites, income inequality, and degree of racial segregation as indicators of the presence and distribution of threatening people.

Three of the studies (Jacobs 1979, Jackson & Carroll 1981, Liska et al 1981) examine civil disorders and fail to find an effect. This is not surprising. If the civil disorders affect police size, the process probably operates at the regional or national level. Disorders in any one city may affect police size, not only locally but also in comparable and neighboring cities.

All four studies examine the effect of the percentage of poor and the percentage of nonwhites on the size of the police force. The findings are consistent. They report no effect on police size of the percentage of poor but a substantial effect of the percentage of nonwhites. This effect is stronger in 1970, following the civil disorders, than in 1960 or 1980 and is stronger in South than the non-South.

Three of the studies examine income inequality, and one examines racial segregation. Empirical support for the effect of income inequality on police size is inconsistent. Jacobs (1979) reports a positive effect, but Jackson & Carroll (1981) and Greenberg et al (1985) are unable to replicate his results. Liska et al (1981) report that segregation has a negative effect on the size of the police forces, which like the effect of the percentage of nonwhites, is stronger in the South than in the non-South and increases from 1950 to 1970. They argue that the segregation of problematic populations, such as nonwhites, into urban ghettos functions as a vehicle of social control, thereby lessening the need for more overt forms of social control.

Generally, economic structures (e.g. the percentage of poor and the degree of income inequality) appear to have less effect on police size, than do racial structures (e.g. percentage of nonwhites and degree of segregation). To explain this, Liska et al (1981) argue that the white poor are viewed as respectable, while nonwhites are believed to be associated with crime. This perceived association was strengthened during the 1960s and early 1970s, the time of racial disorder in the United States, and has always been stronger in the South than in other regions. Liska et al (1982) support this argument through survey data. After controlling for the crime rate, research shows that the fear of crime is strongly associated with the percentage of nonwhites in a city. Hence, they argue that the effect of the percentage of nonwhites is an expression not of economic repression but of racial stereotypes that link nonwhites with crime.

Liska & Chamlin (1984) and Liska et al (1985) extend this work to study actual crime control activities, such as arrests. Clearly, the arrest rate of nonwhites is higher than that of whites. However, contrary to the threat hypothesis (that an increase in the proportion of nonwhites increases people's sense of threat and thus the arrest rate of non-whites), the findings show that as the percentage of nonwhites increases, the arrest rate of nonwhites decreases. Liska & Chamlin argue that the latter occurs because as the percentage of nonwhites increases, the victims of nonwhite offenders also tend to be nonwhite. Nonwhite victims may be less able to define their misfortunes and victimizations as crimes deserving of police attention; crimes between nonwhites may be treated more like personal than legal problems by police. Hence, not only may nonwhites be linked with the threat of crime, they may also find authorities insensitive to their legitimate needs for protection from crime.

Economic Control (Welfare)

Welfare is frequently conceptualized within conflict theory as a form of social control. Piven & Cloward (1971) have stimulated considerable controversy by arguing that the welfare expansion in the United States during the mid and late 1960s was a response to the urban riots during that period—an attempt to pacify an economically deprived and threatening population.

Various studies provide some support for this thesis. In what is perhaps the first major systematic study, Isaac & Kelly (1981) report that no relationship between riots and welfare exists at the city level, but that a strong relationship exists at the national level from 1947 to 1974. They argue that the political processes that affect welfare policy operate at the national level; it is federal policy that drives the welfare system. Jennings (1983) arrives at a similar conclusion, although he respecifies Isaac & Kelly's model and changes the measures of some of the variables. Schram & Turbett (1983) report that riots affect welfare policy in two stages. Riots during the mid-1960s prodded the Federal government to liberalize welfare policies generally; these policies were then most likely to be implemented in the late 1960s and early 1970s by those states that experienced the most rioting. These initial studies provide a foundation for understanding welfare as a form of social control and direct our attention to the importance of the proper unit of analysis.

The Emerging Conflict Model

The conflict theory of crime control consists of a set of loosely interrelated and ideologically charged ideas. Major concepts, such as interest and power, are not clearly defined independent of what those concepts are supposed to explain; thus, the definitions frequently yield tautological propositions. That is, law formulation and enforcement, thought to be explained by ruling class interests, are frequently used to infer those interests in concrete historical cases in either the short (Quinney 1977) or the long (Beirne 1979) term. Consequently, conflict theory is only loosely linked to research in various substantive areas, and conflict research on crime control consists of a loosely interrelated set of studies, more linked to various substantive "sociology of" areas, such as race relations, criminology, stratification, and penology, than to each other. Conceptual integration across these substantive areas and a tightening of theoretical and epistemic connections are clearly needed.

As a working strategy toward these goals, this paper has categorized crime control strategies along a dimension ranging from the stick (deadly force) to the carrot (economic controls); it has categorized the macro causes of threat into actions (crime and riots), and people (the proportion of nonwhites and of unemployed, and the degree of racial segregation and of income inequality). It has further emphasized the central role of "threat" in conceptually organizing and integrating the above macro conditions and in linking them to various forms of crime control. See Figure 1D.

The explication of the causal structure underlying the threat hypothesis of conflict theory serves two important functions. First, tightening the theoretical linkages between various and diverse research literatures (e.g. welfare, arrests, and lynching) both enlarges the empirical scope of the theory to include various forms of control and stimulates researchers to examine the interrelationships among these forms. The perception of threat may not lead necessarily to all forms of control; many forms of control require use of economic resources. Both imprisonment and welfare cost money—a special instance of the classic "guns and butter" issue. To the extent that social units expend their economic resources for imprisonment, they may not be able to afford welfare. The perspective also does not predict what types of threat lead to what forms of crime control. Some research (Kluegel & Smith 1981) suggests that authorities and the public believe that some categories of the poor (nonwhites) are less deserving of financial support than are others (whites)—the respectable poor. Hence, an increase in the proportion of nonwhite poor may lead to more forceful forms of crime control, such as arrests, rather than to more beneficial forms, such as welfare.

Second, tightening the epistemic and theoretical linkages clarifies the implications of research for theory. Traditionally, because of loose linkages, crime control research has not had much feedback on conflict theory, that is, the theory has not grown and developed as a result of this research; instead, the research has been merely used to illustrate the theory.

What are the implications of macro research for the conflict theory of crime control? Perhaps the major finding across these research areas is that racial distributions of people and actions (percentage of nonwhites, degree of segregation, number of riots) have more effect than do economic distributions (percentage poor, percentage unemployed, and extent of income inequality) on forms of crime control, at least in the United States. Liska et al (1985) interpret the strong racial effect to mean that the threat of crime, rather than a general threat to the economic order, is the catalyst to crime control. Non-whites in contemporary United States are culturally associated with crime; thus, an increase in the percentage of nonwhites in a given area and a decrease in segregation increases the visibility of nonwhites, which in turn increases the perceived threat of crime. Crime control is what it seems to be—a response to the perceived threat of crime, not a strategy to manage the economic order.

Research on the fear of crime also raises some question as to whose interests are served by crime control. The traditional conflict perspective suggests that crime control serves the interests of the ruling or property class. Yet, survey research (Garofalo 1979, Liska et al 1983) shows that fear of crime is inversely related to income and education and is higher for nonwhites than whites, and that demand for law and order is strongest among low and middle income groups. This is quite understandable. High income groups can afford to reside and even to locate their businesses in low crime neighborhoods and to insure and secure their property.

Contemporary conflict theories of crime control have not been informed by this research. Rather, they have been based on images of class structure and crime control drawn from eighteenth and nineteenth century Western societies undergoing industrialization—at a time when the class structure was comparatively simple, class conflict was blatant, and bureaucratization of crime control was just beginning (Harring 1983). Thus, crime control theory has been couched and framed in terms of conflict between clearly defined economic classes. In postindustrial societies, the class structure is more complex and the emergence of a middle class of managers, technicians, and bureaucrats has made class conflict less open and explicit. On the other hand, racial stratification remains explicit, and racial conflict may have even intensified, particularly during the 1960s and 1970s.

CONCLUSION

Economists argue that the level of crime control is a response to the aggregate demand for crime control, which in turn reflects the aggregate economic cost of crime. These costs are assumed to be rationally calculated and to be directly linked to the crime rate; and the aggregate demand is thought to be expressed in crime control policy through elections, which are equated with an economic market where people choose between candidates with different positions on crime control. While these propositions are tightly interwoven into a general theory of crime control that can be logically derived from a more general economic theory of collective behavior, this theory is built on some questionable assumptions.

If the economic perspective can be characterized as a logically tight set of propositions derived from explicit but questionable assumptions, then the sociological perspectives—structural functionalism and conflict—can be characterized as loose sets of propositions based on implicit and vague assumptions. Social processes are vaguely described in the theoretical propositions, and linkages between operational indicators and theoretical concepts are vaguely specified. This has led to the formulation of teleological and tautological propositions and to research literatures that are only loosely integrated with each other and to a common body of theory.

The structural-functional perspective on crime control, from Durkheim to Blumstein, contains strains of teleology. The persistence of crime control is explained by its functions or consequences for the survival of society. The processes or mechanisms by which the consequences of crime control, such as boundary maintenance and solidarity, somehow influence crime control are not clearly specified. These teleological propositions frequently degenerate into empty tautologies. They do not show empirically that patterns of crime control persist because they maintain and bolster social states necessary for survival. Rather, the persistence of crime control is frequently used to infer the presence of functions, which in turn are used to explain the persistence.

What is needed is the specification of causal feedback loops through which the observable consequences of crime control act upon crime control. Social systems with such feedback processes tend toward stability. External shocks vibrate through them and dampen with time. The postulation of unobservable goals, targets, or needs is simply unnecessary to explain stability in crime control.

These theoretical problems are no different for the conflict perspective. Conflict theorists, particularly Marxists, have not been overly concerned with theory construction and testing. Major concepts, such as interest and power, are not clearly defined independent of the phenomena they are supposed to explain; thus, they frequently yield tautological propositions. That is, law formulation and enforcement, thought to be explained by ruling class interests, are also frequently used to infer them. Some researchers (Greenberg 1980, Jacobs 1980) have been sharply critical of this manner of conceptualizing conflict theory, and in their own research they have tried to define and infer ruling class interests independent of the conditions such interests are supposed to explain. Yet, rather than measuring ruling class interests and threats to these interests directly, by measuring people's perceptions and beliefs, researchers measure them indirectly by the structural conditions (economic inequality, crime rates, and percentage nonwhite) assumed to threaten these interests. Such indirect measures of the central theoretical concept yield only weak tests of the central theoretical propositions.

As a result of tautological propositions and weak epistemic correlations, conflict theory is frequently able to explain everything and predict nothing; conflict research is loosely organized around substantial problems in different "sociology of" areas, rather than tightly linked to a general conflict theory of crime control. We have reviewed these areas, ranging from welfare dependence to deadly force, as a common body of research in order to develop "a literature" and explicate its implications for conflict theory.

Where, then, do we stand today? Most macro sociological research on crime control consists of historical and contemporary case studies constituted in a tradition of illustrating rather than testing theory. Sociological perspectives on crime control are composed of loosely linked theoretical propositions and weak linkages between theoretical concepts and empirical indicators. This has frequently led to teleological and tautological propositions and to isolated research traditions more closely tied to different "sociology of" areas than to crime control theory. What is now needed is a clear articulation of the causal processes and structures implied in sociological perspectives on crime control, to provide a focal point for organizing and integrating theory testing research.

ACKNOWLEDGMENTS

I thank the following individuals for ideas and comments on earlier drafts of this paper: Barbara Duffee, Marvin Krohn, David McDowall, Steven Messner, Mark Reed, and James F. Short, Jr.

Literature Cited

Bagozzi, R. 1977. Populism and lynching in Louisiana. (Comment on Inverarity, ASR April 1976) *Am. Sociol. Rev.* 42:335–58

Becker, G. 1968. Crime and punishment: An economic approach. *J. Polit. Econ.* 76:169–217

Beirne, P. 1979. Empiricism and the critique of marxism on law and crime. *Soc. Probl.* 26:373–85

Ben-Yehuda, N. 1980. The European witch craze of the 14th to 17th centuries: A sociologist's perspective. *Am. J. Sociol.* 86:1–31

Berk, R. A. 1977. Proof? No. Evidence? No. A skeptic's comment on Inverarity's use of statistical inference. (Comment on Inverarity ASR April 1976) *Am. Sociol. Rev.* 42:625–55

Berk, R., Messinger, S. L., Rauma, D., Berecochea, J. E. 1983. Prisons as self-regulating systems: A comparison of historical patterns in California for male and

female offenders *Law Soc. Rev.* 17:547–86

Berk, R. A., Rauma, D., Messinger, S. L., Cooley, T. F. 1981. A test of the stability of punishment hypothesis: The case of California, 1851–1970. *Am. Sociol. Rev.* 46:805–29

Blalock, H. M. Jr. 1967. *Toward a Theory of Minority Group Relations.* New York: Wiley

Blumstein, A., Cohen, J. 1973. A theory of the stability of punishment. *J. Crim. Law Criminol.* 64:198–207

Blumstein, A., Cohen, J., Nagin, D. 1978. *Deterrence and Incapacitation: Estimating the Effects of Criminal Sanctions on Crime Rates.* Washington, DC: Natl. Acad. Sci.

Blumstein, A., Moitra, S. 1979. Growing or stable incarceration rates: A comment on Cahalan's trends in incarceration in the United States since 1880. *Crime Delin.* 25:91–94

Blumstein, A., Cohen, J., Nagin, D. 1976. The dynamics of a homeostatic punishment process. *J. Crim. Law Criminol.* 67:317–34

Bohrnstedt, G. W. 1977. Use of the multiple indicators multiple causes (MIMIC) model. (Comment on Inverarity ASR, April 1976) *Am. Sociol. Rev.* 42:656–63

Box, S., Hale, C. 1982. Economic crisis and the rising prisoner population in England and Wales. *Crime Soc. Justice* 13:20–35

Carr-Hill, R. A., Stern, N. H. 1979. *Crime, the Police, and Criminal Statistics* New York: Academic Press

Connor, W. D. 1972. The manufacture of deviance: The case of the Soviet Purge, 1936–1938. *Am. Sociol. Rev.* 37:403–13

Cook, P. J. 1977. Punishment and crime: A critique of current findings concerning the preventive effect of criminal sanctions. *Law Contemp. Probl.* 41:164–204

Corzine, J., Creech, J., Corzine, L. 1983. Black concentration and lynchings in the South: Testing Blalock's power-threat hypothesis. *Soc. Forces* 61:774–96

Currie, E. P. 1968. Crimes without criminals: Witchcraft and its control in renaissance Europe. *Law Soc. Rev.* 3:7–32

Dentler, R. A., Erikson, K. T. 1959. The functions of deviance in groups. *Soc. Probl.* 7:98–107

Durkheim, E. 1938. *The Rules of Sociological Method* (Transl. S. A. Solovay, J. H. Mueller, ed. G. E. G. Catlin). Glencoe, Ill: Free Press

Ehrlich, I. 1973. Participation in illegitimate activities: A theoretical and empirical investigation. *J. Polit. Econ.* 81:521–64

Erikson, K. T. 1966. *Wayward Puritans: A Study in the Sociology of Deviance.* New York: Wiley

Foucault, M. 1978. *Discipline and Punish.* (Transl. A. Sheridan) New York: Pantheon

Fyfe, J. J. 1982. *Readings on Police Use of Deadly Force.* Washington, DC: Police Found.

Galster, G. C., Scaturo, L. H. 1985. The U.S. criminal justice system: Unemployment and the severity of punishment. *J. Res. Crime Delin.* 22:163–90

Garofalo, J. 1979. Victimization and the fear of crime. *J. Res. Crime Delin.* 16:80–97

Greenberg, D. F. 1977. The dynamics of oscillatory punishment processes. *J. Crim. Law Criminol.* 68:643–51

Greenberg, D. F. 1980. A critique of the immaculate conception: A comment on Beirne. *Soc. Probl.* 27:476–77

Greenberg, D., Kessler, R. C., Loftin, C. 1985. Social inequality and crime control. *J. Crim. Law Criminol.* 76:684–704

Greenwood, M. J., Wadychi, W. J. 1973. Crime rates and public expenditures for police protection: Their interaction. *Rev. Social Econ.* 31:138–51

Harring, S. L. 1983. *Policing A Class Society.* New Brunswick, NJ: Rutgers Univ. Press

Ignatieff, M. 1978. *A Just Measure of Pain: The Penitentiary in the Industrial Revolution, 1850–1950.* New York: Pantheon

Inverarity, J. M. 1976. Populism and lynching in Louisiana, 1899–1896: A test of Erikson's theory of the relationship between boundary crises and repressive justice. *Am. Sociol. Rev.* 41:262–80

Isaac, L., Kelly, W. R. 1981. Racial insurgency, the state, and welfare expansion: Local and national level evidence from the postwar United States. *Am. J. Sociol.* 86:1348–86

Jackson, P. I., Carroll, L. 1981. Race and the war on crime: The sociopolitical determinants of municipal expenditures in 90 nonsouthern U.S. cities. *Am. Sociol. Rev.* 46:290–305

Jacobs, D. 1979. Inequality and police strength: Conflict theory and coercive control in metropolitan areas. *Am. Sociol. Rev.* 44:913–25

Jacobs, D. 1980. Marxism and the critique of empiricism: A comment on Beirne. *Soc. Probl.* 27:467–70

Jacobs, D., Britt, D. 1979. Inequality and police use of deadly force: An empirical assessment of a conflict hypothesis. *Soc. Probl.* 26:403–12

Jankovic, I. 1977. Labor market and imprisonment. *Crime Soc. Justice* 8:17–37

Jennings, E. Jr. 1983. Racial insurgency, the state and welfare expansion: A critical comment and reanalysis. *Am. J. Sociol.* 88:1220–36

Kania, R., Mackey, W. C. 1977. Police violence as a function of community characteristics. *Criminology* 27:27–48

Kluegel, J., Smith, E. R. 1981. Beliefs about stratification. *Annual Rev. Sociol.* 7:29–56

Lauderdale, P. 1976. Deviance and moral boundaries. *Am. Sociol. Rev.* 41:660–76

Lauderdale, P., Parker, J., Smith-Cunnien, P., Inverarity, J. 1984. External threat and the definition of deviance. *J. Personality Soc. Psychol.* 46:1058–68

Liska, A. E., Baccaglini, W. 1983. Fear of crime. *In Encyclopedia of Crime and Justice,* ed. Sanford H. Kadish 2:765–68. New York: Free Press

Liska, A. E., Chamlin, M. B. 1984. Social structure and crime control among macro social units. *Am. J. Sociol.* 90:383–95

Liska, A. E., Chamlin, M. B., Reed, M. 1985. Testing the economic production and conflict models of crime control. *Soc. Forc.* 63:119–38

Liska, A. E., Lawrence, J. J., Benson, M. 1981. Perspectives on the legal order: The capacity for social control. *Am. J. Sociol.* 87:412–26

Liska, A. E., Lawrence, J. J., Sanchirico, A. 1982. Fear of crime as a social fact. *Soc. Forc.* 60:760–71

Loftin, C., McDowall, D. 1982. The police, crime and economic theory. *Am. Sociol. Rev.* 47:393–401

McPheters, L. R., Stronge, W. B. 1974. Law enforcement expenditures and urban crime. *Natl. Tax J.* 27:633–44

Phillips, L., Votey, H. L. Jr. 1981. *The Economics of Crime Control.* Beverly Hills: Sage

Piven, F. F., Cloward, R. A. 1971. *Regulating the Poor: The Functions of Public Welfare.* New York: Vintage

Pope, W., Ragin, C. 1977. Mechanical solidarity, repressive justice, and lynchings in Louisiana (Comment on Inverarity ASR April 1976). *Am. Sociol. Rev.* 42:2:363–68

Quinney, R. 1977. *Class, State and Crime.* New York: McKay

Rauma, D. 1981a. Crime and punishment reconsidered: Some comments on Blumstein's stability of punishment hypothesis. *J. Crim. Law Criminol.* 72:1772–98

Rauma, D. 1981b. A concluding note on the stability of punishment: Reply to Blumstein, Cohen, Moitra, and Nagin. *J. Crim. Law Criminol.* 72:1809–12

Reed, J. S. 1972. Percent black and lynching: A test of Blalock's theory. *Soc. Forc.* 50:356–60

Rusche, G., Kirchheimer, O. 1939. *Punishment and Social Structure.* New York: Russell & Russell

Schmidt, P., Witte, A. D. 1984. *An Economic Analysis of Crime and Justice.* New York: Academic Press

Schram, S. F., Turbett, J. P. 1983. Civil disorder and welfare explosion: A two-step process. *Am. Sociol. Rev.* 48:408–14

Scott, R. A. 1976. Deviance, sanctions and integration in small scale societies. *Soc. Forc.* 54:604–20

Sherman, L. W., Langworthy, R. H. 1979. Measuring homicide by police officers. *J. Crim. Law Criminol.* 70:546–60

Spitzer, S. 1975. Toward a marxian theory of deviance. *Soc. Probl.* 22:638–51

Stinchcombe, A. L. 1968. *Constructing Social Theories.* New York: Harcourt, Brace & World

Turk, A. T. 1969. *Criminality and Legal Order.* Chicago: Rand McNally

Wasserman, I. M. 1977. Southern violence and the political process (Comment on Inverarity, ASR April 1976). *Am. Sociol. Rev.* 42:359–62

Weicher, J. C. 1970. Determinants of central city expenditure, some overlooked factors and problems. *Natl. Tax J.* 23:379–96

Yeager, M. G. 1979. Unemployment and imprisonment. *J. Crim. Law Criminol.* 70:586–88

Ann. Rev. Sociol. 1987. 13:89–108
Copyright © 1987 by Annual Reviews Inc. All rights reserved

THEORY AND RESEARCH ON INDUSTRIALIZATION

John Walton

Department of Sociology, University of California, Davis, California 95616

Abstract

Sociological approaches to industrialization are framed by two major theories: social differentiation, based on classical liberalism and Durkheimian sociology, and uneven development, derived from the critical work of Marx and Weber. Although social differentiation continues to influence general treatments of the subject, uneven development has proven more fruitful in research. Important themes in recent research are reviewed by means of a property space based on epochs and processes of industrialization. A summary of five key research areas describes the important issues in current work and, by way of conclusion, suggests some convergence.

INTRODUCTION

Industrialization plays a central, yet ambiguous, role in social theory. On the one hand, industrialization is often understood as the principal agent in the making of modern society: "The industrial revolution marks the most fundamental transformation of human life in the history of the world recorded in written documents" (Hobsbawm 1968:13). On the other hand, industrialization is sometimes construed as simply one element in a set of changes, such as urbanization and rationalization, which combine in a broader evolutionary transformation: "The industrialization process . . . is an expression of a complex of forces that are really rooted in more general processes, in what are most aptly characterized as the processes of modernization" (Berg 1979:6). Most features of modern society are traced to the influence of industrialization

89

in some theory. Yet in the theorizing about industrial society, the interconnections and causal relations among these processes are matters of considerable debate. Controversy surrounds such basic questions as these: When did industrialization begin? Has it ended in some "post-industrial" societies? How is it causally and temporally related to urbanization? Has it developed along one path or many? How does it affect the family and social classes?

Such ambiguities are common in social theory, and when they force themselves upon us as distressing anomalies, they facilitate critical research. In the last two decades sociological theories of industrialization have been hounded by anomaly. For example, growth models of industrial takeoff that posit a repetition of Western development have not reflected reality in the Third World. Industry has come to many less developed countries without initiating growth in other sectors of the economy and society. Developed countries once assumed to be sailing smoothly on a course of sustained growth are now suffering the effects of decline in heavy industry and the internationalization of production in many aspects of high technology. Plants close, industrial communities wither, and "sunrise" industries seem unable to reabsorb workers. Conventional sociological wisdom cannot account for the change. Yet refutation of standard models has stimulated and coincided with a rekindled interest in comparative and historical research. The combined result of these circumstances (ambiguity, anomaly, and new research) is a reinterpretation of the industrialization process that carries fundamental implications for social theory.

This chapter is intended to show that current sociological theories do not explain what we have recently learned from history and what we are now witnessing in the development of industrialization. The argument relies on resurgent historical and comparative research that challenges the old theories and suggests some convergence on new explanations. Finally, I shall venture some generalizations drawn from the confrontation of theory and research and suggest that the themes for a new theoretical interpretation are at hand. The argument, accordingly, proceeds in three steps. First, I characterize two major and sharply contrasting theoretical traditions that have shaped sociological thinking about industrialization. Although these theories are now in doubt, they have effectively stimulated critical research, and they still retain many adherents. Second, I develop a purely heuristic property space within which the sprawling research literature can be organized and critical foci highlighted. The purpose here is to show in exemplary detail how current theory fails us and what alternative interpretations demand attention in a more complete explanation. Third, I propose a synthesis of current research and the nascent theory it implies.

CONVENTIONAL INTERPRETATIONS

In succinct form, sociological theory divides into two camps on the meaning and development of industrialization: first, the classic liberal theory of an evolving division of labor generalized to social differentiation and, second, the critical theory of uneven development. The paradigms are fully contrasted in Durkheim and Marx respectively, although each perspective antedates these writers and has been reformulated in relation to succeeding generations of industrial society. Liberal theory combines assumptions from laissez faire economics and the theory of comparative advantage from the late eighteenth century with the biological and evolutionary metaphors that appear in Durkheim and Spencer. These are carried into contemporary thinking by Parsons and his followers. The theory of uneven development begins with the misgivings of St. Simon and is amplified in the varied, yet related, criticisms of industrial capitalism developed by Marx (1867), Weber (1946), Schumpeter (1935), Polanyi (1944), and Thompson (1963). In the most general terms these orientations to industrialization highlight fundamental differences and the competing images that have prompted critical research. The terms "social differentiation" and "uneven development," are shorthand, of course, and might be hyphenated—in the first instance with specialization and integration or, in the second, with exploitation and contradiction.

Social Differentiation

Social differentiation, at bottom, combines classical liberalism and evolutionary precepts in a theory of social change aimed primarily at explaining the consequences of major transformations—in the modern era, that is, the consequences of industrialization. Durkheim granted that Adam Smith and John Stuart Mill had correctly identified a new division of labor as the outstanding fact of eighteenth-century society; they failed only to understand "that the law of the division of labor applies to organisms as to societies . . . the more specialized the functions of the organism, the greater its development. . . . The division of labor in society appears to be no more than a particular form of this general process" (Durkheim 1893:41). Durkheim posed "the problem" of industrial society in terms of fragmentation.

> We need have no further illusions about the tendencies of modern industry; it advances steadily toward powerful machines, towards greater concentrations of forces and capital, and consequently to the extreme division of labor. Occupations are infinitely separated and specialized, not only inside the factories, but each product is itself a speciality dependent on others . . . the principal branches of the agricultural industry are steadily being drawn into the general movement. Finally, business itself is ingeniously following and reflecting in all its shadings the infinite diversity of industrial enterprise. (Durkheim 1893:39)

Fragmentation and the dissolution of older forms of social solidarity produced the need for a new basis of social integration, a need that Durkheim reasoned could only be met by occupational groups. Whatever the merits of this proposal, subsequent formulations of the social differentiation approach have continued to emphasize the question of integration. Indeed, the most influential modern statements of the theory by Parsons and Smelser identify the "structural differentiation" of social systems with evolutionary stages and economic development, taking the "functional requirement" of new forms of social integration at each stage as the key to institutional life (Parsons & Smelser 1956; Smelser 1963; Parsons 1966).

Moore's (1965) volume on *The Impact of Industry* summarizes the theory under three general headings. These are "conditions for industrialization," "first order consequences," and "reverberations." The "conditions for industrialization" correspond to liberal prescriptions for economic development: rational organization, alienable property, wage labor, political order, and entrepreneurial values. The "first-order consequences" of economic growth show a "remarkably high degree of uniformity in the industrial system": productive organizations in which work relationships are technologically determined and therefore functionally specific, impersonal, and affectively neutral; administrative hierarchies in which rational authority is organized on a pyramid principle; sectoral relocation of the labor force that follows modal shifts from agriculture to manufacturing and to services; a varied association between urbanization and industrialization that moves in time from industrialization without urbanization to their close correlation and, later, to overurbanization. Finally, among the "reverberations" produced by industrialization, Moore includes: predominance of the nuclear family; urban social disorganization; the substitution of formal for informal control; and complex stratification on the axes of occupation, skill, and economic criteria as the primary determinants of status.

Moore's model defies summary in a short space, in part because it allows for wide variation across time and space. The key analytic point, however, is that where a generalization (e.g. sequential changes in the sectoral distribution of the labor force) is first identified and then qualified, the factors that explain variations are themselves closely tied to the liberal evolutionary approach (e.g. technological changes in production, markets and communication, or an upgrading of skill levels).

Although the model of social differentiation is derived mainly from a reading of the Western industrial experience, it has been extended in two directions. First, it has been applied as a diagnostic and explanation for underdevelopment. On the assumption that development follows the same path in all societies, structural differentiation is construed as a set of requirements that Third World countries must satisfy. "The concept of structural differentiation can be employed to encompass many of the structural changes that accompany the movement from pre-industrial to industrial society . . . In the transition from domestic to factory industry, the division of labor increases, and the economic activities previously lodged in the family move to the factory . . . Empirically we may classify underdeveloped or semi-developed economies according to how far they have moved along this line of differentiation" (Smelser 1963:106–7). Second, present trends such as advances in information technology, service sector expansion, and labor professionalization are projected in the concept "post-industrial society [which] emphasizes the centrality of theoretical knowledge as the axis around which new technology, economic growth and the stratification of society will be organized" (Bell 1973:113).

Although the theory of social differentiation has recently come under attack, it is far from moribund. Much research is still animated by its claims, and it continues to be accepted as textbook sociology (e.g. Berg 1979).

Uneven Development

Critical theories of industrialization are fundamentally concerned with the historical process as it reveals the "laws of motion" of capitalist development. The distinctly modern phase of this process involves the advent of what Marx called "large-scale industry," itself an outgrowth of agriculture and "domestic industry" (sometimes "handicrafts"). The process is complex, a choice example of the uneven nature of capitalist development. On one hand, "machinery does away with co-operation based on handicrafts, and with manufacture based on the handicraft division of labor"; on the other hand "(w)ith the development of the factory system and the revolution in agriculture that accompanies it, production in *all* the other branches of industry not only *expands,* but also alters its character" (Marx 1977:588–90, emphasis added). Elsewhere, Marx describes a process in which capitalist manufacture may at first "formally" subsume noncapitalist labor in independent workshops, merely annexing it without changing its social relations of production, and later may move to its "real subsumption" in which work and industrial organization are integrated with fully capitalist forms.

Marx's point, of course, is that industrial development is an uneven and contradictory process: "large-scale industry, by its very nature, necessitates variation of labor" and so at times it even "reproduces the old division of labor with its ossified particularities" (Marx 1977:617). Uneven development is not random, however. The basic law governing these varied appearances is the drive for profit in a competitive economy: "the division of labor in manufacture is merely a particular method of creating relative surplus-value" (Marx 1977:486). Having established the intricacies of this process, Marx moves to the familiar features and consequences of large-scale industry. In brief, three major tendencies characterize the transformation: concentration-centralization, proletarianization, and crisis.

Concentration is the process in which capitalist enterprises become large as a result of growth based on economies of scale. Centralization is bigness resulting from the acquisition of other less competitive enterprises. Both tendencies describe the long-run direction of industrialization, although they, too, exhibit unevenness and contradiction. Bigness as a result of concentration entails the destruction of small-scale enterprise and the incorporation of labor in large firms with a detailed division of labor and hierarchical control structure. Bigness stemming from centralization means oligopoly. Among the manifold consequences of both tendencies Marx identified a "new and international division of labor . . . suited to the requirements of the main industrial countries [that] converts one part of the globe into a chiefly agricultural field of production for supplying the other part, which remains a pre-eminently industrial field" (Marx 1977:579–80).

Proletarianization is defined by the steady decline of independent production and self-employment and a correlative increase in the numbers of wage laborers or workers dependent on the sale of their labor to capitalists. In tandem with other changes, wage labor in the mature stage of capitalist development is absorbed mainly in large-scale industry where conditions (density, exploitation, alienation) are ripe for the creation of a self-conscious, militant working class.

The meaning of crisis in Marxian theory is manifold and controversial (Mandel 1975, O'Connor 1984). Here, it suffices to say that Marx understood capitalist development as inherently crisis prone. Crises vary in magnitude in the sense that some are overcome in the adaptation of capitalist development to changing conditions (overproduction, underconsumption, falling rates of profit, etc), yet in the long run capitalism undermines itself through the antagonistic forces it generates. Inherent crisis implies that change is a conflictual process (rather than a steady evolutionary upgrading through differentiation) and that industrialization will take distinctly different forms under different historical conditions. Early and late (or European and Third World) industrialization will not follow the same pattern.

Although Marx was the earliest and most prolific exponent of the theory of uneven development as it is understood today, the perspective was never uniquely Marxian, and much of its appeal stems from other critics of capitalist society. Weber (1946:196) identified industrial capitalism as the principal force behind the bureaucratic rationalization of modern society. Where Marx treated bourgeois thought almost exclusively as an expression of class-based ideology, Weber saw its deeper penetration to the institutional foundations and individualistic ethic of contemporary society. Yet Weber's critique extended beyond a restoration of the analysis of idealism which Marx had rejected. In concrete empirical work, Weber addressed the uneven development of the agrarian and industrial regions of Germany. He carried this analysis to the key role of the modern state, which grows through the expropriation of private holders of power: "The whole process is a complete parallel to the development of the capitalist enterprise through the gradual expropriation of the independent producers" (Weber 1946:82). Polanyi (1944:40) drew on Marx and Weber for his analysis of exploitation under the market economy as a product of the industrial revolution: "how shall this revolution itself be defined? We submit . . .[that] one basic change, [is required:] the establishment of market economy, and that the nature of this institution cannot be fully grasped unless the impact of the machine on a commercial society is realized."

Recent contributions to the theory of uneven industrial development have taken several directions and different stances toward the classic texts. Baran & Sweezey (1966) emend Marx's theory to explain a posited trend toward monopoly capitalism in the United States; they argue that giant U.S. corporations have rates of profit that do not fall owing to state support. Among other things, this thesis rejects the notion of a "managerial revolution" and the claim that the control of industry has shifted to a class of administrative experts whose methods differ from owners. In some ways Dahrendorf (1959) takes the other side of this argument by rewriting Marx in a Weberian manner. He claims that the political and industrial realms are separate and, therefore, that class conflict focuses on delimited issues of authority in the enterprise and unions.

Contemporary emphases in the theory of uneven development are drawn alternately from Marx and Weber. Braverman (1974) develops the radical alternative: He argues that monopoly capitalism degrades and deskills labor, first in industry and later in services, in the interests of management control and with the support of the state. In a related and more sophisticated vein, Mandel (1975) argues that under "late capitalism" industrialization spreads to all branches of the economy in a pattern of "complete," rather than post, industrialism. Neo-Weberian treatments of industrial society stress power and authority, state autonomy, and class determination in market situations that go beyond the sphere of production (e.g. Giddens 1973). Finally, perhaps the most synthetic application of the theory of uneven development has been in studies of the Third World that examine the intersection of global economic forces, the state, and individual societal conditions of class struggle, all of which combine in patterns of "associated dependent development" (e.g. Cardoso & Faletto 1979). As in the case of social differentiation theory, uneven development has its classical expression and a variety of reformulations designed for specific times and topics.

EPOCHS AND PROCESSES

Social differentiation and uneven development together effectively frame current research on industrialization. Each theory has stimulated waves of research that sometimes undercut its own foundation and reveal the bedrock beneath. The theory of uneven development has proven more fruitful, particularly in the continuing importance of its emendations, but it is far from complete or definitive. The two paradigms, however, are seldom directly comparable because they focus on different periods of time, explore different ramifications of industrialization, and describe in different vocabularies events that are not themselves in dispute—although the significance and causal relations surrounding those events usually are issues for contention.

The theories differ on conceptual and substantive issues. Among the principal points of conceptual disagreement is, first, the very nature of industry and industrialization. Social differentiation stresses technology, the factory, and the industrial revolution, beginning in the late eighteenth century. "*Industry* refers to the fabrication of raw materials into components or finished products by primarily mechanical means dependent on inanimate sources of power" (Moore 1965:4). To the extent that Marx speaks for the uneven development school, ("domestic") industry is taken as beginning long before the advent of "large-scale industry" in Britain; and two eminently social, rather than technological, conditions establish its distinctive character. "The *collective worker,* formed out of the combination of a number of specialized workers, is the item of machinery specifically characteristic of the manufacturing period . . .[and the] division of labor in manufacture requires that a *division of labor in society* should have attained a certain degree of development" (Marx 1977:468, 473, emphasis added). In the first case, industry is a temporally specific and essentially technological phenomenon; in the second, it is fundamentally social and broadly historical.

With regard to substantive questions, second, social differentiation posits a general model of industrialization (the term is used synonomously with economic development) applicable to separate societies in different periods of time. Essentially the same conditions must be met everywhere to initiate development, and the same kinds of general consequences are expected to follow. Uneven development is historically specific. The social organization of domestic industry differs dramatically from large-scale industry in capitalist society, just as today's Third World confronts a new social form in dependent development. Third, social differentiation has promoted research centered mainly on the consequences of industrialization, changes in institutions such as "mass society," bureaucracy, and the family (e.g. Smelser 1959). Uneven development has focused heavily on labor, class conflict, and underdevelopment.

These differences in theory and research suggest the need for a schema for organizing the study of industrialization, especially the recent work that has moved beyond conventional paradigms. The discussion so far provides a necessary first approximation based on major theoretical orientations and the empirical avenues they have opened. To complete a delineation of the field, we now reverse the logic by examining exemplary recent research and asking what theoretical themes animate the work. Some guidelines are needed, however, and here the first approach abets the second by suggesting underlying dimensions.

Drawing on the previous discussion, I propose a property space based on key moments in the development of industrialization and on central analytic issues: epochs and processes. The property space is substantive in the sense that the categories subdividing epochs and processes are informed by the research literature rather than by any logical presumptions of exclusivity or exhaustiveness. The epochs are less chronological than distinctive historical experiences, according to research. The processes constitute a considered sampling of major preoccupations in research, and the list could easily be extended or reorganized. One more proviso: The property space, abbreviated as it is, still includes 25 cells or distinct historical expressions of industrialization.

In the space available here, just 5 of those cells will be discussed, and each one briefly. The 5-part exposition attempts to describe some of the most salient areas of current research on industrialization, but the remaining 20 cells designate lively fields of inquiry. The diagonal intersection of epochs and processes is labeled for the 5 discussion topics: protoindustrialization, culture and class struggle, control structures, proletarianization and the informal sector, and deindustrialization. These designate active research issues, but not the only kind of work described by the intersection. The cells not discussed here also represent important research topics. For example, the cell labeled "V" would include the enormous literature on the causes of the industrial revolution (e.g. Hobsbawm 1968); "W" would embrace studies of social class under conditions of "late" industrialization such as those in the United States and Germany (e.g. Moore 1978); "X" includes the forms of enterprise in developing areas, such as the multinational corporation and its novel patterns of control (e.g. Arrighi 1970); "Y" addresses the sectoral organization of work and casual labor under "mature" industrialization (e.g. Stedman-Jones 1971); "Z" focuses on the crisis of feudalism that helped precipitate industrial revolution (e.g. Anderson 1974). In short, the property space provides one way of organizing and highlighting a very large subject.

Protoindustrialization

Recent research has reopened the question of when and how industrialization began. Conventional interpretations hold that the industrial revolution was an abrupt and qualitative change in social organization that commenced around

Table 1 Epochs and processes of industrialization

	I. Origins	II. Industrial revolution	III. Late industrialization	IV. Newly industrializing societies	V. Postindustrial society
1. Growth and transition	A. Protoindustrialization	V.			
2. Class formation		B. Culture and class struggle	W.		
3. Authority and enterprise			C. Control structures	X.	
4. Labor force			Y.	D. Proletarianization and the informal sector	
5. Contradiction and crisis	Z.				E. Deindustrialization

1760 with the steam engine and mechanized factory production. In the main, sociological theory has accepted this view, conceiving of the industrial revolution as a discontinuous "big bang" that reorganized modern society along the lines of a rational and technical division of labor. Despite his appreciation for the steady evolution of domestic industry, even Marx saw the late eighteenth century as a watershed.

Research over the last several decades questions the timing and discontinuity of industrial development. From the standpoint of technology alone, the Egyptians invented steam power and the Romans the water wheel. Roughly 50 years ago, Carus-Wilson (1941) argued that England's "first industrial revolution" took shape between the eleventh century and the thirteenth century with the advent of milled cloth production, and Nef (1934) marshalled evidence to show that the foundations of modern industry were created between 1540 and 1640, when machinery, coal consumption, large workshops, capital investment, and the domestic market all expanded dramatically. Braudel's (1984:556) review of this research concludes that "the English industrial revolution of the eighteenth century had already begun in the sixteenth century and was simply making progress by stages."

Convincing as these empirical demonstrations may have been, they did not attack the theories behind conventional interpretations (e.g. Cipolla 1980). Anomalies accumulated until the early 1970s when the term "protoindustrialization" (Mendels 1972) and its theoretical implications (Tilly & Tilly 1971) began to be developed. Tilly (1983:129) defines protoindustrialization as "the increase in manufacturing activity by means of the multiplication of very small producing units and small to medium accumulations of capital." The considerable significance of research on protoindustrialization lies in its demonstration that widespread industrial production existed in small towns and rural villages long before the mechanized urban factory; that the labor force was reorganized and proletarianized from 1500 onward; and that industry migrated between regions and urban and rural settings, creating an early pattern of uneven development.

The theoretical implications of protoindustrialization have been aimed at both liberal and Marxian interpretations. Tilly (1983:124) argues that it was the movement of capital, rather than the urbanization and mechanization of large-scale industry, that continuously reshaped industrial society: "The farther the inquiry goes, the more it appears that redeployment of capital and labor makes the big difference, and that mechanization is only one of several means by which that redeployment occurred in Europe." Stated differently— conventional theories are spuriously preoccupied with technology and the division of labor in manufacture, but these are simply particular industrial forms that appear in a longer series of changes explained by capital flows and the uses of labor.

Kriedte et al (1981) extended protoindustrialization to a more focused and controversial revision of Marxian theory in which urban industry of the middle ages and the social division of labor between town and countryside began to collapse under the weight of guild monopoly. "Merchant capital solved this problem by shifting industrial production from the town to the countryside where the process of differentiation and polarization had created a resource in the form of labor power which could easily be tapped by merchant capital. Thus, proto-industrialization, due to its timing, belonged to the second phase of the great transformation from feudalism to capitalism" (Kriedte et al 1981:7). Interregional trade and the world market figured significantly in the successful transition to protoindustrialization, leading these authors (1981:209–10) to stress the theoretical importance of a capitalist world system. Their conception, however, differs in many ways from that in the work of Wallerstein (1974).

Protoindustrialization has recently suffered a barrage of theoretical and factual criticism (e.g. Coleman 1983, Berg et al 1983). Strictly speaking, "proto" (meaning "original") industrialization dates from long before the sixteenth and seventeenth centuries although that period is the focus of this work. The theory behind protoindustrialization, it is alleged, does not really deal with the origins of large-scale industry because it fails to explain why protoindustrialization developed far in some places and collapsed in others (Coleman 1983). On closer examination, most of the work on protoindustrialization is based exclusively on cottage textile production; it does not fit the pattern of other early industrial experience in mining, mills, smelting, or for that matter, in anything but fabrics. Nevertheless, the value of this debate lies in its interpretive contributions which are concerned less with quaint descriptions of rural industry than with theoretical explanations: The concept of protoindustrialization undermines simplifications about the discontinuous character of industrialization that were based on foreshortened time horizons. Recent research demonstrates the value of closer connections between social theory and historical research and suggests new explanations for the longer and more winding course in industrialization.

Culture and Class Struggle

Twenty years ago, when the paradigms described previously dominated thinking about industrialization, the concept of social class was in disrepute. On one hand, theories of social differentiation rejected the term. "As industrialization advances, the skills of manual workers become more differentiated, and still more kinds of managers, technicians, and professionals are added to the productive organization . . . these distinctions cannot be meaningfully equated with 'class' " (Moore 1965:93). On the other hand, Marxian theory had made few advances beyond an economic interpretation of class formation in which a self-conscious and acting proletariat appears only under the conditions of large-scale industry. Either there were no classes, or else the ones that existed did not act like classes.

No single work did more to reverse this situation than Thompson's (1963) *The Making of the English Working Class*. Thompson's singular achievement was to portray the working class as a historical actor rather than a descriptive category. Classes appear when people commence to struggle against exploitation, mainly but not exclusively in relations of production, and their struggles draw on cultural traditions as much as on political rights and economic opportunity. Thompson's approach has influenced a great many students of industry (e.g. Gutman 1966), just as it has provoked criticism, for example, of its blurred distinctions between action stemming from traditional community organization and from class as such (Calhoun 1982). In both cases, Thompson's work has become the pivot of recent research on industry and class formation.

The most important work in the Marxist tradition is John Foster's (1974) study of *Class Struggle and the Industrial Revolution* in three English towns. Foster explains the rise of revolutionary class consciousness in Oldham during the 1820s and its subsequent demise by 1850. In the first period Oldham workers attained a high degree of organization and awareness because people in various occupations were linked through neighborhood ties, and they intermarried at a high rate. Social solidarity enabled them to gain political control of town government and the police. Two other towns experienced the same working class grievances, but less occupational intermarriage, community cohesion, and unity. As the English economy passed through successive crises, Oldham's bourgeois liberalization and industrial reorganization created a labor aristocracy that combined to defeat working class militance. Although Foster's study ultimately supports a Leninist interpretation of worker cooptation, its analysis rests on a broadly sociological account of changes in the community, religion, politics, and the workplace.

Similar analytic strategies inform recent research aimed less at formulating neo-Marxian theory than at evaluating rival explanations of class formation and action. Aminzade (1984) compares Marxian and research mobilization theories of industrial protest in three French towns with varied economic structures. In the town dominated by mechanized factory production, grievances were keen, but the capacity for collective protest was undermined by workers' competition with available unskilled labor. Conversely, in towns with labor concentrated in household production or in handicrafts, protest was more frequent and vigorous owing to the capacity for action developed in workers through more autonomous community and class arrangements. Aminzade (1984:451) concludes that "contrary to Marx's expectations . . . there was a disjuncture between the conditions within which interest polarization was sharpest and the conditions under which class capacities were strongest." The incidence and form of protest are explained by the intersection of industrial pattern, national-level political changes, and the resolution of grievance-capacity conditions. Katznelson's (1985) study of class formation in the United States and England neatly parallels the previous examples. Here the issue is "state- and economy-centered explanations" of national differences in working class consciousness and political action. The argument reviews the labor aristocracy thesis and the spatial transformation of urban communities but concludes that key differences stem from the interplay of state and class. In the United States the vote was granted without struggle, and communities became the base for interclass political parties that appealed to nonclass solidarities. Unions were a separate locus for working class action. Public policy and union repression in England led to a fusion of all aspects of working-class action in locality-based organizations of workers with a deeply felt consciousness of class.

As in the case of protoindustrialization, controversy surrounds some of the recent work on class formation. Stedman-Jones (1983) complains of reductionism in the research exemplified by Foster and Aminzade, although this debate has more to do with the differences between historians and sociologists over the nature of explanation than with the accuracy of specific interpretations. In general, class is back in studies of industrialization, but class in a broader Weberian sense that incorporates political and market power. Recent research emphasizes different conditions of class formation and action—variation, in each case, that is affected by the interaction of industrial organization, community, interclass politics (e.g. reform or repression), technology (cf Cohen, 1985), and the state.

Control Structures

The modern sociological classic on control structures in enterprise is Bendix's (1956) *Work and Authority in Industry*. Bendix observes that a central problem for any industrial society is the development of both the techniques for managing large-scale coordinated enterprises and the ideologies that justify those methods. Management ideologies vary along many dimensions that Bendix seeks to encompass in a comparative study of countries classified by characteristics of early or late industrialization and laissez-faire or state-managed economies. The resulting analysis of England, Russia, the United States, and East Germany, however, focuses more on particular historically evolved ideologies than on cross-national generalizations. At the other extreme, Chandler's (1977, 1984:475) research on managerial capitalism in the United States, England, Germany, and Japan claims that each country arrived, by different routes, at a common pattern of integrated hierarchical organization. This convergence, moreover, occurred "at almost exactly the same time" for each country—except Japan "only because it was later to industrialize." Chandler thus concluded that market forces such as transportation and competitive costs explain the singularly efficient result.

The Bendix-Chandler dispute is only a contemporary version of the debates that Marx and Weber conducted with liberal social and economic theorists. Recent research is beginning to provide some answers. Hamilton & Biggart (forthcoming) evaluate three theories of industrial organization and growth in a comparative study of Japan, South Korea, and Taiwan. Market and cultural explanations of enterprise growth prove useful, but the third approach based on authority relations in society supersedes the first two in some ways and proves uniquely fit for explaining the organizational form of industrial firms.

Complementing this work on the "top down" determinants of industrial organization are studies of authority in relation to people who are the objects of control. Recent research has moved beyond worker satisfaction and staff-line interaction to an analysis of production politics (Sabel 1982), notably in Burawoy's work. The central idea here is that a distinction must be drawn between authority relations that govern the labor process and "the *factory regime,* understood as the institutions that regulate and shape struggles in the workplace" (Burawoy 1984:250). Factory regimes help explain the Marxian paradox of how workers can transform the very structures that oppress them and how changing patterns of authority respond to workers' struggles. Comparative study of the United States, England, and Russia shows that distinctive factory regimes are explained by the interplay of market forces, labor process and reproduction, and the state. Production politics vary from Marx's portrait of coercive "market despotism" to "hegemonic" regimes in which consensus and coordination of the interests of labor and capital are promoted, particularly by state regulation and protections. A new form of "despotic-hegemonic" politics is emerging as enterprises enforce control through threats and acts of plant closure, runaway shops, and substitution of cheap labor (Burawoy 1983).

Research on industrial relations has been revitalized of late through reconceptualizing of authority in its broader social context and through evaluations of competing theories.

Proletarianization and the Informal Sector

Conventional theories are similar in one respect: Both project the experience of European industrialization on the present course of Third World development. Social differentiation envisions a progressive shift in the sectoral distribution of the labor force from primary agricultural activities to secondary manufacture and tertiary commerce and services. In contrast, uneven development theories describe the same general process as an ineluctable trend toward a fully proletarianized labor force. Recent research shows that both scenarios are mistaken.

Browning & Roberts (1980:89) have examined the sectoral distribution of labor in the long-industrialized countries of Europe, in late-industrializing North America, and in the recently industrializing Latin America. "Only Europe has followed the sequence by which employment is first greatest in agriculture, then in manufacturing, and finally in services. In both North America and Latin America employment in the services has always been greater than in manufacturing." The service economies of North and South America, moreover, are structurally distinct. The former is characterized by distributive services for a mass internal market, by high productivity, and by concentrated finance capital. The latter is distinguished by overurbanization, domination by foreign enterprise, and self-employment that subsidizes the modern capitalist sector. These distinct patterns require historical explanation, particularly in the Latin American case, based on analysis of the varied consequences of British and United States imperialism.

In a compact theoretical analysis of the Latin American case, Veltmeyer (1983) argues that labor is not in a state of transition between familiar, developed-nation patterns. Rather, the precise nature of peripheral underdevelopment is due to persistence of precapitalist relations, to surplus labor in the tertiary sector, a proliferation of petty production, and "active semiproletarianization." Although opinion is divided about whether this semi-proletarianized labor force represents a different form of venerable casual labor (Bromley & Gerry 1979) or an etiologically distinct "informal sector" (Portes & Walton 1981), most observers agree that it encompasses the growing bulk of Third World labor.

Defined as paid work that is unregulated and unprotected by the state, the informal sector is growing (Portes & Benton 1984). Not merely in "marginal" self-employment such as street vending (Armstrong & McGee 1985), this growth is occurring across all branches of underdeveloped economies from middle class services to traditional industries such as construction to the most advanced multinational enterprises employing contract out workers or "disguised wage labor" (Birbeck 1978, Redclift & Mingione 1985).

With research expanding rapidly in this field, newly discovered patterns contribute to a lively theoretical dialogue. The prominent role of women workers in the informal economy raises questions about whether the divisions are essentially sectoral or gender-related and whether they recreate nineteenth-century patterns of female proletarianization (Armstrong & McGee 1985). The increase of informal work in the United States raises questions as to whether it is a phenomenon of peripheral or of international capitalism (Sassen-Koob 1982). Whatever the outcome of these issues, it is now clear that sectoral changes are distinctive for different periods of industrialization, that proletarianization is an uneven and dialectical process, and that the sequence Marx envisioned from formal to real subsumption of labor is reversible.

Deindustrialization

In a field where few broad generalizations are safely ventured, we can affirm that today's industrial world is a closely integrated international system. Industrialization relied on international trade from the beginning. Regional shifts in production sites and declines in manufacturing process were known in the periods of protoindustrialization (Tilly 1983). Apropos of current concern about the runaway shop, Landes (1969:116) reports that it was "in the late eighteenth century when, with the power loom not yet practicable and English weavers enjoying the unprecedented demand consequent on the introduction of machine spinning, it began to pay to ship British yarn to central Europe, there to be woven by peasants accustomed to a far lower standard of living than Englishmen." Thus, these days the existence of a world system is less novel than is its growing scale and integration in a pattern of global interdependence.

Operating through large transnational corporations, global industry produces a "new international division of labor" (Frobel et al 1980) that reserves research and development for the advanced nations and less skilled production work for cheap labor enclaves in underdeveloped areas. The "deindustrialization of America" (Bluestone & Harrison 1982) affects heavy industry and blue-collar workers. US production (e.g. steel) is a abandoned for foreign imports, and easily transported products (e.g. footwear, textiles, electronic components) are fabricated in export-oriented Third World sites or assembled in US runaway shops that reimport to the developed economies, often under programs of state support. The familiar consequences of deindustrialization, such as unemployment, displaced and degraded labor, income inequality, and declining unionization, all combine to produce major alterations in the class structures of the advanced societies (Portes & Walton 1981)—as well as the bloating of the tertiary sector in underdeveloped economies, discussed previously.

This, naturally, is a highly schematic picture of a complex process. The internationalization of capital varies with exchange rates, concessions from domestic labor, public policy (e.g. on social insurance, the environment, protectionism), and market demand—the largest US producer of computer chips, which was exporting jobs five years ago, recently closed its operations in Barbados and Puerto Rico due to a slack domestic market. The failure of economic recovery in many sectors of the US economy has generated a vocal protectionist movement aimed at reducing imports and preventing plant closures. Conversely, in some Third World countries a new alliance of national capital and labor may resist incursions by transnational capital (Singer 1985). For example, Brazil's new democratic government, needing to consolidate its domestic bases of support, is presently locked in a struggle with the US government and transnational corporations to preserve some branches of the Brazilian computer market for national firms (Evans 1985). Although deindustrialization is immediately motivated by competition for markets and labor cost advantages, its concrete expression is ultimately fashioned in a many-sided political struggle.

In summary, it is unwise to project a unilinear trend toward a de-industrialized core and a worldwide recourse to cheap labor on the periphery of the world system. A more realistic expectation is that there will be growing international political conflict around these issues, conflict that may be resolved in a variety of ways. This seems to be the thrust of crisis theories that have profited from the failures of economistic analyses and replaced such analyses with interpretations of how economic contradictions become social crises (O'Connor 1984). At all events, two conclusions are inescapable: One, the advanced industrial societies face a period of continuing and traumatic economic restructuring, and two, far from seeing any post-industrial society, we are witnessing the consolidation of a fully industrialized global economy (Mandel 1975).

CONCLUSION

Sociological understanding of industrialization has advanced greatly in the last two decades under the impact of rapid social change and a new style of research that combines theory, historical inquiry, and a global perspective. As for the paradigms that once guided research—social differentiation has been eclipsed except as a metaphor describing subprocesses, and uneven development has been transformed from an imperfect insight to a broader and empirically more refined framework. From the legacies of these alternatives, a new interpretation of the political economy of industrialization is taking shape. Although this is not yet a coherent theory, it most certainly embodies the elements that will organize one.

A fittingly open-ended conclusion can do no better than to draw these lessons: 1. Industrialization is a continuous process driven by wit and contradiction to successively distinct forms of organization, rather than a revolutionary event that is recapitulated over time in separate societies that put together the necessary prerequisites. 2. Important aspects of this process that relate to technological change and market forces are subsumed in sociological explanations of economic organization based on the social division of labor, group formation, classes, authority, the conditions of work, and social protest. 3. The key institutional mediation of diverse social factors lies with community and culture. 4. The state is an enveloping influence shaping both the organization of classes and communities and the conditions of industrial development. 5. The international division of labor and global industrial system affect decisively the opportunity and organization of local industry. 6. Research and theoretical refinement depend on understanding the patterned interaction of these forces over time. However demanding a complete elaboration of each point may be, together they suggest the substantial progress realized in recent work.

Literature Cited

Aminzade, R. 1984. Capitalist industrialization and patterns of industrial protest: A comparative urban study of nineteenth-century France. *Am. Sociol. Rev.* 49:437–53

Armstrong, W., T. McGee. 1985. *Theatres of Accumulation: Studies in Asian and Latin American Urbanization.* London: Methuen

Anderson, P. 1974. *Lineages of the Absolutist State.* London: New Left Books

Arrighi, E. 1970. International corporations, labor aristocracies, and economic development in tropical Africa. In *Imperialism and Underdevelopment: A Reader,* ed. R. Rhodes, pp. 220–67. New York: Monthly Review

Baran, P., P. Sweezey. 1966. *Monopoly Capital: An Essay on the American Economic and Social Order.* New York: Monthly Review

Bell, D. 1973. *The Coming of Post-Industrial Society: A Venture in Social Forecasting.* New York: Basic Books

Bendix, R. 1956. *Work and Authority in Industry: Ideologies of Management in the Course of Industrialization.* New York: Wiley

Berg, I. 1979. *Industrial Sociology.* Englewood Cliffs, NJ: Prentice Hall

Berg, M., Hudson, P., Sonenscher, M. 1983. *Manufacture in Town and Country Before the Factory.* Cambridge: Cambridge Univ. Press

Birbeck, C. 1978. Self-employed proletarians in an informal factory: The case of Cali's garbage dump. *World Dev.* 6:1173–85

Bluestone, B., Harrison, B. 1982. *The Deindustrialization of America: Plant Closings, Community Abandonment, and the Dismantling of Basic Industry.* New York: Basic Books

Braudel, F. 1984. *The Perspective of the World,* Vol. 3, *Civilization and Capitalism, 15th–18th Century.* New York: Harper & Row

Braverman, H. 1974. *Labor and Monopoly Capital: The Degradation of Work in the Twentieth Century.* New York: Monthly Review

Bromley, R., Gerry, C. 1979. *Casual Work and Poverty in Third World Cities.* New York: Wiley

Browning, H., Roberts, B. 1980. Urbanization, sectoral transformation, and the utilization of labor in Latin America. *Comp. Urb. Res.* 8:86–104

Burawoy, M. 1983. Between the labor process and the State: The changing face of factory regimes under advanced capitalism. *Am. Sociol. Rev.* 48:587–605

Burawoy, M. 1984. Karl Marx and the satanic mills: Factory politics under early capitalism in England, the United States, and Russia. *Am. J. Sociol.* 90:247–82

Calhoun, C. 1982. *The Question of Class Struggle: Social Foundations of Popular Radicalism During the Industrial Revolution.* Chicago: Univ. Chicago Press

Cardoso, F., Falleto, E. 1979. *Dependency and Development in Latin America.* Berkeley: Univ. Calif. Press

Carus-Wilson, E. 1941. An industrial revolution of the thirteenth century. *Econ. Hist. Rev.* XI:39–60

Chandler, A. 1977. *The Visible Hand: The Managerial Revolution in American Business.* Cambridge: Harvard Univ. Press

Chandler, A. 1984. The emergence of managerial capitalism. *Bus. Hist. Rev.* 58:473–503

Cipolla, C. 1980. *Before the Industrial Revolution: European Society and Economy, 1000–1700.* New York: Norton

Cohen, I. 1985. Industrial capitalism, technology, and labor relations: The early cotton industry in Lancashire (1770–1840) and New England (1790–1870). In *Political Power and Social Theory,* ed. M. Zeitlin, 5:89–140

Coleman, D. C. 1983. Proto-Industrialization: A Concept Too Many, *Econ. Hist. Rev.* 36(August):435–48

Dahrendorf, R. 1959. *Class and Class Conflict in Industrial Society.* Stanford: Stanford Univ. Press

Durkheim, E. 1933. *The Division of Labor in Society.* Glencoe, Ill: Free Press. (First English edition 1933)

Evans, P. 1985. *Investigating the computer industry: An illustration of possibilities for collaborative North-South research.* Presented at Workshop on the Impact of the Current Economic Crisis on the Social and Political Structures of the Newly Industrialized Nations, Sao Paulo, Brazil

Foster, J. 1974. *Class Struggle and the Industrial Revolution: Early Industrial Cap-*

italism in Three English Towns. London: Weidenfeld & Nicholson

Frobel, F., Heinrichs, J., Kreye, O. 1980. The New International Division of Labor. Cambridge: Cambridge Univ. Press

Diddens, A. 1973. The Class Structures of the Advanced Societies. New York: Barnes & Noble

Gutman, H. G. 1966. Work, Culture, and Society in Industrializing America. New York: Random

Hamilton, G., Biggart, N. 1987. Market, culture, and authority: A comparative analysis of management and organization in the Far East. Am. J. Sociol. In press

Hobsbawm, E. 1968. Industry and Empire. London: Penguin

Katznelson, I. 1985. Working-class formation and the state: Nineteenth-century England in American perspective. In Bringing the State Back In eds. P. Evans, D. Rueschemeyer, T. Skocpol, pp. 257–84. Cambridge: Cambridge Univ. Press

Kriedt, P., Medick, H., Schlumbohm, J. 1981. Industrialization Before Industrialization: Rural Industry and the Genesis of Capitalism. Cambridge: Cambridge Univ. Press

Landes, D. 1969. The Unbound Prometheus: Technological Change and Industrial Development in Western Europe from 1750 to the Present. Cambridge: Cambridge Univ. Press

Mandel, E. 1975. Late Capitalism. London: New Left Books

Marx, K. (1867) 1977. Capital. New York: Vintage

Mendels, F. 1972. Proto-industrialization: The first phase of the industrialization process. J. Econ. Hist. 32:241–61

Moore, B. 1978. Injustice: The Social Bases of Obedience and Revolt. White Plains, NY: Sharpe

Moore, W. 1965. The Impact of Industry. Englewood Cliffs, NJ: Prentice Hall

Nef, J. 1934. The progress of technology and growth of large-scale industry in Great Britain, 1540–1640. Econ. Hist. Rev. V:3–24

O'Connor, J. 1984. Accumulation Crisis. London: Basil Blackwell

Parsons, T. 1966. Societies: Evolutionary and Contemporary Perspectives. Englewood Cliffs, NJ: Prentice Hall

Parsons, T., Smelser, N. 1956. Economy and Society. New York: Free Press

Polanyi, K. 1944. The Great Transformation: The Political and Economic Origins of Our Time. (Paperback edition, 1957.) Boston: Beacon

Portes, A., Walton, J. 1981. Labor, Class, and the International System. New York: Academic Press

Portes, A., Benton, L. 1984. Industrial development and labor absorption: A reinterpretation. Pop. Dev. Rev. 10:589–611

Redclift, N., Mingione, E. 1985. Beyond Employment: Household, Gender, and Subsistence. London: Basil Blackwell

Sabel, C. 1982. Work and Politics: The Division of Labor in Industry. Cambridge: Cambridge Univ. Press

Sassen-Koob, S. 1982. Recomposition and peripheralization at the core. Contemp. Marxism 5:88–100

Schumpeter, J. A. 1935. The Theory of Economic Development. Cambridge: Harvard Univ. Press

Singer, P. 1985. Capital and the nation state: A historical interpretation. In Capital and Labor in the Urbanized World, ed. J. Walton. London: Sage

Smelser, N. 1959. Social Change and the Industrial Revolution. Chicago: Univ. Chicago Press

Smelser, N. 1963. The Sociology of Economic Life. Englewood Cliffs, NJ: Prentice Hall

Stedman-Jones, G. 1971. Outcast London: A Study in the Relationship Between Classes in Victorian Society. Oxford: Oxford Univ. Press

Stedman-Jones, G. 1983. Languages of Class: Studies in English Working Class History, 1832–1982. Cambridge: Cambridge Univ. Press

Tilly, C., Tilly, R. 1971. Agenda for European economic history in the 1970s. J. Econ. Hist. 31:184–98

Tilly, C. 1983. Flows of capital and forms of industry in Europe, 1500–1900. Theor. Soc. 12:123–42

Thompson, E. P. 1963. The Making of the English Working Class. New York: Vintage

Veltmeyer, H. 1983. Surplus Labor and Class Formation on the Latin American Periphery. In Theories of Development: Mode of Production or Dependency?, ed. R. Chilcote, D. Johnson, pp. 201–30. Beverly Hills: Sage

Weber, M. 1946. From Max Weber: Essays in Sociology. Ed. H. Gerth, C. W. Mills. New York: Oxford Univ. Press

Wallerstein, I. 1974. The Modern World System: Capitalist Agriculture and the Origins of the European World-Economy in the Sixteenth Century. New York: Academic Press

Ann. Rev. Sociol. 1987. 13:109–28
Copyright © 1987 by Annual Reviews Inc. All rights reserved

THEORIES OF THE WELFARE STATE

Jill Quadagno

Department of Sociology, University of Kansas, Lawrence, Kansas 66045

Abstract

In the post–World War II era the apparent success of Keynesian economic principles in evening out the instabilities of the business cycle stimulated rapid growth in public welfare expenditures in Western capitalist democracies. For social science, welfare state expansion was not a puzzle but a given. When the economic crisis of the 1970s undermined faith in permanent and sustained growth in welfare programs, the new agenda for social theory concentrated upon the conditions that hindered or favored development. Ironically, both neo-Marxists and conservative economists reached the same conclusion: Welfare programs undermined profitability. The first half of this paper traces these theoretical developments, both in relation to internal debates among social scientists and in regard to external social and economic conditions that shaped the context of theorizing about the welfare state.

Underlying the broader debates about the factors influencing welfare state development has been a more specific concern with the exceptionalism of the American welfare state. Here the central agenda has been to explain why the United States was late in developing national welfare programs and why the programs that did arise contained a bifurcated structure that separated benefits for the poor from those available to all citizens as a right. Three explanations have emerged: the failure of organized labor, the legacy of American politics and the dualism of the American economy. This paper critically assesses the theoretical relevance of these arguments and their implications for recent attacks on benefit programs.

109

0360-0572/87/0815-0109$02.00

INTRODUCTION

Public welfare expenditures in Western capitalist democracies showed a rapid growth, beginning immediately after World War II and slackening only in the 1970s. Welfare state expansion was for social science not a puzzle but a given. With the West in the lead, it seemed only a matter of time before less developed nations would modernize sufficiently to develop the economic surplus and bureaucratic capacity that would allow them to initiate similar programs.

Strengthened by the Keynesian hypothesis that social expenditures for public welfare could stimulate aggregate demand and even out the instabilities and fluctuations of the business cycle, confidence in continuous expansion shaped theories of the welfare state around the issues of origins and growth (Janowitz 1976). Not until the energy crisis of the mid-1970s and subsequent stagflation triggered a questioning of the Keynesian consensus did a decline in welfare state expansion begin (Myles 1984a). Some economists, long persistent critics of welfare programs, attributed the economic crisis to excessive government spending. Their core argument was that the welfare state impinged on the profitability of the capitalist sector by acting as a disincentive both to work and to investment (Bosworth 1980, Fiedler 1975, Haveman 1978, McCracken et al 1977). Both welfare and macroeconomic control, these critics concluded, retarded growth by paralyzing markets. Governments increasingly accepted the monetarist economic doctrines and cut back on public expenditures, especially social benefits (Champagne & Harpham 1984, Gough 1979, Joe & Rogers 1985, Piven & Cloward 1982).

As the economic crisis undermined faith in permanent and sustained growth in welfare programs, social scientists no longer accepted welfare expansion as an inevitable concomitant of economic development or as a satisfactory solution to economic stabilization. Rather, the puzzling aspects of the welfare state became the new agenda for social theory, which now concentrated upon the conditions that hinder or favor development (Myles 1984a). Those still convinced that industrialization was the major factor in creating the welfare state now viewed those same variables that had previously explained program expansion—demographic change, need predicated upon dislocation—as impediments to growth (Gronbjerg 1977; Wilensky 1975). It is surprising that the neo-Marxists came to agree with the conservative viewpoint that welfare programs undermine profitability (Bowles & Gintis 1982, Gough 1979, Offe 1984a, b, Piven & Cloward 1982). In this paper I trace these theoretical developments, both in relation to internal debates among sociologists, economists, and political scientists and in regard to external social and economic conditions that shaped the context of theorizing about the welfare state.

WELFARE STATE GROWTH AND DEVELOPMENT

Prior to World War II, a few nations (Germany, the first) implemented welfare programs based on a social insurance model. In most Western nations, however, national welfare differed little from traditional relief systems, providing minimum benefits to ease the extreme poverty of the least privileged (Heclo 1974, Perrin 1969, Quadagno 1982, Rimlinger 1971). But in the postwar era, social programs were transformed into more comprehensive systems of universal benefits, guaranteeing workers a basic standard of living (Myles 1984b). Sweden implemented major pension reform after World War II, indexing its program of demogrants and making it universally available, then adding a family allowance system in 1947 (Tomasson 1984). In England the 1942 Beveridge report, proposing a national minimum benefit to guarantee freedom from want for all citizens, stimulated legislation for family allowances, old age pensions, and health insurance (Myles 1984c). Germany's 1957 pension legislation contained three programs that covered the vast majority of the West German population (Tomasson 1984). By contrast, the United States still lacks a comprehensive national welfare system. Although the Social Security Act was passed in 1935, only old age insurance was a national program. Unemployment insurance, old age insurance, old age assistance, and aid to dependent children were all joint federal-state programs, which left the determination of eligibility criteria to the states. Most states maintained traditional relief requirements, including local administration, means tests, and family responsibility clauses (Quadagno 1984b, Skocpol & Ikenberry 1983). Not only was the American welfare state less generous than its European counterparts, its programs were bifurcated: social insurance for the majority; social assistance for the poor.

Why welfare states expanded in the postwar period is open to debate, but three factors seem most salient. The welfare state rests, first and foremost, on the availability of some form of reallocable economic surplus. The high level of economic development between 1945 and 1973 provided the economic means, Keynesian economics provided the rationale, while the centralization of the federal government during national wartime mobilization expanded national bureaucratic capacity (Janowitz 1976). For the next 25 years, Keynesian economic principles overrode the conservative view that a deflationary budget and tight monetary policies represented the road to prosperity (Kirchheimer 1965, Marwick 1968, Titmuss 1958).

In this era of post-war prosperity, Lipset (1960, 1974) concluded that the tension between the principles governing a capitalist society and political democracy had been eliminated, replaced by "the democratic class struggle," which made all social arrangements contingent on democratic mass politics.

Concepts of class and state, and the tensions between them, were submerged in the new consensus. Studies of welfare state formation reflected this perspective, minimizing the impact of class and state. The theory that evolved to explain welfare state development mimicked history, including a notion of continuous expansion and a basic optimism that welfare state programs and economic growth were in harmony.

The core argument of this thesis, sometimes termed "the logic of industrialism," is that all industrializing nations, regardless of their historical and cultural traditions or present political and economic structures, become similar through an evolutionary process resulting from the impact of economic and technological growth on the occupational system (Kerr et al 1964, Lerner 1958). As industrialization proceeds, it creates new needs for public spending by reducing the functions of the traditional family and by dislocating certain categories of individuals whose labor becomes surplus—the very young, the old, the sick, and the disabled (Cowgill 1982, Form 1979, Pampel & Weiss 1983). Because traditional societal institutions are unable to meet the needs of these vulnerable individuals, the state expands more or less automatically (Cutright 1965; Jackman 1974, 1975; Wilensky 1975). As Wilensky (1975:xiii) explains, "Economic growth and its demographic and bureaucratic outcomes are the root causes of the general emergence of the welfare state."

Adherents to the logic-of-industrialism thesis do recognize heterogeneity in national welfare programs, which they attribute to variations in surplus wealth, in thresholds of economic development, in the longevity of programs, in the representativeness of government, and in the ability of the state to extract resources (Flora & Albers 1981). But for the initial formulation of the thesis, heterogeneity was not an issue because researchers presumed that Westernization was inevitable. Not until the Keynesian consensus unraveled did explaining heterogenity become a part of the intellectual program.

What makes it possible for industrializing nations to develop national welfare benefits? According to the logic of industrialism, social benefits became feasible because of the new wealth and expanded surplus created by the industrialization process and because of the development of an enhanced organizational structure—a massive state bureaucracy—through which benefits could be delivered (Goldthorpe 1969). Only nations at a particular level of social and economic development can develop welfare programs (Cutright 1965, Pryor 1968).

Studies questioning the inevitability of the relationship between development and the initiation of benefit programs forced industrialism theorists to qualify their conclusions (Williamson & Weiss 1979). In an analysis of 59 nonsocialist nations, Collier & Messick (1975) found little support for the argument that welfare states emerge as a by-product of industrialization. The least modernized nations in their sample initiated social security with less than 5% of the workforce in industry and less than $51 per capita income. Social security was implemented at lower levels of development in later-developing countries, according to Collier & Messick, because the state played a larger role, discovering in such measures an easy way to tax citizens and a means of weakening labor movements. Similarly, in a comparative study of welfare state formation in Germany, Britain, France, and Italy, Hage & Hanneman (1980) concluded that the development of new vulnerabilities in the population does not, in itself, automatically lead to increased welfare expenditures. These needs must be translated into policy through some mechanism, the choice of which is related to the level of political development. Comparing 39 nations at various stages of development, Williamson & Weiss (1979) found that socialist party strength or labor union strength had a significant, indirect effect on the development of a welfare bureaucracy. Thus, the addition of class and political system variables undermined the argument that economic development alone can explain welfare state formation.

What ultimately wreaked greater havoc on the "logic of industrialism" were concerns regarding its basic assumptions. Formulated in a period when there appeared to be an organic unity between the welfare state and an industrialized market economy, the theory had until the 1970s an apparently solid empirical basis. The logic of the argument reflected the growth in both national GNPs and welfare state expenditures associated with the Keynesian welfare state. A distinct change of circumstances in the mid-1970s—the massive inflation following the Vietnam war, OPEC price policies, the collapse of detente—signaled the end of the Keynesian consensus (Myles 1984a, Offe 1984a). No longer, it seemed, were government expenditures able to bring about a balance between unemployment and inflation. For the first time since the Depression, high unemployment and unprecedented inflation persisted, with government seemingly helpless to control either (Offe 1984a, Piven & Cloward 1981). Conservative economists and neo-Marxists, strange bedfellows indeed, found themselves agreeing that the tenuous compromise between capitalism and democracy forged by the Keynesian welfare state had broken down and that public social benefits had become a fetter on the economy. The logic of industrialism contained a critical gap in its portrayal of historical development—it could not explain the struggle for power resources between classes and the political conflicts that arise from these struggles. Neo-Marxist theorists developed a new set of arguments to fill that gap.

THE CONTRADICTION BETWEEN CAPITALISM AND DEMOCRACY

Historically, there is nothing new in the liberal-Marxist consensus that capitalism and democracy represent contradictory principles of social organization. Such nineteenth-century liberal theorists as Mill and de Tocqueville feared that democratic mass politics would lead to class legislation by the propertyless, uneducated majority. Marx, too, recognized that the French democratic constitution of 1848 would withdraw political guarantees from the dominant class and give political power to the subordinate (Offe 1984a).

Yet capitalism and democracy have coexisted, and the central question has become: How is this possible? How can equality of citizenship coexist with capitalism, a system based on social class inequality (Marshall 1950)? Why hasn't the working class, now granted the full and equal franchise, translated its numerical strength into a revolutionary transformation of the state? The answer is twofold. First, class politics were transformed into competitive party politics and thus deradicalized. Deradicalization occurs because the prerequisites of mass democratic politics include the development of a bureaucratized and centralized organization, the expansion of the political base to include a more heterogenous group of supporters, and the consequent erosion of collective identity (Offe 1984a). These manifestations of party politics limit the range of political aims and provide a virtual guarantee that the structure of political power will not deviate from the structure of economic power.

Second, the institutionalization of welfare programs transformed the prewar pattern of industrial class conflict and led to "more economistic, distribution-centered and increasingly institutionalized class conflict" (Offe 1984a:193). The welfare state dispels the motives for class conflict otherwise implicit in the commodification of labor by granting concessions to both capitalists and workers. Workers must accept the legitimacy of the capitalist system, because a sufficient level of profitability and investment ensures an economic surplus that can be used to initiate welfare benefits. Capitalists, in turn, accept the need for basic wages and welfare state expenditures, because these benefits ensure a healthy and complacent working class (Offe 1984a). Thus, public social benefits represent a real gain for the working class, even though welfare programs also benefit capital.

Other neo-Marxist theorists take a more unidimensional view, emphasizing the functions of welfare benefits for capital. In their analyses, social welfare programs are the outgrowth of the basic imperatives that mold the activities of the state in capitalist society—the need to maintain profitability and the need to ensure social harmony. Welfare programs contribute to profitability by lowering the employer's costs of maintaining a healthy and skilled labor force. By subsidizing the social expenditures formerly borne by the private sector, the state thus acts in the interest of capital. Welfare programs also contribute to the legitimation function of capital by containing worker unrest (O'Connor 1973, Olson 1982, Phillipson 1983, Trempe 1983).

According to neo-Marxist theory, the state can never develop a set of policies truly designed to meet human needs because these policies will invariably encounter the constraints of the capitalist economic system (Gough 1979). For example, if the state attempted to eliminate poverty by providing a higher minimum wage, this wage would soon surpass the wages paid to low-wage workers. If we assume that men and women prefer benefits over low-wage labor, then welfare would become a disincentive to work and would eliminate a source of cheap labor. Because it always has the potential to interfere with the free operation of the labor market, the welfare state embodies the contradictions of the capitalist mode of production.

A major gap in the logic-of-industrialism thesis was its inability to specify the mechanism by which benefit programs get enacted. This gap has been filled in what Shalev (1983) terms the "social democratic" model, whose basic premise is that "the growth of the welfare state is a product of the growing strength of labor in civil society" (Stephens 1979). Labor gains strength in a series of historical stages associated with the development of capitalism. Because capitalism requires a free labor market where labor can be bought and sold for a wage, the first right of labor is legal emancipation (Myles 1984c, Therborn 1977). From this fundamental cleavage, between those who sell labor and those who purchase it, the capitalist economy emerges. An emancipated labor force first organizes in the marketplace to demand wages beyond those prevailing in a free market and then carries the struggle to the state, where unionized workers capture the state through electoral struggle and use it as a vehicle to modify distributional inequalities (Cameron 1978, Shalev 1983).

A substantial body of evidence supports the social democratic view (Korpi 1978, 1980; Furniss & Tilton 1977). In many European nations, workers organized into political parties to implement aggressive social spending measures (Bjorn 1979, Cameron 1978, Stephens 1979). Further, numerous quantitative, cross-national analyses verify the thesis that nations with high union mobilization and stable leftist governments have the highest levels of welfare spending (Cameron 1978, Castles 1983, Castles & McKinlay 1979). Yet contradictory evidence undermines the power of the social democratic argument. Many studies, for example, concede that state power through social democracy is not the only route to welfare state growth and that socialist impact on welfare is at least somewhat conditioned by economic conditions and political system characteristics (Shalev 1983). Further, although the social democratic model only applies to advanced industrial democracies, nondemocratic and noncapitalist societies also establish welfare states (Flora & Heidenheimer 1981). Another anomoly is that the social democratic agenda in welfare spending is not always consistent. As Parkin (1971:121) notes, "Social democrats have been more willing to broaden the social base of recruitment to privileged positions than to equalize rewards attached to different positions."

Parkin's argument does not undermine the social democratic position so much as it reflects the political realities of mass democratic politics. As organized labor attempts to implement socialist goals through competitive political parties, it is constrained by the need to expand the party base beyond the working class. As the party becomes more heterogeneous, it erodes the sense of collective identity of party members and limits the range of political goals (Offe 1984b). The inherent dynamic of the party system limits the content of all politics and "makes democracy safe for capitalism" (Macpherson 1977).

A basic social democratic principle is that in capitalist democracies the state and the economy are separate. Because of this separation, workers are able "to alter the distributional process in a manner that is independent of market criteria and the class principle; in effect, the market can be bypassed, and its rules of distribution made irrelevant" (Myles 1984c). In a more radical neo-Marxist view of the welfare state, the state and the economy are inextricably intertwined. The state is not, in this perspective, a neutral state, but rather a capitalist state that serves the interest of the dominant capitalist class (Gough 1979, Miliband 1969).

Why should the state act in the interests of capital rather than reflect impartially the interests of all groups in society? One answer is that members of the capitalist class dominate government and are thus able to act in their own best interests (Miliband 1969; Domhoff 1972, 1979). But different and potentially conflicting elements exist within this class, and the state cannot act on behalf of the long-term interests of the capitalist class as a whole unless it possesses a degree of autonomy. One way it achieves autonomy is through a division of labor between those who accumulate capital and those who manage the state apparatus (Block 1977, 1980). While capitalists are generally not conscious of what is necessary to reproduce the social order, state managers must be, for their continued power rests on political and economic order. The central constraint on the decision-making power of state managers is "business confidence." Individual capitalists make investment decisions on the basis of such tangibles as the price of labor and the size of the market as well as such intangibles as the political and economic climate. Business confidence falls during political turmoil and rises when there is a restoration of order. Since state managers are dependent on the investment accumulation process, they must use whatever resources they possess to aid that process (Block 1977).

Another perspective sees the state as the very embodiment of class contradictions (Carnoy 1984, Poulantzas 1978). As Poulantzas (1978:133) explains:

Each state branch or apparatus and each of their respective sections and levels frequently constitutes the power-base and favored representative of a particular fraction of the bloc, or of a conflictual alliance of several fractions opposed to certain others.

The contradictions between the dominant fractions imbedded in the state make it necessary for the state to perform an organizing function. The state thus becomes a mediating body, weighing priorities, filtering information, and integrating contradictory measures into state policy (Poulantzas 1978). But it can never be a neutral state, because it embodies class relations in its very structure (Carnoy 1984).

Some research supports the neo-Marxist view that the welfare state is largely a repressive social control mechanism. The German pension program established by Bismarck in 1889 served a dual purpose: It checked the threat of the working class and contained the power of the bourgeoisie (Rimlinger 1971, Tomasson 1984). Others have demonstrated that employers' organizations have sometimes initiated social benefit programs and that social expenditures by right wing parties are sometimes greater than those under left-leaning governments (Quadagno 1984a, Shalev 1983:). The apparently conflicting evidence over who initiates welfare programs can be resolved by recognizing that since these programs benefit both capital and labor, either class faction may be in a structural position at a given historical moment to establish them (Offe 1984a).

In Bismarckian Germany, state authority was the key factor in welfare state development; in France, too, the state bureaucracy maintained a balance between industrialists and agrarian groups (Rimlinger 1971). Yet a third perspective focuses on the state, emphasizing the influence of the state bureaucracy in initiating and expanding social welfare programs and the impact of existing social policies on subsequent policy decisions. In a period when state authority has become a powerful instrument for shrinking welfare benefits, it is not surprising to find convincing those arguments that redirect attention toward the state. As Skocpol (1980:200) contends:

States and political parties within capitalism have cross-nationally and historically varying structures. These structures powerfully shape and limit state interventions in the economy, and they determine the ways in which class interests and conflicts get organized into (or out of) politics in a given time and place.

STATES, PARTIES, AND POLICY PRECEDENTS

Adherents to the logic-of-industrialism thesis view the state largely as a passive instrument, which responds to the demands of various citizen groups or to those made needy by the dislocations of industrialism (Gronbjerg 1977, Pampel & Williamson 1985). Social democratic theorists also see the state as manipulable, not by all citizen groups, but by labor unions organized into class-based political parties. Marxists, by contrast, view the state as an instrument of the ruling class. Yet a substantial and expanding body of research has demonstrated that the state is not merely a passive instrument through which various interest groups can press their demands; it is rather a major force in shaping the directions of social legislation (Amenta & Skocpol 1986).

At its most basic level, the state is defined in terms of the activities of the state bureaucracy. Several studies have found the state bureaucracy to be an important component of the policy formation process. In a comparative study of policy formation in Britain and Sweden, Heclo (1974) finds that policy innovations came primarily from civil servants. Two case studies of the development of the American program of old age insurance also indicate the importance of the state bureaucracy. Derthick (1979) examined the actions of program administrators in the Social Security Administration from its founding years to the late 1970s. She found a high degree of administrative autonomy in establishing and implementing program priorities, within limits circumscribed by the orientation of the party in power. Similarly, Cates (1983) found that program administrators contributed to the expansion of social insurance through concerted and ultimately successful efforts to contain the public old age assistance program.

Quantitative measures of state capacity support these case studies. Comparing twenty democratic capitalist nations, DeViney (1983) found that the degree of bureaucratization and centralization and reliance on direct taxation were the best predictors of welfare program expansion. DeViney's findings are backed by Flora & Alber (1981), who conclude that a strong state bureaucracy significantly influences the initiation of welfare programs.

A second thrust of the state-centered approach has been an emphasis on political learning. Policymakers do not base their agendas primarily on external demands; rather prior state actions shape future goals (Heclo 1974, Shefter 1977, Skocpol & Finegold 1982). As Heclo (1974:315) explains:

> What is normally considered the dependent variable (policy output) is also an independent variable (in an ongoing process in which everything becomes an intervening variable) . . . policy inevitably builds on policy, either in moving forward what has been inherited, or amending it, or repudiating it.

The impact of policy legacies was one factor shaping the American welfare state. According to one interpretation, the prior existence of state-level initiatives in unemployment insurance, old age pensions, and mother's pensions prevented the Social Security Act of 1935 from being legislated as a single national program (Skocpol & Ikenberry 1983). Thus, state activity is not merely a reflection of socioeconomically rooted demands, needs, and preferences, given expression by organized groups. Rather, policymaking is an inherently historical process in which "all actors consciously build upon or react against, previous governmental efforts dealing with the same sorts of problems" (Orloff 1985:27).

A third component of the state-centered approach asserts that historical variations in state structures shape the content and timing of policy initiatives (Skocpol 1980). The sequence of the timing of democratization and bureaucratization is a key determinant of the timing of benefit programs (Orloff & Skocpol 1984). The British welfare state developed early because Britain had a centralized state bureaucracy and credentialed civil service prior to mass democratization. Because of this juxtaposition of structural factors, political parties in Britain moved toward programmatic appeals to the electorate, among them social benefits. In the United States, in contrast, full democratization preceded bureaucratization. Until the struggle against political corruption achieved significant regulatory breakthroughs in the Progressive Era, public distrust for patronage-based parties obstructed major administrative reform.

The major criticism of the state-centered approach is that it deemphasizes the class nature of the state (Carnoy 1984); the impact on social policy of both labor and capital are minimized or discounted. Ruggie (1984) compensates for this theoretical gap by assessing state capacity through a typology, ranking what she terms the "liberal welfare state" low on state capacity and the "corporatist welfare state" high. In a liberal welfare state, "the proper sphere of state behavior is circumscribed by the functioning of market forces," and the function of public welfare is to ameliorate market dysfunctions (Ruggie 1984:15). The result is incremental public policy measures and a fragmented structure. By contrast, a corporatist welfare state defines the parameters of market forces a priori, intervening not simply to compensate for inequality but to institutionalize equality. The result is a blurring of the boundaries between state and society. What determines state capacity, according to Ruggie, is the position of labor within the state. Thus, state capacity is not an abstract concept but evolves within a particular power nexus.

Although the state-centered approach provides a welcome corrective to the view that social insurance innovations were simply responses to socioeconomic dislocation or concessions to demands by trade unions, the hegemonic role of the administrative and coercive institutions of the state over its representative institutions needs to be treated as a variable that requires explanation rather than as an explanatory constant (Myles 1984a).

All of the theories discussed above deal either implicitly or explicitly with the present "crisis of the welfare state." Yet, with the exception of the industrialism thesis, none takes seriously the consequences of demographic change, or, more specifically, the issue of population aging. For most countries, pension expenditures are the most expensive of government social welfare costs, and the expansion of the aged population in the West has undeniably increased the welfare burden (Pampel & Williamson 1985). What social democratic and neo-Marxist theorists alike need to assess is whether the expansion of the older population, independent of conflict between workers and capitalists, has contributed to the present perception of crisis.

THE EXCEPTIONALISM OF THE AMERICAN WELFARE STATE

Whereas other nations have developed comprehensive national welfare systems, the United States still has not established national standards for most kinds of benefits, has maintained a bifurcated program of benefits distinguishing the deserving majority from the nondeserving poor, and has been unable or unwilling to coordinate social welfare taxing and spending with deliberate public interventions in the economy (Skocpol & Ikenberry 1983). Why the United States was late in developing national welfare programs and why those programs have been relatively inadequate has become a topic of debate among scholars intrigued by the broader issue of welfare state development in Western capitalist democracies (Orloff 1985; Orloff & Skocpol 1984; Quadagno 1988a, b; Skocpol 1984; Skocpol & Ikenberry 1983; Zald 1985). Three explanations provide some insight into the American case.

The Failure of Organized Labor

One explanation, stemming from the social democratic premise, is that the weakness of the American labor movement impeded the development of a national welfare state. Organized labor never formed a political party through which to press its demands, and American labor leaders adopted a philosophy of voluntarism that rejected social insurance (Rimlinger 1971).

The weak labor hypothesis is part of a broader argument about the absence of class-based politics in America. What is distinctive about American political development that has undermined a class-based political movement? Why did a labor movement that was once the most radical and violent in history never form an independent political party through which to advocate a socialist agenda (Oppenheimer 1985)? The answers have been diverse: opportunities on the frontier that diffused class conflict, the absence of a feudal past, racial and ethnic diversity that splintered the labor movement, early suffrage that demobilized working-class consciousness, the presence of an egalitarian, achievement-oriented ethos, and the greater opportunities for upward mobility available to the American worker (Davis 1980; Hartz 1974; Karabel 1979; Katznelson 1981; Laslett 1979; Lipset 1974; Sombart 1976).

Although the American labor movement did not form a political party, it has not received credit for much of the concerted and successful political action it did engage in. Most analyses of organized labor have concentrated upon the stance of the national leadership, in particular the voluntaristic philosophy of American Federation of Labor President, Samuel Gompers. Yet most of labor's political activity prior to 1935 took place at the state rather than the national level, a natural product of the federalized structure of government (Fink 1975, Orloff & Skocpol 1984; Quadagno 1988b). And at the state level, labor unions did engage in political action. In the battle for old age pensions, for example, state federations, central labor bodies, and locals of the United Mine Workers worked for legislation for more than 20 years (Anglim & Gratton 1987, Quadagno 1988b). The greatest impediment to labor's political effectiveness in the pre–New Deal era was its persistent need to focus on organizational maintenance, rather than broader social issues because of employers' efforts to defeat the labor movement (Griffin et al 1986, Quadagno 1988b).

The lack of unionization among mass production workers, the source of much pro-welfare activism in European politics, must also be taken into account. Prior to the New Deal, the AFL showed little interest in organizing industrial workers, but the most significant effort for state welfare legislation arose from the one strong industrial union, the United Mine Workers (Quadagno 1988). After World War II, however, the CIO's newly won collective bargaining rights directed the union's attention toward private rather than public sector benefits (Piore & Sabel 1984, Quadagno 1988b, Tomlins 1985). To the extent that industrial workers influenced the expansion of the American welfare state, their impact was indirect, as increases in private sector benefits reduced employer resistance to public sector expansion. The intersection of public and private sector benefits, a topic that has received little attention in the literature on the welfare state, deserves further exploration.

Finally, several studies indicate that the most militant expression of working class unrest has come not from organized labor but from racial insurgency and urban riots (Griffin et al 1983; Isaac & Kelly 1981). In the US post–World War II era, mass insurgency has contributed to increased levels of welfare spending; in this the state shows its central concern for the maintenance of order and social harmony.

The Legacy of American Politics

A second line of argument attributes the underdevelopment of the American welfare state to the legacy of previous policy precedents. According to Orloff & Skocpol (1984), the early democratization of the US electorate created a patronage system in which government outputs took the form of distributional policies. Patronage spending peaked under the Civil War pension system, when a substantial portion of the federal budget was expended on a corruptly administered program. With the central government weak and the state bureaucracy virtually undeveloped, reformers doubted that social spending measures could be implemented honestly. Fears by citizens of further patronage abuses in benefit programs undermined public support for national social programs and thus delayed the onset of the American welfare state (Orloff 1985).

Previous policy precedents also influenced the structure of the Social Security Act and set limits on subsequent policy developments (Skocpol 1984, Skocpol & Amenta 1985, Skocpol & Ikenberry 1983). As Skocpol (1984 : 9) argues, New Deal reformers were strongly influenced by Wisconsin policymakers, who believed that "open-ended governmental handouts to citizens must be avoided, for these could fuel political corruption and unbalanced budgets." Wisconsin policymakers were committed to keeping public assistance programs for the poor separate from social insurance programs that workers would earn as a matter of right. Of all the programs enacted under the Social Security Act, only old age insurance became a national program. The others—old age assistance, unemployment insurance, and aid to dependent children—were legislated as joint federal-state initiatives because existing state programs and policy initiatives in these areas undercut efforts for a totally national agenda (Skocpol & Ikenberry 1983). Once the programs were in place, administrators in the expanding state bureaucracy, imbued with the Wisconsin ethos, resisted expanding the old age assistance program for fear it would become a viable alternative to old age insurance (Cates 1983).

All Western capitalist nations are cognizant of "the fiscal crisis of the welfare state." In the United States, however, the bifurcated structure of the American welfare state has focused attacks on welfare spending primarily on programs for the poor. The New Deal legacy created a virtually untouchable old age insurance program for the majority. By excluding agricultural workers from coverage in OASI and unemployment insurance, however, the Social Security Act left most blacks uncovered. This initial program structure left the assistance programs for the poor politically vulnerable, and it continues to affect the adequacy of protection for blacks (Skocpol 1984).

The Dualism of the American Economy

Yet a third argument links welfare to the labor process. Employers have traditionally used welfare to manipulate the labor supply. For example, the key features of the English poor law—local autonomy in administration and the requirement of local residency—allowed landlords in their dual capacity as poor law authorities to maintain a local labor force by controlling the relationship between wages and relief benefits (Quadagno 1982). Benefits were kept below wages so as not to undermine work incentives, while workers could be removed from relief whenever they were needed to work the fields or harvest the crops. Similar uses of welfare can be found in relief programs in the United States in the early poor laws (Quadagno 1984b), in old age assistance (Quadagno 1988a) and in AFDC (Bell 1965, Piven & Cloward 1982). Thus, relief programs have historically maintained a pool of marginally employed, low-wage workers.

In the United States industrialization progressed at an uneven pace. In the North it created a labor force of semiskilled and unskilled workers, who formed into national labor unions and negotiated with employers for improved working conditions, higher wages, and social benefits (Gordon et al 1982). Northern workers also formed a coalition with the Democratic party in the years following the New Deal to press for supportive labor legislation and to demand benefits from the state (Bensel 1984). In contrast, until midway through the twentieth century, the South had few of the characteristics identified as necessary for welfare state development: industrialization, democracy, political parties, and a working class capable of pressing for social benefits. Economically and politically isolated from the rest of the nation, members of the Southern planter class took advantage of the peculiar structure of the American political system to form what Southern statesman John Calhoun termed a "concurrent majority," that is, a minority able to exercise negative power over the majority (Sydnor 1948). In the twentieth century, they used this negative power to impede national welfare programs (Alston & Ferrie 1985, Quadagno 1988a).

Why did the South resist national welfare legislation? The answer lies in the political economy of the cotton South. As the North industrialized, the South remained primarily agricultural, with Southern cotton planters dependent on massive numbers of unskilled black workers. The system of tenancy, which developed after slavery was abolished, guaranteed planters control over a subservient, primarily black labor force (Mandle 1978). Any flow of benefits into this system would have disrupted the planter-tenant relationship and undermined the planter's paternalistic control (Alston & Ferrie 1985).

How did the South, a region which contained less than 25% of the total population until 1969, exert a controlling, negative influence on national legislation (Potter 1972)? The answer lies in the organizational and procedural structure of the congressional committee system and in the status of democracy in the South. When we speak of the early democratization of American society, we tend to forget that full democracy did not exist in the South until the Voting Rights Act of the 1960s. The turn-of-the-century disenfranchising conventions had reduced the Southern electorate to less than 20% and in some states to less than 12% (Woodward 1951, Key 1949). Disenfranchisement also effectively eliminated two-party democracy in the South. As a result,

Southern politics were conducted by amorphous factions within the Democratic party (Key 1949).

One-party democracy, Southern-style, also gave Southern congressmen
enormous political power on the national scene. The right granted committees
to refuse to report a bill out, and the seniority system which served as the basis
for selecting committee chairmen, gave Southern congressmen control over
key congressional committees for decades—Southern congressmen who often
ran unopposed were consistently reelected to office (Potter 1972). All social
benefit programs had to pass through the House Ways and Means and the
Senate Finance committees, both Southern-controlled until the 1960s. Two
studies of the Social Security Act conclude that Southern congressmen impeded the establishment of more generous benefit programs by insisting that
agricultural workers be excluded from the national old age insurance program
and by eliminating federal controls and regulations from the joint federal-state
programs (Alston & Feree 1985, Quadagno 1985, 1988a, b). It was not until
the Civil Rights movement undermined the coalition of urban labor and
Southern politicians in the Democratic party that the influence of Southern
congressmen on national legislation was reduced.

The three perspectives on American political development discussed above
are not necessarily contradictory. Rather, each addresses different influences
on welfare state formation. Any comprehensive analysis of the development
of social benefits in the United States must include analyses of the impact of
organized labor, of policy legacies, and of the existence of two distinct
economic formations within a single nation state.

CONCLUSION

Welfare programs are not a unique feature of advanced capitalist nations,
although they are sometimes treated as such. Since at least the sixteenth
century, all Western societies have developed methods of dispensing sustenance to their more vulnerable members. What has changed is the method of
providing social benefits, as welfare was transformed from locally financed
and administered systems of labor control befitting a rural, labor-dependent
society to nationally financed and administered programs of benefits for
citizens of industrialized nations. The transformation of form, however, does
not mean that the labor control functions have disappeared. Rather, they have
been structured to fit the logic of the new industrial order. In seeking an
explanation of "the welfare state," we would do best to reconstruct our
understanding of social welfare. Instead of looking for correlations between
variables, we must examine the underlying functions welfare programs provide. Thus, one agenda for future research might be to examine how changes
in benefit programs are related to changes in the labor process.

Although many countries in the Western world are presently weighing the relative costs and benefits of welfare state programs, in the United States these attacks have focused most intensely on the income maintenance programs for the poor, most of which disproportionately aid women and minorities. The bifurcated structure of the American welfare state is not predicated solely on class but also on race and gender. The legacy of the South partially explains why blacks have fared poorly under public programs in the United States, but much of the research on women's welfare has not been incorporated into debates about the welfare state (O'Rand & Henretta 1982; O'Rand & Landerman 1984; Pearce 1978; Pearce & McAdoo 1981; Scott 1984; Treas 1981). Future research on the welfare state must begin to take both race and gender into account as major variables that cut across class-based divisions. To the extent that monopoly capital and organized labor have achieved some consensus in American society, it has come about at the price of excluding workers, often women and minorities, in low-wage, nonunionized industries, from equal access to full social insurance benefits (Friedland 1976).

ACKNOWLEDGMENTS

I am grateful to John Myles for providing comments and suggestions for revisions on an earlier draft of this manuscript and to Charles Tilly for helping to focus the direction of the essay.

Literature Cited

Alston, L., Feree, J. 1985. Labor costs, paternalism, and loyalty in Southern agriculture: A constraint on the growth of the welfare state. *J. Econ. Hist.* 45:95–117

Amenta, E., Skocpol, T. 1986. States and social policies. *Ann. Rev. Sociol.* 12:131–57

Anglim, C., Gratton, B. 1987. Organized labor and old age pensions. *Int. J. Aging Hum. Dev.*

Bell, W. 1965. *Aid to Dependent Children.* New York: Columbia Univ. Press

Bensel, R. F. 1984. *Sectionalism and American Political Development.* Madison: Univ. Wisc. Press

Bjorn, L. 1979. Labor parties, economic growth and redistribution in five capitalist democracies. *Comp. Soc. Res.* 2:93–128

Block, F. 1977. Beyond corporate liberalism. *Soc. Probl.* 24:352–61

Block, F. 1980. Beyond relative autonomy: State managers as historical subjects. In *The Socialist Register,* ed. R. Miliband, J. Saville, pp. 227–62 London: Merlin

Bosworth, B. 1980. "Re-establishing an economic consensus: An impossible agenda." *Daedalus* 109:59–70

Bowles, S., Gintis, S. 1982. The crisis of liberal democratic capitalism: The case of the United States. *Polit. Soc.* 11:51–93

Cameron, D. 1978. The expansion of the public economy. *Am. Polit. Sci. Rev.* 72:1243–60

Carnoy, M. 1984. *The State and Political Theory.* Princeton: Princeton Univ. Press

Castles, F. 1983. *The Impact of Parties.* Beverly Hills, Calif: Sage

Castles, F., McKinlay, R. 1979. Public welfare provision and the sheer futility of the sociological approach to politics. *Br. J. Polit. Sci.* 9:157–72

Cates, J. 1983. *Insuring Inequality, Administrative Leadership in Social Security, 1935–54.* Ann Arbor: Univ. Mich. Press

Champagne, A., Harpham, E. J. 1984. *The Attack on the Welfare State.* Prospect Heights, Il: Waveland

Collier, D., Messick, R. 1975. Prerequisites versus diffusion: Testing alternative explanations of social security adoption. *Am. Polit. Sci. Rev.* 69:1299–1315

Cowgill, D. 1980. The aging of populations and societies. In *Aging, the Individual and Society,* ed. J. Quadagno, pp. 15–33. New York: St. Martin's

Cutright, P. 1965. Political structure, economic development, and national social security programs. *Am. J. Sociol.* 70:537–48

Davis, Mike. 1980. Why the U.S. working class is different. *New Left Rev.* 123:3–44

Derthick, M. 1979. *Policymaking for Social Security.* Washington, DC: Brookings Inst.

DeViney, S. 1983. Characteristics of the state and the expansion of public social expenditures. *Comp. Soc. Res.* 6:151–74

Domhoff, W. 1972. *The Higher Circles.* New York: Random

Domhoff, W. 1979. *The Powers That Be.* New York: Vintage

Fiedler, E. 1975. Economic policies to control stagflation. In *Inflation: Long-term Problems: Proc. Acad. Polit. Sci.* ed., C. Harriss, 31:169–78

Fink, G. 1975. *State Labor Proceedings: A Bibliography of the AFL, CIO and AFL-CIO Proceedings, 1885–1974.* Westport, Conn: Greenwood

Flora, P., Alber, J. 1981. Modernization, democratization and the development of welfare states in Western Europe. See Flora & Heidenheimer 1981, pp. 37–80

Flora, P., Heidenheimer, A. 1981. *The Development of Welfare States in Europe and America.* New Brunswick, NJ: Transaction

Form, W. 1979. Comparative industrial sociology and the convergence hypothesis. *Ann. Rev. Sociol.* 5:1–25

Friedland, R. 1976. Class power and social control: The War on Poverty. *Polit. Soc.* 6:459–89

Furniss, N., Tilton, T. 1977. *The Case for the Welfare State: From Social Security to Social Equality.* Bloomington, Ind: Ind. Univ. Press

Goldthorpe, J. 1969. Social stratification in industrial society. In *Structured Social Inequality,* C. Heller, ed., London: Macmillan

Gordon, D. M., Edwards, R., Reich, M. 1982. *Segmented Work, Divided Workers.* Cambridge: Cambridge Univ. Press

Gough, I. 1979. *The Political Economy of the Welfare State.* London: Macmillan

Griffin, L., Devine, J., Wallace, M. 1983. On the economic and political determinants of welfare spending in the post-World War II era. *Polit. Soc.* 12:331–72

Griffin, L., Wallace, M., Rubin, B. 1986. Capital resistance to the organization of labor before the New Deal. Why? How? Success? *Am. Sociol. Rev.* 51:147–67

Gronbjerg, K. 1977. *Mass Society and the Extension of Welfare 1960–1970.* Chicago: Univ. Chicago Press

Hage, J., Hanneman, R. 1980. The growth of the welfare state in Britain, France, Germany and Italy: A comparison of three paradigms. *Comp. Soc. Res.* 3:45–70

Hartz, L. 1974. The liberal tradition. See Laslett & Lipset 1974, pp. 397–408

Haveman, R. 1978. Unemployment in Western Europe and the United States: A problem of demand, structure, or measurement. *Am. Econ. Rev.* 68:44–50

Heclo, H. 1974. *Modern Social Politics in Britain and Sweden.* New Haven, Conn: Yale Univ. Press

Held, T., Anderson, J., Gieben, B., Harris, L., et al. 1983. *States and Societies.* New York: New York Univ. Press

Hewitt, C. 1977. The effect of political democracy and social democracy on equality in industrial societies: A cross-national comparison. *Am. Sociol. Rev.* 42:450–64

Isaac, L., Kelly, W. 1981. Racial insurgency, the state, and welfare expansion: Local and national level evidence from the postwar United States. *Am. J. Sociol.* 86:1348–86

Jackman, R. 1974. Political democracy and social equality: A comparative analysis. *Am. Sociol. Rev.* 39:29–45

Jackman, R. 1975. *Politics and Social Equality: A Comparative Analysis.* New York: Wiley

Janowitz, M. 1976. *Social Control of the Welfare State.* Chicago: Univ. Chicago Press

Joe, T., Rogers, C. 1985. *By the Few for the Few, The Reagan Welfare Legacy.* Lexington, Mass: Lexington

Karabel, J. 1979. The reasons why. *NY Rev. Books* 29:22–27

Katznelson, I. 1981. *City Trenches, Urban Politics and the Patterning of Class in the United States.* New York: Pantheon

Kerr, C., Dunlop, J., Harbison, F., Myers, C. 1964. *Industrialism and Industrial Man: The Problems of Labor and Management in Economic Growth.* New York: Oxford Univ. Press

Key, V. O. 1949. *Southern Politics in State and Nation.* New York: Knopf

Kirchheimer, O. 1965. Confining conditions and revolutionary breakthroughs. *Am. Polit. Sci. Rev.* 59:964–74

Korpi, W. 1978. *The Working Class in Welfare Capitalism: Work, Unions and Politics in Sweden.* London: Routledge Kegan Paul

Korpi, W. 1980. Social policy and distributional conflict in the capitalist democracies. *West Eur. Polit.* 3:296–315

Laslett, H. M. 1979. The American tradition of labor theory and its relevance to the contemporary working class. In *The American Working Class,* ed. I. L. Horowitz, J. C. Leggett, M. Oppenheimer, pp. 3–30. New Brunswick, NJ: Transaction

Lerner, D. 1958. *The Passing of Traditional Society.* Glencoe, Il: Free Press

Lipset, S. M. 1960. *Political Man.* Garden City, New York: Doubleday

Lipset, S. M. 1974. The labor movement and

American values. See Laslett & Lipset 1974, pp. 553–72

Macpherson, C. 1977. *The Life and Times of Liberal Democracy.* New York: Oxford Univ. Press

Mandle, J. 1978. *The Roots of Black Poverty, The Southern Plantation Economy After the Civil War.* Durham, NC: Duke Univ. Press

Marshall, T. 1950. Citizenship and social class. See Held et al 1983, pp. 248–260

Marwick, A. 1968. *Britain in the Century of Total War: War, Peace, and Social Change 1900–1967.* Boston: Little Brown

McCracken, P. 1977. *Towards Full Employment and Price Stability.* Paris: Org. Econ. Coop. Dev.

Miliband, R. 1969. *The State in Capitalist Society.* London: Weidenfield & Nicolson

Myles, J. 1984a. *State structures and the structure of the welfare state: Comment on Skocpol.* Presented at the Conf. Polit. Econ., Dept. Polit. Sci., Univ. Minn., Minneapolis

Myles, J. 1984b. *The retirement wage in postwar capitalist democracies.* Presented at Ann. Meet. Am. Sociol. Assoc., San Antonio

Myles, J. 1984c. *Old Age in the Welfare State.* Boston: Little Brown

O'Connor, J. 1973. *The Fiscal Crisis of the State.* New York: St. Martin's

Offe, C. 1984a. *Contradictions of the Welfare State.* Cambridge, Mass: MIT Press

Offe, C. 1984b. Competitive party democracy and the Keynesian welfare state: Factors of stability and disorganization. In *The Political Economy,* ed. T. Ferguson, J. Rogers, pp. 349–67. Armonk, NY: Sharpe

Olson, L. 1982. *The Political Economy of the Welfare State.* New York: Columbia Univ. Press

Oppenheimer, M. 1985. *White Collar Politics.* New York: Monthly Rev.

Orloff, A. 1985. *The politics of pensions: A comparative analysis of the origins of pensions and old age insurance in Canada, Great Britain and the United States, 1880s–1930s.* PhD thesis. Princeton Univ. Dep. Sociol. Princeton, NJ 326 pp.

Orloff, A., Skocpol, T. 1984. Why not equal protection? Explaining the politics of public social spending in Britain, 1900–1911, and the United States, 1880s–1920. *Am. Sociol. Rev.* 49:726–50

O'Rand, A., Henretta, J. 1982. Midlife work history and retirement income. In *Women's Retirement: Policy Implications of Recent Research,* ed. M. Szinovacz, pp. 25–44. Beverly Hills, Calif: Sage

O'Rand, A., Landerman, R. 1984. Women's and men's retirement income status. *Res. Aging* 6:25–44

Pampel, F., Weiss, J. 1983. Economic de-

velopment, pension policies, and the labor force participation of aged males: A cross-national, longitudinal analysis. *Am. J. Sociol.* 89:350–72

Pampel, F., Williamson, J. B. 1985. Age structure, politics, and cross-national patterns of public pension expenditures. *Am. Sociol. Rev.* 50:782–98

Parkin, F. 1971. *Class Inequality and Political Order.* New York: Praeger

Pearce, D. 1978. The feminization of poverty: Women, work and welfare. *Urban Soc. Change Rev.* (Feb) 11:1–36

Pearce, D., McAdoo, H. 1981. *Women and Children: Alone and in Poverty.* Washington, DC: Ctr. Natl. Policy Rev.

Perrin, G. 1969. Reflections on fifty years of social security. *Int. Labor Rev.* 99:249–89

Phillipson, C. 1983. The state, the economy and retirement. See Guillemard 1983, pp. 127–42

Piore, M., Sable, C. 1984. *The Second Industrial Divide.* New York: Basic

Piven, R., Cloward, R. 1971. *Regulating the Poor: The Functions of Public Welfare.* New York: Random

Piven, F., Cloward, R. 1982. *The New Class War.* New York: Pantheon

Potter, D. 1972. *The South and the Concurrent Majority.* Baton Rouge, La: La. State Univ. Press

Poulantzas, N. 1978. *State, Power, Socialism.* London: New Left Books

Pryor, F. 1968. *Public Expenditures in Communist and Capitalist Nations.* Homewood, Ill: Irwin

Quadagno, J. 1982. *Aging in Early Industrial Society, Work, Family and Social Policy in Nineteenth Century England.* New York: Academic Press

Quadagno, J. 1984a. Welfare capitalism and the Social Security Act of 1935. *Am. Sociol. Rev.* 49:632–47

Quadagno, J. 1984b. From poor laws to pensions: The evolution of economic support for the aged in England and America. *Milbank Mem. Fund Q.* 62:417–46

Quadagno, J. 1985. Two models of welfare state development: Reply to Skocpol and Amenta. *Am. Soc. Rev.* 50:575–77

Quadagno, J. 1988a. From old age assistance to supplemental security income: The political economy of relief in the South. In *The Politics of Social Policy in the United States,* ed. A. Orloff, M. Weir, T. Skocpol.

Quadagno, J. 1988b. *Labor's Benefits in the Welfare State: The Transformation of Old Age Security.* Chicago: Univ. Chicago Press.

Rimlinger, G. 1971. *Welfare Policy and Industrialization in Europe, America and Russia.* New York: Wiley

Ruggie, M. 1984. *The State and Working*

Women: A Comparative Study of Britain and Sweden. Princeton, NJ: Princeton Univ. Press

Scott, H. 1984. *Working Your Way to the Bottom, The Feminization of Poverty*. London: Pandora

Shalev, M. 1983. The social democratic model and beyond: Two generations of comparative research on the welfare state. *Comp. Soc. Res.* 6:315–51

Shefter, M. 1977. Party and patronage: Germany, England, and Italy. *Polit. Sci. Q.* 98:459–83

Skocpol, T. 1980. Political response to capitalist crisis: Neo-Marxist theories of the state and the case of the New Deal. *Polit. Soc.* 10:155–201

Skocpol, T. 1984. *America's incomplete welfare state: the limits of New Deal reforms and the origins of the present crisis*. Presented at Ann. Meet. Amer. Soc. Assoc., San Antonio

Skocpol, T., Amenta, E. 1985. Did capitalists shape social security? *Am. Sociol. Rev.* 50:572–75

Skocpol, T., Finegold, K. 1982. State capacity and economic intervention in the early New Deal. *Polit. Sci. Q.* 97:255–78

Skocpol, T., Ikenberry, J. 1983. The political formation of the American welfare state in historical and comparative perspective. *Comp. Soc. Res.* 6:87–148

Sombart, W. (1906) 1976. *Why Is There No Socialism in the United States*. White Plains, NY: Sharpe

Stephens, J. 1979. *The Transition from Capitalism to Socialism*. London: Macmillan

Sydnor, C. S. 1948. *The Development of Southern Sectionalism*. Baton Rouge, La: La. State Univ. Press

Therborn, G. 1977. The rule of capital and the rise of democracy. See Held et al 1983, pp. 261–71

Titmuss, R. 1958. *Essays on the Welfare State*. London: Allen & Unwin

Tomasson, R. 1984. Government old age pensions under affluence and austerity: West Germany, Sweden, the Netherlands and the United States. *Res. Soc. Probl. Public Policy* 3:217–72

Tomlins, C. 1985. *The State and the Unions, Labor Relations, Law and the Organized Labor Movement in America, 1880–1960*. Cambridge: Cambridge Univ. Press

Treas, J. Women's employment and its implications for the status of the elderly of the future. In *Aging, Social Change*, ed. S. Kiesler, J. Morgan, V. Oppenheimer, pp. 561–85, New York: Academic Press

Trempe, R. 1983. The struggles of French miners for the creation of retirement funds in the nineteenth century. See Guillemard 1983, pp. 101–4

Wilensky, H. 1975. *The Welfare State and Equality: Structural and Ideological Roots of Public Expenditures*. Berkeley: Univ. Calif. Press

Williamson, J., Weiss, J. 1979. Egalitarian political movements, social welfare effort and convergence theory: A cross-national analysis. *Comp. Soc. Res.* 2:289–302

Woodward, C. V. 1951. *Origins of the New South, 1877–1913*. Baton Rouge, La: La. State Univ. Press

Zald, M. 1985. Political change, citizenship rights and the welfare state. *Ann. Am. Acad. Polit. Soc. Sci.* 479:48–66

Ann. Rev. Sociol. 1987. 13:129–47

GENTRIFICATION: CULTURE AND CAPITAL IN THE URBAN CORE

Sharon Zukin

Department of Sociology, Brooklyn College, City University of New York, Brooklyn, New York 11210, and City University Graduate Center, New York, New York 10036

Abstract

Gentrification, the conversion of socially marginal and working-class areas of the central city to middle-class residential use, reflects a movement, that began in the 1960s, of private-market investment capital into downtown districts of major urban centers. Related to a shift in corporate investment and a corresponding expansion of the urban service economy, gentrification was seen more immediately in architectural restoration of deteriorating housing and the clustering of new cultural amenities in the urban core.

Research on gentrification initially concentrated on documenting its extent, tracing it as a process of neighborhood change, and speculating on its consequences for reversing trends of suburbanization and inner-city decline. But a cumulation of 10 years of research findings suggests, instead, that it results in a geographical reshuffling, among neighborhoods and metropolitan areas, of professional, managerial, and technical employees who work in corporate, government, and business services.

Having verified the extent of the phenomenon, empirical research on gentrification has reached a stalemate. Theoretically interesting problems concern the use of historic preservation to constitute a new urban middle class, gentrification and displacement, the economic rationality of the gentrifier's behavior, and the economic restructuring of the central city in which gentrification plays a part.

Broadening the analytic framework beyond demographic factors and neo-classical land use theory is problematic because of serious conceptual and methodological disagreements among neo-Marxist, neo-Weberian, and main-

0360-0572/87/0815-0129$02.00

stream analysts. Yet efforts to understand gentrification benefit from the use of economic paradigms by considering such issues as production, consumption, and social reproduction of the urban middle class, as well as the factors that create a supply of gentrifiable housing and demand for it on the part of potential gentrifiers.

An emerging synthesis in the field integrates economic and cultural analysis. The mutual validation and valorization of urban art and real estate markets indicates the importance of the cultural constitution of the higher social strata in an advanced service economy. It also underlines how space and time are used in the social and material constitution of an urban middle class.

INTRODUCTION

During the 1970s, throughout North America and Western Europe, new residential patterns in many old cities appeared to contradict the long-term decline of their inner core. These patterns emerged in a wave of capital reinvestment in deteriorating housing that was concentrated near central business districts (CBDs). Although some of the rehabilitation was publicly subsidized, most was financed by the private market, and a significant portion was carried out by do-it-yourself or "sweat equity" part-time workers. The progenitors of this urban "renaissance"—as magazines and newspapers termed it—had white-collar jobs. In many cases, too, they had markedly nontraditional households and styles of life. Together with a surge in service-sector employment and corresponding cultural and commercial amenities, their presence as a newly minted urban "gentry" gave the downtown a different form.

Much of the initial sociological research on gentrification concentrated on documenting its extent, tracing it as a process of neighborhood change, and speculating on its consequences in terms of both displacement of an existing population and reversal of trends toward suburbanization and urban decline. This general approach was especially characteristic of sociologists in the United States, who were still strongly influenced by positivism and the empirical tradition.

Gradually, however, the work of Marxist and left-Weberian urban sociologists and geographers broadened the study of gentrification by emphasizing an underlying dynamic of economic restructuring. The most relevant processes, in this view, were a regional and metropolitan de-industrialization and a concentration of professional and technical jobs and cultural markets in the urban core. Consequently, gentrification was subsumed under the rubrics of production and consumption rather than of demographic structure or individual choice.

Although empirical research on gentrification has repeatedly verified the extent of the phenomenon, the effort to establish a broader analytic framework is problematic. Disagreement on an underlying structure deepens the methodological schisms dividing neo-Marxist, neo-Weberian, and mainstream sociologists. Nevertheless, further research on gentrification may overcome these issues by investigating urban morphology—the shape the city takes—in terms of economic and cultural analysis. Both large and small investors are constrained by the availability of capital and the housing supply. Yet since the 1960s, the expansion of cultural patronage among middle class social strata has shown that investment in culture may augment limited means. Therefore, the accumulation strategies of large investors in central-city real estate are supported by smaller investors' patterns of cultural and social reproduction.

THE EMPIRICAL STALEMATE

From the moment an English sociologist invented the term "gentrification" to describe the residential movement of middle-class people into low-income areas of London (Glass 1964), the word evoked more than a simple change of scene. It suggested a symbolic new attachment to old buildings and a heightened sensibility to space and time. It also indicated a radical break with suburbia, a movement away from child-centered households toward the social diversity and aesthetic promiscuity of city life. In the public view, at least, gentrifiers were different from other middle-class people. Their collective residential choices, the amenities that clustered around them, and their generally high educational and occupational status were structured by—and in turn expressed—a distinctive *habitus,* a class culture and milieu in Bourdieu's (1984) sense. Thus, gentrification may be described as a process of spatial and social differentiation.

Early research denied that most gentrifiers moved "back to the city" from suburban housing (Laska & Spain 1980). Recent work confirms that they tend to come from other urban neighborhoods and large metropolitan areas (McDonald 1983, LeGates & Hartman 1986).

Yet there is much disagreement about the sources of these shifts, as well as their empirical referent. While some of the literature focuses on gentrifiers, other studies examine property that is gentrified.

In both cases, "supply-side" interpretations stress the economic and social factors that produce an attractive housing supply in the central city for middle-class individuals, and "demand-side" interpretations affirm a consumer preference, for demographic or cultural reasons, for the buildings and areas that become gentrified. Other problems are introduced by considering housing tenure—specifically, the different interests of homeowners and renters—when gentrification by both groups causes property values to rise.

Moreover, case studies that include the local political context of gentrification document the contributions of financial and political elites who seem, at first, not to be directly involved. Conflict over zoning laws, historic district designations, and property tax assessments indicates how important may be the state's role in defining the economic and social value of an urban area. Strategic shifts in government policy from 1970 to 1975 supported gentrification at the very time that rising inflation rates, fuel costs, and construction prices made rehabilitation in the center city an economically viable alternative for both homeowners and real estate developers.

At that time, local and national governments in both the United States and Western Europe shifted from supporting the demolition required by urban renewal to giving incentive grants for housing improvement. This facilitated the small-scale building rehabilitation on which gentrification depends. And though gentrification remains predominantly a privately financed action, a strong expression of local government support has generally been a precondition for the participation of lending institutions.

Little wonder, then, that British geographers call gentrification a "chaotic" concept (Rose 1984, after Sayer 1982) or that this observation has become the *cri de coeur* of some thoughtful writers (e.g. Smith & Williams 1986).

For several years, a large portion of every article on gentrification has been devoted to a literature review. Although this may suggest a welcome quality of introspection, it more likely indicates a worrisome stasis in the field.

Descriptive Overview

By all accounts, a small wave of private-market capital reinvestment in deteriorating central-city housing began in the 1960s. Both early and recent studies correctly associate it with the "vitality" of an urban core (Frieden 1964, Bradbury et al 1982). But this investment shows a high degree of selectivity. There are important regional variations in its strength, and an intra-urban concentration occurs in areas of "historic" significance (Black 1975). Moreover, highly visible reinvestment and rehabilitation by upper-income residents take place alongside continuing deterioration of inner-city housing, disinvestment in the CBD, and suburbanization of most new housing construction for the private market (Clay 1979).

In no way but proximity does gentrification counteract the economic and racial polarization of most urban populations. In big cities as different as New York and San Francisco, it fails to raise median family income or to reverse a secular decrease in the number of high-status census areas; nor does gentrification always spread beyond a street or neighborhood to an entire census tract (Lipton 1977, Baldassare 1984, Marcuse 1986). At least initially, housing reinvestment may be concentrated in "pockets" or at the edges of declining districts (Schaeffer & Smith 1986, Marcuse 1986). In fact, the effects of gentrification at the "extreme micro-level" show much divergence:

What appears as ethnic, racial, and economic integration at the neighborhood level may be disaggregated into traditionally segregated enclaves within the census tract, the block, and individual buildings (LeGates & Hartman 1986:195).

The gentrifiers' choice of neighborhood does not imply their social integration with existing neighbors of a different race, ethnicity, and socio-economic status. In street encounters, they approach each other warily until familiarity with neighborhood routine ensures politeness (Anderson 1985). New middle-class residents often expect crime to be as prevalent as "background noise" (McDonald 1983:292, Anderson 1985). For their part, existing residents may resent the superimposition of an alien culture—with different consumption patterns and an accelerated pace of change—on their community.[1]

While residents' associations sometimes mobilize to fight "developers" (Chernoff 1980, Weiler 1980), they really confront the whole set of economic and social processes that underlie "development" (Zukin 1982). This makes for an uneven social contest. In general, community mobilization cannot do battle with "the abstract logic of the private market"; and in particular, "the institutionalized procedures for responding to gentrification are weaker, more fragmented, and more costly to engage in" than those that respond to coherent public policies (Henig 1982:353–54).

Moreover, people who live in a gentrifying neighborhood have different interests. Pre-gentrification residents, as already partly noted, are likely to have consumption patterns of a lower social class, constitute a different ethnic and racial community, and an older age group (Spain 1980, Henig 1984, LeGates & Hartman 1986). When they mobilize to defend a neighborhood "as it is," they exclude the "improvements" identified with gentrification. Chief among these improvements, in the gentrifiers' view, is the restoration of historic architectural detail. Yet if existing residents join gentrifiers in associations that support the "historic" community, they may be aiding a process that causes property values to rise and leads to their own displacement. Existing homeowners, however, may have reason to do so. In economic terms, they forsake sentiment, or attachment to the community, for exchange values (Logan & Molotch 1987).

Among gentrifiers, renters have significantly lower incomes than homeowners (DeGiovanni & Paulson 1984). Thus, a cleavage develops between these groups when neighborhood associations pursue improvement strategies that cause rents to rise. Moreover, gentrifiers who buy and maintain multifamily dwellings are torn between a landlord's interest in getting higher

[1]An early view of the implicit and explicit conflicts in this sort of neighborhood improvement is Lyford's (1966) study of Manhattan's Upper West Side. As various factors, including community resistance to dislocation and resulting investor uncertainty, prolonged the process of "revitalization" and reduced the public sector's role, urban renewal in the area was succeeded by gentrification.

rents and a resident's desire to keep the neighborhood unpretentious, afford-able, and somewhat socially diverse (McDonald 1983).

Community organizations may mediate residents' conflicting interests in unexpected ways. In a gentrified area near downtown Brooklyn, for example, the gentrifiers' association pursued a strategy of historic preservation—to the extent of creating a "historic" neighborhood name—that permitted them to define and appropriate the area (Kasinitz 1984). Gradually, their Puerto Rican neighbors responded by mobilizing on the basis of ethnicity. Another situa-tion emerged in Philadelphia, when gentrifiers joined existing white ethnic residents in excluding blacks from the neighborhood (Cybriwsky 1978).[2]

When community organizations impose social and cultural homogeneity on a gentrifying neighborhood, they act as a "vanguard of the bourgeoisie" (Logan & Molotch 1987). They seem to be able to carry out their aims regardless of local government involvement or the degree to which they fabricate the area's historic past (Cybriwsky et al 1986).

While studies of gentrification agree on many of these key points, they indicate four contentious—and suggestive—areas of analysis: the use of historic preservation in constituting a new urban elite, gentrification's con-tribution to homelessness and displacement, the economic rationality of the gentrifier's role, and the relation between gentrification and economic transformation.

Historic Preservation

It is tempting to associate contemporary gentrifiers, as part of a new middle class, with the appropriation of Victorian style (Jager 1986). Certainly the industrial bourgeoisie of the late nineteenth century bequeathed a major portion of the buildings now gentrified in North American, British, and Australian cities. But gentrifiers' tastes are conditioned by the availability and affordability of older buildings. Their aesthetic tastes may be diverted by either new construction in an older mode, like the current vogue in London of new neo-Georgian houses (Wright 1985a), or newer, perhaps Edwardian, old building styles (Williams 1984:212). Similarly, gentrification applies to a taste for restored brownstone, red brick, or gingerbread houses as well as manufacturing lofts that are converted to residential use (Zukin 1982).[3]

---

[2]Nevertheless, such strategies do not inevitably result in gentrification. In the Brooklyn community described by Krase (1982), white middle-class gentrifiers mobilized for historic preservation, yet by the time the study was published, the neighborhood was known again as a black ghetto. Also see Williams (1985).

[3]McDonald (1983), however, claims that gentrifiers' choices may be specific to certain neighborhoods. In Boston—a city where older central-city housing is in short supply—his survey of new South End residents found that 39% had looked for housing only in that area. Yet again, the large number of multifamily dwellings in the South End that gentrifiers use for rental income suggests an economic choice.

More significant than the impression of architectural homogeneity is the emphasis on culture in constructing new middle-class consumption patterns. By means of historic preservation, the new middle classes parlay a relatively modest investment of time and money into a quasi-bourgeois *habitus* (Williams, 1986). They are able to enjoy a solid building stock, often individualized to specific spatial requirements—notably, space that supports working at home. They also participate in the creation in their neighborhood of "a critical mass of pleasant amenity" (Logan & Molotch 1987), where shopping and housing provide serious social and cultural experiences (Beauregard 1986).

There is some question, however, about whether historic preservation really confers or affirms more "distinction" than the modern style of most new construction. In contrast to widespread assumptions, gentrifiers have the same income level and educational background as other middle-class people who live downtown in either new or rehabilitated apartment buildings (Ford 1978). In the same ways they also resemble the middle-class residents of affluent, older suburbs (McDonald 1983).[4]

A quest for historic districts implies more, of course. It confronts the plane of modernity with the rich and varied temporality of the past—but which past, and whose? "In this new perspective [a gentrified area] is not so much a literal place as a cultural oscillation between the prosaic reality of the contemporary inner city and an imaginative reconstruction of the area's past" (Wright 1985b:228–29).

Gentrification and Displacement

In a subtle way, the ideology of historic preservation facilitates the removal of a pre-gentrification population, especially those residents whose modernization of their homes is incongruous with the spirit of authenticity in the gentrifiers' own restoration. But the pragmatic wedge of their displacement is rising rents and higher sale prices for homes in gentrifying neighborhoods.

All studies of gentrification confirm that a fairly homogeneous group of in-movers reduces residential density and replaces an existing population. The out-movers, however, are a relatively heterogeneous group (LeGates & Hartman 1986). They can be characterized as economically vulnerable though not always disadvantaged. At least through the early 1970s, white-collar workers were affected by gentrification more than blue-collar workers, with whites displaced more frequently than members of other races. After 1973, revitalization in several major US cities accelerated the displacement of blacks by whites in certain neighborhoods (Gale 1984:24). In somewhat

---

[4]McDonald's (1983) survey, however, shows a larger standard deviation in gentrifiers' household income, especially among single-person households.

smaller cities, also, upper-income households showed greater willingness to move into lower-class areas and racial ghettos (Henig 1984:178).

Yet to some degree, race and class may still be a barrier to gentrification. Whites and most middle-class blacks have not gentrified lower-class black areas, such as Harlem and Newark, despite a building stock and a cost structure equivalent to other areas' (Schaeffer & Smith 1986, Beauregard 1986:39).

It is generally agreed that gentrifying neighborhoods produce higher tax yields. For this reason, among others, gentrification elicits the approval of local political leaders, who correspondingly moderate their support for displacees.

In reality, the relation between gentrification and property taxes is more complex. Increases in assessed property values in gentrifying areas may not be significantly greater than in other neighborhoods; they also lag behind increases in market values (DeGiovanni 1984). Nevertheless, once assessments have been raised to reflect some rehabilitation activity, the assessed value of unimproved properties in the neighborhood also rises. So gentrifiers carry their less affluent neighbors with them on a rising tide of property tax assessments.

A more severe blow against an existing population is effected by the removal of low-price rental housing from the city's building stock (Gale 1984, Marcuse 1986). Single-room-occupancy hotels, where tenants pay by the night or week, are a vivid victim (Kasinitz 1983), but the general problem is one of *housing* rather than *household* dislocation (Gale 1984:164). As a rule, low-income residents are displaced farther from the CBD. And no matter where they move, displacees usually pay a higher rent (Kain & Apgar 1985, LeGates & Hartman 1986).

Efforts have been made to qualify these stark changes. An examination of one year's tenant out-movers from "revitalizing" areas in five US cities found the costs of displacement to be outweighed by "benefits" (Schill & Nathan 1983). Similarly, a simulation of displacement in several revitalizing low-income neighborhoods in Chicago speculated that many low-income tenants regularly move out of their neighborhood with or without gentrification; at any rate, Kain & Apgar (1985) consider that the benefits to the area and the residents who continue to live there—in improvements to capital stock—exceed the costs of displacement.

It is more worrisome to consider that spatial differentials—that is, conditions in specific neighborhoods—do not have much effect on rates of displacement (Lee & Lodge 1984). If displacement in the face of mounting rents is an important national trend, then the whole structure of housing markets and their fit with social needs should be revised.

These findings suggest that the gentrifiers' aesthetic hallmark—their investment in rehabilitation—has less of an impact on other people than does their property investment. This calls into question the relative weights of "sentiment and symbolism" (*pace* Firey 1945) and economic rationality in the gentrifiers' role.

Economic Rationality

Throughout North America and Western Europe, gentrification has occurred together with a shift toward new homeownership and condominium conversion in traditionally low-rent areas of the central city. Generally these forms of housing reinvestment—rehabilitation, on the one hand, and homeownership, on the other—have to clear historical barriers posed by tenants' property rights and the taxation and credit systems (Gale 1984, Williams 1984, Hamnett & Randolph 1986). Once they do, however, they open up an avenue of speculation for both gentrifiers and real estate developers.

The small scale of gentrifiable property and the cost of rehabilitation, relative to new construction, do not attract large-scale investors. Nevertheless, the low cost of entry into this market, at least in its early years, propels significant numbers of professional, managerial, and technical employees into becoming part-time developers and landlords (Zukin 1982, McDonald 1983).

Much emphasis has been placed on the apparent lack of interest in speculation on the part of early, "risk-oblivious" gentrifiers or "urban pioneers" (Berry 1985:78–79). Yet they are hardly insensible to the rationality of a housing investment. Indeed, economic contingencies may "encourage [them to take] defensive actions to protect [themselves] against the vagaries of the housing market and, at the same time, to avoid the ravages of the effects of inflation on [their] salary" (Beauregard 1986:45). Early gentrifiers find the niche they can afford in urban housing markets.

Although respondents often fail to cite economic reasons for their involvement in gentrification (Berry 1985), some surveys have confirmed the importance to them of both investment potential and housing prices (McDonald 1983, Gale 1980:100, 1984:16). Despite this general effect, however, the decision to buy property in a gentrifiable area may reflect different material priorities.

Some gentrifiers may be most influenced by the rent gap, i.e. the difference between ground-rent levels at various locations in a metropolitan area (Smith 1979). The devalorization of capital (the decrease in the economic value of property) in the inner city offers them a fairly low-cost opportunity to get involved in its restructuring. This is especially important when a central-city location already offers some advantages. Although the rent gap introduces a mechanistic and somewhat circular argument, it does accord with real locational choices. What must be remembered is that the increases in investment and property values associated with gentrification represent only one part of a range of possible outcomes in the inner city (Beauregard 1986).

Low-income gentrifiers may have other motives for making a housing investment in gentrification. In their case, a marginal investment may ensure the conditions they require for their social reproduction (Rose 1984). Residence in a gentrified area may be especially important to single mothers, who try to stabilize their position in urban housing markets and to locate near support services by buying a low-cost, inner-city apartment.[5] Similarly, unemployed and informally employed workers, particularly in the creative and performing arts, may try to cluster in inner-city neighborhoods in order to maintain access to information, training, and markets for their work.

Thus, the economic rationality of gentrification is subject to finely tuned variations. Different forms of capital have a different relation to space and time, and the division of labor within white-collar sectors of the work force shapes both a dispersal and a concentration of middle-class residence (Smith 1986). The new middle classes' insertion into the metropolis takes place at the micro-level of both the suburb and the gentrified neighborhood. The overlay of these insertions on urban, regional, national, and international scales calls our attention to spatial switches even as they are being produced for a variety of economic and social reasons (Smith 1984, Massey 1984).

Economic Restructuring

A major focus of economic shifts since the 1960s has been the recentralization of corporate investment in selected metropolitan cores (Fainstein & Fainstein 1982, Smith 1986). This process involves new uses of space and new spatial forms, as the city is restructured to suit corporate needs. While office towers sprout in underutilized or devalorized downtown districts, a new hierarchy of urban neighborhoods reflects different corporate uses. Headquarters and "back offices" no longer share space; each stratum of white-collar work generates in its proximity the amenities that suit its status, salary levels, and office rents. Manufacturing activity and blue-collar residence are displaced beyond the heart of the city (Zukin 1982).

Gentrification as a white-collar residential style reflects the agglomeration of large companies—or mainly their professional, managerial, and technical staffs and related business services—in the downtown area. Whether the crucial factor is the number of corporate headquarters in a metropolitan area (Palmer & Roussel 1986) or the presence of just a few key corporate employers (Gale 1984:155), this capital presence draws new investors and consumers. The city's population may still be polarized between rich and poor, with

---

[5]Using a broader sample, however, a 1978 survey by the US Department of Housing and Urban Development found that women may be satisfied by suburban services (Fava 1985).

the poor providing personal and domestic services for the rich and working in the remaining labor-intensive manufacturing sectors (Portes & Walton 1981, Sassen-Koob 1984). But high-status gentrification, as well as other relatively affluent residential styles, reflects the expansion of high-income personnel in corporations and government and producers' services.[6]

In any city, gentrification correlates *grosso modo* with "administrative activity" (Lipton 1977) and new office construction in the CBD (Berry 1985).

Yet many analyses of gentrification persist in stressing noneconomic factors. One such factor—social solidarity—is indicated by the residential clustering of visible, highly singular social groups, such as gay householders, who constitute a plurality of residents in some gentrifying neighborhoods (McDonald 1983, Castells 1983:ch.14). Nevertheless, the creation by gays of new spatial communities in gentrifiable areas—in contrast to the older spatial division between special entertainment districts and residence submerged in heterosexual society—may be related to the participation of gay men in an expanding service economy (Fitzgerald 1986).

Most mainstream analysts still consider economic restructuring secondary to demographic, i.e. generational, life-style and life-cycle factors that have created consumer demand for new residential styles. In this view, gentrification is the mark of the zeitgeist borne by the baby-boom generation. In the spirit of synthesis, however, a recent examination of gentrification emphasizes both economic restructuring and demographic factors, without giving priority to either (London et al 1986).[7]

Proponents of demographic explanations of gentrification are not persuaded that economic restructuring constitutes a necessary and a sufficient cause. In fact, if values had not changed to accept smaller families, two-earner households, and single parents, most of the gentrifying population would lack either the means or the motivation for city living. Yet gentrifiers' residential choices are ultimately conditioned by material factors. These include the expansion of middle-class social strata because of an increase in white-collar jobs, especially in regional, national, and international business services; a secular withdrawal of investment capital from urban manufacturing, thus freeing industrial sites for redevelopment; and a recentralization of corporate activity in selected CBDs and suburban towns.

Nevertheless, the struggle to reconcile economic and demographic analysis

---

[6]Like gentrification, the expansion of jobs in producers' services has no effect on metropolitan median income; neither reduces metropolitan income inequality (Nelson & Lorence 1985).

[7]Using quantitative analysis and survey methods, this study offers a smorgasbord of findings. Gentrification is correlated positively with the size of the baby-boom cohort and the proportion of professional to other jobs. It is correlated negatively with young children and the percentage of the labor force employed in manufacturing. Historical preservation, culture, and corporate presence are also important (London et al 1986).

raises the question, whether the concept of gentrification is really significant, and if so, on which level of analysis. Without conceptual agreement, empirical studies of gentrification have reached a stalemate.

METHODOLOGICAL SCHISMS

Conceptual divergence is reflected in serious disagreements on methodology. A preference for materialism on the one hand or positivism on the other leads to dichotomous views of gentrification. It is described in terms of either structural causality or individual choice (i.e. structure vs agency), cultural style or economic necessity (choice vs need), or consequences that carry greater or lesser costs (displacement vs revitalization).

The broadest analyses of gentrification (hence, those with the most interesting theoretical implications) are influenced in some way by economic paradigms. Two of these refine the Marxist emphasis on production by also considering social reproduction and consumption. A third reformulates the neoclassical model based on supply and demand.

Production/Reproduction

From the outset, the Marxist epistemological critique of gentrification has targeted positivism in general and neoclassical land-use theory in particular. "Positivist approaches to gentrification," in this view, "have remained ad hoc, full of exceptions, and frequently contradictory to other people's positivist explanations" (Rose 1984). Lacking uncontestable criteria for either outcomes or causes, the concept of gentrification, as mainstream analysts use it, suffers from disorganization. Moreover, as Damaris Rose insists, what we observe as the unified phenomenon of gentrification may really result from several causes (1984).

Rose also takes issue with the dominant Marxist approach. Accepting its emphasis on structural causes and economic necessity, she nonetheless criticizes its tendency to stress a single causal factor: the production of gentrified dwellings as commodities. Besides the rent gap, the falling rate of profit, or corporate investment, all else is relegated to a residual category, "a scratch on the surface of underlying capital."

In place of a single resource-maximizing strategy that historically results in gentrification, Rose credits a number of different strategies. And in lieu of production, Rose stresses the importance of social reproduction. Thus, she accords a central role in gentrification processes to marginally employed but highly educated individuals who seek a central-city *and* low-cost residence for social or ecological reasons. Moreover, by considering social reproduction as a separate factor, Rose avoids conflating reproduction and consumption, as both positivists and Marxists tend to do.

Production/Consumption

Rose's critique has influenced other Marxists to the extent that they now seek to give full weight to consumption, though not necessarily to "reproduction" (Smith & Williams 1986). Meanwhile, they continue to study processes of production and devalorization: the first, in order to identify potential gentrifiers, and the second, in order to understand how certain housing becomes gentrifiable.

A major focus of Marxist analysis is the social location of gentrifiers. Because most of them are in the new middle classes, with professional, technical, or managerial jobs, they are identified with corporate reinvestment in the CBD and the growth of local, regional, and national services. This situation has two related effects. On the one hand, whether gentrification is considered an investment for capital accumulation or an investment in social reproduction, it helps promote capital's long wave of expansion. On the other hand, ideological support for gentrification helps legitimize corporate expansion throughout the central city.

As Neil Smith (1986) points out, the ideology of gentrification often describes it as a process of *spatial* expansion—notably, as settlement on an urban "frontier." But the changes in the use of downtown space that result from corporate investment really illustrate *capital* expansion. In our time, capital expansion has no new territory left to explore, so it redevelops, or internally redifferentiates, urban space. Just as the frontier thesis in US history legitimized an economic push through "uncivilized" lands, so the urban frontier thesis legitimizes the corporate reclamation of the inner city from racial ghettos and marginal business uses.

Yet no structural process can disregard institutional constraints. Downtown reinvestment must take account of urban real estate markets, forms and degrees of government intervention, and local politics and social forces. In the United States, social support for gentrification also reflects a response to racial conflict and fiscal crisis (Williams 1986). In that sense, too, gentrification is compatible with a broad movement away from collective consumption.

In fact, much US urban redevelopment during the two decades following World War II could be called "demand-led urbanization" (Harvey 1985b). Although this differs from a process that might be "consumption led," it calls attention to shifting patterns of consumption, their basis in the public or private sector, and their material representation in urban forms.

Economic restructuring changes the basis of consumption for different social classes and also shapes their social and spatial differentiation. Consequently, in contrast to the ghettoization of large areas of the central city, gentrification represents a filtering *up* of housing. Conversely, in contrast to corporate redevelopment of the CBD, gentrification of downtown neighborhoods represents a filtering *down* of investment opportunity (Smith, forthcoming).

Supply/Demand

In an attempt to infuse some of these distinctions into the neoclassical model, Brian J. L. Berry has devised a new supply-side interpretation of gentrification (Berry 1985). In Berry's view, the necessary but not sufficient conditions for gentrification are the "contagious abandonment" of large inner-city areas and a dynamic suburban housing market in new construction. Further, the catalyst of gentrification is significant corporate redevelopment of the CBD, especially office construction that locates professional and white-collar jobs downtown. "To turn the supply-side argument around, the nation's key 'command and control' centers provide a sufficient demand-side trigger for gentrification, provided that the necessary supply-side housing market characteristics also are present" (p. 95).

Berry's "new" interpretation adopts several of the neo-Marxist and neo-Weberian key assumptions: corporate centralization in a small number of urban cores (cf Cohen 1981), widespread devalorization and underutilization of inner-city property, a resulting rent gap between the inner city and the periphery, and new consumption patterns that follow the expansion of white-collar jobs. While this corrects Berry's earlier tendency to see housing in terms of rational choice (cf Gale 1984:158), it offers a descriptive rather than an analytic model.

Berry's model does highlight the historical contingency of gentrification, a point on which most Marxist analyses also agree. Moreover, it emphasizes the simultaneity of continued growth in the suburbs, and both abandonment and redevelopment of the inner core. Berry's "islands of renewal in seas of decay" are the metaphorical equivalent of the Marxists' "polarization of urban populations."

SYNTHESIS: CULTURE AND CAPITAL

By upsetting expectations about unrelieved deterioration of the central city, gentrification was initially received as a revelation. But recent analysis by sociologists and geographers emphasizes several constraints. The area transformed in gentrification's penumbra is limited by strategies for capital accumulation on the part of dominant social and economic institutions, and the related strategies of "consumption sectors" (Saunders 1984) that support the internal redifferentiation of urban space.

The emphasis on capital investment calls into question gentrifiers' identification with, and mobilization for, historic preservation. Clearly, they share with others in society a generalized appreciation of the material and aesthetic qualities that old buildings and old neighborhoods evoke. Further, their support of historic preservation and contemporary urban restorations recalls the patrician sponsorship of art and architecture in US cities in the late nineteenth century, as well as urban professionals' advocacy of "City Beautiful" programs for rebuilding cities at that time (Boyer 1983). But affluent gentrifiers' cultural appropriations do not lack economic rationality. Cultural validation helps valorize their housing investment, and activism on behalf of historic property eases the transition, for some of them, into semiprofessional and part-time real estate development.

Indeed, political mobilization for the legal status of a historic landmark designation typically unifies people with different aesthetic and material interests. While historic preservation enables some of them to satisfy civic pride, others profit by producing goods and services for a "preservationist" mode of consumption.

Yet cultural consumption also offers other dividends. Culturally validated neighborhoods automatically provide new middle classes with the collective identity and social credentials for which they strive (cf Logan & Molotch 1987). Moreover, the ideology of gentrification legitimizes their social reproduction, often despite the claims of an existing population. This is especially important when appeals are made to public opinion and municipal authorities to decide between the claims of different residential and commercial groups.

With some paradoxical results, support for gentrification also channels support to producers of cultural goods and services who seek housing in central-city areas. In the short run, proximity to markets for their services eases their insertion into the urban economy. In the long run, however, their contribution to the downtown's cultural capital may raise housing prices so high that they no longer can afford to live there.

In general, the presence of cultural markets both validates and valorizes business investment in major corporate cities. While the cultural constitution of new urban middle classes has ironically been termed an "Artistic Mode of Production" (Zukin 1982), a study by the National Endowment for the Arts found that cities with the highest percentage of artists in the labor force also had the highest rates of downtown gentrification and condominium conversion (Gale 1984:155).

Gentrification thus appears as a multidimensional cultural practice that is rooted on both sides of the methodological schisms that we have reviewed. As a form of homeownership, gentrified dwellings are both a means of accumulation and a means of social reproduction for part of the highly educated middle class. Moreover, as a reference to specific building types in the center of the city, gentrification connotes both a mode of high-status cultural consumption and the colonization of an expanding terrain by economic institutions associated with the service sector.

In the long run, economic institutions establish the conditions to which gentrifiers respond. Secular trends of disinvestment in urban manufacturing destroy the viability of industrial areas and blue-collar neighborhoods. The recent resurgence of investment in American cities by major lending institutions reflects, on the one hand, their reduction of foreign loans and, on the other, their participation in an expanding service economy. The office construction that they finance eventually provides jobs for potential gentrifiers, but it is not matched by an interest in building new housing most of these people can afford.

To some extent, also, gentrifiers' locational preferences reflect their withdrawal from a transportation and distribution infrastructure that they perceive as being archaic. Many of them prefer walking or bicycling to work instead of making a long journey to the city by car or train. Similarly, they abandon suburban shopping centers for the smaller scale of shops and the range of goods and services available in the city.

Property values rise in middle-class residential areas, reflecting increased competition for a milieu that unifies proximity to professional, managerial, and "creative" jobs; opportunities for specialized high-status consumption; and the combination of population density and individualized facilities that can support independent, quasi-bourgeois social reproduction by people who are not really rich. Thus, gentrifiers are caught between the expansion of middle-class styles of life and a market situation that makes it harder to realize such lifestyles without compromise.

Microlevel studies of gentrified neighborhoods cannot address these issues. But there are at least three alternate ways to frame a study of gentrification that would integrate cultural and economic analysis. First, the synergy between gentrification and deindustrialization suggests a comparative study of housing and labor markets in metropolitan areas. Second, the long-term plans of local financial, political, and social elites—including their investment projects and their own residential quarters—focus attention on "downtown" interests, whether they momentarily support urban renewal, gentrification, or new private-market construction (cf Ballain et al 1982, Fainstein et al 1986, Hartman 1984). And third, the morphology of urban areas—both their changing form and the way this form inserts itself into the city as a whole—shows how the spatial and built environment concretizes, transmits, and transforms the city's constituent social interests (cf Zunz 1970, Harvey 1985a, Pred 1985).

These proposals may shock traditional urban sociologists, as well as those whose reading in the field ended with the Chicago School. To them it may seem as though urban sociology has been engulfed by political economy, and the study of cities subordinated to economic processes and social class (Zukin 1980).

In fact, a number of sociologists have recently refocused the discipline's attention on economic institutions (Zukin & DiMaggio 1986). Moreover, there is a growing movement in sociology to incorporate the analysis of space and time (Giddens 1985). These interests should infuse more rigor into urban sociologists' efforts to describe the "post-industrial city," which, like "gentrification," really refers to existing patterns of social, spatial, and economic restructuring of the central city.

Literature Cited

Anderson, E. 1985. Race and neighborhood transition. See Peterson 1985, pp. 99–128

Baldassare, M. 1984. Evidence for neighborhood revitalization: Manhattan. See Palen & London 1984, pp. 90–102

Ballain, R., Bobroff, J. Courant, G., Darris, G. et al 1982. *Evolution des Quartiers Anciens*. Paris: Plan Construction, Bilan Thématique

Beauregard, R. A. 1986. The chaos and complexity of gentrification. See Smith & Williams 1986, pp. 35–55

Berry, B. J. L. 1985. Islands of renewal in seas of decay. See Peterson 1985, pp. 69–96

Black, T. J. 1975. Private-market housing renovation in central cities: An Urban Land Institute Survey. *Urb. Land* 34 (November):3–9

Bourdieu, P. 1984. *Distinction: A Social Critique of the Judgement of Taste*, tr. R. Nice. Cambridge, Mass: Harvard Univ. Press

Boyer, M. C. 1983. *Dreaming the Rational City: The Myth of American City Planning*. Cambridge, Mass: MIT Press

Bradbury, K. L., Downs, A., Small, K. A. 1982. *Urban Decline and the Future of American Cities*. Washington, DC: Brookings

Castells, M. 1983. *The City and the Grassroots*. Berkeley, Calif: Univ. Calif. Press

Chernoff, M. 1980. Social displacement in a renovating neighborhood's commercial district: Atlanta. See Laska & Spain 1980, pp. 204–19

Clay, P. L. 1979. *Neighborhood Renewal*. Lexington, Mass: Lexington

Cohen, R. B. 1981. The new international division of labor, multinational corporations and urban hierarchy. In *Urbanization and Urban Planning in Capitalist Society*, ed. M. Dear, A. J. Scott, pp. 287–315. London/New York: Methuen

Cybriwsky, R. A. 1978. Social aspects of neighborhood change. *Ann. Assoc. Am. Geogr.* 68:17–33

Cybriwsky, R. A., Ley, D., Western, J. 1986. The political and social construction of revitalized neighborhoods: Society Hill, Philadelphia, and False Creek, Vancouver. See Smith & Williams 1986, pp. 92–120

DeGiovanni, F. 1984. An examination of selected consequences of revitalization in six U.S. cities. See Palen & London 1984, pp. 67–89

DeGiovanni, F., Paulson, N. 1984. Housing diversity in revitalizing neighborhoods. *Urb. Aff. Q.* 20(2):211–32

Fainstein, N. I., Fainstein, S. S. 1982. Restructuring the American city: A comparative perspective. In *Urban Policy Under Capitalism*, ed. N. I. Fainstein, S. S. Fainstein, pp. 161–89. Vol. 22, Sage Urb. Aff. Ann. Rev. Beverly Hills, Calif: Sage

Fainstein, S. S., Fainstein, N. I., Hill, R. C., Judd, D. R., Smith, M. P. 1986. *Restructuring the City*. New York: Longman. Rev. ed.

Fava, S. F. 1985. Residential preferences in the suburban era: A new look? *Soc. Forc.* 18(2):109–17

Firey, W. 1945. Sentiment and symbolism as ecological variables. *Am. Sociol. Rev.* 10(2):140–48

Fitzgerald, F. 1986. A reporter at large (San Francisco—Pt. I). *The New Yorker*, July 21, pp. 34–70

Ford, K. 1978. *Housing Policy and the Urban Middle Class*. New Brunswick, NJ: Cent. Urb. Policy Res.

Frieden, B. 1964. *The Future of Old Neighborhoods*. Cambridge, Mass: MIT Press

Gale, D. E. 1980. Neighborhood resettlement: Washington, D.C. See Laska & Spain, 1980, pp. 95–115

Gale, D. E. 1984. *Neighborhood Revitalization and the Postindustrial City: A Multi-*

national Perspective. Lexington, Mass: Lexington

Giddens, A. 1985. Time, space and regionalisation. See Gregory & Urry 1985, pp. 265–95

Glass, R. 1964. Introduction. In *London: Aspects of Change,* ed. Centre for Urban Studies, pp. xiii–xlii. London: MacGibbon and Kee.

Gregory, D., Urry, J. 1985. *Social Relations and Spatial Structures.* New York: St. Martin's

Hamnett, C., Randolph, B. 1986. Tenurial transformation and the flat break-up market in London: The British condo experience. See Smith & Williams 1986, pp. 121–52

Hartman, C. 1984. *The Transformation of San Francisco.* Totowa, NJ: Rowman & Allanheld

Harvey, D. 1985a. *Consciousness and the Urban Experience.* Baltimore: Johns Hopkins Univ. Press

Harvey, D. 1985b. *The Urbanization of Capital.* Baltimore: Johns Hopkins Univ. Press

Henig, J. R. 1982. Neighborhood response to gentrification: Conditions of mobilization. *Urb. Aff. Q.* 17(3):343–58

Henig, J. R. 1984. Gentrification and displacement of the elderly: An empirical analysis. See Palen & London 1984, pp. 170–84

Jager, M. 1986. Class definition and the esthetics of gentrification: Victoriana in Melbourne. See Smith & Williams 1986, pp. 78–91

Kain, J. F., Apgar, W. C. Jr. 1985. *Housing and Neighborhood Dynamics: A Simulation Study.* Cambridge, Mass: Harvard Univ. Press

Kasinitz, P. 1983. Gentrification and homelessness: The single room occupant and the inner city revival. *Urb. Soc. Change Rev.* 17(1):9–14

Kasinitz, P. 1984. *Neighborhood change and conflicts over definitions: The "gentrification" of "Boerum Hill."* Presented at 54th Ann. Meet. East. Sociol. Assoc., Boston

Krase, J. 1982. *Self and Community in the City.* Washington, DC: Univ. Press

Laska, S. B., Spain, D. 1980. *Back to the City: Issues in Neighborhood Renovation.* New York: Pergamon

Lee, B. A., Lodge, D. C. 1984. Spatial differentials in residential displacement. *Urb. Stud.* 21(3):219–32

LeGates, R. T., Hartman, C. 1986. The anatomy of displacement in the United States. See Smith & Williams 1986, pp. 178–200

Lipton, S. G. 1977. Evidence of central-city revival. *J. Am. Plan. Assoc.* 43 (April):136–47

Logan, J., Molotch, H. 1987. *Urban For-*

tunes. Berkeley, Calif: Univ. Calif. Press. In press

London, B., Lee, B. A., Lipton, S. G. 1986. The determinants of gentrification in the United States: A city-level analysis. *Urb. Aff. Q.* 21(3):369–87

Lyford, J. P. 1966. *The Airtight Cage: A Study of New York's West Side.* New York: Harper & Row

Marcuse, P. 1986. Abandonment, gentrification, and displacement: The linkages in New York City. See Smith & Williams 1986, pp. 153–77

Massey, D. 1984. *Spatial Divisions of Labor: Social Structures and the Geography of Production.* New York: Methuen

McDonald, S. C. 1983. *Human and market dynamics in the gentrification of a Boston neighborhood.* PhD thesis. Harvard Univ., Cambridge, Mass.

Nelson, J. I., Lorence, J. 1985. Employment in service activities and inequality in metropolitan areas. *Urb. Aff. Q.* 21(1):106–25

Palen, J. J., London, B. 1984. *Gentrification, Displacement and Neighborhood Revitalization.* Albany, NY: State Univ. NY Press

Palmer, D., Roussel, A. 1986. *Corporate headquarter presence and business service activity in U.S. central cities.* Presented at 81st Ann. Meet. Am. Sociol. Assoc., New York

Peterson, P. E. 1985. *The New Urban Reality.* Washington, DC: Brookings Inst.

Portes, A., Walton, J. 1981. *Labor, Class, and the International System.* New York: Academic

Pred, A. 1985. The social becomes the spatial, the spatial becomes the social: Enclosures, social change and the becoming of places in the Swedish province of Skane. See Gregory & Urry 1985, pp. 337–65

Rose, D. 1984. Rethinking gentrification: Beyond the uneven development of marxist urban theory. *Soc. Space* 1:47–74

Sassen-Koob, S. 1984. The new labor demand in global cities. In *Cities in Transformation: Class, Capital, and the State,* ed. M. P. Smith, pp. 139–71. Vol. 26, Sage Urb. Aff. Ann. Rev. Beverly Hills, Calif: Sage

Saunders, P. 1984. Beyond housing classes: The sociological significance of private property rights in means of consumption. *Int. J. Urb. Reg. Res.* 8(2):202–27

Sayer, A. 1982. Explanation in economic geography: Abstraction versus generalization. *Progr. Hum. Geog.* 6 (March):68–88

Schaeffer, R., Smith, N. 1986. *The gentrification of Harlem?* Ann. Assoc. Am. Geogr. 76:347–65

Schill, M. H., Nathan, R. P. 1983. *Revitalizing America's Cities: Neighborhood, Rein-*

vestment and Displacement. Albany, NY: State Univ. NY Press

Smith, N. 1979. Gentrification and capital: Theory, practice and ideology in Society Hill. *Antipode* 11(3):24–35

Smith, N. 1984. *Uneven Development.* Oxford: Basil Blackwell

Smith, N. 1987. Of yuppies and housing: Gentrification, social restructuring, and the urban dream. *Soc. Space.* In press

Smith, N. 1986. Gentrification, the frontier, and the restructuring of urban space. See Smith & Williams 1986, pp. 15–34

Smith, N., Williams, P. 1986. *Gentrification of the City.* Boston: Allen & Unwin

Spain, D. 1980. Indicators of urban revitalization: Racial and socioeconomic changes in central-city housing. See Laska & Spain 1980, pp. 27–41

Weiler, C. 1980. The neighborhood's role in optimizing reinvestment: Philadelphia. See Laska & Spain 1980, pp. 220–35

Williams, B. 1985. Owning places and buying time: Class, culture, and stalled gentrification. *Urb. Life* 14(3):251–73

Williams, P. 1984. Gentrification in Britain and Europe. See Palen & London 1984, pp. 205–34

Williams, P. 1986. Class constitution through spatial reconstruction? A re-evaluation of gentrification in Australia, Britain, and the United States. See Smith & Williams 1986, pp. 56–77

Wright, P. 1985a. Ideal homes: A return to the classical past. *New Socialist,* October, pp. 16–21

Wright, P. 1985b. *On Living in an Old Country: The National Past in Contemporary Britain.* London: Verso

Zukin, S. 1980. A decade of the new urban sociology. *Theory Soc.* 9(4):575–601

Zukin, S. 1982. *Loft Living: Culture and Capital in Urban Change.* Baltimore: Johns Hopkins Univ. Press

Zukin, S., DiMaggio, P. 1986. *Structures of Capital: The Social Organization of Economic Institutions.* Submitted for publication

Zunz, O. 1970. Etude d'un processus d'urbanisation: Le quartier du Gros-Caillou à Paris. *Annales, E.S.C.* 25:1024–65

Ann. Rev. Sociol. 1987. 13:149–64

TIME BUDGETS AND THEIR USES

Rudolf Andorka

Karl Marx University of Economics, Department of Sociology, Budapest 5. Pf. 489. H1828 Hungary 175-172

Abstract

The paper summarizes the state of the art of time budget surveys and analyses. It first treats the new methodological developments, than reviews the different fields of utilization of time budget data: mass media contact, demand for cultural and other leisure goods and services, urban planning, consumer behavior, needs of elderly persons and of children, the sexual division of labor, the informal economy and household economics, social accounting, social indicators, quality of life, way of life, social structure. It deals also with the lessons from intertemporal and international comparisons of the results of time budget surveys.

INTRODUCTION

The first time budget surveys were performed in the interwar period, e.g. by S. G. Strumilin (1961) in a Soviet town in 1924 (Szalai 1966), and by Lundberg and coauthors in the 1930s in their Westchester Country Survey (Lundberg et al 1934). In 1939, Sorokin & Berger published an important book about the methods of analysis of time budgets. The great upsurge of time budget surveys and analyses, however, began in the 1960s, essentially with a 12-nation international comparative survey (Szalai 1972). The results of this survey seem to have convinced sociologists and statistical agencies that the time budget survey was feasible and might provide valuable new information for many different purposes, ranging from very practical social planning questions (e.g. the demand for urban mass transport) to sophisticated theoretical problems (e.g. the stratification of a given national society).

149

0360-0572/87/0815-0149$02.00

In the past 20 years, time budget surveys have been carried out in many countries, including developing countries, by both academic researchers and statistical agencies. The time budget method has been included in the works of statistical organizations of the United Nations and other international agencies. Researchers in the field established in 1970 an association, the International Research Group on Time Budgets and Social Activities, the secretariat of which is at Saint Mary's University, Halifax, Canada, and which has regular meetings. The vast scientific literature on time budgets is difficult to review and even to systematize. This review article first briefly discusses some methodological developments and then examines the purposes or uses of the surveys, beginning with the simplest practical utilizations and progressing to increasingly complex theoretical uses.

METHODOLOGY

The methods of time budget surveys and of their analysis were elaborated by the participants of the 12-nation time budget survey of 1965–1966 (Szalai 1972). The daily activities of a sample of the population are registered from midnight to midnight (in the case of the abovementioned multinational survey, the population included only individuals who were aged 18–64). This activity record can be attained in two ways: (*a*) by diaries filled out by the persons in the sample, or (*b*) by interviews with the persons. Either the exact times of beginning and finishing the activities are recorded, or the activities are inserted in short time slots (of 10–15 minutes, e.g. from 10:00 to 10:15). For each activity, times, places and other participants are also registered. Usually it is possible to note secondary activities, e.g. listening to the radio while doing housework.

Three main indexes are calculated and used in the analysis: (*a*) the average duration of each type of activity during the day (or the week) for all persons interviewed, (*b*) the percentage of all persons who participated in the given activity on the selected day, (*c*) the average duration of the activity for those who actually participated in it on the given day. Given these indexes, investigators compare various demographic groups and social strata by different nations and cohorts from different historical periods in a given society (Harvey et al 1977). For international and intertemporal comparison, the crucial problem is obviously the use of a common or at least comparable lists (*a*) of demographic and social categories, (*b*) of activities, and (*c*) of codes for the location of activities and for the other participants (Harvey 1984). Most surveys have, in fact, used slightly different lists of activities due to the particular purposes of the study and the conditions of a particular society. However, most often the categories in the list can be collapsed and so made comparable to the list of 37 activities or a grosser list from the 12-nation international time budget survey of 1965–1966.

Maintaining this basic technique, investigators have added some important new developments and methodological investigations. Concerning the sample, it is usually considered desirable to extend the age limits, since it is important to obtain knowledge about the daily activities of aged persons, in order to ascertain their needs for care. It is also interesting to have information on the time of children (Zimmer et al 1985). The sampling of the days for which time budget diaries are collected is also an issue. In the case of the international time budget survey, the only requirement was to perform the interviewing within two months—these two months should not include summer time, time at Christmas, nor the period of very cold weather. In addition, both weekdays and weekend days should be included in the sample, more or less according to their actual proportion. Some recent surveys have attempted to embrace a complete year by distributing the days of interviewing throughout the year. In this case multiple interviews for each respondent are considered to be advantageous, since the quality of responses tends to improve over time. However, not more than four interviews per person (distributed usually at equal intervals during the year) are recommended (Kalton 1985).

The quality of time budget data has been investigated by different methods. On the one hand, responses were checked against actual behavior. On the other hand, some "rules of thumb" were established, e.g. that the less valid diaries tend to have fewer activities, a smaller variety of activities, fewer secondary activities, more "not ascertained" time, and more activities beginning exactly on the hour or half hour (Juster 1985a). It is also possible to compare the time budget data to the responses given to so-called "stylized questions," i.e. the respondent is asked about how much time he has devoted to certain activities or how often he was engaged in various activities (e.g. watching television). The time budget diaries provide valid and reliable data, and the time budget is "the only viable method of obtaining valid and reliable data on activities" (Robinson 1985a:). Therefore, time budget methods ought to be preferred, in spite of higher costs, to the method of "stylized questions."

For analytical purposes it is often desirable to condense the great amount of data contained in the time-budget diaries. A four-category classification of activities was proposed (Ås 1978), namely, (a) necessary time/physiological needs, (b) contracted time/paid work and studying in regular schools, (c) committed time/other work, usually not paid, the time obligations of which are less precise, e.g. household work, (d) free time/to be distinguished from leisure, which means some subjectively gratifying activity, (free time means the time left over after the activities in a-c). Clark et al (1982) proposed hypercodes and composite variables to analyze the time budget diaries.

FIELDS OF UTILIZATION

Mass Media Contact, Demand for Cultural and Other Leisure Goods and Services

About 20–30 years ago it was expected that parallel with the rapid growth of productivity and the rise in the standard of living, the amount of leisure time would increase sharply. It was predicted that in the near future an average person would not work more than 40,000 hours in a lifetime (Fourastie 1965). The question was raised whether we were heading for a "civilization of leisure" (Dumazedier 1962). This possibility was not considered an undisputed blessing by all authors (Anderson 1962, Riesman 1964). The recognition of its likelihood, however, directed sociological research toward leisure activities. The companies selling leisure goods and services and organizations involved in planning were equally interested in these studies. They expected these studies to yield practical guidelines for the development of the production and marketing of leisure goods and for the building of a leisure infrastructure. Surveys on the utilization of the newly introduced work-free Saturdays are obviously useful examples (Szanto 1972).

The most developed field of leisure time research involves determining the length of time and the exact time slots of radio listening and television viewing. These data provide helpful information for designing programs for these mass media. In some countries, radio and television companies have their own public opinion research institutions which perform time budget surveys regularly. Examples of such countries are Japan (Nakanishi 1982), Hungary (Tomka 1978), and Korea (Kim et al 1982). Long-range plans for the mass media "contact time" can be constructed on the basis of these surveys. Originally, many longitudinal analyses indicated that time devoted to viewing television programs was increasing (Robinson & Converse 1972, Robinson 1985b). Recently, however, both an American follow-up survey in 1981–1982 (Juster 1985a, b, c, d) and a Japanese survey in 1985 (Nakanishi & Suzuki 1986) indicate a turning point in this pattern of growth. The earlier increase in time devoted to television viewing observed in some advanced societies and the parallel decrease in several other cultural activities (e.g. reading) as well as social contacts outside the home obviously reflected transformations in everyday life (Robinson 1969, 1977). These transformations can be evaluated both positively and negatively.

Urban Planning

One of the oldest theses of urban sociology is that the larger urban areas provide many more numerous and diversified possibilities for working, shopping, and entertainment than do the traditional rural areas. The way of life of the urban populations therefore differs strongly from that of the rural populations. A corollary of this thesis states that human contacts in cities are more numerous but much less deep. Time budget surveys offer possibilities to verify these theses (Harvey & Procos 1974).

Urban sociologists are also interested in the time budget technique for urban planning. From the point of view of the development of urban infrastructures, it is obviously interesting to discover where people do their shopping, where they go for recreation, which kind of transport they use, etc. The usual time budget questionnaire is often supplemented for these purposes by including questions (a) on the exact location of activities in the cities, so that the movement of persons can be traced geographically, and (b) on the time of these movements, in order that data on congestion can be provided (Gutenschwager 1973, Elliot et al 1973, Chapin 1974, Walldén 1975, Clar et al 1979). This method can be employed to evaluate the impact of urban policies (Cullen 1982).

Consumer Behavior

Time budget studies have also proven useful in the area of consumer behavior research (Venkantesan & Anderson 1986). Such analyses have addressed both practical policy issues such as the implications of compulsory closing hours in Norway (Grønmo 1978) and more academic and yet still practical issues such as social interaction and shopping behavior (Grønmo & Lavik 1986). Additionally, time budget surveys can be used to evaluate the demand of households for electricity during different parts of the day and the possibility of influencing this demand by pricing policies (Atkinson 1978, Hill, 1985).

The Needs of Elderly Persons and the Care of Children

As the population of all advanced societies is aging and, in particular, as the percentage of persons living to attain very old age increases, there is increased interest in the way these elderly persons live, in their demands and interests, and in their eventual need for care by social institutions. On the other hand, it is considered desirable that they continue to live in their accustomed milieu. Still, their demands for assistance and care increase with age. If these demands are not satisfied, the aged might become completely isolated and forced to live in very difficult circumstances, especially if they are relatively poor. Time budget surveys provide valuable ways to investigate the changes in the way the elderly live and changes in their needs. It is also possible to investigate the existence or nonexistence of personal contacts and of relatives who are able to provide help. Additionally, the relationship of activity patterns and human contacts to the general well-being of elderly persons can be studied by including supplementary questions (Altergott 1982a, 1986; Little 1984; Ujimoto 1984).

The time parents and others devote to the care of children is of particular interest. It is useful to secure information on the type of persons who care for the children, especially given the growing employment of married women with children. Because the labor force participation among married women has increased, the care of the children needs to be reorganized in some way. The level of help provided by grandparents and by other private persons (partly on the basis of mutual help, partly for pay) is not well known in many societies, although this knowledge is necessary to plan for the development of kindergartens and day schools. On a more theoretical level, parental care might be considered an important—or perhaps the most important—form of human investment (Hill & Stafford 1985) on which the quality of the future adult generations depends.

From other research there is some evidence that the amount of parental care is indeed positively correlated with the cognitive development of the children and also with the future economic status of the children. The American time budget survey of 1975–1976 demonstrated very important differences in the per-child parental care time according to the education of the mother, suggesting that highly educated parents transfer in this way important advantages to their children (Hill & Stafford 1985).

The Sexual Division of Labor

At least since the advent of industrialization, a characteristic pattern of division of labor between husbands and wives has developed. The men at first were the ones primarily engaged in paid work outside the home, while the married women were responsible for most of the household work and care of the children. This division of tasks is clearly reflected in the time budget survey in 1965–1966 (Szalai 1975). These surveys are often referred to in debates about the emancipation of women and about the equalization of the conditions of the two sexes.

Several developments in advanced societies may help to equalize the division of tasks and lead to a more "symmetrical family." Grønmo & Lingsom (1982) mention five such tendencies when comparing Norwegian time budget data from 1971–1972 and 1980–1981: (a) the social movement emphasizing the values of women's liberation, (b) the increase of the general level of education and the fact that more educated men spend more time in household chores, while more educated women spend more time in paid work and less in the household than do less educated women (c) the increase in women's participation in the active labor force, (d) the reduction in the average number of children per family, (e) the acquisition and use of more household appliances that enhance the productivity of household work. Comparing the data from the 1971–1972 and 1980–1981 time budget surveys, they found that the sexual differences of participation in household work had diminished. Similar tendencies were found in other countries, e.g. Hungary (Andorka & Falussy 1982). Nevertheless, the change toward sexual equalization of household chores is very slow. This area seems to be very resistant to change.

Another important aspect of the male-female differences involves the discrepancy between the total contracted (market work) and committed (household and child care) time. In Hungary, where a very large and growing proportion of women are employed fulltime, the average of this time was more than 30 min longer per day for women 15–69 years old than for men (men: 8hr, 27 min; women, 9 hr, 1 min, on an average day in 1976–1977). This difference did not appreciably decline since the first survey in 1963; in fact, it has increased from some minutes to more than half an hour. The reason for this increase involves the growth of full-time employment for women, which counterbalanced the reduction of contracted working hours and the shortening of household work of women. Thus, it could be concluded that in Hungary the major part of the burden of work is on the shoulders of the women, in spite of (or in consequence of) the complete legal equalization of the position of women and men (Andorka & Falussy 1982). The difference of the total contracted and committed time of men and women was almost identical in Finland (Niemi et al 1979) and even more so in Poland (Adamczuk 1978), but somewhat less so in the United States (Hill 1985). Thus the overburdening of women seems to be nearly universal.

The Informal Economy and Household Economics

It was originally assumed that economic activities would be steadily transposed from the household to the industrial production system, as was convincingly described by Polanyi in his *Great Transformation*. Therefore, both social scientists and the general public were greatly surprised when it was discovered in the 1970s that instead of declining, many types of small scale production activities were increasing in some advanced societies, e.g. Hungary. Such activities were conducted in the household, partly in other small units, for the market; but also to a large extent they occurred outside the market in the framework of mutual help simply for household consumption. As noted by Zapf (1984), under the conditions of both "market failure" (unemployment, etc) and "state failure" (problems of the welfare state), the other two producers of welfare—voluntary associations and the households—stepped in and increasingly assisted the members of the society to satisfy their material and nonmaterial (e.g. personal care) demands. Gershuny (1978, 1979) assumes that instead of a service economy (where the employment in services will grow at the expense of industrial and agricultural employment in the near future we will witness the emergence of a self-service economy where more and more service demands will be satisfied on a "do-it-yourself" basis and by moonlighting. Such predictions are based on the rising costs of services purchased from large organizations and the parallel decline of the price of the capital goods necessary to perform these service activities at home. If this tendency proves to be true, it would result in a future quite different from that predicted by the "post-industrial society" hypothesis.

All these productive or income-generating activities in the households and in small units are difficult to measure by traditional statistical techniques. As Gershuny (1979) stated, estimates of these household and communal activities may be made on the basis of the time devoted to them, and the best way to obtain this information is the time budget survey.

Hungary is an interesting example of the existence of these activities and of the attempts to measure them by time budgets. Since the introduction of reforms in 1968, governmental policy gradually changed from tolerance and legalization to the stimulation of these supplementary income–producing activities. The most widespread form of them is the small-scale agricultural production on household and auxiliary plots, i.e. in the courtyard and on small plots in the villages and in the smaller towns. A time budget survey of the households having such a plot in 1972–1973 showed on the one hand that not only peasants but also half the workers participated in small-scale agricultural production and that their time input was substantial. The data on the working time put into these small plots has led to the conclusion that the income per hour generated was relatively low, certainly lower than the hourly wage rate in the large agricultural production units (Oros & Schindele 1977).

Contrary to general expectations, the national time budget survey of 1976–1977 in Hungary demonstrated that the total work time input of the population (2.7 thousand million working hours per year for a population of about 10.6 million) had in fact not changed since the survey of 1972–1973 and has increased since the previous national time budget of 1963 (Andorka et al 1982). The new time budget survey of the households having household and auxiliary plots (Oros & Schindele 1985) confirmed this estimate and proved the continuing stability of the working time input, in spite of the fact that the number of persons employed in agriculture and the number living in villages declined and the number of peasants having experience in private agriculture diminished. Hungarian agriculture was completely collectivized in 1961.

Two other productive activities performed outside the big productive organizations, namely private housebuilding (carried on mostly in the framework of mutual help) and the repair and maintenance of consumer durables were also found to be important in Hungary (Andorka 1984). Repair and maintenance activities in the household were registered also by the American survey of 1975–1976, and a model was developed to explain the amount of these activities (M. S. Hill 1985).

Although the informal economy seems to be expanding in many advanced societies, the Hungarian case is considered to be special in many respects. First of all the combination of employment in the so-called "socialist" sector, i.e. in enterprises in state ownership and in cooperatives, with work done after the regular working hours in the informal sector proved to be more widespread than in Poland, and this "doubling" of work for income hardly exists in Finland (Adamczuk et al 1984). Thus it seems that if there exists a general tendency toward a more important role of the informal economy and "self-service" society, its actual forms are very different in the particular societies.

Time budget data might be used also to estimate the actual amount of time of labor force participation, or it might be used to control for the data obtained by other methods, e.g. by household sample surveys. The American time budget survey of 1975–1976 found that the hours of work per week obtained from these latter mentioned sources were substantially overstated as compared to the time budget data (Juster 1985b).

Time budget surveys providing data on the time devoted to market work, household work, and other activities provide the posibility to study empirically the relationships proposed by the economic theory of household behavior (Becker 1965, 1977; Ghez & Becker 1975). According to this theory, persons and households allocate their total available time—not only during the shorter periods but over the life cycle—on the basis of economic calculations so that they produce the maximum of benefit for themselves. Thus, it is argued that the division of labor between the spouses follows economic rationality: The husband usually engages more in market work because he can attain a higher wage than his wife, who therefore takes over most of the household chores. The alternative sociological theory stresses the importance of roles embedded in values and norms, i.e. the husband is expected to play the role of breadwinner and the wife is expected to do the role of the housewife. Hill & Juster (1985) were able to model the household division of labor tasks on the basis of American data from 1975–1976. Both market wage rates and stereotypes were shown to influence the division of tasks between the spouses; the role expectations, however, seem to be stronger. Analysts have attempted to construct an econometric model of lifetime fertility, childcare, and labor supply of the household (Hill & Stafford 1985).

Social Accounting, Social Indicators, Well-Being, Quality of Life

In the 1960s, statisticians, economists, and sociologists became more and more dissatisfied with the use of national income and the gross domestic product as measures of well-being and of economic and social developments. There were, therefore, endeavors to enlarge the number of indicators, for example, the work of housewives. Systems of social accounting and studies of social indicators and of quality of life increased. The results of time budget surveys were taken into consideration by these new research directions.

Time budget surveys might obviously be used to determine the length of household working time for various members of the household. If the value or shadow price of an hour of household work can somehow be estimated, it might be included in the national income, avoiding in that way the old and justified critique pointing out that the work of the domestic servant is part of the national income, whereas the work of the wife is not.

The social indicators movement tries to give a more realistic view of welfare by acknowledging that welfare is a multidimensional concept and income is only one of its dimensions. It has been proposed that the amount of leisure time ought to be included in measures of welfare (Beckerman 1978). Eight types of social indicators were proposed (Ås 1982) to be based on time budgets: (*a*) the amount of free time, (*b*) the amount of free time spent on various activities, (*c*) the amount of free time spent outside the home, (*d*) the amount of free time spent alone, with members of own household, and with others, (*e*) the rate of participation (percentage of persons) in selected free time activities over a given period, (*f*) the geographical accessibility to selected leisure facilities, (*g*) the flexibility of working hours, (*h*) subjective measures of problems in relation to daily time allocations—e.g. is there enough time for certain activities?

A related but somewhat different and more ambitious approach was proposed by R. Stone (1974). He constructed a set of social and demographic statistics and presented a series of tables that demonstrated the flows of the population among different categories during the period of observation. Time budgets and models of the allocation of time were mentioned as possible elements of such a system.

Recently Juster et al (1981a, b) proposed a much more elaborate accounting system that included time allocation. According to these authors, the time devoted to different activities influences the well-being of individuals in three ways: (*a*) activities produce flows of material goods, (*b*) activities alter the levels of resources and their contexts—e.g. the social and political environment—which have a strong impact on the well-being, and (*c*) activities themselves have positive or negative "process benefits"—some activities are enjoyable while other cause a feeling of discomfort.

Juster (1985d) tried to measure these process benefits by data collected in the 1975–1976 time budget survey in the United States. Respondents were asked to record their level of enjoyment of some 22 activities on a scale ranging from 10 to 0. The activities with own children (talking, trips, games) got the highest scores and household chores usually low scores. The most remarkable finding seems to be that working at the job received a relatively high score.

Michelson (1986) attempted to measure the subjective aspects of daily life by another method, namely by asking the respondents to evaluate each activity in their time budget on two scales. One of the scales measured the tension involved in the activity, the other assessed the degree that respondents viewed the activities as voluntary or involuntary.

Patrushev (1982) tried to measure the general satisfaction with free time in the Soviet Union by asking whether the respondent would prefer (a) to have more free time with the existing working hours and wages, (b) to have more free time with a shorter working day and lower wages, (c) to have less free time and earn more. Remarkably, few workers preferred higher wages at the expense of less free time. Therefore, he concluded that in the Soviet society an increased demand for free time is developing.

Campbell et al (1976) integrated the evaluation of the time budget into their methodology of quality of life surveys. Andrews & Withey (1974) also included questions on the use of time in the methodology of investigating the perceived quality of life. Szalai (1980) considered that the individual use of time is an indicator of the quality of life of the given person.

The Exploration of the "Style of Life"

Although the "way of life" or "style of life" is a concept used in sociology at least since Max Weber *(Lebensführung)*, it came to the forefront of sociology in European socialist countries around 1970. The greater interest was justified by stating that the material standard of living had attained such a level that it became increasingly more important to consider how the increased income was spent and how the increased free time was used (see e.g. Bolgov 1964, Patrushev 1969, Gordon & Klopov 1972, USSR Academy of Sciences 1981, Lippold & Manz 1982). The operationalization of the theoretical concept of "style" or "way" of life was, however, difficult. Hungarian sociologists defined the "way of life" as the system of activities of the members of the society (Kulcsár 1976). This definition seems to be more or less accepted by the sociologists in the European socialist societies. From this definition it follows that the time budget survey is one of the principal techniques to investigate the contours of citizens' way of life.

The research involving way of life is similar to the somewhat vague research into everyday life in the Western societies (Weigert 1981). Although this research direction intends to embrace the meaning given to the everyday activities in addition to the allocation of time and the movements in space (Douglas 1970), the core of the empirical investigations seems to involve the pattern of activities.

Social Structure

In the famous three dimensional scheme of Max Weber, the "Stände" dimension (translated into English as "status," although the exact meaning is nearer to "estate" in the feudal sense) is manifested by esteem and by the way of life or style of life. Thus, differences in the way of life can help to locate the boundaries between status groups.

Therefore, time budget survey data recommend themselves for the investigation of status differences as an element of social structure. Ferge (1972) emphasized this point in the analysis of data of the 12-nation international time budget survey, stating that the more privileged strata show a more variated use of their free time. Also, Wnuk-Lipinski (1972) found that in Poland the more privileged groups devoted more time to cultural activities and to active sports, although the difference in free time activities among various social strata was not very large. The Hungarian survey of 1975–1976, however, demonstrated a surprising trend: The differences of total contracted and committed time had increased since the first survey in 1963 (Andorka et al 1982). The main reason for this result was the great difference in the time devoted to activities outside the main working place producing supplementary income, e.g. the time spent in small-scale agricultural production. It might be concluded that in Hungary there is a slow tendency toward the reduction of the differences in income and living conditions, due to the fact that many citizens were spending increased time in agricultural activities outside the work place. This great extra work input occurred mainly in the lower strata of society, first of all among the peasants and the semi- and unskilled workers residing in the rural areas. The less free time for individuals in the lower strata obviously resulted in a much lower participation in cultural activities and less time for recreation in general. Therefore, it was concluded that it is not possible to get a realistic picture of the present Hungarian society without taking into consideration the differences in ways of life. In other advanced countries like Finland, the amount of free time is usually less differentiated by social categories, but the use of this free time, the leisure activities, seem to be similar within particular social strata (Adamczuk et al 1984).

Intertemporal and International Comparison

As several countries have already conducted two or more national time budget surveys, the possibility exists to make intertemporal comparisons, to analyze the changes in time use. Although Gutenschwager's (1973) statement that time budgets may ultimately be the only way of truly assessing social change seems to be somewhat exaggerated, the comparison of the results of several time budget surveys in a given society provides a good basis to ascertain some important social changes. Patrushev (1979) could do the comparison for one town in the Soviet Union for a 47-year period (1924–1971), by using the survey of Strumilin in the 1920s. The Japanese have data since 1960 (Furuka-wa 1976).

When comparing the time use data of the United States, Robinson & Converse (1972) stated 14 years ago that prophecies that America was turning into a "leisure society" were at least premature, if not inaccurate. In the 1960s, American people seemed to have even less free time than in earlier decades. The comparison of the 1965–1966 and the 1975–1976 survey, however, showed some decline in the time spent in work-related activities for employed men and women, an important decline in the household work of women, an increase of about 10% in free time, in which the sharply increasing time spent in television viewing was predominant (Robinson 1985b). On the basis of the follow-up survey in 1980–1981, Juster (1985c) found a trend toward more nearly equal division of labor between husbands and wives, as wives worked more at the market and less in the household, while their husbands worked somewhat shorter hours at the market and longer time in the household. The increase in television viewing time seems to have stopped, maybe even to have reversed.

As the introduction indicated, the upsurge of time budget analysis was initiated by the international survey of 1965–1966. Some interesting, although tentative conclusions of the international comparison of time budgets were the following: 1. Industrialization has a considerable impact of the use of time of societies, i.e. on their everyday life (Robinson et al 1972). On the basis of pairwise country-by-country comparions of the differences of time budgets a remarkable "map" of the investigated societies could be constructed: the first axis of this "map" ordered the countries in an East-West dimension from the USSR and Bulgaria to the German Federal Republic and the United States; the second axis ordered them in a North-South dimension from the United States and the USSR to Peru. The East was characterized by more work at the main working place, more reading of books, more cinema attendance, the West by more television viewing and more social contacts, etc. The North-South dimension was differentiated most of all by the place where the free time was spent: in the North more time was spent at home, in the South on the street (Converse 1972). Recently some bilateral and trilateral comparisons were made on the basis of the more recent national surveys (Adamczuk et al 1984, Harvey & Grønmo 1986). These introduced other variables in the analysis—e.g. per capita national income, employment by branches, income inequality, social mobility, ownership of consumer durables—and demonstrated that the differences among time budgets exist between societies at similar levels of development and that these might well be interpreted in terms of the economic and sociological characteristics of the societies. A new international time budget survey, however, seems to be highly desirable.

CONCLUDING REMARKS

The study of time budgets appears to be a research direction with many potential uses. Its future development and spread will depend probably on the willingness of the members of societies to be engaged in rather long and complicated interviews (or in rather time-consuming work, if they prepare the diaries themselves), on the development of more refined methods for analyzing and modelling data, and on the ability to include a wider spectrum of sociological variables in the analysis. International cooperation was an important factor stimulating development in this field, and it is hoped that such cooperation will continue.

Literature Cited

Adamczuk, L., 1978. *Budzett. Czasu Mieszkancow Polski.* Warszawa: GUS.

Adamczuk, L., Andorka, R., Harcsa, I., Niemi, I. 1984. *Modernization and time budget in Hungary, Poland and Finland.* Presented at the Conference of the International Research Group on Time Budgets and Social Activities, Helsinki

Altergott, K. 1982a. *Observing family life: A methodological assessment of time budgets.* Presented at 10th World Congress of Sociology, Mexico City

Altergott, K. 1982b. Role-relationships across the life span: A secondary analysis of a national study. Preliminary Report. See Staikov 1982. pp. 123–36

Anderson, N. 1962. *Work and Leisure.* New York: Free Press

Andorka, R. 1984. Elements of private welfare production in Hungary. *Social Indicators Research.* 14:235–40

Andorka, R., Falussy, B. 1982. The way of life of the Hungarian society on the basis of the time budget survey of 1976–1977. *Social Indicators Research.* 11:31–74

Andorka, R., Falussy, B., Harcsa, I. 1982. *Idömérleg. Részletes adatok.* Vols. 1, 2. Budapest: Central Statist. Off.

Andrews, F. M., Withey, S. B. 1974. Developing measures of perceived life quality: Results from several national surveys. *Soc. Indic. Res.* 1:7–9

Atkinson, S. E. 1978. A comparative analysis of response to time-of-day electricity pricing: Arizona and Wisconsin. In Aigner, D., ed. *Modeling and the Analysis of Electricity Demand by Time-of-Day.* Palo Alto: Electric Power Research Inst.

Becker, G. S. 1965. A theory of the allocation of time. *Econ. J.* 75:493–517

Becker, G. S. 1977. *The Economic Approach to Human Behavior.* Chicago: Univ. Chicago Press

Beckerman, W. 1978. *Measures of Leisure, Equality and Welfare.* Paris: OECD

Bolgov, V. I. 1964. *Vnerabocsee vremia i uroven zhizni trudiaisia.* Novosibirski. AN SSSR Sibirskoe Otdel

Campbell, A., Converse, P., Rodgers, W. 1976. *The Quality of American Life.* New York: Russell Sage

Chapin, S. 1974. *Human Activity Patterns in the City.* New York: Wiley Intersci.

Clar, M., Friedrichs, J., Hempel, W. 1979. *Zeitbudget und Aktionsräume von Stadtbewohnern.* Hamburg: Christians Verlag

Clark, S., Elliott, D., Harvey, A. 1982. Hypercodes and composite variables: Simple techniques for the reduction and analysis of time budget data. See Staikov 1982, pp. 66–92

Converse, P. E. 1972. Country differences in time use. See Szalai 1972, pp. 145–77

Cullen, I. 1982. Measuring the impact of urban social policies. See Staikov 1982, pp. 329–48

Douglas, J. ed. 1970. *Understanding Everyday Life.* Chicago: Aldine

Dumazedier, J. 1962. *Vers une civilisation du loisir?* Paris: Seuil

Elliott, D. H., Harvey, A. S., Procos, D. 1973. *An Overview of the Halifax Time-Budget Study.* Halifax: Regional and Urban Studies Centre. Ms.

Ferge, S. 1972. Social differentiation in leisure activity choices: An unfinished experiment. See Szalai 1972, 213–28

Fourastié, J. 1965. *Les 40000 heures. Le travail d'une vie, demain.* Paris: Denoel

Furukawa, M. 1976. *How Japanese People Spend Their Time, 1960–1975.* Tokyo: Public Opinion Res. Inst. Japan Broadcast. Corp.

Gershuny, J. I. 1978. *After Industrial Society? The Emerging Self-Service Economy.* London: Macmillan

Gershuny, J. I. 1979. The informal economy. Its role in post-industrial society. *Futures* 12:3–15

Ghez, G. R., Becker, G. S. 1975. *The Allocation of Time and Goods Over the Life Cycle.* New York: Columbia Univ. Press

Gordon, A. A., Klopov, E. V. 1972. *Chelovek posle raboty. Szocialnye problemy byta i vnerabochego vremeni.* Vol 1, 2. Moscow: Nauka

Grønmo, S. 1978. *Handling og samhandling. Lørdagshandelens befydning for norske forbrukere.* Prosjektrapport nr. 17. Oslo: Fondet for markeds- of distribusjonsforskning

Grønmo, S., Lavik, R. 1986. *Consumer behaviour and social interaction: An analysis of Norwegian time budget data.* Presented at the 11th World Congress of Sociology, New Delhi

Grønmo, S., Lingsom, S. 1982. *Sexual differences in household work: Patterns of time use change in Norway.* Presented at the 10th World Congress of Sociology, Mexico City

Gutenschwager, G. 1973. The time-budget-activity systems perspective in urban research and planning. *J. Am. Inst. Planners* 39:378–87

Harvey, A. S. 1984. *Proposal for multinational cooperation in time: budget research.* Halifax: Saint Mary's Univ.

Harvey, A. S., Gronmo, S. 1984. *Social contact and use of time. Canada and Norway.* Presented at the conference of the Int. Res. Group on Time Budgets and Soc. Activities, Helsinki

Harvey, A. S., Procos, D. 1974. *Suburb and satellite contrasted: An exploration of activity patterns and urban form.* Presented at the Third Advanced Studies Institute in Regional Science, Karlsruhe

Harvey, A. S., Szalai, A., Elliott, D. H., Stona, P. J., Clark, S. 1977. Cross national time budget analysis: A workbook draft. Halifax: Inst. Public Affairs, Dalhousie Univ.

Hill, C. R., Stafford, F. P. 1985. Parental care for children: Time diary estimates of quantity, predictability, and variety. See Juster & Stafford 1985. pp. 415–37

Hill, C. R., Stafford, F. P. 1985. Lifetime fertility, child care, and labor supply. See Juster & Stafford 1985, pp. 471–92

Hill, D. H. 1985. Implications of home production and inventory adjustment processes for time-of-day demand for electricity. See Juster & Stafford. 1985, pp. 493–513

Hill, M. S. 1985. Investments of time in houses and durables. See Juster & Stafford 1985, pp. 205–43

Hill, S. M., Juster, F. T. 1985. Constraints and complementarities in time use. See Juster & Stafford 1985, pp. 439–470

Hill, S. M. 1985. Patterns of time use. See Juster & Stafford 1985, pp. 133–76

Juster, F. T. 1985a. The validity and quality of time use estimates obtained from recall diaries. See Juster & Stafford 1985, pp. 63–91

Juster, F. T. 1985b. Conceptual and methodological issues involved in the measurement of time use. See Juster & Stafford 1985, pp. 19–31

Juster, F. T. 1985c. A note on recent changes in time use. See Juster & Stafford 1985, pp. 313–32

Juster, F. T. 1985d. Preferences for work and leisure. See Juster & Stafford 1985, pp. 333–51

Juster, F. T., Courant, P. N., Dow, G. K. 1981a. A theoretical framework for the measurement of well-being. *Rev. Income Wealth.* 27:1–31

Juster, F. T., Courant, P. N., Dow, G. K. 1981b. The theory and measurement of well-being: A suggested framework for accounting and analysis. See *Social Accounting Systems: Essays on the State of the Art.* ed. F. T. Juster, K. C. Land, New York. Academic Press

Juster, F. T., Stafford, F. P. eds. 1985. *Time, Goods, and Well-Being.* Ann Arbor. Survey Res. Center Instit. Soc. Res. Univ. Mich.

Kalton, G. 1985. Sample design issues in time diary studies. See Juster & Stafford 1985, pp. 93–112

Kim, K-W., Oh, I-H., Choo, K-Y., Kang, D-I., Park, H-S., Yang, S-M. 1982. A survey of time budgeting by Korean people. Presented at the 10th World Congress of Sociology, Mexico City

Kulcsár, K. 1976. *A szocialista életmód formálásának feltételei és politikai problémái.* Budapest: Kossuth

Lipphold, G., Manz, G. 1982. The use of time categories for an outline of the mode of life. See Staikov 1982, pp. 166–87

Little, V. C. 1984. An overview of research using the time-budget methodology to study age-related behaviour. *Aging Soc.* 4:3–20

Lundberg, G., Keonavouski, M., McInery, M. 1934. *Leisure: A Suburban Study.* New York: Columbia Univ. Press

Michelson, W. 1977. *Environmental Choice, Human Behavior, and Residential Satisfaction.* New York:

Michelson, W. 1984. *The empirical merger of objective and subjective aspects of daily life.* Presented at Conference Int. Res. Group on Time Budgets and Social Activities, Helsinki

Nakanishi, N. 1982. *Changes in mass media contact times. Analysis of results of national time use survey.* Presented at 10th World Congress Sociol. Mexico City

Nakanishi, N., Suzuki, Y. 1986. Japanese time use in 1985. Presented at the 11th World Congress of Sociology, New Delhi

Niemi, I., Kiiski, S., Liikkanen, M. 1979. Use of time in Finland. Helsink: Central Statistical Office of Finland

Oros, I., Schindele, M. 1977. Idömérleg a háztáji és kisegitö gazdaságokban. *Statisztikai Szemle*. 55:846–63

Oros, I., Schindele, M. 1985. A háztáji és kisegitö gazdaságokban végzett emberi munka. *Statisztikai Szemle*. 63:968–87

Patrushev, V. A. ed. 1969. *Budzet vremeni, planirovanie i soversestvovanie organizacii svobodnogo vremeni*. Novosibirsk

Patrushev, V. 1979. Changes in leisure time activities. *Soviet Stud. Sociol*. Moscow. USSR Acad. Sci. 179–187

Patrushev, V. D. 1982. Satisfaction with free time as a social category. See Staikov 1982, pp. 259–67

Riesman, D. 1964. *Abundance for what? and other essays*. Garden City: Doubleday

Robinson, J. P. 1969. Television and leisure time: Yesterday, today and/maybe/tomorrow. *Public Opin. Q*. 33:210–222

Robinson, J. P. 1985a. The validity and reliability of diaries versus alternative time use measures. See Juster & Stafford 1985, pp. 33–62

Robinson, J. P. 1985b. Changes in time use: An historical overview. See Juster & Stafford 1985, pp. 289–311

Robinson, J. P., Converse, P. 1972. Social change reflected in the use of time. In *The Human Meaning of Social Change*, ed. A. Campbell, P. Converse, pp. 17–68. New York: Russell Sage Found.

Robinson, J. P., Converse, P., Szalai, A. 1972. Everyday life in twelve countries. See Szalai 1972, 113–44

Sorokin, P., Berger, C. 1939. *Time-Budgets of Human Behavior*. Cambridge: Harvard Univ. Press

Staikov, Z. ed. 1982. It's about time. Sofia: Inst. Sociol. Bulgarian Acad. Sci.

Stone, R., 1974. *Towards a System of Social and Demographic Statistics*. New York: United Nations

Strumilin, S. G. 1961. *Problemy socializma i kommunizma v SSSR*. Moscow: Ekonomizdat

Szalai, A. 1966. Trends in comparative time budget research. *Am. Behav. Sci*. 29:3–8

Szalai, A. ed. 1972. *The Use of Time*. The Hague: Mouton

Szalai, A. 1975. *The situation of women in the light of contemporary time budget research*. Presented World Conf. Int. Women's Year, Mexico City

Szalai, A. 1980. *Quality of life and the individual use of time*. Presented Conf. Fundación Bariloche.

Szántó, M. 1972. A szabad szombat bevezetése és a városokban élö ipari munkavállalók életmódjában vekövetkezett változások. In *Szabadidö és müvelódés*, ed. B. Falussy, pp. 33–61. Budapest. TIT

Tomka, M. 1978. *A tévénézés és a rádióhallgatás a napi tevékenvségek rendszerében*. Budapest. Tömegkomminukációs Kutatóközpont

Ujimoto, K. V. 1984. *Time use in comparative gerontological research*. Presented Conf. Int. Res. Group on Time Budgets and Soc. Activities, Helsinki

USSR Academy of Sciences. 1981. *Socialist Way of Life: Problems and Perspectives*. Moscow: USSR Acad. Sci.

Venkantesan, M., Anderson, B. B. 1986. Time budgets and consumer behavior. Presented 11th World Congr. Sociol., New Delhi.

Walldén, M. 1975. *Individers aktivitetsmöster. Del 3. Tidsanvändning*. Stockholm: Statens rad för byggnadsforskning

Weigert, A. J. 1981. *Sociology of Everyday Life*. New York: Longmans

Wnuk-Lipinski, E. 1972. Praca i wypoczynek w budzecie czasu. Wroclaw. Ossolineum

Zapf, W. 1984. Welfare production: public versus private. *Social Indicators Research*. 14:263–74

Zimmer, S. G., Eccles, J., O'Brien, K. 1985. How children use time. See Juster & Stafford 1985, pp. 353–87

Ås, D. 1978. Studies of time use: Problems and prospects. *Acta Sociol*. 15:125–41

Ås, D. 1982. Designs for large scale time use studies of the 24-hour day. See Staikov 1982, pp. 17–53

Ås, D., Harvey, A. S., Wnuk-Lipinski, E. eds. 1986. *Time use studies: Dimensions and applications*. Helsinki: Central Statistical Office of Finland

Ann. Rev. Sociol. 1987. 13:165–92

DECISION-MAKING AT THE TOP OF ORGANIZATIONS

David J. Hickson

University of Bradford Management Centre, Bradford BD9 4JL England

Abstract

Strategic decision-making processes at the top of organizations are examined. Research is reviewed on types of process movement, on the matters under decision, the problems raised, the interests implicated, the rules of the game, and its outcomes and implementation. Methodology is found to have gone through a conventional sequence of development from the small-scale intensive study to the large-scale extensive study, the latter very recently. Methodology has been catching up with theory, which has long been well developed. There are three main theories, overlapping and complementary—the incrementalism theory, the garbage-can theory, and the dual rationality theory. Five areas for further research are indicated.

WHAT THEY LOOK LIKE: THE MAKING OF STRATEGIC DECISIONS

From the vantage point of some researchers, the making of big decisions by those at the top of organizations appears like a football game. But which kind of football? By some, it has been seen as an "unconventional soccer match" (Weick 1976). Instead of the usual oblong soccer pitch, the field is round. Instead of two teams each attacking a goal at the other end, goals are scattered around haphazardly, and people can come on and off as they please and aim at any goals they like. The field is sloping. And yet "the game is played as if it made sense" (Weick 1976, and also March & Romelaer 1976).

While some Americans have this view of decision-making as a kind of

0360-0572/87/0815-0165$02.00

crazy European soccer, those on the other side of the Atlantic see it as a sort of riotous American football! It is seen as a game of powerful groups in which some teams are much bigger and have "thicker protective padding and harder helmets" (Hickson et al 1986). Boundaries are elastic, the field is bumpy, and the number of teams in play fluctuates. They disagree as to where the ends of the field are, but eventually "one team or coalition of teams pushes its way through holding the ball to where it says the end is" (Hickson et al 1986). This is a game in which the heavier or better protected players have a greater chance of shaping what is going on and where it is going to. The shape of the ball itself can be changed.

Whichever of these two fanciful analogies may be the more fitting, they have in common the view that what happens on the way to a decision is not always straightforward. The matter under decision may bounce around from hand to hand in a way that can be difficult to follow. So this essay is an attempt to discuss, in a more or less orderly way, processes that may not take place in an orderly way, and to discuss one by one things that may happen all together.

Admitting that, then it begins by examining the main features of strategic decision-making: The kinds of processes that occur, the strategic matters that come up for decision, the uncertainty encountered, and the influence of interests; the basic rules of the game, its outcomes, and their implementation. The doubts and divisions over research methodology are then commented upon, and its historical development is reviewed. Some of the principal concepts and theories are discussed, and a new maturity is discernable in both methods and ideas. Finally, some of the least known and least understood aspects are pointed out as possible areas for future research. However, this is an essay, and it does not pretend to be an encyclopedia of absolutely everything that has ever been done on decision-making.

The Process in Motion

Just as the ball moves across a football field toward a goal, so the matter under consideration moves toward a decision. The answer to the question "what is process" is that process is movement. The process of strategic decision-making moves a strategic matter from A to B through an organization through time.

The difficulty is in defining A and B. Where is the start and where is the finish? Ultimately this is asking where are the ends of time, for there are no finite beginnings and endings. Everything can be traced back further and further and further. As historians know, periods have to be chopped out of the human saga at junctures that help to make sense of it, and that is sufficient justification. Most students of decision-making at the top of organizations have chopped out periods of overt and acknowledged decision-related activity. Typically, "the decision process encompasses all those steps taken from the time a stimulus for an action is perceived until the time the commitment to the action is made" (Mintzberg 1979:58), that is from "first proposal" to "final decision outcome" (Hage 1980:117). Such periods do not include the whole story. There is much to tell both beforehand and afterwards (and this is referred to later in this essay), but these periods of deliberate managerial movement towards a decision are the focus of the tale.

How long are they? How long does it take to reach a major decision? Not very long as a rule. Most of the big choices are made in two years or less. The mean period is about a year, and such decisions are quite commonly made in a few months since there is a modal point around six months (Hickson et al 1986, Mallory 1986). On the other hand, a few are prolonged indeed. While a new dean was chosen in an American university in just nine months (March & Olsen 1976: Chapters 6 & 15), many matters are undecided for up to four years (Mintzberg et al 1976, Hickson et al 1986, Mallory 1986). Some persist even longer—as did the maneuverings over computer equipment in a British retail business, which went on for seven years (Pettigrew 1973).

As Hage (1980:110) visualizes it, this movement through time towards a decision follows a "trajectory" which bounces around like that of a molecule in a bubble chamber. Certainly the trajectories often do bounce to and fro in a lively, though not necessarily erratic, manner. Those concerned may well feel that they know what they are doing, at the time anyway, even if hindsight brings second thoughts. But what they do can twist and turn and repeat itself. This has been nowhere better revealed than by Mintzberg et al (1976) who studied 25 cases of decision-making, one each in a variety of Canadian organizations. They identified no less than seven kinds of processes: simple impasse, political design, basic search, modified search, basic design, blocked design, and dynamic design processes. Of the 25 processes, 15 were broken up by "interrupts" ("sudden events that interrupted them and caused changes in pace or direction"), and all showed cycling and recycling, that is the reassessing of information and alternatives again and again. Mintzberg and his coworkers (1976) faced quite a problem in trying to diagram these uneven and repetitive sequences of events! The same sort of thing is suggested by Nutt (1984) from the analysis of a decision process in each of 73 health-related service organizations in the United States. Burgelman (1983) noted that new product proposals were forced up through a business corporation until they reached the attention of those at the top. In the course of this they were the subject of repetitive entrepreneurial moves from below and administrative manipulations from above, with feed-forward and feed-backward loop effects.

So those at the pinnacle of the hierarchy often run into delays or doubts about the available information or opposition, many of which either give them the chance to go over the ground again or force them to do so. [Hickson et al (1986) enumerate nine kinds of impediments of this nature.] Even if they follow a textbook course that begins by identifying a problem, goes on to search for pertinent information, evaluates alternative solutions to find which is best, and finally makes a choice—they are not very likely to move step by step through these phases in a neat orderly way once and for all. They may do so, but more often they will repeat some phases or parts of phases more than once before they come to a conclusion.

"Muddling through" the process in this fashion is "disjointed" partly because it looks for solutions bit by bit, that is, as a succession of limited "incremental" comparisons (Lindblom 1959, Braybrooke & Lindblom 1963). Since to attempt to achieve the "rational deductive ideal" of amassing and evaluating all possible information on all possible alternatives would be mind blowing, decisionmakers content themselves with enough information to make limited comparisons between alternative decisions, most of which would be mere increments added on tentatively at the point where the last decision finished off. Disjointed processes move first one way, then another, feeling the way ahead in small steps. Most senior managers and administrators are likely to approach decisions this way. For even though Lindblom first saw these characteristics in public administration (Lindblom 1959), Quinn argues persuasively that a similar "logical incrementalism" pervades private industry (Quinn 1978, 1980).

Of course, these insights indicate broad tendencies, a matter of degree in many instances but not all. Some decisions can be all or nothing, too indivisible to be tackled incrementally (Schulman 1975, Lustick 1980).

Indeed, it has to be asked whether the whole image of a volatile molecule—or football—bouncing sideways and backwards as often as forwards, and making progress only little by little in fits and starts, is not too lurid. It is a brilliant and invaluable cartoon which describes what happens in a way that gives penetrating understanding, although while it may well hold much of the truth much of the time, there is strong evidence that it does not represent all of the truth all of the time.

The Bradford studies of decision-making by my colleagues and myself (Hickson et al 1985, 1986) derived a characterization of the movement of strategic decision-making processes from 150 cases, 5 each in 30 diverse organizations in Britain. The most distinctive summary features of these cases were their discontinuity and their dispersion. That is, they differed first in the extent to which they had proceeded steadily and continuously, and second in the extent to which they had proceeded throughout the organization or were relatively confined. While many were *dis*continuous or, in more colorful terms, did seem to bounce around, many were comparatively continuous; and they varied similarly in *dispersion*.

Three types of movement emerged from an analysis of 136 cases that had the necessary data. There were *sporadic processes,* "informally spasmodic and protracted", as when in a state-owned industry a decision to buy a one-third share in a large customer firm was taken over a period of a year and a half, in irregular bursts of activity and flurries of negotiation with other interested corporations. There were *fluid processes,* "steadily paced, formally channelled, speedy," as when in a city government, a decision to launch a lottery, an unprecedented and potentially controversial source of funds at the time, was rushed through the framework of municipal committees in a month or so. And there were *constricted processes,* "narrowly channelled", as when in an insurance company, a decision was taken to defend its autonomous existence via an updating and centralizing of its data handling, a decision-making process that revolved around the chief executive in a tried and recognized manner. Some matters for decision and kinds of organizations are prone to one type of process rather than another.

Although the sporadic processes showed symptoms of the discontinuous excitation that the general image of decision-making leads one to expect, the fluid processes showed far fewer symptoms of this. The constricted group were divided either way but, more significantly, were the opposite of dispersed, as the word constricted denotes. The process moved in well-worn channels under the control of a chief executive or similar figure and did not flow around the organization as sporadic and fluid processes tended to do. In short, the salient impression given by at least a half the cases (the fluids and many of the constricteds) was of smooth continuity or limited movement or both. We should avoid drawing an over-excited image of what goes on along the corridors of decision.

The Strategic Matter in Motion

Impressions of what strategic decisions are about can also be unbalanced. Media stories focus attention on the big product launch successes and failures, such as the well-known cases, in American industry, of IBM's computer, Du Pont's Corfam shoe, and Ford's Edsel car which Hage (1980) cites as examples of high risk decisions. Yet among decisions that have been studied, those chosen by executives as being strategic matters, new products in manufacturing are only one category (Quinn 1978). In published comparative research (Drenth et al 1979, Nutt 1984, Mintzberg et al 1976, March & Olsen 1976, Hickson et al 1986: see Table 2.2 in the last reference), new technology and investments in buildings and equipment, internal reorganizations, and electronic data processing and related planning, all bulk large among topics for decision (computers and the like have been a favorite among researchers ever since the early case histories published by Cyert et al (1956), Cyert & March (1963), Carter (1971), and Pettigrew (1973). Decisions to introduce new services in private commerce and in the public sector are quite common, even more so than new product designs in manufacturers. Then there are a range of less frequent topics such as market and price decisions, personnel grading schemes, takeovers and mergers, the raising of capital, and whether to move the main organization to a fresh location. In summary, the principal strategic preoccupations of those at the top appear from research coverage to be: how the organization is to be equipped (by investment in productive technology or in data processing equipment), what the best structure is for the organization, and what the organization is to do. This is reassuringly obvious. These are the sorts of topics that governing elites would be expected to be dealing with.

The matter in hand is labeled as the new plant decision or the merger question, or whatever it is, by those involved in the process. This topic label identifies it at the time and subsequently but does not necessarily convey all that is at stake. Any matter is liable to be the surface expression of long-standing underlying issues—such as how far to go in diversifying a firm, or what the balance should be between research and teaching in a university—issues not signified by the simple topic label that the matter acquires.

Even so, the ostensible topics do offer a first grasp on what is afoot. They frequently embody intentional managerial strategies that can be seen in the way in which one decision leads to another (Hickson et al 1986). However, it is questionable whether the decisions actually carried out are always the same as the intended strategy. "A pattern in a stream of decisions" (Mintzberg 1978) can expose the actual strategy that has emerged in practice. Mintzberg & Waters (1982) show this in the patterns of store openings and closings, of financing, and of related activities over many decades in a Canadian retail chain. After tracing in the same way the patterns of films that have been produced by the National Film Board of Canada, Mintzberg & McHugh (1985) go further and suggest that strategies emerge from all the "grass-roots" operating decisions in organizations as well as from deliberate strategic decisions higher up.

The Problems Raised

The handling of each matter for decision is partly shaped by the problems it raises; the uncertainty these problems bring is thought to be especially telling. All strategic matters are by definition largely beyond the routines evolved to deal with repetitive matters in a programmed way. They are comparatively nonprogrammed because of the uncertainty about how to deal with them and what conclusion to reach (Simon 1960). There may be no accepted assumptions about cause and effect, so that the consequences of choosing this alternative rather than that are unforeseeable (Thompson & Tuden 1964). The factors to be weighed may be numerous, varied, and changing, as they were in the Swedish schools and colleges investigated by Axelsson & Rosenberg (1979).

It is contended that organizations attempt to avoid uncertainty so that their central activities can continue undisturbed (Thompson 1967, Cyert & March 1963). The word "avoid" is misleading if it is taken to mean that executives always run away from anything uncertain; indeed, many major decisions, particularly reorganizations and relocations, are "an unprecedented step into the unknown" (Hickson et al 1986). The point is more accurately understood as meaning that executives take risks only so far as they must and at a time when they hope their organizations can hold down the uncertainty. Specialist departments gain influence from developing a capacity to cope with areas of uncertainty (March & Simon 1958, Hickson et al 1971, Hinings et al 1974), and they feed in information and recommendations during the making of strategic decisions.

"Problemistic search" spurred by the immediate problem is more important than is the steady routine accumulation of information on, say, sales or costs (Cyert & March 1963). By sorting through case material on decisions in 73 hospitals and governmental agencies, insurance companies, and consulting firms in the health field, Nutt (1984) discerned 5 ways in which ideas were sought (and 11 subvariations on these 5 ways). Most common (41%) was the "historical process" which used "concepts drawn from the practices of others." Almost as common (30%) was the "off-the-shelf" process in which "aggressive and overt search" attempted to find "the best available ideas." "Nova" processes (15%) deliberately aimed at innovation. In other words, if what appeared to happen in these health related organizations can be generalized, the thrust of the search for ideas is about evenly divided between looking backward at what has been done before and more energetically looking forward and outward to what might be done. Nutt (1984) found also a minority of more defensive "search" processes which "lacked a workable idea," and "appraisal" processes which assessed "an idea that has an unknown or contentious value."

Whether or not this typology is exactly transferable to other kinds of organization, there is no doubt of either the limited capacity of the human mind or its susceptibility to believing what it wants to believe. Cognitive limits set a "bounded rationality" within which things make reasoned sense, though looked at in a wider context they make no sense at all (March & Simon 1958, Simon 1960, Cyert & March 1963). Motivation limits bias the acquisition of information, so that those concerned go for the most easy to come by and least controversial information which they come to treat as more certain that it originally was (O'Reilly 1983). Thus, decisions ensue from narrow perspectives and distorted data!

Despite this, organizations survive, and these pages are written by an employee of one. Even though the makers of decisions grope around in a probabalistic world in a selective self-justifying way and there is always an element of chaos as a result, coherence persists in most organizations and most societies most of the time.

The Interests Implicated

Within each organization, as within a whole society, this coherence must somehow contain multiple interests. In the understanding of decision-making in organizations, the early brilliance of the ideas from the "Carnegie school," principally those of Cyert, and of March, and of Simon (for examples, March & Simon 1958; Simon 1945, 1960; Cyert & March 1963), outshone all else and led to an emphasis on the information processing aspect of decision-making rather than the political aspect. This was not an altogether fair reflection of the Carnegie school which comprehended both aspects, even if its writings did not make this sufficiently plain, but probably it was more a reflection of the selective perception of academics in business education at the time. Since then, through the 1970s and 1980s, greater attention has come to be paid to the political nature of strategic decisions. It is well recognized that the way each matter is handled is shaped by the interests it implicates as well as by the problems it raises.

Each interest exerts influence or "kinetic power," as it has been called (French & Raven 1959), in the "bureaucratic politics" (Allison 1969) of decision-making. "Politics refers to the active influence process, but power is latent, referring to the ability or capacity to influence" (Miles 1980). Departments submit reports, consultants make recommendations, suppliers indicate possible prices, and so on. The more influential the interest, the more likely it is that the information and/or views it offers will be acted upon (O'Reilly 1983). The timing of an intervention is crucial, since everyone cannot attend to everything at once, and so there are right moments and wrong moments: "Every entrance is an exit somewhere else" (March & Olsen 1976). Thus, timing when to come in and when to stay out demands political judgment. There is "fluid participation" (Cohen et al 1972). It has been suggested that while most of the action takes place during the middle phase of a decision-making process (DIO International Research Team 1983), it is vital to influence the start and the finish (Heller et al 1987).

Each decision-making process involves a subset, or "decision-set" (Hickson et al 1986) of the interests in the "organizational coalition" (Cyert & March 1963, Pfeffer & Salancik 1977) of the internal and external interests that sustain the organization in being. An average of about seven "interest units" per decision has been found, including both "heavyweights" and "lightweights" in terms of the influence they exert and the number of decisions they become involved with (Hickson et al 1986). Among the heavyweights are production departments (and the equivalent in service organizations), sales and marketing, and accounting; from outside the organization the customers or clients may be involved, although only now and again. Governmental departments and agencies, and trade unions, are relatively uninfluential lightweights. On rare occasions, however, when the moment and the circumstances are right, a governmental interest may bring pressure to bear for a particular decision and it then may manage to exert considerable influence.

Games of position are played in which interests are protected in a "concatenation of maneuver" (March 1981) across "bargaining zones" (Abell 1975). Indeed, an organization can be regarded as an "ensemble des jeux" (Crozier & Friedberg 1980). Two memorably vivid case histories come from British experience. One, mentioned earlier, describes the manipulation of information and of access to authority figures in the retail business (Pettigrew 1973). The other tells how an otherwise smooth process in a chemicals producer was inflamed by a career struggle between the two directors, both of whom used it in their endeavors to attain the managing directorship (Wilson 1982, Hickson et al 1986). In the American corporation studied by Burgelman (1983), if a product innovation were to become part of the corporation's strategy it had to be thrust upwards by its "champion" until it secured a positive top-level decision, a process in which "gatekeeping, idea generating and bootlegging activities" could all be found. Political success allowed initial "strategic forcing" of the product into the market by its supporters; this, if successful, won sustained corporate management support.

There is a sense in which the political game turns a decision-making process around back to front. Interests in its outcome are already there before the process begins, insofar as most of those whose interests may be implicated know their objectives, their preferences, and their *logiques d'action* (Karpik 1972, Weiss 1981) irrespective of which topic arises. Thus, solutions exist *before* problems arise, and the game is to find a problem to which you can attach your solution (Cohen et al 1972, March & Olsen 1976).

In a decision-making process, therefore, the search is not only for problem-solving information but for interest-accommodating alternatives. Cognitive limits are paralleled by acceptability limits. Since there are multiple interests, all of which cannot be met at once, there is "sequential attention to goals" (Cyert & March 1963) with first one and then the other claiming priority. Since differing interests are built into an organization—sales versus production, surgical versus medical, sociology versus biology, and so on—each decision is only a "quasi-resolution of conflict": The differences remain and will come out again next time (Cyert & March 1963). Grandori (1984) puts forward a rather simplistic classification of procedures that logically should fit different levels of conflict and uncertainty, running from "computation" of value maximizing choices when there is agreement and certainty, to random casting around when there is a great deal of disagreement and uncertainty.

A prime social mechanism for the management of potentially conflicting interests is the committee by whatever name (the council, board, senate, committee, subcommittee, working party, project team, etc). A committee makes political behavior less obtrusive and more legitimate, and it diffuses responsibility (Miles 1980). Universities probably have more of these creations than any other known form of organization but, strangely, they do not seem to slow decision-making in universities nor anywhere else despite the popular impression that they clog it up (Hickson et al 1986).

The contemporary view of the making of a strategic decision therefore sees it as an essentially political process (Pfeffer & Salancik 1974) in which problems are defined and information is used with the interests of a range of insiders and outsiders in mind implicitly, if not explicitly. Emphasizing this in American private industry, Donaldson & Lorsch (1983) make what is nevertheless a general point about "unlimited ambition, limited choice": "Top management's freedom to set strategic direction in the mature industrial corporation is significantly constrained."

Even so, "the managerial prerogative is in no danger of being usurped" (Heller et al 1986). Power and counter-power offset one another (Rus 1980), and by and large the multiple interests are contained within a "malleable constrained domination" by the general executives at the top (Hickson et al 1986).

The Rules of the Game

Most of the time, then, the elite keep a grip on what is going on, though no one would suggest that it is entirely within their control. Behind this grip lie the rules of the game as these are expressed in the constitution and structure of the organization itself. Whether the organization is in a relatively 'capitalist' or a relatively 'communist' state, (for what these terms are worth), those who have power to do so set it up on a legal basis with basic resources that frame their intentions on what should and should not be done.

Overtly, the management of an organization has a given autonomy to make decisions to the extent that its position in any owning group allows and within the laws of the state. Thus, in business firms with a divisional structure, the divisional and even departmental managements are able to play a part in initiating and pushing through proposals requiring major investments that is greater than would be feasible in more centralized structures (Ackerman 1970). Further, the more independent an organization is of external entanglements the wider the range of decisions open to its management. The more it is dependent upon others (e.g. suppliers or customers or, most obviously, owners such as another corporation or a government), the less autonomy it is likely to have in decision-making and, in addition, the more centralized it is likely to be within itself (Pugh et al 1969, Pugh & Hickson 1976). The ultimate in dependence is the small subsidiary unit that takes all its inputs from others within the same group and sends them all its outputs, and whose managers are that in name only, locked within either a private or a state-owned corporation or government administration.

Covertly, beneath this overt exclusion of some matters for decision from the legitimate authority of the management of the organization in question, there are several further levels of "nondecision" (Bachrach & Baratz 1962), if that expression may be stretched to cover them all. First there is what has been called "quasi-decision making", where the forms of decision-making must be proceeded with even though it is apparent to some or all of those involved that the decision has already been made (Hickson et al 1986). A good third of decision-making seems to be like this. Then there are the potential issues that are never allowed to break the surface to become labeled as matters for decision (Abell 1977, Lukes 1974): "I wouldn't bring that up if I were you." Higher levels control lower levels by "structuring an internal selection environment" (Burgelman 1983). Beneath this again lie the taken-for-granted values and managerial language that may divert or suppress the formulation by powerless interests of matters they would otherwise bring forward (Lukes 1974, Clegg 1975). Taken together, all these levels of "nondecision" mean that each decision-making process must wend its way between a series of unquestionable assumptions and unthinkable options. Power rests as much in "its ability to be the natural convention" as in any overt action (Clegg 1977).

Insightful though this comment is on the nature of what is happening, it rests more on supposition than on empirical research. For instance, if there are different rules of the game, should this not be apparent in differences in the decision-making in different organizations? There is very little to go on here, and what there is seems ambiguous. March & Olsen (1976) titillate us with colorful visions of "organized anarchy" in universities and colleges that "do not know what they are doing". Yet what they are doing in decision-making mostly goes through in comparatively smooth "fluid" or "constricted" processes, that are not conspicuously anarchical (Hickson et al 1986). Again, while, in general, public ownership is held to load the chances in favor of a greater proportion of comparatively agitated "sporadic" processes (Hickson et al 1986) and probably prolongs them (Mallory 1986), the aims of managers under public ownership look much the same as their aims under private ownership (Aharoni & Lachman 1982). That could be held to mean the opposite, that public sector processes should not differ much from those in the private sector.

Outcomes and Implementation

There is a similar lack of research on which kinds of processes lead to what outcomes. Indeed, it may be questioned whether processes lead to outcomes at all (*outcome* here meaning the choice made between alternatives, the formal decision)? If interested parties already know their preferred choices before the process begins, as suggested earlier, and if during the process all sorts of problems and choices intermingle, then how far can a decision-making process be thought logically to lead to a choice? It has been asked whether a process can be partly "decoupled" from its outcome (Cohen et al 1972, March & Olsen 1976)? If it can be, then there is no manifest rational link between the decision made and the ostensible moves that look as if they lead up to it?

Perhaps not, but even if the precise choice made is therefore something of a surprise, the alternative chosen is unlikely to be very novel. Some argue that a search for a solution seems rarely to look far away from the point reached by the last decision. It is a "simple-minded" (Cyert & March 1963) examination of the simpler alternatives about which a lot is known already and will not disturb the status quo very much. Each step in this "incrementalism" (Lindblom 1959, Braybrooke & Lindblom 1963) adds just an increment to the previous conclusion, thereby avoiding too much uncertainty and the need for overmuch information. The small step is more common than the big leap.

A small step can be in a new direction, of course, and it has been argued that a succession of small steps is easier to make than one big one because the risk is less. Thus, changes can be made as rapidly by a series of small steps as by drastic but infrequent steps (Lindblom 1959). Empirical research does suggest that in a substantial proportion of cases decisionmakers do search for novel ideas or at least for fresh ideas taken "off-the-shelf" (Nutt 1984), and they do reach "custom-made" solutions much more often than "ready-made" ones (Mintzberg et al 1976).

However, if the recorded discussions between President Kennedy's advisers in 1962, when Soviet missiles were discovered on Cuba, are anything to go by, reaching a decision is less a weighing up of the merits of possible alternatives than it is an acknowledging of objections to them. It is likely to be "decision making by objection" (Anderson 1983). In this, alternatives are sought that are least likely to make things worse, and they are objected to iteratively, one by one, until the sequence of binary yes/no choices is brought to an end by finding one that is more or less acceptable. "Acceptable level decision rules" (Cyert & March 1963) mean that the search stops when a solution is found which is just about compatible with other decisions and will do for the time being. Such an outcome is "satisficing," the term coined by Simon (1960) to describe decisions that are neither wholly satisfactory nor wholly sufficing but which will get by with a little of both. It is the reverse of optimizing, that almost mythical outcome which all managers and administrators are supposed to strive for but which the Carnegie school shrewdly suspect is hardly ever achieved. In their famous analogy, which never loses its impact, decision-making is not about searching for the sharpest needle in a haystack but about finding one that is sharp enough to sew with (March & Simon 1958).

It is easy to take from published research the mistaken impression that all strategic decisions are positive. They are not. Although the majority are positive, such as to extend buildings, to reequip, to raise capital, or to buy a subsidiary, a minority of decisions are negative. They either decide to do nothing and leave the situation as it is (not to make a takeover bid, not to enter a market), or they decide to undo something (to shut down shops, to close hospitals). Of the 150 cases covered by the Bradford studies, as many as 12 (8%) were negative (Hickson et al 1986).

Whether positive or negative, once a decision has been made it represents such an accumulated effort, and probably such a careful reconciliation of interests, that there is great reluctance to change it. Indeed, even if when it is implemented it turns out to have been a bad decision, there is a pronounced tendency to keep going and "pour good resources after bad," in the hope that all that is needed to pull things round is a little more money or time or effort, less than would be needed to start all over again in another direction. There is an "escalation of commitment" (Staw 1981).

After all, everything is not cut and dried once the decision is taken. Great uncertainty may exist about implementation (Mumford & Pettigrew 1975), and this can be frustrated not only by unforeseen difficulties but by un-reconciled interests. Perhaps these interests failed to stop the decision during the decision-making process, or perhaps they were never in on the process because they were kept out or because they kept themselves out. For example, trade unions in Britain are both kept out and keep out; as a result their influence on the process of making a major decision is relatively negligible (Wilson et al 1982). They do not count. They make themselves felt, if at all, after the decision is taken, during its implementation. At this stage they can slow down and mollify what is done, in defence of what they see as their members' interests. But they cannot change the decision.

In fact, Heller et al (1987) conclude that the importance of the implementation stage has been underestimated. Even in terms of time it takes much longer than they had believed. Certainly executives do try and peer through the uncertainty a long way ahead when making strategic decisions. They do not anticipate the first effects of their decision to show up for a couple of years (Mallory 1987), and they expect the effects to last many years beyond that. They anticipate that the overall consequences will endure for around eight years on average, and even longer for reorganization and relocation decisions because they are especially tricky to change or to supersede until many years have passed (Hickson et al 1986).

METHODOLOGY

The Doubts and the Data

Humankind's study of itself has always been beset with doubts and divisions over how it should be done. Should such study be more an artistic distillation of impressions or a scientistic interpretation of data? The study of elite strategic decision-making processes poses this puzzle as acutely as anything does. The description of decision-making given here (perhaps a caricature of it in some respects) is wholly the result of the methods that produced it. So what methods have been and are feasible and acceptable?

The crux of the difficulty for researchers is the vaporous quality of a decision-making process. Its outcome, the decision itself, can usually be found in the deliberations of a board or council meeting, and the resulting new product or share issue or reorganization or whatever can be seen to have happened. But where is, or was, the *process* of reaching the decision? Workers or clerks can be studied, after a fashion, because where they are, or are supposed to be, is known and the researcher can go there and talk to them or watch them or even work with them. They can be got at. So can an individual manager, though not so readily since a manager moves about more. Still, spot checks and self-recorded diaries yield a fairly standard picture (for example, Mintzberg 1973, Stewart 1976). But the social process of moving toward a decision is located nowhere in particular. Put the other way around, it can be anywhere in general.

Does it then require its own special methods of study? Here there is great appeal in data for data's sake. The story of what happens is itself interesting— with luck sensational—in a way that a story of workers working or clerks clerking or lecturers lecturing is unlikely to be. Here is power with the lid off! What may be the best record ever made was produced in the early 1970s not by researchers but by television camera crews filming hundreds or maybe thousands of hours of meetings and conversations in the offices and corridors of the nationalized steel corporation in Britain. Cut down to a remarkable couple of hours, this was an inside view of a cliffhanger plant investment decision. It went out on the public television network and has been widely used for teaching ever since. It was and is absorbing data, showing as nothing else can do how the process does become manifest in a phone call, a few words around an executive desk, a conflict of views in the board, or a nod in the chairman's room. Yet even this is inevitably a small selection of all that occurred and, most significantly, in the television rendering there is nothing that an academic researcher would call analysis. It is data and only data.

Researchers have never equalled what the resources of a television company can do, but they have often tried to go as far as they can. An inclination to tell all is distinctive to this field of work. Cyert et al (1956) reported their

"Observation of a Business Decision," and this was followed by some more case histories in Cyert & March (1963). In the 1970s Pettigrew's (1973) well-known case story centered on the manager "Kenny" in a retail firm; some detailed Scandinavian descriptions were collected in March & Olsen (1976). Most recently, each stage of each of the 73 cases studied by Nutt (1984) is set out in a summary page after page. The Canadian National Film Board is exposed at great length by Mintzberg & McHugh (1985), and the book in which the bulk of the results of the Bradford studies are presented begins with the "tale of Toxicem" on its first page, an instant immersion in data (Hickson et al 1986). These few examples suggest that, in the study of decision making at this elevated level in organizations, not only do researchers like to tell their stories they also seem to feel that readers need to be convinced. Not many of them personally inhabit the more rarified layers of a hierarchy and unless given a mass of description, they may not understand what it is like there, nor will they credit the researcher with having found out. The case study method is not special to decision-making research, of course, but the urge to regale the reader with the data it produces is pronounced.

Researchers have tended not to venture outside the bounds of the case study method, but understandably so. Long ago, Bachrach & Baratz (1962) criticized political scientists for concentrating on what did happen rather than what did not (what they called the "non-decisions"); their point has been uncomfortably at the back of researchers' minds ever since. It was restated and reinforced (for instance by Lukes 1974 and Clegg & Dunkerley 1980) under the impulse in the 1970s of radical and ethnomethodological criticisms of the sociology of organizations and organization theory (for example, Silverman 1970; Zey-Ferrell & Aiken 1981). The feeling persists that if any method has a chance of getting underneath the decision-maker's carpet, it is the close personal familiarity of the intensive case history. An associated fear has been that to move so far out of the case narrative as to apply variables to cases would somehow "de-nature" the data itself.

But ideas and not data are the prize. In decision-making research, as elsewhere, data for data's sake is sterile. While descriptive data are absolutely indispensable to revealing the human experience as a basis for understanding it, ultimately data are the means to the end of devising concepts with which to interpret that data.

To this end researchers need not only the case study method and the narrative history but any and every other method of data collection and data analysis to use alongside it. Among others, Galtung (1967) wrote of the "data matrix" in which one axis was the number of dimensions or variables—or concepts—employed, from one to many, and the other axis was the number of units or cases studied, also from one to many. Research on decision-making should not pay undue attention to the advantages to be gained by working on one side of the matrix, the part with just a few cases, without making an equal effort to see what can be gained from the other side, many cases. And on both sides, the more ideas the better.

Coming of Age

Research on decision-making seems to be beginning to spread more evenly across the data matrix than hitherto. Indeed, research on decision-making may not be special at all and has probably been developing through a most conventional scientistic progression—not from bad to better but from the cautious use of some methods to the ability to work anywhere across Galtung's (1967) data matrix according to the needs of the research and the researcher.

Take three elements of empirical method—sample, data collection, and data analysis and presentation. There has been an extension from small samples with some form of intensive case study data collection (personal observation and conversation) and narrative presentation, through various middling approaches, to comparatively large samples with some form of structured interview or questionnaire and analysis by variables. At the smaller scale and narrative end, illustrative examples are the description by Cyert et al (1956) of an electronic data processing decision, accounts by Cyert & March (1963) of four cases including a similar electronic data processing decision, and the intricate story of a computer purchase decision, told by Pettigrew (1973), all of which have already been referred to. A number of case histories are included in March & Olsen (1976), such as decisions on departmental changes in a university, and one (never implemented) on racial desegregation and on a new open class structure in schools. Latterly, Wilson (1982) reviews the Toxicem case that has been mentioned here and Wilson et al (1986) compare it and another in the same company with cases in a university. Hence, the classic case study method is in no sense being supplanted. But researchers have been successfully trying out other possibilities as well, and these enable a wider coverage.

The collection of data on as many as 25 cases by Mintzberg and his students (Mintzberg et al 1976) was "historically a milestone" (Butler et al 1979–1980), opening the way to larger numbers and heartening others working in the same direction. Quinn (1980) tackled nine privately owned manufacturers of household-name repute and Nutt (1984) subsequently followed up with data from no less than 73 health-related service organizations as mentioned before. The characteristic of the middling approach taken by these studies is the collection of data by substantial interviews, moderately structured, and the analysis of the data by comparison of cases in words and diagrams, rather than by numbers.

Numerical analysis, and the definition of variables as explicit means of comparison, has become prominent in print during the 1980s, reflecting research launched in the 1970s. For instance, Heller and his colleagues (Drenth et al 1979, DIO International Research Team 1983, Heller et al 1987) have used unstructured and structured interviews to obtain data on 217 decisions in 7 companies, 102 of which were classed as strategic. They compared these by a combination of verbal case discussion and the numerical analysis of variables such as influence, satisfaction, and trust. Yet another example is the progression of the Bradford studies over ten years from intensive case studies, both concurrent and historically traced, to substantial structured interviews commencing with case histories and moving eventually to mailed questionnaires. With 6 early depth cases as a base (Wilson 1980, Wilson et al 1982), the research amassed a further 146 cases of strategic decisions in 30 organizations by interview alone (including covering the original six again, a total of 150), and then applied comparative analysis by variables to processual data (Hickson et al 1986). The variables included, for instance, disruption by delays, formality and informality of interaction, and the number of sources of information, as well as the seriousness of the matter and the contention of interests. Although a prior attempt by Stein (1981a, b) had not seemed at all encouraging, Mallory (1986) went on to "do the impossible" by producing process data on a further 56 cases not merely by questionnaire but by a *mail* questionnaire covering four sides of paper. The likely validity of this is attested by the results available which so far match those from the study of 150 cases in places where the two studies coincide. One extraordinarily precise example is the duration (as defined at the beginning of this essay) of the processes in the two studies which were (Mallory figures second): means 12.4 months and 12.4 months, standard deviations 10.6 months and 10.9 months, ranges 1–48 months and 2–48 months!

Clearly, therefore, it is possible to apply the customary range of social science methods of data collection and analysis to these kinds of decision-making processes, however vaporous such processes might seem to be. Equally clearly, the methods of data collection differ in what they rely upon. The depth case study relies on the personality and accuity of what is usually a lone researcher. This method is limited because the researcher, or even a small team of researchers, cannot be everywhere all at once; they often have to make do with being told what has happened rather than with being on the spot as it happens. The interview and the questionnaire rely even more on the executive as a recording device. That is, they are limited by reliance on the informant's longer term memory; in the depth case, the memory is usually more recent, of course. On the other hand, the interview or questionnaire does get an overview of the basic events and the character of a completed story.

Essentially the methodological pros and cons are those of any other area of study. In this sense, the field has come of age.

Common Difficulties

Coming of age does not remove the difficulties that affect sampling, data collection, and data analysis—e.g. difficulties in collaboration, costs, and classification, respectively.

Sampling is hampered by the difficulty of persuading top executives to collaborate by giving up their time and, especially, giving it up to talk of something about which they feel apprehensive, lest they betray some innermost managerial secret. It is difficult to gain permission to follow one case in detail, or to question many managers in many organizations briefly, in person or by questionnaire. Frequently researchers obtain collaboration by exploiting a teaching or a consulting type link (for example, Nutt 1984, Quinn 1980) but this carries the inevitable risk of compromising the research relationship. Otherwise, the form of words and the appropriate degree of confidence with which to present researcher and research in a way that is understandable and appealing has to be found by trial and error. Random sampling or any other deliberate selection has so far been out of the question: A third at least of those contacted are likely to say no (Hickson et al 1986).

Even when collaboration is achieved, costs hamper data collection. Following a process along as it happens is enormously expensive in researcher time, and there is always the risk that the researcher may have to finish—or be shown the door—before a decision is reached. Extensive interviewing is also expensive in time and travel; this tends to force expedients such as using students as interviewers (Mintzberg et al 1976) (when each different case may be perceived through the medium of different and relatively inexperienced individuals) or relying on comparatively few principal informants (for example, Nutt 1984; Hickson et al 1986) when more would be more readily and manifestly persuasive, even given the reassurance of various cross-checks (Hickson et al 1986).

Thirdly, the difficulty of classification is shared with every other field of study, social science and otherwise. How many categories make sense? Too few cases in too many categories makes classification complicated and unrevealing, adding little to leaving the cases separate and unclassified. Categories have utility when each contains a substantial number of cases. On the other hand, too few categories could result in over simplification. The classification of decision-making processes has sharp contrasts in this respect. For instance, Stein (1981b) construed as many as 16 categories from 63 questionnaires (only 4 cases per category, on average); Mintzberg et al (1976) proposed 7 process categories (and a range of possible "routines" within each) for 25 cases; Nutt (1984) suggested 5 types and 11 subvarieties to cover 73 cases, and Hickson et al (1986) arrived at 3 types covering 53, 42, and 41 cases in a total of 136 processes.

First and foremost, however, the value of a classification is in the insightfulness and generalizability of the concepts that define the categories. This essay now turns to concepts and theories.

CONCEPTS AND THEORIES

Concepts

The comprehension of strategic decision-making began with concepts of its problems and their solutions. The emphasis then gradually shifted to the politics and movement of the process. These two emphases are not mutually exclusive. The one grew to complement the other, and both are indispensable to any full comprehension.

The most penetrating and lively concepts of decision-making problems and solutions have come from March and Simon and their colleagues of the one-time "Carnegie school," and from those who think likewise. Among their illuminating concepts included in this essay are the notions of *sequential attention to goals* (that decisionmakers cannot balance everything at once but turn first one way and then the other); of *uncertainty avoidance* (whereby decisionmakers seek ways to protect and stabilize their organization); and of *simpleminded search* (whereby decisionmakers prefer alternatives that are not far away from what is being done already) (Cyert & March 1963). These lead to *satisficing* decisions, it has been said, rather than to optimizing ones, on the more consequential and more novel *non-programmed matters* (Simon 1960).

Those whose contribution has been rather more to concepts of the *politics and movement* of decisionmaking have not yet equalled this Marchian flair for evocative terminology! Had they done so we might have had a spectacular vocabulary with which to appreciate its political essence and action.

Nevertheless, we do have *"ensembles des jeux"* (Crozier & Friedberg 1980), a conception of an organization as a setting for political games and, in horseracing parlance, jockeying for position. These games are played across *bargaining zones* (Abell 1975) to protect or promote *interests*. Movement toward a decision is broken by *interrupts,* and it often *cycles* back upon itself (Mintzberg et al 1976). It has both *duration* in chronological time and *pace* in the eyes of those involved, and the two are not at all the same (Mallory 1987). Its character may be *sporadic, fluid,* or *constricted* (Hickson et al 1986).

These concepts and others (this does not pretend to be a complete list) are the basis for the main theories that have been put forward to explain what happens in decision-making.

Theories

The study of decision-making has been the playground of contestants who, with a little license, might be called either the "managerial systemetizers" or the "behavioral debunkers." The managerial systematizers are those whose necessary normative mission it must be to advocate to managers, and to students aspiring to be managers, the means to an orderly controllable world. Decision trees, planning charts, cost-benefit analyses, and the like are aimed at easing the manager's lot when confusing and worrisome decisions have to be taken. Against these, the behavioral debunkers have delighted in pointing out the mental and political limits that hinder their use. Just as psychologists have relished citing articles showing poor human reasoning and decision-making rather than good (Christensen-Szalanski & Beach 1984), so the debunkers of managerial decision making have bolstered their own position by puncturing managerial reasoning!

The contest has been productive, nonetheless. From it have emerged three ways of thinking about and explaining decision-making that have appeared again and again in this essay. These three theories are *incrementalism,* the *garbage-can model,* and *dual rationality.*

Incrementalism originates very obviously in the contest between systematizers and debunkers. Incrementalism contrasts the "synoptic" approach, that aims at the "rational deductive ideal," with the mundane practicabilities of "successive limited comparisons" of information and alternatives, and with compromises by "mutual partisan adjustment," (Lindblom 1959, Braybrooke & Lindblom 1963). This bit by bit approach, or "disjointed incrementalism," is explained by the limited information handling capacities of the decision-makers and by their need to pick a way through the "partisan" viewpoints. Doing a bit at a time in this way is said to be the most generally applicable and successful tactic.

The second theory, the *garbage-can model,* rests on the same assumptions about mental and political limits. Its evocative terminology conjures up the tangled innards of a garbage can as an alternative to the vision of rational orderliness (Cohen et al 1972, March & Olsen 1976, March & Olsen 1984). Inside the can, there are quite a few oddities, or so they appear. Individuals fight for the right to participate and then do not exercise it; information that is available is ignored, more is requested, and then that too is ignored; there is acrimonious contention over the adoption of policies, but relative indifference to whether policies are implemented; and so on. To account for what goes on, the model turns the conventional view back to front. Instead of assuming that one thing causally leads to another in a logical "consequential order," which is not the way things seem to happen, it postulates *"temporal order"* as being the more apposite.

Into the can tumble streams of problems, solutions, and participants. It is not their logical ordering but their temporal simultaneity that accounts for decision-making. When compatible problems and solutions coincide in time, then there is a choice opportunity that may enable a decision. Whether it does so or not depends upon who has time and attention to give to it, since no one can attend to everything all at once; in short, "the process is sensitive to load" (March & Olsen 1984).

The model is flexible and can be adjusted to different streams of problems, solutions, and participants, and to different conditions of time and attention. It shares with incrementalism the explanation that what happens is due to the possibilities being bounded both cognitively and politically, but it reverses the presumed order of things. Solutions come *before* problems, in the sense that participants know what they want and await a chance to get it, and the occurrence of a chance that catches their attention is the necessary circumstance. Among the handy inferences drawn are that participants should choose their time, should persist if they fail since another chance may come, should give due import to symbolic issues, and should "overload the system" with proposals since even if one proposal misses its moment another may succeed (March & Olsen 1984).

The model goes so far and no further, of course—as those who devised it frankly say. It does not encompass the powers that define what streams of problems, solutions, and participants may flow and that set the situation so that some are more likely to coincide than others. Empirically, the theory is grounded in the experience of educational organizations, but in other organizations decision-making may be less like this.

Thirdly, in a more prosaic manner, the *dual rationality theory* is an attempt to draw together the ingredients that appear commonly in one form or another in research in this field. These ingredients so permeate thought that it is tempting to indulge current fashion and refer to them as the dominant paradigm. Very simply, they are the assumptions—inherent in both the incrementalism and the garbage can explanations—that decision-making is a process of handling both problems and politics.

Beginning as a "dual explanation" (Hickson et al 1981, Astley et al 1982, Hickson et al 1986), this may better be termed a dual rationality theory. It argues that every matter that arises for decision must *both* raise problems and implicate interests. Because the problems raised and the interests implicated by one matter are not the same as those encountered by the previous one, nor will they be the same as those in the next, the process of arriving at each decision will differ. Greater complexity of problems and greater politicality of interests ginger up activity and involvement; lesser complexity and lesser politicality allow a more quiescent process.

Three prevalent combinations of complexity and politicality have been identified empirically. Most complex and political are the "weighty and controversial" *vortex* matters. Less complex and least political are the "unusual but non-controversial" *tractable* matters. Least complex, but rather more political than tractable matters, are the "normal and recurrent" *familiar* matters. Each combination tends to generate a typical kind of movement towards a decision. A vortex matter is likely to generate a sporadic process, a tractable matter a fluid process, and a familiar matter a constricted process.

Each matter is approached by the élite of the hierarchy in accordance with dual implicit managerial or administrative rationalities. On the one hand, they aspire to handle its complexities by the classic problem-solving rationality whose limitations the incrementalism and garbage-can theories expose so piercingly, yet which remains a guide to action. On the other hand, although there is no equivalent explicit model in the literature for handling politicality, there is an implicit interest-accommodating rationality that weighs up what is at stake for each interested party and what the range of acceptable alternatives may be. However, the product of two different rationalities is not necessarily "rational" in the original textbook sense of that word, since the solving of the problems is shaped by the accommodating of the interests.

In this formulation, both the definition of the matter on hand and the guiding rationalities derive from the rules of the game inherent in the organization itself. A framework of power prescribes what an organization is for and who in the last resort determines what it is for. That framework sets the rules for what can and cannot be decided and how it may be decided. Managerial focusing upon the matter in hand means that "the matter for decision matters most" for the character of overt decision-making processes, but for covert nondecision processes—if processes is the right word—it is the power that frames the organization which matters even more.

What do these three theories try to explain? In a uniquely stringent assessment of what passes for theory about decisions, Mohr (1982) argues that there is no theory adequate to the explanation of why one choice is made rather than another. No theory gives reasons for the decision or *outcome* in which the decision-making process culminates. Neither a variance explanation nor a processual explanation is offered. The former kind of explanation, "variance theory," would attempt to explain the variance in a dependent variable. Since variables of the decision or outcome are not specified, however, nor are independent variables, this is not accomplished. The latter kind of explanation, "process theory"—or is it processual theory?—would attempt to explain a phenomenon as the result of "a series of occurrences in a sequence over time," but decisions or outcomes have not been defined in a way that enables this to be done, except perhaps at too particular or too general a level.

Rather than attempting either of these kinds of explanation of the outcomes of decision-making, research has concentrated on *describing* decision-making processes. In the same way that "description is often called theory in science not because it is an explanatory generalization or set of interrelated laws but because it is both important and conjectural" (Mohr 1982:160), this has produced valuable descriptive theory, full of inspired conjectures about what goes on as decisions are made.

However, although the three theories summed up here as incrementalism, garbage-can model, and dual rationality may not have yielded explanations of the outcomes of decision-making processes, they do explain the *processes*. Process is and should be the focus of research, says Mohr (1982).

All three theories are putative explanations of the managerial social processes in which decisions are formed. The first, incrementalism, suggests that the more complex and indefinable is the matter for decision, the more disjointedly incremental the process of deciding is likely to be. The second, the garbage-can model, suggests that the more "loosely coupled" an organization is, and the more "anarchic," the more the model will account for what occurs. In other words, in organizations that lack tight hierarchical control, where means and ends are not clear, garbage-can style processes are more likely to be characteristic—for example, in universities and colleges in the Western world.

Most recently, the dual rationality theory brings prior thinking together, doing so because of a fresh step, namely, the application to process data of what Mohr (1982) calls variance theory. Variable characteristics of organizations (e.g. ownerships and functions), and of the problems raised and the interests implicated by the matters on hand (e.g. their consequentiality and influence) are used to explain the probabilities that one type of decision-making process will occur rather than another. Dual rationality theory attempts explicit explanation, over and above description. Dual managerial problem-solving and interest-accommodating rationalities are inferred to account for the relationships between the variables that make up the explanation.

These three theories are not in competition. They are overlapping and complementary. Between them, the explanation of decision-making processes is well advanced. In this field, theory has been ahead of the methodology rather than lagging behind. It is the methodology that has to catch up, and it is doing so.

SOME GROUND TO BE COVERED

All research is bad research, inasmuch as it could always be done better and there is always more to do. The ground to be covered is infinite. And those who study decision-making have been accused of devoting too much intellectual energy to a priori modelling and too little to empirical enquiry (Smith & May 1980). From the infinity, five areas of empirical interest will be picked out here as possibilities for further research—namely nondecisions, organizational and decisional differences, the matter for decision, successful decision-making, and societal differences.

Nondecisions

The covert side to decision-making may be described as being at three levels of nondecision: (*a*) quasi–decision making, where it is tacitly accepted that the decision has already been made, (*b*) the suppression of issues that then do not become matters for decision, and (*c*) the establishing of taken-for-granted values and language that obscure some matters and promote others. The difficulty is that the scanty publications about this aspect of decision-making have an air of the dark thriller about them, the lights low and the language mysteriously multisyllabic. They are fascinating, they are suggestive, but they do not rip the curtain aside and reveal all. Where are the researchers who can find means to confirm empirically that nondecisions at any level are all they are said to be?

Since organizations constitute the rules of the game for strategic decision-making, the study of any form of nondecision almost certainly requires the investigation of more than one organization, otherwise the rules may not be noticed by the researcher. They are more likely to be detected in the contrasts.

Organizational Differences and Decisional Differences

While the study of nondecisions might be aided by comparison between organizations, the study of overt decisions requires also the comparison of different decisions within any one organization. There is a glaring empirical gap here. Most explanations of decision-making are weakened because they say nothing about what may be due to the nature of the organization as against the nature of the matter for decision. The overwhelming portion of empirical research is one-in-one, that is, one case of decision-making in one organization. This prevents any comparison of different decisions in the same organization or of the same kinds of decision in different organizations. It confounds organizational and decisional explanations. They should be disentangled.

What Is The Matter?

The question "What is the matter?" needs asking more bluntly and answering more clearly. This essay began lightheartedly by wondering whether decision-making is more like soccer football or American football, and in the terms of that analogy we need to know more about the shape of the ball. In other words, what is the shape of the matter under decision? How does the incipient matter for decision begin to form during what has been called the gestation period prior to its surfacing as the subject for overt decision making? Indeed, does this reveal the rules for nondecisions? Once surfaced, how does the matter get redefined along the way, and how likely is it to finish as it began? Much of this appears in many case narratives, but rarely is it brought to the forefront of interest in the analysis.

Asking about the matter for decision confronts us with the problem of comparing like with like. This essay purports to be about "strategic" decisions. Yet who knows whether one researcher's strategic decision is the same as another's? The word is appealing to researchers who by using it imply that the research is really up there in the big time, but there is hardly any discussion of how different grades of decision might be operationally defined, and no way of knowing how far different studies are about the same or somewhat different classes of decision. A thoughtful, laborious, but important task of definition has yet to be done.

What Works Best?

Which kind of process leads to the best decision is a question bound to arise in any discussion of decision-making, whether with students or faculty or managers and administrators. Everyone in their heart of hearts hopes to find a clue to how they could do it better or see that it was done better. So far the question has no straight answer.

In fact, it is not one question but several. If processes are partly uncoupled from decisions, then which are more uncoupled and which more logically connected, and is it best to be uncoupled or coupled? Further, does the kind of process affect how and how fully the decision is implemented? Is the process an end in itself? There is some evidence for this in universities and hospitals, at least, where participation in the process of making a decision can be as important, even more important, than whether there is any means to implement it (Rodrigues 1980)!

The definition of a good decision is relative, of course. Are the criteria the costs, or profits, or the greatest satisfaction of the greatest number, or what? And what are the evaluations of those who participated in the decision-making process, of those who had most influence and those who had least, of those who formally "made" the decision by authorizing implementation, and of those affected by implementation?

Whose Processes Are They Anyway?

It must be confessed that this essay has been written as if the people taking part in decision-making processes are everywhere the same, in the same economic and political circumstances. Obviously they are not! They are American or Chinese or Russian or Indian or Arabic or Germanic or Latin European, and so on. Yet it has not been possible to review research on the *processes* of making strategic decisions in such a way as to show differences between national or cultural settings. This is because the available published material on which this essay has had to rely is solidly "Anglo-Nordic," that is, it comes from empirical work in Canada, the United States, Britain, Scandinavia, and The Netherlands. Nothing has been used from African, Arabic, Asian, East European, or Latin lands.

Within the Anglo-Nordic sphere, nothing has stood out sharply as a feature that characterizes one nation or one culture (or is it subculture?) more than another, but then the published work pays no attention to this possibility. Yet it is impossible to believe that social processes, including those decision-making processes that take place at the apex of an organization's hierarchy, are not deeply affected by national wealth and economic structure and by culture. Even though person-to-person interaction, which might reveal cultural differences most vividly, has not been directly dealt with here, the process properties that have been discussed must surely be affected? After all, the incessant comparisons of American and Japanese management practice suggest more prolonged and consultative processes among Japanese executives. Decisions in Africa have to be made in particular national political contexts which must affect their making. Those in Latin countries cannot be unaffected by hierarchies where blockages to vertical communication are frequent. In the People's Republic of China, centralization of decisions recurs despite efforts to decentralize. Indeed "socialist" economies typically struggle with endemic centralist tendencies and with what the role of the ruling party should be in strategic decision-making.

So although research on processes of decision-making at this level has a history of vigorous theoretical development, and it is maturing methodologically, there is as always much to be done and nowhere more so than in cross-national and cross-cultural investigation and explanation.

ACKNOWLEDGMENTS

Although all omissions and commissions herein are my own, I could never have attempted the task but for what I learned in the Bradford studies of decision-making from my colleagues, notably Richard Butler, David Cray, Geoffrey Mallory, David Wilson, Runo Axelsson, and Graham Astley.

Literature Cited

Abell, P. 1975. Organizations as bargaining and influence systems: Measuring intraorganizational power and influence. In *Organizations as Bargaining and Influence Systems,* ed. P. Abell, pp. 10–40. London: Heinemann

Abell, P. 1977. The many faces of power and liberty: Revealed preference, autonomy and teleological explanation. *Sociology* 11(1):3–24

Ackerman, R. W. 1970. Influence of integration and diversity on the investment process. *Admin. Sci. Q.* 15(3):341–53

Aharoni, Y., Lachman, R. 1982. Can the manager's mind be nationalized? *Organ. Stud.* 3(1):33–46

Allison, G. T. 1969. Conceptual models and the Cuban missile crisis. *Am. Polit. Sci. Rev.* 63(3):689–718

Anderson, P. A. 1983. Decision making by

objection and the Cuban missile crisis. *Admin. Sci. Q.* 28(2):201–22

Astley, W. G., Axelsson, R., Butler, R. J., Hickson, D. J., Wilson, D. C. 1982. Complexity and cleavage: Dual explanations of strategic decision making. *J. Manage. Stud.* 19(4):357–75

Axelsson, R., Rosenberg, L. 1979. Decision-making and organizational turbulence. *Acta Sociol.* 22(1):45–62

Bachrach, P., Baratz, M. S. 1962. The two faces of power. *Am. Polit. Sci. Rev.* 56: 947–52

Braybrooke, D., Lindblom, C. 1963. *A Strategy of Decision.* New York: Free Press

Burgelman, R. A. 1983. A process model of internal corporate venturing in the diversified major firm. *Admin. Sci. Q.* 28(2):223–44

Butler, R. J., Astley, W. G., Hickson, D. J., Mallory, G. R., Wilson, D. C. 1979–1980. Strategic decision making: Concepts of content and process. *Int. Stud. Manage. Organ.* 9(4):5–36

Carter, E. E. 1971. The behavioral theory of the firm and top-level corporate decisions. *Admin. Sci. Q.* 16(4):413–28

Christensen-Szalanski, J. J. J., Beech, L. R. 1984. The citation bias: Fad and fashion in the judgment and decision literature, *Am. Psychol.* 39(1):75–78

Clegg, S. 1975. *Power, Rule and Domination.* London: Routledge & Kegan Paul

Clegg, S. 1977. Power, organization theory, Marx, and Critique. In *Critical Issues in Organizations*, ed. S. Clegg, D. Dunkerley, pp. 21–40. London: Routledge & Kegan Paul

Clegg, S., Dunkerley, D. 1980. *Organization, Class, and Control.* London: Routledge & Kegan Paul

Cohen, M. D., March, J. G., Olsen, J. P. 1972. A garbage can model of organizational choice. *Admin. Sci. Q.* 17:1–25

Crozier, M., Friedberg, E. (1977) 1980. *Actors and Systems,* Chicago: Univ. Chicago Press

Cyert, R. M., Simon, H. A., Trow, D. B. 1956. Observation of a business decision. *J. Bus.* 29:237–48

Cyert, R. M., March, J. G. 1963. *A Behavioral Theory of the Firm.* Englewood Cliffs: Prentice Hall

DIO International Research Team. 1983. A contingency model of participative decision making: An analysis of 56 decisions in three Dutch organizations. *J. Occup. Psychol.* 56(1):1–18

Donaldson, G., Lorsch, J. G. 1983. *Decision Making at the Top.* New York: Basic Books

Drenth, P. J. D., Koopman, P. L., Rus, V., Odar, M., Heller, F., Brown, A. 1979. Participative decision making: A comparative study. *Ind. Relat.* 18(3):295–309

French, J. R. P., Raven, B. 1959. The bases of social power. In *Studies in Social Power*, ed. D. Cartwright, pp. 150–67. Ann Arbor: Univ. Mich. Press

Galtung, J. 1967. *Theory and Methods of Social Research.* Oslo: Universitetsforlaget

Grandori, A. 1984. A prescriptive contingency view of organizational decision making. *Admin. Sci. Q.* 29(2):192–209

Hage, J. 1980. *Theories of Organizations: Form, Process and Transformation.* New York: Wiley

Heller, F., Drenth, P., Koopman, P., Rus, V. 1986. *Decisions in Organizations: A Three Country Longitudinal Study.* New York: Wiley

Hickson, D. J., Astley, W. G., Butler, R. J., Wilson, D. C. 1981. Organization as power. In *Research in Organizational Behavior, Vol. 3,* ed. L. L. Cummings, B. Staw, pp. 151–96. Greenwich, Conn: JAI

Hickson, D. J., Butler, R. J., Cray, D., Mallory, G. R., Wilson, D. C. 1985. Comparing 150 Decision Processes. In *Organization Strategy and Change,* J. M. Pennings and associates, pp. 114–43. San Francisco: Jossey-Bass

Hickson, D. J., Butler, R. J., Cray, D., Mallory, G. R., Wilson, D. C. 1986. *Top Decisions: Strategic Decision Making in Organizations.* Oxford: Blackwell; San Francisco: Jossey-Bass

Hickson, D. J., Hinings, C. R., Lee, C. A., Schneck, R. E., Pennings, J. M. 1971. A strategic contingencies theory of intraorganizational power. *Admin. Sci. Q.* 16(2):216–29

Hinings, C. R., Hickson, D. J., Pennings, J. M., Schneck, R. E. 1974. Structural conditions of intraorganizational power. *Admin. Sci. Q.* 19(1):22–44

Karpik, L. 1972. Les politiques et les logiques d'action de la grande enterprise industrielle. *Sociol. Travail* 1:82–105

Lindblom, C. 1959. The science of muddling through. *Public Admin. Rev.* XIX(2):79–88

Lukes, S. 1974. *Power: A Radical View.* London: Macmillan

Lustick, I. 1980. Explaining the variable utility of disjointed incrementalism: Four propositions. *Am. Polit. Sci. Rev.* 74:342–53

Mallory, G. R. 1987. *The Speed of Strategic Decisions.* PhD thesis. University of Bradford, Yorkshire

March, J. G. 1981. Decisions in organizations and theories of choice. In *Perspectives on Organization Design and Behavior*, ed. A. H. Van de Ven, W. F. Joyce, pp. 205–44. New York: Wiley.

March, J. G., Olsen, J. P. 1984. *Garbage can models of decision making in organizations.* Presented to a workshop on Decision Making in Military Organizations. Montreal, Canada

March, J. G., Olsen, J. P. 1976. *Ambiguity and Choice in Organizations.* Bergen, Oslo, & Tromso: Universitetsforlaget

March, J. G., Romelaer, P. J. 1976. Position and presence in the drift of decisions. In *Ambiguity and Choice in Organizations,* ed. J. G. March, J. P. Olsen, pp. 251–76. Bergen, Oslo and Tromso: Universitetsforlaget

March, J. G., Simon, H. A. 1958. *Organizations,* New York: Wiley

Miles, R. H. 1980. *Macro organizational Behavior,* California: Goodyear

Mintzberg, H. 1973. *The Nature of Managerial Work.* New York: Harper & Row

Mintzberg, H. 1978. Patterns in strategy formation. *Manage. Sci.* 24(9):934–48

Mintzberg, H. 1979. *The Structuring of Organizations.* Englewood Cliffs, NJ: Prentice-Hall

Mintzberg, H., McHugh, A. 1985. Strategy formation in an Adhocracy. *Admin. Sci. Q.* 30(2):160–97

Mintzberg, H., Raisinghani, D., Theoret, A. 1976. The structure of "unstructured" decision processes. *Admin. Sci. Q.* 21:246–75

Mintzberg, H., Waters, J. A. 1982. Tracking strategy in an entrepreneurial firm. *Acad. Manage. J.* 25(3):465–99

Mohr, L. B. 1982. *Explaining Organizational Behavior.* San Francisco: Jossey-Bass

Mumford, E., Pettigrew, A. 1975. *Implementing Strategic Decisions.* London: Longman

Nutt, P. 1984. Types of organizational decision processes. *Admin. Sci. Q.* 29(3):414–50

O'Reilly, C. A. 1983. The use of information in organizational decision making: A model and some propositions. In *Research in Organizational Behavior, Vol. 5,* ed. L. L. Cummings, B. M. Staw, pp. 103–40. Greenwich, Conn: JAI

Pettigrew, A. 1973. *The Politics of Organizational Decision Making.* London: Tavistock

Pfeffer, J., Salancik, G. R. 1974. Organizational decision making as a political process: The case of a university budget. *Admin. Sci. Q.* 19:135–51

Pfeffer, J., Salancik, G. R. 1977. Organization design: The case of a coalitional model of organizations. *Organ. Dynam.* 6:15–29

Pugh, D. S., Hickson, D. J. 1976. *Organizational structure in its context: The Aston Programme I.* Farnborough: Gower (and formerly D. C. Heath)

Pugh, D. S., Hickson, D. J., Hinings, C. R., Turner, C. 1969. The context of organization structures. *Admin. Sci. Q.* 14:91–114

Quinn, J. B. 1978. Strategic change: Logical incrementalism. *Sloan Manage. Rev.* Fall 1978:7–21

Quinn, J. B. 1980. *Strategies for Change: Logical Incrementalism.* Homewood, Ill: Irwin

Rodrigues, S. B. 1980. *Processes of Successful Managerial Decision Making in Organizations.* PhD thesis. University of Bradford, Yorkshire

Rus, V. 1980. Positive and negative power: Thoughts on the Dialectics of Power. *Organ. Stud.* 1(1):3–20

Schulman, P. R. 1975. Nonincremental policy making: Notes towards an alternative paradigm. *Am. Polit. Sci. Rev.* 69:1354–70

Smith, G., May, D. 1980. The artificial debate between rationalist and incrementalist models of decision making. *Policy Polit.* 8(2):147–61

Silverman, D. 1970. *The Theory of Organizations.* London: Heinemann

Simon, H. A. 1945. *Administrative Behavior* New York: Free Press 2nd Ed.

Simon, H. A. 1960. *The New Science of Management Decision.* New York: Harper & Row

Staw, B. M. 1981. The escalation of commitment to a course of action. *Acad. Manage. Rev.* 6(4):577–87

Stein, J. 1981a. Contextual factors in the selection of strategic decision methods. *Hum. Relat.* 34(10):819–34

Stein, J. 1981b. Strategic decision methods. *Hum. Relat.* 34(11):917–33

Stewart, R. 1976. *Contrasts in Management: A Study of Different Types of Managers' Jobs.* New York: McGraw Hill

Thompson, J. D. 1967. *Organizations in Action.* New York: McGraw Hill

Thompson, J. D., Tuden, A. 1964. Strategies, structures and processes of organizational decision. In *Readings in Managerial Psychology,* ed. H. J. Leavitt, R. Pondy, pp. 195–216. Chicago: Univ. Chicago Press

Weick, K. E. 1976. Educational organizations as loosely coupled systems. *Admin. Sci. Q.* 21(1):1–19

Weiss, J. W. 1981. The historical and political perspective on organizations of Lucien Karpik. In *Complex Organizations: Critical Perspectives,* ed. M. Zey-Ferrell, M. Aiken, pp. 382–96. Glenview, Ill: Scott, Foresman

Wilson, D. C. 1980. *Organizational Strategy.* PhD thesis. University of Bradford, Yorkshire

Wilson, D. C. 1982. Electricity and resistance: A case study of innovation and politics. *Organ. Stud.* 3(2):119–40

Wilson, D. C., Butler, R. J., Cray, D., Hickson, D. J., Mallory, G. R. 1982. The limits of trade union power in organizational decision making. *Br. J. Ind. Relat.,* 20(3):322–41

Wilson, D. C., Butler, R. J., Cray, D., Hickson, D. J., Mallory, G. R. 1986. Breaking the bounds of organization in strategic decision making. *Hum. Relat.* 39(4):309–32

Zey-Ferrell, M., Aiken, M. 1981. *Complex Organizations: Critical Perspectives.* Glenview, Ill: Scott, Foresman

Ann. Rev. Sociol. 1987. 13:193–216

CHANGING PERSPECTIVES ON THE AMERICAN FAMILY IN THE PAST

Susan M. Juster

Department of History, University of Michigan, Ann Arbor, Michigan 48109

Maris A. Vinovskis

Department of History and Center for Political Studies of the Institute for Social Research, University of Michigan, Ann Arbor, Michigan 48109

Abstract

Past reviews of American family history, while providing useful information about certain aspects of family life in the past, have inadequately addressed the conceptual framework informing the discipline. This article begins by reviewing four approaches developed by social scientists for studying the family: household composition, generations, family cycle, and life-course. The life-course perspective seems the most promising for a dynamic, complex view of families that links changes in the domestic sphere to wider societal trends and concerns. Using the analytical perspective of the life-course, we then examine significant historiographical contributions in four areas of family life—childbearing, early child development, adolescence, and old age.

INTRODUCTION

While the study of American family history dates back to the early twentieth century, a dramatic increase has occurred in the number of articles and research monographs devoted to this topic during the past 20 years. This expansion has been accompanied by considerable disagreement over how to analyze the family as well as how to interpret specific aspects of American family life in the past.

0360-0572/87/0815-0193$02.00

Several useful review essays cover American family development (Degler 1980a, Gordon 1978), but most do not consider the methodological and conceptual issues involved in using a particular analytical framework. Therefore, we begin by reviewing several different analytical approaches developed by historians and other social scientists: household composition, generational shifts, family cycle, and life-course perspective. Then we consider a few of the more interesting and important substantive findings from the study of the American family by examining recent work on childbearing, early child development, adolescence, and old age. Given the limitations of space, we cannot address several other important topics such as the middle years of the life course—a topic generally neglected by historians of the family but one which should be more thoroughly researched in the future.

ANALYTIC APPROACHES TO THE STUDY OF FAMILY LIFE

During the late 1960s the study of American family history was focused almost entirely on colonial New England (Demos 1970, Greven 1970, Lockridge 1970). Since then most of the attention has shifted to the colonial southern family (Lewis 1983, Smith 1980) or the nineteenth-century family (Hareven 1982b, Lebsock 1984). Although there have been some historical studies of family life in the twentieth century (Elder 1974), this area still remains relatively underdeveloped.

The initial investigations of family life in colonial New England usually were undertaken in the context of larger local community studies of social, political, and economic developments within a particular town. Using family reconstitution methods, researchers concentrated on analyzing the interplay of demographic events such as births, marriages, and deaths with such social events as the transmission of property from parents to their children and the control fathers tried to exert over the behavior of their offspring (Greven 1970). The American historians who undertook these early studies did not have any formal training in the social sciences and therefore improvised the demographic indexes they employed. Although no overall analytical scheme guided their study of family life, these scholars frequently used generations as their organizing principle. Greven (1970), for example, studied changing relations between parents and children from the first generation of settlers in Andover, Massachusetts, in the mid-seventeenth century, through those of their descendants in that community in the second, third, and fourth generations.

The employment of generations to study the initial settlement of an area or the transmission of property from fathers to children can be useful, but the concept of generations loses much of its analytical rigor and meaning if one tries to study family life over longer periods of time (Kertzer 1982). Indeed, by the early eighteenth century in Andover such a chronological overlap exists between members of the second and third generations that Greven's analysis becomes confusing and misleading (Vinovskis 1977). Thus, while one can use generations to investigate a specific aspect of family life, it is not a very useful or robust framework in general for analyzing family development historically.

English family historians, meanwhile, embarked on an ambitious project to disprove those sociologists (Parsons & Bales 1954) who had argued that industrialization transformed the extended family into a nuclear one. Led by the Cambridge Group for the History of Population and Social Structure, European historians (Laslett 1972) relied on the consistently small mean size of households in the past to demonstrate that preindustrial Western European families had always been nuclear. The use of mean household size to index family life historically became very popular among historians in the late 1960s and early 1970s as this measure was readily available in many local censuses throughout Western Europe and the United States and could be quickly and easily calculated.

The widespread use of mean household size to measure family composition by European historians did not go unchallenged. Several scholars (Anderson 1980) questioned the usefulness and meaning of a measure that encompassed a broad range of members other than those of the immediate family (e.g. boarders and lodgers, servants). Even more troubling was Berkner's (1972) attack on this approach for failing to take into account the dynamics of family life. He argued that although at any given moment only a small minority of families were nuclear, a much higher proportion of them were extended at some time. Using computer simulations of the demographic dynamics of preindustrial life, however, scholars (Wachter et al 1978) have demonstrated that even a more developmental approach to family life does not suggest that many households were extended in preindustrial England. Nevertheless, the conceptual and methodological challenges to analyses of mean household size have succeeded, and almost no one uses this approach anymore.

As historians abandoned the mean household size as a way of organizing their data on families, they looked for a more dynamic approach. American historians took the lead in this shift by drawing upon the work of sociologists (Duvall 1967, Hill 1964) who pioneered the concept of a family cycle with eight or nine stages depicting mainly the childbearing and childrearing experiences of a couple. Hareven (1974, 1978a) recognized the limitations of using a contemporary model of the family life cycle for historical analysis and called upon historians to develop a model more appropriate for the past that would account for the presence in households of nonkin members such as boarders and lodgers.

Despite Hareven's (1974) challenge over 10 years ago for historians to develop a broader and more flexible family cycle model, she has not been able to devise one herself because of the inherent difficulties in such an approach. Any family cycle model necessarily greatly constricts the factors that describe the development of the family. The Duvall model (1967), for example, focuses heavily upon the impact of the birth and development of the eldest child but ignores the effects of other children on that family. Attempts to expand the family cycle model to take into account the youngest as well as the eldest child have resulted in an unwieldy 24-stage family cycle model (Rodgers 1962). The family cycle model also fails to recognize the importance of differences in the timing of events such as first having an out-of-wedlock child and then marrying (Elder 1978). Furthermore, the family cycle model assumes the presence of both parents during the period of childrearing and cannot incorporate the effects of the higher rates of adult deaths in the colonial South (Vinovskis 1978) or the increasing likelihood of divorce in the twentieth century (May 1980).

The family cycle approach has been heavily criticized by both sociologists (Elder 1978, Nock 1979, Spanier et al 1979) and historians (Vinovskis 1978, in press). Nevertheless, some historians (Chudacoff 1978a, b; Haines 1981; Ryan 1981) continue to use that concept casually, and a few (Katz et al 1982; Wells 1985) have even developed more elaborate models. Katz and his associates (1982) created a 12-stage family cycle model for their study of Hamilton, Ontario, in the second half of the nineteenth century. Whereas the age of the husband is used by most other historians to denote the stages of the family cycle, this model uses the age of the wife instead and focuses on the presence or absence of children of different age-groups as an indication of the financial strain on the family.

The family cycle model developed by Katz and his colleagues (1982) illustrates the shortcomings of this approach for the analysis of family life in the past. Since their family cycle model is intended to reflect the economic strains on the family, perhaps the age of the father rather than that of the mother should have been used since few white married women worked outside the home in the nineteenth century (Mason et al 1978). In addition, by not taking into account the exact number or ages of children in each family or whether they were employed or in school, Katz's family cycle model tells us very little about the actual impact of children on the economic welfare of the family. Finally, since a sizable proportion of families were female-headed at some time, any model purporting to capture the economic situation of the family over time should at least try to incorporate that situation.

The most popular and widely accepted alternative to the family cycle is the life-course approach. The life-course perspective was introduced to historians through the work of Elder (1974) on family life during the Great Depression in the 1930s, and he remains its most articulate and prominent spokesperson (1981, 1983).

The advantage of the life-course approach is that it takes the individual as the unit of analysis rather than the family, and embeds the development of the individual within the changing context of family, neighborhood, and community. Unlike family cycle models which tend to constrain the number and type of issues a researcher can consider, the life-course approach invites a much broader and more complex interpretation of human development and behavior. The life-course approach also recognizes that family members may continue to play an important role in the lives of individuals even when they are not living in the same household. In addition, while it is almost impossible in practice to study families or households over time because of the many changes in their membership and geographic location, it is much easier to trace the lives of individuals. As a result, the life-course approach is very interested in the transitions of individuals and pays particular attention to the timing and sequencing of events such as finishing school, marrying, and having children. The life-course approach also concerns the interactions of the individual with social institutions such as churches and schools and how these relationships are mediated by the family. The disadvantage of the life-course approach, however, is that it resembles more a theoretical perspective or general research guide than a definite prescription for analysis.

Many American family historians (Hareven 1977, 1978, 1982a; Vinovskis 1977, in press) are now advocating the use of life-course analysis, but only a few have incorporated it so far into their own research. Studies of school attendance (Kaestle & Vinovskis 1980), women in the labor force (Mason et al 1978), and aging (Chudacoff & Hareven 1978) have used the life-course perspective. Yet many of these studies are based only on cross-sectional manuscript census data and do not have the type of longitudinal data really necessary for life-course analysis. The shift toward a life-course perspective among American family historians probably will necessitate the assembling of longitudinal information, which will improve the quality of the data but at the same time greatly increase the cost of doing historical research on the family. Furthermore, life-course analysis encourages researchers to focus upon particular aspects of an individual's life such as childbearing, caring for young children, raising adolescents, and growing old rather than trying to analyze the development of the family as a whole from its formation to its dissolution.

CHILDBEARING

The central event in American family history in the nineteenth century was the gradual but sustained decline in the national birthrate (Degler 1980b). In the seventeenth and eighteenth centuries, birth rates in America were much higher than those for Western European countries. By the time of the American Revolution, however, couples in the United States began to limit their fertility at a pace not experienced in most of Europe until the middle of the nineteenth century. Fertility dropped by 30% nationally between 1800 and 1860 (Vinovskis 1981a). The historiographical debate on the origins of fertility decline has proven a rich opportunity for interdisciplinary research into the economic, cultural, and sexual habits of early nineteenth-century American families.

In the literature on fertility decline, a gradual shift is evident away from macro-level economic analyses toward micro-level studies of individual households which emphasize the interaction of socioeconomic conditions with cultural attitudes. The ongoing efforts of historical demographers and historians of the family to isolate the economic determinents of fertility decline in America have been thoroughly discussed elsewhere (Vinovskis 1978, 1984) and so are only briefly reviewed here. In directing attention first to the spread of industrialization and urbanization (Potter 1965), and more recently toward the problem of reduced land resources in rural areas (Yasuba 1962; Easterlin 1976, 1977a, b; Easterlin et al 1978; Forster & Tucker 1972; Schapiro 1982; Laidig et al 1981), historians have identified factors such as the depressed labor value of children to the urban household and reduced availability of farmland as key variables in the demographic transition to low fertility. Yet they have shown little understanding of how these economic conditions became translated into actual preferences or how they interacted with structural changes in other areas such as education and religion to form attitudes toward childbearing. While we now know that restricted economic opportunity is associated with declining fertility levels, we do not yet understand the decision-making process by which economic considerations were transformed into a preference for fewer children or even whose preference it was (Vinovskis 1984). The assumption implicit in the economic approach, that an economic rationalism (the balancing of estimated costs against expected gains) motivated fertility decisions, presumes a certain mentality that cannot be taken for granted, but rather is the proper object of study. Wells (1975) has argued that without a prior change in attitudes, families confronted with declining resources would most likely have acquiesced passively in their fate rather than taking active measures to change it. How, when, and among which groups this change in mental outlook first developed has become the focus of recent research into fertility decline.

The inadequacy of economic explanations of the decline in fertility prompted historians to look for patterns of cultural change that cut across socioeconomic boundaries. In the United States, this effort has most often been directed at identifying trends toward "modernization" in all spheres of American life: education, employment, communication, religion, and gender relations (Vinovskis 1981a, Brown 1976, Wells 1975, Degler 1980b). In Europe, the term "secularization" has been employed to describe a similar cultural reorientation whose roots lie in the liberalization of religious habits (Lesthaeghe & Wilson 1986, Lockridge 1983). In either case, the key factor in the development of a "modern" or "secular" perspective is the belief that change is both possible and desirable (Knodel 1977).

Several recent studies of fertility decline nicely illustrate the growing sensitivity to the issues of cultural change. In a study of fertility patterns in the commercial center of Nantucket, Massachusetts, over the period 1680–1840, Byers (1982) concluded that the increasing absorption of Nantucket families into the commercial economy led couples to limit family size deliberately as early as the 1740s. Although this interpretation has been sharply criticized (Logue 1985, 1986; Byers 1986), the debate has continued to center around the link between the spread of commercialization and changing reproductive behavior. Byers associates growing commercialization with the erosion of a mental outlook characterized by "fatalism, improvisation, and passivity," changes in the economic activities and independence of women within the family, and the prevailing religious milieu. Quaker beliefs in the spiritual equality of women and the innocent nature of children interacted with structural conditions which favored smaller families to produce a new cultural context in which family limitation was perceived as both possible and advantageous.

In their study of Sturbridge, Massachusetts, Osterud & Fulton (1976), similarly link the expansion of the market economy in the early nineteenth century to the spread of new ideas about childbearing and family relations. They dispute the claim of economic historians that the growth of commercial and industrial capitalism altered the relative contribution of children and adults to the family labor supply or income pool. Rather, economic developments influenced fertility behavior on the level of "mentalite," by making reproductive strategies a matter of conscious awareness and planning. The notion of "family economy," they stress, was not created by industrial capitalists but rather was advocated by middle-class reformers early in the century for families in both urban and rural sectors.

The role of religion in the formation of cultural attitudes toward childbearing has only recently been addressed. While the relationship of religious affiliation and fertility has been extensively studied by contemporary sociologists (Chamie 1981, Bouvier & Rao 1975), it has been almost entirely neglected in nineteenth-century studies. In a household-level study of fertility differentials among religious groups in one Michigan community in 1860, Juster (1985) argues that the theological and social reorientation of evangelical religion in the antebellum period helped liberalize couples' attitudes about children and contributed to the acceptance of family limitation as a permissible strategy. Using only aggregate data on church seating capacity recorded in the federal census, Leasure (1982) has attempted to correlate fertility decline with the strength of liberal denominations on the county level. The inaccuracy of church seating capacity as an index of religious strength has been a stumbling block in the effort to measure the relationship of religious beliefs and fertility behavior in the nineteenth century. We need more micro-level studies that link church membership records with census or other nominal listings to develop an accurate profile of the demographic character-istics of various religious subgroups.

Perhaps one of the most promising areas of analysis, combining both cultural and economic considerations, is the role of education in reducing fertility. Studies of nineteenth-century fertility differentials at the state (Vinovskis 1976a; Ransom & Sutch 1986), county (Vinovskis 1976b), city (Guest & Tolnay 1983a, Vinovskis 1981a), and individual (Guest & Tolnay 1983b) levels have found a strong inverse relationship between fertility and education. Indeed, education is often found to be the single best predictor of fertility levels even though these analyses are usually hampered by the lack of adequate data on education. In addition, it is not clear exactly how education affects fertility. The educational level of the mother or father may affect how they perceive the world (Vinovskis 1981a) or their own employment oppor-tunities (Vinovskis & Bernard 1978, Mason et al 1978). The notion of universal education also greatly increased the cost of raising children, who were expected to enter school at older ages, attend more regularly, and acquire more formal training (Kaestle & Vinovskis 1980).

Changing relations between parents and children and between husbands and wives have also been explored as a possible factor in fertility decline. The transformation of the traditional, patriarchal family into the modern, affec-tionate family has been widely discussed by family historians, but the im-plications of this shift for demographic behavior remain to be fully drawn out. Smith (1973a,b) has detailed the growing autonomy of children from parental intervention in decisions concerning their marital and sexual behavior and has posited the existence of a kind of "domestic feminism" in the early nineteenth century to explain the increasing independence of women within the home. Degler (1980b) in his study of the rise of the modern family has suggested that the ideology of "individualism" which emerged out of Enlightenment philoso-phy and revolutionary rhetoric led women to assert a personal and collective interest that was qualitatively different from that of men. Other efforts to integrate changes in gender relations into the historiographical debate over fertility decline have been hampered by an uncritical acceptance of the historical construct of "separate spheres" (Cott 1977), which has obscured the interrelatedness of men's and women's social, economic, and domestic activities in the nineteenth century. Rather than being construed as a male- or female-initiated decision (Degler 1980b), family limitation should be viewed in the context of mutual negotiation between husbands and wives (Mohr 1978).

The cultural interpretation of fertility behavior, which places primary emphasis on the attitudinal shift toward rational planning of reproductive behavior, has not been without its critics. Caldwell (1982), in particular, has questioned the assumption that fertility behavior was not rationally (i.e. economically) motivated in premodern populations. He argues instead that childbearing has always been subject to rational considerations of an economic nature; as economic conditions change, the optimum level of fertility changes as well. In traditional, agricultural societies, it was in a family's best interest to have as many children as possible because the direction of wealth transfers was from children to parents. In an industrialized society, on the other hand, wealth flows from parents to children, and the rational strategy then becomes one of family limitation. American researchers are only beginning to explore the issue of intergenerational exchanges in the context of fertility limitation (David & Sundstrom 1985, 1986; Nugent 1985; Shammas 1985), though this promises to be one of the most exciting areas of future study.

RAISING YOUNG CHILDREN

Child psychologists and sociologists often assume that young children are the same in different cultures and times and that information about child development today is thus a reliable guide to their behavior in the past. Historians of the family are discovering considerable variation over time in how children have been perceived and treated by adults. Whether this reflects a much greater plasticity in the nature of early child development than we had imagined or merely more variation in adult attitudes and actions towards young children is not entirely clear at this time.

More than 50 years ago Fleming (1933) declared that New England Puritans regarded their children as miniature adults rather than as a separate and distinct set of developing individuals. This notion did not become widely known or accepted among scholars until Aries (1962), in his influential work on family life in early modern Europe, popularized the idea that medieval parents did not perceive young children as different from adults. Subsequently, many American historians (Demos 1970, 1974; Degler 1980b; Wells 1982) have adopted his interpretation by arguing that colonial Americans viewed and treated their offspring as miniature adults.

Several historians (Axtell 1974, Stannard 1977, Kaestle & Vinovskis 1980) have challenged the view that early Americans ever regarded their children as miniature adults. New England Puritans did see their children as more capable intellectually than many of us see our own children today, but they did not regard them as indistinguishable from adults. Children were regarded as a separate and identifiable group of individuals, with different abilities and temperaments, who required careful and specialized nurturing (Moran & Vinovskis 1986). Indeed, the Puritans even wrote special catechisms for young children rather than assuming that both children and adults could learn and recite from the same texts.

Early Americans believed that children were capable of learning to read at very early ages. English educators like John Locke assumed that children should be taught to read as soon as they could talk and the Puritans encouraged children to learn to read the Bible at a very early age. The enthusiasm for early education was greatly stimulated in the 1820s and 1830s when special infant schools were established in the United States to teach children aged two, three, or four their alphabet and how to read (May & Vinovskis 1977). Initially, the infant schools were intended to help poor children overcome their disadvantages, but once middle-class parents saw the success of these special institutions they insisted that their own children be admitted as well. It is estimated that 40–50% of all three-year-old children in Massachusetts in 1840 were enrolled in a public or private school—a figure unmatched by Headstart and other early education programs until very recently (Kaestle & Vinovskis 1980).

During the first 150 years of our history, teaching very young children to read was considered normal. But during the 1830s and 1840s a major shift occurred in attitudes as physicians and educators came increasingly to believe that early childhood education could be harmful to the child. They based their opposition to early learning on the notion that any overstimulation of the mind would divert vital energy necessary for normal growth and eventually would lead to insanity. These new ideas about child development were quickly accepted by some of the leading doctors and educators who then led the fight against early education and the infant schools. By 1860 there were almost no three- or four-year-olds in Massachusetts schools, and efforts were even underway to discourage children aged five or six from enrolling prematurely (Kaestle & Vinovskis 1980).

Thus, within a couple of decades, adult perceptions of the intellectual capabilities and needs of young children were greatly changed, leading to a marked deemphasis on early schooling. When kindergartens were established later in the second half of the nineteenth century in the United States, most of them excluded very young children and did not attempt to teach their pupils how to read. The infant schools soon became so forgotten that a 125 years later Americans thought they had invented early childhood education through the Headstart Program.

Just as adult perceptions of early child development have altered, so have our views of the roles of the mother and the father in the rearing of young children. The Puritans emphasized the importance of the father as the head of the household in educating his children (Cremin 1970). While the mother was regarded as his assistant, fathers were assigned the primary responsibility for teaching children how to read and instructing them in their catechisms. That a man was much more likely to be literate than a woman in the seventeenth century simply reinforced the assigned role of men in the education of children (Lockridge 1974).

The primacy of the father as the educator of his own children faced an unexpected challenge in the second half of the seventeenth century when many second-generation male settlers did not join the church in New England. Since education was intimately tied to religious instruction, the refusal of males to join the church made it necessary to find other means of catechizing the young. The Puritans experimented with several alternatives such as assigning the task to primary school teachers or to local ministers (Axtell 1974). Gradually and somewhat reluctantly they came to accept the idea that women, who continued to join the church in higher proportions than men, should be given the responsibility for educating and catechizing young children at home (Moran & Vinovskis 1986).

The transition from the father to the mother as the primary socializer and educator of young children was completed by the nineteenth century. The mother was now regarded as the "natural" caretaker of the child, and the father's role was limited in practice to that of a supervisor or the ultimate dispenser of discipline in the home (Cott 1977, Demos 1982a, Ryan 1981). One consequence of this shift in roles was the necessity for women to become more literate, which justified the expansion of female schooling in the eighteenth and nineteenth centuries (Kerber 1980). The growing identification of mothers with early childhood education also helped to pave the way for the replacement of males by females as primary school teachers, and this provided new employment opportunities for antebellum women. In 1860 approximately 20% of all native-born Massachusetts women had taught school at some time in their lives (Kaestle & Vinovskis 1980, Vinovskis & Bernard 1978).

Today we are experiencing considerable change in how we perceive and treat young children. A much greater emphasis is placed on early education, and some public school systems are now opening their doors to all four-year-olds rather than just to those enrolled in special programs like Headstart. The responsibility of the father in the rearing of young children is also being reappraised as many child developmental experts try to redefine his role within the family. While these changes may seem disturbing and "unnatural" to some in our society, they should be seen as part of an ongoing and neverending reconsideration and reordering of the roles of mothers and fathers in the care and socialization of children throughout our history.

ADOLESCENCE

In contrast to the literature on early child development, the study of adolescence in the past has received much more attention, yet considerable disagreement still exists on the major points of debate. Historians have been strongly influenced in this area by the work of Aries (1962) and Erikson (1968). Those who follow in Aries' footsteps argue that the concept of adolescence is a temporally bounded one, whose history corresponds to the social and economic history of the family. Those who adhere to the Eriksonian model of psychological development, on the other hand, see adolescence as a universal stage in human development which transcends any cultural and historical context. In part, this debate turns on how adolescence is to be defined; if conceived as the transition to biological and physical maturity, then the potential for cultural variation in the experience of adolescence is more limited. If defined, on the other hand, as the achievement of social maturity, then the historic dimensions of adolescence become much more important. American historians of the family are sharply divided on the question of when adolescence as a distinct phase first emerged. While some argue that it was the creation of late nineteenth-century industrial society (Demos & Demos 1969, Kett 1977), others locate its origins in the seventeenth (Thompson 1984) and eighteenth (Hiner 1975, Beales 1975) centuries.

In their search for evidence of an adolescent culture in colonial America, several historians have pointed to the presence of widespread generational tensions throughout this period. Morgan (1966) suggested that the nearly universal custom of "putting out" older children to service in other households may have served to defuse potential conflicts between parents and children in a society where aggressive impulses were generally sublimated. Greven (1970) argued that the patriarchal practice of delayed property transmission to sons constituted a kind of preemptive move by fathers against the opportunities for greater independence offered young men by the abundant resources of the New World. Greven (1970) pointed to the late age of marriage of sons as an index of patriarchal control, but Farber (1972) surprisingly used the late age of marriage in Salem as evidence of the decline in patriarchal power.

While the relationship of fathers to sons has most often been the focus of attention, Demos (1971, 1982b), in a rare attempt to examine the situation of adolescent girls, has suggested that witchcraft accusations in seventeenth-century New England reflected in part the repressed hostility of young girls (for whom social and familial responsibilities were severely constrained) toward their mothers. Others (Elliott 1975, Morgan 1961, Murrin 1972) have presented the religious controversy over the adoption of the Half-Way Covenant in late seventeenth-century New England as both a political and a spiritual struggle between the founding settlers and their less pious offspring. Hiner (1975) similarly argues that the refusal of early eighteenth-century youth to convert implied an assertion of independence from adult authority.

This collection of studies, diverse in scope yet linked by a common concern for relations between parents and children, reflects the influence of the generational model of family history that prevailed early in the discipline's history. As historians have moved toward a life-course perspective, their focus has accordingly shifted toward an examination in the lives of individuals of certain turning points that mark the transition from one phase of the life course to another. We have chosen to review three events which have been identified as demarking passage from adolescence to adulthood in the past: religious conversion, the transition from school to work, and sexual activity.

The notion that religious conversion became a predominantly adolescent rite of passage with the evangelicalization of Protestantism in the eighteenth and nineteenth centuries has until recently been accepted with little dissent. Substantiating the claims of the evangelical clergy, historians of colonial religion (Walsh 1971, Greven 1972, Moran 1972) presented the shift toward youthful conversions as a key feature of the First Great Awakening in the 1740s. While the trend toward earlier conversion was temporarily reversed in the second half of the eighteenth century, teenage conversion, it is argued, became the norm during the revivals that swept the country from the 1790s through the 1830s (Kett 1977, Cott 1975, Ryan 1981).

This interpretation has been challenged on several fronts. First, Smith (1982) has warned against interpreting a drop in the mean age of conversion during revival seasons as indicating a qualitative shift in the nature of religious conversion from an adult to an adolescent phenomenon. Rather, this quantitative change may in part be a statistical artifact; as the number of church members rose, new converts had to be drawn from an ever smaller pool of potential members, a pool in which the young tended to be disproportionately represented. The sufficiency of a single measure such as mean age of conversion for capturing the essence of religious experience has been further questioned by Grossbart (1984) and Shiels (1985), in two studies of religious conversion in eighteenth-century New England. Following in the steps of Modell et al (1976), they present a series of indexes (spread, timing, congruence with other transitional events) that suggest that the experience of conversion in the eighteenth century was too diffused and ill-defined to constitute a meaningful rite of passage. In a study of conversion narratives published in the evangelical press, Juster (1986) disputes the claim (Kett 1977) that the anger and hostility expressed in these spiritual accounts represent a premodern form of adolescent identity crisis. She argues rather, that they should be understood as the psychological fall-out of the clash of adult personalities with the evangelical demand for complete self-renunciation. These studies demonstrate the complexity of rites of passage and the need for a more precise methodology in mapping such life-course transitions.

The historiographical literature on the transition from school to work has emphasized the expansion of employment options available to youth in the past through the impact of industrialization, on the one hand, and the restriction of school attendance to certain age-groups on the other. Initially, historians turned their attention to identifying the ethnic and socioeconomic variables that predisposed nineteenth-century parents to send their children to school or into the labor force. Thernstrom (1964) argues that the lower school attendance of children from foreign-born households in Newburyport, Massachusetts, can be explained by the cultural preference of the largely Irish community for home ownership over education. Katz & Davey (1978), on the other hand, point to the greater economic dependency of immigrant families on the supplementary income of children as the primary factor inhibiting school attendance. Later studies which employed multivariate techniques to measure the relationship of ethnicity and occupation with school-leaving (Kaestle & Vinovskis 1980) found that both variables influenced the decision to remove a child from school to provide extra income to the household.

Recently, studies of school-leaving and labor force participation among the young have moved beyond examining the influence of family environment to exploring the parameters of this shift as a life-course transition. Kett (1977) has suggested that school and work in the nineteenth century did not represent opposing modes of occupation that were mutually exclusive; rather, they adhered to seasonal patterns of attendance which allowed teenagers to move back and forth between the two. Like religious initiation, joining the labor force as a permanent member was a long, drawn out process for many youths and not the sharply defined transition it has become in the twentieth century. Similarly, school attendance did not abruptly end at a particular age in nineteenth-century America but rather was spread out over a long period of time. Often within a single classroom could be found children of three and four and young adults of twenty. Given the protracted and imprecise nature of these adolescent experiences, Kett (1977) prefers to distinguish life-stages in terms of degrees of dependency rather than age-groups. The emergence of age-graded criteria for the transition from one life-course event to another is mainly a twentieth-century phenomenon (Modell et al 1978).

By definition, the achievement of sexual maturity among adolescents has always been subject to more narrowly circumscribed age limits than other transitional events. Yet changing sexual behavior among the young historically reflects cultural shifts in attitudes more than biological changes in the age of maturity. While the age of menarche has dropped steadily from approximately 17–18 in the seventeenth century in Western Europe (Laslett 1971, Tanner 1962) and 15–16 in colonial America (Vinovskis 1986) to 12–13 in this century, levels of sexual activity among teenagers have not conformed to this trend but rather have followed their own cyclical pattern. Smith & Hindus (1975) have divided the history of premarital pregnancy rates in America into four phases: two troughs, occurring in the seventeenth and mid-nineteenth centuries, and two peaks, occurring in the second half of the eighteenth and mid-twentieth centuries. They conclude that periods of sexual restraint were marked by harmonious intergenerational relations and a well-defined institutional framework of control, while periods of high premarital conceptions indicate strained relations between parents and children and a breakdown in the social and familial systems of control.

While Smith & Hindus use premarital pregnancy as a proxy for adolescent sexual activity, Vinovskis (1981b) has argued that adolescent sexuality should also be analytically and conceptually broken down into its marital and non-marital components if its development over time is to be fully understood. He points out that while in the twentieth century the adolescent pregnancy rate has actually declined since 1957 (contrary to public and private opinion), the incidence of out-of-wedlock births has increased dramatically and should be the proper focus of concern for policymakers. Building on the work of Vinovskis, Brumberg (1984), suggests that social responses to the problem of illegitimacy have not been constant over time but rather became privatized in the late nineteenth century as the Victorian "code of silence" removed the issue of sexuality from the public forum.

Within this diverse body of literature on the historical experiences of youth, most historians now agree that adolescence in the past was a much more loosely defined stage of life than it is today. As their activities became more age-graded and institutionally bounded in contemporary America, twentieth-century youth lost much of the flexibility that characterized the lives of their preindustrial counterparts.

OLD AGE

The conceptual framework surrounding the study of old age and attitudes toward the elderly is strikingly similar to that which informs the historiographical debate over the decline in fertility. The literature on childbearing patterns and that on the position of the elderly in society have both struggled to come to terms with the relative influence of structural and attitudinal variables on developments within the family. As in studies of the origins of fertility decline, the process of modernization has been proposed by some scholars as the key transforming event in the lives of elderly Americans (Gratton 1986, Cowgill & Holmes 1972); for others, changes in the status of the elderly are due to cultural factors that operate independently of structural changes in the economy (Achenbaum 1978, Fischer 1978, Cole 1986). Today scholars are working to combine the two perspectives in a way that is neither economically deterministic nor ideologically naive.

The focus on modernization as a transforming process has tended to polarize the history of the age into two periods: a "before" period when the aged were revered, respected, and powerful; and an "after," in which attitudes toward the elderly deteriorated and old age was increasingly seen as a stage of dependence, debility, and impotence. However, historians differ on exactly when the shift from a "golden age" of influence and affluence to an institutionalized existence of poverty and loneliness took place. Fischer (1978) has pinpointed the critical period as the post-revolutionary era, from roughly 1770 to 1820. Later studies have pushed this transition further into the nineteenth century, with varying beginning and end points: Rosenkrantz & Vinovskis (1978) suggest that the change took place in the years 1840–1860; Achenbaum (1978) argues for the period 1860–1914; Gruman (1978), for 1890–1930; and Smith (1986), for the post-1940 era. Within this diversity, the latter half of the nineteenth century has emerged as a crucial period of change in both attitudes toward and conditions of the elderly (Haber 1983). The fact that the spread of industrialization and urbanization was the most visible social development in these years has given the modernization theory much of its analytical persuasiveness. Yet neither structural nor attitudinal shifts have yet been empirically established as contributing to the growth of "age-ism," that is systematic discrimination against the elderly (Gratton 1986), and the field remains open to new interpretations.

The studies cited above, while disagreeing on periodicity, concur that, at some point in the past, the elderly were an influential and venerated segment of society and that this advantaged position was reversed at a later date. This "before and after" approach has been questioned by scholars (Haber 1983) who posit a more fundamental ambiguity in the status of the elderly that has persisted throughout American history. Demos (1983), Smith (1978), Vinovskis (1982), and Keyssar (1974) have argued that the status of the elderly in colonial society was tied to economic position; only those old people who retained control over households and economic resources commanded the respect of the community. For the poor and dependent elderly, such as widows, old age brought only social denigration and financial duress. For example, Vinovskis' study (1982) of aged ministers in seventeenth- and eighteenth-century New England finds a steady deterioration in social status and wealth from the first generation through eighteenth-century cohorts and a corresponding rise in disputes between ministers and congregations over salary matters. As the financial position of ministers became more insecure, elderly "servants of the Lord" were less likely to serve for life or to be self-sufficient in their old age. Communal responses to old age were not constant, in other words, but fluctuated according to economic pressures.

Respect for the elderly in traditional societies has been linked to the numerical absence of large numbers of aged in the population. Because people over age 60 formed such a small proportion of the population, Fischer (1978) has argued that the few old people who survived wielded great power. Demos (1983), however, has calculated that the proportion of elderly in society and their proximity to other members of the community was significantly great to assure that old age was a common and visible experience in New England. Over 90% of the children under 20 in one New Hampshire town in the seventeenth century had at least one grandparent living; no child under age five was without grandparents. More damaging to Fischer's argument is the evidence that real political and economic power in colonial America was held by middle-aged men, not by the elderly. Smith (1978) and Demos (1983) both report that the majority of office holders in colonial New England were in their 40s and 50s (a finding supported by Fischer's own data), and few served into old age—the average interval between the final term in office and death was over 11 years (Demos 1983). Voluntary retirement from both work and public service was not uncommon.

Studies of aging in the nineteenth century have been strongly influenced by the life-course perspective. Examinations of adult transitions from middle age to old age have discovered no sharp discontinuities in the lives of aging men and women (Chudacoff & Hareven 1978, 1979; Hareven 1986; Smith 1979). Like the experiences of adolescents described by Modell et al (1976), adult transitions in the nineteenth century were erratic, took a long time to complete, and were less rapidly timed than today (Chudacoff & Hareven 1979). Several key events have been identified as signifying passage from middle to old age: loss of household headship, widowhood, retirement from work, and the end of childbearing or the "empty nest" syndrome. Withdrawal from labor force participation and the empty nest stage seem not to have affected most nineteenth-century elderly; over 90% of the men over age 55 in Chudacoff & Harven's study (1978) were still employed, while a majority of aged couples never experienced the departure of all their children from the household (1979). Widowhood, on the other hand, was common in the nineteenth-century for many elderly, especially women. Of the women in their late 60s and early 70s, 60% were widows, as compared to 15% of men under 70 (Chudacoff & Hareven 1979). The prevalence of widowhood as a life-course event for women constitutes a major continuity with the twentieth-century family.

One of the most important findings from this body of research has been that loss of household headship in the nineteenth century did not customarily entail institutionalization in old-age homes (as has increasingly occurred in the twentieth century) but rather coresidence with adult children. Haber (1983) found that by 1910 only 2% of the elderly she studied lived in institutions; Chudacoff & Hareven's study (1978) of Essex County, Massachusetts, in the period 1860–1880 puts that figure at less than 1%. The importance of coresidence as a family strategy to mitigate the effects of dependence in the elderly has led scholars to focus greater attention on intergenerational relations in the nineteenth century. While Chudacoff & Hareven (1978, 1979) argue that coresidence was achieved by adult children remaining at home, or returning home, after having once left, to care for their parents, Smith (1979) finds that most of the increasing complexity in household arrangements in the late nineteenth century resulted from older people moving into the households of their married children. The distinction is important, for it bears on the question of the waning influence of the aged within the family after industrialization and urbanization. Chudacoff & Hareven (1978) suggest that the elderly remained an important source of financial and emotional assistance for their offspring in these critical years, whereas Smith's (1979) analysis posits a loss of status for aged parents as they succumbed to the necessity of relinquishing household headship. This pattern of coresidence was significantly reversed in the twentieth century when the proportion of elderly living alone or with spouses only jumped dramatically (Smith 1986). Rather than a steady deterioration in the status of the aged since the nineteenth century, then, Smith suggests increasing autonomy for older Americans in the post-1940 era.

Most recently, discussions of the relation between the desire for security in old age and declining fertility rates have contributed a new perspective to the question of intergenerational relations. Explicitly rejecting Easterlin's (1976) notion that parents in nineteenth-century America based property transfers to children on altruistic motives, David & Sundstrom (1985, 1986) have argued that farm parents made childbearing decisions on the basis of self-serving concerns about their own future security. The model of intergenerational exchange offered by David & Sundstrom or Nugent (1985) is built around the concept of an ongoing struggle for power between parents and children in which competing interests must be resolved. Caldwell's (1982) pioneering work on intergenerational exchange, as noted earlier in the section on childbearing, presents the balance of power as shifting more toward children under the impact of industrialization. In this approach, the conclusion of the modernization proponents that the elderly gradually lost status is given added support.

The literature on the need for security in old age and on intergenerational conflicts is based on an underlying premise that nineteenth-century Americans anticipated spending a considerable portion of their lives as dependent elderly members of the household (David & Sundstrom 1985). This assumption has been challenged by several scholars. Stearns (1980) argues that in the nineteenth century men and women had difficulty imagining their own old age. Given the prevalence of high death rates, few people believed it likely that they would reach 60 or 65. David & Sundstrom (1985) have countered this objection by reference to the impressively high life expectancies of those who survived childhood throughout the eighteenth and early nineteenth centuries in America; yet, as Vinovskis (1979) has cautioned, attitudes toward death may differ significantly from actual levels and trends in mortality. He suggests that in early America most colonists had a skewed perception of high mortality that did not coincide with demographic reality. Evidence from diaries of New Englanders shows an obsession with death that persisted at least until the early nineteenth century.

Smith (1979) has further questioned the validity of the generational model underlying the old-age security literature. In a sample of households from the 1900 federal census, he found no significant relationship between the number of living children reported by a couple and the probability of a child coresiding with his or her widowed mother. As far as intergenerational exchanges were concerned, one child was as useful as five. In the absence of cultural norms prescribing assistance for elderly parents, adult children were equally likely (or unlikely) regardless of birth order to return voluntarily to their family of origin to care for an aged parent. Smith's work offers a persuasive reminder that structural and attitudinal perspectives must be combined in interpreting changes in the status and behavior of the elderly in the past.

CONCLUSION

As we have seen, the study of the American family in the past has really only matured in the last 20 years. Yet it is now one of the most exciting and active areas of historical research and has profoundly affected how we view both contemporary and historical developments within the family in the United States.

Largely because of the newness of the discipline, there has been considerable confusion over the proper conceptual approach to employ in analyzing families. In the late 1960s many historians used measures of household composition to analyze family life, but today this approach has been largely discredited. Instead, the profession seems split between those using the family cycle models and those using a life-course perspective, with the latter attracting the most attention and support. Nevertheless, much work remains to be done as historians try to find more appropriate and effective ways of studying family life in the past.

Beyond these methodological debates, there exists even greater diversity in our interpretations of specific areas of family life as illustrated by the ongoing efforts of scholars to understand childbearing, raising young children, adolescence, and old age in their historical context. Indeed, most of the recent work on family life has focused on addressing particular facets of that experience rather than on trying to resolve the methodological problems involved in studying families. While the results of these investigations are often still quite inconclusive and even contradictory, they do demonstrate the importance and the great promise that this area of historical analysis holds for the future.

Literature Cited

Achenbaum, A. 1978. *Old Age in the New World: The American Experience Since 1970.* Baltimore: Johns Hopkins Univ. Press. 237 pp.

Anderson, M. 1980. *Approaches to the History of the Western Family, 1500–1914.* London: MacMillan. 96 pp.

Aries, P. 1962. *Centuries of Childhood: A Social History of Family Life.* Transl. Robert Baldick. New York: Vintage. 447 pp.

Axtell, J. 1974. *The School Upon a Hill: Education and Society in Colonial New England.* New Haven, Conn: Yale Univ. Press. 298 pp.

Beales, R. Jr. 1975. In search of the historical child: Miniature adulthood and youth in colonial New England. *Am. Q.* 27:379–98

Berkner, L. 1972. The stem family and the developmental cycle of the peasant household: An eighteenth-century Austrian example. *Am. Hist. Rev.* 77:398–418

Bouvier, L., Rao, S. L. N. 1975. *Socioreligious Factors in Fertility Decline.* Cambridge, Mass: Ballinger. 204 pp.

Brown, R. D. 1976. *Modernization: The Transformation of American Life, 1600–1865.* New York: Norton. 229 pp.

Brumberg, J. J. 1984. "Ruined" girls: Changing community responses to illegitimacy in upstate New York, 1890–1920. *J. Soc. Hist.* 18:247–72

Byers, E. 1982. Fertility transition in a New England commercial center: Nantucket, Massachusetts, 1760–1840. *J. Int. Hist.* 13:17–40

Byers, E. 1986. Putting history back in historical demography: Nantucket re-examined. *J. Int. Hist.* 16:683–90

Caldwell, J. 1982. *Theory of Fertility Decline.* London: Academic Press. 286 pp.

Chamie, J. 1981. *Religion and Fertility: Arab-Christian-Muslim Differentials.* Cambridge: Cambridge Univ. Press. 150 pp.

Chudacoff, H. P. 1978a. New branches of the tree: Household structure in early stages of the family cycle in Worcester, Massachusetts, 1860–1880. In *Themes in the History of the Family,* ed. T. K. Hareven, pp. 55–72. Lunenburg, Vt: Stinehour. 72 pp.

Chudacoff, H. P. 1978b. Newlyweds and family extension: The first stage of the family cycle in Providence, Rhode Island, 1864–1865 and 1879–1880. In *Family and Population in Nineteenth-Century America,* ed. T. K. Hareven, M. A. Vinovskis, pp. 179–205. Princeton: Princeton Univ. Press. 250 pp.

Chudacoff, H. P., Hareven, T. K. 1978. Family transitions into old age. See Hareven 1978b. pp. 217–43

Chudacoff, H. P., Hareven, T. K. 1979. From the empty nest to family dissolution: Life course transitions into old age. *J. Fam. Hist.* 4:69–83

Cole, T. R. 1986. "Putting off the old": Middle-Class morality, antebellum Protestantism, and the origins of ageism. See Van Tassell 1986, pp. 49–65

Cott, N. F. 1977. *The Bonds of Womanhood: "Woman's Sphere" in New England, 1780–1835.* New Haven: Yale Univ. Press. 225 pp.

Cott, N. F. 1975. Young women in the Second Great Awakening. *Am. Q.* 3:15–29

Cowgill, D. O., Holmes, L. D. 1972. *Aging and Modernization.* New York: Appleton-Century-Crofts. 331 pp.

Cremin, L. A. 1970. *American Education: The Colonial Experience, 1607–1783.* New York: Harper & Row. 688 pp.

David, P., Sundstrom, W. 1985. *Intergenerational exchange, the aged, and fertility decline in antebellum America.* Presented at Soc. Sci. Hist. Assoc. Meet. Chicago, Ill

David, P., Sundstrom, W. 1986. *Old age security motives, labor markets, and farm family fertility in antebellum America.* Presented at 10th Conf. Univ. Calif. Intercampus Group Econ. Hist. Laguna Beach, Calif.

Degler, C. N. 1980a. Women and the family. In *The Past Before Us: Contemporary Historical Writing in the United States,* ed. M. Kammen, pp. 308–26. Ithaca, NY: Cornell Univ. Press. 524 pp.

Degler, C. N. 1980b. *At Odds: Women and the Family in America from the Revolution to the Present.* New York: Oxford Univ. Press. 527 pp.

Demos, J. 1970. *A Little Commonwealth: Family Life in Plymouth Colony.* New York: Oxford Univ. Press. 201 pp.

Demos, J. 1971. Underlying themes in the witchcraft of seventeenth-century New England. In *Colonial America: Essays in Politics and Social Development,* ed. S. Katz, pp. 113–33. Boston: Little Brown. 491 pp.

Demos, J. 1974. The American family in past time. *Am. Schol.* 43:422–46

Demos, J. 1982a. The changing faces of fatherhood: A new exploration in American family history. In *Father and Child: Developmental and Clinical Perspective,* ed. S. H. Cath, A. R. Gurwitt, J. M. Ross, pp. 425–45. Boston: Little Brown. 636 pp.

Demos, J. 1982b. *Entertaining Satan: Witchcraft and the Culture of Early New England.* New York: Oxford Univ. Press. 543 pp.

Demos, J. 1983. Old age in early New England. In *The American Family in Social-Historical Perspective,* ed. M. Gordon, pp. 269–305. New York: St. Martin's. 531 pp. 3rd ed.

Demos, J., Demos, V. 1969. Adolescence in historical perspective. *J. Marriage Fam.* 31:632–38

Duvall, E. M. 1967. *Family Development.* Philadelphia: Lippincott. 532 pp. 3rd ed.

Easterlin, R. A. 1976. Population change and farm settlement in the northern United States. *J. Econ. Hist.* 36:45–75

Easterlin, R. A. 1977a. Population issues in American economic history: A survey and critique. In *Research in Economic History, Suppl. 1,* ed. P. J. Uselding, pp. 133–58. Greenwich, Conn: JAI. 305 pp.

Easterlin, R. A. 1977b. Population change and farm settlement in the northern United States. *J. Econ. Hist.* 36:45–75

Easterlin, R. A., Alter, G., Condran, G. A. 1978. Farm families in old and new areas: The northern states in 1860. In *Family and Population in Nineteenth-Century America,* ed. T. K. Hareven, M. A. Vinovskis, pp. 22–84. Princeton: Princeton Univ. Press. 250 pp.

Elder, G. H. Jr. 1974. *Children of the Great Depression: Social Change in Life Experi-*

ence. Chicago: Univ. Chicago Press. 400 pp.

Elder, G. H. Jr. 1978. Family history and the life course. See Hareven 1978b, pp. 17–64

Elder, G. H. Jr. 1981. History and the family: The discovery of complexity. *J. Marriage Fam.* 43:489–519

Elder, G. H. Jr. 1983. The life-course perspective. In *The American Family in Social-Historical Perspective,* ed. M. Gordon, pp. 54–60. New York: St. Martin's. 531 pp. 3rd ed.

Elliott, E. 1975. *Power and the Pulpit in Colonial New England.* Princeton: Princeton Univ. Press. 240 pp.

Erikson, E. H. 1968. *Identity: Youth and Crisis.* New York: Norton. 336 pp.

Farber, B. 1972. *Guardians of Virtue: Salem Families in 1800.* New York: Basic Books. 228 pp.

Fischer, D. J. 1978. *Growing Old in America.* New York: Oxford Univ. Press. 292 pp. Rev. ed.

Fleming, S. 1933. *Children and Puritanism: The Place of Children in the Life and Thought of the New England Churches, 1620–1847.* New Haven, Conn: Yale Univ. Press. 236 pp.

Forster, C., Tucker, G. S. L. 1972. *Economic Opportunity and White American Fertility Ratios, 1800–1860.* New Haven: Yale Univ. Press. 121 pp.

Gordon, M. 1978. *The American Family: Past, Present, and Future.* New York: Random. 400 pp.

Gratton, B. 1986. The new history of the aged: A critique. See Van Tassell 1986, pp. 3–29

Greven, P. J. Jr. 1970. *Four Generations: Population, Land, and Family in Colonial Andover, Massachusetts.* Ithaca, NY: Cornell Univ. Press. 329 pp.

Greven, P. J. Jr. 1972. Youth, maturity, and religious conversion: A note on the ages of converts in Anover, Massachusetts, 1711–1749. *Essex Inst. Hist. Coll.* 108:119–34

Grossbart, S. 1984. *The parameters of religious conversion in eighteenth century Canterbury, Connecticut.* Presented at the Soc. Sci. Hist. Assoc. Meet., Toronto, Canada

Gruman, G. R. 1978. Cultural origins of present-day "age-ism": The modernization of the life-cycle. See Spicker et al 1978, pp. 359–87

Guest, A. M., Tolnay, S. 1983a. Urban industrial structure and fertility: The case of large American cities. *J. Int. Hist.* 3:387–409

Guest, A. M., Tolnay, S. 1983b. Children's roles and fertility: Late nineteenth-century United States. *Soc. Sci. Hist.* 7:355–80

Haber, C. 1983. *Beyond Sixty-Five: The Dilemma of Old Age in America's Past.*

214   JUSTER & VINOVSKIS

Cambridge, England: Cambridge Univ. Press. 181 pp.

Haines, M. R. 1981. Poverty, economic stress, and the family in a late nineteenth-century American city: Whites in Philadelphia, 1880. In *Philadelphia: Work, Space, Family, and Group Experience in the Nineteenth Century: Essays Toward an Interdisciplinary History of the City,* ed. T. Hershberg, pp. 240–76. New York: Oxford Univ. Press. 525 pp.

Hareven, T. K. 1974. The family process: The historical study of the family cycle. *J. Soc. Hist.* 7:322–29

Hareven, T. K. 1978a. Cycles, courses and cohorts: Reflections on the theoretical and methodological approaches to the historical study of family development. *J. Soc. Hist.* 12:97–109

Hareven, T. K., ed. 1978b. *Transitions: The Family and the Life Course in Historical Perspective.* New York: Academic Press. 304 pp.

Hareven, T. K. 1982a. The life course and aging in historical perspective. In *Aging and the Life Transitions: An Interdisciplinary Perspective,* ed. T. K. Hareven, K. J. Adams, pp. 1–26. New York: Guilford. 281 pp.

Hareven, T. K. 1982b. *Family Time and Industrial Time: The Relationship Between the Family and Work in a New England Industrial Community.* Cambridge: Cambridge Univ. Press. 474 pp.

Hareven, T. K. 1986. Life-course transitions and kin awareness in old age: A cohort comparison. See Van Tassell 1986, pp. 110–26

Hill, R. 1964. Methodological issues in family development research. *Fam. Process* 3: 186–206

Hiner, N. R. 1975. Adolescence in eighteenth-century America. *Hist. Childhood Q.* 3:253–80

Juster, S. 1986. *"In a different voice": Male and female narratives of conversion.* Unpubl. paper. Univ. Mich. Ann Arbor

Juster, S. 1985. *Religion and fertility in nineteenth-century America.* Presented at Great Lakes Am. Stud. Assoc. Meet., Oct., South Bend, Ind.

Kaestle, C. F., Vinovskis, M. A. 1980. *Education and Social Change in Nineteenth-Century Massachusetts.* Cambridge: Cambridge Univ. Press. 349 pp.

Katz, M. B., Davey, I. 1978. School attendance and early industrialization in a Canadian city: A multivariate analysis. *Hist. Educ. Q.* 18:271–93

Katz, M. B., Doucet, M. J., Stern, M. J. 1982. *The Social Organization of Early Industrial Capitalism.* Cambridge, Mass: Harvard Univ. Press. 444 pp.

Kerber, L. K. 1980. *Women of the Republic: Intellect and Ideology in Revolutionary America.* Chapel Hill, NC: Univ. Press. 304 pp.

Kertzer, D. I. 1982. Generation and age in cross-cultural perspective. In *Aging from Birth to Death: Sociotemporal Perspectives,* Vol. 2, ed. M. W. Riley, R. P. Abeles, M. S. Teitelbaum, pp. 27–50. Boulder, Colo: Westview. 228 pp.

Kett, J. 1977. *Rites of Passage: Adolescence in America, 1790 to the Present.* New York: Basic Books. 327 pp.

Keyssar, A. 1974. Widowhood in eighteenth-century Massachusetts: A problem in the history of the family. *Perspectives Am. Hist.* 8:83–119

Knodel, J. 1977. Family limitation and the fertility transition: Evidence from the age patterns of fertility in Europe and Asia. *Pop. Stud.* 31:219–49

Laidig, G. L., Schutjer, W. A., Stokes, C. S. 1981. Agricultural variation and human fertility in antebellum Pennsylvania. *J. Fam. Hist.* 6:195–204

Laslett, P., ed. 1972. *Household and Family in Past Time.* Cambridge: Cambridge Univ. Press. 623 pp.

Laslett, P. 1971. Age at menarche in Europe since the eighteenth century. *J. Int. hist.* 2:221–36

Leasure, W. 1985. La baisse de la fecondite aux Etats-Unis de 1800 a 1860. *Population* 37:607–22

Lebsock, S. 1984. *The Free Women of Petersburg: Status and Culture in a Southern Town, 1784–1860.* New York: Norton. 326 pp.

Lesthaeghe, R., Wilson, C. 1986. Modes of production, secularization, and the pace of the fertility decline in western Europem, 1870–1930. In *The Decline of Fertility in Europe,* ed. A. J. Coale, S. C. Watkins, pp. 261–92. Princeton: Princeton Univ. Press. 484 pp.

Lewis, J. 1983. *The Pursuit of Happiness: Family and Values in Jefferson's Virginia.* Cambridge: Cambridge Univ. Press. 290 pp.

Lockridge, K. A. 1983. *The Fertility Transition in Sweden: A Preliminary Look at Smaller Geographic Units, 1855–1890.* Umea, Sweden: Demographic Data Base, Umea Univ. 135 pp.

Lockridge, K. A. 1974. *Literacy in Colonial New England: An Enquiry into the Social Context of Literacy in the Early Modern West.* New York: Norton. 164 pp.

Lockridge, K. A. 1970. *A New England Town: The First Hundred Years: Dedham, Massachusetts, 1636–1736.* New York: Norton. 208 pp.

Logue, B. J. 1986. Of sound history and

sound methodology: A rejoinder. *J. Int. Hist.* 16:691–99

Logue, B. J. 1985. The case for birth control before 1850. Nantucket re-examined. *J. Int. Hist.* 15:371–91

Mason, K. O., Vinovskis, M. A., Hareven, T. K. 1978. Women's work and the life course in Essex County, Massachusetts, 1880. See Hareven 1978b, pp. 187–216

May, D., Vinovskis, M. A. 1977. "A ray of millenial light": Early education and social reform in the infant school movement in Massachusetts, 1826–1840. In *Family and Kin in American Urban Communities, 1800–1940,* ed. T. K. Hareven, pp. 62–99. New York: Watts. 214 pp.

Modell, J., Furstenberg, F., Hershberg, T. 1976. Social change and transition to adulthood in historical perspective. *J. Fam. Hist.* 1:7–32

Mohr, J. 1978. *Abortion in America: Origins and Evolution of National Policy, 1800–1900.* New York: Oxford Univ. Press. 331 pp.

Moran, G. F. 1972. Conditions of religious conversion in the First Society of Norwich, Connecticut, 1718–1744. *J. Soc. Hist.* 5:331–43

Moran, G. F., Vinovskis, M. A. 1986. The great care of Godly parents: Early childhood in Puritan New England. In *History and Research in Child Development: In Celebration of the Fiftieth Anniversary of the Society,* ed. J. Hagen, A. Smuts, 50:24–37. Chicago: Univ. Chicago Press

Morgan, E. S. 1961. New England Puritanism: Another approach. *William Mary Q.* (3rd Ser.) 18:236–42

Morgan, E. S. 1966. *The Puritan Family.* New York: Harper & Row. 196 pp. Rev. ed.

Murrin, J. 1972. Review essay. *Hist. Theory* 11:226–75

Nock, S. L. 1979. The family life cycle: Empirical or conceptual tool? *J. Marr. Fam.* 41:15–26

Nugent, J. B. 1985. The old-age security motive for fertility. *Pop. Dev. Rev.* 11:75–97

Osterud, N., Fulton, J. 1976. Family limitation and age at marriage: Fertility decline in Sturbridge, Massachusetts, 1730–1850. *Pop. Stud.* 30:481–94

Parsons, T., Bales, R. F. 1954. *Family, Socialization and Interaction Process.* New York: Free Press. 422 pp.

Potter, J. 1965. The growth of population in America, 1700–1860. In *Population in History: Essays in Historical Demography,* ed. D. V. Glass, D. E. C. Eversley, pp. 631–88. Chicago: Aldine. 692 pp.

Ransom, R. L., Sutch, R. 1986. *Did rising out-migration cause fertility to decline in antebellum New England? A life-cycle per-*

spective on old-age security motives, child default, and farm-family fertility. *Soc. Sci. Work. Pap. 610.* Pasadena: Calif. Inst. Technol.

Rodgers, R. H. 1962. *Improvements in the Construction and Analysis of Family Life Cycle Categories.* Kalamazoo, Mich: West. Mich. Univ. 244 pp.

Rosenkrantz, B. G., Vinovskis, M. A. 1978. The invisible lunatics: Old age and insanity in mid–nineteenth-century Massachusetts. See Spicker et al 1978, pp. 95–126

Ryan, M. P. 1981. *Cradle of the Middle Class: The Family in Oneida County, New York, 1790–1865.* Cambridge: Cambridge Univ. Press. 321 pp.

Schapiro, M. O. 1982. A land availability model of fertility change in the rural northern United States, 1760–1870. *J. Econ. Hist.* 42:577–600

Shammas, C. 1985. *Family egalitarianism and intergenerational wealth transfers in nineteenth-century America.* Presented at Soc. Sci. Hist. Assoc. Meet. Nov., Chicago, Ill.

Shiels, R. 1985. The scope of the Second Great Awakening: Andover, Massachusetts, as a case study. *J. Early Republic* 5:223–46

Smith, D. B. 1980. *Inside the Great House: Planter Family Life in Eighteenth-Century Chesapeake Society.* Ithaca, NY: Cornell Univ. Press. 305 pp.

Smith, D. S. 1973a. Parental power and marriage patterns: An analysis of historical trends in Hingham, Massachusetts. *J. Marriage Fam.* 35:419–28

Smith, D. S. 1973b. Family limitation, sexual control, and domestic feminism in Victorian America. *Feminist Stud.* 1:40–57

Smith, D. S. 1978. Old age and the "great transformation": A New England case study. See Spicker et al 1978, pp. 285–302

Smith, D. S. 1979. Life course, norms, and the family system of older Americans in 1900. *J. Fam. Hist.* 4:285–98

Smith, D. S. 1982. A perspective on demographic methods and effects in social history. *William Mary Q.* (3rd Ser.) 3:442–68

Smith, D. S. 1986. Accounting for change in the families of the elderly in the United States, 1900-present. See Van Tassell 1986, pp. 87–109

Smith, D. S., Hindus, M. S. 1974–1975. Premarital pregnancy in America, 1640–1975: An overview and interpretation. *J. Int. Hist.* 5:537–70

Spanier, G. B., Sauer, W., Larzelere, R. 1979. An empirical evaluation of the family life cycle. *J. Marriage Fam.* 41:27–38

Spicker, S. F., Woodward, K. M., Van Tassell, D., eds. 1978. *Aging and the Elderly:*

Humanistic Perspectives in Gerontology. Atlantic Highlands, NJ: Humanities Press. 406 pp.

Stannard, D. E. 1977. *The Puritan Way of Death: A Study in Religion, Culture, and Social Change.* New Haven, Conn: Yale Univ. Press. 236 pp.

Stearns, P. 1980. Old women: Some historical observations. *J. Fam. Hist.* 5:44–57

Tanner, J. M. 1962. *Growth at Adolescence.* Oxford: Oxford Univ. Press. 325 pp. 2nd ed.

Thernstrom, S. 1964. *Poverty and Progress: Social Mobility in a Nineteenth-Century City.* Cambridge, Mass: Harvard Univ. Press. 286 pp.

Thompson, R. 1984. Adolescent culture in colonial Massachusetts. *J. Fam. Hist.* 9: 127–44

Van Tassell, D., ed. 1986. *Old Age in a Bureaucratic Society.* Westport, Conn: Greenwood. 259 pp.

Vinovskis, M. A. 1976a. Socioeconomic determinants of interstate fertility differentials in the United States in 1850 and 1860. *J. Int. Hist.* 6:375–96

Vinovskis, M. A. 1976b. *Demographic History and the World Population Crisis.* Worcester, Mass: Clark Univ. Press. 94 pp.

Vinovskis, M. A. 1977. From household size to the life course: Some observations on recent trends in family history. *Am. Behav. Sci.* 21:263–87

Vinovskis, M. A. 1978. Recent trends in American historical demography: Some methodological and conceptual considerations. *Ann. Rev. Sociol.* 4:603–27

Vinovskis, M. A. 1979. Angels' heads and weeping willows: Death in early America. In *Studies in American Historical Demography,* ed. M. A. Vinovskis, pp. 181–210. New York: Academic Press. 530 pp.

Vinovskis, M. A. 1981a. *Fertility in Massachussets from the Revolution to the Civil War.* New York: Academic Press. 253 pp.

Vinovskis, M. A. 1981b. An "epidemic" of adolescent pregnancy? Some historical considerations. *J. Fam. Hist.* 6:205–30

Vinovskis, M. A. 1982. "Aged servants of the Lord": Changes in the status and treatment of elderly ministers in colonial America. In *Aging from Birth to Death: SocioTemporal Perspectives,* ed. M. W. Riley, R. P. Abeles, M. S. Teitelbaum, 2:105–38. Boulder, Colo: Westview. 228 pp.

Vinovskis, M. A. 1984. Historical perspectives on rural development and human fertility in nineteenth-century America. In *Rural Development and Human Fertility,* ed. W. A. Shutjer, C. S. Stokes, pp. 77–96. New York: Macmillan. 318 pp.

Vinovskis, M. A. 1986. Adolescent sexuality, pregnancy, and childbearing in early America: Some preliminary speculations. In *School-Age Pregnancy and Parenthood: Biosocial Dimensions,* ed. J. B. Lancaster, B. A. Hamburg, pp. 303–22. New York: Aldine. 403 pp.

Vinovskis, M. A. 1987. The historian and the life course: Reflections on recent approaches to the study of American family life in the past. In *Life-Span Development and Behavior,* vol. 8, ed. D. Featherman, R. Lerner. In press

Vinovskis, M. A., Bernard, R. M. 1978. Beyond Catherine Beecher: Female education in the antebellum period. *Signs* 3:856–69

Wachter, K. W., Hammel, E. A., Laslett, P. 1978. *Statistical Studies of Historical Social Structure.* New York: Academic Press. 229 pp.

Walsh, J. 1971. The Great Awakening in the First Congregational Church of Woodbury, Connecticut. *William Mary Q.* (3rd Ser.) 28:543–62

Wells, R. V. 1985. *Uncle Sam's Family: Issues in and Perspectives on American Demographic History.* Albany, NY: State Univ. New York Press. 184 pp.

Wells, R. V. 1982. *Revolution in Americans' Lives: A Demographic Perspective on the History of Americans, Their Families, and Their Society.* Westport, Lonni Greenwood. 311 pp.

Wells, R. V. 1975. Family history and demographic transitions. *J. Soc. Hist.* 9:1–20

Yasuba, Y. 1962. *Birth Rates of the White Population in the United States, 1800–1860: An Economic Study.* Baltimore: Johns Hopkins Univ. Press. 198 pp.

Ann. Rev. Sociol. 1987. 13:217–35

EVERYDAY LIFE SOCIOLOGY

Patricia A. Adler and Peter Adler

Department of Sociology, Washington University, St. Louis, Missouri 63130

Andrea Fontana

Department of Sociology, University of Nevada, Las Vegas, Nevada 89154

Abstract

Everyday life sociology comprises a broad spectrum of micro perspectives: symbolic interactionism, dramaturgy, phenomenology, ethnomethodology, and existential sociology. We discuss the underlying themes that bind these diverse subfields into a unified approach to the study of social interaction. We outline the historical development of everyday life sociology, indicating the individuals, ideas, and surrounding context that helped to shape this evolving theoretical movement. We then examine three contemporary developments in everyday life sociology that represent significant theoretical, substantive, and methodological advances: existential sociology, the sociology of emotions, and conversation analysis. Within these areas, we outline major themes, review recent literature, and evaluate their contribution to sociology. Everyday life sociology has had influence outside its arena, stimulating grand theorists to create various micro-macro syntheses. We consider these and their relation to the everyday life themes. We conclude by discussing the major critiques and assess the future promise and problems of this perspective.

INTRODUCTION

Any attempt to offer a brief but thorough outline of the focus and scope of everyday life sociology is difficult because of its diversity and the lack of systematic integration among its subfields. In fact, the sociology of everyday

217

0360-0572/87/0815-0217$02.00

life is an umbrella term encompassing several related but distinct theoretical perspectives: symbolic interactionism, dramaturgy, labeling theory, phenomenology, ethnomethodology, and existential sociology. The questions arise, then: Is everyday life sociology merely a collection of fragmented parts, arbitrarily referred to as a single perspective for the sake of maintaining proprietary interests? Is there anything that characterizes the everyday life perspective as a distinctive body of theory? We argue that everyday life sociology does represent a theoretical arena (although it is often associated with certain methods[1] and substantive interests) characterized by a climate of intellectual compatibility and eclectic synthesis among sociological thinkers using a micro perspective. Within this overarching approach, individual practitioners can seek relevance for their empirical findings by drawing on a variety of interrelated perspectives, incorporating ideas from diverse camps into their own theoretical formulations. The everyday life field has thus been one of evolving adaptation, with new subfields emerging out of ideas creatively drawn from both within and outside of micro sociology.

MAJOR TENETS OF EVERYDAY LIFE SOCIOLOGY

The Critique of Macro Sociology

A central impetus to the development of everyday life sociology was the growing dissatisfaction in mid-twentieth century American social thought with the approach contained in classical and contemporary macro theory. Both positivism and critical sociology were seen as overly deterministic in their portrayal of the individual in society: The actor was depicted as either a *tabula rasa,* internalizing the norms and values of society out of a desire for group membership, or as a *homo economicus,* developing social, political, and ideological characteristics as a result of his/her class membership. As a result, these traditional approaches generated an overly passive and constrained view of the actor. In its determinism, macro sociology also tended to be a monocausal gloss, failing to capture the complexity of the everyday world. Some of the early critiques of macro sociology from the everyday life perspective include Douglas (1970a), Filmer et al (1972), Lyman & Scott (1970), Psathas (1968, 1973), Tiryakian (1962, 1965, 1968), Wilson (1970), and Zimmerman & Wieder (1970).

Everyday life sociologists critiqued traditional sociology epistemologically for its "absolutist" stance toward studying natural phenomena (Douglas 1970a, 1976; Douglas & Johnson 1977; Feyerabend 1972; Johnson 1975;

---

[1]For a fuller discussion of the various epistemological stances associated with symbolic interactionism, ethnomethodology (with respect to ethnography), and existential sociology, see Adler & Adler (1987).

Kauffman 1944; Manning 1973; Mehan & Wood 1975; Phillips 1974). They rejected the premise of *subject-object dualism:* the belief that the subject (knower) and the object (known) can be effectively separated through scientific principles. Procedures such as the objectification, detachment, control, and manipulation of abstracted concepts and variables violate the integrity of the phenomena under study (Cicourel 1964; Douglas 1970a, 1976; Schutz 1962, 1964).

Contextuality

Everyday life sociologists sought to respect this integrity by studying people in their *natural context:* the everyday social world (Cicourel 1964; Denzin 1970; Douglas 1970a, 1976; Garfinkel 1967; J. Lofland 1971, 1976). This is the most fundamental and central emphasis of everyday life sociology. Naturally occurring interaction is the foundation of all understanding of society. Describing and analyzing the character and implications of everyday life interaction should thus serve as both the beginning and the end point of sociology. This includes the perceptions, feelings, and meanings members experience as well as the micro structure they create in the process.

Model of the Actor

Everyday life sociologists move from studying interaction and communication in two directions. First, they move inward, toward consciousness, deriving a model of the actor based on people's everyday life attitudes and behavior. This includes the interactionist view of the self, the ethnomethodological view of cognitive structure, and the existential view of brute being. To a degree, the relationship between consciousness and interaction is seen as reflexive: people are shaped or socialized by interaction as well as instrumental in shaping the character of interaction.

Social Structure

Second, they employ a view of social structure and social order that derives from interaction and is also characterized by a reciprocal relation to it. Social structure, organization, and order do not exist independent of the people that interact within them (Blumer 1969). Rather, they are endogenously constructed, or constituted, as people negotiate their way through interactions (Garfinkel 1967; Heritage 1984; Maines 1977, 1982; Strauss 1978). The rituals and institutions they thus create then influence the character of their behavior through the expectations and micro social norms they yield (Goffman 1967). Interaction is thus both voluntaristic and structured (but not completely determined) because of this reflexivity.

HISTORICAL DEVELOPMENT OF EVERYDAY LIFE SOCIOLOGY

The groundwork for the development of everyday life sociology was laid in the 1920s and 1930s in two philosophical traditions that established an ideological foundation and direction for micro sociological theory. At the University of Chicago, Mead was forging a pragmatic social behaviorism that would ultimately evolve into symbolic interactionism (Bulmer 1984, Rock 1979). In Germany, Husserl and Schutz were creating the emerging phenomenological perspective (Wagner 1983). During this era, however, phenomenology and social behaviorism were fairly disparate and isolated, with little reciprocal or combined influence.

By the 1950s and 1960s this isolation began to abate. Schutz came to the New School for Social Research where his influence spread among American scholars. Blumer moved from the University of Chicago to the University of California, Berkeley, and brought with him symbolic interactionism, his revision of Mead's behaviorism. Shortly thereafter he was joined by Goffman.

Blumer's interactionism (1969) took shape in California, where he incorporated Mead's conceptions of the rationally voluntaristic actor, reflexivity, and role-taking, with an emphasis on the way actors construct their worlds through subjective meanings and motivations. He therefore directed his students to look toward shared meanings established in social interaction and to explore various "meaning worlds" (J. Irwin, personal communication). His work was a critical impetus to the everyday life perspective in sociology.

Goffman's new subfield, dramaturgy, was launched with *The Presentation of Self in Everyday Life* (1959). Influenced by the works of Blumer, Burke, and Durkheim, Goffman offered an analysis of the individual in society which made the arena of interaction the locus of reality, of socialization, and of societal regeneration. Goffman's work speaks to both roles (the nature of the self) and rules (micro-social norms). Instead of role-taking for the purpose of cooperatively aligning their actions with others, Goffman's actors intentionally and manipulatively role-play for the purpose of managing others' impressions of them. This occurs through the interaction rituals of everyday life—rituals that shape the individual's inner self by externally imprinting their rules on him or her at the same time they ensure the self-regulatory character of society (Collins 1980, Fontana 1980, Lofland 1980, Vidich & Lyman 1985).

Garfinkel broadened the everyday life perspective with his *Studies in Ethnomethodology* (1967). Garfinkel's ethnomethodology addressed Parsons' grand questions about social order and social structure, using Schutz's (1962, 1964, 1966, 1967) hermeneutical perspective of the actor as a vocabulary for answering them. He directed practitioners to study the mundane routines of everyday life through which social order is created and maintained. He drew on Husserl (1970a, 1970b, 1973) to focus on the rationality and commonality within people that underlies the situational contextuality of behavior. Ethnomethodology thus differs from other everyday life sociology by being less interested in how situations are defined and how subjective meanings emerge.[2] It focuses, rather, on how people negotiate and apply rules which embody the social structure on an everyday level (Heritage 1984, Zimmerman & Wieder 1970).

The 1960s and 1970s brought a surge of sociological interest in phenomenology due to the English translation of Schutz's and Husserl's work. Sociologists applied these philosophical ideas to an empirical plane and evolved another everyday life perspective: phenomenological sociology.[3] Early works in this tradition include Berger & Luckmann (1967), Douglas (1970b), and Psathas (1973). The former tied phenomenology's emphasis on consciousness as the locus of reality to a social constructionist view of society. Douglas' edited volume contained seminal theoretical essays advancing, critiquing, and synthesizing the ethnomethodological, symbolic interactionist, and phenomenological/existential perspectives. This work was one of the first applications of the term "everyday life" to the new sociologies.[4] Psathas' book further discussed and empirically applied the phenomenological sociology perspective.

Everyday life sociology thus had its birth during these decades. It emerged in an atmosphere, especially in California, of eclectic synthesis and excitement about the creation and synthesis of new ideas (Manning 1973). Everyday life sociology was also nurtured and shaped by the surrounding background of California's secularism, heterogeneous beliefs, and pluralistic subcultures, fostering an atmosphere of innovation, divergence, and freedom (Vidich & Lyman 1985). From Berkeley, use of the everyday life perspective spread to the other sociology departments of the University of California system, where compatible thinkers were located. Unfortunately, this burgeoning perspective was somewhat marred by the in-fighting and drift which effectively prohibited "everyday life" from becoming the focal theme of these

[2]For a distinction between ethnomethodology and phenomenological sociology, see Rogers (1983) and Zimmerman (1979). For the difference between ethnomethodology and symbolic interactionism, see Gallant & Kleinman (1983) and Zimmerman & Wieder (1970). See Johnson (1977) for a contrast between ethnomethodology and existential sociology. Finally, Perinbanayagam (1974) contrasts ethnomethodology and dramaturgy.

[3]Zaner (1970) has suggested that we should speak of phenomenologically derived sociology rather than of phenomenological sociology, for the goals of phenomenology as a philosophy are different from those of its sociological derivatives.

[4]Douglas first used the term everyday life phenomena in his (1967) work, where he distinguished between "everyday" and "anyday" phenomena.

theorists. While a unified concept remained, no movement developed to press for the identification and recognition of all this work under the everyday life rubric. As a result, individual practitioners chose freely from among the various theories, used and combined them as they saw fit, and made their own decisions as to whether they wanted to affiliate themselves with the everyday life label.

The late 1970s and 1980s brought a new generation of everyday life sociologists. In this era, we have seen a continuation of both the unity and diversity of the everyday life perspective. On the one hand, there has been a growing awareness of the overarching everyday life label. More people identified their work with everyday life sociology, and a number of books appeared that addressed this theme. Morris (1977) produced a theoretical treatise offering comparisons, contrasts, critiques, and historical discussions of the various "creative," or everyday life perspectives. Mackie (1985) employed a phenomenological/existential perspective to analyze the drift of the modern everyday world and the individual's alienated role within it. Textbooks were offered by Douglas and his colleagues (1980), Weigert (1981), and Karp & Yoels (1986). A number of empirical works, drawn from the various subfields, all explored the problematic and mundane features of everyday life. Among these are L. Lofland (1973), Irwin (1977), Cohen & Taylor (1976), and the collected works found in Brissett & Edgley (1975), J. Lofland (1978), and Psathas (1973, 1979).

During this period the diversity of everyday life studies in sociology also continued in a variety of directions. For this forum we have selected three to explore more fully: existential sociology, the sociology of emotions, and conversation analysis. These three arenas represent the major successes of everyday life sociology that emerged from the churning dissension and consensus of the 1960s and 1970s. We have chosen them because they represent recent advances in, respectively, theoretical, substantive, and methdological arenas of everyday life sociology.

EXISTENTIAL SOCIOLOGY

Existential sociology is located within a philosophical tradition that dates back to the ancient Greek culture. Early Greek existentialists include both Thrasymachus, the sophist from Chalcedon who rejected Socrates' rational search for an understanding of human beings within the cosmos, and the god Dionysus, who represented the inner feelings and situated expressions of human beings, unbridled by any rational restrictions. More recently and directly, this tradition draws on the existential philosophy of Heidegger, Camus, Sartre, and Merleau-Ponty, the phenomenology of Husserl and Schutz, and the hermeneutics of Dilthey (Fontana 1980).

Existential sociology is the most recent of the everyday life theoretical perspectives. It shares with the others a common critique of the absolutist sociologies and an orientation toward the same set of focal concerns and beliefs. It goes beyond them in integrating subfields, combining them with a more complex, contradictory, and multidimensional view of the actor and the social world. Existential sociology also differs from other everyday life theories in its view of human beings as not merely rational or symbolic, or motivated by the desire to cooperate by interlinking actions. Instead, its proponents believe that people have strong elements of emotionality and irrationality, and that they often act on the basis of their feelings or moods. People are simultaneously determined and free, affected by structural constraints while remaining mutable, changeable, and emergent (see Zurcher 1977, for a fuller discussion of the relationship between social change and the existential self).

At the same time, existential sociologists view society as complex and pluralistic, divided by power struggles between different groups (see Douglas, 1971, for an existential analysis of American social order). Torn by the loyalties of their multiple memberships, people experience inner conflict. Since most groups in the society have things they want to hide from other groups, people present fronts to nonmembers. This creates two sets of realities about their activities: one presented to outsiders, the other reserved for insiders. Drawing on the perspectives of Goffman (1959) and Machiavelli (1532), existential sociologists also believe that people manage the impressions they present to others. Researchers, then, must penetrate these fronts to find out about human nature and human society (Adler & Adler 1987, Douglas 1976). The main theoretical works in this tradition include Lyman & Scott (1970), Manning (1973), Douglas & Johnson (1977), and Kotarba & Fontana (1984).

A number of empirical works illustrate the application and analytical value of this perspective. These works share a focus on individuals' search for meaning and self in an increasingly bureaucratized modern society. They also emphasize the importance of individuals' core feelings and emotions in guiding their perceptions, interpretations, and lives. *The Nude Beach,* by Douglas & Rasmussen (1977), offered a multi-perspective view of the complexity of feelings, motivations, rationalizations, behaviors, fronts, and micro and macro politics associated with public nudity and sexuality. In *Wheeling and Dealing,* P. A. Adler (1985) portrayed the greed and narcissism, rationality and irrationality, hedonism and materialism, secrecy and exhibitionism, and the alienation and involvement associated with the fast life of upper level drug dealers and smugglers. Kotarba's (1983) study, *Chronic Pain,* described the anxiety and uncertainty faced by chronic sufferers as they confront the futility of their search for solutions that will both alleviate their pain and provide viable meanings for their experience. *The Last Frontier,* by Fontana (1977), explored the emotional issues, loneliness, and existential identity changes that underlie and render insignificant the rational meaning of growing old. In P. Adler's (1981) book, *Momentum,* he analyzed the dynamics and self-reinforcing excitement and depression caused by momentum-infused individuals, groups, and masses. Last, a series of articles that address the existential self in society are noteworthy: Altheide (1984) on the aggrandized nature of the media self; Ferraro & Johnson (1984) on the victimized self of the organizational member, and Warren & Ponse (1977) on the stigmatized, conflictful, and dramaturgical nature of the gay self.

THE SOCIOLOGY OF EMOTIONS

For many years the topic of emotions was ignored or addressed only tangentially by sociologists. Recently, however, a newfound interest in the emotions has spawned a spate of articles, books, sessions, and a section of the American Sociological Association devoted to this substantive arena. Most of this interest has come from everyday life sociologists. Their perspective is well suited to generate understanding about emotions because sentiments occur within the interactional realm and its correlates: inward to the self and outward to what Maines (1982) has called the mesostructure. The recent literature on the sociology of emotions can be divided according to these two main themes.

Organistic/Voluntaristic

The first of these approaches focuses on the organic foundation of emotion. Emotions are considered to exist apart from and prior to introspection and are motored by instinct rather than by cognition. Social experiences trigger emotions that derive from inner sources. This is, thus, a conception of behavior which emphasizes individuals' inner-directed character. Its practitioners build from this base to show how individuals' emotions ultimately work upward to reconfirm, maintain, and change society and social structure (Franks 1985, Hochschild 1983).

Using an organic perspective, Kemper (1978) has emphasized how the power and/or status inherent in social relationships influence body chemistry. Scheff (1979) proposed a "need theory" of emotional catharsis where individuals undergo arousal, climax, and the resolution of feeling states through a biological reflex sequence. Hochschild's (1983) work on airline stewardesses has attempted to show that emotions are an organically based sixth sense that serve, as Freud (1923) first suggested, a critical signal function. The work of the existential sociologists (see Douglas 1977 and Johnson 1977 for their programmatic statements on emotions), too, falls into this approach, as they have ascribed a critical emotional dimension to the individual's inner "brute being." For them, feelings are not only independent of rational thought and values but ultimately dominate them.

Constructionist

The second everyday life approach to the study of emotions does not rule out a biological component but focuses instead on how these physiological processes are molded, structured, and given meaning. Emotions do not exist independent of everyday life experiences, they argue; rather, these experiences call out, modulate, shape, and ultimately create feelings. These are then labeled, assessed, and managed through and by interaction. Structural and cultural factors influence the feeling and interpretation of various emotions due to the way they constrain possibilities and frame situations (Franks 1985, Hochschild 1983).

Constructionist analysts include Goffman (1967), who discussed the link between situations and institutions and proposed that emotions are determined by the rules and micro acts that comprise situations. Hochschild (1979, 1983) discussed the types of "feeling rules" which are structurally mandated onto interactions and relationships through social guidelines. People then try to make their feelings coincide with these rules by doing cognitive, bodily, or expressive "emotions work." Emotion work can become commercialized when it is co-opted by business, leading to a "commoditization of feeling." Shott (1979) focused on role-taking emotions, suggesting that our empathy for the feelings of others is a mechanism ensuring the maintenance of social order and social control. Her discussion of the social processes common to diverse emotional experiences also accentuated structurally derived display rules. Gordon's (1981) approach to emotions focused on sentiments, learned in enduring social relationships, whose differentiation, socialization, management, and normative regulation are structurally dictated. Building on Hochschild, Heiss (1981) discussed "emotion rules" which are shaped through interaction by individuals' definitions of the situation, role-taking, self-concepts, and self-presentations, leading to the formation of "emotion roles" [i.e. Clark's discussion of sympathizers (1987)]. Averill (1980) proposed that during states of heightened emotional arousal we experience passivity and enact socially prescribed behavior. Zurcher (1982, 1985) and L. Lofland (1985) have suggested that emotions are scripted by structural and interactional contexts. Finally, Denzin (1984) has suggested that emotions are shaped through the direct experience of practical activities in the processes of the obdurate social world. In sum, understanding emotions enriches our perspective on the actor's voluntarism and illustrates further one means by which society motivates individuals to conform to its rules.

CONVERSATION ANALYSIS

Conversation analysis is a method of data gathering and analysis that is informed by the theoretical beliefs of ethnomethodology. Like other ethnomethodologists, conversation analysts have largely abandoned the earlier ethnomethodological concern with studying the contextual particularity of subjective meanings because endless indexicality refuted any intersubjectivity and became "a phenomenologically inspired but sociologically aimless empiricism" (Zimmerman 1979:384). Drawing on Parsons through Garfinkel and Durkheim through Goffman (Heritage 1985), conversation analysts have embraced a structural interest that makes them more closely aligned with and acceptable to the interests of positivist mainstream sociologists (see Boden 1986; Collins 1981a,b).[5]

Conversation analysts study language because they regard "natural language" as an everyday-life social system that is (a) external, existing prior to and independently of any speaker, and (b) constraining, obligatory rather than preferential in its framing. Natural language as a "mode of doing things" (Austin 1961, Wittgenstein 1953) is thus reviewed as an interactional object, a widespread, general, abstract system that is both immediate (situational) and transcendent (transsituational). As such, it exhibits the objective properties of a Durkheimian social fact (Zimmerman 1979).

Conversation analysts are concerned with both the competencies and the structure underlying ordinary, everyday social activities. They therefore study the production of natural language in situ, as it occurs spontaneously in the everyday world. They regard conversation as both context-shaped and context-renewing, influenced by and contributing to the context shaped by interaction. Disdaining "premature" theory construction, they have focused on tape recording minute, detailed "instances": the raw, primary data of actual conversation (Heritage 1984, 1985, Schegloff 1980, Schegloff & Sacks 1973).

In their studies, conversation analysts began by concentrating on action sequences of talk. An interest in turns-within-sequences developed out of the early work of Sacks et al (1974) on the management of conversational turn-taking. It was soon discovered that such structural analyses of talk served as a guideline for interpersonal interaction and its analysis.

Further conversation analysis has focused on a number of topics. First, Sacks, Schegloff, and others continued to investigate turn-taking, observing the recurrence of the question-response format they termed the "adjacency pair" (Schegloff 1968, Schegloff & Sacks 1973), "preference organization"

---

[5]Conversation analysis articles are increasingly beginning to appear in establishment journals, such as Maynard & Zimmerman (1984), Maynard (1985), and Molotch & Boden (1985).

(the tendency of respondents to select the preferred alternative) (Davidson 1984, Pomerantz 1984, Sacks & Schegloff 1979, Schegloff et al 1977, Wooton 1981), and "topic organization" (the continuation of conversation around the same topic) (Button & Casey 1984, Maynard 1980).

Second, conversation analysts have examined the use of non- or quasi-lexical speech objects such as laughter and head nods that show the listener's continuing participation in the interaction (C. Goodwin 1980; Jefferson 1979, 1984; Schegloff 1982).

A third area of inquiry has been the integration of vocal and nonvocal activities, such as gazing and body movements (C. Goodwin 1981; M. Goodwin 1980; Heath 1982a, 1984).

Last, a number of excellent studies have examined interaction in institutional settings. These works build on the foundation of knowledge about mundane conversations, seek variations from that structure, and attribute it to the institutional context. As such, this body of work represents a more contextual approach and moves away from pure empiricism toward the beginnings of theoretical development. Institutional settings that have yielded fruitful research include courts (Atkinson & Drew 1979, Dunstan 1980, Maynard 1984, Pomerantz & Atkinson 1984), classrooms (Cuff & Hustler 1982, Mehan 1979), and medical encounters (Heath 1981, 1982b; West 1983, 1984b, 1985). Several studies have also addressed the impact of gender on institutional interaction (French & French 1984, West 1984a).

While focused on naturally occurring, mundane communication observed in situ, conversation analysis diverges sharply in its orientation from the remaining corpus of everyday life sociology. It is more structural in interest and formal in analysis. Conversation analysis is also more objectively oriented, treating conversation as external to individuals, encouraging the replication and testing of its findings, and addressing the context of verification. In this way it departs from the customary hallmarks of everyday life sociology—subjectivity and discovery. Yet at the same time as it diverges, conversation analysis broadens the base of the everyday life perspective. Its radically micro and radically empiricist approach translates the product of interaction into a form that can be built upon by macro sociologists interested in an objective micro base for grand structural analysis (Collins 1981a, 1981b).

INFLUENCES ON MACRO THEORY

With the onslaught on macro theory by the early sociologies of everyday life, the schism between the macro and micro perspectives widened. Recently, however, in response to the challenges presented by everyday life sociologists, certain macro theorists have begun to incorporate some of the micro concepts discussed earlier. Prominent among these new "integrationists" have been several important neo-Marxists in Europe (especially the French everyday life sociologists, or *sociologiests de la vie quotidienne*), and in England and America, a small group of neofunctionalists and eclectic, synthetic thinkers. In attempting to bridge the micro-macro gap, these grand theorists have begun to integrate the diametrically opposed positions of absolutist and everyday life sociology (for a further discussion see Alexander et al 1987, Collins 1981a, Knorr-Cetina & Cicourel 1981).

One of the most significant concepts adapted from everyday life sociology is *voluntarism* and its related dimensions. These newer macro theorists, as Parsons once did, are recognizing the importance of the individual, or active agent, within the structure of society. While they view individuals as constrained by social structure, they of course recognize them as not determined by it. Their portrayals of social life and ultimately society thus incorporate an element of unpredictability (Alexander 1982, Bourdieu 1977, Collins 1975, Giddens 1979, 1984, Touraine 1984), a feature lacking in the Parsonian formulation. In addition, embedding voluntaristic action in structure leads to a view of society as both context-shaped and context-forming. This draws on the ethnomethodological concept that interactions are embedded in their context of occurrence while at the same time they reflexively constitute these contexts. It also uses the symbolic interactionist view that we live in a negotiated order and cause our subjective perceptions to become real by acting on their imagined consequences. Macro theorists have transformed this into a dialectical relationship between action and order: society both creates the historical, social, and cultural orientations that evoke behavior and at the same time serves as an agent of its own self-production (Alexander 1982, Bourdieu 1977, Giddens 1979, 1984, Lefebvre 1971, Touraine 1977).

Modern integrationist theorists also try to avoid totally objectivist approaches by incorporating an element of *subjectivism* from everyday life sociology. Rather than proposing models of generative mechanisms or deep structures invisible to the acting agents, they incorporate a view of the actor who understands and reflects upon his or her behavior as he/she is engaged in it (Collins 1975, 1981a; Giddens 1979, 1984).

Another departure from traditional macro sociology is the formulation of perspectives "propelled by a combination of theoretical and empirical argument" (Alexander 1982:30). Instead of merely looking to the idealistic logic of reason and philosophy for explanatory hypotheses, these new theorists are turning to the material reality of what Blumer (1969) has called the "obdurate" empirical world. This integrates an awareness of the everyday life actor's "natural attitude" (Schutz 1962) with the "theoretic stance" (Douglas 1970a) employed by the social science analyst. In this way irrational and emotional dimensions can be introduced into the overall perspective (Alexander 1982; Bourdieu 1977, 1984; Collins 1975, 1981a; Giddens 1979, 1984; Lefebvre 1971; Touraine 1977, 1984).

Finally, these theorists have looked to everyday life *interaction*, searching for a hidden unity beneath the surface. They have found everyday life to be organized, even repetitive, to the point of being ritualistic. Goffman's analysis of micro social norms, Garfinkel's discovery of the moral character undergirding the routines of everyday life interaction, and the conversation analytic view that natural language embodies the structural organization of social reality have been especially influential. The organized character of everyday life has been used in two ways: as a base for building an "aggregation" (Knorr-Cetina 1981) of micro interactions into a macro reality (Collins 1975, 1981b), and as a point of mediation between the individual and social structure so that the feedback at the interactional level leads to their reciprocal influence (Bourdieu 1977, Giddens 1984, Lefebvre 1971).

It is in these micro-macro syntheses that many of the most far-reaching theoretical advances of everyday life sociology can be found.

CRITIQUES AND ASSESSMENTS

The critiques of everyday life sociology are legion. Research guided by this perspective has been condemned as astructural or acontextual (Coser 1975, Gouldner 1970, Horowitz 1971, Reynolds & Reynolds 1973, Zeitlen 1973), incapable of addressing political factors (Gouldner 1970), ahistorical (Bernstein 1976, Gouldner 1970, Ropers 1973, Smith 1973, Zeitlen 1973), and generally trivial in its focus and findings (Coser 1975, Gellner 1975), to name the major ones.

While several of these critiques may have been accurate during the early years of the field, there have been movements in the last decade to address these criticisms. The area where the greatest advances have been made is structural analysis. Some practitioners have addressed the topics of social organization and social structure directly, theorizing about the macro implications of micro models of interaction and communication (Hall 1986; Maines 1977, 1982; Maynard & Wilson 1980; Schegloff 1987). Other everyday life sociologists have studied specific organizations or industries and written about their structural characteristics (Denzin 1977, Farberman 1975). Last, research into the structure and content of organizational culture has been fruitful (Fine 1984, Rohlen 1974, Schein 1983, Van Maanen 1973).

The political arena has also attracted increased attention from everyday life sociologists. Some researchers have addressed organizational or governmental power and politics (Clegg 1975; Hall 1972, 1985; Kinsey 1985; Klatch 1987; Molotch & Boden 1985), while others have focused on interpersonal political dimensions (Fisher & Todd 1983, Kramarae et al 1984), especially those related to gender politics (Thorne & Henley 1975, West 1979).

Everyday life sociology can still be considered largely ahistorical because of its emphasis on the contemporary. Some research is historically embedded though (Ball & Lilly 1982; Galliher & Walker 1977; Gusfield 1963, 1981), and the aggregation of micro interactions may build to an understanding of historicism (Collins 1981b).

Last, everyday life sociology may appear trivial to outsiders who are unfamiliar with the theoretical issues it addresses. The strength of everyday life sociology lies in generating sociological concepts or insights from seemingly trivial settings, such as the notion of idioculture from Little League baseball (Fine 1987), emotion work from airline stewardesses (Hochschild 1983), and lust and deceit from nude beaches (Douglas & Rasmussen 1977), and from the minutiae of everyday life, such as telephone openings (Schegloff 1979), interruptions (West & Zimmerman 1983), and gazing (C. Goodwin 1980). Beyond this, the study of everyday life lays a foundation for understanding the basis of social order, social action, and the social construction of reality (Collins 1981b).

FUTURE

Everyday life sociology is at a crossroads. It has a rich heritage of making valuable theoretical, epistemological, and substantive contributions to social science. It also has continuing potential to fill lacunae in empirical knowledge and conceptual understanding of the everyday world. It has a secure foothold in the discipline as an established alternative approach. Everyday life sociology is routinely published by university presses, its own journals, and to a lesser degree, by mainstream journals. Last, some of its subfields have lost their cultlike isolation and become increasingly integrated into the discipline.

Yet several dangers lie ahead. First, the field must continue to advance new perspectives on substantive, epistemological, and theoretical issues rather than merely applying existing ones. Second, with the imminent retirement of many of its founders, leadership must emerge from within its ranks. Third, there is a near absence of research centers with the critical mass of faculty necessary to train the next generation of everyday life sociologists. Without this regenerative capacity, everyday life sociology may have a limited future and faces a bankruptcy that threatens not only itself but the insight it brings to the entire discipline.

ACKNOWLEDGMENTS

We would like to thank Deirdre Boden, John Johnson, Ralph Turner, and an anonymous reviewer for their help in preparing this manuscript.

Literature Cited

Adler, P. 1981. *Momentum*. Beverly Hills, Calif: Sage

Adler, P. A. 1985. *Wheeling and Dealing*. New York: Columbia Univ. Press

Adler, P. A., Adler, P. 1987. *Membership Roles in Field Research*. Beverly Hills, Calif: Sage

Alexander, J. 1982. *Theoretical Logic in Sociology: Positivism, Presuppositions and Current Controversies*. Berkeley: Univ. Calif. Press

Alexander, J., Giesen, B., Munch, R., Smelser, N. 1987. *The Micro-Macro Link*. Berkeley: Univ. Calif. Press

Altheide, D. L. 1984. The media self. See Kotarba & Fontana 1984, pp. 177–95

Atkinson, J. M., Drew, P. 1979. *Order in Court*. London: Macmillan

Atkinson, J. M., Heritage, J. C., eds. 1984. *Structures of Social Action: Studies in Conversation Analysis*. Cambridge, Cambridge Univ. Press

Austin, J. L. 1961. *Philosophical Papers*. London: Oxford Univ. Press

Averill, J. R. 1980. A constructivist view of emotion. In *Emotion: Theory, Research, and Experience*, ed. R. Plutchik, H. Kellerman. V. I. New York: Academic Press

Ball, R. A., Lilly, J. R. 1982. The menace of margarine: The rise and fall of a social problem. *Soc. Probl.* 29:488–98

Berger, P., Luckmann, T. 1967. *The Social Construction of Reality*. New York: Doubleday

Bernstein, R. J. 1976. *The Restructuring of Political Theory*. New York: Harcourt Brace & Jovanovich

Blumer, H. 1969. *Symbolic Interactionism*. Englewood Cliffs, NJ: Prentice-Hall

Boden, D. 1986. Talking with doctors: Conversation analysis in action. *Cont. Sociol.* 15:715–18

Bourdieu, P. 1977. *Outline of a Theory of Practice*. Cambridge: Cambridge Univ. Press

Bourdieu, P. 1984. *Distinction*. London: Routledge & Kegan Paul

Brissett, D., Edgley, C., eds. 1975. *Life as Theater*. Chicago: Aldine

Bulmer, M. 1984. *The Chicago School of Sociology*. Chicago: Univ. Chicago Press

Button, G., Casey, N. 1984. Generating topic: The use of topic initial elicitors. See Atkinson & Heritage 1984, pp. 167–90

Cicourel, A. V. 1964. *Method and Measurement in Sociology*. New York: Free Press

Clark, C. 1987. Sympathy biography and sympathy margin. *Am. J. Sociol.* In press

Clegg, S. 1975. *Power, Rule and Domination: A Critical and Empirical Understanding of Power in Sociological Theory and Everyday Life*. London: Routledge & Kegan Paul

Cohen, S., Taylor, L. 1976. *Escape Attempts*. Harmondsworth, Eng: Penguin

Collins, R. 1975. *Conflict Sociology*. New York: Academic Press

Collins, R. 1980. Erving Goffman and the development of modern social theory. In *The View from Goffman*, ed. J. Ditton, pp. 170–210. London: Macmillan

Collins, R. 1981a. On the micro-foundations of macro-sociology. *Am. J. Sociol* 86:984–1015

Collins, R. 1981b. Micro-translation as a theory-building strategy. See Knorr-Cetina & Cicourel 1981, pp. 81–108

Coser, L. A. 1975. Two methods in search of a substance. *Am. Sociol. Rev.* 40:691–700

Cuff, E. C., Hustler, D. 1982. Stories and story-time in an infant classroom. *Semiotica* 42:119–54

Davidson, J. A. 1984. Subsequent versions of invitations, offers, requests, and proposals dealing with potential or actual rejection. See Atkinson & Heritage, 1984, pp. 102–28

Denzin, N. K. 1970. *The Research Act*. Chicago: Aldine

Denzin, N. K. 1977. Notes on the criminogenic hypothesis: A case study of the American liquor industry. *Am. Sociol. Rev.* 42:905–20

Denzin, N. K. 1984. *On Understanding Emotion*. San Francisco: Jossey-Bass

Douglas, J. D. 1967. *The Social Meanings of Suicide*. Princeton, NJ: Princeton Univ. Press

Douglas, J. D. 1970a. Understanding everyday life. See Douglas 1970b, pp. 3–44

Douglas, J. D., ed. 1970b. *Understanding Everyday Life*. Chicago: Aldine

Douglas, J. D. 1971. *American Social Order*. New York: Free Press

Douglas, J. D. 1976. *Investigative Social Research*. Beverly Hills, Calif: Sage

Douglas, J. D. 1977. Existential sociology. See Douglas & Johnson 1977, pp. 3–73

Douglas, J. D., Adler, P. A., Adler, P., Fontana, A., Freeman, C., Kotarba, J. 1980. *Introduction to the Sociologies of Everyday Life*. Boston: Allyn & Bacon

Douglas, J. D., Johnson, J. M., eds. 1977. *Existential Sociology*. New York: Cambridge Univ. Press

Douglas, J. D., Rasmussen, P. 1977. *The Nude Beach*. Beverly Hills, Calif: Sage

Dunstan, R. 1980. Contexts for coercion: Analyzing properties of courtroom questions. *Br. J. Law Society* 6:61–77

Farberman, H. A. 1975. A criminogenic market structure: The automotive industry. *Sociol. Q.* 16:438–57

Ferraro, K. J., Johnson, J. M. 1984. The victimized self: The case of battered women. See Kotarba & Fontana 1984, pp. 119–30

Feyerabend, P. F. 1972. *Against Method*. London: New Left Books

Filmer, P., Phillipson, M., Silverman, D., Walsh, D. 1972. *New Directions in Sociological Theory*. Cambridge, Mass: MIT Press

Fine, G. A. 1984. Negotiated orders and organizational cultures. *Ann. Rev. Sociol.* 10:239–62

Fine, G. A. 1987. *With the Boys*. Chicago: Univ. Chicago Press

Fisher, S., Todd, A. D., eds. 1983. *The Social Organization of Doctor-Patient Communication*. Washington, DC: Cent. Appl. Linguis.

Fontana, A. 1977. *The Last Frontier*. Beverly Hills, Calif: Sage

Fontana, A. 1980. Toward a complex universe: Existential sociology. See Douglas et al 1980, pp. 155–81

Franks, D. 1985. Introduction to the special issue on the sociology of emotions. *Symb. Interact*. 8:161–70

French, J., French, P. 1984. Gender imbalances in the primary classroom: An interactional account. *Educ. Res.* 26:127–36

Freud, S. 1923. *The Ego and the Id*. London: Hogarth

Gallant, M. J., Kleinman, S. 1983. Symbolic interactionism vs. ethnomethodology. *Symb. Interact.* 6:1–18

Galliher, J. F., Walker, A. 1977. The puzzle of the social origins of The Marijuana Tax Act of 1937. *Soc. Probl.* 24:267–76

Garfinkel, H. 1967. *Studies in Ethnomethodology*. Englewood Cliffs, NJ: Prentice-Hall

Gellner, E. 1975. Ethnomethodology: The reenchantment industry of the California way of subjectivity. *Phil. Soc. Sci.* 5:431–50

Giddens, A. 1979. *Central Problems in Social Theory: Action, Structure and Construction in Social Analysis*. Berkeley: Univ. Calif. Press

Giddens, A. 1984. *The Constitution of Society*. Berkeley: Univ. Calif. Press

Goffman, E. 1959. *The Presentation of Self in Everyday Life*. New York: Doubleday Anchor

Goffman, E. 1967. *Interaction Ritual*. New York: Doubleday Anchor

Goodwin, C. 1980. Restarts, pauses and the achievement of mutual gaze at turn beginning. *Sociol. Inq.* 50:272–302

Goodwin, C. 1981. *Conversational Organization: Interaction between Speakers and Hearers*. New York: Academic Press

Goodwin, M. H. 1980. Some aspects of processes of mutual monitoring implicated in the production of description sequences. *Sociol. Inq.* 50:303–17

Gordon, S. L. 1981. The sociology of sentiments and emotions. In *Social Psychology*, ed. M. Rosenberg, R. H. Turner, pp. 562–92. New York: Basic Books

Gouldner, A. 1970. *The Coming Crisis of Western Sociology*. New York: Basic Books

Gusfield, J. 1963. *Symbolic Crusade*. Urbana, Ill: Univ. Ill. Press

Gusfield, J. 1981. *The Culture of Public Problems*. Chicago: Univ. Chicago Press

Hall, P. M. 1972. A symbolic interactionist analysis of politics. *Sociol. Inq.* 42:35–75

Hall, P. M. 1985. Asymmetric relationships and processes of power. In *Foundations of Interpretive Sociology*, ed. H. Farberman, R. Perinbanayagam, pp. 309–44. Greenwich, Conn: JAI Press

Hall, P. M. 1986. *Interactionism and the study of social organization*. Presented at Ann. Meet. Midwest Sociol. Society, Des Moines, Iowa

Heath, C. C. 1981. The opening sequence in doctor-patient interaction. In *Medical Work: Realities and Routines*, ed. P. Atkinson, C. C. Heath, pp. 71–90. Farnborough, Eng: Gower

Heath, C. C. 1982a. The display of recipiency: An instance of a sequential relationship between speech and body movements. *Semiotica* 42:147–67

Heath, C. C. 1982b. Preserving the consultation: Medical record cards and professional conduct. *J. Sociol. Health Illness* 4:56–74

Heath, C. C. 1984. Talk and recipiency: Sequential organization in speech and body movement. See Atkinson & Heritage 1984, pp. 247–65

Heiss, J. 1981. *The Social Psychology of Interaction*. Englewood Cliffs, NJ: Prentice-Hall

Heritage, J. C. 1984. *Garfinkel and Ethnomethodology*. Cambridge, Eng: Polity

Heritage, J. C. 1985. Recent developments in conversation analysis. *Sociolinguistics* XV:1–18

Hochschild, A. R. 1979. Emotion work, feeling rules and social structure. *Am. J. Sociol.* 85:551–75

Hochschild, A. R. 1983. *The Managed Heart*. Berkeley: Univ. Calif. Press

Horowitz, I. L. 1971. Review of Howard S. Becker's sociological work: Methods and substance. *Am. Sociol. Rev.* 36:527–28

Husserl, E. 1970a. *Logical Investigations*. New York: Humanities Press

Husserl, E. 1970b. *The Crisis of European Sciences and Transcendental Phenomenology: An Introduction to Phenomenological Philosophy*. Evanston, Ill: Northwestern Univ. Press

Husserl, E. 1973. *Experience and Judgment*. Evanston, Ill: Northwestern Univ. Press

Irwin, J. 1977. *Scenes*. Beverly Hills, Calif: Sage

Jefferson, G. 1979. A technique for inviting laughter and its subsequent acceptance/declination. See Psathas 1979, pp. 79–96

Jefferson, G. 1984. On stepwise transition

from talk about a trouble to inappropriately next-positioned matters. See Atkinson & Heritage 1984, pp. 1919–222

Johnson, J. M. 1975. *Doing Field Research*. New York: Free Press

Johnson, J. M. 1977. Ethnomethodology and existential sociology. See Douglas & Johnson 1977, pp. 153–73

Karp, D., Yoels, W. 1986. *Sociology and Everyday Life*. Itasca, Ill: Peacock

Kauffman, F. 1944. *Methodology of the Social Sciences*. New York: Humanities

Kemper, T. D. 1978. *A Social Interactional Theory of Emotions*. New York: Wiley

Kinsey, B. 1985. Congressional staff: The cultivation and maintenance of personal networks in an insecure work environment. *Urban Life* 13:395–422

Klatch, R. 1987. *Women of the New Right*. Philadelphia: Temple Univ. Press

Knorr-Cetina, K. 1981. The microsociological challenge of macro-sociology: Towards a reconstruction of social theory and methodology. See Knorr-Cetina & Cicourel 1981, pp. 1–47

Knorr-Cetina K., Cicourel, A. eds. 1981. *Advances in Social Theory and Methodology*. London: Routledge & Kegan Paul

Kotarba, J. A. 1983. *Chronic Pain*. Beverly Hills, Calif: Sage

Kotarba, J. A., Fontana, A., eds, 1984. *The Existential Self in Society*. Chicago: Univ. Chicago Press

Kramarae, C., Schulz, M., O'Barr, W., eds., 1984. *Language and Power*. Beverly Hills, Calif: Sage

Lefebvre, H. 1971. *Everyday Life in the Modern World*. London: Penguin

Lofland, J. 1971. *Analyzing Social Settings*. Belmont, Calif: Wadsworth

Lofland, J. 1976. *Doing Social Life*. New York: Wiley

Lofland, J., ed., 1978. *Interaction in Everyday Life*. Beverly Hills, Calif: Sage

Lofland, J. 1980. Early Goffman: Style, structure, substance, soul. In *The View from Goffman*, ed. J. Ditton pp. 24–51. London: Macmillan

Lofland, L. H. 1973. *A World of Strangers*. New York: Basic

Lofland, L. H. 1985. The social shaping of emotion: The case of grief. *Symb. Interact.* 8:171–90

Lyman, S. M., Scott, M. B. 1970. *A Sociology of the Absurd*. New York: Appleton

Machiavelli, N. [1532] 1970. *The Prince*. New York: Wash. Square

Mackie, F. 1985. *The Status of Everyday Life*. London: Routledge & Kegan Paul

Maines, D. R. 1977. Social organization and social structure in symbolic interactionist thought. *Ann. Rev. Sociol.* 3:75–95

Maines, D. R. 1982. In search of mesostructure. *Urban Life* 11:267–79

Manning, P. K. 1973. Existential sociology. *Sociol. Q.* 14:200–25

Maynard, D. W. 1980. Placement of topic changes in conversation. *Semiotica* 30:263–290

Maynard, D. W. 1984. *Inside Plea Bargaining*. New York: Plenum

Maynard, D. W. 1985. Social conflict among children. *Am. Sociol. Rev.* 50:207–23

Maynard, D. W., Wilson, T. P. 1980. On the reification of social structure. In *Current Perspectives in Social Theory*, ed. S. G. McNall, G. N. Howe, 1:287–322. Greenwich, Conn.: JAI Press

Maynard, D. W., Zimmerman, D. H. 1984. Topical talk, ritual and the social organization of relationships. *Soc. Psych. Q.* 47: 301–16

Mehan, H. 1979. *Learning Lessons*. Cambridge, Mass: Harvard Univ. Press

Mehan, H., Wood, H. 1975. *The Reality of Ethnomethodology*. New York: Wiley

Molotch, H. L., Boden, D. 1985. Talking social structure: Discourse, domination, and the Watergate hearings. *Am. Sociol. Rev.* 50:273–88

Morris, M. B. 1977. *An Excursus into Creative Sociology*. New York: Columbia Univ. Press

Perinbanayagam, R. 1974. The definition of the situation and an analysis of the ethnomethodological and dramaturgical view. *Sociol. Q.* 15:521–42

Phillips, D. 1974. Epistemology and the sociology of knowledge. *Theory and Society* 1:59–88

Pomerantz, A. M. 1984. Pursuing a response. See Atkinson & Heritage 1984, pp. 152–63

Pomerantz, A. M., Atkinson, J. M. 1984. Ethnomethodology, conversation analysis and the study of courtroom instruction. In *Topics in Psychology and Law*, ed. D. J. Muller, D. E. Blackman, A. J. Chapman, pp. 283–94. Chichester, Eng: Wiley

Psathas, G. 1968. Ethnomethods and phenomenology. *Soc. Res.* 35:500–20

Psathas, G., ed. 1973. *Phenomenological Sociology*. New York: Wiley

Psathas, G., ed. 1979. *Everyday Language: Studies in Ethnomethodology*. New York: Irvington Press

Reynolds, L., Reynolds, J. 1973. Interactionism, complicity and the astructural bias. *Catalyst* 7:76–85

Rock, P. 1979. *The Making of Symbolic Interactionism*. Totowa, NJ: Rowman & Littlefield

Rogers, M. F. 1983. *Sociology, Ethnomethodology and Experience*. New York: Cambridge Univ. Press

Rohlen, T. 1974. *For Harmony and Strength: Japanese White-Collar Organization in Anthropological Perspective*. Berkeley: Univ. Calif. Press

Ropers, R. 1973. Mead, Marx and social psychology. *Catalyst* 7:42–61

Sacks, H., Schegloff, E. A. 1979. Two preferences in the organization of reference in conversation and their interaction. See Psathas 1979, pp. 15–21

Sacks, H., Schegloff, E. A., Jefferson, G. 1974. A simplest systematics for the organization of turn-taking for conversation. *Language* 50:696–735

Scheff, T. 1979. *Catharsis in Healing, Ritual and Drama.* Berkeley: Univ. Calif. Press

Schegloff, E. A. 1968. Sequencing in conversational openings. *Am. Anthropol.* 70:1075–95

Schegloff, E. A. 1979. Identification and recognition in telephone openings. See Psathas 1979, pp. 23–78

Schegloff, E. A. 1980. Preliminaries to preliminaries: Can I ask you a question? *Sociol. Inq.* 50:104–52

Schegloff, E. A. 1982. Discourse as an interactional achievement: Some uses of "uh-huh" and other things that come between sentences. *Georgetown Univ. Roundtable on Language and Linguistics,* pp. 71–93. Washington, DC: Georgetown Univ. Press

Schegloff, E. A. 1987. Between macro and micro: Contexts and other connections. See Alexander et al 1987. In press

Schegloff, E. A., Jefferson, G., Sacks, H. 1977. The preference for self-correction in the organization of repair in conversation. *Language* 53:361–82

Schegloff, E. A., Sacks, H. 1973. Opening up closings. *Semiotica* 7:289–327

Schein, E. 1983. The role of the founder in creating organizational culture. *Organ. Dynam.* 12:5–23

Schutz, A. 1962. *Collected Papers I: The Problem of Social Reality.* The Hague: Martinus Nijhoff

Schutz, A. 1964. *Collected Papers II: Studies in Social Theory.* The Hague: Martinus Nijhoff

Schutz, A. 1966. *Collected Papers III: Studies in Phenomenological Philosophy.* The Hague: Martinus Nijhoff

Schutz, A. 1967. *The Phenomenology of the Social World.* Evanston, Ill: Northwestern Univ. Press

Shott, S. 1979. Emotion and social life: A symbolic interactionist analysis. *Am. J. Sociol.* 81:1265–86

Smith, D. L. 1973. Symbolic interactionism: Definitions of the situation from H. Becker and J. Lofland. *Catalyst* 7:62–75

Smith, R. W. 1984. An existential view of organizations: Is the member condemned to be free? See Kotarba & Fontana 1984, pp. 100–18

Strauss, A. 1978. *Negotiations.* San Francisco: Jossey-Bass

Thorne, B., Henley, N. eds. 1975. *Language and Sex: Difference and Dominance.* Rowley, Mass: Newbury House

Tiryakian, E. 1962. *Existentialism and Sociologism.* Englewood Cliffs, N.J.:Prentice-Hall

Tiryakian, E. 1965. Existential phenomenology and sociology. *Am. Sociol. Rev.* 30:647–88

Tiryakian, E. 1968. The existential self and the person. In *The Self in Social Interaction,* ed. K. J. Gergen, C. Gordon, pp. 75–86. New York: Wiley

Touraine, A. 1977. *The Self-Production of Society.* Chicago: Univ. Chicago Press

Touraine, A. 1984. *Le Retour de l'Acteur: Essai de Sociologie.* Paris: Fayard

Van Maanen, J. 1973. Observations on the making of policemen *Hum. Organ.* 32:407–18

Vidich, A., Lyman, S. M. 1985. *American Sociology.* New Haven: Yale Univ. Press

Wagner, H. 1983. *Alfred Schutz: An Intellectual Biography.* Chicago: Univ. Chicago Press

Warren, C. A. B., Ponse, B. 1977. The existential self in the gay world. See Douglas & Johnson, pp. 273–89

Weigert, A. J. 1981. *Sociology of Everyday Life.* New York: Longman

West, C. 1979. Against our will: Male interruptions of females in cross-sex conversation. In *Language, Sex and Gender,* M. K. Slater, L. L. Adler, pp. 81–97. New York: Ann. New York Acad. Sci.

West, C. 1983. Ask me no questions . . . an analysis of queries and replies in physician-patient dialogues. See Fisher & Todd 1983, pp. 75–106

West, C. 1984a. When the doctor is a "lady": Power, status, and gender in physician-patient encounters. *Symb. Interact.* 7:87–106

West, C. 1984b. Medical misfires: Mishearings, misgivings and misunderstandings in physician-patient dialogues. *Discourse Processes* 7:107–34

West, C. 1985. *Routine Complications.* Bloomington, Ind: Indiana Univ. Press

West, C., Zimmerman, D. H. 1983. Small insults: A study of interruptions in cross-sex conversations between unacquainted persons. In *Language, Gender and Society,* ed. B. Thorne, C. Kramarae, N. Henley, pp. 102–17. Rowley, Mass: Newbury House

Wilson, T. P. 1970. Normative and interpretive paradigms in sociology. See Douglas 1970, pp. 57–79

Wittgenstein, L. 1953. *Philosophical Investigations.* London: Basil Blackwell.

Wooton, A. 1981. The management of grantings and rejections by parents in request sequences. *Semiotica* 37:59–89

Zaner, R. 1970. *The Way of Phenomenology.* New York: Pegasus

Zeitlen, I. M. 1973. *Rethinking Sociology.* New York: Appleton-Century-Crofts

Zimmerman, D. W. 1979. Ethnomethodology. In *Theoretical Perspectives in Sociology,* ed. S. G. McNall, pp. 381–96. New York: St. Martins

Zimmerman, D. W., Wieder, D. L. 1970. Ethnomethodology and the problem of order: Comment on Denzin. See Douglas 1970, pp. 285–98

Zurcher, L. A. 1977. *The Mutable Self.* Beverly Hills, Calif: Sage

Zurcher, L. A. 1982. The staging of emotions: A dramaturgical analysis. *Symb. Interact.* 5:1–22

Zurcher, L. A. 1985. The war game: Organizational scripting and the expression of emotion. *Symb. Interact.* 8:191–206

Ann. Rev. Immunol. 1987. 5:237–57

PARENTHOOD AND PSYCHOLOGICAL WELL-BEING

Sara McLanahan and Julia Adams

Department of Sociology, 1180 Observatory Drive, University of Wisconsin, Madison, Wisconsin 53706

Abstract

Recent studies suggest that parenthood may have negative consequences for the psychological well-being of adults. Adults with children at home report that they are less happy and less satisfied with their lives than other groups. They also appear to worry more and to experience higher levels of anxiety and depression. The overall difference between parents and nonparents appears to be small, although it has increased during the past two decades. Differences between parents and nonparents stem from economic and time constraints, which in turn arise from general social trends such as the increase in women's labor force participation and the increase in marital disruption and single parenthood. We expect these trends to continue in the near future, reducing the desire for children and increasing gender conflict over the division of parental obligations. Parental strain might be alleviated by some form of state-supported childcare or child allowance.

INTRODUCTION

The research on the psychological consequences of parenthood is of interest to the broader community of sociologists for a number of reasons. First, the finding that parents are less well off than nonparents is inconsistent with some theories about sources of social identity and self image. The parental role serves a function—societal reproduction—that is putatively of great value. How can we reconcile the fact that parenthood, a highly valued social position, is associated with lower levels of psychological well-being? Further,

237

0360-0572/87/0815-0237$02.00

theorists have argued that multiple role identities form the basis for more positive self images. Is the parent role somehow different? How does this alter our understanding of the construction of social identity?

Second, the subjective effects of being a parent have implications for the current debate among demographers over recent trends in fertility: will fertility in fact level off in the near future or continue to decline. While researchers agree that the economic value of children has decreased during the past century, some have argued that this decline is offset by the social rewards that accrue to those who abide by pronatalist norms. If the subjective benefits of parenthood are also declining, does this suggest that normative pressures are no longer powerful enough to counteract perceived economic costs? Will this have an impact on fertility trends?

Finally, the studies described below are relevant to our understanding of gender relations and the struggle over gender inequality. Feminist scholars have long argued that the mother/housewife role, at least as it is currently structured, is a fundamental element in women's oppression inasmuch as it underpins women's economic dependence on men. The research on the psychological consequences of motherhood provides empirical evidence that there are psychic as well as economic costs associated with motherhood and that these costs are related to the unequal division of responsibility for children.

We begin this review by discussing the social trends that have occurred during the past century that we believe are directly related to changes in the experience of parenthood. Next we examine the empirical literature on the psychological effects of children, including studies of happiness and satisfaction as well as studies of anxiety and depression. We also look at research that asks adults about the costs and benefits of children and the overall consequences of parenthood. In the final section, we speculate on what all this means for future fertility and gender relations, and how changes in social policy might alter current trends.

TRENDS AFFECTING THE EXPERIENCE OF PARENTHOOD

During this century, a number of changes have occurred in the social organization of society and in the behavior of individuals that have had a profound effect on the meaning and experience of parenthood. These include the decline in the economic value of children, the increase in women's labor force participation, and the increase in marital instability and single parent families. We are especially interested in changes during the past 30 years, the period during which the empirical research on parenthood and psychological well-being has been carried out. These changes can provide important clues to our understanding of the specific forces underlying recent declines in parents' well-being, and they can help us determine whether current trends will continue in their present direction or reverse.

The first change affecting the experience of parenthood is the decline in the economic value of children. Whereas at one time children were clearly an economic asset to their parents—both as children who contributed to the family income and as adults who provided care for elderly parents—their value as sources of economic support has eroded during the twentieth century. Initially, the decline was due to the passage during the early 1900s of child labor laws which transformed children from producers into dependents. The passage of the Social Security Act in 1935 further reduced their value by providing parents with old age pensions. Most recently, a series of amendments between 1965 and 1972 approximately doubled the real value of benefits to the elderly, making older parents even less dependent on their children for economic support.[1]

A second major trend affecting parenthood is the growth of women's labor force participation. Labor force participation increased gradually for all new cohorts of women since the early 1900s and grew markedly for married women with children during the 1960s and 1970s. Whereas in 1950 only 24% of married women were in the labor force, by 1980 over 50% were working. For mothers with young children the change was even more dramatic. Of mothers with children under six, 12% were employed in 1950 as compared with 45% in 1980 (England & Farkas 1986). The increase in women's labor force participation had several consequences for the family roles of men and women, and these were especially acute for women. First, the trend reflected the growing independence of women and, in particular, the increase in opportunities outside the housewife/mother role. Increases in employment opportunities mean increases in opportunity costs for women who choose not to work in the paid labor force. These costs are greatest for women with a college education, which suggests that parenthood may be viewed more negatively by adults with college degrees. In addition to opportunity costs, the increase in women's employment has caused conflict over the traditional gender-based division of labor, especially among parents. At present, working mothers appear to bear a greater burden than fathers or nonworking mothers, in that they work about 5–15 hours more per week (market work plus housework) than other parents (Vanek 1974, Cain 1984). We should note that the increase in wives' employment during the 1970s was partly in response to a decline in husbands' income, suggesting that wives' working may be associated with greater economic strain as well as greater marital conflict.

[1]For discussions of the changing value of children see Bumpass 1985, Butz & Ward 1979, Huber 1980, Ryder 1979, Westoff 1978.

The increase in marital instability is the third trend. The divorce rate increased steadily over most of the twentieth century and accelerated in the 1960s and 1970s. By the 1980s, one out of two couples who married was expected to divorce. The increase in marital disruption has altered the experience of parenthood in several ways (Cherlin 1981). It has led to the formation of single parent families, which are subject to numerous forms of economic and psychological stress (Garfinkel & McLanahan 1986), and to the creation of noncustodial parents, whose contact with their children is often irregular and unrewarding (Furstenberg et al 1983). Increases in divorce have led to increases in remarriage, which means that a larger proportion of families include stepparents as well as stepchildren. Although remarriage generally reduces the economic problems of single parent families, parent-child relationships in such families are often difficult (Cherlin 1978). Given the increase in nontraditional families, we would expect parents to experience more psychological distress today than they did in the fifties when family relationships were more stable and less complex.

A final factor that is relevant to interpreting the relationship between parenthood and psychological well-being is the decline in the importance of the parent role as a central focus of identity. Although one might argue that changes in attitudes about parenthood simply reflect the rising opportunity costs of raising children, they also play an independent role in lowering the relative well-being of parents vis-à-vis nonparents. First, they affect the selection into the nonparent category. The relaxation of norms against voluntary childlessness means that a greater proportion of those in the nonparent status are there by virtue of their own choice (Veevers 1980). Today the childless category is made up of a large number of adults who either have a strong preference against parenthood or a preference for some other activity that interferes with parenthood. Because of greater selectivity, we would expect these adults to be more satisfied with their status and more satisfied with their lives in general than were childless adults in the fifties. Second, changes in parental norms should affect the willingness of adults to admit to negative feelings about their own children and about parenthood in general. To the extent that normative constraints have led to an overvaluation of children in the past, a shift in norms will deflate these evaluations. If this holds true, an increase in negative perceptions will reflect a change in response bias rather than a change in the experience of parenthood.[2]

---

[2]We do not believe that changes in attitudes about parenthood can account for all of the change in well-being. First, response bias might account for observed changes in perceptions of children, but it is unlikely to explain changes in direct measures of well-being and distress, e.g. happiness, anxiety. Changes in selectivity are also unlikely to account for all of the decline in parents' well-being since the increase in voluntary childlessness is a fairly recent phenomenon and could not account for dissatisfaction or unhappiness among older cohorts of parents.

PARENTHOOD AND SUBJECTIVE WELL-BEING

Three areas of research are pertinent to the question of whether parenthood enhances or reduces subjective well-being: the research on happiness and quality of life, the research on psychological distress, and studies of adults' perceptions of children. In the first two areas respondents' well-being is measured directly, and comparisons are made to determine whether parents are psychologically better off (or worse off) than nonparents. In the research on perceptions of children, respondents are asked about their overall evaluations of parenthood and about the specific costs and benefits of children.

The major dependent variables in the quality of life research are global indicators of well-being, such as satisfaction with life, happiness, and worries, and domain-specific indicators, such as marital happiness, satisfaction with friends, etc. According to Campbell et al (1976), questions on satisfaction tend to evoke a cognitive judgment based on external standards, whereas questions about happiness or worries tend to pinpoint an absolute emotional state. It is arguable that satisfaction questions serve as more cumulative measures, asking respondents to reflect on their past experiences, whereas the questions about worries and happiness focus on the present and are more sensitive to current stress.

The two most commonly used constructs in the psychological distress research are depression and anxiety, the former being measured by a set of questions about feelings and perceptions of the self (e.g. the Center for Epidemiological Studies Depression Scale (CES-D), Radloff 1975) and the latter by questions about psycho-physiological symptoms such as a fast heartbeat, loss of appetite, or nervous stomach—e.g. the Gurin Psychological Symptoms (PPS) scale, Gurin et al 1960.[3] A few researchers have examined both well-being and distress (Alwin et al 1984, Gurin et al 1960, Veroff et al 1981), but most have concentrated exclusively on one or the other of the constructs. In fact, researchers who study well-being rarely cite the work of those who study distress.

The Quality of Life

The research on the quality of life has focused on variation in parents' well-being over the life course and on specific transitions, such as the birth of the first child and the departure from home of the last child. Generally, parenthood is broken down into multiple categories that represent distinct phases in the family life cycle and are intended to capture the context in which parenthood is experienced. Life cycle categories typically consist of a period

---

[3]Neither of these measures claims to make clinical diagnoses, but both have been shown to distinguish between healthy and nonhealthy persons in the general population.

without children, a period with preschool children, a period with school age children, and an "empty nest" stage, after the children have grown and gone.

Many researchers have commented on the apparent U-shaped curve in marital well-being that is associated with the sequence of life cycle stages for couples who become parents (Aldous 1978, Figley 1973, Rollins & Cannon 1974, Rollins & Feldman 1970). These authors claim that marital satisfaction drops with the advent of the first child, continues to decline up to the first child's adolescence, and then begins to increase as the children leave the home. Some have found that this life cycle variation is especially strong for wives (Rollins & Feldman 1970).

These studies have been criticized on several grounds. First, there is some disagreement as to the prevalence of the U-shaped pattern and how it should be interpreted. Spanier et al (1975), for example, have argued that the patterns are evident for working-class but not for middle-class respondents.[4] Second, some researchers have contended that the life cycle approach has no noticeable advantage over the use of separate variables to measure each stage (Menaghan 1982, Nock 1979, Spanier et al 1979, Spanier & Lewis, 1980). They conclude that it is more useful to examine the effects of the presence and age of children independent of the effects of age of respondent, duration of marriage, etc.

In addition to the cross-sectional studies described above, a few researchers have looked at particular transitions such as the birth of a child (generally the first birth) and the departure of the last child (which marks the beginning of the "empty nest" phase of the family life cycle).[5]

Much of the work in this area has shown that the quality of married life declines after the birth of the first child (Belsky 1985, Miller & Sollie 1980, Russell 1974, Waldron & Routh 1981). Recently, however, these results have been challenged by researchers who argue that the effects of duration of marriage have been confounded with births of children. White & Booth (1985) report that marital quality declines sharply during the first few years of marriage, for nonparents as well as for parents, and that this decline has often been attributed to the transition to parenthood. Studies of the transition to the "empty nest" are less common than studies of the first birth, but again the evidence available suggests that the departure from home of the last child has

---

[4]Rollins & Galligan (1978) try to explain this discrepancy by arguing that only families with few resources would be affected by high-demand family stages, but others have objected to this line of reasoning. For example, Oppenheimer's (1982) description of the life cycle squeeze on economic resources applies to middle-class as well as working-class families.

[5]Note that some studies are described as "transition studies" when in fact they are based on cross-sectional data. (See for example Harkins 1978.) In this review, however, we use the term transition to refer specifically to studies of changes in well-being over time.

very little effect on the psychological well-being of the parents (Menaghan 1982, Mullan 1981, Pearlin & Lieberman 1979).[6]

Many of the studies described above are based on small and nonrepresentative samples of married couples taken for the explicit purpose of studying marital quality and family relationships. Moreover, at least in the early work, statistical analyses tended to be rather crude.[7] A second group of studies based on data from large national surveys has extended this research in several ways: by including nonmarried as well as married respondents in the samples, by using multivariate models that control for exogenous variables, and by attempting to explain the conditions under which parenthood is associated with lower levels of well-being (Alwin et al 1984; Andrews & Withey 1976; Bradburn 1969; Campbell et al 1976; Glenn & McLanahan 1981, 1982; Glenn & Weaver 1978, 1979; Marini 1980; McLanahan & Adams 1984, 1985).[8]

This second group of studies finds that parents with children at home are psychologically less well off than nonparents on a wide range of indicators. Parents report less satisfaction with their lives and with other domains, such as friends, marriage, and health. They are also less happy and appear to worry more than adults without children. The overall contrast between parents and nonparents appears to be small, with the greatest differences appearing for marital happiness and worries. [Several researchers have reported no differences between parents and nonparents, or at least no difference on some indicators of well-being (Alwin et al 1984, Andrews & Withey 1976, Marini 1980, McLanahan & Adams 1984), but no one has found that parents are better off than nonparents on any of the conventional measures of well-being.] Some researchers have found that mothers, especially those with young children, are less happy and less satisfied than other groups (Campbell 1976, Glenn & Weaver 1978, Glenn & McLanahan 1982, Hoffmann & Manis 1978), whereas others report no gender differences (McLanahan & Adams 1985). At least one study has looked at race and found that the effects of children on marital happiness are similar for blacks and whites (Glenn & McLanahan 1982).[9]

---

[6]Mullan found that parental distress declined after the children had been gone for a while, whereas marital well-being showed no improvement. Menaghan found that the transition to the empty nest was associated with a small positive shift in feelings of marital equity but had no impact on another indicator of marital quality. Finally, Pearlin & Lieberman reported that parents showed no change in psychological distress as a result of their children leaving home. All of these analyses were based on the same data, but the researchers used different indicators of well-being.

[7]The studies by Pearlin & Lieberman, Mullan & Menaghan are exceptions. For more information on this point, see the review by Hicks & Platt (1970).

[8]Andrews & Withey, Bradburn & Campbell et al generally look at bivariate relationships, but they meet the other two criteria for inclusion in the second group of studies.

The later studies are consistent with the earlier research in showing that parents with children living at home are neither as happy nor as satisfied with their lives as other groups (Glenn & McLanahan 1981, McLanahan & Adams 1985). There is mixed evidence on whether the absolute number of children is important,[10] and disagreement regarding whether spacing and density of offspring affect well-being.[11] Overall, the presence of children appears to be more consistently important than either number, spacing, or gender of child (Polit 1982).[12]

In addition to specifying family structure characteristics, several studies have looked at how marital status, women's employment, and socioeconomic status moderate the consequences of children. Not surprisingly, those that examine marital status have found that single parents (nonmarried adults living with children) report more worries and less happiness than other groups (Alwin et al 1984, Andrews & Withey 1976, Glenn & Weaver 1979, McLanahan & Adams 1984). Furthermore, divorced fathers—both those who are currently divorced and those who have remarried—appear to worry more and to be less satisfied with themselves than other groups (McLanahan & Adams, 1985).

The consequences of children are also related to whether or not the mother works outside the home. McLanahan & Adams (1985) found that employed mothers with young children worried much more than employed women without children. This does not mean that working itself has negative consequences. In fact, working appears to increase the psychological well-being of women. Rather, mothers do not obtain the psychological benefits from

---

[9]See Reskin & Coverman (1985) for conflicting results. They find that the effects of children on psychological distress are less negative for blacks.

[10]There is particular contention over the issue of the impact of the number of children on marital satisfaction or happiness. Some studies have indicated that marital happiness declines as number of children increases (Campbell et al 1976, Glenn & McLanahan 1982, Miller 1975), whereas other researchers have found no effect (Marini 1980, Polonko et al 1982, Renne 1970). Finally, Abbott & Brody (1985) suggest that there is an interaction of number and gender of children, arguing that the lower marital adjustment of wives with children is accounted for by the problems of those women with preschool children and/or more than one male child.

[11]Again, the issue of marital well-being serves as an exemplar. Most argue that these variables are not important (Figley 1973, Marini 1980, Miller 1975), but Rollins & Galligan (1978) attribute the absence of findings to a failure to include desire for children as an intervening variable.

[12]We should note that the relative well-being of parents in the empty nest stage may have as much to do with the fact that their children are now managing their own lives, for the most part successfully, as it has to do with the stabilization of the household. American parents are made to feel responsible for how their children "turn out," and yet they have few indicators as to how they are doing as parents. Once children are on their own, parents are better able to evaluate their past efforts and to feel greater satisfaction with themselves.

employment that accrue to fathers and to women without children.[13] Perceived economic strain also appears to be an important factor in accounting for the lower levels of well-being among men as well as women (Bradburn 1969, Campbell et al 1976), but education does not (Glenn & McLanahan 1982).

Since most of the empirical research on the effects of parenthood is based on data collected in the late sixties and seventies, the question arises as to whether or not the relative disadvantage of parents who are living with children is a fairly recent phenomenon or whether it has existed for some time. As noted above, single parenthood detracts from the well-being of mothers, whereas working enhances the well-being of women without children relative to that of mothers. Since both single parenthood and working wives have become more common in recent years, we would expect parents, and especially mothers, to have become relatively less well off than they were previously.

The two "Americans View Their Mental Health" surveys provide information on the contrast between parents and nonparents at two time periods: 1957 and 1976. Analyses based on these data indicate that parents with children at home worried more and were less happy with their marriages in the seventies (relative to nonparents) than in the fifties (McLanahan & Adams 1984, Veroff et al 1981).[14] They also show a relative decline in the satisfaction of parents in the empty nest stage. The latter finding may be due to the increase in the economic and social independence of the older cohorts and to the decline in the need for children as a source of support.

Parenthood and Psychological Distress

Most of the early research on psychological distress emerges from the debate over the importance of the housewife role in explaining gender differences in the mental health of married men and women. This debate was initiated by Bernard (1972) and Gove (1972), and followed up by Gove & Tudor (1973). Bernard's widely influential work argued that housekeeping has a "pathogenic" effect on wives. According to Gove, keeping house is unstructured and may lead to perceptions of poor performance. Moreover, housewives have

---

[13]Wright (1978) found no significant differences in happiness or life satisfaction between housewives and women who work outside the home. However, his data exclude working women with preschool children, nonwhite women, students, and retired, disabled, and nonmarried women. Wright controls only for whether the woman's spouse was employed in blue- or white-collar work, and he does not examine the general impact of parenthood or number of children on his general measures of well-being.

[14]We should note that marital happiness increased absolutely for both groups between 1957 and 1976, which is what one would have expected, given the greater freedom to divorce.

fewer sources of gratification than husbands. Married men have both a family role and an employment role. When things go badly in one domain (the family), they may compensate by investing more heavily in the other role (career). Housewives have no such alternative, Gove argued, and therefore they are more vulnerable to the problems associated with family life.[15]

This description of the housewife role and its implications for mental health stimulated a large body of research during the seventies, most of which was designed to test hypotheses about the nature of the role and whether women's employment would reduce gender differences in mental health. The overall findings have been mixed. Some researchers found that employment reduced depression, although not as much for women as for men (Gove & Geerken 1977, Radloff 1975). Other researchers reported no differences between employed and nonemployed women (Pearlin 1974). Although Pearlin found no direct relationship between employment and depression, he did find that women who were disaffected with the homemaker role were more likely to be depressed than other women. This experience was further differentiated by class. For middle-class women, the meaning of their job was the main factor in predicting disaffection—career-oriented women felt torn between two sets of ambitions. For working-class women, family demands were the most important factor.

Strictly speaking, motherhood is not a necessary component of the home-maker role. In the process of specifying the latter, however, researchers incorporated parental status into their models, and thus the literature on gender differences in psychological distress provides information on the relationship between parenthood and mental health. All of the studies discussed above found that parents experienced more depression and anxiety than adults without children. Pearlin (1974) found that maternal responsibilities, measured by number of children at home and age of youngest child, were major factors in determining disaffection with the maternal role, which in turn increased depression for women. Others found that parenthood increased depression for fathers as well as mothers (Gove & Geerken 1977, Radloff 1974). Gove & Geerken also looked at the effects of family size and age of children on parents' feelings about (a) experiencing too many demands from others, (b) needing to be alone, and (c) loneliness. For men, the presence of children increased perceived demands, whereas for women, the number and ages of children increased perceived demands and also increased the desire to be alone.[16]

---

[15]Gove also noted that even when married women work, they usually have badly paid jobs and very often carry the burden of two jobs: homemaker and worker. Moreover, they are apt to view their careers as contingent on their husband's career—or family goals—rather than in terms of their own needs.

[16]Gove and Geerken's study did not show parenthood to be related to loneliness.

A problem with these studies is that couples with children at home are compared to other married couples, including parents in the empty nest stage as well as adults who never had children. Thus, it is difficult to determine whether the negative effects of living with children arise from the comparison with empty nest parents or the comparison with childless couples. Only in Radloff's study can we distinguish between the three groups, and her results indicate that it is the empty nest parents rather than the childless couples who are less depressed than parents with children at home. When empty nest parents were compared with childless couples of similar age, Radloff found that the former were slightly less depressed, although the difference was not statistically significant.

Since the late seventies, researchers have expanded their focus to include nonmarried adults as well as married couples. The issue of women's waged work continues to be a major concern, but the questions posed are somewhat different. Whereas early studies concentrated on married women and whether employment reduces the stress associated with the homemaker role, recent studies have focused on employment in general and have examined whether women with children garner the same benefits from work as childless women. As with the quality of life research, the later work on distress is based on more sophisticated methodologies and more complex models.

The recent work is less conclusive than the early studies with respect to the effect of children on psychological distress, and especially with respect to depression. Gore & Mangione (1983) found that having children at home increased the anxiety of married women but did not affect depression. Cleary & Mechanic (1983) also found that parenthood was not related to depression, except among employed mothers.

At least two researchers have reported that parents are better off than childless adults. Kandel and her colleagues (1985) found that parenthood reduced the incidence of depression in women, and Aneshensel et al (1981) reported similar results for men as well as women. The latter two studies defined parenthood as having ever had children rather than as living with children, and therefore their comparisons were between parents and childless adults. Although they did not test for within-group differences, their results indicate that parents with children at home were not as well off as parents whose children were grown.[17] Thus, the main reason for the contradictory findings in these studies may be the difference in comparison groups.

The most consistent finding in this research is that single mothers are much more distressed than other groups. Pearlin noted this in the early seventies, as did Brown & Harris (1978). It has since been verified by numerous other researchers (Alwin et al 1984, Aneshenshel et al 1981, Guttentag et al 1980,

---

[17]Kandel, for example, reported that the bivariate relationship between number of children at home and depression was positive.

Kandel et al 1985). Kandel et al who found that parenthood reduced depression, also reported that nonmarried mothers were more depressed than other groups.

In addition to qualifying our thinking about the overall effects of children, the more recent reseach has contributed to our understanding of the mechanisms by which children increase distress. Ross & Huber (1985) found that having children at home leads to economic strain, which in turn increases depression for men as well as women. They also found that after controlling for economic strain, children actually increased well-being for women. Ross & Huber note that direct and indirect effects may cancel one another out, which could explain why some studies find no relationship between children and women's depression. The weight of economic strain in parents' well-being supports Campbell & Bradburn's similar findings in the quality of life literature.

Finally, the research on distress has extended our knowledge about the interaction of employment and parental status. As noted above, those who followed up on Bernard and Gove found that working reduced mothers' distress, but not enough to close the gap with men. It now appears that employment has positive effects for women without children and under certain conditions for women with children. At least two studies have shown that employment has a positive effect for married women if their husbands help with childcare and housework (Kessler & McRae 1982, Ross et al 1983). Ross et al found that the benefits of work depended on the couple's preferences about whether the wife should work. If they preferred a "traditional" division of labor, working had no psychological benefits for the wife.[18]

Several generalizations can be drawn from the studies reviewed in the previous two sections. First, the presence of children appears to be associated with lower levels of happiness and satisfaction and with higher levels of psychological distress for both women and men. There is some evidence that effects of parenthood are more negative for women. The differences between parents and nonparents are small although they appear to have increased since the late 1950s.

Second, single mothers are clearly worse off than other groups. Third, parents whose children have grown and left home (empty nest parents) are no different than adults of similar age who have never had children. Fourth, working outside the home improves the psychological well-being of women without children, and it improves the well-being of mothers *if* husbands help with childcare and *if* both partners approve of her dual role as homemaker and

---

[18]Ross et al combine housework and childcare into one measure of domestic work, whereas Kessler & McRae look at the two types of help separately. The latter find that help with childcare is more important than help with housework.

breadwinner. Finally, perceptions of economic strain and personal demands are important factors in accounting for the negative psychological effects of children.

Parents' Perceptions of Children

The findings described above are based on studies that examine the correlation between parental status (the independent variable) and psychological well-being (the dependent variable). A second major approach to determining the consequences of parenthood studies parents' perceptions of children: This approach questions respondents about the costs and benefits of children or asks them to evaluate how children alter the lives of adults.

Not surprisingly, parents appear to have more positive perceptions of children than do nonparents. Moreover, parents' responses vary over the life course (Blake & del Pinal 1981, McLanahan & Adams 1985, Veroff et al 1981). Looking just at parents, Veroff and his colleagues found that younger couples were less positive and viewed parenthood as more restrictive than couples over 50. These results were confirmed by McLanahan & Adams (1985), who distinguished between parents with children at home and empty nest parents, controlling for age.

Veroff et al (1981) also found that mothers were slightly less positive than fathers in their evaluations of children and reported more parental problems as well. Tolerance (patience) was the major concern of mothers whereas fathers were more bothered by financial problems. The finding that mothers' perceptions were less positive than fathers should be qualified, however, Hoffman & Manis (1978) found that the former reported more parental satisfaction than the latter, and Campbell et al (1976) found no gender differences in parental satisfaction.

In her extensive review of the research on parental satisfaction, Goetting (1986) suggests that such inconsistent results reflect the multidimensional and gender-specific nature of the construct: Motherhood brings both greater role fulfillment and more restrictions than fatherhood. This argument is tacitly supported by Veroff et al (1981) in their investigation of the salience of parenthood. When asked about fulfillment associated with the parent role, mothers were more likely than fathers to say that parenthood gave them a great deal of fulfillment. Blake & del Pinal also found that women were more likely to view children as a "social investment."

Women's perceptions also vary according to whether or not they work outside the home (or plan to work) and whether they see parenthood as entailing conventionally structured gender roles. (Blake & del Pinal 1981). Blake & del Pinal found that women who were currently employed, part- or full-time, were twice as likely as homemakers to say that the costs of children outweighed the benefits. Similarly, women who believed that men were unlikely to share in housework and childcare were much more likely to emphasize the direct costs of children: being tied down, being subject to burdensome demands, and having difficulty organizing one's time. These findings dovetail nicely with what we have learned about the joint effect of employment and motherhood.

Several studies show that being divorced has negative consequences for adults' perceptions of children, at least among women. Blake & del Pinal found that divorced women were much more likely than married women to say that the costs of children exceeded the benefits, whereas divorced men were more sanguine than their married counterparts. According to Veroff et al, single mothers reported the most problems of all subgroups and reported economic problems twice as often as married men. Overall, however, their evaluations were no less positive than those of married women, and they viewed children as no more restrictive. The latter study also found that divorced fathers had unusually positive perceptions. Evaluations were about 1.5 times as positive as those of other parents, and they reported fewer restrictions and problems. The discrepancy between the rosy perceptions of divorced fathers and their experience of living apart from their children may account in part for this group's extremely low levels of subjective well-being (McLanahan & Adams 1984).

The research on perceptions of children shows that women who do not graduate from high school are more likely to report that the benefits of children outweight the costs than are women with a high school or college degree. Blake & del Pinal (1981) found that women with limited schooling were more likely to view children as a social and financial investment, especially compared to women who had attended college. Veroff and his colleagues (1981) also reported that mothers with only a high school education were more likely than other groups to say that parenthood gave them a great deal of fulfillment.

The fact that women with less education have more positive views about children than women with college degrees is consistent with the argument that groups with fewer social and economic alternatives will value children more highly (Hoffman et al 1978). It is also consistent with the argument that the opportunity costs of children are lower for women with only a high school education. Ironically, these are the women whom we might expect to experience the greatest economic strain.

Finally, parental satisfaction appears to have declined over time. Veroff et al's bivariate analysis indicated that parents in 1976 felt significantly less positive about parenthood than they did in 1957. These results were confirmed by McLanahan & Adams (1984), who found that the variation among parents was consistent with the trends in the well-being indicators: The relative decline in perceptions of children was greater for parents with children at home than for parents whose children were grown and gone.

Explanations for Why Children Are Stressful

The quality of life literature tends to be atheoretical, with researchers concentrating primarily on describing the effects of children on different indicators of well-being for different subgroups of adults. The studies of psychological distress, on the other hand, contain a variety of explanations for why parenthood has negative consequences. This research traces variations in individuals' subjective well-being to variations and changes in the linked roles that compose institutions. Two major perspectives inform this research: One holds that by accumulating roles, individuals gain sources of identity and self-esteem, and one argues that multiple roles are potentially incompatible, and that role incompatibilities may undermine psychological well-being. In this section, we clarify the arguments underlying this research and evaluate them in light of the empirical evidence.

The first perspective holds that individuals who take on additional roles are accumulating further bases on which to build identity and self-esteem (Marks 1977).[19] If an individual with multiple roles finds that one ceases to be gratifying, it is argued, she or he can draw on other roles for support. If someone has few roles, and things are going badly in one domain, there are no alternative sources of esteem. This view predicts that parents have higher well-being than nonparents and that employed parents are better off than childless workers. It also predicts that the well-being of women in particular, should have improved over time. This framework is implicitly adopted by Gove (1972), who states that the parental role is negative for women because it limits access to other roles.[20]

The empirical evidence does not support the simple "role accumulation" argument. Nearly all of the research suggests that parenthood does not increase psychological well-being or self-satisfaction. Moreover, it appears that motherhood and paid employment do not mix well for women (Ryder 1979), insofar as occupying or managing both roles offers women no additional subjective benefits over occupying one or the other. One might point out that employment enhances the well-being of fathers and that marriage enhances the well-being of mothers. However, the additional benefits deriv-

---

[19]In a sophisticated example of this approach, Thoits (1983) argues that there is a curvilinear relationship between the numeric accumulation of roles and psychological well-being.

[20]Similarly, Brown & Harris (1978) emphasize that having a limited number of roles restricts access to social support, which has both preventive and curative functions in maintaining mental health.

ing from these roles would appear to result more from their association with success in the parent role than from their provision of additional sources of identity. The only evidence that parents are psychologically better off than nonparents comes from two studies of depression whose findings are not statistically significant (Aneshensel et al 1981, Kandel et al 1985).[21]

The second predominant explanation argues that individuals may experience strain, and a consequent drop in subjective well-being, by trying to link incompatible roles (Goode 1960). "Role strain" actually contains two concepts, role overload and role conflict, not systematically separated by Goode (Sieber 1974). Role overload denotes problems generated by accumulating too many roles, given time constraints. The overload hypothesis states that effects will be most negative when the ratio of demands to resources is highest. The hypothesis incorporates role characteristics that result in financial or emotional demands into a more general model that includes the availability of resources.[22] The parent role should prove burdensome for those with too much other work and too few resources to meet its demands. Role conflict, on the other hand, refers to discordant expectations that exist irrespective of time pressures. The conflict hypothesis states that problems arise when an individual fills two roles that have conflicting expectations, or when individuals disagree over the expectations of a particular role. The concept was adopted by Bernard (1972) and Pearlin (1975) as the basis for an explanation of the impact of women's experience of competing commitments to work and home. It also applies to situations in which couples disagree over spousal roles, such as whether wives should work outside the home or how housework should be divided.

The empirical findings discussed above are more consistent with the role strain than the role accumulation perspective, and in particular are consistent with the role overload hypothesis. The ratio of demands to resources is highest for parents with young children, parents with large numbers of children, single parents, and low-income working mothers, all of whom report higher levels of distress and lower levels of well-being. Moreover, the central role of economic strain and demands in accounting for parental stress has been documented directly by several researchers (Cleary & Mechanic 1983, Gove & Geerken 1977, McLanahan & Adams 1985, Ross & Huber 1985). McLanahan & Adams also show that the drop over time in mothers' relative well-being can be explained by increases in single parenthood and employment.

---

[21]The Aneshensel study finds no significant difference for parental status, and the Kandel study does not test for whether parents are less depressed than nonparents.

[22]In this way it is similar to the notion of the family "life cycle squeeze" discussed by Oppenheimer (1982).

Role conflict may also be a factor in accounting for parental distress, but the evidence suggests that this is more important for middle-class women than for working-class women. Pearlin's work shows that middle-class mothers are more likely to feel torn between two careers, whereas working-class mothers are more likely to feel overloaded. Additional evidence for the role conflict argument comes from the research on married couples which shows that both partners are less depressed when husbands help with housework and childcare (Kessler & McRae 1982, Ross et al 1984). Although some might argue that the wife is better off because she has less work (the overload hypothesis), husband's help may also be symptomatic of his acceptance of her dual role.[23]

Two key objections exist to the role-theoretic analytical perspective in which much of the distress literature is couched. First, the framework is theoretically weak. The relationship between concepts and indicators is not always adequately specified. A single empirical phenomenon, such as the impact of husbands' housework on wives' depression described above, can be used to substantiate different causal arguments. More fundamentally, sociologists working within this tradition conceptualize the individual as an assortment of roles, and they ignore the rigidity or flexibility of role allocation and differences in the degree of internalization of different roles. As Turner has noted, when a role is deeply merged with the person, socialization in that role structures the individual's personality. The differences in the degree to which role and person are merged should have a profound effect on the adoption and performance of other roles, and on responses to role strain and role conflict (Turner 1978).

Second, the role perspective fails to situate in a broader social-structural context its arguments about the individuals who manage or occupy various roles. The research on parenthood and psychological well-being suggests that the higher levels of stress reported by parents stem from the more general social trends that were discussed in the section on Trends Affecting the Experience of Parenthood. All of the studies indicate that single mothers experience more psychological distress than other groups, and at least one study has shown that the increase in single motherhood can account for a substantial part of the increase in mothers' distress between 1957 and 1976. Evidence also suggests that the subjective well-being of divorced fathers has deteriorated more than other groups. Thus, the increase in marital disruption and in numbers of families headed by women arguably has played a significant role in undermining parental well-being during the past 30 years.

In addition, the change in women's labor force participation has been critical in the relative decline in mothers' subjective well-being. Women are

---

[23]Since the amount of housework husbands do is very small, the symbolic interpretation may be more accurate than the overload explanation (England & Farkas 1986).

much more likely to be employed today than they were in the past, and working has substantial psychological benefits for women without children. Working mothers, on the other hand, do not receive equivalent benefits from work, and therefore their well-being has declined relative to that of non-mothers. Mothers clearly face a dilemma: If they work, they reduce their opportunity costs, but they simultaneously increase the demands on their time.

These patterns testify to the causal links between macro-structural developments and parents' well-being. Researchers using concepts from role theory to assess parents' subjective well-being, and hypothesizing role overload and conflict, should situate their arguments within the ambit of more general patterns of social change.

IMPLICATIONS AND CONCLUSIONS

To date, researchers have concentrated on documenting the impact of parental roles on psychological well-being of parents and their perceptions of children. They will also need to chart the reciprocal influence of these effects on individuals' actions. There are at least two key areas which are closely related to parental status and which should be foci of further research: namely, gender relations and fertility behavior. With respect to gender relations, we expect a continuation of the struggle over the division of domestic responsibilities and, among divorced parents, over the division of financial responsibilies as well. The flow of women into the labor market during the past two decades has meant a decline in the time available for childcare, and we expect that couples will continue to contest the division of parental responsibilies. Husbands will resist in part because of self interest and in part because norms are slow to change, even in the face of changing circumstances. Moreover, although some husbands are assuming a greater share of household responsibilities, it is doubtful that a satisfactory resolution to this struggle can be obtained simply through a readjustment of gender roles on an individual or couple basis, given the time demands on two working parents.

With respect to fertility, we expect that childless adults, or couples that have not reached their desired fertility, will anticipate the problems partially captured in the concept of role strain and therefore have fewer children. This means simply that negative perceptions regarding the psychological costs of children will have a feedback effect on the more general decline in fertility that has been occurring throughout the twentieth century. This effect should be especially great among couples with higher levels of education for whom the perceived costs of parenthood may appear greater than the benefits. Changes in gender roles might mitigate perceptions of costs among women. However, such a shift would place a greater burden on men, which might reduce their desire for children. Conflicting preferences generally lead to lower fertility (Thomson et al 1984).

Many of the problems associated with parenthood result from a lack of family resources (time and money), and these problems are amenable to public solutions. Numerous other industrialized countries have a child allowance and/or some form of subsidized childcare, and some support exists for such policies in this country, especially for the latter (Kamerman & Kahn 1978). Public solutions would reduce economic strain for both men and women and would have a beneficial effect on their mental health. They should also increase fertility by removing some of the disincentives to rearing children. The consequences for gender relations would probably not be unequivocal and would depend on the precise nature of state policies. A child allowance, for example, has no direct implications for the sexual division of labor and might actually buttress traditional gender roles in the household. State-supported childcare, on the other hand, is more likely to free women from traditional role obligations and to reduce their economic dependence on men.

Literature Cited

Abbott, D. A., Brody, G. H. 1985. The relation of child age, gender, and number of children to the marital adjustment of wives. *J. Marriage Fam.* 47:77–84

Aldous, J. 1978. *Family Careers: Developmental Change in Families.* New York: Wiley

Alwin, D. F., Converse, P. E., Martin, S. S. 1984. *Living arrangements, social integration and psychological well-being.* Presented at Ann. Meet. Midwest Sociol. Assoc. Chicago, Ill.

Andrews, F. M., Withey, S. B. 1976. *Social Indicators of Well-being: Americans' Perceptions of Life Quality.* New York: Plenum

Aneshensel, C. S., Frerichs, R. R., Clark, V. A. 1981. Family roles and sex differences in depression. *J. Health Soc. Behav.* 22:379–93

Belsky, J., Lang, M. E., Rovine, M. 1985. Stability and change in marriage across the transition to parenthood. *J. Marriage Fam.* 27:855–67

Bernard, J. 1972. *The Future of Marriage.* New York: World

Blake, J., del Pinal, J. H. 1981. The childlessness option: Recent American views of nonparenthood. In *Predicting Fertility: Demographic Studies of Birth Expectations,* ed. G. E. Hendershot, P. J. Placek, pp. 235–61. Lexington, Mass: Lexington

Booth, A., Johnson, R., White, L., Edwards, J. N. 1984. Women, outside employment, and marital instability. *Am. J. Sociol.* 90:567–83

Bradburn, N. 1969. *The Structure of Psychological Well-Being.* Chicago: Aldine

Brown, G. W., Harris, T. 1978. *Social Origins of Depression.* New York: Free Press

Bumpass, L. 1985. *Marriage and childbearing "after" the demographic transition.* Paper for Pop. Stud. Cent. 25th Reunion Symp.

Butz, W. P., Ward, M. P. 1979. Will US fertility remain low? A new economic interpretation. *Pop. Dev. Rev.* 5:663–88

Cain, G. 1984. *Women and Work: Trends in Time Spent in Housework. Inst. Res. Poverty Discuss. Pap.* 747–84. Univ. Wisc. Madison

Campbell, A. 1981. *The Sense of Well-Being in America.* New York: McGraw-Hill

Campbell, A., Converse, P. E., Rogers, W. L. 1976. *The Quality of American Life.* New York: Russell Sage

Cherlin, A. 1978. Remarriage as an incomplete institution. *Am. J. Sociol.* 84:634–50

Cherlin, A. 1981. *Marriage, Divorce and Remarriage.* Cambridge: Harvard Univ. Press

Cleary, P. D., Mechanic, D. 1983. Sex differences in psychological distress among married people. *J. Health Soc. Behav.* 24:111–21

England, P., Farkas, G. 1986. *Households,*

256   McLANAHAN & ADAMS

Employment, and Gender. New York: Aldine

Figley, C. R. 1973. Child density and the marital relationship. *J. Marriage Fam.* 35:272–82

Furstenberg, F. F. Jr., Nord, C. W., Patterson, J. L., Zill, N. 1983. The life course of children of divorce: Marital disruption and parental contact. *Am. Sociol. Rev.* 48:656–68

Garfinkel, I., McLanahan, S. 1986. *Single Mothers and Their Children: A New American Dilemma.* Washington, DC: Urban Inst.

Glenn, N. D., McLanahan, S. 1981. The effects of children on the psychological well-being of older adults. *J. Marriage Fam.* 43:409–21

Glenn, N. D., McLanahan, S. 1982. Children and marital happiness: A further specification of the relationship. *J. Marriage Fam.* 44:63–72

Glenn, N. D., Weaver, C. N. 1978. A multivariate, multisurvey study of marital happiness. *J. Marriage Fam.* 40:269–81

Glenn, N. D., Weaver, C. N. 1979. A note on family situation and global happiness. *Soc. Forc.* 57:269–82

Goetting, A. 1986. Parental satisfaction: A review of research. *J. Fam. Iss.* 7:83–109

Goode, W. 1960. A theory of role strain. *Am. Sociol. Rev.* 25:483–96

Gore, S., Mangione, T. 1983. Social roles, sex roles and psychological distress: Additive and interactive models of sex differences. *J. Health Soc. Behav.* 24:300–13

Gove, W. R. 1972. The relationship between sex roles, marital status, and mental illness. *Soc. Forc.* 51:34–44

Gove, W. R., Geerken, M. R. 1977. The effect of children and employment on the mental health of married men and women. *Soc. Forc.* 56:66–76

Gove, W. R., Hughes, M., Style, C. 1983. Does marriage have positive effects on the psychological wellbeing of the individual?" *J. Health Soc. Behav.* 24:122–31

Gove, W. R., Tudor, J. F. 1973. Adult sex roles and mental illness. *Am. J. Sociol.* 98:812–35

Gurin, G., Veroff, J., Field, S. C. 1960. *Americans View Their Mental Health.* New York: Basic Books

Guttentag, M., Salasin, S., Belle, D. 1980. *The Mental Health of Women.* New York: Academic Press

Harkins, E. B. 1978. Effects of empty nest transition on self-report of psychological and physical well-being. *J. Marriage Fam.* 40:549–56

Hicks, M., Platt, M. 1970. Marital happiness and stability: A review of the research in the sixties. *J. Marriage Fam.* 32:553–74

Hoffman, L. W., Manis, J. B. 1978. Influences of children on marital interaction and parental satisfactions and dissatisfactions. In *Child Influences on Marital and Family Interaction,* ed. R. M. Lerner, G. B. Spanier, pp. 165–214. New York: Academic Press

Hoffman, L. W., Thornton, A., Manis, J. B. 1978. The value of children to parents in the United States. *J. Pop.* 1:91–131

Huber, J. 1980. Will US fertiity decline toward zero? *Sociol. Q.* 21:481–92

Kamerman, S., Kahn, A., eds. 1978. *Family Policy.* New York: Columbia Univ. Press

Kandel, D. B., Davies, M., Raveis, V. H. 1985. The stressfulness of daily social roles for women. *J. Health Soc. Behav.* 26:64–78

Kessler, R., McRae, J. Jr. 1981. Trends in sex and psychological distress. *Am. Sociol. Rev.* 46:443–52

Kessler, R., McRae, J. Jr. 1982. The effects of wives' employment on the mental health of married men and women. *Am. Sociol. Rev.* 47:216–27

McLanahan, S., Adams, J. 1984. *The changing effect of children on subjective well-being.* Univ. Wisc.-Madison Center Demogr. Ecol. Work. Pap. 84–16

McLanahan, S., Adams, J. 1985. *Explaining the decline in parents' psychological well-being: The role of employment, marital disruption and social integration.* Univ. Wisc.-Madison Center Demogr. Ecol. Work. Pap. 85–25

Marini, M. 1980. Effects of the number and spacing of children on marital and parental satisfaction. *Demography* 17:225–42

Marks, S. 1977. Multiple roles and role strain: Some notes on human energy, time, and commitment. *Am. Sociol. Rev.* 42:921–36

Menaghan, E. G. 1982. Assessing the impact of family transitions on marital experience. In *Family Stress, Coping, and Social Support,* ed. H. I. McCubbin, A. E.. Cauble, J. M. Patterson, pp. 90–108. Springfield, Ill: Charles C. Thomas

Miller, B. C. 1975. Child density, marital satisfaction, and conventionalization: A research note. *J. Marriage Fam.* 37:345–47

Miller, B. C., Sollie, D. L. 1980. Normal stresses during the transition to parenthood. *Fam. Relat.* 29:459–65

Mullan, J. T. 1981. *Parental distress and marital happiness: The transition to the "empty nest."* PhD thesis. Univ. Chicago, Chicago

Nock, S. L. 1979. The family life cycle: Empirical or conceptual tool? *J. Marriage Fam.* 41:15–27

Oppenheimer, V. 1982. *Work and Family: A Study in Social Demography.* New York: Academic Press

Pearlin, L. I. 1974. Sex roles and depression.

In *Life Span Developmental Psychology Conference: Normative Life Crises,* ed. N. Datan, L. Ginsberg, pp. 191–207. New York: Academic Press

Pearlin, L. I., Lieberman, M. A. 1979. Social sources of emotional distress. In *Research in Community and Mental Health: An Annual Compilation of Research,* ed. R. G. Simmons, 1:217–48. Greenwich, Conn: JAI

Polit, D. F. 1982. *Effects of family size: A Critical Review of Literature Since 1973.* Washington, DC: Am. Inst. Res.

Polonko, K. A., Scanzoni, J., Teachman, J. D. 1982. Childlessness and marital satisfaction. *J. Fam. Iss.* 3:545–73

Radloff, L. S. 1975. Sex differences in depression: The effects of occupation and marital status. *Sex Roles* 1:249–65

Renne, K. S. 1970. Correlates of dissatisfaction in marriage. *J. Marriage Fam.* 32:54–66

Reskin, B. F., Coverman, S. 1985. Sex and race in the determinants of psychophysical distress: A reappraisal of the sex-role hypothesis. *Soc. Forc.* 63:1038–59

Rollins, B. C., Cannon, K. 1974. Marital satisfaction over the family life cycle: A reevaluation. *J. Marriage Fam.* 36:271–82

Rollins, B., Feldman, H. 1970. Marital satisfaction over the family life cycle. *J. Marriage Fam.* 32:20–28

Rollins, B., Galligan, R. 1978. The developing child and marital satisfaction of parents. In *Child Influences on Marital and Family Interaction,* ed. R. M. Lerner, G. B. Spanier, pp. 71–106. New York: Academic Press

Ross, C. E., Huber, J. 1985. *Hardship and depression. J. Health Soc. Behav.* 26:312–27

Ross, C., Mirowsky, J., Huber, J. 1983. Marriage patterns and depression. *Am. Sociol. Rev.* 48:809–23

Rossi, A. 1968. Transition to parenthood. *J. Marriage Fam.* 30:26–39

Russell, C. S. 1974. Transition to parenthood:

Problems and gratifications. *J. Marriage Fam.* 36:294–302

Ryder, N. B. 1979. The future of American fertility. *Soc. Probl.* 26:359–69

Sieber, S. D. 1974. Toward a theory of role accumulation. *Am. Sociol. Rev.* 39:567–578

Spanier, G. B., Lewis, R. A. 1980. Marital quality: A review of the seventies. *J. Marriage Fam.* 42:825–39

Spanier, G. B., Lewis, R. A., Cole, C. L. 1975. Marital adjustment over the family life cycle: The issue of curvilinearity. *J. Marriage Fam.* 37:263–75

Spanier, G. B., Sauer, W., Larzelere, R. 1979. An empirical evaluation of the family life cycle. *J. Marriage Fam.* 41:27–38

Thoits, P. A. 1983. Multiple identities and psychological wellbeing: A reformulation and test of the social isolation hypothesis. *Am. Sociol. Rev.* 48:174–87

Thomson, E., Czajka, J. L., Williams, R. 1984. *Wives' and husbands' demand for children.* Univ. Wisc.-Madison Cent. Demogr. Ecol. Work. Pap. 84–6

Turner, R. H. 1978. The role and the person. *Am. J. Sociol.* 84:1–23

Vanck, J. 1974. Time spent in housework. *Sci. Am.* 231:116–20

Veevers, J. E. 1980. *Childless By Choice.* Toronto: Butterworth

Veroff, J., Douvan, E., Kulka, R. 1981. *Mental Health in America: Patterns of Help-Seeking from 1957–1976.* New York: Basic Books

Waldron, H., Routh, D. K. 1981. The effect of the first child on the marital relationship. *J. Marriage Fam.* 43:785–88

Westoff, C. F. 1978. Some speculations on the future of marriage and fertility. *Fam. Plan. Perspectives* 10:79–83

White, L., Booth, A. 1985. The transition to parenthood and marital quality. *J. Family Iss.* 6:435–50

Wright, J. D. 1978. Are working women really more satisfied? Evidence from several national surveys. *J. Marriage Fam.* 40:301–13

Ann. Rev. Sociol. 1987. 13:259–88
Copyright © 1987 by Annual Reviews Inc. All rights reserved

THE EFFECT OF WOMEN'S LABOR FORCE PARTICIPATION ON THE DISTRIBUTION OF INCOME IN THE UNITED STATES

Judith Treas

Department of Sociology, University of Southern California, Los Angeles, California 90089-0032

Abstract

Because the wives of highly paid men participate less in the labor force, the earnings of working wives make the distribution of pretax, money income more equal for families than it might otherwise be. Although there is considerable speculation that future developments in women's labor force participation may foster greater inequality, the empirical results are mixed. To assess the impact of women's labor force participation on the distribution of well-being, future research will need to consider the implications of taxes, job-related expenses, fringe benefits, and the value of homemaker services. Future research would also benefit from linking empirical research to an implicit sociological theory of family income-getting—one that recognizes the motivational structure of household decision-making as well as the changing environment that families face. Rising housing costs, poorer economic prospects of young men, and women's higher wage rates, for example, make wives' paychecks more salient, but family dependence on married women's earnings means secondary earners become a less viable way of coping with unemployment.

0360-0572/87/0815-0259$02.00

INTRODUCTION

Few trends in American society are as striking as the postwar rise in women's labor force participation. This development is driven largely by the entry into the labor force of women who traditionally worked only in their own homes—wives, mothers, and, more recently, mothers of preschool children. In 1984, 52.8% of married women worked in the marketplace as compared to only 22.5% in 1947 (US Bureau of the Census 1984). Many empirical studies document these trends and identify the determinants of this growing work force involvement (Bowen & Finegan 1969; Cain 1966; Sweet 1973; Kreps & Clark 1975; Waite 1976, 1981; Oppenheimer 1970, 1982). Among the consequences studied are the effects of women's employment on children (Hoffman 1974, Leibowitz 1977), on the division of labor between husbands and wives (Huber & Spitze 1983, Geerken & Gove 1983, Farkas 1976, Berk & Berk 1979), and on spouses mental health (Kessler & McRae 1981). No consequence is as immediate as the impact of the wife's paycheck on family finances. Sociologists, economists, and demographers have offered both speculation and empirical evidence on how working wives affect the distribution of income among families.

Writing in a 1960 Census monograph, Herman Miller (1966:22) was among the first to consider the impact on family income inequality of increasing labor force participation by women. Observing that families with working wives have more nearly equal incomes than families without working wives, he reasoned that "the sizeable increase in the proportion of families with working wives has therefore tended to decrease income inequality. . . ." Although others (e.g. Sweet 1971) have pointed out that the dynamics of family income inequality are a good deal more complicated than Miller's logic implied, a growing body of research agrees with his basic conclusion: Married women's rising labor force participation has been a force for equalizing the pretax money income of husband-wife families. Many unanswered questions remain about the broad implications of women's labor force participation for the distribution of economic well-being.

To lay the groundwork for later discussions, this paper begins by summarizing the technical studies on how women's labor force participation has affected the distribution of income among husband-wife families. The overall conclusion is that working wives have reduced income inequality to date. Turning to studies forecasting future inequality, however, there is some support for the notion that higher rates of involvement of married women in the work force eventually will lead to greater income disparities among white husband-wife families. These generalizations, however, do not hold for black families; a separate section deals with black working wives.

While informative, these studies have a number of limitations, which are detailed in the second half of this paper. We note, for example, that projections have rested on tenuous assumptions about the future course of women's labor force participation and the future wage rates of husbands and wives. To simplify analysis, studies have often limited attention to husband-wife earnings to the exclusion of other income sources and while ignoring the value of homemaker's services. Given the limitations of empirical studies, we open up the discussion to examine the widespread contention that working wives are propping up the middle class, cushioning unemployment, and offsetting effects of inflation. Lastly, we address the implications of women's labor force participation for the economic situation of female-headed families.

NINE STUDIES CONFIRM AN EQUALIZING EFFECT

Study after study agrees that greater work force involvement by married women has had an equalizing influence on family incomes in the United States. This consensus is all the more impressive because the different studies tackle the research question with different data, measures, and methodologies. Table 1 summarizes nine investigations, their approaches, and findings. Each arrives at the conclusion that working wives equalize income—at least among the white population.

The diversity among these studies cannot be overemphasized. Despite a common focus on married couples, several studies restrict the population in one way or another. Lehrer & Nerlove (1984), for instance, limit consideration to couples where the wife is less than 45 years old and either has had or plans to have children. Horvath (1980) excludes families without earnings and those where the husband is self-employed, a student, a farmer, 65 or older, or without earned income.

Measures of inequality employed range over the Gini coefficient, Theil's information-based measure, the standard deviation, the coefficient of variation, and the log variance of income. All these studies use inequality measures like the Gini coefficient that summarize income dispersion at all points on the income distribution. The fortunes of the rich, the poor, and those in between are evaluated with reference to the entire distribution of income. This is in contrast to the poverty line or interquartile range—measures that focus on only one point or segment on the overall distribution. The Gini coefficient, for example, plots cumulative shares of income against cumulative shares of families; the resulting Lorenz curve is then compared with the 45° line of perfect equality (i.e. where 10% of families get 10% of income, 20% get 20%, and so on). Many other inequality measures exist, although the others lack the intuitive appeal of the Gini. The definitions and properties of various inequality measures are reviewed by Allison (1978) and Kakwani (1980). Since the studies in Table 1 use many different measures, it is important to

Table 1 Effect on family income inequality of wife's employment in the United States

Study	Population	Data	Design	Income distribution	Inequality measure	Results
Betson & van der Gaag 1984	Nonaged, married households with one or two earners	1968–1980 CPS	Time series	Household income & wife's earnings	Theil's coefficient	Equalized Blacks larger equalization
Harris & Hedderson 1981	Married couples	1968–1977 PSID	Panel	Earnings of husband & wife	Coefficient of variation	Equalized
Horvath 1980	Spouse present, husband-wife families except those with no earnings or with a self-employed, farmer, student, 65+, or zero-earner husband	1978 CPS	Cross-section	Earnings of husband & wife	Standard deviation	Equalized
Lehrer & Nerlove 1984	Married couples, wife < 45, who have or ex-pect to have children	1973 National Survey of Family Growth	Cross-section	Earnings of husband & wife	Coefficient of variation	Whites: equalized Blacks: unequalized if no children and less equalized if children

Mincer 1974	Married spouse present families	1960 PUS 1/1000	Cross-section	Family income & husband's earnings	Log variance	Equalized
Smith 1979	Husband-wife families	1960, 1970 PUS 1/100	Cross-section	Earnings of husband & wife	Log variance	Whites: equalized Blacks: slightly equalized
Sweet 1971	Nonfarm married couples, wife < 60	1960 PUS 1/1000	Cross-section	Family income & family income less wife's earnings	Gini	Nonblacks: equalized Blacks: No effect
Treas 1983	Husband-wife families	1948–1977 CPS	Time series	Total family income	Theil's coefficient	Equalized
Treas & Walther 1978	Husband-wife families	1951–1974 CPS	Time series	Total family income	Theil's coefficient	Equalized

CPS: Current Population Survey; PSID: Panel Study of Income Dynamics; PUS: Public Use Sample of the Decennial Census.

note that the measure itself can lead to different conclusions regarding trends and differentials in inequality, if only because different measures assign different weights to different points on the income distribution. In Table 1, however, the results are very consistent.

The studies draw on diverse data sources spanning different years and including the Public Use Samples from the Decennial Censuses, published tabulations from the replicated cross-sectional Current Population Surveys, the longitudinal Panel Study of Income Dynamics, and the specialized 1973 National Survey of Family Growth. The diverse data sets employed by the studies have given rise to different analytic strategies and methods, too.

With individual-level data, researchers call on two strategies. One strategy asks whether total income for families with working wives is more equally distributed than is the income of their husbands alone or, alternately, of total family income less wife's earnings (Sweet 1971, Danziger 1980, Betson & van der Gaag 1984, Horvath 1980). A second strategy decomposes overall family income inequality into that due to wife's earnings and that due to other family income sources (Mincer 1974, Harris & Hedderson 1981, Lehrer & Nerlove 1984, Smith 1979, Shorrocks 1983).

With aggregated data, two other approaches apply. First, observed inequality may be compared with an "expected" measure of inequality; this expected measure is calculated by weighting family income distributions for working wives and homemakers according to the proportions of wives working and not working in an earlier, baseline year (Treas & Walther 1978). Second, the measure of inequality for husband-wife families may be regressed on annual time series of women's labor force participation rates and other explanatory variables (Treas 1983).

Despite their differences in data, time frames, populations, inequality measures, and analytic approaches, these studies reach the same conclusion. All agree that American working wives make the distribution of income among husband-wife families more nearly equal than it might otherwise be. Other researchers report compatible results for Israel (Gronau 1982) and Great Britain (Layard & Zabalza 1979).

This is not to say that family income inequality has actually declined as women's labor force participation has increased. Most evidence suggests that inequality has been fairly stable since World War II. Regressing Theil's measure of inequality for husband-wife families on time, Treas & Walther (1978) find only glacial change between 1951 and 1974; the regression results imply an annual decline of only .001 for husband-wife families as contrasted with a more substantial .005 drop for female-headed families. Charting trends in the Panel Study of Income Dynamics, Harris & Hedderson (1981) even report a slight increase in inequality for husband-wife units between 1968 and 1977. Although women's growing labor force involvement did not result in major reductions in inequality, it blunted the impact of other factors which, if unchecked, might have led to widening income differences among husband-wife families. Such unequalizing forces include the declining labor force participation of older men (Treas 1983) and growing inequality in male earnings (Dooley & Gottschalk 1982).

HOW WORKING WIVES AFFECTED INEQUALITY

Understanding inequality for husband-wife families depends on knowing something about husband's earnings, wife's earnings, and the relation between them. Mincer (1974) put this rather formally, showing that family income inequality could be expressed as a function of the variances and covariance of two sources:

$$\sigma_F^2 = \sigma_H^2 + \sigma_W^2 + 2\text{Cov}_{HW},$$

where F is the family income, H is the husband's earnings, and W is the wife's earnings.

This sort of decomposition of overall family inequality by income source calls attention to the factors that may reshape the distribution of income. The dispersion in husbands' earnings, for example, may be sensitive to shifts in their age structure, changes in the education and experience of this workforce, transformations of the economy, altered patterns of labor supply, and economic cycles. The dispersion for women is dominated by the zero earnings of homemakers and the part-time employment of many working wives. Factors influencing the labor force participation of married women overwhelm wage rate determinants as influences on inequality. The covariance for spouses' earnings is influenced by trends in marital homogamy and in the selective labor force participation of wives. Beginning with the association of husband-wife earnings, let us consider each of the three components of family inequality in turn and relate them back to studies in Table 1.

The Association of Husband-Wife Earnings

Two contradictory determinants are at work in the covariation of husbands' and wives' earnings. As Mincer (1974:122–3) points out, "The sign of the covariance depends partly on the correlation between the earning power . . . of family members, and partly on their labor supply functions. The correlation between earning power, which is positive . . . , tends to impart a positive sign to the covariance; however, . . . the labor supply relation tends to influence the covariance in the opposite direction." In other words, men with high earnings tend to be married to women with relatively good earnings prospects, but their wives are less likely to be working than women married to less well paid men.

A positive association of spouses' wage rates has been long observed (Carroll 1962). On the one hand, it reflects marital homogamy, the tendency of men and women of similar schooling and social origins to wed one another (Blau & Duncan 1967). On the other hand, it reflects the fact that husbands and wives share the labor market advantages and disadvantages of their common social network and community of residence (Sweet 1973). Educational homogamy complicates the relation of spouses' earnings. Attenuating the positive correlation in earning power is the fact that highly educated professional men have often married women with less education (Oppenheimer 1982). Attenuating the negative labor supply relation is the fact that the positive effect of the wife's education on her labor force participation offsets the negative influence of her husband's earnings (Waite 1976).

The observed correlation between the earnings of husbands and wives is miniscule, as shown by the .08 reported for spouses' incomes in 1978 (Harris & Hedderson 1981). Even with the labor supply relation taken into account, the correlation is modest. Jencks and associates (1972:233) found a correlation of .19 between the 1959 earnings of northeastern husbands and wives who worked full-time and full-year. Lehrer & Nerlove (1984) estimate the correlation of spouses' latent earning capacity (i.e. what they would make if each worked full-time) to range from .10 to .25 over various race and life cycle groups.

There are some reasons to suspect that the covariation in spouses' earnings might increase. The rising age at marriage, for example, means that men and women have better information on which to gauge potential mates' earning power. Higher divorce rates might promote a higher covariation both by removing the more divorce-prone heterogamous couples from the married population and by fostering second marriages where men wed working partners who can pay their own way (Oppenheimer 1982). Using an alternative decomposition for the coefficient of variation for family income, Harris & Hedderson (1981) did find that the correlation between husband's and wife's income increased between 1967 and 1976. The correlation was only one component of inequality, however. Also contributing to the observed increase in inequality were widening income disparities among husbands, but women's labor force participation partially offset these unequalizing developments.

The Dispersion in Husband's Earnings

Several analyses of income inequality (Miller 1966, Treas & Walther 1978, see also Bartlett & Poulton-Callahan 1982) have rested on the simplifying assumption that families with and without working wives have very similar income distributions before the wife's earnings are added in. Since husband's earnings dominate family income, this assumption is akin to saying that the same earnings disparities exist for the husbands of working women as for those of homemakers. Drawing on individual level data from the 1960 Census of Population, Sweet (1971) shows that this is not the case. The families of nonblack, married women in the labor force have incomes that are more equal to start with—a conclusion that holds whether one compares just husband's income or total family income less wife's earnings. This finding is not unanticipated. Husbands with high incomes are underrepresented in the group of families with a working wife, because their wives are less likely to be in the labor force. To be sure, married women's labor force participation does have some equalizing effect; total family income for these women is more equally distributed than is the income of their husbands or, indeed, family income less wives' earnings. However, wives' earnings alone do not account for the greater equality of families with working wives; they were more equal to start with.

Betson & van der Gaag (1984) update these results. Between 1968 and 1980, the equalizing impact of married women's labor force participation actually increased, offsetting a noteworthy rise in the inequality of household income before wife's earnings. Not counting the wife's paycheck, household inequality increased for families whether or not the wife worked. While Betson & van der Gaag do not address husband's earnings inequality per se, their results are compatible with studies showing growing dispersion in the inequality of men's earnings (Dooley & Gottschalk 1985). While inequality was growing among families of both working wives and homemakers, the overall income distributions of the two groups became more similar; and between-group differences made less contribution to overall inequality among husband-wife families. Presumably, as working women became more ubiquitous, other household income became less and less of a predictor of who worked and who did not. The working and nonworking groups encompassed more socioeconomic diversity and resembled one another more in terms of other income.

Dispersion in Wives' Earnings

In Mincer's formulation, the wife's earnings, themselves unequally distributed, contribute to the observed inequality of income among families. In general, the earnings of women are less equally distributed than those of men (Henle & Ryscavage 1980), because homemakers have zero earnings. Even when comparisons are limited to those who are working, women display more dispersion in earnings, because many women have low earnings due to part-time employment. When this tendency toward part-time jobs is taken into account by looking only at full-time workers, women are more, not less, equal in income than men are (Horvath 1980). This is because few women have high earnings and because women have tended to work in occupations (e.g. clerical) where the income range is fairly narrow (Henle & Ryscavage 1980). As more women enter the labor force or work more hours, one component of overall inequality—the variance of their earnings—could be expected to narrow. This assumes, of course, that the rising number of women in the labor force does not affect the basic distribution of their wage rate.

When we consider the components of inequality, it is clear that both equalizing and unequalizing factors have been at work. This may be described in terms of a declining variance in women's earnings partially offset by increases in both the variance in husband's earnings and the correlation between spouse's earnings. Alternatively, it may be phrased in terms of a narrowing family income gap between homemakers and working wives offset by growing disparities within the two groups in family income before wife's earnings. Recent dynamics in the income distribution are a matter of record. In the coming decade, however, the rising numbers of working women (previously an equalizing force) may come to exacerbate inequality.

INEQUALITY IN THE FUTURE

Everyone agrees that married women's labor force participation has had an equalizing influence on the distribution of family income. Many suspect that future developments in women's work and wages may lead to more inequality, not less. A number of sociologists, economists, and demographers have joined this speculation over the years.

Much of the concern centers on the prospect that the women who will be drawn into the labor force in the years ahead will be those already married to men with high earnings. Because these women can probably command relatively high wages themselves, their earnings could double the advantage of couples at the upper tail of the income distribution. Ross & Sawhill (1975:120, see also Ignatius 1978, Thurow & Lucas 1972:8) articulate this reasoning:

> If there is an influx of relatively well-educated, high earning women into the labor force—women who in the past have married well and worked less frequently than wives in lower income families—then greater inequality would ensue in the future.

Yet another pessimistic prospect is voiced by Rivlin (1975:2) who suggests that the distribution of income for working women could become even more unequal as women adopt career patterns more like men.

> As long as wives have been secondary earners in every sense of the word, their earnings have had a generally equalizing effect on family income. But this effect would be reversed if a major increase occurred in the proportion of wives with a permanent, lifelong

attachment to the labor force and an earnings distribution similar to that of their husbands, and this tendency might well be increased if job status became a more central part of the average woman's life.

England & Farkas (1986:182) predict that the work force involvement of women could lead to a stronger association between the earning power of spouses due, in part, to greater age similarity between spouses.

To the extent that women's employment and earnings continue to increase, they may come to weigh men's earning power less heavily, and place greater importance on emotional or sensual attributes. Men may pay greater attention to a woman's earning power, leading them to weigh youth, beauty, and traditionally feminine emotional qualities less heavily. By this reasoning, as well as by a simple extrapolation of recent trends, we predict that the ages of men and women at first marriage will continue to converge. As these changes occur, the positive correlations between partners' traits that are the hallmark of assortative mating will increase. Applying this to earnings suggests increased inequality in the distribution of family incomes as the tendency for high-earning women and men to marry one another increases.

Only Jencks and associates (1972:211) dismiss such concerns, arguing that the distribution of income for all wives, as opposed to working wives, would be more equal were all zero earners to bring home a paycheck.

If all wives worked, the distribution of income would probably be more equal than it is now. This is because the elimination of nonearners would make the distribution of income between wives more equal than it is now. In addition, husbands with high incomes would often have wives with low incomes and vice versa.

Few scholars have ventured beyond speculation. Bergmann and associates (1980), however, chart the course of future inequality. Their findings lend support to those who expect that further growth of the female labor force would cease to promote family income equality. They begin with the strong assumption that the ratio of wives' earnings to other family income is constant across time and income groups. While dubious, this assumption permits a straightforward simulation of the path of inequality under two different scenarios.

In the first, wives, ranked by other family income, enter the labor force in descending order with the richest going first. In the second, the poorest go first in ascending order—a pattern closer to documented trends in women's labor force participation. When the poor go first, the Gini coefficient falls until it reaches the point at which 60% of women are working, and then it rises. When the rich go first, inequality rises until 40% of wives are in the labor force, and then it declines. These rises and falls are more pronounced if wives are assumed to contribute more to overall family income. The two scenarios predict the same level of inequality, of course, when 100% of wives work.

Rather than imposing assumptions about how much wives will contribute to family income, one can ask what wages homemakers might command if they were employed. Smith (1979) takes this tack. Since working wives are a select group, their wage experience is not an unbiased indicator of what nonworking wives could hope to earn. Correcting for this censoring bias using the technique suggested by Heckman (1976), Smith produces hourly wage rate estimates for all women based on education, Southern residence, and market experience. At least for whites, it appears that there would be greater variance in working wives' earnings, a larger positive correlation between spouses' wages, and thus, more overall family inequality if all married women worked.

Lehrer & Nerlove (1984) use a similar methodology to estimate what women and their husbands could earn if they each worked full-time. They consider three life cycle stages—before the first birth, while there are preschool children, and after all children are school age. Because men tend to work less at higher income levels, actual earnings for men are more equally distributed than their earnings capacity. Because women who can earn more work more, the distribution of female earnings is markedly less equal than their earnings capacity. Were their full earnings capacity realized (i.e. if they both worked full-time), the combined earnings of husbands and wives would be more unequally distributed *only* among couples with preschool children. This, of course, is the life cycle stage where women with relatively good wage prospects and the richest husbands are likely to opt out of the labor force.

In sum, there is mixed support for the notion that higher and higher levels of labor force participation will lead eventually to greater inequality in family incomes. As with all efforts to foresee the future, these estimates and projections are only as good as the assumptions on which they are built. At a later point, we examine these assumptions more critically.

RACIAL DIFFERENCES IN THE EFFECT OF WIVES' WORK

Black husband-wife families are distinguished by higher rates of women's labor force participation and by income disadvantages. They also evidence more income inequality than do white families. This inequality reflects the greater income disparities among black men, the greater income disparities among black women, and the larger positive correlation between black spouses' earnings. Since the income and labor supply of black families is distinctive, many researchers have undertaken separate analyses of whites and blacks. Their conclusions suggest that black wives' labor force participation reduces inequality (although this may be a recent phenomenon).

Sweet (1971) finds that wives' employment had almost no effect on black family income inequality in 1960. Other income received by these families (e.g. earnings by other family members, social welfare, income from investments) actually leads to more inequality, especially for couples without children under 18. Smith (1979) finds that earnings of wives promoted greater inequality among black families in both 1960 and 1970. Lehrer & Nerlove (1984) do report some reduction in black family inequality for those families of working wives, but this reduction is smaller than that for white families and does not occur at all for couples who have not yet had children.

If wife's employment equalizes income for black families (and the evidence is mixed), this is apparently a recent development. Between 1967 and 1976, black wives' income contributions shifted from unequalizing to equalizing influences, with year-to-year movements proving sensitive to the correlation observed between spouses' incomes (Harris & Hedderson 1981). Using different data, Danziger (1980) documents a similar reversal in the influence of wives' earnings between 1967 and 1974. The equalizing impact of wife's earnings also drifts upward between 1968 and 1980 in the figures presented by Betson & van der Gaag (1984).

The earnings of black women and their husbands evidence a higher, positive correlation than is the case for white spouses (Lehrer & Nerlove 1984; Smith 1979). The potential earning power of black partners seems to be more highly correlated to begin with—a finding that has been attributed to stronger assortative mating by schooling among blacks (Lehrer & Nerlove 1984). This association of latent wage capacities expresses itself more readily in observed wages, because black women are not deterred from working even if their husbands have high incomes.

Smith (1979) argues that wives' employment fulfills different functions in black than in white families. White working wives compensate for their husbands' earning inadequacies, but black wives seem not to base decisions about how much they will work on their husband's paycheck. Since black married women's labor force participation is not currently selective of women with highly paid or poorly paid spouses, universal work force involvement would have little effect on overall black family inequality. If all black women worked, it is estimated that the log variance in black family income would be virtually the same as that actually observed for all black families today (Smith 1979). The black population has much lower rates of marriage and higher rates of marital dissolution than does the white population. This may contribute to the distinctive labor force behavior of black wives, but it also suggests they are a more selective group—one whose earnings might be quite sensitive to changes in marriage patterns.

LIMITATIONS OF STUDIES

Sociologists, economists, and demographers agree that married women's labor force participation has narrowed income differentials among husband-wife families. The women who have yet to be drawn into the labor force, however, tend to be married to the more successful husbands and might command relatively good wages themselves by virtue of advantages in education, social networks, and so on. Were all these wives to work, labor force participation of wives could emerge as a cause of greater inequality, rather than a means to spread income more evenly across American families. This result, however, is by no means inevitable. Although empirical studies reaching these conclusions differ in many ways, they share some common limitations. Their conclusions should not be accepted without question or qualification.

Consider efforts to project the future course of women's labor force participation and inequality.

How realistic is it to assume that all wives could work (Bergmann et al 1980) or that all wives might work full-time (Smith 1979, Lehrer & Nerlove 1984)? Although "what if" exercises are instructive, these extreme case assumptions pose scenarios that will never be played out. While the course of women's labor force participation continues upward, other societal developments assure that not all wives will be working wives.

Labor force projections for married women are not readily available. For all women 25–54, the Bureau of Labor Statistics forecasts 1995 participation rates in the range of 73.6 to 86.9, depending on economic growth assumptions (Fullerton & Tschetter 1983). Since work rates for younger, older, and married women will undoubtedly be lower, universal employment of women does not seem to loom on the horizon. Even in the long run, it seems highly unlikely that all wives will be full-time workers for several reasons.

First, women are going to school longer or returning to school later in life (US Bureau of the Census 1984). Second, the 1970s saw the emergence of a trend to early retirement among women (Treas 1981). Labor force participation rates for women between 55 and 64 years of age fell off, particularly among women with 16 or more years of schooling. Relatively well-educated women married to well-paid men, of course, are just the sort slated for higher work rates under scenarios predicting an unequalizing impact of wives' labor force participation. Third, macroeconomic cycles are apt to determine women's employment by affecting their job opportunities and the opportunity costs of staying home to keep house and raise children (Butz & Ward 1979). Fourth, the factors that inhibit women's labor force participation today will continue to discourage women's labor force participation in the future (although the influence of these factors may decline over time). There will always be women whose family situation cannot accommodate the demands of a full-time job, who are too sick to work, who cannot command employment commensurate with their family's social standing, and so on.

Even if we assume all wives will work, how well can we estimate the wage rates of women who may enter the labor force in coming decades? Smith

(1979) and Lehrer & Nerlove (1984), for example, both rely on Heckman's (1976) technique in correcting for censoring in order to estimate the wage prospects of wives who are not now working. Although the wage rates nonworking women might receive are not knowable, Ferber & Green (1985) asked homemakers how much they thought they could earn if they had a job. Although homemakers do not expect to earn as much as their counterparts in the labor force, they do report anticipated wages that are higher than estimated with the Heckman technique.

Of course, if all wives went to work tomorrow, all bets about their wage rates would be off. To date, studies of family income inequality have not incorporated changes in the female income distribution that might result as a consequence of higher work rates. The experience of the baby boom demonstrates that a glut of new job seekers translates into lower and less equal earnings for men—at least in the short run (Welch 1979). Something similar might be expected if women were to surge into the workplace. Women's wages have long been depressed by their "crowding" into traditionally female occupations (Bergmann 1974), but as Oppenheimer (1972) noted, these occupations could not be expected to grow fast enough to absorb all the women who might enter the job market. Female workers have already begun to move into traditionally male jobs (Rytina & Bianchi 1984)—a development that might raise their incomes and alter their income distribution.

Women workers might well depress the incomes of men with whom they compete. Dooley & Gottschalk (1985:31) invoke this explanation to account for growth at the lower tail of the male earnings distribution. There is evidence that declines in men's earnings are associated with occupations with growing numbers of women (Snyder and Hudis 1976). Furthermore, as more wives become workers, men's income distribution could also be affected, because some husbands adjust their labor supply. On the one hand, husbands might work less—passing up overtime in favor of leisure, adapting their schedules to work more around the house, or dropping out of the work force to enroll in school for a time. On the other hand, husbands may work more, putting off retirement until the wife is eligible (Clark et al 1980).

Aside from labor supply effects, employed wives may give more men the luxury of working in jobs like farming that pay poorly and involve an element of risk (Rosenfeld 1985). Pfeffer & Ross (1982) argue that men's wage rates may be depressed to the extent that working wives thwart social expectations, are too busy to help the husband with his career, or eliminate financial need appeals in salary-setting practices. Although the authors find no evidence for an effect on husbands' occupational status, their analysis of annual salaries and wages may confound labor supply and wage rate effects. Although one study of academia shows that spouse's employment is associated with lower salary, net of other factors (Gregorio & associates 1982), wives may work because husbands have low incomes, rather than vice versa. Certainly, working wives might lower their husbands' wages to the extent they discourage geographic mobility (Lichter 1982). We can only speculate about how men's labor supply and their employers' wage policies might respond to universal labor force participation of married women. Men's income distribution might well be affected by working women—a prospect not addressed by the existing literature gauging the distributional impact of more working wives.

If rising work rates for women feed back to affect the earnings distributions of husbands and wives, the relationship of spouses' earnings could also change. The correlation would probably rise above its currently low level. If women take home paychecks comparable to men's, a woman's earnings could become a more valued asset in the marriage market—facilitating a better match. At first blush, it would seem that the correlation would be attenuated were higher earnings to prompt more divorce by making women more independent financially. Second marriages are not as homogamous (e.g. by age). The potential economic contributions of a wife, however, seem to factor even more heavily in the marriage market calculations of divorced men who must often support two households (Oppenheimer 1982).

In short, neither the variation nor the covariation of spouses' earnings can realistically be assumed to be constant. Both may change if women's labor force involvement changes. These changes augur changes in the distribution of family income which are not addressed by mechanistic exercises estimating future levels of inequality.

Even efforts to evaluate the present are fraught with problems. To simplify analysis, studies have typically restricted attention to the earnings of husbands and wives. Other influences on the money income distribution—welfare and entitlement benefits, private transfers (e.g. gifts and child support payments), and returns on investments—receive no more than passing mention. Decomposing household inequality, Shorrocks (1983) shows that income from capital ranks ahead of wives' income as a component of income differences. Indeed, investment income, pensions, and taxable income of family members besides the head and wife all drifted upwards as components of inequality between 1967 and 1976. Studies that have failed to take account of these developments are obviously incomplete.

First, unless the husband's earnings are highly correlated with the omitted income sources, the results of these analyses are problematic. Studies show that married women's labor force participation has contributed to earned income equality because the wives of men with low earnings are more likely to work. Working wives would not necessarily be giving a boost to low income households if these men and their families had substantial unearned income that went uncounted. Men with low or zero earnings are, indeed, good candidates to be receiving some types of unearned income; unemployment insurance, retirement pensions, and even very high investment income come to mind.

Second, other income cannot be assumed to be independent of the wife's work effort. Wife's employment could be a substitute for the employment of teenage children and other family members. It could make the family ineligible for social welfare benefits on which they might otherwise draw. Thus, neither husband's earnings nor family income less wife's earnings are completely reliable indicators of the income working wives' families might have if they did not work. Conclusions regarding the distributional impact of wives' work might or might not be invalidated were analyses to include other income sources and to model their dependence on the labor force participation of married women. Certainly, the substantial underreporting of unearned income poses barriers to such analyses (Radner 1982). Current studies, however, have been incomplete and may well err in estimating the magnitude of the equalizing effect.

THE DISTRIBUTION OF FULL INCOME

In most instances, we are interested in the distribution of money income for what it tells us about the distribution of economic well-being. How well off a family is depends on both the time and the money it has at its disposal. Economists have lumped these two resources together under the rubric of "full income." Studies of the impact of women's labor force participation on the distribution of family income have largely sidestepped the question of full income.

Obviously, working women trade off time for money. Women perform many valued services around the home (e.g. housekeeping, meal preparation, child care, entertaining, emotional support). When the wife goes to work, the family must either forego some of these services, find another family member to provide them, or spend money to purchase them in the marketplace (e.g. on restaurant meals, babysitters). The wife also incurs job-related expenses for union dues, transportation, clothing, and the like. Focusing only on the wife's earnings without recognizing lost services and extra expenses leads to an overestimation of the advantages of working (and perhaps to an overestimation of the equalizing impact of women's labor force participation). Although no study has undertaken a comprehensive examination of the impact of women's labor force participation on the distribution of full income, existing research is suggestive.

Working women spend less time on housework than do homemakers (Walker & Woods 1976, Farkas 1976, Berk & Berk 1979, Geerken & Gove 1983). They typically cut down on leisure time to get chores done, they may manage to become more efficient at some tasks, and they skip some jobs altogether. They don't succeed at getting their husbands to shoulder much of the burden of housekeeping, however. Their families wind up doing without some services taken for granted by the homemaker's family or settling for services of lower quality. Following economic theory, women would not be working if they and their families valued their home contributions more highly than their earnings. The poor, however, may not have the luxury of weighing a home-cooked meal against a restaurant meal, because the alternative is apt to be no meal at all. The working wife's family does without some services; especially at the bottom of the income distribution, where women's labor force participation is less discretionary and money less available to purchase substitutes, valued services may be foregone altogether, with significant implications for economic well-being.

Costing out the value of wives' services has pitfalls, because results are sensitive to different approaches and assumptions. For example, estimates of what it might cost to replace the wife's services with market substitutes are apt to lead to a different figure than would estimates of the opportunity costs of homemaking in terms of foregone earnings. Evaluating the cost of home-produced commodities, Gronau (1980) reports that household production of goods and services suffers little if the working woman has no small children in the home; when there are youngsters, however, losses in home production virtually wipe out the wife's extra earnings. Lazear & Michael (1980) use a "revealed preference" approach that uses direct information on market expenditures to derive dollar amounts necessary to make the families of working wives and homemakers equivalent. They are more pessimistic about the value of working for the young, childless renters whom they study. They estimate that dual earner couples receive 20% more income after taxes, but they would need 30% more to achieve the same standard of living as comparable couples without a working wife!

These findings suggest that working wives do not move up as far in the distribution of economic well-being as money income would suggest—a clear break in the equalizing potential of women's paid employment. Gronau's estimates show that the wives of better educated men are more productive in the home and have more to lose by working. If the overstatement of gains from working is greatest for the well-to-do, fears about working women fostering growing inequality are overblown. These estimates, of course, are only suggestive and point to the need to bring household services into the distributional picture in an explicit way. They are also cross-sectional. A life cycle perspective will be necessary to assess whether short-run losses are offset later in a career by higher pay resulting from continuous job experience.

Working wives incur extra expenses, too. Vickery (1979) used the 1972 Consumer Expenditure Survey to estimate how families with and without working wives compared in their spending patterns. The two groups were very much alike although the families of working women had fewer assets and were less likely to own a home. Taking account of assets, taxes, children, and life cycle stage, working wives spent more on transportation, clothing, and Social Security—expenses related to the job. It is interesting that Vickery does not find much indication that working wives buy market substitutes for their work at home. They may spend slightly more on meal preparation and dry cleaning, but not, apparently, on child care.

Gains from married women's employment are also overstated if taxes are not taken into account. If we accept the assumption that wives are secondary workers predicating their employment on their husband's employment situation, then the extra dollars working wives contribute to the family are taxed at a higher marginal rate than their husbands' earnings. Social security taxes present another complication (Treas 1981, Gordon 1979). If the one-earner and the two-earner couple have the same total earnings and if that total exceeds the ceiling above which no extra payroll taxes are levied, the single-earner couple escapes taxes that their two-earner counterpart must pay. As Gronau (1982) has demonstrated for Israel, the particulars of the tax structure (joint versus separate income tax filing, for example) can substantially modify the distributional impact of married women's labor force participation.

Although focusing on pretax money income may ignore some of the costs of women's employment, it also misses noncash benefits such as health coverage, free or subsidized meals, and pensions. Two-earner couples may have some duplication of benefits, gaining little, if anything, from a second health insurance plan, but counting fringe benefits would undoubtedly raise the incomes of working wives and their families. Working women in higher income classes would probably gain more than less well-paid women. When these fringe benefits are added in, women's labor force participation is probably a less progressive force for income equalization. These benefits typically go to full-time workers in the core sector of the economy who have worked for the same employer for some minimum period of time. In short, they go disproportionately to high-income groups (Smeeding 1985).

Pensions are a case in point. As more women work and as their worklives lengthen, women will increasingly qualify for public and private retirement benefits in their own right (Treas 1981). This suggests a scenario of greater late-life income disparities. Although social security favors the low-income worker in benefit calculations, private pensions do not. Women who qualify for second pensions are apt to be those in stable, highly capitalized sectors of the economy where firms can afford to pay their workers well and to fund and administer pension plans. Given educational similarities between spouses and their common residence in a local labor market, the husbands of these women are also likely to work for firms with pensions. Because of these factors—the nonprogressive nature of private pensions, the limited eligibility of low-paid workers, and the similarity of spouses' employment—it is easy to imagine a polarization between affluent, dual-earner couples with two or more second pensions and other couples (either single-earner or dual-earner in peripheral industries) who get by on little more than social security.

Empirical investigations of the effect of women's labor force participation on the distribution of family income have focused almost exclusively on pre-tax, money income. Until researchers take account of taxes, noncash benefits, employment-related expenses, and the value of homemaker's services foregone when the wife takes a job, the real impact of working wives on equality of economic well-being will be largely a matter of speculation.

THE MIDDLE CLASS

To this point, we have focused largely on fairly mechanical decompositions of changing inequality measures. These changes, however, transpired within a dynamic demographic and economic context. In the 1970s and 1980s, American families were buffeted by several forces undermining their financial security. Runaway inflation of the 1970s priced some goods and services, particularly home ownership, out of the reach of many. Coupled with an on-going restructuring of the American economy, the recessions of 1980–1982 cost many workers their jobs. Surprising numbers of men, especially young men, found themselves with low earnings. A polarization of the income distribution seemed to be endangering the middle class.

While the wife's employment is a time-honored mechanism for meeting economic adversity at all income levels, there is a growing sentiment that the wife's paycheck is what enables many families to maintain a toehold on the middle rungs of the income ladder (Levy & Michel 1985; Steinberg 1983). The fate of the middle class extends beyond concerns with an equitable distribution of economic rewards. The middle class is popularly identified with the mass market that fuels prosperity and the mass citizenry that promotes democracy. How well women's paid employment enables families to maintain middle class consumption standards, to respond to the loss of a breadwinner's income, and to cope with men's lower wages is a matter of considerable interest.

A mounting body of evidence establishes that the wage distribution has become more polarized. For example, the proportion of men with low earnings rose between 1967 and 1978 (Dooley & Gottschalk 1985). Lawrence (1984) reports that the proportion of workers with middle class earnings fell from 50% to 46% between 1969 and 1983. Of these, a group amounting to 3% dropped into the lower earnings class and a group amounting to 1% climbed into the upper class. Any decline from the middle class, however, was limited to men. Women actually shifted into the middle class from the ranks of low earners (Lawrence 1984). Although income gains for women are a very recent phenomenon (Smith & Ward 1984), earnings inequality for men is documented for earlier decades as well (Henle & Ryscavage 1980, Hirschman 1977).

Both a fundamental restructuring of the economy and demographic changes in the workforce are blamed for men's eroded earnings.

The "deindustrialization of America" is thought to be menacing middle-income workers in particular (Bluestone & Harrison 1982). Well-paid, unionized jobs in manufacturing are lost to countries with lower labor costs. Plant closings ripple across hard-hit communities, leading local businesses and government to lay off still more workers. Rather than creating new jobs, capital investment is either siphoned off into unproductive corporate acquisitions (Bluestone & Harrison 1982) or spent on robots, computers, and automation that cost workers' jobs (Leontief 1983).

Although the service sector is booming, many people doubt that service industries will be able to prop up the middle of the income distribution. The recent growth in service sector employment was fueled not by workers moving out of dying industries but rather by new entrants to the labor force (Kutscher & Personick 1986, Urquhart 1984). Future growth of the service sector seems sure to slow (Leontief 1983). Even if service jobs continue to be created at a fast clip, wages in these industries have usually been lower than in manufacturing (Kuttner 1983). In fact, service industries are often portrayed as a "two-tier" system of jobs and pay (*Population Today* 1985). Beneath the well-paid professional and managerial jobs are armies of fast-food workers, hospital orderlies, and office clerks.

An alternative explanation for men's worsening income position emphasizes demographic changes in the composition of the male workforce. Specifically, the big cohort of baby boomers competing for entry-level jobs has driven down the earnings of young men (Welch 1979, Russell 1982, Freeman 1979). The growth in the low-earner population was, indeed, concentrated among young men (Dooley & Gottschalk 1985). Young men's relative earnings vis-a-vis those of middle-aged men in the same occupation also declined for the 1959–1969 period (Oppenheimer 1982).

Since earnings disadvantages are concentrated among the young, this raises the hope that men's earnings picture will improve as the baby boomers work their way past the bottle-neck of entry-level positions (Welch 1979, Smith & Welch 1978) or are succeeded by other, smaller cohorts (Easterlin 1980). In emphasizing a fundamental transformation of the economy, sectoral explanations hold out little encouragement that the trend to lower earnings will soon be reversed.

Empirical studies offer surprisingly little support for the idea that a restructuring of industry is behind declines in earnings. Rosenthal (1985) insists that the earnings distribution did not become polarized. Analyzing 416 detailed occupations between 1973 and 1982, he found that the whole dis-

tribution of employment shifted up from lower and middle earning occupations to better-paid ones. Lawrence (1984) discounts sectoral explanations for
the fate of men's wages, too. Industries with few middle-class jobs did not
grow faster than other industries. While sectoral explanations meet with some
skepticism, neither have demographic explanations proven entirely satisfying.
Dispersion in men's annual earnings increased even *within* education and
experience categories, and more and more men reported no earnings at all
during the year (Dooley & Gottschalk 1982).

Whatever the reason, men's earnings have been under assault, young men
have been particularly hard hit, and it is not certain that an end to this trend is
in sight.

Family income has fared better than have men's earnings. Initial impressions that middle-class families were losing ground were based, in part,
on an error in the income tabulations published by the US Bureau of the
Census (Levy & Michel 1985). A mistake in converting to real, inflation-
adjusted dollars led to the erroneous conclusion that the middle-income ranks
were shrinking. The percent of families in the middle income categories did
decline slightly between 1979 and 1983 but subsequently stabilized—a development that Levy & Michel (1985) attribute to the influence of two-earner
families.

If trends in men's earnings put family income under pressure, changes in
women's earnings may have worked to fill the gap between income and
aspirations. From 1980 to 1984, the wages of working women rose from 60%
of men's to 64%, a development Smith & Ward (1984) attribute largely to an
increase in the schooling and work experience of women in the labor force.
Studies of occupational sex segregation have also commented on the movement of women into fields that have been dominated by men—a development
likely to raise female earnings (Rytina & Bianchi 1984, Treiman & Hartman
1981, Beller 1982).

Wage improvements were greatest for young women (Smith & Ward
1984)—those whose spouses were presumably feeling the brunt of male
earnings declines. Among two-earner married couples in 1983, one third of
those earning more than their husbands were 25–34 (US Bureau of the Census
1986:7).

Bearing in mind that middle-aged women have dominated the postwar rise
in women's labor force participation, the impetus for younger wives to work
becomes apparent. Young husbands, who can expect only entry level wages
in any case, have had the bad fortune to be born in a large cohort reaching
working age in an era of economic dislocation. If this did not place them at a
serious enough disadvantage, vis-à-vis their middle-aged counterparts, the
older families also typically draw on the earnings of a wife whose children no
longer require her attention (Oppenheimer 1982). Lastly, improved earnings

prospects offer an additional incentive for women's paid employment (Smith & Ward 1984).

INFLATION AND UNEMPLOYMENT

Wives work not to achieve a certain level of income but rather to insure a suitable standard of living. Aspirations for middle-class living standards were thwarted in the late 1970s when rapid inflation outpaced wage gains (Schumann 1984). Home ownership came to be priced beyond the means of more and more families. The young, facing their first home purchase, were especially vulnerable. As the cost of owning a home rose faster than the typical incomes of young married couples, the working wife became essential if the couple was to afford a house. Estimating a logistic model of home purchases by couples in which the wife was between ages 25 and 30, Myers (1985) finds that the net effect of wife's earnings on home-buying increased between 1974 and 1980.

Working wives are also thought to have cushioned the impact of unemployment in the 1980s. In 1984, for example, 67% of unemployed husbands could count on at least one family member, usually the wife, to have a job (US Bureau of the Census 1984:407). In 1960, the comparable figure had been only 40%. Unfortunately, a female employment pattern designed to meet the family's day-to-day consumption requirements is ill-suited to cushion family finances against unanticipated contingencies. As more couples work, married couples' dual employment has become a less and less effective means of coping when one partner is out of a job or unable to work.

First, the family is apt to have pegged its living standard to two incomes. When families come to rely on the wife's income for essentials, her paycheck is a necessary complement to, not a substitute for, her spouse's earnings. The dominance of dual-earner couples, according to Carlson (1986), even undermines the historical "family wage" concept (i.e. the idea that breadwinners' earnings ought to be adequate to support a family). Two-earner families imply a dependence not only on a certain level of income, but also on a given patterning of expenditures. They are apt to commit to lifestyles that make them somewhat more dependent on purchased goods and services (Vickery 1979). The working family may lack the time and even experience to practice small economies—darning socks or shopping garage sales. Other spending patterns can be changed only at the cost of disrupting family routine; few would want to give up the family car or take the kids out of nursery school just to meet a short-run shortfall of income.

Second, women experience joblessness, too. Unemployment is more likely to strike married women than married men although the differential has narrowed in recent years (Klein 1983). To be sure, men's unemployment rates are more sensitive to a downturn in the economy (Klein 1983), and future growth projected for industries employing women is apt to insulate women workers still further from joblessness (De Boer & Seeborg 1984). Today, however, families are about as likely to face the loss of the wife's pivotal paycheck as the husband's. When the husband is out of work, there is no guarantee that the wife will be able to keep her job either. Unemployment runs in families. Because of assortative mating and coresidence, couples typically share the disadvantages of limited schooling, a depressed local labor market, and the like. In fact, the unemployment rate is three times higher for those whose spouse is unemployed rather than employed (Klein 1983).

Third, many wives with reasonable earnings prospects are working full-time already. Perhaps for this reason, unemployed husbands in 1984 were slightly less likely than their employed counterparts to have a wife in the labor force—a reversal of the earlier pattern (US Bureau of the Census 1984:399). When the husband loses his job, relatively few homemakers are available to be drawn into the workforce anew, and working wives cannot greatly increase their economic contributions to the family.

Empirical evidence supports the notion that wives' labor force participation does relatively little to make up for income losses when the husband is out of work. Gramlich & Laren (1984) draw on 1967–1980 data from the Panel Study of Income Dynamics to estimate the extra earnings generated by other family members in response to the unemployment of the head. They report that unemployment has only weak effects on the labor incomes of secondary earners. Indeed, these effects are largely swamped by the discouraged worker effect whereby high unemployment keeps other family members from venturing into the work force. Also using the Panel Study of Income Dynamics, Nakamura & Nakamura (1985) find that a drop in husband's income from the previous year has no statistically significant effect on hours of work by wives who were not already working.

To sum up, the economic prospects of young men deteriorated at a time when young women commanded higher wages than ever. Labor force participation by married women undoubtedly permitted young families to achieve middle class consumption standards that would have been impossible on one paycheck alone. The trade-off was that families lost some of their flexibility to field additional earners, should the the main bread winner become unemployed.

IMPACT ON WOMEN NOT IN HUSBAND-WIFE FAMILIES

The implications for inequality of women's labor force participation reach beyond the consequences for husband-wife families. The relative economic situation of female-headed families (and, indeed, women living apart from families) has also been shaped by women's greater involvement in paid employment. Consider the feminization of poverty. Poverty rates among female-headed families stood at a startling 35 per 100 in 1984 (US Bureau of the Census 1985). Women's growing labor force participation did little for the economic situation of these women. Indeed, the feminization of poverty was due to two factors in which women's employment was at least indirectly implicated (Garfinkel & McLanahan 1985).

First, other groups moved out of the poverty population, leaving women behind. For example, the poverty rate for persons in male-headed families was cut in half—from 18.2 in 1959 to 9.3 per hundred in 1983 (Hare 1985:17). The rate for those in families headed by women declined only modestly from 49.4 to 40.5. Male-headed families fared better over the long haul because men's earnings are higher and more responsive to economic growth than are women's (Plotnick & Skidmore 1975). The wife's earnings also increasingly buoyed husband-wife families. If working wives narrowed the gap between homemakers' families and their own, they undoubtably placed female-headed families at an even greater relative disadvantage.

Second, women's share of the poverty population grew because female-headed families became more prevalent among all families. Although no one cause of the growth of female-headed families can be singled out, many researchers have pointed to an "independence effect" of married women's labor force participation (Cherlin 1979, Hannan et al 1977). If a job gives a woman the financial means to end an unhappy marriage and avoid a precipitous remarriage, rising employment rates of wives are apt to have contributed to the increase in divorce and the growth of female-headed families.

Married women's labor force participation has been a social innovation narrowing income disparities among husband-wife families. From the perspective of female-headed families, however, the rise in working women may exacerbate inequality. On the one hand, higher work rates for women add extra earners to the already advantaged husband-wife units. On the other hand, women's paid employment contributes to divorce and the formation of new, characteristically low-income, female-headed families.

A FINAL ASSESSMENT

Research is clear on one point. Working wives have been an equalizing influence on the pretax, money income of husband-wife families. This influence has probably become even more significant in the face of other, unequalizing developments—older men's declining labor force participation, young men's earnings disadvantage, and general cutbacks in social welfare benefits. Besides blunting overall inequality, women's greater work force involvement has worked to smooth out income disparities between age groups, between generations, and even over the life cycle. For example, young families, facing the high cost of a first home and relatively low male wages, have benefited especially from women's rising wage and work rates. As more and more women work, however, the working wife doesn't help a family move up financially so much as she keeps it from losing ground to others.

We have noted deficiencies in existing studies of the distributional impact of women's labor force participation. In moving beyond previous work, future researchers face three challenges.

First, consideration of the distribution of well-being calls for moving beyond pretax money income to considering a full range of costs and benefits associated with working. Basic conclusions about the equalizing role of working wives would undoubtedly be altered were studies to incorporate taxes, the value of homemakers' services, job-related expenses, and fringe benefits. The issue is not merely one of improved measurement of economic well-being. Valuing the homemaker's work hinges on the resolution of theoretical and conceptual questions about how families and individuals come to define "the good life" and go about achieving it.

Second, a satisfying theoretical account would place women's economic activities within a broad social and economic context. To date, studies of the impact of women's labor force participation on the distribution of income have been largely descriptive exercises—informative, technically competent, and even sophisticated, but largely atheoretical. Theory driven analyses would require firmer understanding of the recruitment, allocation, and remuneration of women workers in the marketplace as well as the effect of women workers on the employment opportunities and wage rates of men. The changing opportunity structure for earnings and other income (e.g. social welfare benefits) facilitates and constrains family efforts to generate income. Given this context, a theoretical perspective on women's work and family income inequality calls for a unified theory of family income-getting.

Although the limitations of the "new home economics" are now widely recognized by sociologists and others (Berk & Berk 1983, Hannan 1982, Sawhill 1977), microeconomic theory has provided key notions such as those of rational decision-making, opportunity costs of employment, and benefits from task specialization. In sociology, work by Oppenheimer (1982) has focused attention on the uniquely sociological components of female work force decisions. For instance, she emphasizes the occupational reference group which shapes consumption aspirations; the taken-for-granted strategies of income-getting in response to predictable imbalances between peak career earnings and peak family needs; and the importance of social status considerations in women's labor force participation.

Another useful element in a theory of income-getting takes account of the unobserved heterogeneity of women's work force decisions. Whether women work or not depends on how highly they value housekeeping activities, workplace friendships, having a "career," and other personal preferences reflecting gender socialization, cultural norms, and the like. Nakamura & Nakamura (1985), for example, distinguish wives who see themselves working only temporarily to meet short-run needs; wives who are motivated by the family's economic need but expect to work most of their lives, and wives who are motivated not by financial need but rather by a desire for a career or an avocation. Since differing orientations are likely to influence whether a woman works and how much she earns if she does, motivational aspects of family income-getting would ideally figure in efforts to unify the macro and micro contexts of family decision-making giving rise to the distribution of income.

Third, descriptive studies make clear that the distributional effect of working wives varies by race and life cycle stage. Racial differences in particular have been changing over time. Especially within the context of the theoretical and measurement advances we forecast for studies of family inequality, subgroup analyses are a very promising avenue for research.

Literature Cited

Allison, P. 1978. Measures of inequality. *Am. Sociol. Rev.* 43:685–80

Bartlett, R. L., Poulton-Callahan, C. 1982. Changing family structures and the distribution of family income: 1951 to 1976. *Soc. Sci. Q.* 63:29–47

Beller, A. H. 1982. Occupational segregation by sex: Determinants and changes. *J. Hum. Resour.* 17:371–91

Bergmann, B. R. 1974. Occupational segregation, wages and profits when employers discriminate by race and sex. *East. Econ. J.* 1:103–10

Bergmann, B. R., Devine, R. D., Gordon, P., Reedy, D., Sage, L., Wise, C. 1980. The effect of wives' labor force participation on inequality in the distribution of family income. *J. Hum. Resour.* 15:452–56

Berk, R. A., Berk, S. F. 1983. Supply side sociology of the family: The challenge of the new home economics. *Ann. Rev. Sociol.* 9:375–95

Berk, S. F., Berk, R. A. 1979. *Labor and Leisure at Home: Content and Organization of the Household Day.* Beverly Hills, Calif: Sage

Betson, D., van der Gaag, J. 1984. Working married women and the distribution of income. *J. Hum. Resourc.* 19:532–43

Blau, P. M., Duncan, O. D. 1967. *The American Occupational Structure.* New York: Wiley

Bluestone, B., Harrison, B. 1982. *The De-industrialization of America.* New York: Basic Books

Bowen, W. G., Finegan, T. A. 1969. *The Economics of Labor Force Participation.* Princeton, NJ: Princeton Univ. Press

Butz, W. P., Ward, M. P. 1979. The emergence of countercyclical U.S. fertility. *Am. Econ. Rev.* 69:318–28

Cain, G. 1966. *Married Women in the Labor Force.* Chicago: Univ. Chicago Press

Carlson, A. C. 1986. What happened to the "family wage"? *Public Inter.* 83:3–17

Carroll, M. S. 1962. The working wife and her family's economic position. *Mon. Labor Rev.* 85:866–74

Cherlin, A. 1979. Work life and marital dissolution. In *Divorce and Separation,* ed. G. Levinger, O. C. Moles, pp. 151–66. New York: Basic Books

Clark, R. L., Anderson, K., Johnson, T. 1980. Retirement in dual-career families. In *Retirement Policy in an Aging Society,* ed. R. L. Clark, pp. 109–27. Durham, NC: Duke Univ. Press

Danziger, S. 1980. Do working wives increase family income inequality? *J. Hum. Resour.* 15:446–51

De Boer, L., Seeborg, M. 1984. The female-male unemployment differential: Effects of changes in industry employment. *Mon. Labor Rev.* 107:8–15

Dooley, M., Gottschalk, P. 1982. Does a younger male labor force mean greater earnings inequality? *Mon. Labor Rev.* 107:42–45

Dooley, M., Gottschalk, P. 1985. The increasing proportion of men with low earnings in the United States. *Demography* 22:25–34

Easterlin, R. A. 1980. *Birth and Fortune: The Impact of Numbers on Personal Welfare.* New York: Basic Books

England, P., Farkas, G. 1986. *Households, Employment, and Gender: A Social, Economic, and Demographic View.* New York: Alpine

Farkas, G. 1976. Education, wage rates, and the division of labor between husband and wife. *J. Marriage Fam.* 41:473–83

Ferber, M. A., Green, C. A. 1985. Homemakers' imputed wages: Results of the Heckman technique compared with women's own estimates. *J. Hum. Resour.* 20:90–99

Freeman, R. B. 1979. The effect of demographic factors on age-earnings profiles. *J. Hum. Resour.* 14:289–318

Fullerton, H. N., Tschetter, J. 1983. The 1995 labor force: A second look. *Mon. Labor Rev.* 106:3–10

Garfinkel, I., McLanahan, S. 1985. The feminization of poverty: Nature, causes and a partial cure. *Institute for Poverty Discussion Paper No.* 776–85. Madison, Wisc: Univ. Wisc.

Geerken, M., Gove, W. R. 1983. *At Home and At Work: The Family's Allocation of Labor.* Beverly Hills, Calif: Sage

Gordon, N. M. 1979. The institutional responses: The Social Security system. In *The Subtle Revolution: Women at Work,* ed. R. E. Smith, pp. 223–55. Washington, DC: Urban Inst.

Gramlich, E. M., Laren, D. S. 1984. How widespread are income losses in a recession? In *Aims and Outcomes of President Reagan's Social Welfare Policy,* ed. D. L. Bawden, pp. 157–80. Washington, DC: Urban Inst.

Gregorio, D. I., Lewis, L. S., Wanner, R. A. 1982. Assessing merit and need: Distributive justice and salary attainment in academia. *Soc. Sci. Q.* 63:492–516

Gronau, R. 1980. Home production—a forgotten industry. *Rev. Econ. Stat.* 62:408–13

Gronau, R. 1982. Inequality of family income: Do wives' earnings matter? *Pop. Dev. Rev.* 8:119–136 (Suppl.)

Hannan, M. T. 1982. Families, markets and social structure: An essay on Becker's "A Treatise on the Family." *J. Econ. Lit.* 20:65–72

Hannan, M. T., Tuma, N. B., Groenveld, L. P. 1977. Income and marital events: Evidence from an income maintenance experiment. *Am. J. Sociol.* 82:1186–1211

Harris, R. J., Hedderson, J. J. 1981. Effects of wife's income on family income inequality. *Sociol. Meth. Res.* 10:211–32

Heckman, J. 1976. The common structure of statistical models of truncation, sample selection and limited dependent variables and a simple estimator for such models. *Ann. Econ. Soc. Measur.* 5:475–92

Henle, P., Ryscavage, P. 1980. The distribution of earned income among men and women, 1958–77. *Mon. Labor Rev.* 103:3–10

Hirschman, C. 1977. *The distribution of the secular rise in earned income.* Presented Ann. Meet. Pop. Assoc. Am. St. Louis, Mo.

Hoffman, L. W. 1974. Effects of maternal employment on the child: A review of the research. *Dev. Psychol.* 10:204–28

Horvath, R. W. 1980. Working wives reduce inequality in the distribution of family earnings. *Mon. Labor Rev.* 103:51–3

Huber, J., Spitze, G. 1983. *Sex Stratification: Children, Housework, and Jobs.* New York: Academic Press

Ignatius, D. 1978. The rich get richer as well-to-do wives enter the labor force. *Wall Street J.,* Sept. 8.

Jencks, C., Assoc. 1972. *Inequality: A Reassessment of the Effect of Family Schooling in America.* New York: Harper

Kakwani, N. C. 1980. *Income Inequality and Poverty: Methods of Estimation and Policy Applications.* Oxford: Oxford Univ. Press

Kessler, R. C., McRae, J. A. Jr. 1981. Trends in the relationship between sex and psychological distress: 1957–1976. *Am. Sociol. Rev.* 46:443–52

Klein, D. P. 1983. Trends in employment and unemployment in families. *Mon. Labor Rev.* 107:21–25

Kreps, J., Clark, R. 1975. *Sex, Age, and Work: The Changing Composition of the Labor Force.* Baltimore, Md: Johns Hopkins Univ. Press

Kutscher, R. E., Personick, V. A. 1986. Deindustrialization and the shift to services. *Mon. Labor Rev.* 109:3–13

Kuttner, B. 1983. The declining middle. *Atlantic Mon.* 252:60–72

Lawrence, R. Z. 1984. Sectoral shifts and the size of the middle class. *Brookings Rev.* 3:3–11

Layard, R., Zabalza, A. 1979. Family income distribution: Explanation and policy evaluation. *J. Polit. Econ.* 87:S133–61 (Suppl.)

Lazear, E. P., Michael, R. T. 1980. Real income equivalence among one-earner and two-earner families. *Am. Econ. Rev.* 70:203–8

Lehrer, E., Nerlove, M. 1984. A life-cycle analysis of family income distribution. *Econ. Inq.* 22:360–74

Leibowitz, A. 1977. Parental input and children's achievement. *J. Hum. Res.* 12:242–51

Leontief, W. 1983. Technological advance, economic growth, and the distribution of income. *Pop. Dev. Rev.* 9:403–10

Levy, F., Michel, R. C. 1985. Are the baby boomers selfish? *Am. Demogr.* 7:38–41

Lichter, D. T. 1982. The migration of dual-worker families: Does the wife's job matter? *Soc. Sci. Q.* 63:48–57

Miller, H. P. 1966. *Income Distribution in the United States*. Washington, DC: USGPO

Mincer, J. 1974. *Schooling, Experience, and Earnings*. New York: Nat. Bur. Econ. Res.

Myers, D. 1985. Wives' earnings and rising costs of home ownership. *Soc. Sci. Q.* 66:319–29

Nakamura, A., Nakamura, M. 1985. *The Second Paycheck: A Socioeconomic Analysis of Earnings*. New York: Academic Press

O'Hare, W. P. 1985. Poverty in America: Trends and new patterns. *Pop. Bull.* Vol. 40, No. 3. Washington, DC: Pop. Ref. Bur.

Oppenheimer, V. K. 1970. *Female Labor Force in the United States: Demographic and Economic Factors Governing Its Growth and Changing Composition*. Berkeley, Calif: Inst. Int. Stud.

Oppenheimer, V. K. 1972. Rising educational attainment, declining fertility and the inadequacies of the female labor market. In *Demographic and Social Aspects of Population Growth*, Vol. 1, 9 ed. C. F. Westoff, R. Parke, Jr., pp. 305–28. Washington, DC: USGPO

Oppenheimer, V. K. 1982. *Work and the Family: A Study in Social Demography*. New York: Academic Press

Pfeffer, J., Ross, J. 1982. The effects of marriage and a working wife on occupational and wage attainment. *Admin. Sci. Q.* 27:66–80

Plotnick, R. D. 1982. Trends in male earning inequality. *South. Econ. J.* 48:724–32

Plotnick, R. D., Skidmore, F. 1975. *Progress Against Poverty: A Review of the 1964–1974 Decade*. New York: Academic Press

Population Today. 1985. After manufacturing, what? (Demographically speaking) *Population Today* 13:2,10

Radner, D. B. 1982. Distribution of family income: Improved estimates. *Soc. Security Bull.* 45:13–21

Rivlin, A. 1975. Income distribution: Can economists help? *Am. Econ. Rev.* 55:1–15

Rosenfeld, R. A. 1985. *Farm Women: Work, Farm, and Family*. Chapel Hill, NC: Univ. NC Press

Rosenthal, N. 1985. The shrinking middle class: Myth or reality? *Mon. Labor Rev.* 108:3–10

Ross, H. L., Sawhill, I. 1975. *Time of Transition: The Growth of Families Headed by Women*. Washington, DC: Urban Inst.

Russell, L. B. 1982. *The Baby Boom Generation and the Economy*. Washington, DC: Brookings Inst.

Rytina, N. F., Bianchi, S. M. 1984. Occupational reclassification and changes in distribution by gender. *Mon. Labor Rev.* 107:11–17

Sawhill, I. V. 1977. Economic perspectives on the family. *Daedalus* 106:115–25

Schumann, R. 1984. Workers purchasing power rises despite slowdown in wage and salary gains. *Mon. Labor Rev.* 107:10–14

Shorrocks, A. 1983. The impact of income components on the distribution of family incomes. *Q. J. Econ.* 98:311–26

Smeeding, T. M. 1985. Approaches to measuring and valuing in-kind subsidies and the distribution of their benefits. In *Economic Transfers in the United States*, ed. Marilyn Moon, pp. 139–171. Chicago, Ill: Univ. Chicago Press

Smith, J. P. 1979. The distribution of family earnings. *J. Polit. Econ.* 87:S163–92 (Suppl)

Smith, J. P., Ward, M. P. 1984. *Women's Wages and Work in the Twentieth Century*. Santa Monica, Calif: Rand Corp.

Smith, J. P., Welch, F. 1978. The Over-educated American? A review article. Rand Paper Series P-6253. Santa Monica, Calif: Rand Corp.

Snyder, D., Hudis, P. M. 1976. Occupational income and the effects of minority competition and segregation: A reanalysis and some new evidence. *Am. Sociol. Rev.* 41:209–34

Steinberg, B. 1983. The mass market is splitting apart. *Fortune* 108:76–82

Sweet, J. A. 1971. The employment of wives and the inequality of family income. Soc. Stat. Sect. Proceed. Am. Stat. Assoc.: 1–5

Sweet, J. A. 1973. *Women in the Labor Force*. New York: Seminar

Thurow, L. C., Lucas, R. E. B. 1972. *The American Distribution of Income: A Structural Problem*. Washington, DC: USGPO

Treas, J. 1981. Women's employment and its implications for the economic status of the elderly of the future. In *Aging: Social Change*, ed. S. B. Keisler, J. N. Morgan, V. K. Oppenheimer, pp. 561–85. New York: Academic Press

Treas, J. 1983. Trickle down or transfers? Postwar determinants of family income inequality. *Am. Sociol. Rev.* 48:546–59

Treas, J., Walther, R. J. 1978. Family structure and the distribution of family income. *Soc. Forc.* 56:866–80

Treiman, D. J., Hartman, H. I. 1981. *Women, Work, and Wages*. Washington, DC: Nat. Acad.

Urquhart, M. 1984. The employment shift to services: Where did it come from? *Mon. Labor Rev.* 107:15–22

U.S. Bureau of the Census. 1984. *Statistical Abstract of the U.S.* Washington, DC: USGPO

U.S. Bureau of the Census. 1985. P. 28. USGPO

U.S. Bureau of the Census. 1986. Earnings in 1983 of married couple families, by characteristics of husbands and wives. *Curr. Pop. Rep.* P-60, No. 153

Vickery, C. V. 1979. Women's economic contribution to the family. In *The Subtle Revolution: Women at Work*, ed. R. E. Smith, pp. 159–200. Washington, DC: The Urban Institute.

Waite, L. 1976. Working Wives: 1940–1960. *Am. Sociol. Rev.* 41:61–80

Waite, L. J. 1981. U.S. women at work. *Pop. Bull.*, Vol. 36, No. 2. Washington, DC: Pop. Ref. Bur.

Walker, K. E., Woods, M. 1976. *Time Use: A Measure of Household Production and Family Goods*. Washington, DC: Am. Home Econ. Assoc.

Welch, F. 1979. Effects of cohort size on earnings: The baby boom babies' financial bust. *J. Polit. Econ.* 87:S65–S97

Ann. Rev. Sociol. 1987. 13:289–312

JAPANESE INDUSTRIAL ORGANIZATION IN COMPARATIVE PERSPECTIVE

James R. Lincoln

Department of Management and Department of Sociology, University of Arizona, Tucson, Arizona 85721

Kerry McBride

Department of Sociology, Indiana University, Bloomington, Indiana 47401

Abstract

This review examines theory and research on Japanese patterns of work and industrial organization in broad comparison with the United States and other Western societies. Four topics are considered: labor markets, internal organization structure, employee work attitudes, and industrial organization. Two issues that pervade the discussion are: (*a*) the extent to which real differences exist between Japan and Western industrial economies in the orientations of workers and the structure of labor markets, firms, and industries; (*b*) the extent to which such differences can be explained within general theories of social and economic organization, as opposed to heavily culturalist or historicist claims for Japanese uniqueness. Our general stance is that while internal labor market theory and other rationalist models of Japanese work organization have considerable explanatory power, there are limits to their capacity to account for Japanese distinctiveness.

INTRODUCTION

The study of Japanese industrial and work organization presents more than the usual obstacles to newcomers. The problem is not simply that the literature in Japanese is inaccessible to most, owing to the difficulty of the language and the scarcity of good translations. The last 10 years have brought an inundation

289

0360-0572/87/0815-0289$02.00

of the field with mass media and quasi-scholarly attempts, along with a sprinkling of serious research efforts, to describe and explain the distinctive features of Japanese institutions and their role in Japan's phenomenal economic performance. Separating the hearsay from the evidence, the slogans from the scholarship, and the redundant from the new is no mean feat even for the handful of Western social scientists who have followed these issues since the quieter days preceding the Japanese management boom.

This review by no means provides an exhaustive coverage of published writing or relevant issues pertaining to Japanese work organization. Moreover, rather than attempt to acknowledge all minimally relevant work, we have tried to find common threads and explanatory themes that illuminate the descriptive observations. This is an area in which large bodies of systematic research simply do not exist, although there is a great deal of speculation, qualitative observation, and (more or less) informed opinion. We have chosen to discuss four topics: labor markets, internal organization structure, employee work attitudes, and industrial organization.

JAPANESE LABOR MARKETS AND INDUSTRIAL RELATIONS

Among the numerous distinctive features of Japanese work organization perhaps the most conspicuous and publicized are the labor market patterns of lifetime employment and the *nenko* or seniority-based wage and promotion system (Cole 1972, Eisuke 1984, Galenson 1976, Levine 1965). The former refers to the practice in Japanese industry of selectively recruiting new school graduates and retaining them until a relatively early mandatory retirement age. The latter concerns the practice of heavily basing internal promotion and pay decisions on the employee's age, seniority, and life-course circumstances such as marriage and childrearing.

To those finding economic rationality in the treatment of labor as a variable cost and the association of wages with marginal productivity, these patterns have long seemed an anachronistic drag on Japan's drive to economic modernity which would someday be jettisoned (Abegglen 1958, Aoki 1984). Indeed, the once orthodox interpretation of the Japanese employment system, only recently fallen out of favor, is that its inner logic is a paternalism rooted in traditional Japanese collectivist values (Bennett & Ishino 1963, Shimada 1983). From this perspective, the distinctive features of Japanese work organization—lifetime employment, *nenko,* welfarism, employee loyalty, consensus decision-making, and participatory work structures—are all expressions of a corporate familism carried over from Japanese feudalism into the modern industrial era. The reasons for the decline of this view are, we think, three: (*a*) historical distortions in the accounts of some proponents that label as "traditional" some practices actually of recent origin (Cole 1972, Shimada 1983); (b) indications that such practices have hardly hurt and may even have advanced the performance and competitiveness of Japanese firms (Koike 1983a, Thurow 1985); (c) the rise of sociological theories of organizational control and economic theories of institutional rationality that reinterpret Japanese work structures as efficient, modern developments, conspicuous in Japan but also at the cutting edge of Western economic trends (Cole 1979, Dore 1973, Ouchi 1980).

Considerable debate has centered on whether tenure, pay, and mobility patterns are in fact substantially different between Japan and Western industrial countries. Though few in number, some careful studies have addressed this question (Gordon 1982; Hashimoto & Raisian 1985; Koike 1983a,b; Cole 1979). They generally indicate that Japanese labor markets *are* distinctive, but not so much as some had thought. Moreover, they suggest that crude attempts to contrast Japan with the "West" can be seriously misleading because European and North American modes of work organization are themselves spaced along a continuum on which Japan also falls. Japanese practices may seem particularly exotic to Americans because on many dimensions of workplace and labor market structuring the United States is itself an extreme case and polar opposite of Japan (Cole 1979, Koike 1983a).

Permanent Employment

This is particularly true of tenure with an employer. Under the permanent employment system with its prohibitions on layoffs and mid-career recruiting, one would certainly expect low turnover and high tenure in the Japanese workforce. The data consistently show this to be the case, although the differences do not always appear large. One reason is that the labor force survey data used to make these assessments are often aggregated over industrial and labor market segments whose participation in the permanent employment system is highly uneven. The jobs of temporary workers including many women and retirees, *shokaido* or subcontract workers, plus regular employees in small and peripheral firms are vulnerable to buffeting by market forces from which regular workers in large firms are protected. The existence of these classes of employees has led some writers to put the proportion of the Japanese work force covered by permanent employment guarantees at no more than 30–40% (Hashimoto & Raisian 1985:721, Galenson 1976). Such attempts to draw a sharp boundary around the "permanently employed" seem in general ill-founded. As Cole (1972) has noted, permanent employment is not a contractual state, but a pervasive norm affecting the treatment of regular employees in Japan. Large firms in growing industries more easily abide by it than do small, dependent companies and firms in stagnant or declining markets.

Nenko

Moreover, evidence that the *nenko* system produces distinctive wage determination and mobility processes in Japanese industry is fairly consistent and unambiguous, although it also cautions against the tendency to view Japanese patterns as wholly unique (Kalleberg & Lincoln 1987; Koike 1983a,b; Hashimoto & Raisan 1985). Like permanent employment, the *nenko* practice of life-cycle and seniority-based wage and promotion has its roots in early post–World War II industrial relations, when the newly formed unions demanded that corporations take responsibility for the well-being of employees and their families in a period of economic chaos. Despite the recent emergence of these practices it would be a mistake to wholly discount the role of Japanese culture and tradition in rendering them legitimate solutions to current economic problems. As Cole (1972) has argued in a thoughtful essay, innovations in industrial relations and employment practice aimed at resolving specific labor conflicts and tensions are selected and legitimated within a framework of cultural values and institutional pressures. Though not a simple survival from the past, their apparent congruence with tradition may be a crucial factor in winning them acceptance and ensuring their institutionalization over time (Shimada 1983).

Some fairly systematic analysis demonstrates that wages in Japanese industry do indeed show greater dependence on the seniority of the worker than is the case in the United States (Nakamura 1980, Hashimoto & Raisian 1985, Koike 1983a, Kalleberg & Lincoln 1987). Moreover, consistent with the view that the distinctive features of Japanese labor markets are confined to the "core" firms in the dual economy, the differences are most apparent in the largest firms. Koike (1983a) finds, however, that Japanese distinctiveness exists only for blue-collar workers: The age and seniority-wage profiles for white collar workers in a number of Western countries are not materially different from the Japanese norm. In his view, Japanese production workers have undergone a process of "white-collarization" which in several respects differentiates them from blue-collar employees in other countries while causing the conditions of their employment to converge toward those experienced by white-collar colleagues. This view is consistent with numerous examples of how Japanese companies strive to reduce the gap in status and working conditions between blue- and white-collar workers (Dore 1973). All employees are on salary; there are no segregated parking lots and cafeterias for production workers; the company union includes lower supervisors and other white collar workers; and the management/worker wage gap is considerably smaller than in the United States (Pucik 1984). Moreover, as a matter of historical fact, Japanese unions in the early postwar era bargained explicitly with management for employment status and benefits comparable to those enjoyed by white-collar workers (Koike 1983a, Ono 1980).

Job-Based Compensation

The relatively low significance of the blue-collar/white-collar distinction for labor markets in Japan is a specific manifestation of the more general tendency for occupational differences to be minor criteria in the allocation of wages and other job rewards. This, of course, represents a sharp contrast with the norm in the United States, where job classification systems are a high profile feature of workplace organization and figure centrally in wage and status determination. The small influence of occupational roles in Japanese society has often been noted in "culturalist" arguments that Japanese social organization rests on a tradition-rooted group-centeredness which discounts strong attachments to within-group positions or strata (Abegglen 1958, Nakane 1970, Cole & Tominaga 1976, Dore 1973, Shimada 1983).

Although the merits of detailed job classifications are a continuing topic of Japanese debate, both workers and managers have resisted major moves in this direction. Workers and unions fear the erosion of the principles of seniority and "reproduction costs" which guarantee a rising standard of living for employees with increasing maturity and family responsibilities (Galenson 1976, Ono 1980). Managers are concerned with the constraints on task design and allocation implied by a rigid job classification system (Daito 1984). Job rotation and flexible labor assignments are a characteristic feature of the Japanese workplace and an important mechanism in reducing the strains and costs imposed by the permanent employment system (Hatvany & Pucik 1981). Although many companies have introduced some form of job classification, several studies note that these are often simply another guise for what remains essentially a seniority and age-graded system (Abegglen 1958, Marsh & Mannari 1976).

To our knowledge, there are few careful studies of the contribution of job differences to earnings determination in the Japanese workforce. Cole & Tominaga (1976) analyzed aggregate data on the Japanese labor force in a wages-by-occupation and firm-size table. They find the occupational variance to be small and conclude that their findings underscore the low occupation-consciousness of the Japanese. In a large survey of Japanese and US manufacturing employees, Kalleberg & Lincoln (1987) report strong evidence that the *nenko*-related determinants—age, seniority, and marital status—have a far greater influence on earnings in a Japanese sample, whereas job attributes and managerial rank play the larger role in determining pay in a comparable American sample.

Enterprise Unions and Industrial Relations

A striking institutional contrast between Japan and the United States with numerous implications for the structure of labor markets and industrial relations concerns the organization of unions. A legacy of the postwar Occupation reforms, Japanese unions are organized on a per-enterprise basis, concentrated in the largest firms, and formed into weak federations at higher levels (Kawada 1973, Shirai 1983). They organize all regular (blue- and white-collar) employees, including first and second-line supervisors. These arrangements have provoked much speculation that Japanese unions are highly dependent upon and easily coopted by the company. They avoid strong confrontations to advance their members' interests, and, indeed, function as yet another Japanese device for solidifying the bond between worker and firm (Burawoy 1983, Galenson 1976). Observers on the other side argue that, despite these constraints, Japanese unions bargain hard on wage and benefit issues, and have effectively coordinated their militancy in the annual "Spring offensives" which present selected groups of employers with a set of unified wage demands (Hanami 1981:94). Hard evidence is scarce, but a careful empirical analysis of the effects of Japanese unions on productivity (Freeman 1984, Muramatsu 1984) yields estimates strikingly similar to those obtained with US data. Moreover, a study by Koshiro (1983) concludes that union militancy (as indicated by the Spring strike offensives) has been an important force behind rising aggregate wage levels in the Japanese economy. Yet a recent employee-level investigation of the impact of unionism in 100 Japanese and US factories does provide substantial support for the "cooptation" hypothesis. Lincoln & Kalleberg (1985) find that American unions have a markedly more negative effect on employee job satisfaction and commitment to the firm than do Japanese unions. Kalleberg & Lincoln (1987), moreover, find no evidence in the same sample that Japanese union plants pay higher wages than their nonunion counterparts, although such an effect is clearly evident in US data (Freeman & Medoff 1984).

The Internal Labor Market Hypothesis

As we have noted, an idea which in recent years has gained considerable ground among students of Japanese economic organization is that the distinctive features of the Japanese employment system can be understood within a firm internal labor market (FILM) logic. Since FILMs are viewed by many labor theorists as an emergent form in the evolution of work organization and labor control, this represents a significant shift in perspective, for phenomena once seen as nonrational anachronisms are now cast as cutting-edge developments. In light of Japan's extraordinary economic success, Western theorists have, of course, been under considerable pressure to find the economic and administrative rationality in practices once disparaged as feudal and paternalistic. The firm internal labor market model does provide a compelling explanation of many elements of the Japanese employment system, although probably not all, and some high-quality evidence disputes several of its predictions for Japan.

In a firm internal labor market, employees are recruited at relatively low-level ports of entry into the organization, receive on-the-job training in enterprise-specific skills and values, and compete solely with one another for promotion into higher positions (Doeringer & Piore 1971). Several of the attributes of Japanese labor markets are predicted by FILM theory. Careful screening of new recruits for entry level positions, long tenure with the same firm, intensive in-house instruction and on-the-job training, and filling higher positions through internal promotion are patterns common in Japan which also number among the defining characteristics of FILMs. Moreover, seniority-based compensation and promotion have been given a FILM interpretation: When skills are enterprise-specific, then external training, experience, and certification no longer signal competence and performance potential. Seniority becomes the best indicator of skill and familiarity in the ways of the particular company. Furthermore, Doeringer & Piore (1971) have argued that when knowledge and skills are enterprise-specific, seniority-based internal promotion is further necessary to induce older workers to conduct on-the-job training of younger ones, for they would otherwise be in the position of training potential replacements for themselves.

Many theorists link the origin of FILMs to organizations' drive for control of the motives and behaviors of their members (Burawoy 1979, Edwards 1979). By encouraging lifetime careers within the same firm, competition for promotion among the presently employed, and skills not valued in the external labor market, companies foster dependence and loyalty in a workforce. Thus, FILMs in Japanese companies represent one of numerous Japanese work structures that appear to be designed according to a "commitment-maximizing" logic. That the organizational commitment and loyalty of Japanese employees is widely thought to be among the highest of industrial workers anywhere in the world is often taken as testimony for the effectiveness of FILMs and other Japanese-style control structures for realizing these employee-level outcomes (Cole 1979, Hatvany & Pucik 1981, Lincoln & Kalleberg 1985, Ouchi 1980, Ouchi & Johnson 1978).

Even enterprise unionism in Japan has been explained as another manifestation of internal labor markets in Japanese companies. Since workers acquire much of their training, pursue their careers, and obtain their wages and welfare benefits within the setting of a single firm, Shirai (1983:125) argues that: "An enterprise union becomes the logical form of organization for Japanese workers because they find their common interests as industrial workers within a particular enterprise."

Despite the seemingly impressive congruence between the FILM model and aspects of the Japanese employment system, some pieces of the puzzle do not fit. Other aspects of *nenko,* such as bonuses and salary increments occasioned by marriage and childbearing, do not have the same FILM rationality as seniority-based pay. Furthermore, the assumption that FILMs have further evolved in Japanese industry leads, as Cole (1979) has argued, to a prediction that more internal job changing should complement lower rates of interfirm labor mobility in Japan. His comparative study of Detroit and Yokohama workers found both intra- and interfirm mobility to be lower in Japan. Similarly, Lincoln & Kalleberg's (1985) survey of manufacturing employees in the two countries showed no difference in individual employees' promotion expectations between the American and Japanese samples. Hatvany & Pucik (1981) argue, however, that slow promotion is the norm in Japanese companies, and lateral job rotation functions to provide variation in reward and experience without an upward shift in formal job status.

INTERNAL ORGANIZATIONAL STRUCTURES

If labor market structures and processes rank first in Western eyes among the seemingly exotic features of Japanese industrial organization, internal organization runs a close second. The two, in any case, are closely linked, for permanent employment, *nenko*, and other elements of Japanese internal labor markets impose severe constraints on the organization of firms. Moreover, recent students have made similar arguments about the external organization of industries and markets as manifested in the enterprise groupings *(keiretsu)* that populate the Japanese economic landscape.

Large sample labor force surveys have generated the data base for some fairly fine-grained analyses of employment tenure, mobility, and wage patterns in the Japanese economy. Given obvious problems of access and measurement, the same cannot be said of the internal structuring of Japanese companies. Yet some of the richest and most fascinating accounts of the Japanese workplace are the qualitative and impressionistic descriptions of authority, division of labor, interaction, and supervision that appear in such classics of the genre as Abegglen (1958), Dore (1973), Clark (1979), Cole (1971, 1979), Rohlen (1974), and others. Moreover, it is the Japanese leadership styles and organizational designs, much more than the concrete personnel matters of job security and compensation, which have been promoted in the management-oriented writings of Ouchi (1981) and Pascale & Athos (1981) as stimulants to employee motivation and cures for American industrial doldrums. Japanese organizational structures, then, have attracted intense interest, wide discussion, and a myriad of attempts at imitation, but an unfortunately small body of systematic empirical research.

Division of Labor

Still, there is sufficient consistency in the qualitative reports that, with some supporting quantitative evidence, a fairly clear picture of a Japanese organizational form has evolved—one seemingly built around the immediate imperative of maintaining internal labor markets and the longer-run one of maximizing commitment to the firm (Dore 1973, Hatvany & Pucik 1981). Its central elements involve division of labor, status hierarchy and span of control, and the structure of authority and decision-making.

Consider division of labor—the first step in organizing. In Western—especially American—organizations, job titles proliferate, and individuals generally pursue careers within occupational specialties (Ouchi 1981). One oft-noted reason is the attempts by American labor unions to preserve control over task assignments and labor supply by insisting on detailed job classifications and workrules (Cole 1979, Piore & Sabel 1984). More generally, a case could be made that occupational consciousness and organization play an unusually central role in American culture and social structure, owing to a variety of institutional processes, such as the strength of the professions, the vocational emphasis of American education, and relatively weak attachments to employing organizations and local communities (Cole & Tominaga 1976). Japanese organizations, as we have said, tend not to use detailed job and occupational classifications, and in both blue- and white-collar strata, promote job rotation and generalist careers (Lincoln et al 1978, Ouchi & Johnson 1978, Sasaki 1981). A common characterization is that Americans pursue careers within occupations that cut across firms, while the opposite pattern holds in Japan. A variety of evidence seems consistent with this view (Cole 1979, Cole & Tominaga 1976, Kalleberg & Lincoln 1987).

If the individual incumbents of occupational positions are not the primary functional units in Japanese organizations, what are? The obvious answer is the work group. The cohesion, loyalty, and cooperation associated with work groups in Japanese companies are often cited in qualitative studies (Cole 1971, Dore 1982, Pucik & Hatvany 1983, Osako 1977, Rohlen 1974). Although group leaders may make symbolic gestures at accepting responsibility for failures (Clark 1979), real responsibility is diffused among and born by the members of the group (Nakane 1970). It is this collective sharing of responsibility and accountability that motivates and complements the absence of functional and authority role assignments to individuals and the positions they occupy. Several observers (Abegglen 1958:79, Yoshino 1968:206) argue that, in accord with this system of allocating responsibilities to collective units, organizational subunits proliferate in Japanese companies, although Lincoln et al (1986) find little evidence for this hypothesis in a sample of 106 Japanese and US firms. The proliferation of highly cohesive subunits does invite the risk of rivalry among them and disintegration for the organization as a whole. These tendencies have been associated in particular with the informal cliques (habatsu) that arise from common cohort membership and school ties (Yoshino 1968:208).

Hierarchy

The forms taken by authority and status hierarchies in Japanese firms and bureaus, the social relations between superiors and subordinates, and the distribution and dynamics of decision-making represent a bundle of organizational structures and processes that have struck numerous observers as particularly distinctive in Japan and again seem instrumental in producing the cohesion and commitment associated with the Japanese workforce. Some observers of Japanese corporate organization hold that, in contrast with the bloated middle-management ranks of US firms, Japanese companies have "lean" structures and flatter administrative pyramids (Child 1984, Pucik 1984). To the degree such differences exist, they may reflect the smaller size and greater specialization of Japanese corporations (Caves & Uekusa 1976, Clark 1979), and their lower reliance on such high-level staff departments as planning and finance.

At the plant or establishment level, on the other hand, a number of studies find just the opposite: Japanese hierarchies are on the average taller than the management pyramids of Western organizations (Dore 1973, Azumi & McMillan 1975a; Lincoln et al 1986). Tall hierarchies are a form of organization consistent with the constraints on structure imposed by internal labor markets. They imply long job ladders, hence opportunities for upward mobility and careers within the organization. Developing an argument earlier made by Blauner (1964) and later by Edwards (1979), Dore (1973:257) also contends that the tall and finely graded hierarchies of Japanese organizations work to avert the class consciousness and alienation typical of British plants with their short, squat authority pyramids. Instead of monolithic "classes" faced off across a chasm of privilege and reward inequities, Japanese employees are linked to one another in long chains of superior-subordinate relations. In such a structure, status equals are scarce, and the bulk of interpersonal transactions involve a status difference. Nakane (1970) has broadened this view into a general theory of the Japanese collectivity-orientation. For her, the vertical structure of Japanese society is the mechanism that motivates the strong bonds enmeshing individuals in groups.

Another feature of Japanese authority/status hierarchies, as described by Clark (1979), is their high degree of institutionalization in a set of "standard ranks." The hierarchical structure and the labels given to different levels show remarkable similarity across Japanese organizations of many different types. The titles (*hancho, bucho, kakaricho,* etc) have considerable status significance not only in the company but in the wider society and are used in everyday discourse outside the workplace (Clark 1979:106). Like civil service and military ranks, they designate status more than function, such that positions denoting leadership of a unit may in fact entail little real responsibility (Dore 1973, Hatvany & Pucik 1981). To Clark (1979:107), the standard ranks have a unifying influence on the Japanese company, for all employees occupy them—hence climb the same ladder—and they provide a common frame of reference across functionally disparate departments. Thus, the institutionalized quality of Japanese rank systems, along with their finely graded structure, may be expressions of Nakane's "vertical principle" motivating groupism in Japanese firms.

Spans of Control

Tall hierarchies imply narrow spans of control, and a number of accounts put Japanese spans at smaller numbers of subordinates than typically prevail in Western companies (Dore 1973, Pascale 1978b, Yoshino 1968). Small spans low in the management hierarchy are also thought to be consistent with the work-group organization of the Japanese workplace and the highly distinctive leadership styles of Japanese supervisors. At least one large-sample study, however, finds no significant difference in the first-line spans of Japanese and US factories (Lincoln et al 1986). On the other hand, the tendency for higher-level Japanese managers to have a number of non-line assistants reporting to them broadens spans of control (Pucik 1984:89, Lincoln et al 1986). Whether structural spans do in fact differ between Japanese and US organizations, relations between supervisors and subordinates tend to have a quality different from that commonly found in, say, the American or British workplace. Participant observation studies document the strong bonds, on and off the job, between Japanese employees and their supervisors (Cole 1971, Dore 1973, Rohlen 1974). Labor force surveys have turned up striking evidence of "paternalistic" attitudes and preferences held by Japanese workers toward their superiors (Lincoln et al 1981, Marsh & Mannari 1976, Whitehill & Takezawa 1968).

Decision-Making

As much as any aspect of organization, Japanese decision-making styles have captured the interest of Westerners and figure prominently in the array of Japanese methods that popular business writers have energetically marketed to Western companies. Japanese decision-making is commonly cast as participatory and consensual, with the initiative coming from lower levels ("bottom-up") and the responsibility for outcomes lying with groups instead of individuals (Sasaki 1981: Ch. 4; Vogel 1975, Yoshino 1968). In these respects, it reflects the broader Japanese patterns of assigning role responsibilities to groups and relying on strong vertical bonds to motivate desired actions on the part of subordinates (Hatvany & Pucik 1981, Clark 1979). Once again, the fostering of commitment appears to be the underlying rationale.

Participatory, consensus-oriented decision-making operates at both management and direct worker levels in Japanese organizations. For management-level decisions, the specific practices that have drawn the closest scrutiny are *ringi-seido* and its attendant process of *nemawashi* (Uchida 1985, Vogel 1975). The *ringi* system concerns the making of decisions through a process initiated by a lower- or middle-echelon manager who drafts a petition *(ringi-sho)* and sees that it wends its way up the hierarchy, acquiring in the process the "chops" of other relevant officials. By requiring that all proposals go to the top, the chief executive bears symbolic responsibility for every decision, and the organization averts a formal delegation of authority to lower management positions (Allston 1986, Clark 1979). Several scholars (Dore 1973, Vogel 1975, Yoshino 1968) see Japanese authority structures combining high concentration of formal authority with decentralization of de facto participation. However, as Uchida (1985) points out in a thoughtful study of decision-making in the *sogo shosha* (Japanese trading companies), the circulation of a *ringi-sho* is just the formal manifestation of a process of consensus-building through informal networking termed *nemawashi* (root-binding). By the time the *ringi-sho* is drafted, the proposal has been communicated to all affected parties, and their general acquiescence is assured (Hatvany & Pucik 1981).

The presumption that *ringi* and *nemawashi* produce consensus is widely accepted, but more debate surrounds the question of how truly "bottom-up" Japanese decision-making really is. A clever chief executive can mobilize the strong vertical ties within Japanese companies to ensure that loyal subordinates send up proposals advancing his aims (Clark 1979, Craig 1975). Moreover, given the relative youth of many Japanese corporations, founding entrepreneurs are often still alive and (aided by their glorification as corporate heroes in Japanese organizational culture) able to retain considerable control over company affairs (Clark 1979, Uchida 1985).

At the rank-and-file level, the corresponding decision-making structure that has attracted the interest of Westerners is quality circles (QC), and related small group programs, for engaging workers in decision-making. QC programs have become near-universal in Japanese industry and are rapidly expanding in American companies as well (Thomas & Shimada 1983). It seems clear, however, that there is considerable variation in the structure and functioning of QC circles. Cole (1979) gives a detailed case study description of an ideal QC program in Toyota Auto Body. Workers volunteer for participation, receive extensive training in statistical quality control techniques, are motivated to participate in lengthy meetings largely on their own time, and have the autonomy to implement their proposals. Other programs, however, may be little more than collective suggestion-making exercises, imposed by management, for which workers receive little training (Cole 1980). The diffusion of QC clearly illustrates an institutionalization process in the spread of organizational forms (DiMaggio & Powell 1983): While the jury remains out on their effectiveness, QC programs establish a company in the eyes of relevant audiences as one abreast of current developments and quick to implement progressive management trends. The institutional perspective on organization stresses the diffusion of organizational structures and practices, not as a function of technical efficiency requirements, but in response to external demands for legitimacy and conformity to prevailing "rationalized" norms and expectations.

While one might well expect QC programs in the United States to be generally weak gestures at shop-floor participation, a number of observers find the Japanese programs also failing, particularly as their novelty wears off, to hold the interest of workers. Cole (1980) notes that workers have come to perceive QC participation as one more chore demanded by management. A personnel manager in a showcase automobile plant informed us in a personal interview that attendance at circle meetings had fallen to roughly 50%, and the state of the program was a matter of serious concern to the company. Odaka (1982:232) quotes Japanese workers' complaints that management is often lax in providing the training, time, and facilities necessary for QC operations. Tokunaga (1983:323) argues that the participation of Japanese workers in QC circles and Zero Defect groups is semicompulsory and is often considered in personnel evaluations. He cites a 1970 survey of union members showing that only 7–10% of the workers responding felt a "sense of active involvement in the work," as opposed to feeling burdened by it. Yet the survey of Japanese and US manufacturing employees by Lincoln & Kalleberg (1985) and their colleagues found significant positive relationships in both samples between QC circle membership and employee commitment to the organization. The effect was somewhat larger in the Japanese sample, which may testify to the currently greater novelty value of QC in US work settings. Cole (1985) provides a useful essay on contrasts in the institutionalization of quality circles and other small group programs in Japan, the United States, Sweden, and China.

Quantitative Evidence

There is considerable anecdotal, impressionistic, and case study evidence for this general picture of the internal structuring of Japanese vis-á-vis, US organizations. Systematic quantitative data from large samples of organizations is, however, scarce. Yet a tradition of quantitative cross-national organizational research, including Japanese comparisons, has grown out of replications of the British "Aston" studies of organizational structure. One such study of Japan/Western differences in formal organization was Azumi & McMillan's (1975a) comparison of a sample of 50 Japanese factories with the two British samples of organizations surveyed by the Aston group (Pugh et al 1968) and Child (1972). Although the samples in each country differed in industrial composition and were obtained at different times by different investigators, the results were suggestive. The Japanese organizations had more vertical levels, assigned fewer specialized functions to individuals, were more centralized (in terms of formal authority), and more formalized than the British units. This pattern conforms closely to the expectations generated by qualitative studies—even regarding formalization, which may surprise some readers. Dore (1973:244) reported greater file-keeping and paper processing in the Hitachi plants he studied than in the English Electric factories. Such bureaucratization is a key element in his model of Japanese "welfare corporatism."

Virtually identical findings are reported by Lincoln et al (1986) in their comparative survey of 55 US and 51 Japanese manufacturing plants. However, these researchers obtained separate measures of the centralization of *formal authority* (the usual Aston index) and *de facto decision-making*. A very strong pattern in their data was the tendency, observed in prior qualitative work (e.g. Dore 1973:227), for higher formal centralization in the Japanese organizations to combine with greater dispersion of de facto influence.

Another study using the Aston measures which yielded results generally consistent with this pattern was Lincoln et al's (1978) survey of Japanese-owned firms in the US: With increases in the percentage of Japanese employed, they found reductions in functional specialization and some evidence of rising centralization of authority.

Yet a comparison using a subset of factories from Azumi's sample produced divergent findings. Horvath et al (1981) contrasted matched organizations, 12 each from Japan, Britain, and Sweden. The Japanese companies again proved more formalized, but in this case centralization was highest in the Swedish firms (followed by the Japanese) and the lowest level of specialization was found in the British sample. This last result is somewhat suspect, for the mean specialization score for the British firms was much lower than that observed in previous British surveys (see also Marsh & Mannari 1981, Hsu et al 1983).

Evidence against the hypothesis of a distinctive configuration of Japanese organizational traits also appears in Pascale & Maguire's (1980:440) survey of Japanese and US organizations, which revealed no significant differences between firms in the two countries in vertical differentiation, number of functional departments, or in a formalization measure. Their sample was unusual, however, in that it included companies with operations in both countries. They do, however, report more lateral and bottom-up communication in the Japanese organizations. Further, while Pascale (1978a:105) finds no significant differences by ownership or site (Japan vs the United States) in decision-making style, a more detailed comparison of decision-making in the

US-based Japanese and American-managed firms reveals clear evidence of more consultative, participatory decision-making by the Japanese (Maguire & Pascale 1978).

A large comparative study of organizational structure and performance in 110 US factories with an equal number of Japanese factories has recently been completed by Azumi and his colleagues. Although written reports are only now appearing, this very large sample promises some significant insights into the nature and consequences of Japanese organizational structures (see, e.g., Wharton et al 1986).

Task Environment and Organizational Structure

A key issue in quantitative cross-national research has been whether country differences are limited to *levels* of variables (as indexed, say, by means or proportions), or whether they extend to the causal relationships among those variables (e.g. as indexed by regression slopes; Przeworski & Teune 1970). Given the Western origins and biases of most organizational theory and research, there are indeed grounds for anticipating that the task contingency variables specified in mainstream rationalist theory may relate to organizational structures differently in Japan and in the West. Yet some researchers have concluded that task contingency factors such as scale and technology have effects on organizational structures similar to those reported in the West. In a case study of four Japanese factories with widely varying technologies, Marsh & Mannari infer support for eight of thirteen hypotheses, derived from Western theory and research, relating technology to dimensions of structure, staffing, and employee attitudes. Similarly, Tracy & Azumi's (1976) study of 44 Japanese manufacturing plants found (among other results) formalization falling with task variability and automaticity while rising with size—a pattern consistent with the results of numerous Western studies. A subsequent more extensive survey of Japanese plants by Marsh & Mannari (1981, Hsu et al 1983), however, reports technology effects generally weaker and even contrary to those revealed by Western studies. Their results are corroborated by Lincoln et al (1986), who find substantial evidence of a greater role for technology in the determination of American organization structures. Such patterns are unsettling to writers searching for "universal" tendencies in the dependence of organization on task environment states (Hickson et al 1979). They are, however, quite compatible with the emerging "institutional" perspective on organizations which seeks the antecedents of structure in organizations' efforts to achieve a "fit" with cultural and political elements in their environments (DiMaggio & Powell 1983, Meyer & Rowan 1977). Lincoln et al (1986) speculate that technology may be a weaker determinant of factory organization in Japan because the institutional environment in that country exerts a greater influence on organizing modes than in the culturally heterogeneous and politically decentralized United States.

Employee Work Orientations

We have noted at several junctures that the social and economic organization of Japanese firms and industries seems to follow a commitment-maximizing logic. This, of course, is consistent with the popular impression of Japanese workers as wholly devoted to their companies and with the anecdotal and qualitative evidence produced in case study accounts. As measured by concrete behavioral indicators of labor commitment such as absenteeism, turnover, and militancy, or tendencies to participate in company affairs and develop strong bonds with coworkers, there is abundant evidence of organizational commitment among the Japanese (Allston 1986; Cole 1971, 1979; Galenson 1976). But in terms of the kinds of work attitude survey evidence that sociologists and psychologists have long analyzed as clues to the motivations, orientations, and values of a workforce, the picture is less clear.

A particularly perplexing but strong and consistent finding from numerous work attitude surveys is the low level of job satisfaction reported by the Japanese. A Japanese government-sponsored survey of youth in England, West Germany, France, the United States, Switzerland, Sweden, Yugoslavia, India, and the Philippines found job satisfaction to be lowest in Japan: 60% as compared to 82% in the United States (cited in Cole 1979:232). Other national surveys of the Japanese likewise put the proportion of workers who say they are satisfied with their jobs at 50–60%, as compared with consistent findings of over 80% satisfied in the United States. In a study of 3000 manufacturing workers in two Japanese plants, Odaka (1975b) found that 45% were satisfied with their jobs. Azumi & McMillan's (1975b) survey of Japanese, British, and Swedish workers in 12% plants in each country found only 39% of the Japanese to be satisfied with their jobs as contrasted with 70% of the British and 83% of the Swedish workers. Additional comparisons of Japanese and Western workers by Dore (1973:216), Pascale & Maguire (1980), and Naoi & Schooler (1981) also show the Japanese reporting significantly lower job satisfaction. Using somewhat more "behavioral" indicators, Cole (1979:233) found considerably higher percentages of his Detroit than Yokohama respondents reporting they would do the same work again or would recommend the job to a friend.

In attempting to explain these findings, Cole (1979:238) has argued that lower job satisfaction in Japan is no surprise given the high value, and hence the high expectations, which the Japanese place on work activities. This explanation suggests that low satisfaction may be coupled with high commitment: High motivation and a willingness to invest heavily in the fortunes of a work organization are orientations of workers who want more from their work lives and the employment relationship than they presently experience. Evidence contrary to this hypothesis appears, however, in Haire et al's (1966) finding that the Japanese managers scored no lower than managers from other industrial countries on a series of explicit indicators of worklife "need satisfaction"; i.e. expectations-fulfillment congruence.

A number of attitude surveys have indeed produced findings consistent with the behavioral evidence for a strong Japanese commitment to work and company, although it also appears that such values are declining over time and are less prevalent in young Japanese cohorts (see e.g. Lincoln & Kalleberg 1985; Social Policy Bureau 1981:83, 102; Takezawa & Whitehill 1981:213). Cole (1979), for example, notes that "diligence" is the national character trait that the Japanese most often ascribe to themselves in national sample surveys. Whitehill & Takezawa's (1981) survey of manufacturing workers produced responses that suggested both greater commitment to work and identification with the company in Japan: A far higher percentage of the Japanese (73%) than the Americans (21%) rated their company lives as equal to or greater in importance than their personal lives.

Yet other survey evidence seems at odds with this general portrait of intensely committed Japanese workers. From his labor force survey of Detroit and Yokohama, Cole (1979:234) calculated that the mean of a three-item work commitment index was *lower* by a small but significant margin in the Japanese sample. The studies of Japanese workers by Odaka (1975:146) and Marsh & Mannari (1976:113) have also yielded evidence disputing the presumption of a strong commitment to work among the Japanese. Finally, recent comparative studies of Japanese and American work attitudes by Naoi & Schooler (1985:740) and Lincoln & Kalleberg (1985) report either no mean difference on items measuring commitment or small differences favoring American respondents. Yet Lincoln & Kalleberg find that a statistical adjustment for the US/Japan satisfaction gap raises the Japanese' commitment to a level significantly higher than that of the US. Their analysis also indicates that, while job satisfaction makes a very large positive contribution to commitment, the reverse relation (in two out of three model specifications) was that predicted by Cole: a negative net effect of commitment on satisfaction.

Thus, the much-discussed question of whether commitment to work and to the company is greater in the Japanese workforce (and is thus perhaps a factor in the Japanese productivity edge) has evoked no clear answers from survey research. One has the strong suspicion that problems in the cross-national measurement of work values and attitudes are reflected in these findings. It seems doubtful that job satisfaction is truly as low in the Japanese workforce as the attitude surveys suggest. Rather, there appear to be cultural biases operating, as other observers have suspected (e.g. Blauner 1960, Dore 1973:218), to generate overly positive assessments of worklife by American employees and understatements by the Japanese. A study by Lincoln et al (1981) finds a clear pattern in a sample of employees from the same US-based, Japanese-owned firms, that Japanese nationals express lowest job satisfaction and Americans highest, with Japanese-Americans falling in between. Since these groups were represented in the same organizations, it appears that cultural dispositions produced the apparent differences in work attitudes (see also Kelley & Reeser 1973). Although references to cultural response biases abound in comparative research, modern social science has yet to devise effective procedures for adjusting them in order to obtain unbiased estimates of cross-national differences in survey responses (Przeworski & Teune 1970). We suspect that, were such biases controlled, the data would in fact indicate that commitment to the company is genuinely higher in Japan and job satisfaction is comparable to other industrial countries.

INDUSTRIAL ORGANIZATION

The last topic we address in this review is the organization of Japanese industries and markets. Like other facets of Japanese economic organization, they have distinctive qualities, to which much attention, if less systematic research, has been directed. We focus on the organization of Japanese firms in industrial groupings and its implications for the broader issue of dualism in the Japanese economy.

As laid out in a number of useful accounts, a key feature of the Japanese industrial economy since its inception in the designs of the Meiji rulers is the clustering of firms in interdependent enterprise groups or *keiretsu* (Abegglen & Stalk 1985, Aoki 1984, Clark 1979, Gerlach 1986, Itami 1985, Wallich & Wallich 1976, Yoshino 1968). Such groupings are of two kinds: (*a*) bank-centered groups; and (*b*) groups formed of subcontract relationships. The bank-centered groups are the present-day incarnations of the large industrial combines or *zaibatsu* that were dissolved by the Supreme Command of the Allied Powers at the end of World War II. Each group comprises commercial banks, manufacturers, and trading companies. The groups are bound together by financial obligations, joint stock ownership, and directorship exchanges. At the heart of these interdependencies are the loan transactions between member banks and corporations. A much-noted feature of the capital structure of Japanese companies is their high debt-to-equity ratios, which in turn are often linked to the long-run, market-share strategies pursued by Japanese firms. This pattern is in part due to the willingness of *keiretsu* banks to absorb the risks of member firms, and of the Bank of Japan to ensure in turn the solvency of the banks (Wallich & Wallich 1976).

The second form of industrial grouping derives from the subcontracting relationships that exist between large "parent" firms and their smaller, dependent subsidiaries (Clark 1979). Like the bank-centered groups, these ties are reinforced by mutual stockholding, interlocking directorates, and perceptions of common interest. Large Japanese companies farm out much of their production—and from time to time their redundant labor—to subcontractors whose business is almost exclusively limited to the parent firm. Like the bank-centered *keiretsu,* these arrangements function to diversify risk for the parent firm and buffer it from labor and product market uncertainties. From the perspective of the subcontractor, then, these can be highly asymmetric, even exploitative, transactions between corporate majors positioned at the core of the Japanese economy and their dependent satellites on the periphery.

Subcontracting groups in Japan represent a functional alternative to conglomerate organization in the US economy (Clark 1979). Both, as Gerlach (1986) puts it, represent "administered markets." In the highly diversified American corporation, however, the participating units are internalized as divisions under the financial control of a central headquarters staff. The operations of Japanese companies are highly concentrated in particular industries. Diversification takes the form of establishing subsidiaries in new markets which are administered separately from the parent firm. Hostile takeovers are all but nonexistent in the Japanese economy, and friendly mergers and acquisitions typically do not cross industry boundaries (Clark 1979, Yoshino 1968).

The existence of both kinds of *keiretsu* contribute to "dualism" in the Japanese economy, or what Clark (1979) prefers to call "graded hierarchy," so as to avoid the implication of a sharp division between "core" and "peripheral" sectors (Broadbridge 1966). The bank-centered groups funnel inexpensive capital to large corporations with the risk being born by the large "city" banks, which in turn, are backed by the Bank of Japan. This gives a tremendous competitive edge to large, established firms (Wallich & Wallich 1976). Transactions within the subcontracting groups seem clearly to favor the core, parent company at the expense of the satellite suppliers, who absorb economic shocks that would soon imperil the privileged market positions of the majors.

There is no clear consensus on the functions of *keiretsu* in the Japanese economy. Some writers, taking the perspective of Oliver Williamson's (1975) organizational economics, have argued that enterprise groups, by effectively internalizing market exchanges, economize on transaction costs (Gerlach 1986). Nakatani (1984) contends, however, that this argument founders on empirical evidence that profit margins are lower in affiliated firms (Caves & Uekusa 1976). One reason may be their higher leveraging, feasible because of the favorable financing made available by member banks. But growth rates also appear lower in *keiretsu* firms (Nakatani 1984:236). What group affiliation does appear to increase, according to Nakatani's analysis, is the wage levels of the company's workforce. This suggests an intriguing link between the structure of Japanese labor markets and industrial organization. As Gerlach (1986) puts it, employees are the raison d'etre of the Japanese firm, and concern for their welfare (vis-à-vis that of top management and stockholders) figures more prominently in organizational strategy and design decisions than is typical of the United States. Just as internal labor market processes play a key role in determining the structure of the Japanese firm, so they apparently likewise shape the organization of Japanese industries and capital markets.

CONCLUSIONS

The two key issues in the comparative study of Japanese work and industrial organization have been: (a) the extent to which real differences exist between Japan and other countries in the orientations of workers and the structure of labor markets, firms, and industries; and (b) the extent to which those differences can be explained within general theories of the logic of economic change and organization, as opposed to purely culturalist or historicist assertions of Japanese uniqueness. Firm stands on either question are not easy to come by. Clearly, Japanese labor and economic institutions have their distinctive features, but the same can certainly be said of the United States. When other industrial countries are included in the comparison, moreover, it is not at all clear whether Japan or the United States is the more "unique." Strong conclusions on the nature and magnitude of differences in industrial organization between Japan and other countries remain elusive because of: (a) a still serious lack of large-sample, rigorously collected data; and (b) the limited capacity of contemporary social science research methodology to adjust for cultural response biases in the determination of cross-national differences.

The second issue—finding an appropriate explanatory framework for understanding Japanese organization—has produced some highly interesting and thoughtful, if somewhat ironic, writing. In the face of Japan's seeming invincibility in world markets for manufactured goods, gone are the claims of recent decades that "modernization" would force significant changes in Japanese management and employment systems. Now the alternatives to the "culturalist" model of pure and simple Japanese uniqueness have Japan in the vanguard of current trends toward greater economic and administrative rationality. Internal labor market theory, as we have discussed, offers a rationalist explanation for the distinctive features of Japanese labor markets. In an economy dominated by large, internally complex corporations, FILMs economize on transaction costs and facilitate monitoring and control of performance better than fully competitive labor markets. Several other theories, which usually subsume the internal labor market thesis, illustrate the new convergence thinking with respect to Japan. Dore's (1973) "welfare corporatism," Ouchi's (1981) "Theory Z," Piore & Sabel's (1984) "flexible specialization," even Edwards' (1979) "bureaucratic control" and Burawoy's (1983) "hegemonic despotism" constitute visions of a new stage in the evolution of corporate and industrial organization which, explicitly or implicitly, take Japan as a prototype. Genuine insights are to be found in all these views. Western industry *is* undergoing significant change, and, for whatever reasons (Dore 1973, for example, claims late development), the Japanese have developed forms of organization that seem to fit their culture and at the same time to have brought them enormous economic success. The social and economic conditions leading to productivity and prosperity in the world economy have been considerably transformed since the rapidly fading days of American economic supremacy. Looking to Japan as a model for the future is a natural and probably healthier tendency on the part of American scholars and policymakers than the 1950's and 1960's infatuation with American institutions as the embodiment of rationality in the modern world (Vogel 1979).

Literature Cited

Abegglen, J. C. 1958. *The Japanese Factory: Aspects of Its Social Organization*. Glencoe, Ill: Free Press

Abegglen, J. C., Stalk, G. 1985. *Kaisha, The Japanese Corporation*. New York: Basic Books

Allston, J. P. 1986. *The American Samurai: Blending American and Japanese Managerial Practices*. New York: DeGruyter

Aoki, M., ed. 1984. *The Economic Analysis of the Japanese Firm*. Amsterdam: North-Holland

Aoki, M. 1984. Risk sharing in the corporate group. See Aoki 1984, pp. 259–64

Azumi, K., McMillan, C. J. 1975a. Culture and organization structure: A comparison of Japanese and British organizations. *Int. Stud. Manage. Organ.* 35:201–18

Azumi, K., McMillan, C. J. 1975b. Worker sentiment in the Japanese factory: Its organizational determinants. In *Japan: The Paradox of Progress*, ed. L. Austin, pp. 215–29. New Haven: Yale Univ. Press

Bennett, J. W., Ishino, I. 1963. *Paternalism in the Japanese Economy*. Minneapolis: Univ. Minn. Press

Blauner, R. 1960. Work satisfaction and industrial trends in modern society. In *Labor and Trade Unionism: An Interdisciplinary Reader*, ed. W. Galenson, S. M. Lipset. pp. 339–60. New York: John Wiley

Blauner, R. 1964. *Alienation and Freedom*. Chicago: Univ. Chicago Press

Broadbridge, S. 1966. *Industrial Dualism in Japan: A Problem of Economic Growth and Structural Change*. Chicago: Aldine

Burawoy, M. 1979. *Manufacturing Consent*. Chicago: Univ. Chicago Press

Burawoy, M. 1983. Factory regimes under advanced capitalism. *Am. Sociol. R.* 48:587–605

Caves, R. E., Uekusa, M. 1976. *Industrial Organization in Japan*. Washington, DC: Brookings Inst.

Child, J. 1972. Organization structure and strategies of control. *Admin. Sci. Q.* 17:163–76

Child, J. 1984. *Organization*. London: Harper & Row

Clark, R. C. 1979. *The Japanese Company*. New Haven: Yale Univ. Press

Cole, R. E. 1971. *Japanese Blue Collar: The Changing Tradition*. Berkeley: Univ. Calif. Press

Cole, R. E. 1972. Permanent employment in Japan: Facts and fantasies. *Ind. Labor Relat. R.* 26:612–30

Cole, R. E. 1979. *Work, Mobility, and Participation*. Berkeley: Univ. Calif. Press

Cole, R. E. 1980. Learning from the Japanese: Prospects and pitfalls. *Manage. R.* September:22–42

310   LINCOLN & MCBRIDE

Cole, R. E. 1985. The macropolitics of organizational change: A comparative analysis of the spread of small group activities. *Admin. Sci. Q.* 30:560–85

Cole, R. E., Tominaga, K. 1976. Japan's changing occupational structure and its significance. See Patrick 1976, pp. 53–96

Craig, A. M. 1975. Functional and dysfunctional aspects of government bureaucracy. See Vogel 1975, pp. 3–32

Daito, E. 1984. Seniority wages and labour management: Japanese employers' age policy. In *Industrial Relations in Transition*, ed. S. Tokunaga, J. Bergmann, pp. 119–130. Tokyo: Univ. Tokyo Press

DiMaggio, P., Powell, W. 1983. The iron cage revisited: Institutional isomorphism and collective rationality in organizational fields. *Am. Sociol. R.* 48:147–60

Doeringer, P. B., Piore, M. J. 1971. *Internal Labor Markets and Manpower Analysis*. Lexington, Mass: Heath

Dore, R. P. 1973. *British Factory, Japanese Factory: The Origins of Diversity in Industrial Relations*. Berkeley: Univ. Calif. Press

Dore, R. P. 1982. Introduction. In *Japan in the Passing Lane*, ed. S. Kamata, pp. ix–xl. New York: Pantheon

Edwards, R. 1979. *Contested Terrain*. New York: Basic Books

Eisuke, D., 1984. Seniority wages and labour management. In *Industrial Relations in Transition*, ed. T. Shigeyoshi, J. Bergmann, pp. 119–30. Tokyo: Univ. Tokyo Press

Freeman, R. B. 1984. De-mystifying the Japanese labor markets. See Aoki 1984, pp. 103–24

Freeman, R. B., Medoff, J. L. 1984. *What Do Unions Do?* New York: Basic Books

Galenson, W. 1976. The Japanese labor market. See Patrick 1976, pp. 587–672

Gerlach, M. 1986. Institutionalized markets: Corporate control and large-firm organization in Japan. Unpublished paper, Yale Univ. New Haven, Conn.

Gordon, R. J. 1982. Why U.S. wage and employment behavior differs from that in Britain and Japan. *Econ. J.* 92:13–44

Haire, M., Ghiselli, E. E., Porter, L. W. 1966. *Managerial Thinking: An International Analysis*. New York: McGraw-Hill

Hanami, T. 1981. *Labor Relations in Japan Today*. Tokyo: Kodansha Intl. Ltd.

Hashimoto, M., Raisian, J. 1985. Employment tenure and earnings profiles in Japan and the United States. *Am. Econ. R.* 75:721–35

Hatvany, N., Pucik, V. 1981. An integrated management system: Lessons from the Japanese experience. *Acad. Manage. R.* 6:469–80

Hickson, D. J., McMillan, C. J., Azumi, K., Horvath, D. 1979. Grounds for comparative organization theory: Quicksands or hardcore? In *Organizations Alike and Unlike*, ed. C. J. Lammers, D. J. Hickson, pp. 25–41. London: Routledge & Kegan Paul

Horvath, D., McMillan, C. J., Azumi, K., Hickson, D. J. 1981. The cultural context of organizational control: An international comparison. In *Organization and Nation: The Aston Programme IV*, ed. D. J. Hickson, C. J. McMillan, pp. 173–86. Westmead: Gower

Hsu, C., Marsh, R. M., Mannari, H. 1983. An examination of the determinants of organizational structure. *Am. J. Sociol.* 88:975–96

Itami, H. 1985. The firm and the market in Japan. See Thurow 1985, pp. 69–81

Kalleberg, A. L., Lincoln, J. R. 1987. The structure of earnings inequality in the U.S. and Japan. *Am. J. Sociol.* In press

Kawada, H. 1973. Workers and their organizations. In *Workers and Employers in Japan*, ed. B. Karsh, S. Levine, pp. 217–68. Tokyo: Univ. Tokyo Press

Kelley, L., Reeser, C. 1973. The persistence of culture as a determinant of differentiated attitudes on the part of American managers of Japanese ancestry. *Acad. Manage. J.* 16:67–76

Koike, K. 1983a. Internal labor markets: Workers in large firms. See Shirai 1983, pp. 29–62

Koike, K. 1983b. Workers in small firms and women in industry. See Shirai 1983, pp. 89–116

Koshiro, K. 1983. The quality of working life in Japanese factories. See Shirai 1983, pp. 63–88

Levine, S. B. 1965. Labor markets and collective bargaining in Japan. In *The State and Economic Enterprise in Japan*, ed. W. Lockwood, pp. 633–68. Princeton, NJ: Princeton Univ. Press

Lincoln, J. R., Hanada, M., McBride, K. 1986. Organizational structures in Japanese and U.S. manufacturing. *Admin. Sci. Q.* 31:338–64

Lincoln, J. R., Hanada, M., Olson, J. 1981. Cultural orientations and individual reactions to organizations: A study of employees of Japanese-owned firms. *Admin. Sci. Q.* 26:93–115

Lincoln, J. R., Kalleberg, A. L. 1985. Work organization and workforce commitment: A study of plants and employees in the U.S. and Japan. *Am. Sociol. R.* 50:738–60

Lincoln, J. R., Olson, J., Hanada, M. 1978.

Cultural effects on organizational structure: The case of Japanese firms in the United States. *Am. Sociol. R.* 43:829–47

Maguire, M., Pascale, R. T. 1978. Communication, decision-making, and implementation among managers in Japanese and American managed companies in the United States. *Sociol. Soc. Res.* 63:1–23

Marsh, R. M., Mannari, H. 1976. *Modernization and the Japanese Factory*. Princeton, NJ: Princeton Univ. Press

Marsh, R. M., Mannari, H. 1980, Technological implication theory: A Japanese test. *Organ. Studies*. 1/2:161–83

Marsh, R. M., Mannari, H. 1981. Technology and size as determinants of the organizational structure of Japanese factories. *Admin. Sci. Q.* 26:33–57

Meyer, J. W., Rowan, B. 1977. Institutionalized organizations: Formal structure as myth and ceremony. *Am. J. Sociol.* 83:340–63

Muramatsu, K. 1984. The effect of trade unions on productivity in Japanese manufacturing industries. See Aoki 1984, pp. 103–24

Nakamura, A. 1980. Intra-firm wage differentials. See Nishikawa 1980, pp. 202–15

Nakane, C. 1970. *Japanese Society*. Berkeley: Univ. Calif. Press

Nakatani, I. 1984. The economic role of financial corporate grouping. See Aoki 1984, pp. 227–58

Naoi, A., Schooler, C. 1985. Occupational conditions and psychological functioning in Japan. *Am. J. Sociol.* 90:729–51

Niskhikawa, S., ed. 1980. *The Labor Market in Japan*. Tokyo: Univ. Tokyo Press

Odaka, K. 1975. *Toward Industrial Democracy: Management and Workers in Modern Japan*. Cambridge: Harvard Univ. Press

Odaka, K. 1982. The Japanese style of workers' self-management: From the voluntary to the autonomous group. See Rus et al 1982, pp. 135–48

Ono, T. 1980. Postwar changes in the Japanese wage system. See Nishikawa 1980, pp. 145–76

Osako, M. 1977. Technology and social structure in a Japanese automobile factory. *Sociol. Work Occup.* 4:397–426

Ouchi, W. G. 1980. Markets, hierarchies, and clans. *Admin. Sci. Q.* 25:129–41

Ouchi, W. G. 1981. *Theory Z: How American Business Can Meet the Japanese Challenge*. Reading, Mass: Addison-Wesley

Ouchi, W. G., Johnson, J. B. 1978. Types of organizational control and their relationship to emotional well-being. *Admin. Sci. Q.* 23:293–317

Pascale, R. T. 1978a. Communications and decision-making: Cross cultural comparisons. *Admin. Sci. Q.* 23:91–110

Pascale, R. T. 1978b. Zen and the art of management. *Harv. Bus. R.* 56:153–62

Pascale, R. T., Athos, A. G. 1981. *The Art of Japanese Management: Applications for American Executives*. New York: Simon & Schuster

Pascale, R. T., Maguire, M. 1980. Comparison of selected work factors in Japan and the United States. *Hum. Relat.* 33:433–55

Patrick, H., Rosovsky, H., eds. 1976. *Asia's New Giant: How the Japanese Economy Works*. Washington, DC: Brookings Inst.

Piore, M. J., Sabel, C. F. 1984. *The Second Industrial Divide: Possibilities for Prosperity*. New York: Basic Books

Przeworski, A., Teune, H. 1970. *The Logic of Comparative Social Inquiry*. London: Cambridge Univ. Press

Pucik, V. 1984. White collar human resource management: A comparison of the US and Japanese automobile industries. *Colum. J. World Bus.* Fall:87–94

Pucik, V., Hatvany, N. 1983. Management practices in Japan and their impact on business strategy. *Adv. Strat. Manage.* 1:103–31

Pugh, D. S., Hickson, D. J., Hinings, C. R., Turner, C. 1968. Dimensions of organization structure. *Admin. Sci. Q.* 13:65–91

Rohlen, T. P. 1974. *For Harmony and Strength*. Berkeley: Univ. Calif. Press

Rus, V., Ishikawa, A., Woodhouse, T. eds. 1982. *Employment and Participation*. Tokyo: Chuo Univ. Press

Saski, N. 1981. *Management and Industrial Structure in Japan*. New York: Pergamon

Shimada, H. 1983. Japanese industrial relations—a new general model? See Shirai 1983, pp. 3–27

Shirai, T. 1983. A theory of enterprise unionism. See Shirai 1983, pp. 331–52

Shirai, T. ed. 1983. *Contemporary Industrial Relations in Japan*. Madison: Univ. Wisc. Press

Social Policy Bureau, Economic Planning Agency, Japan. 1981. *Scenarios 1990, Japan*. Tokyo: Japan. Gov. Print. Bur.

Takezawa, S., Whitehill, A. M. 1981. *Work Ways: Japan and America*. Tokyo: Japan Inst. Labor

Thomas, R. J., Shimada, H. 1983. *Work organization and quality control practice in the U.S., Japanese auto industries*. Presented at Ann. Meet. Am. Sociol. Assoc., Detroit

Thurow, L. C. 1985. *The Management Challenge: Japanese Views*. Cambridge: MIT Press

Tokunaga, S. 1983. Marxist interpretation of Japanese industrial relations, with special reference to large private enterprises. See Shirai 1983, pp. 313–29

Tracy, P. K., Azumi, K. 1976. Determinants of administrative control; a test of a theory with Japanese factories. *Am. Sociol. R.* 41:80–94

Uchida, H. 1985. *Nemawashi:* The structure of informal power in the *sogo shosha.* Unpublished paper, Harvard University. Cambridge, Mass.

Vogel, E. F. ed. 1975. *Modern Japanese Organization and Decision-Making.* Berkeley: Univ. Calif. Press

Vogel, E. F. 1979. *Japan as Number One: Lessons for America.* Cambridge, Mass: Harvard Univ. Press

Wallich, H. C., Wallich, M. I. 1976. Banking and finance. In *Asia's New Giant: How the Japanese Economy Works,* ed. H. Patrick, H. Rosovsky, pp. 249–316. Washington, DC: Brookings Inst.

Wharton, R., Hull, F., Azumi, K. 1986. *Market share, organization, and productivity in Japanese factories.* Presented at Ann. Meet. Acad. Manage., Chicago

Whitehill, A. M., Takezawa, S. 1968. *The Other Worker: A Comparative Study of Industrial Relations in the U.S. and Japan.* Honolulu: East-West Center

Williamson, O. E. 1975. *Markets and Hierarchies.* New York: The Free Press

Yoshino, M. Y. 1968. *Japan's Managerial System: Tradition and Innovation.* Cambridge: MIT Press

Ann. Rev. Sociol. 1987. 13:313–34

INCOME INEQUALITY AND ECONOMIC DEVELOPMENT

Giorgio Gagliani

Dipartimento di Economia Politica, Universita' della Calabria, 87036 Arcavacata di Rende (CS), Italy

Abstract

Although good theoretical reasons exist for expecting development to be inegalitarian in its early phase, a reverse-U pattern of change in measured inequality might just as easily derive from a statistical composition effect. That such a pattern occurs in reality, however, is far from certain, and all authors agree on governments' ability to keep inequality in check, if they so desire. The effects of redistribution on income and employment do not seem to be appreciable. All empirical studies, including those offering elaborate models of less developed economies, suffer from the inadequacy of historical data, as well as from unresolved problems in definition, methodology, and measurement. Most authors, but not all, would subscribe to the statement that absolute poverty (which should cause more concern than, and should not be confused with, relative inequality) is reduced by economic development.

INTRODUCTION

It is not surprising that a single comprehensive theory of the effects of development on personal income distribution (PID) is unavailable. No comprehensive PID theory exists even for developed countries. Such a theory should comprise nothing less than an analysis of the determinants of: (*a*) levels of factor incomes, i.e. of factor quantities and prices; (*b*) the allocation of factors to individuals; and, since individuals pool their incomes, (*c*) the distribution of individuals among households. Finally, if we want to analyze the effect of development, we must consider the changes in (*a*), (*b*) and (*c*) resulting from the development process. Practically all the chapters of standard economics textbooks have some relevance to distributional matters.

313

0360-0572/87/0815-0313$02.00

Theories directed toward an explanation of income inequality (INEQ) in developed nations are often thought inapplicable to the less developed countries (LDCs) or to the development process, owing to the absence of competitive conditions in the latter. Many writers feel in fact authorized by the alleged presence of such conditions in the developed nations to adopt a ready-made set of questionable assumptions. Thus, functions behave impeccably, factors are paid their marginal products, individual tastes are represented by homothetic indifference maps and, for a realistic touch, "children . . . are produced without mating" (Becker & Tomes 1979:1161). Noncompetitive groups and the influence of power (as opposed to scarcity) are all too often mentioned as unfortunate practical imperfections, and such problems diverted to sociologists and political scientist. The recurring, though always "surprising" (Becker & Tomes 1979:118) conclusion is that policy-makers had better abstain from intervention because inheritance taxes *may* increase the inequality of wealth (Stiglitz 1978:271) or "progressive taxes and subsidies *may* . . . widen the inequality in the long run equilibrium distribution of income" (Becker & Tomes 1979:1182; my emphasis). The possibility of these perverse results is elegantly proved. Their likelihood is not, however, and that must surely depend on the degree of realism in the assumptions.

More plausible is the view that even before the equalizing effect of taxation on capital income, INEQ in developed countries is mainly due to differences in pay (Tinbergen 1975:31). Thus, PID theories may safely concentrate on wage and salary differentials, leaving treatment of, say, income from property and self-employment to writers on LDCs, where they count considerably more. Unfortunately, this is less a guarantee of the theory's success in one branch of analysis than a symptom of its shortcomings in others.

Interesting hints of the relevance of power appear in Pen (1978), Knight (1976:169), and Lewis (1979:223–28). Analyses by radical, dependency, and world-system writers tend to neglect the relevance of scarcity as if it were a neoclassical totem. On pay differentials, see especially Tinbergen (1975, 1985) and Phelps Brown (1977); on wealth, Meade (1976) and Atkinson (1983); on neoclassical theory and on nonemployment incomes, Lydall (1979a:79–94, 265–77). The literature on PID theory was reviewed by Sahota (1978); that on development and INEQ by Cline (1975) and Bigsten (1983:21–45). This review deals only with PID and with the strictly economic meaning of development. On the relationship between functional and personal distribution, see Krelle (1978:19–23).

THEORIES OF CHANGES IN INEQUALITY WITH DEVELOPMENT

Development must be inegalitarian since "it does not start in every part of the economy at the same time" (Lewis 1976:26). Balanced growth is unrealistic and enclaves unavoidable in the early stages. Economies grow by adopting higher techniques and "only a limited number of people can be transferred from one technique to another in a given period of time. The remainder have to wait their turn; and while they wait they are likely to fall behind" (Lydall 1977:13–14). The case for arguing that INEQ rises as development is set in motion could not be stated better. Another interesting way to put it is in Fields (1980:50–56): Development normally acts by "enlarging" and/or "enriching" the modern sector (MS). Pure modern sector–enlargement is an inflow of workers from the traditional sector at constant average incomes within sectors. Pure modern sector–enrichment implies a *ceteris paribus* rise in average modern sector incomes. Even if INEQ was higher within the traditional sector, overall INEQ would first increase then decrease in pure modern sector enlargement growth. Since development always entails some modern sector enlargement, a reverse-U path of an index of INEQ plotted against income per head is highly likely. Traditional sector enrichment is equalizing but rare.

Kuznets (1955:7–8 and Table 1) was the first to observe that an increasing weight of the urban (relative to the rural) population "means an increasing share for the more unequal of the two component distributions." Together with the possible widening of urban-rural percapita income differentials in early growth, this will increase INEQ. Somewhat puzzling, however, was his discovery that even by assuming a constant urban-rural income margin and identical intrasectoral income dispersion, an inverted-U curve would be generated by the sheer change in the weights (rows 2–7 of Table 1). This may also be thought of in terms of occupational categories. When the nonfarm share of the population (NF) equals 10%, all quintiles except a fraction of the fifth (the top earners) are made up of poor farmers, unpaid family workers and farm laborers. As NF grows, the various categories of urban manual labor and subsequently of nonmanual labor (Gagliani 1985) gradually extend to the fourth quintile, third, and so on. In so doing they at first increase measured INEQ and subsequently reduce it. The point of inversion occurs at different values of NF depending on the hypotheses on income differentials and the measure of inequality used. By using sectoral rather than occupational shifts and various measures of distribution, Swamy (1967), Cline (1975:369), Knight (1976:175–77), Berry & Urrutia (1976:18), Robinson (1976), Lydall (1977:15–22) and Fields (1980:53) all provide us with their own versions of the phenomenon which, as mentioned earlier, would occur even if income dispersion were higher in the traditional than in the modern sector. Opinions vary as to the relevance of the phenomenon, however. While Robinson (1976:439) and Berry & Urrutia (1976:19 and 107) seem not to question, respectively, the log-variance and the Gini-index ability to measure INEQ correctly in this case, Fields (1980:55) clearly states that when purely structural shifts are all that happen, the ensuing changes in measured inequality are not worrisome. Cline (1975:365n) calls them spurious, while Knight

(1976:172–73) wonders whether we should be concerned but does not discount the possible influence of relative deprivation affecting those left behind (see also Lewis 1979:212). The issue might be clarified by assuming a limiting case. Suppose that on a certain date, a fraction of the many poor farmers and artisans withdraw from the labor force due to old age and at the same time some of their children are hired by modern firms at their constant, higher wage. If the modern sector employment share goes up, measured INEQ would rise, but policy advisors who show concern about it should be fired. 'Real' increases in inequality would instead arise for instance, when modern sector wages increase faster than traditional sector self-employment incomes, or worse, when traditional sector incomes actually fall owing to a large number of displaced traditional activities performed by people still in the labor force. This is the kind of INEQ we are talking about. The other one in fact belongs in the section on problems of measurement (below).

Lewis (1976:28–29) presents "a formidable list of adverse possibilities" in which enclave development would actually reduce incomes in the traditional sector. These possibilities range from predatory practices and the destruction of traditional trades via product-price or wage competition, to geographical polarization, to acceleration in population growth due to the reduction in the death rate. Enlightened governments could act to prevent much of this or, at least, much of the suffering thus generated. Within the enclave the share of profits and urban rents will most probably rise at first. At some point, however, downward pressure on INEQ will be generated by "an expansion of the middle," a "huge upward differentiation of the labor force" (Lewis 1976:31) and by a tightening labor market. Lewis' analysis is supported by studies showing: (a) a different asymmetry of Lorenz curves in advanced countries than in LDCs (Kakwani 1980); (b) a composition-effect decrease in the wage-income ratio in labor-abundant development, followed by a stabilization (Lecaillon & Germidis 1977), and then an increase (Gagliani 1981); and (c) a reverse-U pattern of change in regional inequality (Cantarelli & Bressan 1984). Falling intersectoral productivity differentials will contribute as well (Chenery & Syrquin 1975:52).

Changes in INEQ also depend on the pattern of growth which varies in turn with: (a) structural characteristics, such as the original distribution of property, the magnitude of supply and demand elasticities, the proportion of smallscale enterprise, and the availability of local resources (Lewis 1976); (b) private behavior concerning population growth, education, geographical/sectoral concentration of investment; and (c) the government's growth strategy and intervention in all of the above (Adelman & Morris 1973, Lipton, 1977, Fei et al 1979).

Many authors starting from Kuznets (1955:9) make passing remarks on the impact of the political system and of democracy in particular. Indeed, one wonders whether not only specific anti-INEQ government policies but also the establishment of democratic regimes are not a function (via the sectoral and occupational structure of the labor force) of the stage of development. Countries undergoing a process of industrialization by definition acquire an industrial, manual workforce sooner or later. How large this force will be depends among other things on the timing of development, since labor requirements per dollar invested in each production line tend to decline in all countries over time. An industrial workforce does not like wage squeezes and, unless repressed by military juntas, will use its muscle and votes accordingly. It may well be that the 'need' for a junta arises, and its chances of success are greater, when industrial wage-earners are neither too few (i.e. weak) nor too many (i.e. too strong to be held in check) relative to their competitors in the distributive struggle.

Since the organization of farmers is much more difficult, it may be necessary to wait for progressive taxation and social security stemming from the pressure of unionized factory workers before the needs of traditional sector workers are provided for, 'by extension', as it were. By that time, of course, many of those who were displaced will be dead. China and Cuba were not willing to wait and seem to have managed to reduce INEQ (for some data on the former see ILO 1977b; for the latter, Brundenius 1981). Russia, on the other hand, eliminated many of her farmers before she turned to deal with their inequality. The reader will not find here the answer to the question of whether revolutions are feasible or desirable. My point is that the relationships that may exist between the structure of the labor force and variables relating to the political system probably deserve some interdisciplinary effort (two interesting articles on economy and polity are Fossum 1967 and Venieris & Gupta 1983; on democracy and INEQ, see Bollen & Jackman 1985 and the literature cited there).

Agreement on the favorable effects of one of the possible governmental policy instruments, namely land reform, is so wide that one regrets the likely absence of significant overlap between the set of *latifundistas* and that of authors on INEQ. In most cases, no advice is given on how some radical change that is advocated is to be implemented. A. Gunder Frank (1975:105–6) was clear on this, but since a group of nonsocialist peripheral economies started developing rapidly, his own brand of dependency theory has lost momentum (Blomström & Hette 1984:184–85).

Recently Amin (1984) produced an article that must draw on data unavailable to the scientific community. These data would show (as a "fact": p. 25) a secular (1880–1980) "immiseration" in the entire world's periphery. He may be using the term not as a synonym of impoverishment but as meaning a rise in INEQ, in which case it would still be interesting to learn where he uncovered the relevant information, say, for 1880–1950. At any rate, Amin places "this evolution within the framework of the world-system." Thus, "the stability of distribution in the core countries . . . does not exclude, but in fact supposes, a much more unequal distribution in the periphery" (Amin 1984:22). The main problem with Amin's analysis seems to lie in its mixture of "persuasive definitions" (Little 1982:220) and unsubstantiated 'facts.'

Although some dependency writers and some of their critics might not agree (see e.g. Palma 1978:905–6), the attempt to formulate the world-system approach in a statistically testable form must be considered an improvement. The sections in this review on data and measurement show that to expect truth from the facts is at best premature, but at least by confronting the evidence, these authors indicate an alternative path, away from persuasive definitions and intrinsic vagueness. True to their doctrine, they attribute all the many negative things a country's government and ruling classes can do to increase INEQ to one factor, that is, external dependence. This is measured, for instance, by (the log of) profits per capita of population made by foreign direct investment (FDI), as in Chase-Dunn (1975:728). Or it may be measured by (the square root of) the share of FDI-controlled capital in total capital, multiplied by the amount of FDI-capital per unit of labor force or population. Bornschier (1983:19) calls this an index of penetration, but it measures, rather, a mixture of penetration and overall capital intensity. A high degree of penetration increases INEQ in four ways: (*a*) Penetration makes it easier for the ruling national elites to oppose redistributive measures through a more likely and effective alliance with foreign interests and the ensuing enhancement of internal conflict and political instability (Chase-Dunn 1975, Rubinson 1976). (*b*) Penetration aggravates the dualistic features of development and causes wider sectoral inequality (Rubinson 1976, Bornschier & Ballmer-Cao 1978). (*c*) It weakens the bargaining power of labor (Rubinson 1976, Bornschier & Ballmer-Cao 1978), by (*d*) distorting growth towards excessive tertiarization of the labor force (Evans & Timberlake 1980, but see also Fiala 1983). Bornschier (1983; see also Bornschier & Chase-Dunn 1985) attempted a reconciliation of the inverse-U hypothesis with the world-system approach.

Apart from the unreliability of the data which mars all research in this field (see below), the empirical results were recently challenged by Muller (1984; on some methodological points see Rusterholz 1984). On the theoretical level, these studies suffer from the strictures of the *idée fixe*. Many LDC governments do not know whether incoming foreign capital only anticipates domestic investment, and neither of course do we. They often welcome it because, although it is biased toward labor-saving, it nevertheless does create employment in the modern sector. Thus, it is vital for world-system analysis to show that foreign capital hampers growth [Bornschier & Chase-Dunn (1985:80–116) review earlier studies and add new fuel to their thesis]. Other studies show, however, that FDI is attracted by a high GNP per head and by political stability (Schneider & Frey 1985). To prove that this later generates instability and relative stagnation in host countries, one needs a much tighter specification of causality both in the models employed and by means of the time-lags used (this is virtually impossible with cross-sections). Moreover, treating LDC governments as bridgeheads of the multinationals, and conversely, assuming that locally stimulated growth would be inequality-neutral, both appear to be far-fetched. Finally, the possibility that multinationals might be attracted by low INEQ which might imply, after all, a local mass consumption market to be exploited is never analyzed.

THE EFFECTS OF REDISTRIBUTION

If household savings depend on household incomes, the way income is distributed among households has an effect on aggregate savings. If consumption of different classes of commodities also depends on income via some kind of Engel's law, the structure of consumption will vary with distributive changes. And finally, if producing different commodities requires different factor proportions, the structure of consumption will affect employment and incomes. Suppose the goods 'favored' by the poor are relatively labor-intensive: Redistribution of income towards the poor would then generate more employment. The economist's tool-kit for analyzing these possibilities includes: (a) macro growth models à-la-Harrod-Domar, and (b) micro multi-sector input-output models à-la-Leontief. Income redistribution leading to changes in savings and in the structure of consumption would thus be translated into a growth rate of the economy by means of (a) and into a structure of output and—via a set of labor coefficients—of employment by means of (b). Morawetz (1974:503–7) reviews some early attempts along these lines. Most of these [but also later studies by, among others, Figueroa (1975) on Peru, Foxley (1976a:179–200) on Chile, Stewart (1978) on Mexico, and Paukert et al (1981) on four Asian countries] found the simulated effects of redistribution on growth to be small. Ballentine & Soligo (1977) include second-round effects of the generated structure of output on income distribution and again output, and conclude that "they are small and work in the opposite direction from the initial redistribution" (p. 706).

Empirical testing of all models reveals a grossly inadequate supply of appropriate data. One of the statistical deficiencies stems from the independent procedures used to collect information on the structure of production and of consumption (Thirsk 1979). James (1980) shows that more disaggregated data may prove that redistribution is not as ineffectual as it is alleged to be. On redistribution policies see Chenery et al (1974), Ffrench-Davis (1976), Lewis (1976:36–41), Lecaillon et al (1984:159–99).

ECONOMY-WIDE MODELS

The input-output models, more or less closed, of the early 1970s were joined in turn by three other kinds: (*a*) the dynamic ILO-generated 'Bachue' simulation models that concentrate on the interrelationships between the economic and demographic aspects of planning (Rodgers et al 1978 and, for a description, Moreland 1984); (*b*) the linear programming models such as van Ginneken (1980) for Mexico, and (*c*) the computable general equilibrium models (CGEMs) such as Adelman & Robinson (1978) on South Korea and, on Brazil, Taylor et al (1980) and Sahota & Rocca (1985).

In this era of omnipotent, though still unintelligent computers, the issue of how wide a model should be is of some importance. According to Frank & Webb (1977:46), "theoretical models must be designed with a specific and limited purpose in mind. Otherwise, the number of variables and the interrelationships among them become so complicated that analysis is impossible." To think that "any one theory can provide a model for analysing all of [the] factors and policies [related to distribution]" would thus be "foolish." The proponents of large economy-wide models are undeterred by this danger. A common denominator to models such as CGEMs is their endogenization of income distribution, which makes it possible, at least in theory, to quantify the effects of policy measures on INEQ. They contain a mixture of national accounting, growth models and multisector analysis (for a description, Blitzer et al 1975; Dervis et al 1982; for a review, Bigsten 1983). They normally arrive at the determination of functional distribution and, from this (via a set of assumptions about the socioeconomic structure of individuals, about income dispersion within socioeconomic groups, and about household composition), of the distribution by size. Adelman & Robinson conduct a series of experiments to single out the most efficient policy packages for 'permanent' redistribution (over a nine-year time span). Taylor et al (1980) also test the effect of various alternative measures. Sahota & Rocca (1985) aim at an integration of no less than seven partial theories of personal distribution. Once tested on Brazil, their (comparatively small) model churns out 4644 estimated impact elasticities of 43 exogenous variables on 108 endogenous variables.

These models might well "force policy-makers to analyze the implications of policy choices within a consistent analytic and information framework" (Dervis et al 1982:7). Reality is of course far more complex than the most complicated model. Among the more than twenty-dozen equations of Bachue-Philippines (Rodgers et al 1978), there is only one price, namely the terms of trade between agriculture and the rest of the economy. Since relative prices are rather important in distributive matters (Beckerman 1977:672–74), these models might in a sense be criticized for being too small. Their two major drawbacks, however, seem to be associated with their being too large. First, it is very hard for readers to appreciate how some crucial conclusion would be altered by suppression, addition, or modification of any hypothesis. Second, the available data must be manipulated and stretched to the extreme in order to fit the models' very demanding requirements. Short of retracing all over again, the reader will never be able to assess the point at which all this cumulative manipulation and stretching starts to generate unreliable results. The chances are high that those to whom such exercises are directed will fail to grasp their implications and will adhere to those prescriptions which meet common sense while they reject all others. In so doing, they might act for the best. Closer examination of some results does not induce optimism.

A policymaker who "feels" that the nationalization of large firms and the creation of social overhead in rural areas help reduce INEQ would learn in fact from CGEMs that in a Korean-type economy, nationalization would be ineffective (Adelman & Robinson 1978:130 & 163) and, in a Brazilian-type economy, the creation of social overhead would be counterproductive (Sahota & Rocca 1985:173). Further probing makes it clear that nationalizing large firms is (in Adelman & Robinson's world) not just likely to slow productivity, dampen profits, and raise the salaries of an expanding army of white-collar employees. Rather, this package of dubious blessings constitutes the very and the only *definition* of nationalization (p. 159). To define anything by means of what we believe are its negative effects seems to beg the question. But even if these effects are inescapable, a trade-off might exist, or be thought to exist, between the firms' efficiency and the government's ability to influence future investment through such firms and/or to dispose of the power of some pervasive oligarchy. Still more discomfort would probably be generated by the fact that Sahota & Rocca are unable to explain (1985:156) their own findings that a 10% increase in the number of miles of roads per 1000 square hectares of agricultural land would bring about a 2% *decrease* in the amount of cruzeiros earned by the average family in the rural northeast (p. 173, row 106, col. 25). When models are too big they are like the brooms of the sorcerer's apprentice: you cannot use them, as they acquire a life of their own.

SOME EMPIRICAL ISSUES

The Data

The main problems in distributional comparisons arise from wide intercountry variations in the methods employed in collecting the basic data, from the inaccuracy of income statements, and from substantial differences across countries in: household size and composition; age structure; life expectancy; year-to-year income fluctuations; income in kind as a fraction of total income; availability of data on taxes, transfers, and services provided at no cost or at subsidized prices; prices paid by different income classes and in different regions and—if what really matters is the distribution of welfare—amount and type of work devoted to earning individual incomes. According to McGranahan (1979:1 & 45), "there does not exist an adequate conceptual and technical basis for common international measurement of income distribution and cross-national comparisons of it." Thus, "comparative statistics on income distribution are likely to be misleading or mischievous." Even for the same country and year, Gini coefficients may be more than seven points apart depending on the definition of income, the unit of observation, the collection of data, and the method of computation (Smolensky et al 1979:69–70). The reader will find further reasons for concern in Lydall (1979b:28–30) and Menard (1986) regarding the collection of data presented in Jain (1975).

Some consensus has emerged on the need to concentrate on individuals as the proper welfare unit to be analyzed. However, as long as the tendency of individuals to associate in income-pooling groups persists, the proper income unit should be one "within which there is a large degree of pooling" (Lydall 1979b:23), i.e. the family or, better, the household (for a dissenting opinion, Wiles 1978:168). One should then correct for household size and composition by finding an appropriate weight based, for instance, on an equivalence scale "which will tell us how many 'equivalent units' there are in each type of household" (Lydall 1979b:23; Beckerman 1977:672). Recent work conducted within the ILO (van Ginneken & Park 1984) goes in that direction and has produced around two dozen 'comparable' sets of statistics for as many countries. Although some sources of potential problems still remain, improvement is visible on the pioneering efforts by Kuznets (1963), Adelman & Morris (1973), Paukert (1973), Jain (1975) and Sawyer (1976), subsequently incorporated in world tables by Bornschier & Heintz (1979) and Taylor & Jodice (1983). Considering the deficiencies of early data, one wonders whether the considerable resources spent on finding statistical correlations between them and a number of socioeconomic variables of all kinds (as well as in criticizing the results) were not simply wasted.

The Methodology

Since time observations are lacking or unreliable (Berry 1985), the analyst interested in the relationship between development and INEQ has tried to infer it from cross-sectional data. The ensuing problems may be likened to those confronting an extraterrestrial statistician trying to derive some 'law' of human development—say, the relationship between height and age in man—based on data from a one-hour research grant from outer space. Options are reduced to taking a snapshot collection of data on age and height of different human beings. The outcome depends on luck. If the sample contains disproportions of tall people of young age and old people who are short, the resulting 'empirical law' might induce terrestrial shrinking theories in celestial scholars' minds.

When historical data are lacking, we are, as it were, the Martians of our past. The available cross-sectional scatter might perfectly fit an increasing 45° line while each country is silently moving along a 45° *decreasing* one. In the absence of a truly convincing theory, no secular inference should be made to rest on single-observation cross-sections, even if—and this is not the case— data were comparable. At least some comparable observations for the same country at different points in time should be included in the scatter. Excluding multiple data when available, "on the grounds that adding more than one observation for some countries would give too much weight to particular country experience" (Ahluwalia 1976:339), is utterly unjustified (Saith 1983:381–82). A plot of as many time observations as are available for each country, connected by linear segments and presented together in a full world-wide scatter, constitutes the only acceptable procedure to check whether a pattern is discernible not only in the cross-section, but also in time, which is the dimension in which development occurs. Social scientists are aware of this (Firebaugh 1980), as well as of problems related to the noncausal but rather associational character of regression analysis. Most of them tend, however, to be content with a few caveats and disclaimers, while disseminating wrong impressions in the rest of their papers. Examples of this are Evans & Timberlake (1980:538) and Weede & Tiefenbach (1981:276). Stringent criticism of Ahluwalia's neglect of his own calls for caution appears in Saith (1983:372–73).

The Measures

Recent additions to the vast literature on measurement are those by Szal & Robinson (1977), Cowell (1977), Kakwani (1980), Nygård & Sandström (1981). Noneconomists apparently have to be catered to separately by their own specialists; e.g. Allison (1978), who follows in the tradition of Alker & Russett (1966).

This field is a T. S. Eliot world where "everything has already been discovered/ once or twice" and emulation is difficult. "New" measures turn out to have been available since the 1920s, albeit in unusual languages. (Kondor 1971 suggests that Schutz's 1951 measure is actually Bresciani-Turroni's.) But they endure under the new name (or even hide under a distortion of it: Kerbo 1983:164 has, consistently, *Schultz*). An author occasionally discovers that one index is preferable to another (Alker & Russett 1966:372 argue that Schutz is better than Gini), but in perusing the literature, one cannot fail to encounter statements to the contrary (Sen 1973:31 thinks

Gini is preferable to the relative mean deviation—which is, of course, Schutz).

A search for 'the' measure is bound to fail. Given any reasonable-looking index of INEQ it is always possible (Kolm 1976) to find another one providing the opposite answer to the question we normally address. This question (Has the distribution worsened or improved?) cannot be unequivocally answered when Lorenz curves intersect, a defect they often have across both time and space. To all those longing for an 'objective' or at least a 'descriptive' yardstick, Atkinson's (1970) brilliant solution (which, if I read Kolm correctly (1976:416–17) should be called 'Kolm's'), incorporates the welfare function of the user into the measure. This must appear tantamount to saying that if blacks were on average taller than whites and we disliked it, we might as well forget the platinum meter and use an elastic one of our own making. (Oxford aplomb puts it more politely in Sen 1973:39 and 1978.) Although said by some to do "explicitly what other measures do implicitly" (Fields 1980:107), Atkinson's measure is thought by Sen (1978:92) to lead "to a clearcut answer but to a question different from the one that was posed." We should also remember that adding *epsilons* and complicating the formula will never allow one measure to convey more than one piece of information, let alone tell the whole story.

The Gini concentration ratio has passed many tests and is widely used even in a context of growth. As with all other measures, however, it has its problems. Suppose 10 underprivileged individuals earn 100 each, and the remaining 90 members of the population earn 1000 each. Would we consider it a distributional improvement if, say, aggregate income became 88% lower, the persons earning 100 became 90, and the earnings of the 'rich' 10 who are still left were cut to approximately 210? I suspect that Hirschman (1973) would say "no," and that among one's own friends a very egalitarian one could always be found who would be inclined to say "yes." According to the Gini index, however, the two worlds are, distributionally speaking, the same. Equality can mean that there are a lot of rich people or a lot of poor people. Rejecting this verdict does not necessarily imply a concession to Atkinson. If one descriptive measure requires normative additions to be meaningful, two descriptive measures taken together might not. What we may need is an evaluation of the size of the area of concentration, coupled with some synthetic way to describe the shape of the Lorenz curve (such as an index of asymmetry).

In addition, there appears to be almost universal consensus that distributional measures have to be scale invariant. (For some refreshing doubts: Sen 1973:36, Jacobs 1981:242; on the whole issue, Kolm 1976; on how persons having different incomes may perceive equiproportional rises, van Praag 1978:128–30). The Gini index complies with this. Suppose, however, that in the initial situation of the example cited above, all incomes are doubled in real terms, due to a successful take-off, and suppose that an income of 100 was just sufficient to purchase one subsistence-level basket of goods. The post-growth Gini index would not change, but the absolute difference in the number of baskets the poor and the rich could acquire would rise from 9 to 18. This may mean a better education, a suburban home, and salmon for breakfast for the latter and just another subsistence basket for the former. Is this what we mean by constant-inequality growth? Might it not be precisely this kind of effect that makes observers 'register' increasing INEQ in the early phases of development, when indeed—low incomes being near subsistence—absolute differentials appear to weigh more?

Decomposition

Suppose the population is disaggregated into n groups by, say, sector, occupation, or age. A change in measured INEQ in the course of development may be caused by inequality changes within or across groups or both. Quite a number of studies have undertaken the tasks of (a) finding ways of decomposing aggregate indexes (e.g. Pyatt 1976, Rao 1969, Fei et al 1979; Fields 1979; Shorrocks 1980) as well as reasons why other authors' decompositions are wrong (Nelson 1977, Adelman & Levy 1984; Cowell 1985), and (b) applying decomposition methods to actual changes in various countries (for a brief review of some of these studies, see Fields 1980:111–24).

Decomposition by age received much attention, owing to the observation that, even if age-income profiles were identical across individuals, perfect equality would require either that the slope of each profile be zero or that all individuals be of the same age. As these conditions are not verified, Paglin (1975) suggested adjusting measured INEQ by subtracting out the variability across age groups. This point is relevant to our topic as Morrisson (1978) provided data confirming Kuznets' observation that INEQ due to age was much lower in some LDCs than in the United States. Generalization of this result would imply that inequalities are much lower in advanced countries but only slightly so in LDCs when measured over a lifetime (as many say they should be) instead of in a single year. The need to measure INEQ over a lifetime is dubious. First, INEQ by age is one type of inequality; second, it can always be eliminated by decomposition if one so desires; third, if year-to-year fluctuations are considered by some as being no more than "statistical noise," they might be reminded that noise can kill. At any rate, if lifetime distribution is what really matters, then yearly comparisons between the two sets of countries are biased.

Incidentally, the age structure of the population in any given year is the outcome of previous trends in birth and death rates. If those trends are closely related to development, as in some version of demographic transition theory, economic growth might have a predictable influence on INEQ via its effects on population growth and on the age structure. More information is needed on this, however, before the separate effects of changing age structures and age-income profiles on changes in INEQ during growth can be singled out (on demography, growth, and distribution, see: Kuznets 1976, 1980; Repetto 1979; Flegg 1980; Morley 1983; Lam 1984; on household size and INEQ: Kuznets 1982).

POVERTY

Measures of poverty are no less problematic than measures of INEQ. In order to count the poor, they must be defined by means of a poverty line, i.e. an income threshold below which there is poverty. Should this threshold be fixed absolutely on the basis of some nutritional, biological, or "basic needs" standard, and a near-to-zero elasticity with respect to changes in average real income? Or should this elasticity instead approach unity, implying that poverty could only be reduced by lowering INEQ? The answer to this question seems to be subjective; so much so, in fact, that the Dutch (Leyden) school suggests leaving it to surveys (Goedhart et al 1977; a recent pro-absolutist reminder is essay 14 in Sen 1984). Once the choice is made and the number q of those in poverty is found, we end up with a head-count ratio ($H=q/n$, where n is total population) which, although a useful starting point, by itself says little since each income might fall just \$1 short of the poverty line (in this case the so-called poverty gap g would amount to q dollars). Thus, the proper measure should include—or indeed be the product of—both H and (a normalized version of) g. (On different normalization procedures and their implications see Anand 1977 and Sen 1976, 1981:189–90.) As the incomes of the poor are also unevenly distributed, Sen's (1976) measure incorporated their own Gini coefficient: poverty was thought greater, the higher the degree of inequality. Owing to the properties of the Gini, this amounted to a specific (rank-order) method of assigning weights to the sum of all income shortfalls in order to derive the poverty index. These weights could instead be the shortfalls themselves, on the grounds that "deprivation depends on the distance between a poor household's actual income and the poverty line, not the number of households that lie between a given household and the poverty line" (Foster et al 1984:762). This gives rise to at least two classes of measures which may, as usual, give contrasting results (Anand 1977:11; on measurement, see also Hagenaars 1986:119–40).

Fields (1980) had predicted that in modern sector–enlargement growth (see above) absolute poverty would fall, while modern sector enrichment would keep it constant. By using a Todaro (1969) model of migration and by assuming the presence of a group of urban poor earning less than the rural average income (which, also by assumption, is itself below the poverty line), Anand & Kanbur (1985) prove the theoretical possibility of inverse-U shaped poverty trends in modern sector enlargement and of monotonically increasing poverty in modern sector enrichment. The latter result is, of course, particularly worrying. In Todaro's model, if the average income in the modern sector is 200 and rural income is 100, even a 40% urban unemployment rate would not discourage migration to towns since migrants would count on a 60% chance to earn 200, i.e. an expected income of 120, which is still higher than rural income. If one then assumes, with Anand & Kanbur, that the poverty line is at 110, that the underemployed and unemployed of the urban informal sector earn on average 50, and that the informal sector accounts in equilibrium for 50% of total urban labor force, then an increase in modern sector income to 250 would raise the equilibrium level of the informal sector to 60%. This would raise poverty under both classes of measures.

The assumption that rural incomes are on average higher than urban informal sector incomes calls for validation. Some available data tend to show the opposite (Teilhet-Waldorf & Waldorf 1983 for Bangkok; House 1983:298, 302 for Nairobi). On the other hand, rural life may guarantee some forms of income which escape measurement, and urban poverty may imply more hardship and destitution than poverty in the countryside.

SOME EVIDENCE: CROSS-SECTIONS AND TIME SERIES

Several authors have attempted to verify cross-sectionally the existence of a parabolic reverse-U curve christened after Kuznets (Adelman & Morris 1973, Paukert 1973, Chenery & Syrquin 1975, Jackman 1975, Ahluwalia 1976, Lydall 1977, Cromwell 1977, Ward 1978 and, on the sceptical side, Papanek 1978). A review of many of these attempts is found in Bacha (1979). As mentioned earlier, serious criticism was put forward by Saith (1983) against Ahluwalia's estimate of the parabola. Nugent (1983) suggested measurement error as an explanation. Still more recently, Lecaillon et al (1984) reviewed that literature, which they see as overwhelmingly favorable to the curve, and presented new, more comparable data for some 39 LDCs. By using these data and those given in Sawyer (1976), they found that: (a) When countries are aggregated by income group, the group-average Gini behaves according to 'Kuznets law;' but (b) the coefficient of variation of within-group Gini coefficients shows such a dispersion that "any simple model purporting to explain changes in the concentration of incomes solely in terms of product per head" has to be rejected (p. 40).

The lesson deriving from cross-sectional studies seems to be more or less as follows. There is no such thing as an inverted-U curve that developing countries are to follow. Cross-sectional data reveal, indeed, an inverted U-shaped band. Its width, however, implies that different paths are possible; and the shortcomings of cross-sectional inference may even entail that countries can pierce through it.

The evidence from long-run country data is not more conclusive. Contrasts among researchers are nowhere better exemplified than in studies concerning Brazil. For the 1960s such contrasts appear both in reporting the facts and in interpreting them (see Taylor et al 1980:337–42; see also Morley 1983). Recent data, however, seem to show that the (very probable) rise in INEQ came to a halt by the end of the 1970s (Pfefferman & Webb 1983; Denslow & Tyler 1984; World Bank 1984). Might we have a Kuznets' curve for Brazil?

Practically everyone agrees that in Taiwan the ascending part of Kuznets' curve failed to materialize. Fei et al (1979) attribute this achievement mainly to events within the rural sector. First, Taiwan had inherited from the Japanese a substantial agricultural infrastructure which allowed that sector to thrive even during the "import-substitution phase." Second, land reform in the 1950s reduced rural income differences and prevented the formation of a *lumpen* class in the cities. Third, the successful "export-promotion phase" was accompanied by a rapid growth of rural labor-intensive industries and services. Fei et al (1979:317) do appear at times to attribute Taiwan's record to successful policy intervention. There are indeed some problems in the official data (Kuznets in Galenson 1979:103). "Personal observation" is thus called for to state that "Taiwan is, if not the most equal, certainly in a tiny class of very equal developing countries" (Little in Galenson 1979:498). But first, personal observation may be considered 'unscientific' only by those who trust single-figure measurements. As the previous discussion may have shown, the eye-glasses through which one evaluates inequality in practice might not be those manufactured by Gini or Theil. And, second, subsequent data for 1970–1980 seem to confirm that Gini coefficients for Taiwan are low and falling (Kuo 1983:96–103). The unresolved question, however, is whether policymakers could have obtained these results without the unexportable aid of very specific historical and geographical conditions. Readers remain uncertain as to what should and could be done elsewhere (Fei et al 1979:311).

Other instances of 'growth with equity' are hard to come by. Hong Kong may have reduced INEQ in 1961–1971 (Hsia & Chau 1978). Japan is said by some to enjoy a rather low degree of INEQ (Boltho 1975). According to Wada (1974:22), however, inequality there increased in 1956–1971. In Mexico the 20% richest families increased their share most in 1950–1975, although the proportion of poor families (and since 1970, their number) decreased significantly. Overall INEQ rose (van Ginneken 1980:17). On the basis of information given in Lecaillon et al (1984:42) INEQ increased in the

1960s in the Zambia and Ivory Coast, decreased in Sri Lanka, and did not change in the Philippines. According to Koo (1984:1030) the Gini index rose, then fell, then rose again in South Korea in 1965–1980. Something like a reverse-U pattern was registered in Colombia (1934–1964) by Berry & Urrutia (1976:114) and in Puerto Rico (1953–1977) by Mann (1985:489). Most of these data are old, are based on too few observations, and are basically unreliable (Berry 1985).

According to Lipton (1977), excessive concentration on urban growth meant that many poor rural families have become even poorer (see also Griffin & Kahn 1978). ILO (1977a:23) registers a poverty rise in LDCs in 1963–1972 but bases this finding on the absolute number q rather than on the head count ratio H (see above). We have some evidence (ILO 1977b) on increasing rural poverty in Asia. Ahluwalia et al (1979:318) presented data, on an aggregate level, showing that although q rose in 1960–1975 in low income LDCs, H decreased in all LDC income groups. The relevant questions here are whether rural and overall poverty increased where growth was most rapid, or vice versa; and what meaning should be given to a divergent trend in H and q?

CONCLUDING REMARKS

There can be development with increasing INEQ. Since INEQ is obviously not better dealt with by stagnation, one is led to question not development but, rather, its morphology. The factors which seemed to help today's developed (Western) countries most were a tight labor market, educational expansion, and democracy. All of these materialized when the farm labor force share had shrunk considerably. None of them can be forced on LDCs. The Western record on the issue of exporting democracy is far from clean (Fagen 1978 on Chile). Merely imitative educational expansion may not reduce INEQ per se in LDCs.

If one is to believe the figures, the Second World appears more egalitarian than the First. Social scientists disagree no less than the concerned populations as to whether the price to be paid for this should be considered too high. They also disagree on most policy measures that should foster growth with equity in LDCs with the exceptions perhaps of taxing landlords and capitalists to invest the proceeds in productive activities outside the 'enclave', and non output-reducing land reform. At any rate, no advice can be provided on how the political decision to implement such measures can be arrived at.

Development can only occur via extensive restructuring and relocation of activities and occupations. The faster the process, the lower the proportion of relocations deferred to the next generation, and the higher the number of persons affected during their lifetimes who are unable to adjust. These persons are those who are negatively affected by development and who should receive compensation until they find new jobs. Helping them to satisfy their basic needs is a moral duty. Helping them to bequeath their old jobs to descendants may be harmful to the latter.

"Prosperity is the real friend of the women, the ethnics and the *lumpenproletariat*"; "the poor have gained much more from development than it is now fashionable to believe" (Lewis 1979:226, 1976:30).

ACKNOWLEDGMENTS

I thank H.-J. Hoffmann-Nowotny, director of the University of Zurich Soziologisches Institut, for hospitality during the writing of this review. I also thank Volker Bornschier and Francesca Sanna-Randaccio for their helpful comments on a first draft. Research was partly funded by CNR.

Literature Cited

Adelman, I., Levy, A. 1984. Decomposing Theil's index of income inequality into between and within components: A note. *Rev. Income Wealth* 30:119–21

Adelman, I., Morris, C. T. 1973. *Economic Growth and Social Equity in Developing Countries.* Stanford: Stanford Univ. Press. 257 pp.

Adelman, I., Robinson, S. 1978. *Income Distribution Policy in Developing Countries: A Case Study of Korea.* Oxford: Oxford Univ. Press. 346 pp.

Ahluwalia, M. S. 1976. Inequality, poverty and development. *J. Dev. Econ.* 3:307–42

Ahluwalia, M. S., Carter, N. G., Chenery, H. B. 1979. Growth and poverty in developing countries. *J. Dev. Econ.* 6:299–341

Alker, H. R. Jr., Russett, B. M. 1966. Indices for comparing inequality. In *Comparing Nations: The Use of Quantitative Data in Cross-National Research*, ed. R. L. Merritt, S. Rokkan, pp. 349–72. New Haven: Yale Univ. Press. 584 pp.

Allison, P. 1978. Measures of inequality. *Am. Sociol. Rev.* 43:865–80

Amin, S. 1984. Income distribution in the capitalist system. *Rev.* 8:3–28

Anand, S. 1977. Aspects of poverty in Malaysia. *Rev. Income Wealth* 23:1–16

Anand, S., Kanbur, S. M. 1985. Poverty under the Kuznets process. *Econ. J. Conf. Pap.*, pp. 42s–50s

Atkinson, A. B. 1970. On the measurement of inequality. *J. Econ. Theory* 2:244–63

Atkinson, A. B. 1983. *The Economics of Inequality.* Oxford: Clarendon. 330 pp. 2nd ed.

Bacha, E. L. 1979. The Kuznets curve and beyond: Growth and changes in inequalities. In *Economic Growth and Resources*, ed. E. Malinvaud, vol. 1:52–73. London: Macmillan. 278 pp.

Ballentine, J. G., Soligo, R. 1977. Consumption and earnings patterns and income distribution. *Econ. Dev. Cult. Change* 26:693–708

Becker, G. S., Tomes, N. 1979. An equilibrium theory of the distribution of income and intergenerational mobility. *J. Polit. Econ.* 87:1153–89

Beckerman, W. 1977. Some reflections on redistribution with growth. *World Dev.* 5:665–76

Berry, A. 1985. On trends in the gap between rich and poor in less developed countries: Why we know so little. *Rev. Income Wealth* 31:337–54

Berry, A., Urrutia, M. 1976. *Income Distribution in Colombia.* New Haven: Yale Univ. Press. 281 pp.

Bigsten, A. 1983. *Income Distribution and Development: Theory, Evidence and Policy.* London: Heinemann. 192 pp.

Blitzer, C. R., Clark, P. B., Taylor, L. 1975. *Economy-Wide Models and Development Planning.* London: Oxford Univ. Press. 369 pp.

Blomström, M., Hettne, B. 1984. *Development Theory in Transition. The Dependency Debate and Beyond: Third World Responses.* London: Zed Books. 215 pp.

Bollen, K. A., Jackman, R. W. 1985. Political democracy and the size distribution of income. *Am. Sociol. Rev.* 50:438–57

Boltho, A. 1975. *Japan: An Economic Survey, 1953–73.* 1975. New York: Oxford Univ. Press. 204 pp.

Bornschier, V. 1983. World economy, level

of development and income distribution: An integration of different approaches to the explanation of income inequality. *World Dev.* 11:11–20

Bornschier, V., Ballmer-Cao, H.-T. 1978. Multinational corporations in the world economy and national development. *Bull. Sociol. Inst. Univ. Zurich* 32:1–169

Bornschier, V., Chase-Dunn, C. 1985. *Transnational Corporations and Underdevelopment.* New York: Praeger. 180 pp.

Bornschier, V., Heintz, P., eds. 1979. Compendium of data for world-system analysis. (Reworked and enlarged by T.-H. Ballmer-Cao, J. Scheidegger) *Sociol. Inst. Univ. Zurich Bull.* (Special Issue) 297 pp.

Brundenius, C. 1981. Growth with equity: The Cuban experience (1959–1980). *World Dev.* 9:1083–96

Cantarelli, D., Bressan, F. 1984. Disuguaglianze regionali e sviluppo economico: Un'analisi econometrica internazionale. *Giorn. Econom. Ann. Econom.* 43:161–89

Chase-Dunn, C. 1975. The effects of international economic dependence on development and inequality: A cross-national study. *Am. Sociol. Rev.* 40:720–38

Chenery, H., Ahluwalia, M. S., Bell, C. L. G., Duloy, J. H., Jolly, R. 1974. *Redistribution with Growth.* London: Oxford Univ. Press. 304 pp.

Chenery, H. B., Syrquin, M. 1975. *Patterns of Development, 1950–70.* London: Oxford Univ. Press. 234 pp.

Cline, W. R. 1975. Distribution and development, a survey of the literature. *J. Dev. Econ.* 2:359–400

Cowell, F. A. 1977. *Measuring Inequality.* Oxford: Philip Allan. 180 pp.

Cowell, F. A. 1985. Multilevel decomposition of Theil's index of inequality. *Rev. Income Wealth* 31:201–5

Cromwell, J. 1977. The size distribution of income: An international comparison. *Rev. Income Wealth* 23:291–308

Denslow, D., Tyler, W. 1984. Perspectives on poverty and income inequality in Brazil. *World Dev.* 12:1019–28

Dervis, K., de Melo, J., Robinson, S. 1982. *General Equilibrium Models for Development Policy.* Cambridge: Cambridge Univ. Press. 526 pp.

Evans, P., Timberlake, M. 1980. Dependence, inequality and the growth of the tertiary: A comparative analysis of less developed countries. *Am. Sociol. Rev.* 45:531–52

Fagen, R. R. 1978. Equity in the South in the context of North-South Relations. In *Rich and Poor Nations in the World Economy*, ed. A. Fishlow, C. F. Diaz-Alejandro, R.

R. Fagen, R. D. Hansen, pp. 165–214. New York: McGraw-Hill. 264 pp.

Fei, J. C. H., Ranis, G., Kuo, S. W. Y. 1979. *Growth With Equity: The Taiwan Case.* New York: Oxford Univ. Press. 422 pp.

Ffrench-Davis, R. 1976. Policy tools and objectives of redistribution. See Foxley 1976b, pp. 107–34

Fiala, R. 1983. Inequality and the service sector in less developed countries: A reanalysis and respecification. *Am. Sociol. Rev.* 48:421–28

Fields, G. S. 1979. Decomposing LDC inequalities. *Oxford Econ. Pap.* 31:437–59

Fields, G. S. 1980. *Poverty, Inequality and Development.* Cambridge: Cambridge Univ. Press. 281 pp.

Figueroa, A. 1975. Income distribution, demand structure and employment: The case of Peru. *J. Dev. Stud.* 11:20–31

Firebaugh, G. 1980. Cross-national versus historical regression models: Conditions of equivalence in comparative analysis. In *Comp. Soc. Res.* 3:333–44

Flegg, A. T. 1980. The interaction of fertility and size distribution of income: A comment. *J. Dev. Stud.* 16:468–72

Fossum, E. 1967. Factors influencing the occurrence of military coups d'etat in Latin America. *J. Peace Res.* 4:228–51

Foster, J., Greer, J., Thorbecke, E. 1984. A class of decomposable poverty measures. *Econometrica* 52:761–66

Foxley, A. 1976a. Redistribution of consumption: Effects on production and employment. See Foxley 1976b, pp. 179–200

Foxley, A., ed. 1976b. *Income Distribution in Latin America.* Cambridge: Cambridge Univ. Press. 244 pp.

Frank, A. G. 1975. *On Capitalist Underdevelopment.* Bombay: Oxford Univ. Press. 113 pp.

Frank, C. R., Webb, R. C., eds. 1977. *Income Distribution and Growth in the Less Developed Countries.* Washington DC: Brookings Inst. 641 pp.

Galenson, W., ed. 1979. *Economic Growth and Structural Change in Taiwan.* Ithaca: Cornell Univ. Press. 519 pp.

Gagliani, G. 1981. La distribuzione funzionale del reddito nello sviluppo: I problemi delle economie ritardatarie. *Note Econ.* 14:18–60

Gagliani, G. 1985. Long-term changes in the occupational structure. *Eur. Sociol. Rev.* 1:183–210

Goedhart, T., Halberstadt, V., Kapteyn, A., van Praag, B. M. S. 1977. The poverty line: Concept and measurement. *J. Hum. Resourc.* 12:503–20

Griffin, K., Kahn, A. R. 1978. Poverty in the

Third World: Ugly facts and fancy models. *World Dev.* 6:295–304

Griliches, Z., Krelle, W., Krupp, H.-J., Kyn, D., eds. 1978. *Income Distribution and Economic Inequality.* Frankfurt: Campus Verlag. 335 pp.

Hagenaars, A. J. M. 1986. *The Perception of Poverty.* Amsterdam: North Holland. 301 pp.

Hirschman, A. O. 1973. The changing tolerance for income inequality in the course of economic development. *World Devel.* 1:29–36

House, W. J. 1983. Nairobi's informal sector: Dynamic entrepreneur or surplus labor? *Econ. Dev. Cult. Change* 32:277–302

Hsia, R., Chau, L. 1978. *Industrialization, Employment and Income Distribution. A Case Study of Hong Kong.* London: Croom Helm. 205 pp.

ILO. 1977a. *Employment, Growth and Basic Needs: A One-World Problem.* New York: Praeger. 222 pp.

ILO. 1977b. *Poverty and Landlessness in Rural Asia.* Geneva: Int. Labor Office. 288 pp.

Jackman, R. W. 1975. *Politics and Social Equality. A Comparative Analysis.* New York: John Wiley. 225 pp.

Jacobs, D. 1981. On theory and measurement (a reply to McGranahan). *Am. Sociol. Rev.* 46:241–45

Jain, S. 1975. *Size Distribution of Income: A Compilation of Data.* Washington DC: World Bank. 137 pp.

James, J. 1980. The employment effects of an income redistribution. *J. Dev. Econ.* 7:175–89

Kakwani, N. C. 1980. *Income Inequality and Poverty.* New York: Oxford Univ. Press. 416 pp.

Kerbo, H. R. 1983. *Social Stratification and Inequality.* New York: McGraw-Hill. 494 pp.

Knight, J. B. 1976. Explaining income distribution in less developed countries: A framework and an agenda. *Oxford Bull. Econ. Statist.* 38:161–77

Kolm, S.-C. 1976. Unequal inequalities (I). *J. Econ. Theory* 12:416–42

Kondor, Y. 1971. An old-new measure of income inequality. *Econometrica* 39:1041–42

Koo, H. 1984. The political economy of income distribution in South Korea: The impact of the state's industrialization policies. *World Dev.* 12:1029–37

Krelle, W. 1978. Introduction: The theory of personal income distribution. See Krelle & Shorrocks 1978, pp. 1–32.

Krelle, W., Shorrocks, A. F., eds. 1978. *Personal Income Distribution.* Amsterdam: North Holland. 524 pp.

Kuo, S. W. Y. 1983. *The Taiwan Economy in Transition.* Boulder: Westview Press. 362 pp.

Kuznets, S. 1955. Economic growth and income inequality. *Am. Econ. Rev.* 45:1–28

Kuznets, S. 1963. Quantitative aspects of the economic growth of nations: viii. Distribution of income by size. *Econ. Dev. Cult. Change* 11,2 (Part 2):1–80

Kuznets, S. 1976. Demographic aspects of the size distribution of income: An exploratory essay. *Econ. Dev. Cult. Change* 25:1–95

Kuznets, S. 1980. Recent population trends in less developed countries and implications for internal income inequality. In *Population and Economic Change in Developing Countries,* ed. R. A. Easterlin, pp. 471–511. Chicago: Univ. Chicago Press. 581 pp.

Kuznets, S. 1982. Children and adults in the income distribution. *Econ. Dev. Cult. Change* 30:697–738

Lam, D. 1984. The variance of population characteristics in stable populations, with applications to the distribution of income. *Pop. Stud.* 38:117–27

Lecaillon, J., Germidis, D. 1977. *Inégalité des Revenus et Développement Économique.* Paris: Presses Univ. de France. 236 pp.

Lecaillon, J., Paukert, F., Morrisson, C., Germidis, D. 1984. *Income Distribution and Economic Development. An Analytical Survey.* Geneva: Int. Labor Office. 212 pp.

Lewis, W. A. 1976. Development and distribution. In *Employment, Income Distribution and Development Strategy,* ed. A. Cairncross, M. Puri, pp. 26–42. London: Macmillan

Lewis, W. A. 1979. The dual economy revisited. *Manchester School* 47:211–29

Lipton, M. 1977. *Why Poor People Stay Poor: A Study of Urban Bias in World Development.* London: Temple Smith. 467 pp.

Little, I. M. D. 1982. *Economic Development. Theory, Policy and International Relations.* New York: Basic Books. 452 pp.

Lydall, H. F. 1977. *Income Distribution During the Process of Development. Res. Work. Pap. WEP 2-23/WP 52.* Geneva: ILO

Lydall, H. F. 1979a. *A Theory of Income Distribution.* Oxford: Clarendon Press. 326 pp.

Lydall, H. F. 1979b. Some problems in making international comparisons of inequality. See Moroney 1976, pp. 21–37

Mann, A. J. 1985. Economic development, income distribution and real income levels: Puerto Rico, 1953–77. *Econ. Dev. Culture Change* 34:485–502

McGranahan, D. 1979. *International Comparability of Statistics on Income Distribution.* Geneva: Inst. Rech. Nations Un. Développement. 50 pp.

Meade, J. E. 1976. *The Just Economy*. London: Allen & Unwin. 247 pp.

Menard, S. 1986. A research note on international comparisons of inequality of income. *Soc. Forc.* 64:779–93

Morawetz, D. 1974. Employment implications of industrialization in developing countries: A survey. *Econ. J.* 84:491–542

Moreland, R. S. 1984. *Population, Development and Income Distribution: A Modelling Approach. Bachue-International.* Aldershot: Gower. 197 pp.

Morley, S. A. 1983. *Labor Markets and Inequitable Growth: The Case of Authoritarian Capitalism in Brazil*. Cambridge: Cambridge Univ. Press. 316 pp.

Moroney, J. R., ed. 1979. *Income Inequality.* Lexington: Lexington Books 201 pp.

Morrisson, C. 1978. Income distribution in less developed countries: Methodological problems. See Krelle & Shorrocks 1978, pp. 241–59

Muller, E. N. 1984. Financial dependence in the capitalist world economy and the distribution of income within nations. See Seligson 1984 pp. 256–82

Nelson, E. R. 1977. The measurement and trend of inequality: Comment. *Am. Econ. Rev.* 67:497–501

Nugent, J. B. 1983. An alternative source of measurement error as an explanation for the inverted-U hypothesis. *Econ. Dev. Culture Change* 31:385–96

Nygård, F., Sandström, A. 1981. *Measuring Income Inequality*. Stockholm: Almqvist & Wiksell. 436 pp.

Paglin, M. 1975. The measurement and trend of inequality: A basic revision. *Am. Econ. Rev.* 65:598–609

Palma, G. 1978. Dependency. A formal theory of underdevelopment or a methodology for the analysis of concrete situations of underdevelopment? *World Dev.* 6:881–924

Papanek, G. 1978. Economic growth, income distribution and the political process in less developed countries. See Griliches et al 1978, pp. 259–73

Paukert, F. 1973. Income distribution at different levels of development: A survey of evidence. *ILO Rev.* 108:97–125

Paukert, F., Skolka, J., Maton, J. 1981. *Income Distribution, Structure of Economy and Employment*. London: Croom Helm. 169 pp.

Pen, J. 1978. The role of power in the distribution of personal income: Some illustrative numbers. See Krelle & Shorrocks 1978, pp. 335–52

Pfefferman, G., Webb, R. 1983. Poverty and income distribution in Brazil. *Rev. Income Wealth* 29:101–24

Phelps Brown, H. 1977. *The Inequality of Pay*. Oxford: Oxford Univ. Press. 360 pp.

Pyatt, G. 1976. On the interpretation and disaggregation of Gini coefficients. *Econ. J.* 86:243–55

Rao, V. M. 1969. The decomposition of concentration ratios. *J. R. Stat. Soc.* 132:418–25

Repetto, R. 1979. *Economic Inequality and Fertility in Developing Countries*. Baltimore: Johns Hopkins Univ. Press. 186 pp.

Robinson, S. 1976. A note on the U hypothesis relating income inequality and economic development. *Am. Econ. Rev.* 66:437–40

Rodgers, G. B., Hopkins, M., Wéry, R. 1978. *Population, Employment and Inequality: Bachue-Philippines*. Farnborough: Saxon House. 434 pp.

Rubinson, R. 1976. The world-economy and the distribution of income within states. *Am. Sociol. Rev.* 41:638–59

Rusterholz, P. 1984. *External economic dependence and income distribution: Towards a new look at old stuff*. Presented at EADI Conf., Madrid

Sahota, G. S. 1978. Theories of personal income distribution: A survey. *J. Econ. Lit.* 16:1–55

Sahota, G. S., Rocca, C. A. 1985. *Income distribution. Theory, Modeling and Case Study of Brazil*. Ames, Iowa: Iowa State Univ. Press. 236 pp.

Saith, A. 1983. Development and distribution. A critique of the cross-country U-hypothesis. *J. Devel. Econ.* 13:367–82

Sawyer, M. 1976. Income distribution in OECD countries. *OECD Econ. Outlook Occas. Stud.*, Sect.V:3–36.

Schneider, F., Frey, B. S. 1985. Economic and political determinants of foreign direct investment. *World Dev.* 13:161–75

Schutz, R. R. 1951. On the measurement of income inequality. *Am. Econ. Rev.* 41:107–22

Seligson, M. A. ed. 1984. *The Gap between the Rich and the Poor: Contending Perspectives on the Political Economy of Development*. Boulder, Colo: Westview. 420 pp.

Sen, A. K. 1973. *On Economic Inequality*. Oxford: Clarendon. 118 pp.

Sen, A. K. 1976. Poverty: An ordinal approach to measurement. *Econometrica* 44:219–32

Sen, A. K. 1978. Ethical measurement of inequality: Some difficulties. See Krelle & Shorrocks 1978, pp. 81–94

Sen, A. K. 1981. *Poverty and Famines. An Essay on Entitlement and Deprivation*. Oxford: Clarendon. 257 pp.

Sen, A. K. 1984. *Resources, Values and Development*. Oxford: Basil Blackwell. 547 pp.

Shorrocks, A. F. 1980. The class of additively decomposable inequality measures. *Econometrica* 48:613–25

Smolensky, E., Pommerehne, W. W., Dalrymple, R. E. 1979. Postfisc income inequality: A comparison of the United States and Germany. See Moroney 1979, pp. 69–81

Stewart, J. R. 1978. Potential effects of income redistribution on economic growth: an expanded estimating procedure applied to Mexico. *Econ. Dev. Cult. Change* 26:467–86

Stiglitz, J. E. 1978. Equality, taxation and inheritance. See Krelle & Shorrocks, pp. 271–99

Swamy, S. 1967. Structural changes and the distribution of income by size: The case of India. *Rev. Income Wealth* 12:155–74

Szal, R., Robinson, S. 1977. Measuring income inequality. See Frank & Webb 1977, pp. 491–534

Taylor, L., Bacha, E. L., Cardoso, E. A., Lysy, F. J. 1980. *Models of Growth and Distribution for Brazil*. New York: Oxford Univ. Press. 355 pp.

Taylor, C. L., Jodice, D. A. 1983. *World Handbook of Political and Social Indicators*, vol. 1. New Haven: Yale Univ. Press. 305 pp.

Teilhet-Waldorf, S., Waldorf, W. H. 1983. Earnings of self-employed in an informal sector: A case study of Bangkok. *Econ. Dev. Cult. Change* 31:587–607

Thirsk, W. R. 1979. Aggregation bias and the sensitivity of income distribution to changes in the composition of demand: The case of Colombia. *J. Dev. Stud.* 16:50–66

Tinbergen, J. 1975. *Income Distribution: Analysis and Policies*. Amsterdam: North-Holland. 170 pp.

Tinbergen, J. 1985. Theories of income distribution in developed countries. In *Issues in Contemporary Macroeconomics and Distribution*, ed. G. R. Feiwel, pp. 335–65. Albany: State Univ. N.Y. Press. 464 pp.

Todaro, M. P. 1969. A model of labor migration and urban unemployment in less developed countries. *Am. Econ. Rev.* 59:138–48

van Ginneken, W. 1980. *Socio-Economic Groups and Income Distribution in Mexico*. London: Croom Helm. 237 pp.

van Ginneken, W., Park, J. 1984. *Generating Internationally Comparable Income Distribution Estimates*. Geneva: ILO. 176 pp.

van Praag, B. M. S. 1978. The perception of income inequality. See Krelle & Shorrocks 1978, pp. 113–36

Venieris, Y. P., Gupta, D. K. 1983. Sociopolitical and economic dimensions of development: A cross-section model. *Econ. Dev. Cult. Change* 31:727–56

Wada, R. O. 1974. *Changes in the size distribution of income in post-war Japan*. *Work. Pap. WEP 2-23/WP 9*. Geneva: ILO. 145 pp.

Ward, M. D. 1978. *The Political Economy of Distribution*. New York: Elsevier. 188 pp.

Weede, E., Tiefenbach, H. 1981. Some recent explanations of income inequality. *Int. Stud. Q.* 25:255–82

Wiles, P. 1978. Our shaky data base. See Krelle & Shorrocks 1978, pp. 167–92

World Bank. 1984. *Brazil: Economic Memorandum*. Washington DC: World Bank. 313 pp.

Ann. Rev. Sociol. 1987. 13:335–58

ORGANIZATIONAL GROWTH AND DECLINE PROCESSES

David A. Whetten

College of Commerce and Business Administration, University of Illinois, Champaign, Illinois 61820

Abstract

Literature on the application of the life cycles analogy to the study of organizations is reviewed. The controversy over the use of life cycle stages to characterize the evolution of organizations is discussed. Research on the causes and consequences of organizational growth and decline, as well as the effective management of growth and decline processes, is examined in detail. Issues endemic to research on evolutionary processes are discussed, including the definition and operationalization of organizational growth and decline.

INTRODUCTION AND HISTORICAL CONTEXT

The increasing emphasis on the temporal aspects of organizations represents a significant trend in the study of organizations. Authors stress the need to examine dynamic, evolutionary processes within single organizations (Cameron & Whetten 1981, Kimberly & Quinn 1984, Miller & Friesen 1980, Kimberly & Miles 1980, Tushman & Romanelli 1985, Singh et al 1986), as well as in populations of organizations (Freeman & Hannan 1975, Tushman & Anderson 1986). Evidence of this trend is reflected in the extensive use of the organizational life cycles analogy, which focuses on the natural, metamorphic processes associated with birth, maturation, decline, and death in organic systems.

Recent efforts to organize strands of organizational theory taxonomically have made clear that theories can be categorized as either mechanistic or organic. Further, some writers see a general trend in the field from mechanistic to organic views of organizations (Van de Ven & Astley 1981, Perrow 1979, Scott 1981). Although economists have drawn on the biological analo-

335

0360-0572/87/0815-0335$02.00

gies of natural selection and birth and death processes for decades (Marshall 1920, Boulding 1950) and isolated early organizational theorists urged their adoption (Haire 1959, Katz & Kahn 1966, Lippitt & Schmidt 1967), such analogies did not gain widespread use in organization research until the 1970s.

Clearly the most hotly contested issue in the life cycles literature is how literally the biological analogy should be applied to social systems. In his early work, Kenneth Boulding advocated a fairly extreme position in favor of a strong, literal adoption of the biological model (1950). He argued that economics should move beyond its prevailing paradigm, which he characterized as a static equilibrium theory of maximizing behavior, to adopt an ecological approach to economics. He described society as a large "ecosystem," in which every organism (organization) behaves according to the interplay between an "inner law of growth and survival" and "a complex hostile-friendly external environment of other organisms" (p. 6). He further argued that economics should develop a life cycle theory which was cognizant of disequilibrium and "the irreversible processes of (decline) and entropy" (p. 37). Indeed, Boulding argued that for all organisms ("individuals, families, firms, nations, and civilizations") there is an "inexorable and irreversible movement towards the equilibrium of death" (p. 38).

This position prompted a strong rebuttal from an early organizational theorist, Edith Penrose (1952). She argued that "the data" simply do not support organizational analogies either to the natural selection process or to biological life cycles. She maintained that there was no evidence to support the claim that all organizations must die or that life cycle stages are a function of age. She argued that the literal adoption of the biological analogies by social scientists, "suggest[s] explanations of events that do not depend upon the conscious willed decisions of human beings" (p. 808). She argued that the search for general laws predetermining individuals' choices missed the mark, because it would "rid the social sciences of the uncertainties and complexities that arise from the apparent 'free will' of man and would endow them with that more reliable power of prediction which for some is the essence of 'science' " (p. 818).

DEBATE OVER LIFE CYCLE "STAGES"

The debate between voluntaristic and deterministic theories of human behavior within organizations is still active today (Van de Ven & Astley 1981), and it is clearly evident in the unresolved question of how literally the life cycles model should be applied to the study of organizations. The central issues in the current writing on this topic are the number of stages in the life cycles model, and the deterministic nature of these stages, including whether movement through the stages is linear or recursive.

One of the major challenges to a serious discussion of these issues is the proliferation of life cycle models. Quinn & Cameron (1983) and Cameron & Whetten (1983) have published reviews of close to 30 life cycle models from the group development and organizational development literatures. The resulting summary model contains four stages: entrepreneurial (early innovation, niche formation, high creativity), collectivity (high cohesion, commitment), formalization and control (emphasis on stability and institutionalization), and elaboration and structure (domain expansion and decentralization).

The most distinctive feature of this summary model is that it covers only the "growth stages," roughly from birth through maturity. This highlights the lack of attention devoted to the stages of decline and death in these literatures, particularly during the growth oriented decades of the 1960s and 1970s (Whetten 1980). However, it also simplifies the debate over the deterministic nature of OLC stages. Several contemporary authors (e.g. Filley & Aldag 1980, Freeman 1982, Starbuck 1968, Tichy 1980) echo the conviction of Edith Penrose that organizational changes cannot be predicted in advance and that current organizational characteristics do not necessarily foretell future characteristics. Still, a review of this literature by McAvoy (1984) indicates there is considerably more consensus about sequential movement through these early stages of development than through the later stages of decline and death.

Part of the reason for disagreement over this issue is the different interpretations of "stages of development" in the literature. Those who choose a fairly narrow definition, analogous to biological development, are most opposed to its application to social systems. These authors object to the deterministic logic reflected in organizational life cycle models which is based on a dialectical view of problem solving (eg Greiner 1972). They also feel that the summary models of stage development, containing 3–5 stages, are overly simplistic, and therefore, of little predictive value (beyond denoting gross developmental processes approximating common sense views of youth, adolescence, maturity, and old age).

A less controversial view suggests that these "stages" are simply clusters of issues or problems that social systems must resolve, and that the inherent nature of these problems suggests a roughly sequential ordering (Miller & Freisen 1980, Cameron & Whetten 1983, Tushman & Romanelli 1985). That is, problem B logically follows problem A in the evolution of a typical organization. In addition, it is argued that these problem sets should be specified at the level of organizational subsystems (e.g. management, technology, structure) to avoid the implication that all facits of an organization proceed simultaneously, in lock-step fashion, through a small number of organization-level developmental stages. This is especially true of mature organizations in which the subsystems become increasingly loosely coupled. An example of a subsystem evolutionary sequence is the need to solve the problem of poor coordination between several organizational units, or product lines, which logically follows an earlier period of structural expansion.

If we define stages as clusters of subsystem problems or issues that are linked sequentially and embedded within the natural evolutionary processes of organizations, then there is considerable logical, as well as empirical, support for this view of organizational development (Lyden 1975, Kimberly 1979, Quinn & Cameron 1983)—with three important qualifications.

First, critics of social evolution theories have consistently objected to the normative connotation of "more advanced" associated with terms like progression and development (Timasheff 1967). It is, therefore, important to note in the life cycle literature that movement from one stage to the next need not be viewed as progression to a higher, more effective, or more sophisticated level of development.

Second, it is important to distinguish between sequential and nonrecursive development. Linear movement implies one direction only. In the life cycle literature no compelling reason argues that the problems present at one stage can only be resolved by moving toward the next level of development. Research on group stage development has shown that a recycling phenomenon often occurs when groups in their latter stages of development encounter major crises (Cameron & Whetten 1983). A similar phenomenon undoubtedly occurs in organizations. As the result of a merger, a substantial decrease in resources, or the loss of key personnel, a mature institution may appropriately revert to an earlier set of problems.

Third, it is important to differentiate between growth stages, or problems and decline stages. As noted earlier, life cycle stage models to date have focussed primarily on the growth side of the developmental process. There are several possible explanations for this lack of attention to decline processes in the organizational sciences literature (Whetten 1980). These include: (a) the practical problems of gaining access to collect data in dying organizations; (b) researchers' cultural biases stemming from the association between growth processes and our society's preoccupation with youth, vigor and virility; (c) the fact that social science research on organizations is largely supported by an entrenched establishment in which managers are rewarded primarily for their ability to foster and sustain organizational growth; and (d) the obvious conclusion that not all mature organizations decline and die, which has undoubtedly discouraged some authors from adding additional stages to the standard life cycle model.

This reluctance to focus on decline and death stages ignores important findings in the life cycle literature. Research on the effective management of declining organizations has shown that the problems associated with shrinking economic resources and moral support are qualitatively different from problems associated with growth (Cameron, Whetten & Kim 1986, Nystrom & Starbuck 1984). This important observation suggests the need to develop a series of problem sets capturing the essence of organizational decline and recovery, or death, which are not causally linked to the birth and growth stages.

Although a coherent, empirically grounded model of organizational decline and death stages has not been proposed thus far, rudimentary bits and pieces are starting to emerge (Whetten & Cameron 1985, Sutton 1983, DeGreene 1982).

In examining this literature, it is important both to understand the largely unresolved controversy over the empirical support for patterned development and to look beyond it, to examine the theoretical and practical benefits derived from the life cycle stages analogy. The literature has identified four important applications (Cameron & Whetten 1983). First, it serves as a very useful diagnostic tool, in the sense that awareness of an organization's current life cycle stage conveys information about problems and experiences probably encountered previously by organizational members. Second, it sensitizes us to the fact that goals, priorities, and even the appropriate criteria of effectiveness shift over the course of an organization's life span. Third, it is an important source of contextual information that must be factored into the analysis of organizational research results. That is, the structural properties and internal processes observed in rapidly growing organizations are very different from those found in declining organizations. Fourth, at a practical level, an understanding of the clusters of problems one is likely to encounter at different stages of organizational development, as well as insights for effectively managing the transitions between stages, represent important aids for organizational leaders.

In reviewing the life cycles literature, it is apparent that in addition to debating these conceptual issues, the discussion of growth and decline processes has focused on two major themes. A number of authors have examined the *causes and consequences* of organizational growth and decline as one way of assessing the extent to which different life cycles stages are qualitatively different. Others have chosen to focus on the *effective management* of the growth and decline processes—arguing that management initiatives influence the incidence and amplitude of the growth and decline cycles, as well as blunt or exacerbate their natural consequences. We discuss in turn the literature addressing each of these themes.

CAUSES AND CONSEQUENCES OF GROWTH AND DECLINE STAGES

Causes of Growth

Organizations grow for a variety of reasons. However, as Pfeffer & Salancik (1978) point out, it is often difficult to assess the true motivations for growth after the fact. That is, one must avoid the pitfall of attempting to extrapolate causes from consequences. It is, therefore, often difficult to gain consensus regarding the reasons for the observed growth in a specific organization. However, three general explanations for organizational growth have been highlighted in the literature (Child & Kieser 1981).

The first and most straightforward explanation is that growth can result as a by-product of other strategies. As organizations successfully satisfy needs for their services, this success fosters growth.

Second, growth is frequently sought directly because it facilitates the internal management of an organization. Increased surplus resources resulting from growth make it easier to obtain commitment to organizational goals and priorities from various factions and to resolve conflicts between those factions (Pfeffer & Salancik 1978). In addition, growth and expansion increase opportunities for promotion (Dent 1959), provide greater challenge for (and utilization of) managers (Starbuck 1965, Penrose 1959), and satisfy needs for higher salaries and prestige (Roberts 1959).

Third, growth enables an organization to attenuate its dependence on the environment by reducing either uncertainty or external control. Research studies have shown that larger organizations tend to have more consistent, stable performance (Caves 1970, Ferguson 1960, Marris & Wood 1971). The likelihood of an organization being either taken over or allowed to go out of business also declines with size (Singh 1971, Steindl 1945). The strategic advantage of large size stems from a variety of factors. For example, in cases where economies of scale can be achieved in the production process, growth makes the organization more efficient and therefore more competitive. Growth also provides the resources for the diversification that enables an organization to spread its risk across several product lines or even industries. It also provides large organizations with the resources necessary to fund the development of new projects or to produce and market more economically designs pioneered by smaller firms. Taking all these factors into consideration, Child & Kieser have concluded that, "Growth is therefore [pursued by organizations as] a basis for security" (1981:32).

Before leaving this topic, it is important to point out two basic problems with the measurement of size and growth. First, studies often do not differentiate between size and growth (Scott 1981). Size is an absolute measure of the scale of an organization, generally based on number of employees or total revenues (Kimberly 1976). In contrast, growth is a relative measure of size, as observed over time. Consequently, it is important that we treat with caution conclusions about the causes or consequences of growth (like those noted above) based on cross-sectional studies of the correlates of size. Research studies on the correlates of large size represent a fertile ground for extrapolating hypotheses for longitudinal studies of the advantages of growth, but there are a variety of reasons why the two approaches might produce different results.

For example, Filley & Aldag (1978) argue that many of the studies correlating size and various measures of success do not control for type of organization (industry, organizational form, or technology); consequently, the correlation between size and outcomes may be spurious. Penrose (1959) also noted several constraints on growth that must be taken into consideration: (a) some types of business are unsuited to large size, such as service organizations; (b) large firms may protect small operations through protective pricing; (c) situations in which easy entry and exit and high mortality rates preclude the achievement of large size; (d) a large business may ignore certain small businesses who could be driven out of business and thus encourage smallness.

The second problem with the traditional approach to measuring growth is that it typically does not examine what Boulding (1953) calls population growth. Because growth is not randomly distributed across a population of organizations, it is bound to create a differential strategic advantage (or disadvantage), Boulding argues. This line of reasoning anticipated the contemporary population ecology perspective which argues that outcomes or characteristics of population members can be presumed to have strategic value only in reference to others in the population and to the carrying capacity of the ecological niche (Hannan & Freeman 1978, Freeman 1982). This argument demonstrates the need to measure the growth of an organization relative to others in its population, if one is interested in assessing the impact of growth on other organizational properties related to survival.

Consequences of Growth

One of the most controversial issues in the literature on the consequences of growth is whether there is an inevitable point of diminishing returns, past which the advantages of growth become less evident until gradually growth becomes disadvantageous. A common and enduring theme in the sociology of organizations literature has been the dysfunctional consequences of large size. Extremely large organizations are viewed as too complex, too rigid, too impersonal, too inefficient, and too inaccessible to outsiders. Consequently, many researchers view growth as beneficial only up to a point (Perrow 1979, Hedberg et al 1976, Meyer 1977). This view was borne out in Pfeffer &

Salancik's (1978) review of this topic in which they found that profitability increased in growing organizations up to a point and then tapered off. Warwick (1975) also observed a steady decline in flexibility and responsiveness due to bureaucratic growth in the US State Department, despite reforms designed to curb it. This is consistent with Aldrich & Auster's (1986) observations that the rate of innovation diminishes with organizational size.

There are basically three prevailing explanations for these apparent dysfunctional outcomes of large size. First, many point to the diminished capacity for changes, and increased bureaucratic ossification, inherent with the aging process. Because organization age and size are positively correlated, consequences of large size are often confused with advanced age. Inkson et al (1970) found that fourteen organizations in England increased their level of bureaucratization over a four-to-five year period, independent of changes in their size. Starbuck (1965) has argued that this process reflects organizational learning, in which organizations learn to cope with their growth by routinizing and formalizing critical communication and coordination activities. The resulting increased efficiencies encourage further bureaucratization, which over time rigidifies more and more of the organization's processes.

Second, several authors have argued that the loss of responsiveness associated with increased size is the result of the substitution of the personal, self-centered goals of key leaders for the original organizational goals emphasizing service and quality. This argument is exemplified by Michel's (1962) "iron law of oligarchy," which grew out of his investigation of the shift towards more conservative goals in the German Socialist party, in response to its leaders' desire for greater security. A related leader-driven bureaucratization process was proposed by Weber (1947) in his discussion of the "routinization of charisma" process. He argued that as organizations founded by charismatic leaders grew, the founder would institute a system of hierarchical offices as a means of legitimizing his or her power and in order to increase its efficiency and continuity through routinization.

Third, as young organizations mature, their growth often reflects adaptation to the dominant societal institutions. Several studies of the maturation process in reform government organizations have observed a pattern of liberal goals and flexible, open structures transformed by the give-and-take associations with established opposing groups (Selznick 1949, Lipset 1950, Cahn & Cahn 1964).

Fourth, undermanning theory suggests that mature, large organizations tend to become less motivating environments for employees because jobs become highly specialized and so provide less autonomy, variety, and task identity (Wicker et al 1976).

Although this "curvilinear benefits of growth" viewpoint pervades the field, others have argued that the relation between growth and effectiveness is moderated by other organizational factors. For example, organizations with routine technologies can capitalize on growth to increase their economies of scale, but rapid growth in nonroutine job shops creates debilitating coordination problems (Filley & Aldag 1980). Zald & Ash (1966) have made a similar argument for the impact of organizational goals, or domain. Contrary to the prevailing view that growth inevitably leads to increased conservatism in organizations, they argued that social-movement organizations with exclusive membership rules and a remote chance of reaching their goals in the near future will likely adopt very radical organizing processes. Others have also argued that growth produces the serious dysfunctional consequences, connoted by "bureaucracy," only in organizations that are poorly managed. In other words, it is not growth per se that causes the problems, but rather, poor management (Child & Kieser 1981).

Up to this point, we have examined the consequences of growth primarily in terms of their strategic implications, i.e. whether growth increases or decreases an organization's chances of survival. Another segment of this literature focuses on the consequences of growth on internal organizational processes—without reference to their strategic implications. This area has its own controversies, focusing primarily on the causal relationships between size, technology, and structure (Aldrich 1972). However, Child & Kieser identify several commonalities in the literature on the effect of organizational growth on structure. These include: "a rising level of internal differentiation into specialized roles, functions, and divisions; a growing complexity in terms of occupations and skills employed; increased delegation and an emphasis on solving problems through direct, lateral communications rather than hierarchical communications; an increasing use of formal systems and procedures; and a rising proportion of employees concerned with administrative and staff functions" (1981:38). They also observed three general changes in organizational technology associated with organizational growth: a shift to mass production of goods and services, the increased utilization of knowledge technology, e.g. computers, and the application of new specialist techniques (1981:42).

Consequences of Decline

Several authors writing on the topic of life cycles have argued that more attention needs to be given to the nongrowth periods of organizational development and evolution (Whetten 1980a, Greenhalgh 1983, Zammuto & Cameron 1985). In response, an extensive literature on the management of decline has emerged within business administration (Starbuck et al 1978, Taber et al 1978), as well as in the related fields of public administration (Levine 1978, Biller 1980), hospital administration (Jick & Murray 1982) and educational administration (Petrie & Alpert 1983, Cyert 1978, Berger, 1983).

Unfortunately, there is little agreement in this literature on the definition of organizational decline. Authors typically focus on decreases in the number of employees or financial resources. However, some combinations of organizational size, performance, and resource levels are extremely difficult to categorize. For example, if a professional football team's win-loss record drops, but its revenues increase (possibly due to the employment of a star quarterback with broad fan appeal), is the organization declining? And, what about a liberal arts college that reduces its enrollment, culls its course offerings, and fires several of its faculty, in the process of becoming a more prestigious, higher priced institution? Or a drug rehabilitation center whose clientele (and staff) increases while its cure rate drops? The resolution of these issues is beyond the scope of this review. The interested reader is referred to Cameron et al (1987). For our immediate purposes, we will use the common definition of decrease in size and/or budget.

Thus far, little empirical research has investigated the individual and organizational consequences of decline. Writers have limited their discussions largely to case studies, theoretical treaties, model development, or demographic trend analyses (Zammuto & Cameron 1985, Jick & Murray 1982, Whetten 1980, Hirschhorn 1983). With the exception of the research on the impact of retrenchment on administrative ratios (Freeman & Hannan 1975, Ford 1980) relatively little empirical research has examined the antecedents or consequences of decline in organizations. There is virtual consensus in the literature, however, that decline produces dysfunctional consequences at both individual and organizational levels. It is argued that conflict, secrecy, rigidity, centralization, formalization, scapegoating, and conservatism increase, and that morale, innovativeness, participation, leader influence, and long-term planning decrease (Cameron et al 1986). The logic of these dysfunctional "outcomes of decline" is explained as follows.

Conditions of decline inherently involve restricted resources and pressures to retrench. Levine (1978, 1979), Whetten (1980b), Hermann (1963), and others have noted the intensification of conflict under these conditions as fights over a smaller resource base and consequent attempts to protect turf predominate. Pluralism, or the development of organized and vocal special interest groups, increases as organizations become politicized (Pfeffer & Salancik 1978, Pfeffer 1981a, Whetten 1981). Morale worsens as a "mean mood" becomes wide-spread (Bozeman & Slusher 1978, Levine et al 1981, Starbuck et al 1978). Attempts to ameliorate conflict and increase morale often involve the use of slack resources to meet operational needs, hence slack and redundancy (and, therefore, flexibility) are eliminated. Managers generally prefer across-the-board cutbacks, rather than selective, prioritized cuts, to appease conflicting demands and minimize the political fall-out of retrenchment (Whetten 1980b, Cyert 1978, Boulding 1975).

Authors also have suggested that conservatism and a short-term orientation result from decline (i.e. the threat-rigidity response), and efficiency takes priority over effectiveness (Staw et al 1981, Cameron 1983, Whetten 1981, Rubin 1979, Bozeman & Slusher 1979). Innovation is more likely to be blamed for decline than seen as a solution to it. As a result, risk taking and creativity decrease (Boyd 1979, Starbuck & Hedberg 1977). Centralization of decision-making increases because mistakes become more visible and costly when resources are scarce, and decisions are pushed up the hierarchy. Participation consequently decreases. Centralization restricts communication channels and increases the likelihood that leaders will be scapegoated by frustrated organizational members who feel uninformed. Leader credibility suffers, and this often leads to high rates of leader turnover and "leadership anemia" (Whetten 1981, Hermann 1963, Greenhalgh & Rosenblatt 1984, Levine 1979).

In sum, despite the lack of extensive empirical verification, general consensus exists in the literature that declining organizations are characterized by a wide range of dysfunctional organizational processes. These outcomes of decline erode organizational effectiveness and undermine member satisfaction and commitment. The management of decline is characterized, therefore, as both difficult operationally and hazardous politically.

This is not to say that decline cannot stimulate organizational renewal through increased productivity, prioritization of organization commitments, and renewed personal dedication. Indeed, a sizable literature has emerged during the past decade codifying the procedures for turning around declining organizations (Hofer 1980, Schendel et al 1976, Bibeault 1982), and several authors have argued that the key stimulant for major change and innovation in mature organizations is the shock of failure in the marketplace (Nystrom & Starbuck 1984). However, it is evident from this literature that, as its name implies, turnaround management involves taking an organization that has been buffeted by the vagaries of diminished resources and setting it upon a new course. With rare exception, organizations are turned around only after the internal organizational and personal consequences of decline are so pervasive and severe that a consensus around the need for drastic action has grudgingly emerged.

Research on the consequences of organizational decline and death suggests an important linkage between the organizational life cycles and population ecology literatures. To date research on micro (organizational) processes has not linked very well with that on macro (population) birth and death rates. Multilevel studies of organizational morbidity would enable us to examine in fine grained detail the causes of changes in the size and composition of populations of organizations, as well as the aggregate impact of individual organizational processes. They would also allow us to examine important public policy issues, such as: How can the components of defunct organizations be used most efficiently to stimulate the generation of new organizations?

Causes of Decline

In considering the causes of decline, one must keep in mind the distinction between environmental and organizational decline. The model of decline proposed by Zammuto & Cameron (1985) highlights the two major forms of environmental decline: (*a*) decrease in a niche's carrying capacity for current activities and (*b*) a qualitative shift within a niche to support new activities. From a population ecology perspective, these environmental decline conditions will precipitate organizational decline among members of a population who are unable to compete successfully for a shrinking resource base in condition (*a*), or who fail to shift into new activities supported under condition (*b*) (Hannan & Freeman 1984).

This leaves open the question of why some organizations fail to adapt to these shifting environmental conditions, while others hold their own or even flourish. Obviously, we must look at the management practices within organizations to understand fully the causes of organizational decline. Information about environmental conditions is, therefore, necessary but not sufficient for understanding the causes of organizational decline.

The literature on the internal causes of organizational decline tends to focus on two themes. First, Starbuck and his associates (Stabuck & Hedberg 1977, Nystrom & Starbuck 1984) have examined numerous cases of organizational decline within the American and European business community to try to better understand the organizational decline process. They coined the phrase "success breeds failure" to explain a frequently observed pattern of decline. Their argument is that very successful organizations often become over-confident of their ability to dominate a market. This over-confidence is manifest in a reduction in both product development and emphasis on quality, insensitivity to negative feedback from customers, failure to monitor trends in basic research and product innovation, and discounting of the seriousness of short-term drops in sales. In essence, these organizations do a poor job of anticipating problems, or even of responding to them in their nascent stage. Instead, they wait until erosion of their competitive position has reached a crisis level, and then they tend to overreact with draconian actions to save a product or, in some cases, the entire company.

This argument goes further. The tendency to discount pressing environmental problems is not the result of all forms of growth ("success"). Rather it is the natural outcome of earlier spectacular and continuous growth. That is, this dysfunctional over-confident mind-set is brought on by the absence of any disconfirming evidence. In a sense, it is a form of the Midas Touch problem, in that senior officials become convinced that any task they set their mind to will turn to gold, and this egotistical view is reinforced by their very impressive track record.

The second explanation for organizational decline focuses on organizations with a very different growth pattern. These are mature institutions who have maintained a steady, though generally modest, growth rate. However, in the process they have fallen prey to the liabilities of large size and complexity discussed in an earlier section. They have become so cumbersome and rule-bound that they are unable to respond quickly to changing environmental conditions. Furthermore, a feeling of complacency pervades the organization. This condition has been referred to as decline-as-stagnation (Whetten 1980). In contrast to the mercurial rise and precipitous fall of the decline-as-crisis organizations described by Starbuck, most members of these latter organizations are unaware of the slight changes in growth or decline. Whereas, the bottom seems to fall out of the first organization's growth, the second organization slides almost imperceptibly into trouble. An example of this form of gradual erosion is a large state university whose annual increases in operating expenses from the legislature do not keep pace with inflation. In this situation it generally takes several years to detect a significant impact on organizational performance, and even in those cases where an astute administration points to the problem early on, they have difficulty generating a mandate for change.

EFFECTIVE MANAGEMENT OF GROWTH AND DECLINE

Organizational Growth

Thus far we have determined that authors in this field generally agree that members of organizations view growth as a desirable objective to pursue; there is considerably less agreement on the merits of growth once it is achieved. This discussion of motives and consequences still leaves open the question of means, i.e. "How do organizations grow effectively?" In this section we review the most common growth mechanisms, or means, used by organizations. The larger question of how managers can mitigate the organizational and personal dysfunctional consequences of growth (or large size) is beyond the scope of this review. Access to this extensive literature can be gained through the articles proposing life cycle models summarized in Quinn & Cameron (1983), or through DeGreene (1982), Miller & Friesen (1983, 1980), Tushman & Romanelli (1985), or Child & Kieser (1981).

There are at least four distinct vehicles for organizational growth—two strategic and two operational (suggested by Child & Kieser 1981).

The first is growth in an organization's existing domain. The trend towards greater concentration in most industries suggests that many organizations strive for monopoly within their field of activity. This can be done either through competitive or noncompetitive strategies (Pennings 1981). The latter include contracting, co-opting, and coalescing (forming joint partnerships) (Thompson 1967).

Second is growth through diversification into new domains. Diversification is a well-known strategy for spreading risk in business organizations, or for increasing legitimacy (political support) among government organizations (Peabody & Rourke 1965). Aggressive diversification has been particularly characteristic of big businesses and appears in a variety of forms, including development of new products and services, vertical integration, concentric diversification, and conglomerate diversification (Ansoff 1965, Rumelt 1974, Wood 1971).

Third is growth through technological development. The history of organizational development since the industrial revolution has to a large extent been one of adaptation to technological progress. This has resulted in a substantial increase in average firm size (Child & Kieser 1981). The trend is evident in both business and nonbusiness organizations (Perrow 1965), although the causal direction between increases in size and changes in technology is sometimes difficult to determine (Mansfield 1968).

Fourth is growth through improved managerial techniques. As we noted earlier, one of the early explanations for organizational growth was that it served as a means for utilizing excess managerial talent (Penrose 1952). It follows that increases in the efficiency of the management process would provide the impetus for further growth. Again, it is often difficult to separate cause from effect, but there are strong position statements in the literature arguing that improved management fosters organizational development (Hedberg et al 1976, Weick 1977, Staw 1977, Porter 1980, Tushman & Romanelli 1985).

Organizational Decline

Because the literature on the effective management of decline is less well formed than the comparable literature for organizational growth, we review it in more detail. In reviewing the material on this subject, the distinction in the biological ecology literature between r-extinction and k-extinction is a useful organizing device (Wilson 1980). A key concept in the ecology literature is that ecological niches have an inherent carrying capacity. The upper limit "K" represents the maximum population size that can be supported by the resource base in that niche. Organizations that decline short of this upper limit are generally victims of poor management (r-extinction). Their failure to remain competitive is self-induced. In contrast, organizations that decline at the zenith of the carrying capacity curve are victims of a depleted resource pool (k-extinction). They are having problems coping, but so are most other members of the population. In today's economy, the death of a software manufacturing firm would generally represent a case of r-extinction, whereas, the failure of a coal mine would represent k-extinction.

The literature on the management of decline typically addresses one of these two conditions. The extensive treatment of turnaround management typically focuses on the problems of r-decline (Hofer 1980). A single organization has made a serious strategic miscalculation and needs to remedy the situation. One of the early studies on this topic distinguished operational from strategic responses to decline (Schendel et al 1976). These authors found that a common mistake made by businesses is that they respond to strategic (effectiveness) problems with operational (efficiency) remedies. Recent research has underscored the importance of this distinction. Hambrick & Schecter (1983) identified three successful turnaround strategies among a sample of approximately 260 businesses experiencing declines: asset/cost surgery, selective product/market pruning, and piecemeal strategy. All three strategies were used widely in this sample, depending primarily on the business' level of production capacity utilization.

Based on his extensive practical experience with turnaround management, Bibeault (1982) identified a four-stage process: management change, evaluation, emergency actions, and stabilization and return-to-normal growth. This model explicitly argues that successful turnaround strategies can only be implemented by new management. This has been a fairly controversial subject in the literature (Whetten 1984, Starbuck & Hedberg 1977), but the general consensus is that when the cause of an organization's problems is widely attributed to current management, both external and internal support for a turnaround strategy is contingent on a change in top personnel. In other words, problem causers have little credibility as problem solvers (Pfeffer & Blake-Davis 1986, Salancik & Meindl 1984).

The symbolic value of a change in management is emphasized in Chaffee's (1984) work on strategic management in universities and colleges. She distinguishes between the traditional view of strategic management (which she refers to as adaptive) and an interpretive approach. The adaptive strategy for turning around an organization focuses on taking substantive action to reconcile inconsistencies and imbalances between organizational components and environmental conditions. The interpretive approach focuses on the management of meaning and underscores the value of symbolism. While the specific actions may be similar under both approaches, the emphasis of the interpretive approach is on anticipating the ways in which planned actions will be interpreted by critical constituencies (see also Pfeffer 1981b).

Zammuto & Cameron (1985) have used a different approach in analyzing turnaround strategies. Building on a typology of business strategies proposed by Miles & Cameron (1982), they clustered successful turnaround efforts into five categories. Domain defense is oriented towards preserving the legitimacy of the existing domain of activities and buffering the organization from hostile environmental conditions, possibly through the formation of coalitions with similar organizations. Domain offense focuses on expanding those activities that the organization already does well. Domain creation supplements current domain activities with new domains, primarily through diversification. Domain consolidation involves reducing the size of the domain occupied by the organization, by cutting back to the core products or services. Domain substitution involves replacing one set of activities with another; such a substitution occurred when the March of Dimes shifted its orientation from polio to birth defects.

In contrast, the work on managing organizations in declining industries (k-decline) focuses on a different set of issues. The principal theme in this literature is selecting the appropriate response to the dwindling resource base available to the population (Harrigan 1980, Porter 1980). The options typically include: taking a leadership position in terms of gaining a larger share of the dwindling market, creating a specific niche in which the organization can exploit a unique competitive advantage, "harvesting" the organization by managing a controlled divestiture, and exiting quickly through immediate liquidation. In considering these choices, firms must confront several "barriers to exit." There are financial, legal, structural, emotional, and informational obstacles to selling a firm and leaving the industry (Harrigan 1982, Porter 1976).

The literature on managing population decline has stimulated considerable interest in the divestment process in large corporations. Studies have focused on the deterrents to divestiture (Harrigan 1981), factors influencing the divestment decision (Duhaime & Grant 1984), and methods for increasing cooperation between the corporate headquarters and the divesting operation (Nees 1981).

There are two bodies of literature on the management of decline that cross-cut the distinctions between r and k decline. These focus on the effective management of retrenchment (down-sizing), and, when necessary, of organizational death.

ORGANIZATIONAL RETRENCHMENT   The retrenchment literature has primarily dealt with the internal management of decline, rather than with strategic responses to it. It is not suprising that this literature is concentrated in the areas of public, health care, and educational administration. In these contexts the recommendations for turning-around an organization or exiting a domain are generally inappropriate. The administration of a school district with shrinking enrollments can do little to turn that situation around, and many underfunded government agencies cannot ignore their legislative mandate and close their doors. Consequently, the only option left in these situations is to manage the downsizing process effectively.

The recommendations in this literature for managing retrenchment effectively can be grouped into roughly three sequential stages (Whetten 1984, Whetten & Cameron 1985). First, it is proposed that management should strive for "early warning and detection" of the impending problem. Effective anticipation of an emerging budget problem can often allow administrators to conserve resources and thereby brunt the impact of the cuts (Levine 1979). Once the problem has been identified, it is important for management to report an accurate and credible account of the causes of the problem and to seek out the experience of others who have encountered similar problems (Behn 1980). It is also critical for the administration to demonstrate their willingness to come to grips with the problems early on, to avoid the appearance of lack of moral conviction or political courage (Warren 1984).

The second stage involves "seizing the initiative." Once the need for change is clear, leaders are urged to convey a clear message that the organization is capable of handling the crisis (Behn 1980). This helps dispel the confidence-shaking attribution, typical of these situations, that the organization is being buffeted by its environment and has no control over its destiny (Salancik & Meindl 1984, Levine 1978). One way to convey this message is to open up the communication and decision-making processes to include all relevant stake holders in the decision-making process (Gilmore & Hirschhorn 1983). Crises create uncertainty, and uncertainty is reduced by information. Managers are also encouraged to promote critical thinking within the organization regarding alternative courses of action (Warren 1984, Perry 1986). At a time when the normal reaction is to become very conservative and essentially opt for doing less of the same, opportunities for revitalizing and overhauling old organizations are often overlooked (Biller 1980, Whetten 1981). A key element in this process is encouraging the high quality members of the organization to remain. The best way to do this seems to be through co-opting them into key leadership positions (formal or informal) and assuring them that quality will not be compromised during the retrenchment process (Behn 1980). Another aspect of seizing the initiative is creating, and then focusing attention on, a clear vision of the future opportunities within the organization (Cyert 1978). Shifting the attention of members from survival to excellence is a key to circumventing the tendency to mourn one's losses (Sutton et al 1986, Walton 1986).

The final stage in the retrenchment process involves effectively "implementing the downsizing program." It is argued that a key aspect of any retrenchment process is creating incentives for reducing or redirecting organizational activities. The tendency to become defensive and suspicious must be countered by overarching goals, personal incentives to cooperate, and social mechanisms for integrating "winners and losers" (Krantz 1985, Biller 1980). It also appears important during this period to establish mechanisms for helping members cope with their insecurity, stress and anxiety (Gilmore & Hirschhorn 1983, Greenhalgh & Rosenblatt 1984, Brockner et al 1985). A key element in effective retrenchment management appears to be preserving some organizational slack for stimulating ongoing innovation (Behn 1980, Cyert 1978). Innovation is the life blood of most organizations and the source of considerable personal satisfaction and pride. It must, therefore, be sustained during periods of retrenchment (Greenhalgh et al 1986).

ORGANIZATIONAL DEATH   Probably the most under-studied aspect of the growth and decline processes in organizations is organizational death. Although the prediction of bankruptcy is a popular topic in the business finance (Altman et al 1977, Argenti 1976) and business strategy fields (Miller 1977, Sharma & Mahajan 1980), very little research has examined the behavioral aspects of actually managing the close-out process (Slote 1969, Loving 1979, Mick 1975). However, this void is rapidly being filled (Harris & Sutton 1986, Sutton 1983). One of the most important contributions on this topic thus far has come from the research on employee behaviors during the organizational closing process (Sutton 1983). This work has shown that the negative expectations and suspicions held by many managers during this time are incorrect. For example, managers typically believe that once a plant closing has been announced, productivity and quality will plummet, employee sabotage and stealing will increase, the best employees will leave, rumors will abound, anger toward management will become the dominant emotion, conflict will increase, and employees will have difficulty accepting the fact that the closing is going to occur. Sutton reports evidence that some of these anticipated reactions never occur and that others occur only under special circumstances (see also, Nees 1981).

Sutton's (1983) work has also examined the dilemmas and paradoxes encountered by management during the closing process. These include accepting blame versus deflecting it to external causes, disbanding the organization while at the same time needing to sustain high morale and productivity; informing openly and broadly versus shielding interested parties from all but the most essential information; and finally, giving hope versus taking it away. These issues effectively portray the complex challenges facing managers of closing facilities. Fortunately, research on strategies for effectively managing the disengagement process should provide significant aids for these managers. Promising disengagement mechanisms include shared symbolic events, such as "parting ceremonies" (Harris & Sutton 1986, Albert 1984), and the establishment of interorganizational social support and outplacement programs (Taber et al 1979).

A slightly different perspective on the task of closing down an organization is provided in the program termination literature in public administration (Behn 1980, Kaufman 1976). It offers several suggestions for accomplishing the seemingly impossible task of terminating a public policy or program. These include the following. Don't float a trial balloon and give your opposition a chance to muster support against your proposal—act quickly and decisively. Enlarge the policy or program's constituency to incorporate interest groups supporting your position. Focus attention on the policy's harm. Inhibit the natural tendency to compromise with opponents. Recruit an outside administrator/terminator. Buy off the beneficiaries of the current program to reduce their opposition. Advocate the adoption of a new (replacement) program, rather than the abolition of the current one.

There is an important distinction between the close-out literature that has emerged in the private and public sectors. The public administration recommendations tend to focus on the termination decision-making process, specifically, how to achieve consensus for your position, or at least how to minimize opposition to your stated objectives. In contrast, research done on the close-out process in the private sector has tended to focus on the effective implementation of the decision. That is, how to minimize the costs, in terms of human capital, of your decision to close a facility.

One of the more promising new topics for study related to organizational death is employee buy-outs (O'Toole 1979, Hochner & Granrose 1985). This research has thus far examined the effects of employee ownership on employee attitudes (Stern & Hammer 1978) and productivity (Conte & Tannenbaum 1978), and the requirements for effectively initiating employee ownership (Stern & Hammer 1978, Hochner & Granrose 1985, Woodworth 1982), including financial support, adequate leadership and management expertise, favorable responses from the parent organization, and union support. Future work in this area should focus on building bridges to the broader streams of research on management succession, organizational innovation, owner control, and management of change.

CONCLUSION

The organizational life cycles literature to date has focused primarily on the early development phases of growing organizations. This has spawned considerable controversy over the legitimate use of the life cycle stages concept to characterize evolutionary processes in older, larger organizations. Recent writing on this subject suggests that the concept of stages should be loosely interpreted to mean a set of problems that logically follows an earlier set but is not determined by that set. Furthermore, the application of this problem-tracking approach appears to be most useful at the subsystem level of organizations. It is also evident that more effort needs to be focused on identifying the sets of problems unique to organizational decline and death.

The research on the causes and consequences of growth and decline processes in organizations has focused on the role of environmental, structural, and individual factors. Indeed, the distinction between internal and external causes has been particularly problematic in the decline literature. In general, our knowledge of the antecedents and outcomes of growth far surpasses our understanding of organizational decline. Important breakthroughs in this area await the development of comprehensive models, and concrete operationalizations of key terms.

The literature on the management of growth and decline is the least well developed. Here again, our knowledge about the effective management of growth far surpasses what we know about retrenchment or downsizing. Due to the lack of large-scale research on this subject, prescriptions for managers are largely based on sketchy, anecdotal evidence. This is an especially promising area for future research.

Literature Cited

Adizes, I. 1979. Organizational passages: Diagnosing and treating life-cycle problems in organizations. *Organ. Dynam.*, Summer, pp. 3–24

Albert, S. 1984. A delete-design model for successful transitions. In *Managing Organizational Transitions*, ed. J. Kimberly, R. Quinn, pp. 169–91. Homewood, Ill: Irwin

Aldrich, H. E. 1972. Technology and organizational structure: A re-examination of the findings of the Aston group. *Admin. Sci. Q.* 17:26–43.

Aldrich, H., Auster, E. 1986. Even dwarfs started small. Liabilities of age and size and their strategic implications. In *Research in Organizational Behavior*, ed. L. Cummings and B. Staw, 8:165–198. Greenwich, Conn: JAI

Altman, E. I., Haldeman, R., Narayanan, P. 1977. Zeta-analysis: A new model to identify bankruptcy risk of corporations. *J. Bank. Finan.* 1:29–54

Ansoff, H. I. 1965. *Corporate Strategy.* New York: McGraw Hill

Argenti, J. 1976. *Corporate Collapse: The Causes and Symptoms.* New York: Wiley

Behn, R. 1980. How to terminate public policy: A dozen hints for the would be ter-

minator. In *Managing Fiscal Stress,* ed. Charles H. Levine, pp. 313–26. Chatham, NJ: Chatham House

Berger, M. 1983. Retrenchment policies: Their organizational consequences. *Peabody J. Educ.* 60(2):49–63

Bibeault, D. B. 1982. *Corporate Turnaround.* New York: McGraw Hill

Biller, R. P. 1980. Leadership tactics for retrenchment. *Public Admin. Rev.* Nov./Dec., pp. 604–9

Boulding, K. E. 1950. *A Reconstruction of Economics.* New York: Wiley

Boulding, K. E. 1953. Toward a general theory of growth. *Can. J. Econ. Polit. Sci.* 12(3):326–40

Boulding, K. 1975. The management of decline. *Change* 64:8–9

Boyd, W. L. 1979. *Retrenchment in American education: The politics of efficiency.* Presented at Am. Educ. Res. Assoc. Meeting, San Francisco

Bozeman, B., Slusher, E. A. 1978. Scarcity and environmental stress in public organizations: A conjectural essay. *Admin. Soc.* 11:335–56

Brocker, J., Davy, J., Carter, C. 1985. Layoffs, self-esteem, and survivor guilt: Motivational, attitudinal, and affective consequences. *Organ. Behav. Hum. Decision Processes* 36:229–44

Cahn, E. S., Cahn, J. C. 1964. The war on poverty: A civilian perspective. *Yale Law J.* 73:1317–52

Cameron, K. 1983. Strategic responses to conditions of decline: Higher education and the private sector. *J. Higher Educ.* 54:359–80

Cameron, K. S., Sutton, R. I., Whetten, D. A. 1987. Issues in organizational decline. In *Organizational Decline: Frameworks, Research, and Applications*, ed. K. S. Cameron, R. I. Sutton, D. A. Whetten. Cambridge, Mass: Ballinger. In press

Cameron, K. S., Whetten, D. A. 1981. Perceptions of organizational effectiveness over organizational lifecycles. *Admin. Sci. Q.* 26(4):525–44

Cameron, K. S., Whetten, D. A. 1983. Models of the organizational life cycle: Applications to higher education. *Rev. Higher Educ.* 6(4):269–99

Cameron, K. S., Whetten, D. A., Kim, M. 1986. Organizational dysfunctions of decline. *Acad. Manage. J.* In press

Caves, J. 1970. Uncertainty, market structure and performance: Galbraith's conventional wisdom. In *Industrial Organizations and Economic Development*, ed. J. W. Markham, G. F. Paparek, pp. 282–302

Chaffee, E. E. 1984. Successful strategic management in small private colleges. *J. Higher Educ.* 55:212–41

Child, J., Kieser, A. 1981. Development of organizations over time. In *Handbook of Organizational Design*, ed. P. C. Nystrom, W. H. Starbuck. New York: Oxford Univ. Press

Conte, M., Tannenbaum, A. S. 1978. Employee-owned companies: Is the difference measurable? *Monthly Labor Rev.* 101:23–28

Cyert, R. M. 1978. The management of universities of constant or decreasing size. *Public Admin. Rev.* 38:345

DeGreene, K. B. 1982. *The Adaptive Organization. Anticipation and Management of Crisis.* New York: Wiley

Dent, J. K. 1959. Organizational correlates of the goals of business management. *Personnel Psychol.* 12:365–93

Downs, A. 1967. The lifecycle of bureaus. In *Inside Bureacracy*, A. Downs. San Francisco: Little Brown

Duhaime, I. M., Grant, J. H. 1984. Factors influencing divestment decision-making: Evidence from a field study. *Strategic Manage. J.* 5:301–18

Ferguson, C. E. 1960. The relationship of business size to stability: An empirical approach. *J. Ind. Econ.* 9:43–62

Filley, A. C., Aldag, R. J. 1978. Characteris-

tics and measurement of an organizational typology. *Acad. Manage. J.* 21:578–91

Filley, A. C., Aldag, R. J. 1980. Organizational growth and types: Lessons from small institutions. In *Research in Organizational Behavior*, ed. B. M. Staw, L. L. Cummings, 2:279–320. Greenwich, Conn: JAI

Ford, J. D. 1980. The occurrence of structural hysteresis in declining organizations. *Acad. Mgmt. Rev.* 5(4):589–98

Freeman, J. 1982. Organizational lifecycles and natural selection processes. In *Research in Organizational Behavior*, ed. B. M. Staw, L. L. Cummings, 4:1–33. Greenwich, Conn: JAI

Freeman, J. H., Hannan, M. T. 1975. Growth and decline processes in organizations. *Am. Sociol. Rev.* 40:215–28

Gilmore, T., Hirschhorn, L. 1983. Management challenges under conditions of retrenchment. *Human Resourc. Manage.* 22(4):341–57

Greiner, L. E. 1972. Evolution and revolution as organizations grow. *Harvard Bus. Rev.* 4 (July–August):37–46

Greenhalgh, L. 1983. Organizational decline. In *Research in Sociology of Organizations*, ed. S. Bachrach, 2:231–76. Greenwich, Conn: JAI

Greenhalgh, L., McKersie, R. B., Gilkey, R. W. 1986. Rebalancing the workforce at IBM: A case study of redeployment and revitalization. *Organ. Dynam.* (Spring) 30–47

Greenhalgh, L., Rosenblatt, Z. 1984. Job insecurity: Toward conceptual clarity. *Acad. Mgmt. Rev.* 9(3):438–48

Haire, M. 1959. Biological models and empirical histories of the growth of organizations. In *Modern Organization Theory*, ed. M. Haire, pp. 272–306. New York: Wiley

Hambrick, D. C., Schechter, S. M. 1983. Turnaround strategies for mature industrial product business units. *Acad. Manage. J.* 26:231–48

Hannan, M. T., Freeman, J. H. 1978. The population ecology of organizations. In *Environments and Organizations*, ed. M. W. Meyer and associates, pp. 177–99. San Francisco: Jossey-Bass

Hannan, M. T., Freeman, J. 1984. Structural inertia and organizational change. *Am. Sociol. Rev.* 29:149–64

Harrigan, K. R. 1980. *Strategies for Declining Businesses.* Lexington, Mass: Heath

Harrigan, K. R. 1981. Deterrents to divestiture. *Acad. Manage. J.* 24(2):306–23

Harrigan, K. R. 1982. Exit decisions in mature industries. *Acad. Manage. J.* 24(4):707–32

Harris, S. G., Sutton, R. I. 1986. Functions of

parting ceremonies in dying organizations. *Acad. Manage. J*. 29(1):5–30

Hedberg, B. L. T., Nystrom, P. C., Starbuck, W. H. 1976. Camping on see-saws: Prescriptions for a self-designing organization. *Admin. Sci. Q*. 21:41–65

Hermann, C. F. 1963. Some consequences of crisis which limit the viability of organizations. *Admin. Sci. Q*. 16:533–47

Hirschhorn, L. 1983. *Cutting Back*. San Francisco: Jossey-Bass

Hochner, A., Granrose, C. S. 1985. Sources of motivation to choose employee ownership as an alternative to job loss. *Acad. Manage. J*. 28(4):860–75

Hofer, C. W. 1980. Turnaround strategies. *J. Bus. Strategy* Summer, pp. 19–31

Inkson, J. H., Pugh, D. S., Hickson, D. J. 1970. Organizational context and structure: An abbreviated replication. *Admin. Sci. Q*. 15:318–408

Jick, T. D., Murray, V. V. 1982. The management of hard times: Budget cutbacks in public sector organizations. *Organ. Stud.* 3:141–69

Katz, D., Kahn, R. L. 1966. *The Social Psychology of Organizations*. New York: Wiley

Kaufman, H. 1976. *Are Government Organizations Immortal?* Washington, DC: Brookings Inst.

Kimberly, J. 1976. Organizational size and the structuralist perspective: A review, critique and proposal. *Admin. Sci. Q*. 21:571–97

Kimberly, J. R. 1979. Issues in the creation of organizations: Initiation, innovation and institutionalization. *Acad. Manage. J*. 22:437–57

Kimberly, J. R., Miles, R. H. 1980. *The Organizational Life Cycle*. San Francisco: Jossey-Bass

Kimberly, J., Quinn, R. 1984. *Organizational Transitions*. Homewood, Ill: Irwin

Krantz, J. 1985. Group processes under conditions of organizational decline. *J. Appl. Behav. Sci.* 21(1):1–17

Levine, C. H. 1978. Organizational decline and cutback management. *Public Admin. Rev.* 38:316–25

Levine, C. H. 1979. More on cutback management: Hard questions for hard times. *Public Admin. Rev.* 39:179–83

Levine, C. H., Rubin, I. S., Wolohojian, G. G. 1981. *The Politics of Retrenchment*. Beverly Hills, Calif: Sage

Lippitt, G. L., Schmidt, W. H. 1967. Crises in a developing organization. *Harvard Bus. Rev.* 45:417–38

Lipset, S. M. 1950. *Agrarian Socialism*. Berkeley: Univ. Calif. press

Loving, R. 1979. W. T. Grant's last days. In *Life in Organizations*, ed. B. A. Stein, R. M. Kanter, pp. 400–11. New York: Basic Books

Lyden, F. J. 1975. Using Parson's functional analysis in the study of public organizations. *Admin. Sci. Q*. 20:59–70

Mansfield, E. 1968. *Industrial Research and Technological Innovation*. New York: Norton

Marris, R. L., Wood, A. 1971. *The Corporate Economy*. London: Macmillan

Marshall, A. 1920. *Principles of Economics* London: Macmillan. 8th ed.

McEvoy, G. M. 1984. *The organizational life-cycle concept: Approaching adolescence or drawing near death?* Work. Pap. Dep. Bus. Admin. Utah State Univ.

Meyer, M. W. 1977. *Theory of Organizational Structure*. Indianapolis: Bobbs-Merrill

Michels, R. 1962. *Political Parties*. New York: Collier

Mick, S. S. 1975. Social and personal costs of plant shutdowns. *Indust. Relat.* 14:203–08

Miles, R. H., Cameron, K. S. 1982. *Coffin Nails and Corporate Strategies*. Englewood Cliffs, NJ: Prentice Hall

Miller, D. 1977. Common syndromes of business failure. *Bus. Horizons* 20 (December):43–53

Miller, D., Friesen, P. 1980. Archetypes of organizational transition. *Admin. Sci. Q*. 25:268–99

Miller, D., Friesen, P. 1983. Successful and unsuccessful phases of the corporate life cycle. *Organ. Stud.* 4:339–56

Nees, D. 1981. Increase your divestment effectiveness. *Strategic Manage. J.* 2:119–30

Nystrom, P. C., Starbuck, W. H. 1984. To avoid organizational crisis, unlearn. *Organ. Dynam.* Spring: 53–65

O'Toole, J. 1979. The uneven record of employee ownership: Is worker capitalism a fruitful opportunity or an impractical idea? *Harvard Bus. Rev.* 57(9):185–97

Peabody, R. L., Rourke, F. E. 1965. Public bureaucracies. In *Handbook of Organizations*, ed. J. G. March, pp. 802–37. Chicago: Rand McNally

Pennings, J. 1981. Strategically interdependent organizations. In *Handbook of Organizational Design*, ed. P. C. Nystrom, W. H. Starbuck, 1:433–55. London: Oxford Univ. Press

Penrose, E. T. 1952. Biological analogies in the theory of the firm. *Am. Econ. Rev.* 4:804–19

Penrose, E. 1959. *The Theory of the Growth of the Firm*. Oxford: Blackwell

Perrow, C. 1965. Hospitals: Technology, structure and goals. In *Handbook of Organizations*, ed. J. G. March, pp. 910–71. Chicago: Rand McNally

Perrow, C. 1979. *Complex Organizations: A Critical Essay* Glenview, Ill: Scott Foresman. 2nd ed.

Perry, L. T. 1986. Least-cost alternatives to layoffs in declining industries. *Organ. Dynam.* (Spring):48–61

Petrie, H. G., Alpert, D. A. 1983. What is the problem of retrenchment in higher education? *J. Manage. Stud.* 20:97–119

Pfeffer, J. 1981. *Power in Organizations.* Marshfield, Mass: Pitman

Pfeffer, J. 1981b. Management as symbolic action: The creation and maintenance of organizational paradigms. In *Research in Organizational Behavior*, ed. L. L. Cummings and B. W. Staw, 3:1–52. Greenwich, Conn: JAI

Pfeffer, J., Davis-Blake, A. 1986. Administrative succession and organizational performance: How administrator experience mediates the succession effect. *Acad. Mgmt. J.* 29(1):72–83

Pfeffer, J., Salancik, G. R. 1978. *The External Control of Organizations: A Resource Dependence Perspective.* New York: Harper & Row

Porter, M. E. 1976. Exit barriers and strategic organizational planning. *Calif. Manage. Rev.* 19(2):21–33

Porter, M. 1980. Competitive strategy in declining industries. In *Competitive Strategy*, ed. M. Porter, pp. 254–74. New York: Free Press

Quinn, R. E., Cameron, K. 1983. Organizational lifecycles and shifting criteria of effectiveness: Some preliminary evidence. *Mgmt. Sci.* 29(1):33–51

Roberts, D. R. 1959. *Executive Compensation.* Glencoe, Ill: Free Press

Rubin, I. S. 1979. Retrenchment, loose structure, and adaptability in the university. *Sociol. Educ.* 52:211–22

Rumelt, R. P. 1974. *Strategy, Structure and Economic Performance in Large American Industrial Corporations.* Boston: Grad. School Bus. Admin. Harvard Univ.

Salancik, G. R., Meindl, J. R. 1984. Corporate attributions as strategic illusions of management control. *Admin. Sci. Q.* 29(2):238–54

Schendel, D., Patton, G. R., Riggs, J. 1976. Corporate turnaround strategies: A study of profit decline and recovery. *J. Gen. Manage.* 3:3–11

Scott, W. R. 1981. *Organizations: Rational, Natural, and Open Systems.* Englewood Cliffs, NJ: Prentice Hall

Selznick, P. 1949. *TVA and the Grass Roots.* Berkeley: Univ. Calif. Press

Sharma, S., Mahejan, V. 1980. Early warning indicators of business failure. *J. Marketing* 44:80–89

Singh, A. 1971. *Take-overs.* Cambridge, Engl: Cambridge Univ. Press

Singh, J. V., House, R. J., Tucker, D. J., 1986. Organizational change and organizational mortality. *Admin. Sci. Q.* In press

Slote, A. 1969. *Termination: The Closing at Baker Plant.* Indianapolis: Bobbs-Merrill

Starbuck, W. H. 1965. Organizational growth and development. In *Handbook of Organizations*, ed. J. G. March, pp. 451–533. Chicago: Rand McNally

Starbuck, W. H. 1968. Organizational metamorphosis. In *Promising Research Directions*, ed. R. W. Millner, M. P. Hottenstein, pp. 113–32. College Station, Penn: Acad. Mgmt.

Starbuck, W., Greve, A., Hedberg, B. L. T. 1978. Responding to crisis. *J. Bus. Admin.* 9:111–37

Starbuck, W., Hedberg, B. L. T. 1977. Saving an organization from stagnating environments. In *Strategy + Structure = Performance*, ed. H. Thorelli, pp. 249–59. Bloomington: Indiana Univ. Press

Staw, B. M. 1977. The experimenting organization. *Organ. Dynam.* 6(2):30–46

Staw, B. M., Sandelands, L. E., Dutton, J. E. 1981. Threat rigidity effects in organizational behavior: A multilevel analysis. *Admin. Sci. Q.* 26:501–24

Steindl, J. 1945. *Small and Big Business.* Oxford: Blackwell

Stern, R. N., Hammer, T. H. 1978. Buying your job: Factors affecting the success or failure of employee acquisition attempts. *Human Relat.* 31:1101–11

Sutton, R. I. 1983. Managing organizational death. *Human Resource Manage.* 22(4):377–90

Sutton, R. I., Eisenhardt, K. M., Jucker, J. V. 1986. Managing organizational decline: Lessons from Atari. *Organ. Dynam.* (Spring):17–29

Taber, T. D., Walsh, J. T., Cooke, R. A. 1979. Developing a community-based program for reducing the social impact of a plant closing. *J. Appl. Behav. Sci.* 20:133–55

Thompson, J. D. 1967. *Organizations in Action.* New York: McGraw Hill

Tichy, N. 1980. Problem cycles in organizations and the management of change. In *The Organizational Lifecycle*, ed. J. R. Kimberley, R. H. Miles, pp. 164–83. San Francisco: Jossey-Bass

Timasheff, N. S. 1967. *Sociological Theory. Its Nature and Growth.* New York: Random House

Torbert, W. R. 1974. Pre-bureaucratic and post-bureaucratic stages of organizational development. *Interpers. Dev.* 5:1–25

Tushman, M. L., Romanelli, E. 1985. Organizational evolution: A metamorphosis model of convergence and reorientation. In *Research in Organizational Behavior*, ed. B. M. Staw, L. L. Cummings, 7:171–222. Greenwich, Conn: JAI

Tushman, M. L., Anderson, P. 1986. Technological discontinuities and organizational environments. *Admin. Sci. Q.* 31(3):439–65

Van de Ven, A. H., Astley, W. G. 1981. Mapping the field to create a dynamic perspective on organizational design and behavior. In *Perspectives on Organizational Design and Behavior*, ed. A. H. Van de Ven, W. F. Joyce, pp. 409–18. New York: Wiley

Walton, R. E. 1986. A vision-led approach to management restructuring. *Organ. Dynam.* (Spring):4–16

Warren, D. A. 1984. Managing in crisis: Nine principles for successful transitions. In *Managing Organizational Transitions*, ed. J. Kimberly, R. Quinn, pp. 85–106. Homewood, Ill: Irwin.

Weick, K. E. 1977. Organizational design: Organizations as self-designing systems. *Organ. Dynam.* 6(2):30–46

Whetten, D. A. 1980b. Organizational decline: A neglected topic in the organizational sciences. *Acad. Manage. Rev.* 4:577–88

Whetten, D. A. 1980c. Sources, responses, and the effects of organizational decline. In *The Organizational Lifecycle*, ed. J. Kimberly, R. Miles, pp. 342–74. San Francisco: Jossey-Bass

Whetten, D. A. 1981. Organizational responses to scarcity. Exploring the obstacles to innovative approaches to retrenchment in education. *Educ. Admin. Q.* 17:80–97

Whetten, D. A. 1984. Effective administrators: Good management in the college campus. *Change* Nov./Dec., pp. 38–43

Whetten, D. A. 1986. *Effective management of retrenchment*. Work. Pap., Coll. Commerce Bus. Admin. Univ. Ill., Champaign

Whetten, D. A., Cameron, K. S. 1985. Administrative effectiveness in higher education. *Rev. Higher Educ.* 9(1):35–49

Wicker, A., Kirmeyer, S. L., Hanson, L., Alexander, D. 1976. Effects of manning levels on subjective experiences, performance, and verbal interaction in groups. *Organ. Behav. Human Perform.* 17:251–74

Wilson, E. 1980. *Sociobiology*. Cambridge, Mass: Harvard Univ. Press

Wood, A. 1971. Diversifications, mergers and research expenditures: A review of empirical studies. In *The Corporate Economy*, ed. R. Marris, A. Wood, pp. 428–53. Cambridge, Mass: Harvard Univ. Press

Woodworth, W. 1982. *Collective power and liberation of work*. Paper presented Tenth World Congress Sociol., Mexico City

Zald, M. N., Ash, R. 1966. Social movement organizations: Growth, decay and change. *Soc. Forc.* 44:327–41

Zammuto, R. F., Cameron, K. S. 1985. Environmental decline and organizational response. In *Research in Organizational Behavior*, ed. B. M. Staw, L. L. Cummings, 7:223–62. Greenwich, Conn: JAI

Ann. Rev. Sociol. 1987. 13:359–85

MAKING SENSE OF DIVERSITY: RECENT RESEARCH ON HISPANIC MINORITIES IN THE UNITED STATES

Alejandro Portes and Cynthia Truelove

Department of Sociology, The Johns Hopkins University, Baltimore, Maryland 21218

Abstract

This is a review of the principal strands of the sociological literature on Spanish-origin groups in the United States. It emphasizes: (*a*) their labor market characteristics; (*b*) English acquisition; and (*c*) political participation and naturalization. We conclude that the label "Hispanic" is itself problematic because of the diversity of the groups included. There are trends toward convergence in political orientations and voting, but there are major divergences in patterns of social and economic adaptation. The rapid increase of new Latin American immigrant communities is likely to add to the diversity characterizing the major Spanish-origin groups already settled in the country.

INTRODUCTION

Hispanics are those individuals whose declared ancestors or who themselves were born in Spain or in the Latin American countries. Until recently, this rubric did not exist as a self-designation for most of the groups so labeled; it was essentially a term of convenience for administrative agencies and scholarly researchers. Thus, the first thing to be said about this population is that it is not a consolidated minority, but rather a group-in-formation whose boundaries and self-definitions are still in a state of flux. The emergence of a Hispanic "minority" has so far depended more on actions of government and the collective perceptions of Anglo-American society than on the initiative of the individuals so designated.

0360-0572/87/0815-0359$02.00

The principal reason for the increasing attention gained by this category of people is its rapid growth during the last two decades which is, in turn, a consequence of high fertility rates among some national groups and, more importantly, of accelerated immigration. In addition, the heavy concentration of this population in certain regions of the country has added to its visibility. Over 75% of the 14.5 million people identified by the 1980 Census as Hispanics are concentrated in just four states—California, New York, Texas, and Florida; California alone has absorbed almost one third (US Bureau of Census 1983).

The absence of a firm collective self-identity among this population is an outcome of its great diversity, despite the apparent "commonness" of language and culture which figures so prominently in official writings. Under the same label, we find individuals whose ancestors lived in the country at least since the time of independence and others who arrived last year; we find substantial numbers of professionals and entrepreneurs, along with humble farm laborers and unskilled factory workers; there are whites, blacks, mulattoes, and mestizos; there are full-fledged citizens and unauthorized aliens; and finally, among the immigrants, there are those who came in search of employment and a better economic future and those who arrived escaping death squads and political persecution at home.

Aside from divisions between the foreign and the native-born, there is no difference of greater significance among the Spanish-origin population than that of national origin. Nationality does not simply stand for different geographic places of birth; rather it serves as a code word for the very distinct history of each major immigrant flow, a history which molded, in turn, its patterns of entry and adaptation to American society. It is for this reason that the literature produced by "Hispanic" scholars until recently has tended to focus on the origins and evolution of their own national groups rather than to encompass the diverse histories of all those falling under the official rubric.

The bulk of the Spanish-origin population—at least 60%—is of Mexican origin, divided into sizable contingents of native-born Americans and immigrants. Another 14% come from Puerto Rico and are US citizens by birth, regardless of whether they were born in the island or the mainland. The third group in size is made up of Cubans who represent about 5% and who are, overwhelmingly, recent immigrants coming after the consolidation of a communist regime in their country. These are the major groups, but there are, in addition, sizable contingents of Dominicans, Colombians, Salvadoreans, Guatemalans, and other Central and South Americans, each with its own distinct history, characteristics, and patterns of adaptation (Nelson & Tienda 1985, US Bureau of the Census 1983, US Immigration and Naturalization Service 1984).

The complexity of Hispanic ethnicity is a consequence, first of all, of these diverse national origins which lead more often to differences than similarities among the various groups. Lumping them together is not too dissimilar from attempting to combine turn-of-the-century Northern Italian, Hungarian, Serbian, and Bohemian immigrants into a unit based on their "common" origin in various patches of the Austro-Hungarian empire. A second difficulty is that most Spanish-origin groups are not yet "settled," but continue expanding and changing in response to uninterrupted immigration and to close contact with events in the home countries. This dense traffic of people, news, and events between US-based immigrant communities and their not-too-remote place of origin offers a far more challenging landscape than, for example, the condition of European ethnic groups whose boundaries are generally well defined and whose bonds with the original countries are increasingly remote (Glazer 1981, Alba 1985).

THE PRINCIPAL STRANDS OF THE SOCIOLOGICAL LITERATURE ON THE HISPANIC POPULATION

This diversity of phenomena under a common label is reflected in the research literature and makes it, in turn, complex and difficult to summarize. To attempt this task with some hope of success, it is necessary to set limits to the discussion that are perforce narrower than those of the topic as a whole. In this essay, we limit ourselves to reviewing the sociological literature, with only passing reference to that coming from other disciplines, and we do so by deliberately focusing greater attention on some specific areas than on others. Since this choice is necessarily arbitrary, it is only fair to present at the start a brief overview of what the sociological literature on Hispanics encompasses at present.

A first general topic fits within the realm of historical sociology, namely the origins and evolution in time of each national group. As mentioned above, we do not have so far a history of Hispanics as such, but rather histories of individual national groups written, more often than not, by scholars of the same minority. Mexicans are the oldest and largest Spanish-speaking minority, and thus it is not surprising that most of this literature deals with the nineteenth and early-twentieth century origins of this group and its subsequent patterns of adaptation. Julian Samora's *Los Mojados: The Wetback Story* (1971), a text which combines historical material with results of contemporary field research, is perhaps the best and best-known in this tradition, but others come close behind, including the early 1970s review volume *The Mexican-American People* by Grebler et al (1970), the many books on migrant laborers by Ernesto Galarza (1964, 1970, 1977), Mario Barrera's carefully researched, *Labor and Class in the Southwest* (1980), and Alfredo

Mirandé's recent *The Chicano Experience* (1985). With few exceptions, historical accounts of the Mexican-American population are written from a critical perspective, using as a theoretical framework ideas drawn from dependency, internal colonialist, class conflict, and related approaches.

A similar theoretical bent is apparent in the less abundant literature on Puerto Ricans which features as one of its earliest distinguished contributions C. Wright Mills's *The Puerto Rican Journey* (Mills et al 1950). Puerto Rican scholars in the island have tended to focus on the condition and the peculiar political status of their nation, and thus the literature on the mainland minority has been, by and large, the product of US-based scholars. Worthy of mention in this regard are Joseph Fitzpatrick's *Puerto Rican Americans* (1971), Elena Padilla, *Up from Puerto Rico* (1958), Virginia Sánchez-Korrol, *From Colonia to Community* (1983), recent works by Bonilla & Campos (1981, 1982), and the Center of Puerto Rican Studies' *Labor Migration under Capitalism* (1979). In a more anthropological vein, this migrant community was also the subject of Oscar Lewis' famous *La Vida, a Puerto Rican Family in the Culture of Poverty* (1966).

Historical accounts of the Cuban community are still less common, due no doubt to its recent emergence. The gap is being rapidly filled by such works as Boswell & Curtis' *The Cuban-American Experience* (1984), Jose Llanes' celebratory *Cuban-Americans: Masters of Survival* (1982), and Silvia Pedraza-Bailey's (1985a) historical essay on the post-1959 exodus. Contrary to the critical orientation of most histories of Spanish-origin groups, those relating to Cubans tend to be of the struggle-and-success type, reflecting the distinct origin and present condition of this minority. Other groups are mostly too small or too recent to have acquired their own biographers. Among exceptions worth mentioning are Glen Hendricks' *Dominican Diaspora* (1974), focused on the history of migration and current situation of this group in the New York area, and Ramiro Cardona & Isabel Cruz' (1980) Spanish-language study of Colombian migration to the United States and return patterns.

A second related strand is the more recent inquiry into determinants of contemporary out-migration. Unlike the historical literature based, for the most part, on secondary sources, the distinguishing trait of this second line of research is original field work in Mexico, Cuba, Puerto Rico, the Dominican Republic, and other sending countries. The principal example is the study initiated by Reichert & Massey (1979, 1980) and completed recently by Massey (1986, 1987) on determinants of out-migration and return migration from four Mexican communities. A similarly ambitious study on Dominican out-migration by Pessar (1982) and Grasmuck (1984) featured in-depth field research in remote rural areas combined with a large survey of popular neighborhoods in Santiago, the Dominican Republic's second largest city. A somewhat different example is Robert Bach's (1985) insightful analysis of the domestic conditions giving rise to the Mariel exodus of 1980, which is based on personal observation and informant interviews with government officials in Cuba.

These and other studies have done much to dispel prior myths about the origins of migration in economic destitution or individual psychological distress. They have instead consistently supported three themes: first, that the very poor seldom emigrate because they lack the means or the knowledge to undertake such long-distance journeys; second, that the principal causes of migration are rooted in structural contradictions in sending countries reflected, at the individual level, in such situations as underemployment, landlessness, and a growing gap between normative consumption patterns and income; third, that once a migration flow begins, it tends to become self-sustaining through the emergence of strong social networks linking places of origin and destination. (See also Cornelius 1977, Reichert 1981, and Portes & Bach 1985).

A third significant strand of the literature is the study of the demography of the Spanish-origin population, both native and foreign-born, including such aspects as regional distribution, residential segregation, fertility, and rates of intermarriage. Unlike historical studies, demographic research has tended to accept the characterization of this population under a single ethnic label, in part because much of the census data on which it depends is organized in this manner. However, after a number of studies, it has also become clear that differences in population characteristics among groups included under a common term frequently exceed their similarities. Thus, although all Hispanics share a high and increasing urban concentration (US Bureau of the Census 1983c), individual nationalities differ significantly in fertility (Bean et al 1985), intermarriage rates (Fitzpatrick & Gurak 1979), and residential patterns and segregation (Massey 1981, Díaz-Briquets & Pérez 1981). The explanation for these differences must be sought in variables other than those generally available in the census public-use tapes. A recent summary study by Bean & Tienda (1987) reviews the existing literature on the demography of Hispanic-Americans within a broad sociological framework that avoids the facile generalizations of the past.

The remaining three principal areas of study are those to which the rest of the chapter are dedicated. They pertain, respectively, to the economic and labor market situation of the different national groups, their language use, and their patterns of political organization and citizenship. These are the areas where recent sociological research has tended to concentrate and are also those where the distinct characteristics and heterogeneity of the Spanish-origin population emerge most clearly.

LABOR MARKET CHARACTERISTICS AND ATTAINMENT

A good part of the literature on this population focuses on comparisons of its labor market performance and general socioeconomic condition with those of other ethnic groups and the US population at large. The sociological literature on these issues has sought to answer three questions: First, are there significant differences in the condition of Hispanic groups both in comparison with the US population and among themselves? Second, are there significant differences in the *process* by which education, occupation, and income are achieved? And third, if there are differences in this process, what are their principal causes?

Table 1 presents a summary of descriptive statistics, drawn from the 1980 census. Aside from age and nativity, included as background information, the rest of the figures indicate that the socioeconomic performance of Hispanics is generally inferior to that of the US population as a whole and, by extension, that of the white non-Hispanic majority. This is true of education, occupation, income, and entrepreneurship (measured by rates of self-employment), although less so of labor force participation especially among females.

The same figures also indicate major disparities among Spanish-origin groups. In general, mainland Puerto Ricans are in the worst socioeconomic situation, a fact manifested by high levels of unemployment, female-headed families, and poverty, and correspondingly low levels of education, occupation, and income. Mexicans occupy an intermediate position, although one consistently below the US population. To be noted is that the size of this group, which represents the majority of all Hispanics, has a disproportionate weight in aggregate figures that purport to describe the Spanish-origin population as a whole.

A more favorable situation is that of Cubans—whose occupation, family income, and self-employment rates come close to US averages—and of the "Other Spanish" group, which behaves in a similar manner. This last category is a sum of immigrant groups too small to be counted individually, plus those who declared their ancestry as Spanish-origin without further specification. Because of this heterogeneity, it is difficult to provide a meaningful interpretation either of the absolute condition of this category or of the processes that have led to it.

This basic picture of the situation and heterogeneity of the Spanish-origin population is familiar to sociologists working in this field (Nelson & Tienda 1984, Pérez 1986, Pedraza-Bailey 1985b). More interesting is the question of the causal factors that produce the above differences. Here the basic question is whether the condition of a specific minority is explainable entirely on the basis of its background characteristics or whether it is due to other factors. If

Table 1   Selected characteristics of Spanish-origin groups, 1980. (Source: U.S. Bureau of the Census 1983a: Tables 39, 48, 70; 1983b: Tables 141, 166–171.)

Variable	Mexicans	Puerto Ricans	Cubans	Other Spanish	Total US
Number—millions	8.7	2.0	0.8	3.1	226.5
Median age	21.9	22.3	37.7	25.5	30.0
Percent native born	74.0	96.9	22.1	60.5	93.8
Percent female headed families	16.4	35.3	14.9	20.5	14.3
Median years of school completed[a]	9.6	10.5	12.2	12.3	12.5
Percent high school graduates[a]	37.6	40.1	55.3	57.4	66.5
Percent with 4+ years of college[a]	4.9	5.6	16.2	12.4	16.2
Percent in labor force[b]	64.6	54.9	66.0	64.6	62.0
Percent females in labor force[b]	49.0	40.1	55.4	53.4	49.9
Percent married women in labor force[c]	42.5	38.9	50.5	45.7	43.9
Percent self-employed[d]	3.5	2.2	5.8	4.5	6.8
Percent unemployed	9.1	11.7	6.0	8.0	6.5
Percent professional specialty, executive, and managerial occupations—males	11.4	14.1	22.0	19.0	25.8
females[d]	12.6	15.5	17.9	17.2	24.7
Percent operators and laborers—males	30.4	30.9	23.1	23.8	18.3
females[d]	22.0	25.5	24.2	19.9	11.7
Median family income	14,765	10,734	18,245	16,230	19,917
Median income of married couples with own children	14,855	13,428	20,334	16,708	19,630
Percent of families with incomes of $50,000+	1.8	1.0	5.2	3.6	5.6
Percent of all families below poverty level	20.6	34.9	11.7	16.7	9.6

[a] Persons 25 years of age or older.
[b] Persons 16 years of age or older.
[c] Women 16 years of age or older; husband present and own children under 6 years of age.
[d] Employed persons 16 years of age or older.

members of a given group are found to attain socioeconomic positions comparable to native-born Americans with similar human capital endowments, then the observed differences can be imputed to the group's current average levels of education, work experience, and other significant causal variables. If, on the other hand, differences persist after equalizing statistically the minority's background, then other factors must come into play. If the gap is one of disadvantage, discrimination is generally assumed to play a role; if the gap is advantageous to the minority, then collective characteristics of the group are explored in search of a possible explanation.

Several analyses, especially those of educational attainment, tend to support the "no difference, no discrimination" hypothesis. This is the conclusion reached, for example, by Hirschman & Falcón (1985) after a broad-gauged study of educational levels among religio-ethnic groups in the United States. However, these authors also report that, after controlling for all possible relevant predictors, the Mexican educational attainment still falls 1.4 years below the norm.

Similarly, in a study of occupational attainment based on the 1976 Survey of Income and Education (SEI), Stolzenberg (1982) concludes that the causal process is essentially the same among all Spanish-origin groups and that, after standardizing individual background characteristics, no evidence of discrimination remains. However, Stolzenberg includes in the analysis a series of state dummy variables in order to control for the possible confounding of geographic location and ethnicity. What he does, of course, is to insure a priori that ethnic differences would be insignificant because of the high concentration of particular groups in certain states. Including "Florida" as a causal predictor, for example, pretty much eliminates the distinct effect of Cuban ethnicity since this group has chosen to concentrate in that state; the same is true for New York and the Puerto Ricans.

Even with state dummies included, significant ethnic effects on occupational attainment remain in Stolzenberg's analysis of the Mexican and Cuban groups. The Mexican coefficient is negative, indicating lower occupational levels than those expected on the basis of the group's average characteristics; the Cuban effect is, however, positive, indicating above-average attainment, and this becomes much stronger when state controls are deleted. A subsequent and more carefully specified analysis of SEI wage data by Reimers (1985) yields similar conclusions. After controlling for selection bias and human capital predictors, Reimers finds that male Puerto Rican wage levels fall 18% below the average for white non-Hispanic men; those of Mexicans and other Hispanics are 6% and 12% below, respectively. These sizable differences are interpreted as evidence of labor market discrimination. Cuban men, however, receive wages 6% *above* white non-Hispanics of similar human capital endowment. These differences lead the author to conclude: "The major Hispanic-American groups differ so much among themselves . . . that it makes little sense to lump them under a single "Hispanic" or "minority" rubric for either analysis or policy treatment" (Reimers 1985:55).

This basic conclusion is supported by studies based on different and more recent data sets which also tend to replicate the finding of significant disadvantages in occupational and earnings attainment for Mexicans and, in particular, Puerto Ricans and a small but consistent advantage for Cubans, relative to their human capital levels (Nelson & Tienda 1985, Pérez 1986, Jasso & Rosenzweig 1985: Table 4).

These differences lead naturally to the more sociologically intriguing question of their possible cause. The argument that there is discrimination in the labor market will not do because such explanation does not clarify why discrimination operates differentially among presumably similar groups and not at all in certain cases. Thus, there is no alternative but to dig into the particular characteristics and history of each group in search of suitable answers. To do this, we must abandon not only the general label "Hispanic," but also leave behind the residual category "Other Spanish." This is necessary not because of lack of substantive importance of the groups that form it, but because the category is itself too heterogeneous to permit a valid summary explanation. Left are the three major Spanish-origin groups—Mexicans, Puerto Ricans, and Cubans.

When comparing the socioeconomic performance of these groups, two major riddles emerge: First, why is it that Mexicans and Puerto Ricans differ so significantly in such characteristics as labor force participation, family structure, and poverty as well as in levels of wage discrimination. Second, why it is that Cubans register above-average occupations and family incomes relative to their levels of human capital. The below-average socioeconomic condition of the first two groups is *not* itself a riddle since the historical literature above has fully clarified the roots of exploitation and labor market discrimination in both cases. What historical accounts do not explain is why the present condition of these groups should be so markedly different. Similarly, the absolute advantage of Cubans relative to other Spanish-origin groups is not mysterious since it is well known that this minority was formed, to a large extent, by the arrival of upper and middle-class persons who left Cuba after the advent of the Castro Revolution. The riddle in this case is why the collective attainment of Cubans should exceed, at times, what can be expected on the basis of their average human capital endowment.

A fairly common explanation of the latter result is that Cubans were welcomed in the United States as refugees from a communist regime and thus received significant government aid denied to other groups. This explanation is mentioned in passing by Jasso & Rosenzweig (1985:18), among other authors, and is vigorously defended by Pedraza-Bailey (1985b) in her comparative study of Cuban and Mexican immigrants. However, this interpretation runs immediately against evidence from other refugee groups who have received equal or more generous federal benefits than Cubans, but whose socioeconomic condition is more precarious. Southeast Asian refugees, for example, benefitted from the extensive aid provisions mandated by the 1980 Refugee Act, more comprehensive and generous than those made available to Cubans during the sixties; however, levels of unemployment, poverty, and welfare dependence among most Southeast Asian groups continue to exceed those of almost every other ethnic minority (Tienda & Jensen 1985, Bach et al 1984).

The favorable governmental reception of Cubans in the United States is certainly a factor contributing to their adaptation, but it must be seen as part of a complex which may be labelled the distinct *mode of incorporation* of each immigrant minority. This alternative interpretation says that the condition of each group is a function both of average individual characteristics and of the social and economic context in which its successive cohorts are received. A sociological explanation to the above riddles is found in the distinct modes of incorporation of the three major Spanish-origin groups.

Mexican immigrants and new Mexican-American entrants into the labor force tend to come from modest socioeconomic origins and have low average levels of education. In addition, however, they enter labor markets in the Southwest and Midwest where Mexican laborers have traditionally supplied the bulk of unskilled labor. Social networks within the ethnic community tend to direct new workers toward jobs similar to their co-ethnics, a pattern reinforced by the orientation of employers. Lacking a coherent entrepreneurial community of their own or effective political representation, Mexican wage workers are thus thrown back onto their own individual resources, "discounted" by past history and present discrimination against their group (Barrera 1980, Nelson & Tienda 1984). Because many Mexican workers are immigrants and a substantial proportion are undocumented (Passel 1985; Bean et al 1983, 1986; Browning & Rodríguez 1985), they continue to be seen by many employers as a valuable source of low-wage pliable labor. This employer "preference," which may account for the relatively low average rates of Mexican unemployment, creates simultaneous barriers for those with upward mobility aspirations.

Puerto Rican migrants fulfilled a similar function for industry and agriculture in the Northeast during an earlier period, but with two significant differences. First, they entered labor markets which, unlike those of the Southwest, were highly unionized. Second, they were US citizens by birth and thus entitled to legal protection and not subject to ready deportation as were many Mexicans. These two factors combined over time to make Puerto Rican workers a less pliable, more costly, and better organized source of labor. Employer preferences in the Northeast thus shifted gradually toward other immigrant groups—West Indian contract workers in agriculture (De-Wind et al 1977, Wood 1984) and Dominican, Colombian, and other mostly undocumented immigrants in urban industry and services (Sassen-Koob 1979, 1980; Glaessel-Brown 1985; Waldinger 1985). Lacking an entrepreneurial community to generate their own jobs and shunted aside by new pools of "preferred" immigrant labor in the open market, Puerto Ricans in the mainland confronted a difficult economic situation. Record numbers have migrated back to the Island during the last two decades, while those remaining in the Northeast continue to experience levels of unemployment and poverty comparable only to those of the black population (Bean & Tienda 1987: Ch. 1, Centro de Estudios Puertorriqueños 1979).

The Cuban pattern of adaptation is different because the first immigrant cohorts created an economically favorable context of reception for subsequent arrivals. This was due to the fact that the bulk of early Cuban migration was composed of displaced numbers of the native bourgeoisie rather than laborers (Pérez 1986). These refugees brought the capital and entrepreneurial skills with which to start new businesses after an early period of adaptation. Ensuing middle-class waves followed a similar course, leading eventually to the consolidation of an enclave economy in South Florida. The characteristics of the Cuban enclave have been described at length in the sociological literature (Wilson & Portes 1980, Portes & Manning 1986, Wilson & Martin 1982). The strong entrepreneurial orientation of the earlier Cuban cohorts is illustrated by census figures on minority-business ownership, presented in Table 2.

In 1977, when these data were collected, black- and Mexican-owned businesses were the most numerous in absolute terms, reflecting the size of the respective populations. In per capita terms, however, Cuban-owned firms were by far the most numerous and the largest both in terms of receipts and

Table 2   Spanish-origin and black-owned firms in the United States. Sources: Bureau of the Census (1980); *Hispanic Review of Business* (1985)

Variable	Mexicans	Puerto Ricans	Cubans	All Spanish	Black
Number of firms, 1977	116,419	13,491	30,336	219,355	231,203
Firms per 100,000 population	1,468	740	3,651	1,890	873
Average gross receipts per firm ($1000)	44.4	43.9	61.6	47.5	37.4
Firms with paid employees, 1977	22,718	1,767	5,588	41,298	39,968
Firms with employees per 100,000 population	286	97	672	356	151
Average employees per firm	4.9	3.9	6.6	5.0	4.1
Average gross receipts per firm with employees ($1000)	150.4	191.9	254.9	172.9	160.1
Ten largest Hispanic industrial firms, 1984:					
Percent located in area of group's concentration[a]	40	10	50	100	NA
Estimated sales ($1,000,000)	402	273	821	2,317	NA
Number of employees	5,800	1,100	3,175	10,075	NA
Ten largest Hispanic-owned banks and savings banks, 1984:					
Percent in area of group's concentration[a]	40	20	40	100	NA
Total assets ($1,000,000)	1,204	489	934	2,627	NA
Total deposits ($1,000,000)	1,102	434	844	2,380	NA

[a] Southwest locations for Mexicans; New York and vicinity for Puerto Ricans; Miami metropolitan area for Cubans.

number of employees. Figures in the bottom rows of Table 2 suggest that the relative weight of Miami Cuban firms among Hispanic-owned businesses has continued to grow since 1977. By 1984, five of the ten largest Hispanic-owned firms in the country and four of the ten largest banks were part of the Cuban enclave, at a time when this group represented barely 5% of the Spanish-origin population.

For our purposes, the significance of an enclave mode of incorporation is that it helps to explain how successive cohorts of Cuban immigrants have been able to make use of past human capital endowment and to exceed at times their expected level of attainment. Employment in enclave firms has two principal advantages for new arrivals: First, it allows many to put to use their occupational skills and experience without having to wait for a long period of cultural adaptation. Second, it creates opportunities for upward mobility either within existing firms or through self-employment. The bond between co-ethnic employers and employees helps fledgling immigrant enterprises survive by taking advantage of the cheap and generally disciplined labor of the new arrivals. The latter benefit over the long term, however, by availing themselves within the enclave of mobility chances that are generally absent in outside employment.

A longitudinal study of Cuban and Mexican immigrants conducted during the 1970s provides an illustration of different patterns of adaptation, conditioned by the presence or absence of an enclave mode of incorporation. By the early 1970s, the middle-class emigration from Cuba had ceased, and new arrivals came from more modest socioeconomic origins, comparable to those of Mexican legal immigrants. The study interviewed samples of Cuban refugees and Mexican legal immigrants at the time of their arrival during 1973–1974. The study followed both samples for six years, interviewing respondents twice during that interval. Results of the study have been reported at length elsewhere (Portes & Bach 1985). Table 3 presents data from the last follow-up survey which took place in 1979–1980. The first finding of note is the degree of concentration of Cuban respondents, 97% of whom remained in the Miami metropolitan area. By comparison, the Mexican sample dispersed throughout the Southwest and Midwest, with the largest concentration— 24%—settling in the border city of El Paso.

Otherwise, samples were similar in their knowledge of English—low for both groups after six years—and their rates of home ownership. They differed sharply, however, in variables relating to their labor market position. More than a third of 1973 Cuban arrivals were employed by co-ethnic firms in 1979, and one fifth had become self-employed by that time; these figures double and quadruple the respective percentages in the Mexican sample. Despite their concentration in a low-wage region of the United States, the

Table 3 The socioeconomic position of Cuban and Mexican immigrants after six years in the United States. Source: Portes & Bach (1985): Chs. 6–7.

Variable	Mexicans (N = 455)	Cubans (N = 413)
Percent in city of principal concentration	23.7	97.2
Percent who speak English well	27.4	23.7
Percent home owners	40.2	40.0
Percent self-employed	5.4	21.2
Percent employed by other Mexicans/Cubans	14.6	36.3
Average monthly income[a]	$ 912	$1057
Average monthly income of employees in large Anglo-owned firms[a]	$1003	$1016
Average monthly income in small non-enclave firms[a]	$ 880	$ 952
Average monthly income in enclave firms[a]	NA	$1111
Average monthly income of the self-employed, Cubans[a]	NA	$1495

[a] 1979 dollars

Cuban average monthly income after six years was significantly greater than that among Mexicans.

However, a closer look at the data shows that there were no major differences in income among those employed in large Anglo-owned firms, commonly identified as part of the "primary" labor market. Nor were there significant income differences among those employed in the smaller firms identified with the "secondary" sector; in both samples, these incomes were much lower than among primary sector employees. The significant difference between Cuban and Mexican immigrants in the study lies with the large proportion of the former employed in enclave firms where their average income was actually the highest of those in both samples. In addition, Cuban immigrants who had become self-employed exceeded the combined monthly income of both samples by approximately $500 or one half of the total average.

No comparable empirical evidence at present supports the mode-of-incorporation hypothesis as an explanation of the observed occupational and income differences among Mexicans and Puerto Ricans. This is due to the scarcity of comparative studies between Puerto Rican patterns of attainment and those of other minorities. (For a recent exception, see Tienda & Lee 1986). The available information points, however, to the gradual displacement of Puerto Ricans by newer immigrant groups as sources of low-wage labor for agricultural and urban employers in the Northeast (DeWind 1977, Glaessel-Brown 1985). This evidence is congruent with the interpretation of the current situation of one group—Mexicans—as an outcome of its continued incorporation as a preferred source of low-wage labor in the Southwest and Midwest and with that of the other—Puerto Ricans—as a consequence of its increasing redundancy for the same labor market in its principal area of concentration.

KNOWLEDGE OF ENGLISH

In this section, we consider some evidence concerning language use among different Spanish-origin groups. According to the 1980 Census, roughly half of the population of the United States who spoke a language other than English spoke Spanish. The absolute number, 11.5 million, would make the United States one of the largest Spanish-speaking countries in the world although, as with the Spanish-origin population itself, use of the language tends to be highly concentrated in a few states. Seventy percent of Spanish-speakers live in just four states—California, Texas, New York, and Florida. The highest state concentration, however, is in New Mexico where close to one third of the population retains use of the language (Moore & Pachón 1985:119–122).

The data in Table 4 indicate that the major gap in English proficiency is between the native and the foreign-born. Over 90% of native-born Hispanics reported speaking English well, the figure being essentially invariant across major national groups. The proportion among the foreign-born varies however, between one half and two thirds of the respective populations. Note that, because the overwhelming majority of Cubans are foreign-born, the total proportion of this group who reported speaking English well is actually much lower than among the other minorities.

Despite an apparently rapid language assimilation after the first or immigrant generation, there is evidence that self-reports of English proficiency are often exaggerated relative to actual knowledge and that language difficulties are not limited to the foreign-born. According to Moore & Pachón (1985:119), four out of five Hispanics reporting difficulties with English were US citizens. This result is, in part, a consequence of the predominance of the native-born in this population, but this suggests that the process of language acquisition is less than straightforward.

These conclusions are supported by results displayed in the middle rows of table 4, drawn from the longitudinal study of Cuban and Mexican immigrants described above. The data show that levels of English knowledge, as measured by an objective index, changed remarkably little over the six years of the study and were almost as low in 1979 as at the time of arrival in 1973.[1] In addition, self-reports of English competence were much higher than actual performance, a result which casts some doubt on the validity of Census reports, based on subjective evaluations. Similar results, reported in the following rows of the table, were obtained in a survey of 1980 Cuban (Mariel) refugees after three years of US residence.

Although it is almost certain that linguistic assimilation will occur over the long run, the resilience of Spanish over time and the apparent difficulty for many immigrants in learning English even after a substantial period of residence in the country is noteworthy. Three factors seem to play a central role in producing these results. First, the generally low levels of education among most Spanish-origin immigrants tend to make acquisition of new language more difficult. Second, continuing immigration and the ebb-and-flow pattern occurs between countries of origin and US communities of destination (Moore & Pachón 1985:121, Browning & Rodríguez 1985, Massey 1987). Third, the tendency of Spanish-origin groups to concentrate in certain geographic areas and of new immigrants to move into them also lessens the need to learn English for everyday living. The particular characteristics of the Cuban enclave in Miami make it possible for new arrivals to live and work within the confines of the ethnic community, a pattern which significantly contributes to the low levels of English acquisition reported above. Other groups, however, also tend to concentrate in their own neighborhoods; this eases the process of adaptation of newcomers but slows their language learning.[2]

Adaptation studies of immigrants and second-generation natives generally report high levels of satisfaction with life in the United States and commitment to remain in the country. Spanish-origin groups are no exception (Rogg & Cooney 1980, Cardona & Cruz 1980, Browning & Rodríguez 1985). Among immigrants, there is a consistent correlation between length of time in the United States and plans to stay permanently—recent immigrants are more likely to voice return plans, but the proportion of would-be returnees drops rapidly with time (Massey 1986b, Grasmuck 1984, Portes & Bach 1985:273). The bottom rows of Table 4 provide illustrative evidence of these trends.

[1]This measure—the knowledge of English Index (KEI)—consists of translations to nine words and phrases at elementary and junior high school levels of comprehension. Factor analysis performed on each sample at each point of time indicated consistently unidimensional structure. Internal consistency reliability, as measured by Cronbach's alpha, exceeded .90 in every survey.

[2]Of Mexican immigrants interviewed in 1979 for the longitudinal study described above, 70% concentrated in central-city areas and almost the same proportion—66%—reported that their neighborhood was predominantly Mexican or Mexican-American. Thus, the ethnic *barrio* was the place of residence for a majority of this immigrant sample, not only at arrival but after six years of US residence.

Table 4 Self-reports and objective measures of English knowledge. Sources: Nelson & Tienda 1985: Table 1; Portes & Stepick 1985: Table 4; authors' tabulations.

Variable	Cubans		Mexicans		Puerto Ricans	
	Native	Foreign-Born	Native	Foreign-Born	Born in Mainland	Born in Puerto Rico
Percent who report speaking English well, 1980[a]	94.3 (3,503)[b]	58.0 (29,888)	92.6 (177,149)	45.4 (93,422)	96.1 (19,078)	69.5 (43,677)
Percent who report speaking English well—immigrants, 1979[c]		38.3 (413)		46.2 (452)		
Percent scoring high in Knowledge of English Index, 1979[c] 1973		16.0 12.3 (590)		17.3 14.5 (822)		
Percent who report speaking English well—Mariel entrants, 1983[d]		33.7 (558)				
Percent scoring high in Knowledge of English Index, 1983[d]		22.6				

	Cuban Immigrants[c]		Mexican Immigrants[c]	
	1976	1979	1976	1979
Percent satisfied with their present lives	(427)	(413)	(439)	(454)
	81.3	93.7	79.1	78.8
Percent planning to stay permanently in the U.S.	88.5	95.9	85.2	88.3
Major adaptation difficulties experienced in the United States, percent:[e]				
Lack of English	42.3	49.1	43.9	28.7
Unemployment, low wages, etc.	29.4	20.1	30.6	39.6
Customs, cultural adaptation	10.2	6.2	11.0	9.6
Family problems	3.0	3.3	4.2	4.7
Health problems	10.5	17.0	6.1	8.2
Other	4.6	4.3	4.2	9.2

[a] Data from 5 percent Public Use Sample, 1980 Census.
[b] Sample sizes in parentheses.
[c] 1973–1979 longitudinal study of Cuban and Mexican immigrants.
[d] Survey of 1980 (Mariel) Cuban refugees settled in the Miami metropolitan area.
[e] Respondents indicating at least one major problem.

Note, however, that next to the predictable economic difficulties, the principal problem reported by Cuban and Mexican immigrants is lack of knowledge of English. Language problems were the adaptation difficulty mentioned most frequently by both groups after three years in the United States, and this continued to be the modal response among Cuban refugees after six years. Hence, despite the protection and comfort offered by the ethnic community, recent immigrants are subjectively aware of the impairment created in their lives by lack of fluency in the language of the surrounding society.

POLITICAL BEHAVIOR AND CITIZENSHIP

Differences between Spanish-origin groups are again highlighted by their political concerns, organization, and effectiveness. Regardless of national origin, a major gap separates the native-born—whose interests are always tied to their situation in the United States—and immigrants—whose political allegiance and organized actions often relate to events in the country of origin. The political sociology of Hispanic-Americans can thus be conveniently summarized under two main topical categories: first, the goals and actions of established groups, including the native-born and naturalized citizens; and second, the political orientations and, in particular, the problematic shift of nationality among immigrants.

Ethnic Politics

Moore & Pachón (1985: Ch. 10) provide a lucid summary of the politics of major Spanish-origin groups. Their overview can be supplemented by studies of Mexican-Americans by Camarillo (1979), Barrera (1980), Murguía (1975), and de la Garza & Flores (1986); of Puerto Ricans by Falcón (1983), Bonilla & Campos (1981), and Glazer & Moynihan (1963); and of Cubans by Boswell & Curtis (1984), Llanes (1982), and Fagen et al (1968).

The political history of Mexican-Americans bears considerable resemblance to that of American blacks, both in their earlier subordination and disenfranchisement and in subsequent attempts to dilute their electoral power through such devices as literacy tests, gerrymandering, and co-optation of ethnic leaders. The two groups are also similar in their contemporary reactions to past discrimination. Mexican-Americans differ from black Americans, however, in one crucial respect, namely their proximity to and strong identification with the country of origin. Attachment to Mexico and Mexican culture is strongly correlated with a sense of "foreignness," even among the native-born and, hence, with lower rates of political participation (García 1981). This reluctance to shift national allegiances appears to have represented one of the main obstacles in the path of effective organizing by Mexican-American leaders.

Despite these obstacles, a number of organizations did emerge which articulated the interests of one or another segment of the minority. These ranged from the earlier *mutualistas* and the *Orden de Hijos de América* to the subsequent League of United Latin American Citizens (LULAC) and the GI Forum, created to defend the interests of Mexican-American World War II veterans (Moore & Pachón 1985:176–86). The 1960s marked a turning point in Mexican-American politics. Inspired in large part by the black example, a number of militant organizations emerged that attempted to redress past grievances by means other than participation in the established parties. A number of radical student and youth organizations were created and a third party, La Raza Unida won a series of significant electoral victories in Texas.

Although the more militant demands of these organizations were never met and most of them have ceased to exist, the organizations succeeded where more conventional tactics had failed in the past: in mobilizing the Mexican-American population and creating a cadre of politicians who could forcefully defend its interests before national leaders and institutions. Today, the still-existing LULAC and MALDEF (the Mexican-American Legal Defense Fund) are among the most powerful and active Hispanic organizations. By 1984, 10 out of 11 members of the Hispanic Caucus in Congress represented districts with a heavy Mexican-American population (Roybal 1984).

Unlike Mexicans, Puerto Ricans are US citizens by birth and thus do not face the obstacle to political participation posed by naturalization proceedings. In addition, the Puerto Rican migrant population is concentrated in New York, a city and state with a long tradition of ethnic politics. A number of factors have conspired, however, to reduce the political weight of this population over the years. These include lack of knowledge of English, generally low levels of education and occupation among the migrants, and the resistance of established political "clubs"—in the hands of Jews, Italians, and other older immigrants—to admitting Puerto Ricans. In addition, the strong sojourner orientation of many migrants has reduced their interest in and attention to local politics. For many years, Puerto Rican activism on the mainland was targeted on demands for improvements in the economic and political status of the Island rather than of the New York community (Falcón 1983, Jennings 1977).

Although concern for the welfare of Puerto Rico has not been abandoned, events and needs of the mainland communities gradually gained priority during the post-World War II period. Puerto Rican politics paralleled the course followed by Mexicans and blacks during the 1960s. Militant youth organizations like the Young Lords and the Puerto Rican Revolutionary Workers' Organization made their appearance. Significant advances in mainstream politics occurred when a number of Puerto Ricans won local and state offices. Like Mexicans, Puerto Ricans vote overwhelmingly Democratic. By 1982, there were six Puerto Rican state legislators in New York, and a joint

Black and Puerto Rican Caucus had been established. During the 1970s, Puerto Ricans also elected their first state senator and first congressman. At present, Congressman Robert García, elected by the Bronx (18th) District, is the eleventh member of the Hispanic Caucus in the US House and still the sole Puerto Rican representative.

Two other congressional districts in New York City and two in the New Jersey suburbs have concentrations of Hispanic population that would make the election of additional Puerto Rican legislators viable (Moore & Pachón 1985:186–90). This will depend, however, on increasing the levels of registration and voting among Puerto Ricans and on securing the support of naturalized immigrants from other Latin American countries who—like Colombians and Dominicans—compose an increasing proportion of the area's population.

Like Mexicans, first-generation Cuban immigrants face the riddle of naturalization and, like Puerto Ricans, they tend to remain preoccupied with events in their country. Like both groups, Cubans generally speak little English on arrival, and this also conspires against effective participation. Despite these obstacles, Cuban-Americans have become a potent political force in South Florida. The mayors of the largest cities in the area—Miami and Hialeah—are Cuban, as are those of several smaller municipalities, and so are numerous city and county commissioners. Cuban-Americans are influential in the local Republican party and have elected a substantial delegation to the state legislature. Observers agree that it is only a matter of time before this community sends its first representatives to Congress from Florida's 17th and 18th districts. Meanwhile, a political action group funded by exiled businessmen—the Cuban-American National Foundation—has lobbied effectively in Washington for such causes as the creation of Radio Marti and the appointment of Cubans to federal offices (Botifoll 1984, Boswell & Curtis 1984, Ch. 10, Petersen & Maidique 1986).

Until the mid-1960s, the attention of Cuban refugees was riveted on the Island and the hope of return after the overthrow of the Castro regime. Two major events reduced these hopes: first, the defeat of the Bay of Pigs invasion in 1961, and second, the U.S.-U.S.S.R. agreement of 1962 which removed Soviet missiles from Cuba in exchange for an American pledge to prevent the refugees from launching new military attacks. Both events took place under the Kennedy Administration, and Cubans have blamed the Democrats for them ever since. As hopes for return became dimmer and the refugee community turned its attention inwards, Cubans naturalized in record numbers and lined solidly behind the Republican Party. With their support, Republicans— a minor force in Florida politics before that time—have become an increasingly serious power contender (Nazario 1983).

There are recent indications, however, that the monolithic conservatism of the Cuban vote may be more apparent than real. It is true that Cubans overwhelmingly supported President Reagan and other Republican candidates for national office in 1980 and 1984; it is also true that they continue to oppose, almost to a man, any foreign policy initiative perceived as "soft" on Communism. However, the vote in local elections has become more progressive and more likely to be guided by local concerns and issues. For example, during the last mayoral election in Miami, the Republican candidate finished a distant last. The final race was between two Cuban-Americans—a conservative banker supported by the Latin and Anglo business communities and a more progressive Harvard-trained lawyer. The latter won handily, primarily because of the support of the Cuban grassroots vote. Similarly, there are indications that Cuban representatives in the state legislature tend to be more concerned with populist issues, especially those involving ethnic minorities, than are fellow Republicans.[3]

An important topic for future research is the apparent trend toward convergence of the political organizations representing major Spanish-origin groups. As seen above, there is little similarity in historical origins or present socioeconomic situation among these groups. There is, however, the realization among certain political leaders of a basic communality of interests (in such issues as the defense of bilingualism and a common cultural image) and of the significance of strength in numbers. Thus, if the term "Hispanic" means anything of substance at present, it is at the political level. An indication of this trend is the emergence of the National Association of Latin Elected Officials (NALEO), a strong organization which groups Mexican, Puerto Rican, and Cuban congressmen, state legislators, and mayors (Moore & Pachón 1985:194–98).

Citizenship

The first step for effective political participation by any immigrant group is acquisition of citizenship. Table 5 presents data showing how different the rates of naturalization have been among the foreign-born in recent years. During the 1970s, naturalized Mexican immigrants represented only 6% of the total, despite the sizable potential pool of eligible individuals—the largest among all nationalities, representing close to 20% of all legal admissions during the preceding decade. By contrast, Cuban immigrants—a much smaller group—contributed 12% of all naturalizations, exceeding the figure for Canada despite the much larger number of eligible Canadian immigrants. The rest of Latin America contributed only 3%, but this is due to the relative small size of the cohorts of legal immigrants from the region before the 1970s.

The remaining columns of the table present data for the 1970 immigrant cohort that are representative of trends during recent years. Highest rates of naturalization correspond to Asian immigrants—mostly Chinese, Indians,

<hr />

[3]Unpublished material from authors' interviews with community leaders in Miami during 1985. See also Portes (1984).

Table 5   US citizenship acquisition for selected countries and regions, 1970–1980. Source: U.S. Immigration and Naturalization Service, *Annual Reports,* various years

	Naturalized 1971–1980	Percent of total	Cohort of 1970[b]	Naturalized during next decade	Percent of cohort	Peak year during decade[c]
Cuba	178,374	12	16,334	7,621	47	8th (2444)
Mexico	68,152	5	44,469	1,475	3	9th (404)
Central and South America	40,843	3	31,316	6,161	20	9th (1480)
Canada	130,380	9	13,804	856	6	8th (182)
West Europe	371,683	25	92,433	17,965	19	7th (5103)
Asia	473,754	32	92,816	44,554	48	7th (15129)
Totals[a]	1,464,772		373,326	94,532	25	7th (27681)

[a] All countries. Column figures do not add up to row total because of exclusion of other world regions—Africa, Eastern Europe, and Oceania.

[b] Number of immigrants admitted for legal permanent residence.

[c] Year of most numerous naturalizations during the decade after legal entry. Actual number naturalized in parentheses.

South Koreans, and Filipinos—and to Cubans. Citizenship acquisition among these groups represented close to half of the legal admissions from the respective source countries in 1970. Intermediate rates—close to a fifth of the immigrant cohort at the beginning of the period—are found among West Europeans and Central and South Americans. The lowest rates, less than 7%, correspond to immigrants from the two contiguous countries: Mexico and Canada. Mexican immigrants are also the slowest to naturalize, as indicated by their peak year of naturalizations during the decade—the ninth—or two full years behind the norm for all countries (Warren 1979, Portes & Mozo 1985).

The analytical literature on determinants of these differences comprises two separate strands: First, there are studies that attempt to explain variation among nationalities, and second, there are those that focus on proximate causes within a particular group. A pioneer contributer to the first or comparative literature was Bernard (1936), who identified literacy, education, and occupational prestige as major causes of differences in rates of naturalization between "old" and "new" European immigrants, as defined at that time. Subsequent studies have generally supported Bernard's hypothesis.[4]

---

[4] The single exception—a study by Barkan & Khoklov (1980) which specifically addresses Bernard's model—is based on a questionable operationalization of variables and a faulty use of the factor analytic method.

In addition, more recent quantitative studies have identified other variables, such as the political origin of migration and the geographical proximity of the country of origin as causally significant. Refugees from communist-controlled countries naturalize in greater numbers, other things being equal, than do regular immigrants. Those from nearby countries, especially those nations that share land borders with the United States, tend to resist citizenship change more than others. Both results seem to reflect the operation of a more general factor, which may be labelled the potential "reversibility" of migration: Immigrants for whom it is more difficult to return because of political conditions at home or the high cost and difficulty of the journey tend to naturalize at higher rates than those for whom return is but a simple bus ride away (Jasso & Rosenzweig 1985, Portes & Mozo 1985).

Studies of proximate determinants of citizenship have generally focused on those specific minorities with the lowest propensities to naturalize. Mexican immigrants are notorious in this respect; their collective behavior has given rise to a huge gap between the pool of potentially eligible citizens (and voters) and its actual size. Accordingly, several recent studies have sought to identify the principal determinants within the Mexican immigrant population of both predispositions and behaviors with respect to adopting US citizenship. This research comprises both quantitative analyses (García 1981, Grebler 1966) and ethnographic observations (Alvarez 1985, Fernández 1984, North 1985, Cornelius 1981). Several studies have noted a correlation between social psychological variables, such as self-identity as a Mexican, attitudes toward US society, and hopes of returning to Mexico with plans for naturalization. With few exceptions, however, these results are based on cross-sectional data, and hence, it is not possible to determine whether these subjective orientations play a causal role in individual decisionmaking or whether they are simply post-factum rationalizations.

Studies that focus on more objective variables have identified such characteristics as length of US residence, level of education, knowledge of English, age, marital status, citizenship of the spouse, and place of residence as potentially significant. In general, propensity to naturalize emerges from these studies as an outcome of a complex of determinants that include: (a) individual needs and motivations, (b) knowledge and ability, and (c) facilitational factors. Those Mexican immigrants whose stake in America is limited to a low wage job intended to support a family or future investments in Mexico have little motivation to obtain US citizenship. Those, on the other hand, who have acquired property, whose spouses or children are US citizens, and who begin to feel barriers to upward mobility because of their legal status have much greater incentive to initiate the process (Alvarez 1985, Portes & Curtis 1986).

Motivation is not enough, however, because citizenship acquisition is not an easy task. For most immigrants, it requires knowledge of English and some knowledge of US civics in order to pass the naturalization test. Thus, better educated immigrants, those who have lived in the country longer and are more informed about it, tend to face fewer obstacles than do the others. Finally, there is the question of external facilitation. Two factors play the most significant roles in this respect: social networks and the conduct of official agencies in charge of the process. Networks limited to Mexican kin and friends tend to be unsupportive of the naturalization process (García 1981, Fernández 1984), while those that include US-born or US-naturalized relatives and friends may facilitate it.

The key governmental agency involved in this process is the US Immigration and Naturalization Services (INS), and its behavior toward applicants has been found decidedly mixed. Ethnographic research has identified "fear of the INS" as a significant deterrent of naturalization among Mexican immigrants (Alvarez 1985). In *The Long Gray Welcome,* an in-depth study of the agency's naturalization procedures, North (1985) outlines the numerous obstacles—from heavy backlogs to arbitrary examiners—often thrown in the way of poor and little-educated immigrants. Confronted with such barriers, the appropriate question may not be why so few Mexicans naturalize, but why so many decide to and succeed in doing so.

CONCLUSION

Unlike research on European ethnic minorities, where the topic of interest is increasingly historical in orientation, the study of Spanish-origin groups involves very contemporary issues which are likely to persist and gain relevance in the future. An important question is whether the label "Hispanic" itself will endure. As seen above, political leaders from various groups have started to cooperate, at least in a limited manner, in the pursuit of common interests. In addition, governmental, journalistic, and academic use of the term will reinforce its currency. On the other hand, the economic and social conditions of the groups so labelled appear to be evolving in increasingly separate and distinct ways. In addition to differentiation among the major groups discussed above, others—such as Dominicans, Colombians, and Salvadoreans—are growing rapidly and will surely add to the overall complexity of the picture. Whatever the fate of the general term of reference, research on Spanish-origin minorities is likely to become more nuanced and sophisticated as scholars learn to appreciate the distinct identity and economic situation of each and as new groups are targeted for study.

This review of the sociological literature has been neither exhaustive nor representative of all substantive concerns. Readers interested in a more extensive discussion may consult a number of recent book-length summaries including Moore & Pachón's, *Hispanics in the United States* and the demographically oriented but highly readable study, *The Hispanic Population of the United States* by Bean & Tienda (1987). Nevertheless, themes touched in the limited space of this chapter—modes of labor market incorporation and their consequences; language acquisition; naturalization and political participation—are likely to remain central ones for these ethnic minorities and for the roles which, individually and collectively, they will play in American society.

Literature Cited

Alba, R. D. 1985. *Italian Americans: Into the Twilight of Ethnicity*. Englewood Cliffs, NJ: Prentice-Hall

Alvarez, R. R. 1985. *A Profile of the Citizenship Process among Hispanics in the United States: An Anthropological Perspective. Special Rep. Nat. Assoc. Latin Elected Officials*. 34 pp. (Mimeo)

Bach, R. L. 1985. Socialist construction and Cuban emigration: Explorations into Mariel. *Cuban Stud*. 15 (Summer):19–36

Bach, R. L., Gordon, L. W., Haines, D. W., Howell, D. R. 1984. The economic adjustment of Southeast Asian refugees in the U.S. In *U.N. Commission for Refugees, World Refugee Survey 1983*, pp. 51–56. Geneva: United Nations

Barkan, E., Khoklov, N. 1980. Socioeconomic data as indices of naturalization patterns in the United States: A theory revisited. *Ethnicity* 7:159–90

Barrera, M. 1980. *Race and Class in the Southwest: A Theory of Racial Inequality*. Notre Dame, Ind: Notre Dame Univ. Press

Bean, F. D., King, A. G., Passel, J. S. 1983. The number of illegal migrants of Mexican origin in the United States: Sex ratio based estimates for 1980. *Demography* 20:99–109

Bean, F. D., King, A. G., Passel, J. S. 1986. Estimates of the size of the illegal migrant population of Mexican origin in the United States: An assessment, review, and proposal. In *Mexican Immigrants and Mexican Americans: An Evolving Relation*, ed. H. L. Browning, R. de la Garza, pp. 13–26. Austin: Ctr. Mex. Am. Stud., Univ. Tex.

Bean, F. D., Swicegood, C. G., King, A. G. 1985. Role incompatibility and the relationship between fertility and labor supply among Hispanic women. See Borjas & Tienda 1985, pp. 221–42 (Fla:)

Bean, F. D., Tienda, M. 1987. *The Hispanic Population of the United States*. New York: Russell Sage Found.

Bernard, W. S. 1936. Cultural determinants of naturalization. *Am. Sociol. Rev.* 1 (Dec):943–53

Bonilla, F. A., Campos, R. 1981. A wealth of poor: Puerto Ricans in the new economic order. *Daedalus* 110:133–76

Bonilla, F. A., Campos, R. 1982. Imperialist initiatives and the Puerto Rican workers: From Foraker to Reagan. *Contemp. Marxism* 5:1–18

Borjas, G. J., Tienda, M., eds. 1985. *Hispanics in the U.S. Economy*. Orlando, Fla: Academic Press

Boswell, T. D., Curtis, J. R. 1984. *The Cuban-American Experience*. Totowa, NJ: Rowman & Allanheld

Botifoll, L. J. 1984. How Miami's new image was created. *Occas. Pap. #1985-1*, Inst. Interam. Stud. Univ. Miami

Browning, H. L., Rodríguez, N. 1985. The migration of Mexican indocumentados as a settlement process: Implications for work. See Borjas & Tienda, 1985, pp. 277–97

Camarillo, A. 1979. *Chicanos in a Changing Society*. Cambridge. Mass: Harvard Univ. Press

Candace, N., Tienda, M. 1985. The structuring of Hispanic ethnicity: Historical and contemporary perspectives. *Ethnic Racial Stud*. 8(Jan):49–74

Cardona, R. C., Cruz, C. I. 1980. *El Exodo de Colombianos*. Bogota: Ediciones Tercer Mundo

Centro de Estudios Puertorriqueños. 1979. *Labor Migration under Capitalism*. New York: Monthly Rev.

Cornelius, W. A. 1977. *Illegal immigration to the United States: Recent research findings, policy implications and research priorities*. Work. Pap. Ctr. Int. Stud., MIT

Cornelius, W. A. 1981. The future of Mexican immigrants in California: A new perspective for public policy. *Work. Pap. on Public Policy #6*, Ctr. U.S.-Mexico Stud. Univ. Calif.-San Diego

de la Garza, R., Flores, A. 1986. The impact of Mexican immigrants on the political behavior of Chicanos. In *Mexican Immigrants and Mexican Americans: An Evolving Relation*, ed. H. L. Browing, R. de la Garza, pp. 211–29. Austin: Ctr. Mex.-Am. Stud. Univ. Tex.

DeWind, J., Seidl, T., Shenk, J. 1977. Contract labor in U.S. agriculture. *NACLA Rep. Americas* 11 (Nov.–Dec):4–37

Díaz-Briquets, S., Pérez, L. 1981. Cuba: The demography of revolution. *Pop. Bull.* 36 (April):2–41

Fagen, R. R., Brody, R. A., O'Leary, T. J. 1968. *Cubans in Exile: Disaffection and the Revolution.* Stanford, Calif: Stanford Univ. Press

Falcón, A. 1983. Puerto Rican politics in urban America: An introduction to the literature. *La Red* (July):2–9

Fernández, C. 1984. *The causes of naturalization and non-naturalization for Mexican immigrants: An empirical study based on case studies. Rep. Project Participar.* (Mimeo)

Fitzpatrick, J. 1971. *Puerto Rican Americans: The Meaning of Migration to the Mainland.* Englewood Cliffs, NJ: Prentice-Hall

Fitzpatrick, J., Gurak, D. 1979. *Hispanic Intermarriage in New York City.* New York: Fordham Univ. Hispanic Res. Ctr.

Galarza, E. 1964. *Merchants of Labor: The Mexican Bracero Story.* Santa Barbara: McNally & Loflin

Galarza, E. 1970. *Spiders in the House and Workers in the Field.* Notre Dame, Ind: Notre Dame Univ. Press

Galarza, E. 1977. *Farm Workers and Agribusiness in California, 1947–1960.* Notre Dame, Ind: Notre Dame Univ. Press

Garcia, J. A. 1981. Political integration of Mexican immigrants: Explorations into the naturalization process. *Int. Migration Rev.* 15 (Winter):608–25

Glaessel-Brown, E. 1985. *Colombian Immigrants in the Industries of the Northeast.* Ph.D. thesis. Dep. Polit. Sci., MIT

Glazer, N. 1981. Pluralism and the new immigrants. *Society* 19(Nov–Dec):31–36

Glazer, N., Moynihan, D. P. 1963. *Beyond the Melting Pot: The Negroes, Puerto Ricans, Jews, Italians, and Irish of New York City.* Cambridge, Mass: MIT Press

Grasmuck, S. 1984. Immigration, ethnic stratification, and native working-class discipline: Comparisons of documented and undocumented Dominicans. *Int. Migration Rev.* 18 (Fall):692–713

Grebler, L. 1966. The naturalization of the Mexican immigrant in the U.S. *Int. Migration Rev.* 1:17–32

Grebler, L., Moore, J. W., Guzman, R. C. 1970. *The Mexican-American People: The Nation's Second Largest Minority.* New York: Free Press

Hendricks, G. L. 1974. *The Dominican Diaspora: From the Dominican Republic to New York City.* New York: Teacher's Coll. Press Columbia Univ.

Hirschman, C., Falcón, L. M. 1985. The educational attainment of religio-ethnic groups in the United States. *Res. Sociol. Educ. Social.* 5:83–120

Hispanic Review of Business. 1985. *Annual Survey of Hispanic Business, 1984* (June–July)

Jasso, G., Rosenzweig, M. R. 1985. *What's in a name? Country-of-origin influences on the earnings of immigrants in the United States. Bull.* #85-4, Econ. Dev. Ctr., Univ. Minn. (Mimeo)

Jennings, J. 1977. *Puerto Rican Politics in New York City.* Washington, DC: Univ. Press

Lewis, O. 1966. *La Vida: A Puerto Rican Family in the Culture of Poverty.* New York: Random House

Llanes, J. 1982. *Cuban-Americans, Masters of Survival.* Cambridge, Mass: Abt.

Massey, D. S. 1981. Hispanic residential segregation: A comparison of Mexicans, Cubans, and Puerto Ricans. *Sociol. Social Res.* 65:311–22

Massey, D. S. 1986. The settlement process among Mexican immigrants to the United States. *Am. Sociol. Rev.* 51:670–84

Massey, D. S. 1987. Understanding Mexican migration to the United States. *Am. J. Sociol.* 92: Forthcoming

Mills, C. W., Senior, C., Goldsen, R. 1950. *Puerto Rican Journey.* New York: Harper & Row

Mirandé, A. 1985. *The Chicago Experience, an Alternative Perspective.* Notre Dame, Ind: Notre Dame Univ. Press

Moore, J., Pachón, H. 1985. *Hispanics in the United States.* Englewood Cliffs, NJ: Prentice-Hall

Murguia, E. 1975. *Assimilation, Colonialism, and the Mexican American People.* Austin: Ctr. Mex.-Am. Stud. Univ. Tex.

Nazario, S. 1983. After a long holdout, Cubans in Miami take a role in politics. *Wall Street J.* June 7

Nelson, C., Tienda, M. 1985. The structuring of Hispanic ethnicity: Historical and contemporary perspectives. *Ethnic Racial Stud.* 8(Jan) 49–74

North, D. S. 1985. *The Long Gray Welcome: A Study of the American Naturalization Program.* Monogr. Rep. Natl. Assoc. Latin Elected Officials (Mimeo)

Padilla, E. 1958. *Up from Puerto Rico.* New York: Columbia Univ. Press

Passel, J. S. 1985. *Undocumented immigrants: How many?* Presented at Ann. meet. Am. Statist. Assoc., Las Vegas

Pedraza-Bailey, S. 1985a. *Political and Economic Migrants in America: Cubans and Mexicans.* Austin: Univ. Tex. Press

Pedraza-Bailey, S. 1985b. Cuba's exiles: Portrait of a refugee migration. *Int. Migration Rev.* 19 (Spring):4–34

Pérez, L. 1986. Immigrant economic adjustment and family organization: The Cuban success story reexamined. *Int. Migration Rev.* 20 (Spring):4–20

Pessar, P. R. 1982. The role of households in international migration and the case of U.S.-bound migration from the Dominican Republic. *Int. Migration Rev.* 16 (Summer):342–64

Petersen, M. F., Maidique, M. A. 1986. *Success patterns of the leading Cuban-American entrepreneurs.* Innovation and Entrepreneurship Inst., Univ. Miami. (Mimeo)

Portes, A. 1984. The rise of ethnicity: Determinants of ethnic perceptions among Cuban exiles in the United States. *Am. Sociol. Rev.* 49 (June):383–97

Portes, A., Bach, R. L. 1985. *Latin Journey, Cuban and Mexican Immigrants in the United States.* Berkeley: Univ. Calif. Press

Portes, A., Curtis, J. 1986. *Changing flags, naturalization and its determinants among Mexican immigrants.* Unpublished Res. Rep. Program in Compar. Int. Dev., Johns Hopkins Univ.

Portes, A., Manning, R. D. 1986. The immigrant enclave: Theory and empirical examples. In *Competitive Ethnic Relations,* pp. 47–64. ed. J. Nagel, S. Olzak, Orlando, Fla: Academic Press

Portes, A., Mozo, R. 1985. The political adaptation process of Cubans and other ethnic minorities in the United States. *Int. Migration Rev.* 19 (Spring):35–63

Portes, A., Stepick, A. 1985. Unwelcome immigrants: The labor market experiences of 1980 (Mariel) Cuban and Haitian refugees in South Florida. *Am. Sociol. Rev.* 50 (August):493–514

Reichert, J. S. 1981. The migrant syndrome: Seasonal U.S. wage labor and rural development in Central Mexico. *Human Organ.* 40 (Spring):59–66

Reichert, J. S., Massey, D. S. 1979. Patterns of U.S. migration from a Mexican sending community: A comparison of legal and illegal migrants. *Int. Migration Rev.* 13 (Winter):599–623

Reichert, J. S., Massey, D. S. 1980. History and trends in U.S. bound migration from a Mexican town. *Int. Migration Rev.* 14 (Winter):475–91

Reimers, C. W. 1985. A comparative analysis of the wages of Hispanics, blacks, and non-Hispanic whites. See Borjas & Tienda 1985, pp. 27–75

Rogg, E., Cooney, R. 1980. *Adaptation and Adjustment of Cubans: West New York.* New York: Fordham Univ. Hispanic Res. Ctr.

Roybal, E. R. 1984. Welcome statement. In *Proceedings of the First National Conference on Citizenship and the Hispanic Community,* p. 7. Washington, DC: Natl. Assoc. Latin Elected Officials

Samora, J. 1971. *Los Mojados: The Wetback Story.* Notre Dame, Ind: Notre Dame Univ. Press

Sánchez-Korrol, V. 1983. *From Colonia to Community.* Westport, Conn: Greenwood

Sassen-Koob, S. 1979. Formal and informal associations: Dominicans and Colombians in New York. *Int. Migration Rev.* 13 (Summer):314–32

Sassen-Koob, S. 1980. Immigrant and minority workers in the organization of the labor process. *J. Ethnic Stud.* 1 (Spring):1–34

Stolzenberg, R. M. 1982. *Occupational Differences Between Hispanics and Non-Hispanics.* Rep. Natl. Commission Employment Policy. Santa Monica, Calif: Rand

Tienda, M., Jensen, L. 1985. *Immigration and public assistance participation: Dispelling the myth of dependency. Discuss. Pap. #777-85.* Inst. Res. Poverty, Univ. Wisc.-Madison, Mimeo

Tienda, M., Lee, D. T. 1986. *Migration, market insertion, and earnings determination of Mexicans, Puerto Ricans, and Cubans.* Pres. Ann. Meet. Am. Sociol. Assoc. New York

U.S. Bureau of the Census. 1980. *1977 Survey of Minority-Owned Business Enterprises.* Washington, DC: USGPO

U.S. Bureau of the Census. 1983a. *General Population Characteristics, United States Summary.* Washington, DC: USGPO

U.S. Bureau of the Census. 1983b. *General Social and Economic Characteristics, United States Summary.* Washington, DC: USGPO

U.S. Bureau of the Census. 1983c. *Condition of Hispanics in America Today,* Special Release, Sept. 13. Washington, DC: USGPO

U.S. Immigration and Naturalization Service. 1984. *Annual Report.* Washington, DC: USGPO

Waldinger, R. 1985. Immigration and industrial change in the New York City apparel industry. See Borjas & Tienda 1985, pp. 323–49

Warren, R. 1979. *Status report on naturalization rates. Work. Pap. #CO 1326, 6C.* U.S. Bureau of the Census. Washington, DC. Mimeo

Wilson, K. L., Martin, W. A. 1982. Ethnic enclaves: A comparison of the Cuban and black economies of Miami. *Am. J. Sociol.* 88(July):135–60

Wilson, K. L., Portes, A. 1980. Immigrant enclaves: An analysis of the labor market experiences of Cubans in Miami. *Am. J. Sociol.* 86(Sept):295–319

Wood, C. H. 1984. *Caribbean cane cutters in Florida: A study of the relative cost of foreign and domestic labor.* Presented at Ann. Meet. Am. Sociol. Assoc. San Antonio

Ann. Rev. Sociol. 1987. 13:387–415
Copyright © 1987 by Annual Reviews Inc. All rights reserved

THE WELFARE STATE, CITIZENSHIP, AND BUREAUCRATIC ENCOUNTERS

Yeheskel Hasenfeld

School of Social Welfare, University of California, Los Angeles, California 90024

Jane A. Rafferty, Mayer N. Zald

Department of Sociology, The University of Michigan, Ann Arbor, Michigan 48109

Abstract

The growth of welfare state programs inevitably leads to an increase of citizen encounters with bureaucratic agencies. Moreover, theories of the welfare state differ in the extent to which citizenship rights are a central aspect of the explanation of the shape of the welfare state. After reviewing major theories of the expansion of the welfare state, we examine determinants of client encounters. The determinants are framed in a social exchange model that draws upon individual resources and agency and program characteristics. The model predicts differences in power-dependence relations and clientele satisfaction with their encounters. The legitimation and protection of citizenship rights may vary from program to program, may vary over time, and may be differently institutionalized in societies at similar levels of economic development. How rights are linked to citizen obligations is also an historical and sociological issue. The chapter concludes with a discussion of methodological issues in evaluating encounters.

INTRODUCTION

Encounters between citizens and welfare state bureaucracies cannot be understood without recognition that they are an integral component of the very

387

0360-0572/87/0815-0387$02.00

structure of the welfare state. The frequency with which citizens interact with welfare state bureaucracies is a direct function of the rapid growth of the welfare state, in terms of both the scope of its programs and services and the range of their coverage. As a result, a profound change has occurred in the relations between citizens and the state in both the dependence of citizens on the state for protection and the state's obligations toward its citizens. In the first section of this chapter, we discuss the major sociological theories explaining the growth of the welfare state. In the next section we explore the implications of ideas of citizenship for the welfare state and bureaucratic encounters. As conceptualized by Marshall (1964:78), the rise of the welfare state was accompanied by the expansion of citizenship rights from civil and political to social. It is the exercise of these social rights that triggers the bureaucratic encounters.

The extension of social rights in Western democracies has certainly not been inevitable or uniform. In terms of eligibility, a key distinction needs to be made between rights to contributory programs such as old age survivor and disability insurance, and rights to means-tested programs such as public assistance. In the former, citizens earn their rights through their tax contributions to the program. In the latter, they "earn" their right by demonstrating that they are deserving poor. Finally, attention must also be paid to the wide variations in the nature of the goods and services provided by different welfare state bureaucracies. Because of technological requirements, the delivery of these services demands different organizational arrangements. All of these factors result in considerable variation in the types and characteristics of the bureaucratic encounters; these are discussed in the third section.

In the fourth section, we examine the process through which private needs are transformed into bureaucratic encounters. In this process, individual and organizational level variables converge to influence the behavior of both citizens and officials. Four types of encounters are identified according to the ability of each party to control the content of the encounter.

To understand the dynamics of these bureaucratic encounters, we propose, in the fifth section, a social exchange model which views the encounter as a power-dependence relationship between the citizen and the bureaucracy (Hasenfeld 1983).

Because welfare state bureaucracies wield so much power over citizens, the protection of social rights becomes a major concern. Bureaucratic power and its remedies are discussed in the sixth section. Finally, in the seventh section, we review studies that evaluate the nature and outcome of bureaucratic encounters. After noting the conflicting findings that indicate, on the one hand, considerable disaffection with welfare state bureaucracies and, on the other hand, the generally favorable citizen evaluations of their encounters, we then attempt to explain the different results within our general framework.

THE GROWTH OF THE WELFARE STATE

The emergence of the welfare state in Western democracies represents a change in the relationship between the state and its citizens. Obligations and rights nested in feudal, familial, community, or religious institutions are expanded so that the notions emerge of national citizenship and of citizenship rights and obligations to the state. As the welfare state expands and the range of programs encompasses more areas of life, the individual and the members of the household, workplace, and community encounter a greater range of bureaucracies.

Citizenship quite vividly captures a *problematique*. The concept encompasses an evolving and continuing struggle and status within Western countries. Since the decline of feudalism and the "rise of the modern era," citizens have come in direct relation to the national political regime and the economy. During the past 250 years, civil, political, and social rights have been extended. Citizen rights have increasingly taken precedence over property rights and hereditary status. The conferring of civil, political, and social rights and duties has been a slow and uneven process. It is still evolving. Generally speaking, the eighteenth century brought civil rights, the nineteenth century saw the advent of political rights, and the twentieth century has brought the development of social rights.

The following discussion of the rise of the welfare state examines the extent to which students of the welfare state incorporate the concept of citizenship into their analyses. Analysts who view the emergence of social welfare programs as an inevitable response to an increase in GNP, or as a response to demographic shifts and a growth of industrialization, generally ignore the concept of citizenship. Questions regarding the legitimate bounds of the rights of citizens to particular goods and services are generally not discussed (Wilensky 1975, Wilensky & Lebeaux 1958). In sharp contrast are theories explaining the development of the welfare state that assign high causal priority to the political power, or the fear of the political power, of the working class (Esping-Anderson 1978, 1981, Shalev 1983a, b). From this perspective, questions of the rights of workers, the poor, and the elderly to a minimum standard of living and protection from economic hardship are central to an accurate understanding of the dynamics of the welfare state.

Although the term "welfare state" is a loosely used term, it is possible to stake out some general boundaries of the concept. In the definition guiding most empirical research, the welfare state refers to the nonmarket, governmental provision of, or direct funding of, consumption needs in such areas as income, housing, and health care. Core programs are income programs for the elderly, medical care, unemployment subsidies, and various forms of public assistance.

Heclo (1981) demarcates four periods of welfare state development. The experimentation stage extends from 1870 to 1920, the consolidation era dates from 1930 to 1950, the expansion era extends from 1950 to 1970, and the current epoch of reformulation began in 1970.

During the experimentation era there was much chopping and altering of social insurance programs. The criteria for coverage and, hence, the number of persons covered varied. For example, in Germany the criteria for workmans' compensation fluctuated greatly around the turn of the century. The question of "deservingness" was also a prime topic during this period. The entire issue of whether the government should, on a routine and institutionalized basis, help the poor was debated. "Three key values—liberty, equality, and security—appeared to be at odds in the late nineteenth century. Trying to resolve the tensions among these values tended to push each of the prevailing bodies of political opinion into an activist orientation toward government and social policy, although each in a somewhat differing way" (Heclo 1981:388).

The era of consolidation was a stage in which tentativeness gave way to commitment to governmental intervention. It was fairly well agreed that the national government should and could intervene in the private sector. Keynesian economics and full employment goals became accepted. Economic depression caused people to lose faith in party programs which relied too heavily on the private sector to solve social problems.

The era of expansion saw an increasing percentage of GNP absorbed by the public sector, rising governmental deficits, and growing government programs. Heclo summarizes the thrust of the era of expansion as follows:

> Any commitment to struggling with the inevitable tensions among such values went soft. Expansion of the austerity welfare state in a context of sustained affluence was producing not just more of the same, but implicitly a newer way of thinking about the welfare state. Instead of shared risks and vulnerability, its ethic was based on piecemeal compensation for anyone who lagged behind others' gain (1981:398).

In light of the economic recession of the late 1960s and early 1970s there has been some rethinking about the welfare state; hence, the term "era of reformulation." There are new economic permutations: high unemployment and high inflation. The old solutions such as deficit spending do not seem to be working, and pressure is building to reduce social spending.

Heclo's periodization exercise serves as a very brief history of the development of the welfare state. Implicit in Heclo's description is a continual change in citizenship rights and access, which increased in scope with each phase of development until the era of reformulation when some curtailment of entitlements has occurred.

The various frameworks aimed at explaining the development of the welfare state assign causal primacy to different factors. The range of variables includes: economic growth, the structure of the nation's tax structure, the organization of the national bureaucracy, the effect of electoral politics, the strength of labor organizations, and the logic of capitalism. Different surveyors of the welfare state operate out of diverse theoretical frames. We label them as the economic, the political, and political economy. (Of course, these labels oversimplify the matter.)

Economic theories link the rise of the welfare state with economic expansion and development and its social ramifications. Political explanations emphasize party politics, the structure of bureaucracies, and the effect of bureaucratic precedents. Political economy theories explore the interrelationship between political and economic spheres; their proponents argue that, to understand social policy, political and economic variables should not be studied in isolation.

A common thread in economic explanations is an emphasis on the social ramifications of economic growth. Wagner (1883), a contemporary of Bismark, asserted that as a society developed and the economy expanded, two conditions would result: There would be new social problems to solve and new services to provide. With the changing role of such institutions as the church and the family, the state would be expected to provide additional services. The second effect assumes that citizens' willingness to pay for services (through taxation) is income elastic. Therefore, as a society's GDP (Gross Domestic Product) increases, taxes will increase and the scope of government services will expand.

In a vein similar to Wagner's, twentieth century students of the welfare state stress the importance of economic growth (Wilensky 1975, Cutright 1965, Hage & Hannemann 1977, Pryor 1968). Economic development results in new social problems and social surplus to solve social problems. These conclusions are based on quantitative studies predicting either the level of spending or the age of pension programs and using as explanatory variables such indicators as GDP, extent of urbanization, percentage of population over 65, political regime type, and strength of various political parties. The common conclusions within this set of studies are that economic and demographic variables are the stronger predictors, and that political variables do not explain the age of welfare programs or the level of spending.

Political explanations are quite diverse. They include the effect of electoral politics, the structure of the federal bureaucracy, the autonomy of career bureaucrats, and the nature of budgeting.

Extrapolating on Downs' (1960:541) premise that "in a democratic society, the division of resources between the public and private sectors is roughly determined by the desires of the electorate," recent works (Kramer 1971, Nordhaus 1975, Tufte 1975, 1978) suggest that electoral politics influences the level of public spending. The logic of this perspective is that incumbent officeholders are aware of their constituents' demands. These studies identify the existence of political business cycles: increases in public spending just before and just after an election. There is an implicit assumption that constituents always desire spending increases. These studies do not assert a connection between individuals' economic interests, social position, or political interests.

Another set of political studies concentrates on the structure of bureaucracy, its autonomy, and the career and professional interests of senior bureaucrats (Niskanen 1971, Tarschys 1975, Heclo 1974, Skocpol 1980, Weir & Skocpol 1985, Orloff & Skocpol 1984, Skocpol & Finegold 1982, Skocpol & Ikenberry 1983). Although the analyses differ, there is a common assumption that bureaucracies can be viewed as partially autonomous units, relatively insulated from voters' concerns and lobbying groups' pressures. Social policy should be seen not as a reflection of the political power of various groups or as a result of economic growth, but as a result of the structure and internal dynamics of the state and its individual bureaucracies.

Niskanen (1971) and Tarschys (1975) attribute growth in public spending to the structure of decision-making and the nature of the budgeting process. The logic is straightforward: There is an inherent incrementalism in budgets. This effect is compounded when fiscal decision-making is very segmented and decentralized. All other factors being equal, the greater the number of autonomous bureaucratic units, the higher the level of spending.

Basing his conclusions on a comparative study of the emergence of income maintenance programs in Britain and Sweden, Heclo (1974) sees civil servants as crucial actors in the enactment of social programs. Administrators are in a position to identify social conditions in need of correction, to design new policy and to implement it. Heclo conceptualizes social policy as a reflection of administrators learning from past precedents and working within the constraints of the state structure. For example, a centralized state administration such as Sweden's was more conducive to massive policy innovation and implementation than was Great Britain's.

Skocpol and her colleagues advocate a state-centered approach to the analysis of the welfare state. Politicians and bureaucrats have career interests and are involved in struggles among themselves. An important assumption in this framework is that the organizational structures of states influence politicians and also influence the collective action of social groups. Empirically the issue becomes the extent to which state agents choose among policy alternatives that are shaped by past policy choices, and the extent to which power groups and elites play a direct role in choosing the policy option.

The defining characteristics of those works we label as political economic are that they bring politics and economics into sharp relief, and that both are analyzed simultaneously. These works can be divided into two analytical subgroups: One group focuses on the logic of capitalism and the interest of capitalists (O'Connor 1973, Offe 1984, Quadagno 1985), and the second stresses the political power of the working class (Shalev 1983a, b; Korpi 1978, 1980; Esping-Anderson 1978, 1981; Therborn 1984a, b).

Within the logic-of-capitalism subgroup, O'Connor (1973) presents the most deterministic/functional account of social spending. He contends that the capitalist state has two primary functions: accumulation and legitimation. Welfare programs serve the legitimation function. It would be dysfunctional to capitalism if the state just fostered capital accumulation without making any attempts to rectify social inequality.

Offe sets forth a Marxist functional explanation in an essay entitled *Competitive party democracy and the Keynesian welfare state* (1984). He begins by noting that contrary to nineteenth century liberal and classical Marxism, twentieth century history has shown that capitalism and democracy can be compatible. Offe argues that competitive party democracy and the Keynesian welfare state are structures that help cement the political and economic systems. As Offe argues:

> The logic of capitalist democracy is one of mutual contamination: authority is infused into the economy by global management, transfers, and regulations so that it loses more of its spontaneous and regulatory character, and market contingency is introduced into the state, thus compromising any notion of absolute authority of absolute good (1984:182–83).

Quadagno (1984) sees political outcomes and policies as predicated upon the divisions within the capitalist class and the structure of the labor process. The key dynamic of her analysis of the enactment of the Social Security Act of 1935 in the United States is the division of interests between monopoly capitalists and competitive sector capitalists. Monopoly capitalists operate on a multistate level and hence are generally less interested in traditional labor market control strategies. They desire a stable labor force. In contrast, entrepreneurs within the competitive sector are more vulnerable than monopoly capitalists to seasonal and cyclical fluctuations and, therefore, are interested in being able to manipulate the labor force supply. Quadagno argues national level state managers were more responsive to interests of monopoly capitalists, and Congress to those of nonmonopoly capitalists. The crux of the Social Security Act reflects the interests of monopoly capitalists and some compromise with Congress (e.g. keeping the administration of pension programs at the state level). [See debate between Quadagno (1985) and Skocpol & Amenta (1985) on the shaping of the Social Security Act.]

One of the most well-developed approaches to the welfare state has been the social democratic one which focuses on the political strength of the working class (Shalev 1983a, b; Korpi 1980; Esping-Anderson 1978, 1981; Therborn 1984a, b). Defenders of the social democratic model argue that capitalist society is inherently unequal; therefore, the welfare state is a class issue. Welfare state programs generally aim at rectifying social inequities, the argument goes, so the working class should be the most avid proponent of welfare legislation. The scope of welfare programs and the level of social program spending should be correlated with the number of social democratic/pro-labor candidates in the national legislature. There is some support for the idea that working class strength within political parties makes a difference (Castles 1982). In countries where there is greater working class strength in parties, the state has a wider and more diverse role in the economy.

Arguing in a similar vein, Therborn (1984a, b) views the strength of labor as the linchpin in an explanation of the timing and the growth of welfare states. From his perspective, the development of social welfare programs should not be seen as a benevolent gesture nor as an inevitable stage of Western political development. Therborn considers the rise of a country's labor and trade union movements as the major impetus for a country's first major social welfare program, whether or not labor parties take power. In addition, Therborn argues that existing state structures influence the form that social welfare programs take. Federated states with traditions of local autonomy will incorporate those traditions in new programs.

Although the social democratic model has been very influential, it is not without limits. First, it may well be that the *incorporation* of labor into a corporatist ruling structure makes the difference (see Wilensky 1981). Moreover, Jackman argues (1986) that most democracies are not structured to represent preferences for welfare state policies on a continuing basis. Second, although class coalitions may be important in the maintenance and expansion of programs, Pampel & Williamson (1985) present convincing data that the size and percentage of the aged in a population are more important than the labor party's control of government for the expansion of pension expenditures, especially in democracies. They interpret their findings as a reflection of the role of the aged in politics, though they have no direct data on the participation of the aged. Finally, and as a point to be developed below, there are alternative routes to the welfare state. The *shape* of specific programs and procedures (e.g. criteria for eligibility, universality, generosity, relationship to inequality) may be more related to class coalitions and ideological conceptions of citizenship rights than is the sheer size or coverage of the welfare state.

The core elements of these analyses are summarized in Table 1. Note that citizenship issues are ignored in the macroscopic overarching approaches to the welfare state.

Whatever the causal model used to explain the growth and differential institutionalization of the welfare state, the consequences for citizens should be clear. Modern nation states vary in the extent of direct and indirect governmental provision of goods and services for their citizens. The range of

Table 1 Summary of major models of welfare state development

	Central dynamic	Theoretical role of citizenship
Economic	— Increase in GNP — Industrialization — Demographic shifts	— No role
Political	— Electoral politics — Political agendas of politi- cians and bureaucrats — Structure of bureaucracy	— No role
Political economy	— Logic of capitalism — Interests of class fractions — Political power of working class — Ability of working class to form alliances	— Implicit and indirect role: Social rights as placating mechanisms — Citizenship is core of struggle — Debate is framed in terms of what are legitimate rights of citizens— How can needs be accommodated, income re-distributed, and stratifica- tion redefined independent of markets

services and income support programs, the criteria for access to these programs, and the distribution of services by region, class, and position in the
labor force all vary significantly. Citizen claims upon and power vis-à-vis the
governmental bureaucracies vary enormously.

CITIZENSHIP AND THE WELFARE STATE

Research on the welfare state that focuses on the economic and political
determinants of the welfare state or its expansion can often assume the
transformation of citizenship rights and obligations as corollaries of larger
political-economic trends. The more macroscopic and/or abstract the analysis,
the easier it is to ignore issues of eligibility, coverage, and entitlement.
However, the more one deals with the concrete politics of program enactment
and change, or the receipt of services by individuals and families, the more
important it becomes to take into account ideologies of citizenship rights and
obligations, and the legal and administrative allocation of rights and duties.

Although the issue of status in a polity is an ancient one, the notion of
national citizenship began to emerge in the late seventeenth and the eighteenth
century. Nisbet locates the uniqueness of the post sixteenth century Western
political state in the:

> . . . relation between the absolute power [of the state] and the masses of the people under
> it. In the traditional Asiatic state prior to the present era, the state's authority rarely if ever
> touched the individual directly. Between the state and individual lay broad strata of

authority—family, clan, village, guild, sometimes caste—which were not penetrated by the power of the king or emperor (1974:613).

Bendix includes the spread of equal citizenship in his general definition of modernization (1967). But it was T. H. Marshall who most forcefully linked transformation of citizenship to the rise of the welfare state.

Civil, Political, and Social Rights

In his seminal lecture "Citizenship and Social Class" (1964), T. H. Marshall presented a rich analysis of the development of the concept of citizenship. His historical examples are primarily from English history but the concepts and thrust of his argument are meant to be generalizable to Western democracies.

Marshall defines citizenship as membership in a unified community with full and equal rights and duties. The three central areas of citizenship are: civil, political, and social. Civil rights include freedom of speech, the right to choose an occupation, and freedom to travel freely. Political rights range from participation in political decision-making to eligibility to be a member of the national legislative body. The scope of social rights includes protection from the free market in the areas of housing, employment, health, and education. Citizenship evolved slowly. Marshall's time line is roughly as follows: The eighteenth century brought in civil rights, the nineteenth century saw the advent of political rights, and the twentieth century is ushering in social rights.

Marshall recognized that the underlying philosophies of the elements of citizenship were quite antithetical to one another; especially, there were potential conflicts between civil and social rights. Civil rights stress the freedoms of the individual in relation to the state, whereas social rights emphasize the state's responsibility to provide for citizens when the market system is inadequate. (Offe's analysis, cited earlier, parallels Marshall's.)

It is important to note that Marshall's influential paper stresses only one half of the citizenship concept. It deals largely with the extension of rights and ignores the transformation of obligations. It is possible that obligation seemed transparent: Marshall wrote after World War II when the claims of the state on citizens were all too apparent. Indeed, some writers argue that the social solidarity created surrounding periods of war and the nation's need for a productive labor force in such periods together led to large spurts in welfare state programs during and immediately after wars (Janowitz 1976). Clearly, the modern state has demanded that citizens pay taxes, and obey the law. It has often demanded participation in the military and has made claims upon individuals for participation in institutions of education and in the labor force.

Conceptions of Citizenship and Sociological Research

Marshall focused upon the evolution of rights in a broad historical process. He was quite aware that a conflictual political process underlay this long development. Few sociologists have taken up Marshall's challenge to examine the politics of citizenship entitlements. (But see Zald 1985 for a discussion of the interaction of political change and legal entitlement in the American case.) Myles (1984) discusses pension policy in a comparative perspective, focusing upon its contradictory bases. On the one hand, pensions in a capitalist society are a deferred *wage* subject to workers' labor as earning power. On the other hand, in democratic societies with their impulse to equality, the pension is subject to a political process that asserts a citizen's entitlement to equality of status and treatment. Flat rate pensions, pressed by labor, are a reflection of the egalitarian and citizen impulse; the earnings replacement components are related to capitalist logic of distribution. Myles traces the political economy of these claims in different advanced societies.

Starting from the premise that the essence of the welfare state is more than guaranteed entitlements to income and services, Esping-Anderson & Korpi (unpublished paper) have designed a typology to explicate more fully the politics of citizenship within Western welfare states. Their ideal-type typology compares three regime types (conservative, liberal, socialist) on three dimensions: commodification, stratification, and distribution. Commodification is the extent to which income and services are tied to labor market participation rather than to citizenship rights. Stratification represents the crux of a society's status system. Esping-Anderson & Korpi conceptualize three status systems corresponding to the three ideal regime types as follows: hierarchy and corporative dependency correspond to conservatism; achievement and voluntarism, to liberalism; and universalism corresponds to socialism. The third key element to understanding the politics of welfare states, according to Esping-Anderson & Korpi, is the concept of equality. What is the basis of a society's income and reward structure: status/rank-based privilege, supply and demand, or equalization based on citizenship? Esping-Anderson & Korpi contend that debates surrounding the scope of welfare state programs implicitly or explicitly deal with questions regarding commodification, stratification, and equality.

SOCIAL RIGHTS AND WELFARE STATE BUREAUCRACIES

The expansion of social rights has been accompanied by the rise of large-scale welfare state bureaucracies that determine the content of these rights through the programs and services they control. These bureaucracies are mandated to determine eligibility, levels of entitlements, and the actual benefits citizens may receive. As social rights expanded to provide increased protection from poverty, illness, and ignorance for broader segments of the population, so have the welfare state bureaucracies expanded. The institutional rules that manifest these rights have been embodied in new organizational forms such as schools, hospitals, state employment commission offices, social security offices, and welfare departments. As institutional organizations, welfare state bureaucracies are structured to reflect and reaffirm the broad cultural, normative, and symbolic justifications of the welfare state (Meyer & Rowan 1977). A new class of welfare functionaries has emerged, broadly categorized as human service workers. This sector has been growing steadily in most Western democracies, and its growth has been least affected by economic crises (Singlemann 1978). It is through encounters with human service workers that citizens attempt to claim their social rights, and the response of these workers determines in very concrete ways the form and substance of citizens' rights.

In American society, welfare state bureaucracies reflect the reluctant acceptance by the polity of full social rights to its citizens. The ambivalent coexistence of two dominant social ideologies—work ethic and collective responsibility—that underpin welfare policies in the United States is expressed in the ambiguities and contradictions in the organization and operation of these bureaucracies (Gronbjerg et al 1979). First, many of these bureaucracies are highly decentralized, and most have limited jurisdiction restricting services to a defined population with prescribed needs. Second, these bureaucracies generally lack coherent administrative controls. Some must account to all three levels of government—federal, state, and local. Others, in the private sector, must be accountable to a self-selected constituency while still meeting certain government regulations. Third, these bureaucracies are riddled by ambiguous and conflicting goals and procedures. They may espouse self-sufficiency but in fact foster dependency. Fourth, the demand for their services generally exceeds their available resources, and this results in a system of bureaucratic rationing. Fiscal crises and uncertainty are endemic to these organizations. Fifth, in many of these organizations, lower level staff carry the burden of the bureaucratic encounter, thus exerting considerable influence over citizens (Lipsky 1980).

Because social rights are not universally granted to all citizens, nor are benefits equally distributed, welfare state bureaucracies are also differentiated by the level of entitlement of their beneficiaries (Hasenfeld 1985a). Some programs such as old age, survivors and health insurance, veterans benefits or unemployment benefits are contributory in the sense that entitlement to their benefits is based on past contributions through a payroll tax or service to the government. Other programs such as Aid to Families with Dependent children or Supplemental Security Income are means-tested; access is restricted to people in restricted categories of age and family status who fall below an income-wealth cutoff.

Welfare bureaucracies are, therefore, organized into segmented sectors according to the rights and entitlements they accord their recipients, and the corresponding administrative structures and processes. These in turn influence the content and form of the bureaucratic encounter. Four dimensions can be identified: (a) the social correlates of the demand for services that is linked to the extent of rights to and awareness of the sector's services; (b) the sector's structure, which includes the universality of its domain, the scarcity of its services, and the administrative control over them; (c) the sector administration, which refers to the discretion of officials and their level of professionalization; and (d) the norms governing the bureaucratic encounter. At one extreme, we find income security programs such as old age, survivors, and disability insurance. In such a program, beneficiaries automatically qualify if they have sufficient work-contribution history, and public awareness of such services is high. The mandate of the program is universal, the scarcity of the service is low, and the control is centralized. Officials' discretion is minimal, and the level of professionalization is low. The norms governing the encounter stress fairness and equity and do not stigmatize the beneficiaries. In such a sector the bureaucratic encounter is characterized by a high degree of utilization, a sense of power balance between applicants and officials, and a high degree of satisfaction.

At the other extreme are public assistance programs such as Aid to Families with Dependent Children. The rights for their services are circumscribed, and public awareness of their existence is limited. The domain of the program is selective, service scarcity is high, and control over the services is somewhat decentralized. Officials have more discretion, but their level of professionalization is low. The norms governing the encounter are stigmatizing and are often perceived as unfair. The bureaucratic encounter in these programs is characterized by a low rate of utilization, by a sense of powerlessness on the part of the applicant, and by a low degree of satisfaction (Hasenfeld & Zald 1987).

This analysis of the structural context of bureaucratic encounters can also be extended to cross-national comparisons. Studying bureaucratic encounters in the Soviet Union, Gitelman (1987) notes that, in contrast to the United States, the bureaucratic system is highly centralized, citizens' rights are weakly protected by the law, and demands for services far outstrip the supply. Hence, in general, the public view of the Soviet bureaucracy is far more negative than that of United States. Yet even in such a system, pension programs are evaluated more positively than housing departments, mostly because the chronic shortage of housing and its nonmandatory allocation system give officials considerable discretion over applicants. In Israel, although the service bureaucracy is centralized and the demand for services also exceeds their supply, Danet (1973) found that officials "gave the underdog a break" because of the overriding political norm of assisting immigrants to become integrated into society. Norway has an extensive social security system providing broad and universal protection. Its administrative structure is centralized, hierarchical, and the behavior of officials is controlled by a complex set of regulations. Nonetheless, even in such a system, many eligible people fail to use it because of the lack of information and understanding of the complex regulations, the strong prejudice in Norway against people who are dependent, and the long delays in processing claims (Oyen 1980).

The political economy of welfare state bureaucracies plays a significant role in influencing their location on the continuum noted above. It shapes the policies governing the substance and form of citizens' encounters with them. In a study of the administrative evolution of Social Security, Cates (1983) points out that in order to buttress the institutionalization of the organization, its leaders actively pursued the insurance metaphor while attempting to minimize its income protection provisions. Hence, despite the fact that they had control and authority over Aid to Dependent Children and had opportunities to change it into a universal income maintenance program, they opted not to do so for organizational maintenance reasons. Instead, they strengthened the insurance model of old age and survivor benefits in order to enhance the legitimization of the organization, and they shifted the responsibility for the welfare program to the states in order to divorce themselves from the precarious task of building legitimacy for protecting the poor and destitute. As a result, quite opposing definitions of clients and bureaucratic responses have emerged for the two programs.

The translation of social rights into administrative policies and bureaucratic procedures is also subject to the exigencies of both the external and internal political economy of the bureaucracy. These exigencies may include shifts in power of key interest groups, availability of fiscal resources, changes in demand for services, ascension of new administrative ideologies, and changes in service technologies (Wamsley & Zald 1976). These will inevitably have an effect on how the bureaucracy operationalizes its mandate. Therefore, a gap is likely to exist between the legislative intent in setting social rights and the actual implementation of these rights in the bureaucratic context. For example, public assistance programs promulgate benign or restrictive administrative regulations, depending on the extent to which they wish to expand or reduce their pool of applicants. As noted by Ritti & Hyman (1977), welfare departments relaxed their eligibility requirements during periods of economic prosperity and increasing political concern about urban unrest. These requirements, however, became more restrictive when economic conditions deteriorated and adverse political sentiments toward welfare recipients increased.

Lipsky (1984) refers to this process of restriction as bureaucratic disentitlement. He identifies several bureaucratic tactics that can effectively erode the social rights of applicants. These include rationing access to benefits, reducing available material assistance, failure to adjust benefits to prevailing economic conditions such as inflation or high unemployment, reducing the discretion of officials to respond to the needs of applicants, and curbing the influence of recipients and advocacy groups on bureaucratic policies. Similarly, when the politically conservative administrators of the Social Security Disability Insurance and the Supplementary Security Income programs wanted to halt the rise in claims and costs, they relied on the Continuing Disability Review process to terminate an unprecedented number of beneficiaries (Chambers 1985). Despite rulings by the federal courts that the new administrative procedures were in conflict with the Social Security Act, the Social Security Administration "declined to acquiesce" (Mashaw 1983:186).

FROM PRIVATE TROUBLES TO BUREAUCRATIC ENCOUNTERS

One of the paradoxes of the welfare state is that in order to exercise their social rights citizens must disclose their private problems to officials. Private problems and needs have to become public and have to be officially processed in order for applicants to establish an entitlement to welfare programs and benefits. Citizens must, therefore, make the decision about when to shift their problems from the private to the public domain. Such decisions will be greatly influenced by the perceived costs and payoff of publicly disclosing one's needs. To the extent that public disclosure is stigmatizing and the bureaucratic response demeaning, citizens will be reluctant to exercise their rights (Prottas 1981). The underutilization of services may be explained, in part, from this perspective. As noted by McKinlay (1972), in the case of medical services, several factors may contribute to the reluctance to utilize such services: (*a*) economic factors resulting in high access costs; (*b*) social psychological factors such as lack of both motivation to cope with the problems and knowledge about available services; (*c*) cultural beliefs and norms that inhibit public disclosure of need; and (*d*) organizational factors that set barriers to access to services. In general, the rate of utilization of services increases as the rights to them are publicly affirmed (Hasenfeld 1985a, Katz et al 1975).

The official processing of people in need constitutes the core of the bureaucratic encounter between citizens and officials. The processing of people encompasses several bureaucratic activities: (*a*) determination of the organizational jurisdiction over applicants and their needs; (*b*) a determination of eligibility to organizational goods and services; and (*c*) a determination of the amount of goods and services to which the applicant is entitled. In these decisions the interests of applicants and officials may conflict. On the one hand, applicants are motivated by personal needs and circumstances. They tend to apply personalistic and particularistic criteria to define their needs and make their claims. On the other hand, officials are guided by bureaucratic rules and regulations that are based on a set of universalistic criteria applied uniformly to all applicants. While officials may exercise considerable discretion, they are guided by "normal case" conceptions which typify clients into organizationally acceptable categories that selectively recognize or ignore information about the applicant (Hasenfeld 1983). Hence, the nature of the encounter is such that two different sets of values and norms are juxtaposed. The bureaucratic encounter is both an information exchange and a negotiation and conflict management process through which the applicant's normative framework and expectations are brought in line with the organization's.

The compatibility of interests between applicants and officials is significantly influenced by the choice each has to engage in the encounter. Applicants vary in the degree of freedom they may have to initiate the encounter. This ranges from application to an employment placement program, which is voluntary, to an involuntary commitment to a psychiatric hospital. Officials also vary in the discretion they have to engage in an encounter. While fee-for-service physicians have considerable discretion, public school teachers have none. The intersection of these two dimensions produces four different types of bureaucratic encounters that define the position of the applicant vis-a-vis the bureaucracy (for similar typologies see Thompson 1962, Carlson 1964, Lefton & Rosengren 1966). These types, labeled as "customer," "consumer," "client," and "inmate" (see Table 2), affect both the form and content of the encounter.

In the "customer" type, the applicants' main concern is to select the service provider most suitable to their particular needs and interests, while the provider's concern is to attract applicants who are amenable and responsive to its mode of service. The matching process is analogous to an exchange in a free market, and the symmetry in the selection increases the likelihood of high compatibility of interests and mutual satisfaction, as is the case of fee-for-service medical services (Freidson 1970). Yet, both applicants and providers must expend significant resources to attain a satisfactory match.

In the "consumer" type, the bureaucracy faces the burden of requests for service by potentially undesirable applicants who thus increase the service costs to the organization. Because officials, as in the case of hospital emergency room or public employment placement offices, cannot control the

Table 2 Types of bureaucratic encounters

		Applicant's freedom of choice	
		HIGH	LOW
Official's discretion:	HIGH	Customer	Client
	LOW	Consumer	Inmate

input of applicants, they may resort to "cooling out" tactics (Clark 1960) which may include lengthy waiting periods, excessive bureaucratic processing, and provision of low quality services (Hasenfeld & Steinmetz 1981, Schwartz 1975). In these encounters we expect to find a small but significant group of disgruntled applicants.

The "client" mode is particularly common for many publicly administered social services. In these, applicants have little choice because of the organizational monopoly over the services, while officials have significant discretion in determining who qualifies for their services. Applicants must acquiesce to organizational rules over which they have little control if they are to obtain services. Hence, the encounter acquires coercive elements. Social workers administering personal social services can use their monopoly to coerce clients to engage in certain modes of behavior as a precondition for receipt of the services (Handler 1973). Although the potential for conflict and dissatisfaction is fairly high, clients will generally accept these preconditions as a small price for highly needed services for which they have few alternatives.

Finally, the "inmate" type of a bureaucratic encounter is also characteristic of many welfare state bureaucracies, particularly those that are means-tested. In programs such as Aid to Families with Dependent Children or food stamps, the applicants have little chance to resort to alternative services, and officials have little formal control over eligibility. In such encounters the potential for conflict between applicants and officials is particularly high. It is for this reason that the rate of utilization of these services is particularly low and citizens utilize them only as an act of last resort or when coerced to do so.

It should be further emphasized that the protection of the applicant's rights becomes more problematic as the discretion of officials increases and the applicant's choices decrease (Handler 1979). On the one hand, the increased dependency of applicants on officials has a chilling effect on their readiness to challenge the official's actions. On the other hand, the increased discretion of low-level officials reduces the effectiveness of administrative control over their behavior.

BUREAUCRATIC ENCOUNTERS AS POWER-DEPENDENCE RELATIONS

The study of bureaucratic encounters has generally been atheoretical and guided by a potpourri of perspectives ranging from social psychological (Katz & Danet 1973) to political (Lipsky 1980). Danet (1981) in a comprehensive review of the field has proposed the following general model which she used to organize diverse research findings (see Figure 1).

This is clearly a very eclectic approach that does not readily provide for

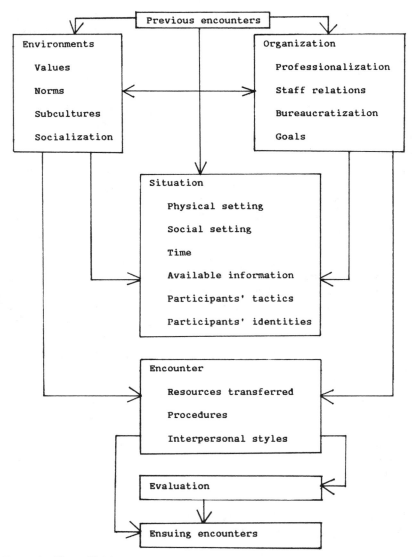

Figure 1   Client-official encounter. (Adapted from Danet 1981:384)

theory building and verification. Nor does it address the context of most bureaucratic encounters—the welfare state. To do that, we begin with another paradox of the welfare state. Paraphrasing Coleman (1974), to gain the benefits of the state, individuals must give over the use of certain rights, resources, and power to welfare state bureaucracies. That is, by vesting welfare state bureaucracies with the power to act on their behalf, individual citizens lose their own power over the direction these organizations may take. Individuals who contribute to Social Security through a payroll tax are assured of certain benefits, but they lose control over their own contributions and have little influence over the administrative policies and regulations of Social Security Administration. As noted by Coleman (1974), vesting the bureaucracy with power in exchange for benefits underlies the contract between the individual and the organization.

Thus, to understand the nature of the bureaucratic encounter, we utilize the theory of power-dependence relations developed by Emerson (1974). We conceive of the bureaucratic encounter as a series of transactions through which resources and services are exchanged between the citizen and the bureaucracy. The citizen seeks to obtain goods and services controlled by the organization, while the organization needs the citizen as a resource to justify its existence, to obtain fiscal resources, to operate its service technology, and to demonstrate its effectiveness. Both parties seek to obtain these resources and services in a manner that optimizes their respective payoff and minimizes their costs (Hasenfeld 1983). The dependence of citizens on the bureaucracy is a direct function of the need they have for the resources and services controlled by it, and it is an inverse function of the availability of these resources and services elsewhere. The power of the organization over the citizen thus equals the dependence of the citizen on the organization. Similarly, the dependence of the bureaucracy on the citizen is a direct function of its needs for the resources the citizen controls and is an inverse function of its ability to obtain these resources elsewhere. The bureaucracy is said to have a power advantage over the citizen when its dependence on the citizen is less than the citizen's dependence on it (Cook & Emerson 1978).

Our basic proposition is that, unless constrained, the party with the power advantage will use it to influence the parameters of the bureaucratic encounter in order to maximize its payoff and to minimize costs. Structurally, welfare state bureaucracies have a considerable power advantage over the beneficiaries of their services. They control a far greater pool of resources than any natural actor; they generally tend to have a monopoly or quasi-monopoly over their services; they enjoy a large pool of potential applicants (particularly since the demand for their services typically exceeds their supply); and citizens seldom control directly the flow of resources to the bureaucracy.

Welfare state bureaucracies will use their power advantage to structure the bureaucratic encounter in a manner that buttresses their political economies, and much of the research on people processing can be understood from this perspective (for a review of these studies see Hasenfeld & Steinmetz 1981). This is manifested in several ways. Welfare state bureaucracies tend to prefer applicants who reflect positively on the evaluative criteria used by the external legitimizing and funding bodies (Greenley 1980). Similarly, these bureaucracies prefer to encourage applicants who can bolster the mobilization of organizational resources and to avoid applicants who drain these resources. Welfare state bureaucracies will structure the encounters so that they reaffirm dominant institutional ideologies (Meyer & Rowan 1977). Thus, organizational definitions of deservingness and worthiness will influence the nature and scope of services that applicants are likely to obtain (Roth 1972, Prottas 1979). Finally, the bureaucracies will develop differential tracking and routing of applicants to facilitate the smooth operation of their service technologies (Lipsky 1980, Hasenfeld & Cheung 1985). The assignment of students to different curriculum tracks epitomizes this process (Rosenbaum 1976).

Citizens, too, have power resources they can use to negotiate favorable outcomes. By withholding their demand for the organization's services, they increase the need of the organization for them as a resource. Hirschman (1970) describes this as the exit option. Citizens may coalesce to put collective pressure on the organization to provide more favorable services. This is the voice option. Citizens may also evoke the power of third parties such as legislative and judicial agencies to pressure the organization to meet their needs. Acquiring knowledge and information about their social rights and making the organization dependent on them for fiscal resources through vouchers also strengthen the negotiation power of citizens vis-à-vis officials.

In general, citizens with greater access to power resources such as income and education are able to negotiate more favorable outcomes, which in turn reinforce their power position. Hasenfeld (1985) found that citizens with higher income have higher expectations regarding the outcome of their bureaucratic encounters, are more likely to interact with contributory programs, and obtain what they want from the bureaucracy. Interacting with contributory, rather than means-tested, programs gives citizens a greater sense of influence over officials and, thus, the perception of getting what they want. As a consequence, the nature and outcome of the encounter with welfare state bureaucracies is sensitive to the citizen's social class. That is, both welfare state bureaucracies and encounters with them are differentiated in quality and results in response to the social differentiation among the citizens. For example, while most citizens have access to health care services, social class position as reflected in the ability to pay, access to medical insurance, and ability to absorb access costs make a significant difference in the nature and quality of care citizens will obtain (Alford 1972, Starr 1985). The same can be said about access to public education or mental health services.

Herein lies another paradox of the welfare state. The expansion of the welfare state has been directed at increasing the scope of its protection to a widening circle of citizens, including those from lower socioeconomic groups. Moreover, the redistributive function of the welfare state attenuates social class differences. Nonetheless, welfare state policy makers and bureaucracies are not immune from the power and influence associated with the social class position of their constituencies. As programs and services are structured to reflect the power of their constituencies, they, in turn, become an indispensable vehicle in the maintenance and advancement of the constituents' social class position.

THE PROTECTION OF SOCIAL RIGHTS

The power advantage of welfare state bureaucracies poses a threat to the social rights of their recipients. That power is enhanced by the administrative discretion enjoyed by officials. Curbing the discretion of officials through detailed rules and regulations (i.e. administrative law) is a remedy that may actually exacerbate the problem because the rules may become so complex and voluminous that they are ignored or not implemented. More seriously, however, excessive rules may actually increase the discretion of low level staff by making it much more difficult and costly to monitor their behavior (Prottas 1979). There is, therefore, a clear recognition in administrative law that "the citizen has a right to keep officials from straying beyond some large and loose requirements of clear statutory language, procedural regularity, and substantive rationality. Within these boundaries there lies a gigantic policy space, invisible to the legal order because devoid of justiciable rights" (Mashaw 1983:9).

To fill this void, welfare state bureaucracies develop what Mashaw (1983) terms "bureaucratic justice" which is based on the following elements: (*a*) It attempts to maximize accuracy and efficiency; (*b*) its main objective is to implement the legislative intent; (*c*) its system of internal control and accountability is based on hierarchical relations; and (*d*) the key aim of the bureaucratic encounter is information processing. The bureaucracy develops a decision-making system that circumscribes but does not eliminate discretion, yet promotes universalism, predictability, and accountability. Such a system attempts to limit intrusion into the personal privacy of the applicant, to promote equality through its decision-making system, and to give applicants some measure of control through an appeal procedure.

Bureaucratic justice works reasonably well as long as there is compatibility of interests between citizens and the bureaucracy. It breaks down when bureaucratic needs emanating from the organizational political economy overwhelm the needs of applicants, as noted in the case of Social Security Disability Insurance. Bureaucratic justice ultimately reflects the values and norms of the dominant interest groups in the bureaucracy, which often do not include the recipients of services.

In the United States, judicial intervention has been a major means to regulate the duties and responsibilities of the welfare state bureaucracies and to define the rights of the recipients of their services. As noted by Cranston (1985:172) "the strength of legal rights depends on the remedies available for their implementation." In reviewing these remedies, Cranston (1985:180) points out that "entitlement to state social welfare benefits is grounded in statute, rather than in contractual, property, equitable, or constitutional principles. Although *Goldberg v. Kelly* granted welfare recipients procedural rights, and hinted toward the desirability of treating welfare entitlements as property rather than gratuity, this concept was never adopted by the courts."

Pearlman (1977) traces changes in judicial and legislative precedence in the arena of public assistance law. In the early 1970s a shift began toward recognizing that the poor had been treated like second-class citizens and that people have a right to public assistance. Some of the early pathbreaking cases involved disputes over regulations governing qualifications for general assistance and AFDC. For example, in 1969 the US Supreme Court decided *Shapiro v. Thompson* in which the judges struck down a one-year residence requirement for welfare assistance, since it violated the right to travel. To quote Pearlman:

> The Court rejected the argument that public assistance benefits are a 'privilege' and not a 'right', and also rejected as a 'compelling interest' preservation of fiscal integrity of state public assistance programs. (1977:38)

Good (1984) argues that even in the mid-1980s, the legal right of the poor to assistance is still a slippery issue. Good delineates some of the legal and procedural obstacles to the extension of the legal rights of the poor. Courts, in general, are quite deferential to legislative decisions. For example, the use of the equal protection clause requires a case to pass one of two tests: the rational relation test, which is very deferential to legislative decisions, or the strict scrutiny test, which requires a state to show that the categories it has created are necessary for achieving a compelling state interest. Discrimination on the basis of race and national origin are suspect criteria, but age and wealth generally are not suspect criteria. Good notes that the US Supreme Court has set some limits on the legitimate grounds for the denial of "vital benefits." For example, states cannot deny welfare benefits to aliens or illegitimate children.

The mentally ill provide an interesting case for a discussion of citizen rights and legal rights within the welfare state. For most potential social welfare program target groups, the relevant analytic and policy-oriented questions include: boundaries of deservingness, and the scope and level of coverage. It is a given that state intervention on behalf of these groups is desirable. The role of the state vis-à-vis the mentally ill involves a broader range of questions—questions involving positive and negative rights. There is the common question (as in the case of all social welfare programs) of whether it is the state's responsibility to provide for the mentally ill. Should this be a public and not private responsibility (i.e. a responsibility of the family)? In addition, there are legal questions concerning the limits of the state's right to intervene.

Specifically, under what conditions can someone be involuntarily committed to a state institution? In line with criminal law, the overriding rationale for involuntary commitment is a perceived potential danger to society. The theoretical and ethical questions are: How accurately can psychiatrists and judges "predict" the potential for dangerous behavior (Gulevich & Bourne 1970, Dershowitz 1973)? To the extent that this is a slippery process, unfavorable light is thrown on the fundamental rationale of civil commitment (Stone 1975).

Once committed, the mentally ill raise another issue in the protection of rights: the right to refuse treatment. The central question is: What are the workable boundaries of competent informed consent? There are precedents that disallow mere commitment to be used to establish incompetency. The critical components of competent informed consent are: that the patient is able to make the decision regarding treatment; that the doctors must give reasonable information regarding what the treatment involves; and that the conditions of consent—patients' consent—should be given freely (Stone 1975).

Legal rights and the role of the courts are especially crucial for the mentally ill since as a group they have very little political power. They must rely heavily on the courts to ensure the protection of their rights.

Aside from use of courts to enforce social rights, mechanisms within organizations such as ombudsman, tribunals, or fair hearing and appeals boards have been established. These have been shown to be of some success (Danet 1981, Hill 1981), but they are limited in their effectiveness. First, they are passive mechanisms which must be activated by citizens. Hence, their use is a function of the knowledge and motivation of the citizens about them. Second, they require commitment of time and resources that not all citizens may be able to afford. Third, citizens may feel intimidated in using them, unless such mechanisms are widely institutionalized. Finally, citizens may be afraid that using such mechanisms may jeopardize future encounters.

One of the chief difficulties in reliance on legal remedies is the fact that individuals do not have equal capacity to invoke them, and those most likely to suffer from bureaucratic injustices are least likely to be able to afford to seek these remedies (Cranston 1985, Handler, 1979). As an adversarial process, the outcome of litigations against the bureaucracy is affected in a major way by the legal resources citizens can marshal.

THE EVALUATION OF BUREAUCRATIC ENCOUNTERS

Reviewing the research on client evaluation of bureaucratic encounters, Nelson (1981) points to a series of substantive and methodological issues. Because many of the studies lack an explicit theoretical framework, it is difficult to assess the results. Studies that rely on measures of client satisfaction are plagued by global and insensitive measures. The results of such studies are also affected by uncontrollable variables such as expectations. Finally, the research focus of the investigator—relationship-centered or problem-centered—influences the results.

Two distinctively different approaches to the evaluation of bureaucratic encounters lead to opposing conclusions (Hasenfeld 1985a). The first, articulated by Lipsky (1980), conceptualizes many welfare state bureaucracies such as welfare departments, public hospitals, and public schools as "street level bureaucracies" that have the following characteristics: (a) The demand for services far outstrips the available supply; (b) service goals are ambiguous and performance measures problematic; (c) applicants must assume a role of a client or inmate; (d) lower level staff have considerable discretion which they use to ration services to applicants; and (e) lower level staff find their work alienating because of their inability to respond to applicant needs.

Case studies employing such a perspective (Roth 1972, Prottas 1979, Lipsky 1984) find that bureaucratic encounters in such organizations are alienating to many applicants, and most importantly, result in inequitable, discriminatory, and unfair distribution of services. It must be emphasized that most of the studies are of involuntary bureaucratic encounters. The difficulty with these studies is twofold. First, the theoretical perspective is anti-bureaucratic and, thus, biases the findings. Second, because of the participant observation methodology, it is possible that mostly the deviant cases were sought out, and thus the generalizability of the findings is problematic.

The second approach to evaluating bureaucratic encounters is based on surveys of recipients of services in a wide range of welfare state bureaucracies. This research concludes that, in general, recipients are quite satisfied with their bureaucratic encounters (Katz et al 1975, Glampston & Goldberg 1976, Nelson 1979, Goodsell 1980, Hasenfeld 1985a). All these studies find that the overwhelming majority of applicants to Social Security are satisfied with their experience (80% and more), while a smaller number are satisfied with their encounter with welfare departments (45% or more). A majority of applicants to these and other programs find officials to be fair and helpful. It is interesting that Glampson & Goldberg (1976) found that while most clients were satisfied with their encounters with their social workers and thought they were treated fairly, the social workers felt more pessimistic about their clients' satisfaction.

Most of these studies are based on attitudes and perceptions of samples of recipients. The difficulty with them is their sole reliance on post factum attitudinal measures of satisfaction without behavioral verification. As Gutek (1978:49) put it: "One reason for distrusting measures of satisfaction is simply that people seem to be satisfied with everything that social scientists ask them about." There is a sense that respondents tend to give answers considered socially acceptable. In addition, these surveys fail to take into account differences among recipients and programs. Hasenfeld (1985a) found that recipients with personal resources tend to be more satisfied with the encounter, and that means-tested programs (which are more like street-level bureaucracies) tend to evoke more dissatisfaction than contributory programs.

The evaluation of bureaucratic encounters requires, therefore, a much more comprehensive and sophisticated research design than has been used so far. It must be based on careful sampling of the four major types of encounters (client, consumer, customer, inmate) with sufficient samples of organizations and recipients. It must combine attitudinal and behavioral measures, and the measures themselves must be specific and detailed. Ideally, the design should be longitudinal in order both to capture applicants' expectations before the encounter and to follow the experience of recipients with the organization.

Still, the case can be made that the underlying reason for the general satisfaction with bureaucratic encounters is the acceptable work of officials providing the services. Although officials may operate under varying constraints, they are generally guided by reasonably uniform and fair standard operating procedures. The bureaucratic structure, in a Weberian sense, is expressly designed to reinforce these standard operating procedures. Although deviations may occur, they are more likely to be the exception than the rule. Therefore, what may be at issue is not the fairness of the procedures and their universalistic application, or the behavior of the officials, but rather the perceived substantive fairness and equity of the rules themselves which may indeed discriminate against certain groups of applicants.

CONCLUSIONS

The growth of the welfare state creates a new set of citizenship entitlements, a set of governmentally allocated quasi-property rights. The scope of the welfare state, the range of the programs, the criteria for access, the legal constraints, and the characteristics of specific "products" delivered, create a variety of bureaucratic encounters. This bureaucratic context can be analyzed in terms of its power-dependence components—the relative strength and options of bureaucrats and clients. The power-dependence balance affects the extent to which citizens achieve entitlements with dignity.

This chapter has reviewed theories and research on the determinants of the expansion of the welfare state, the transformation of citizenship rights, and the evaluation of bureaucratic encounters. But research inevitably lags reality. It is clear that from 1975 onward, the welfare state entered a period of retrenchment. Although budgets for core programs for the aged increased, in many areas the federal presence came under attack. Fiscal constraints and a conservative resurgence led to redirecting the mechanisms for services provisions. Privatization and third-party insurance mechanisms increasingly were used as modes for delivering services (Gilbert 1983). What is unclear is the impact of these changes on the quality and quantity of services in different welfare arenas. The deinstitutionalization movement increases citizen freedom and street destitution (Lerman 1982, 1985); the inclusion of mental health treatment as part of medical insurance massively spreads access to short-term treatment; the variety of after-care programs presents protean problems of organizational control (Vladeck 1980).

Moreover, in an era of retrenchment and disillusion, some contemporary students of social policy in American believe that a balanced conception of citizenship obligation and welfare entitlements can have positive effects on the effectiveness of programs. Garfinkel (1985) argues that programs to enforce parental obligation to support children are an effective way to combat child poverty in America. A combination of state income subsidy and garnished wages can gain public support and achieve adequate child welfare. Mead (1986) shows how precise work expectations for welfare recipients that are, in fact, enforced and reasonably structured lead to higher labor force participation. It is important to note that even if "workfare" programs were not clearly effective in reducing welfare costs or raising labor force participation, in a "liberal" regime, they have greater legitimacy. In a liberal regime, government support is earned on the basis of labor force claims.

What is clear is that citizen obligations and rights are in a changed state of tension as the welfare state is adapted to new political and economic constraints. These changes will be manifested in the bureaucratic encounters between citizens and officials, particularly in regard to access, expectations, and responses. Because bureaucratic encounters are a microcosmic reflection of the relations between citizens and the welfare state, they will mirror the unfolding of these relations.

Literature Cited

Alford, R. 1972. The political economy of health care: Dynamics without change." *Poli. Soc.* 2:127–64

Alford, R., Friedland, R. 1985. *Powers of Theory: Capitalism, the State, and Democracy.* Cambridge: Cambridge Univ. Press

Bendix, R. 1967. Tradition and modernity reconsidered. *Comp. Stud. Soc. Hist.* 9:292–313

Carlson, R. O. 1964. Environmental constraints and organizational consequences: The public school and its clients. In *Behavioral Science and Educational Administration,* ed. D. E. Griffiths, pp. 262–76. Chicago, IL: Natl. Soc. Stud. Educ.

Castles, F. G. 1982. The impact of parties on public expenditures. In *The Impact of Par-*ties: Politics and Policies in Democratic Capitalist States,* ed. F. G. Castles, pp. 21–96. London: Sage

Cates, J. 1983. *Insuring Inequality: Administrative Leadership in Social Security, 1935–54.* Ann Arbor, Mich: Univ. Mich. Press

Chambers, D. E. 1985. Policy weaknesses and political opportunities. *Soc. Serv. Rev.* 59:1–17

Clark, B. 1960. The cooling-out function in higher education. *Am. J. Sociol.* 65:569–76

Coleman, J. 1974. *Power and the Structure of Society.* New York: Norton

Cook, K., Emerson, R. 1978. Power, equity and commitment in exchange networks. *Am. Sociol. Rev.* 43:721–39

Cranston, R. 1985. *Legal Foundations of the*

Welfare State. London: Weidenfeld & Nicolson

Cutright, P. 1965. Political structure, economic development, and national social security programs. *Am. J. Sociol.* 70:537–50

Danet, B. 1973. Giving the underdog a break. In *Bureaucracy and the Public: A Reader in Client Official Relations,* ed. E. Katz, B. Danet pp. 329–37. New York: Basic Books

Danet, B. 1981. Client-organization relationships. In *Handbook of Organizational Design,* ed. P. C. Nystrom, W. H. Starbuck, pp. 382–428. NY: Oxford Univ. Press

Downs, A. 1960. Why the government budget is too small in a democracy. *World Polit.* 12:541–63

Dershowitz, A. 1973. Preventative confinement: A suggested framework for constitutional analyses. *Tex. Law Rev.* 51:1306

Emerson, R. M. 1974. Social exchange theory. *Ann. Rev. Sociol.* 1:335–62

Esping-Anderson, G. 1978. Social class, social democracy, and the state: Party policy and party decomposition in Denmark and Sweden. *Comp. Polit.* 11:42–58

Esping-Anderson, G. 1981. From welfare state to democratic socialism: The politics of economic democracy in Denmark and Sweden. *Polit. Power Soc. Theory* 2:111–40

Freidson, E. 1970. *Profession of Medicine.* New York: Dodd, Mead

Garfinkel, I. 1985. The role of child support insurance in antipoverty policy. *Ann. Am. Acad. Polit.* 479:119–31

Gilbert, N. 1983. *Capitalism and the Welfare State.* New Haven, Conn: Yale Univ. Press

Gitelman, Z. 1987. Unequal encounters: The citizen and the soviet welfare bureaucracies. In *Social Welfare and the Social Services: USA/USSR,* ed. G. W. Lapidus, G. E. Swanson. Berkeley, Calif: Inst. Int. Stud.

Glampson, A. and M. Goldberg. 1976. Post Seebohm social services: The consumer's view point. *Soc. Work Today.* 8:9–14

Good, M. 1984. Freedom from want: The failure of United States courts to protect subsistence rights." *Human Rights Q.* 6:335–65

Goodsell, D. T. 1980. Client evaluation of three welfare programs. *Admin. Soc.* 12:123–36

Goldberg v. Kelly. 1970. 397 U.S. 254

Gronbjerg, K., Street, D., Suttles, G. 1979. *Poverty and Social Change.* Chicago, Ill: Univ. Chicago Press

Greenley, J. R. 1980. Organizational processes and client selectivity in social welfare. In *Welfare or Bureaucracy? Problems of Matching Social Services to Clients' Needs,* ed. D. Grunow, F. Hegrer, pp. Cambridge, Mass: Oelgeschlager, Gunn, & Hain

Gulevich, G. D., Bourne, P. G. 1970. Mental illness and violence. In *Violence and the Struggle for Existence,* ed. D. Daniels, M. Gilula, F. Ochberg, pp. 309–26. Boston, Mass: Little, Brown

Gutek, B. 1978. Strategies for studying client satisfaction. *J. Social Issues* 34:44–56

Hage, J., Hannemann, R. 1977. *The Growth of the Welfare State in Four Western European Societies: A Comparison of Three Paradigms.* Madison, Wisc: Inst. Res. Poverty

Handler, J. 1973. The coercive social worker: British lessons for American social services. Chicago, Ill: Rand McNally

Handler, J. 1978. *Social Movements and the Legal System: A Theory of Law Reform and Social Change.* New York: Academic Press

Handler, J. 1979. *Protecting the Social Service Client: Legal and Structural Controls on Official Discretion.* New York: Academic Press

Hasenfeld, Y. 1983. *Human Service Organizations.* Englewood Cliffs, NJ: Prentice-Hall

Hasenfeld, Y. 1985. Citizens' encounters with welfare state bureaucracies. *Soc. Service Rev.* 59:622–35

Hasenfeld, Y., Cheung, P. 1985. People-processing in the juvenile court. *Am. J. Sociol.* 90:801–24

Hasenfeld, Y., Steinmetz, D. 1981. Client-official encounters in social service agencies." In *The Public Encounter: Where State and Citizen Meet,* ed. C. T. Goodsell, pp. 83–101. Bloomington, Ind: Indiana Univ. Press

Hasenfeld, Y., Zald, M. 1987. Client-organization encounters in the United States' social welfare sector. In *Social Welfare and the Social Services: USA/USSR,* ed. G. W. Lapidus, G. E. Swanson, Berkeley, Calif: Inst. Int. Stud.

Heclo, H. 1974. *Modern Social Politics in Britain and Sweden.* New Haven, Conn: Yale Univ. Press

Heclo, H. 1981. Toward a New Welfare State? In *The Development of Welfare States in Europe and America,* ed. P. Flora, A. J. Heidenheimer, pp. 383–406. New Brunswick, NJ: Transaction

Hill, L. 1981. Bureaucratic monitoring mechanisms. In *The Public Encounter: Where State and Citizen Meet,* ed. C. T. Goodsell, pp. 160–88. Bloomington, Ind: Ind. Univ. Press

Hirschman, A. O. 1970. *Exit. Voice and Loyalty.* Cambridge, Mass: Harvard Univ. Press

Jackman, R. W. 1986. Elections and the democratic class struggle. *World Polit.* 39:123–46

Janowitz, M. 1976. *Social Control of the Welfare State*. New York: Elsevier

Katz, D., Gutek, B. A., Kahn, R. A., Burton, E. 1975. *Bureaucratic Encounters: A Pilot Study in the Evaluation of Government Services*. Ann Arbor, Mich: Inst. Soc. Res.

Katz, E., Danet, B., ed. 1973. *Bureaucracy and the Public: A Reader in Client Official Relations*. New York: Basic Books

Korpi, W. 1978. *The Working Class in Welfare Capitalism: Work, Unions, and Politics in Sweden*. London: Routledge & Kegan Paul

Korpi, W. 1980. Social policy and distributional conflict in capitalist democracies: A preliminary comparative framework. *West. Eur. Polit.* 3:296–316

Kramer, S. 1971. Short-term fluctuations in U.S. voting behavior, 1896–1964. *Am. Polit. Sci. R.* 65:131–43

Lefton, M., Rosengren, W. R. 1966. Organizations and clients: Lateral and longitudinal dimensions. *Am. Sociol. R.* 31:802–10

Lerman, P. 1982. *Deinstitutionalization and the Welfare State*. New Brunswick, NJ: Rutgers Univ. Press

Lerman, P. 1985. Deinstitutionalization and welfare policies. *Ann. Am. Polit.* 479:132–55

Lipsky, M. 1980. *Street-Level Bureaucracy: Dilemmas of the Individual in Public Services*. New York: Russell Sage Found.

Lipsky, M. 1984. Bureaucratic disentitlement in social welfare programs. *Soc. Serv. Rev.* 58:3–27

Marshall, T. H. 1964. *Class, Citizenship, and Social Development*. Garden City, NY: Doubleday

Mashaw, J. 1983. *Bureaucratic Justice: Managing Social Security Disability Claims*. New Haven, Conn: Yale Univ. Press

McKinlay, J. 1972. Some approaches and problems in the study of the use of services—An overview. *J. Health Soc.* 13:115–52

Mead, L. 1986. *Beyond Entitlement: The Social Obligations of Citizenship*. New York: Free Press

Meyer, J. W., Rowan, B. 1977. Institutionalized organizations: Formal structure as myth and ceremony. *Am. J. Sociol.* 83:340–63

Myles, J. 1984. *Old Age in the Welfare State: The Political Economy of Public Pensions*. Boston, Mass: Little Brown

Nelson, R. 1979. Clients and bureaucracies: Applicant evaluation at public human service and benefit programs. Presented at the Ann. Meet. Am. Polit. Sci. Assoc., Washington

Nelson, R. 1981. Client evaluation of social programs. In *The Public Encounter: Where State and Citizen Meet*, ed. C. T. Goodsell,

pp. 23–42. Bloomington, Ind: Ind. Univ. Press

Nisbet, R. 1974. Citizenship: Two traditions. *Soc. Res.* 41:612–37

Niskanen, W. 1971. *Bureaucracy and Representative Government*. Chicago: Aldine

Nordhaus, W. 1975. The political business cycle. *Rev. Econ. Stud.* 42:160–90

O'Connor, J. 1973. *The Fiscal Crisis of the State*. New York: St. Martin's Press

Offe, C. 1984. *Contradictions of the Welfare State*. Cambridge, Mass: The MIT Press

Orloff, A. S., Skocpol, T. 1984. Why not equal protection? Explaining the politics of public social spending in Britain, 1900–1911, and the United States, 1880's–1920." *Am. Sociol. Rev.* 49:726–50

Oyen, R. 1980. Structural rationing of social service benefits in a welfare state. In *Welfare or Bureaucracy? Problems of Matching Social Services to Clients' Needs*, ed. D. Grunow, F. Hegner, pp. Cambridge, Mass: Oelgeschlager, Gunn, Hain

Pampel, F. C., Williamson, J. B. 1985. Public Pension Expenditures. *Am. Sociol. Rev.* 50:782–98

Pearlman, L. A. 1977. Welfare, administration, and rights of welfare recipients. *Hastings Law J.* 29:19–71

Prottas, J. 1979. *People Processing: Street-Level Bureaucracy in Public Service Bureaucracies*. Lexington, Mass: DC Heath

Prottas, J. 1981. The cost of free services: Organizational impediments to access to public services. *Public Admin. Rev.* 41:526–34

Pryor, F. 1968. *Public Expenditures in Communist and Capitalist Nations*. London: Allen & Union

Quadagno, J. S. 1984. Welfare capitalism and the Social Security Act of 1935. *Am. Sociol. Rev.* 49:632–47

Quadagno, J. S. 1985. Two models of welfare state development: Reply to Skocpol and Amenta." *Am. Sociol. Rev.* 50:575–78

Rimlinger, G. 1971. *Welfare Policy and Industrialization in Europe, America, and Russia*. New York: Wiley

Ritti, R. R., Hyman, D. W. 1977. The administration of poverty: Lessons from the welfare explosion. *Soc. Problems* 25:157–75

Rosenbaum, J. 1976. *Making Inequality: The Curriculum of High School Tracking*. New York: Wiley

Roth, J. 1972. Some contingencies of the moral evaluation and control of clientele: The care of the hospital emergency service. *Am. J. Sociol.* 77:839–56

Schwartz, B. 1975. *Queuing and Waiting: Studies in the Social Organization of Access and Delay*. Chicago, Ill: Univ. Chicago Press

Shalev, M. 1983a. Class politics and the Western welfare state. In *Evaluating the Welfare State: Social and Political Perspectives*, ed. S. E. Spiro, E. Yuchtman-Yaar, pp. 27–50. New York: Academic Press

Shalev, M. 1983b. The social democratic model and beyond: Two 'generations' of comparative research on the welfare state. *Comp. Sociol. Res.* 6:315–51

Shapiro v. Thompson. 1969. 394 U.S. 618

Singlemann, J. 1978. *From Agriculture to Services: The Transformation of Industrial Employment*. Beverly Hills, Calif: Sage

Skocpol, T. 1980. Political response to capitalist crisis: Neo-Marxist theories of the state and the case of the New Deal." *Polit. Soc.* 10:155–201

Skocpol, T., Amenta, E. 1985. Did capitalists shape social security?" *Am. Sociol. Rev.* 50:572–75

Skocpol, T., Finegold, K. 1982. State capacity and economic intervention in the early New Deal. *Polit. Sci. Q.* 97:255–78

Skocpol, T., Ikenberry, J. 1983. The political formation of the American welfare state in historical and comparative perspective. *Comp. Soc. Res.* 6:87–148

Starr, P. 1985. *Health Care and the Poor: The Last Twenty Years*. Madison, Wisc: Univ. Wisc. Press

Stone, A. A. 1975. *Mental Health and Law: A System in Transition*. Rockville, Md: Natl. Inst. Mental Health

Tarschys, D. 1975. The growth of public expenditures: Nine modes of explanation. *Scand. Polit. Stud.* 10:9–31

Therborn, G. 1984a. Classes and states: Welfare state developments, 1881–1981. *Stud. Polit. Econ.* 14:7–42

Therborn, G. 1984b. The prospects of labour and the transformation of advanced capitalism. *New Left Rev.* 145:5–38

Tufte, E. 1975. Determinants of the outcome of midterm congressional elections. *Am. Polit. Sci. Rev.* 69:812–26

Tufte, E. 1978. *Political Control of the Economy*. Princeton, NJ: Princeton Univ. Press

Wagner, A. 1883. The nature of the fiscal economy. In *Classics in the Theory of Public Finance* (1958), ed. R. A. Musgrave, A. R. Peacock, pp. 1–8. Boston, Mass: Little, Brown

Weir, M., Skocpol, T. 1985. State structures and the possibilities for Keynesian responses to the great depression in Sweden, Britain, and the United States. In *Bringing the State Back In*, ed. P. B. Evans, D. Rueschemeyer, T. Skocpol. Cambridge: Cambridge Univ. Press

Vladeck, B. C. 1980. *Unloving Care: The Nursing Home Tragedy*. New York: Basic Books

Wamsley, G. L., Zald, M. N. 1976. *The Political Economy of Public Organizations*. Bloomington, Ind: Indiana Univ. Press

Wilensky, H. 1975. *The Welfare State and Equality: Structural and Ideological Roots of Public Expenditures*. Berkeley, Calif: Univ. Calif. Press

Wilensky, H. 1981. Leftism, Catholicism, and democratic corporatism: The role of political parties in welfare state development. In *The Development of Welfare States in Europe and America*, ed. P. Flora, A. J. Heidenheimer, pp. 345–82. New Brunswick, NJ: Transaction

Wilensky, H., Lebeaux, C. N. 1958. *Industrial Society and Social Welfare: The Impact of Industrialization on the Supply and Organization of Social Welfare Services in the United States*. New York: Russell Sage Found.

Zald, M. N. 1985. Political change, citizenship rights, and the welfare state. *Ann. Am. Polit.* 479:48–66

Ann. Rev. Sociol. 1987. 13:417–42
Copyright © 1987 by Annual Reviews Inc. All rights reserved

CLASS MOBILITY IN THE INDUSTRIAL WORLD

Karin Kurz and Walter Müller

Department of Sociology, Universität Mannheim, Seminargebäude A 5, 6800 Mannheim 1, Federal Republic of Germany

Abstract

The main interest of this review is in the developments in social mobility research during the last ten years. These can be characterized as the revitalization of the class perspective, intensive comparative (cross-national and cross-temporal) research efforts, and the large-scale application of the log-linear modeling approach. After discussing the basic ideas of mobility studies conducted in an explicit class framework and the developments regarding class concepts, the review summarizes the major results of empirical research as to intergenerational mobility of men and women. These results are yielded within different conceptual frameworks for several industrialized countries. It continues by examining the constituent worklife processes, stressing the effects of different institutional arrangements and of labor market conditions for intragenerational mobility. Finally, a brief summary of the research desiderata still existing in social mobility research closes the review.

INTRODUCTION

In the years following Blau & Duncan's seminal contribution (1967), the preoccupation with models of status attainment led to a remarkable limitation to one particular perspective on social mobility: namely, the developments in the degree of equality of opportunity and openness of society. This perspective, which is as old as empirical research in social mobility, has been taken from different theoretical positions and political orientations. In a functionalist interpretation, the study of mobility processes should show how efficiently different talents are allocated to positions of unequal rewards. Guided by the political goal of equality of opportunity, measures of social immobility were used to examine how far reality falls short of achieving this goal.

417

0360-0572/87/0815-0417$02.00

Since the late 1970s, another long-neglected perspective has been revitalized. This second view focuses on the implications of mobility for class consciousness and class formation (Goldthorpe 1980, 1984b; but see also Parkin 1971; Giddens 1973; Mann 1975). Its roots can already be found in the work of Marx (cf Goldthorpe 1980, Heath 1981). Mobility does not play a central role in Marx's argumentation (except in the case of collective downward mobility in the Verelendungstheorie). However, in his discussion of the North American class structure, Marx considers mobility as a crucial determinant of working class organization. While the older European countries would possess a mature class structure, he argues, the classes in America—although existing—"have not yet become fixed, but continually change and interchange their elements in a constant flux" (Marx 1852:255), a view later similarly put forward by Sombart (1906). The difference to which Marx refers is simply that between "class in itself" and "class for itself": whereas in North America the working class exists in itself, and a certain degree of immobility is seen as an indispensable prerequisite of the emergence of a class for itself. Moreover, Marx considers in another context the reverse of the coin, arguing that "the more the ruling class is able to assimilate the foremost minds of a ruled class, the more stable and dangerous becomes its rule" (Marx 1894:587). He is applying here a functionalist argument well-known from the later work of Pareto (1916) although it is formulated there with a different political thrust.

Still another one of the founding fathers of sociology dealt with the significance of social mobility for class formation: Max Weber (1968). He defined social class in terms of intra- and intergenerational mobility patterns: Social classes are composed of class situations between which an interchange of individuals in their life course or in the course of generations is readily possible and typically observable. Max Weber evidently recognized immobility as a central determinant for the social and cultural identity of a class. While of course some differences do exist between the Weberian and the Marxist tradition in assessing the status of mobility for class formation, the kernel of the idea is obviously the same. Hence, with the revival of the class perspective in mobility research, the ideas of both traditions serve by now as typical points of reference. Though in a few early empirical studies, a class perspective is mentioned (Sorokin 1927) or adopted (Carlsson 1958), the recent preoccupation has been prompted by Goldthorpe (1980: Ch. 1; 1984b) who argued "that class formation at the demographic level, in which the effect of mobility is crucial, is *prior to* class formation at other levels. Classes, that is to say, must have some degree of demographic identity before they can acquire a socio-cultural identity or provide a basis for collective action" (Goldthorpe 1984b:20).

Even if one does not want to make so far-reaching an assessment, it seems possible that mobility processes are indeed central determinants of the formation of classes. But while non-Marxists have conducted a series of studies to this end (e.g. Goldthorpe 1980; Erikson et al 1979, 1983; Haller 1982a, 1983b; Featherman & Selbee 1986), the proper neo-Marxist school of sociology until recently had remained surprisingly uninterested in mobility studies. The latter usually argued that there is no need for the study of mobility processes since mobility across the fundamental line between capital and labor can be neglected (e.g. Carchedi 1975) and, further, since class formation is seen in the first place as dependent on the class position and not on the individual who occupies it (e.g. Poulantzas 1975). An exception in this tradition is Westergaard & Resler's empirical study of England (1975). Contrary to the mainstream of western Marxists, East European sociologists (especially in Poland and Hungary) have dealt theoretically and empirically with intergenerational mobility (e.g. Zagorski 1976, Wesolowski 1979, Wesolowski et al 1979, Andorka & Zagorski 1978, 1979, Mach & Wesolowski 1986).

The growing interest in social mobility studies carried out in a class framework has profited in its conceptual precision and methodological sophistication by the developments in loglinear modeling techniques advanced primarily by Goodman and Hauser (e.g. Goodman 1969, 1972, 1979a,b; Hauser 1978, 1979). (For summary, see Hout 1983; for computation advice, see Dessens et al 1983, Breen 1984.) Now the whole range of existing theoretical and empirical possibilities can be exhausted to construct the 'space' in which mobility is to be observed. For the loglinear techniques do not presuppose—as the status attainment models did—any hierarchical ordering of the underlying categories.

In the last years two lines of the loglinear approach have been further developed. On the one hand, there are the now widely used 'topological' or 'level' models (Hauser 1978, Hout 1983) that make it possible to model different mobility propensities of the cells in the mobility table. Because these models do not require any assumptions on hierarchical orderings, they have been preferred in studies carried out in a class framework (see e.g. Erikson et al 1979, Goldthorpe 1980). The typical argument there is that on the side of origin different class positions are connected with qualitatively different resources (as capital or special skills) which are the grounds for different mobility chances. And, further, that on the side of destination, different class positions have different attractiveness because of their promise of different rewards.

On the other hand, researchers who start from a socioeconomic hierarchy have argued that mobility processes are predominantly governed by some sort of vertical effects. Assuming that the observed mobility is a function of the distance between the hierarchically ordered categories, social distance and association models have been developed (Duncan 1979; Goodman 1979a,b;

Clogg 1982; Grusky & Hauser 1984; Hope 1982, 1984; Hout 1984b; Breen 1985a,b; Hout & Jackson 1986). Hence, the different kinds of loglinear modeling make it possible to capture vertical and nonvertical effects with the same precision and to test them against each other.

Moreover, comparative (cross-temporal and cross-national) mobility research has much benefitted from the loglinear modeling approach because it opens a way to control adequately for marginal effects in mobility tables. After a long debate that attempted to rescue the old distinction between structural and exchange mobility (Slomczynski & Krauze 1983, Krauze & Slomczynski 1986 a,b), the most convincing argument was to abandon this distinction (Sobel 1983a,b). Hence, following the work of Featherman et al (1975), Hauser & Featherman (1977), and Goldthorpe (1980), the more sensible distinction between absolute and relative mobility rates is now widely accepted. Relative rates are mobility measures net of marginal effects and refer to the competitive advantages of the progeny of one category to that of another category in the competition for different positions (the "odds ratios" in the loglinear model). Relative rates thus are particularly suitable to measure differences or similarities in inequality of opportunity in different countries or at different times, independent of marginal effects.

The absolute mobility rates are appropriate when adopting a class perspective. Absolute rates are the raw flows between origin and destination, i.e. they measure the factual (destination) opportunities of members of a given origin class, and they show how homogeneously or heterogeneously classes recruit their members from different origins. Strongly affected by the size of origin and destination classes, they reflect the factual mobility experiences in a given country at a given time.

Regarding intergenerational mobility on a macrosociological level the rediscovery of the class perspective, the enormous extension of possibilities to analyze the conventional mobility matrix, and finally, the increase of comparative mobility studies are the hallmarks of the recent research efforts. To appreciate the outcomes of these developments we begin with the discussion of attempts to construct differentiated class concepts. In the next step, we summarize the multitude of empirical results regarding intergenerational mobility of men and women in industrial societies. While not all of these studies are based on class concepts (but on concepts of socioeconomic position, too), they have in common the application of loglinear modeling methods. The few studies that are bound to status attainment research we do not take under review. (For reviews of that 'school' see Matras 1980, Mayer 1980, Featherman 1981, Bielby 1981.) In the two sections that follow we turn from the macroperspective on mobility to studies that more closely examine the constituent worklife processes and the institutional arrangements of mobility and, finally, the labor market conditions of intragenerational mobility. We close with a brief overview of research desiderata still existing in social mobility research.

CLASSES AND CLASSIFICATION CONCEPTS

Much of earlier research on social mobility is flawed by the fact that it relies on classifications that scarcely can pretend to be deduced from some explicit theoretical basis. Partly due to constraints imposed by the available data, much of the cross-national comparative work was restricted to the manual/nonmanual/farm distinction. Classifications based on the notions of prestige or socioeconomic status that are theoretically more informed are flawed because they press the structure of inequality in a simple hierarchy. In this respect the categorization of occupations in terms of class has brought decisive progress. It is common practice in sociology to distinguish between class concepts in the Weberian—market based—and the Marxist—production-based—tradition. As we shall see, this distinction does not grasp the essence of the concepts developed during the last years—two of which we discuss: the scheme developed by Goldthorpe (1980, 1982) and the one proposed by Wright (1985).

In the class scheme of Goldthorpe, classes are constructed by combining "occupations whose incumbents share in broadly similar *market* and *work* situations" (Goldthorpe 1980:39). Deeper insight into the leading theoretical rationale is given by Goldthorpe's elaboration of the concept of the 'service class' (1982), which builds on earlier work of Renner (1953) and Dahrendorf (1964). Formulating the concept, Goldthorpe takes into account that class relations in advanced industrial societies are increasingly shaped by the development of large scale organizations and the problem of securing control in such organizations. In the case of the 'typical' wage laborer, direct control is a practicable solution to sustain productivity and discipline in the company. That solution becomes problematic with increasing autonomy and discretion in the tasks of the employees. Thus, mechanisms of direct control are replaced by special exchange relationships suited to create loyalty and moral commitment. These 'bureaucratic' or service relationships are characterized by a generally higher level of remuneration and—more crucial—through the qualitatively different features: salary (instead of wage), fringe benefits, and, in particular, rewards of an essentially prospective kind (salary increments, security in employment, career prospects). These latter constitute the hallmarks of the exchange between employer and employees in service class positions.

The characterization of the service class relationship as opposed to that of the wage laborers is, of course, an ideal typical one. As Goldthorpe (1982) stresses, there are always some gradations between perfect service class and perfect working class conditions. In his class scheme, Goldthorpe therefore distinguishes between the higher and lower levels of the service class and the class position of the routine nonmanual employees who still enjoy to some extent 'bureaucratic' working conditions. He similarly separates three class positions for the 'manual occupations' (supervisors and technicians; skilled laborers; semiskilled and unskilled laborers). Besides the working class and service class positions, he distinguishes the positions of agricultural and nonagricultural small proprietors (Goldthorpe 1980:39–42; for critiques from Marxist points of view, see Crompton 1980, Penn 1981).

Goldthorpe's class scheme obviously captures characteristics of occupational positions that are central in the relation of mobility to processes of class formation: Incumbents of service class positions earn high incomes and most often have attained high educational levels—both important resources for securing the 'inheritance' of an advantageous class position. Further, the attention is directed towards important factors of class formation at the level of the organization of interests: Career prospects, employment security, and salary increments. Finally, Goldthorpe's concept draws a compelling conjunction between market and work situation, a conjunction in which the crucial argument refers to the strategy of the employer to secure internal domination in the company. Links to Weberian theories of bureaucracy and to the "structuralist" school of labor market theory are quite evident. The label "Weberian market based class concept" thus obviously falls short. Perhaps this label is more appropriate for the neo-Marxist account of Wright (1985) (see also Rose & Marshall 1986:452–53). Wright's proposition stands in the long tradition of Marxist scholars who, even if they do not question the primacy of the capital/labor division, try to overcome its insufficiencies. But it must be mentioned that Marx himself had already dealt with differentiated pictures of the class structure in his historical analyses without, however, clarifying the theoretical status of these concrete descriptions (e.g. Marx 1852). And since the days of Marx—largely because of the steadily growing "new middle classes"—Marxists cannot get away from dealing with the role of these categories (e.g. Poulantzas 1975, Carchedi 1977, and most recently Wright 1985). Refuting his earlier concept of "contradictory class locations" (1978) as "domination centered" and thus inherently non-Marxist, Wright now intends to bring the Marxist concept of exploitation back to the analysis of class relationships.

Wright takes over the basic idea from Roemer (1982): In a society several productive assets exist that are unequally distributed and that thus can form the basis of exploitation. For example, one can use scarce skills, often in the form of credentials, exploitatively, to secure rewards greater than the cost of acquiring the skills. In turn, the differential must be drawn from the nonowners of skills (Wright 1985:70, 76). In any given society typically several kinds of exploitation exist, but only one establishes the central class conflict in society. Connected to this hypothesis is a stage theory of societal development: The central basis of exploitation is unequal control of labor power in feudalism, of means of production in capitalism, of organization assets in statism (i.e. in the 'actually existing socialism') and of skills in socialism. From one stage of society to the next, one source of exploitation after the other is eliminated. Thus, in capitalism three exploitative resources exist: means of production, organization assets, and skills. Different combinations and three graduations in each productive asset lead to a twelvefold class scheme (Wright 1985:88)—a class scheme that has obvious resemblances to the multifactorial approaches in the Weberian tradition (assuming, however, not different *market* chances but *exploitation* chances based on different productive resources; cf. see also Rose & Marshall 1986:453).

The striking contrasts to Goldthorpe's scheme are, on the one hand, the additional distinction between managers and experts, both of whom in Goldthorpe's scheme fall into the service class, and on the other, the neglect of the bureaucratic work relationship.

At first Wright's theory that resources create several different antagonistic relationships seems to be plausible, but we think there is one crucial weakness: Wright doesn't analyze the interrelationships between the use of different resources and, although stressing the primacy of the division between capital and labor in capitalism, he does not show how skill and organizational resources are subsumed under the capitalist interest. Such a perspective would perhaps have led to a stance like that of Goldthorpe, who focusses on the capitalist production unit. And in such a perspective it seems reasonable to expect that managers and experts will have more common than divided interests. The arrangements to secure productivity and discipline are rather similar (cf Goldthorpe 1982), and further, management positions are increasingly connected with special qualifications.

The opposite point may be put forward in the case of the missing division between bureaucratic and nonbureaucratic work relationships. In the long run, those in the routine nonmanual occupations may organize along with the manual laborers. But as long as these positions are typically involved in bureaucratic organizational settings, it makes sense to separate out these groups—at least those who are working as clerks or in similar positions. This view is supported by the finding that clerk jobs could—at least some years ago—still hold considerable career opportunities (cf Stewart et al 1980; Goldthorpe 1986, for England; Müller 1977, Mayer & Carroll 1987, for West-Germany).

Up to now we have considered class concepts based on the assumption that classes should be defined a priori on theoretical grounds. Still, starting from Weber's definition of social class, there have been a great many sophisticated attempts to identify classes a posteriori, according to the mobility barriers displayed in the mobility patterns between a larger number of occupational groupings (see Breiger 1981, 1982a,b; Goodman 1981; Clogg 1981; Clogg & Goodman 1983; Marsden 1985; Snipp 1985). While these attempts might be useful for assessing the advisability of collapsing certain categories in a mobility table or even for describing the mobility patterns, it would seem indispensable to have a clear notion of the underlying inequality structure that the class scheme should capture and from which the mobility processes themselves could be understood. One might further ask how useful these models can be for comparative research, if for one country a collapsibility model assigns a given occupation to class A, whereas for another country it identifies it as a member of class B.

CONSTANCIES AND VARIATIONS IN INTERGENERATIONAL CLASS MOBILITY

Defining the class structure a priori most mobility researchers consider social mobility as the dependent variable and, further, as a variable that refers to macrosociological properties of a society. Its very nature implies a comparative framework of mobility studies where both hypotheses about historical constancy or change within a given society and hypotheses about cross-national similarity or variation are of interest.

The pivotal role in shaping the mobility patterns has regularly been attributed to the casting force of industrialism (but other factors—in particular education, historical events, or government policies—have been also taken into account). Goldthorpe (1985) has pointed out two variants of the industrialization thesis: On the one hand, it is claimed that industrialism makes uniform the extent of social mobility (Lipset & Zetterberg 1959, Featherman et al 1975); On the other, industrialism is claimed to be connected with a fundamental trend towards rationalism reflected in universalistic criteria of selection procedures for social positions. In turn, this would lead to a trend of increasing mobility rates in industrialized societies (Blau & Duncan 1967, Treiman 1970). While the former hypothesis requires cross-national comparisons, the latter one implies the examination of the historical development of mobility patterns.

The long history of cumulative research appears now to approach a state of maturity that allows the empirical testing of these hypotheses. With respect to the trend hypothesis, progress has mainly been achieved through the availability of large-scale replicative surveys of high quality in several countries. For cross-national comparisons, the comparability of classifications has been much improved by secondary analysis of the original national data sets rather than comparison of published mobility matrices (Goldthorpe & Müller 1982).

The first hypothesis was related in its original version—advanced by Lipset & Zetterberg (1959)—to absolute mobility rates. The authors assumed that industrialization would lead to the development of similar occupational structures, a process that in turn would result in similar mobility rates. This hypothesis could clearly be rejected precisely since the process of industrialization does not result in a uniform occupational structure. On the contrary, differences in the path of industrial development and differences of the occupational structure in countries of a similar level of industrialization are the main factors producing the differences in the absolute mobility rates between advanced societies.

In the light of this finding, Featherman et al (1975) put forward the hypotheses in a modified version; they argue that although the absolute mobility rates may vary between societies, the underlying mobility regime— captured with *relative* mobility rates—would show a basic similarity in all societies with market economies and nuclear family systems (for further specifications of this thesis, see Grusky & Hauser 1984:20). Inspired by the so-called FJH-hypothesis, (*F*eatherman, *J*ones, & *H*auser 1975), a considerable number of studies were undertaken that yielded not always consistent results. Yet some of these studies were founded on data and classifications of somewhat doubtful quality (e.g. Hazelrigg & Garnier 1976, Tyree et al 1979, McClendon 1980a,b). More recent studies, working for the most part on better empirical grounds, found considerable support for the FJH thesis (McRoberts & Selbee 1981, Erikson et al 1982, Hope 1982, Pöntinen 1983, Portocarero 1983a, Hauser 1984a,b, Erikson & Goldthorpe 1985a,b, Kerckhoff et al 1985, Erikson & Goldthorpe 1986, Jones & Davis 1986).

Using in most cases 'topological models' (cf Hauser 1978, Hout 1983), the basic patterns of relative mobility chances were modelled and repeatedly confirmed: Immobility is greatest among farmers, followed by the petty bourgeoisie and the service class. The immobility at the peak of the socioeconomic hierarchy (or in class terms: in the upper service class) is greater than at the bottom, in the working class. Mobility is more likely in the 'middle' of the socioeconomic hierarchy (or the class structure) than at the peak. Short-range mobility occurs more often than long-range mobility. Still, these are only *general* patterns that need some specifications when looking at particular nations. In other words the FJH-thesis can only be maintained in a weak version, postulating basic similarities.

The question that then obviously arises is: What amount or what kind of differences are necessary to challenge the assumption of basic similarities? The salient point is—as Erikson & Goldthorpe (1985, 1986) have argued— whether the deviations are attributable to national peculiarities or to some macro-sociological variables—"that is, variables referring to generalisable attributes of total societies" (Erikson & Goldthorpe 1986:39). The latter case would lead to the identification of types of societies (apart from their characterization as industrialized) with different patterns of mobility—a result that seriously would call into question the FJH thesis.

But as the examination of the deviations of several nations from a 'core' pattern shows (Erikson & Goldthorpe 1986), this does not seem to be the case: The numerous deviations were largely attributable to nation-specific, historically formed features that affect (im)mobility propensities between some specific class positions (most obviously in West Germany, Hungary, the Republic of Ireland). Only one nation—Sweden—displays a general shift towards greater openness, a pattern that, as Erikson & Goldthorpe (1986) suggest, could be interpreted in the light of the long-standing social democratic government. Yet they are well aware that this single case provides too weak a basis to postulate a type of 'social democratic society' which would regularly yield higher social fluidity. Another problem arose in the case of the socialist countries. Poland shows a marked shift towards greater fluidity in particular between the working class and the intelligentsia, a pattern that is, however, not found in Hungary. (For further results, see Andorka & Zagorski 1978, 1979; Simkus 1981a; Simkus & Andorka 1982; Simkus 1984.) Hence, Erikson & Goldthorpe conclude that it is obviously not possible to postulate a 'socialist mobility regime' as a specific type.

The final assessment of these findings results in the convincing critique that the FJH thesis underestimates the role of 'the political' for the mobility regime—a factor that, however, would not necessarily lead to the distinction between specific types of societies. Political interventions might have very different and uncertain outcomes, so it is difficult to develop hypotheses about expected mobility patterns in advance (Erikson & Goldthorpe 1986:44–45). Other nation-specific factors could be related to institutions that shape mobility processes, such as particular forms of the educational system or labor legislation. In the light of these latter observations, it seems reasonable to expect that microscopic studies focusing on the special historical and institutional conditions of single countries (see e.g. Whelan & Whelan, 1984, for Ireland; Müller, 1986, for Germany) will sharpen our understanding of the individual particularities found within the "family resemblance" (Erikson et al 1982) of the mobility regime in industrialized nations.

With regard to the second—the trend—hypothesis that increasing mobility parallels industrialization, the distinction between absolute and relative rates is again fundamental. Absolute rates are found to increase with industrial development. The transition from an agricultural to an industrial or postindustrial occupational structure results in marked discrepancies in the size of the origin and destination classes. The higher the discrepancy is, the higher the absolute rates of mobility tend to be. Apart from the effects of discrepancies yielded by the structural transformations, industrialization affects absolute mobility through what Simkus (1984) has termed compositional effects. Since in the course of industrialization the classes with the highest immobility rates regularly decrease—namely, the classes of farmers and the nonagricultural petty-bourgeoisie—the composition of an advanced industrial or postindustrial occupational structure should provide an enhanced level of absolute mobility, even if the structural transformation process slows down.

As concerns trend changes in relative rates of mobility, the findings are less clear. For some societies it has been found that the mobility regime has not substantively changed over the last decades (Rogoff-Ramsoy 1977 for Norway, Hope 1981a for England and Wales, Goyder 1985a for Canada, Goldthorpe & Payne 1986 for England and Wales, Jones & Davis 1986 for Australia and New Zealand). In other instances changes towards greater fluidity have been detected, but regularly they are only slight (e.g. Featherman & Hauser, 1978, for the United States Ganzeboom & de Graaf, 1984, for the Netherlands). Moreover, the changes seem to be episodic rather than systematically linked to industrialization. They may reflect a temporal effect of a socialist revolution such as that in Hungary (Simkus 1981a, 1984). They may be related to factors other than industrial development per se (Erikson 1983 for Sweden) or related to a change in the composition and standing of classes, as Thelot (1982) suggested for France (for the latter nation, see also Goldthorpe & Portocarero 1981).

The distinction between absolute and relative mobility rates has also brought greater insight into another much debated topic: the issue of gender inequality. As for men, so for women, mobility opportunities and patterns of mobility depend most importantly on the distribution of the accessible positions. Thus, as a consequence of the occupational segregation and discrimination, the mobility opportunities—in an absolute sense—for women are clearly less advantageous than for men. However, if the differences in the job structure are taken into account, the mobility regime appears to be very similar for both sexes. The relative advantages or disadvantages for women of a given origin class, compared to women from other origins, are much the same as the respective odds for men. Studies from various countries have repeatedly demonstrated that models of common social fluidity for men and women fit the observations quite well (Hauser & Featherman 1977:204–15; Dunton & Featherman 1983 for the United States; Pöntinen 1983:105–7; Erikson & Pöntinen 1985 for the Scandinavian countries; Portocarero 1983b, 1985 for France and Sweden; Handl 1982 for West-Germany; Goldthorpe & Payne 1985 for Great Britain, Goyder 1985b for Canada). If minor deviances from common social fluidity exist, they are related to differences in inheritance of the self-employed categories: The class of the petty bourgeoisie transmit the heritage of business or capital more often to sons than to daughters. Conversely, the daughters of petty bourgeoisie parents have—in relative terms—slightly better opportunities to enter the service class than do the sons of this origin.

The most substantial implication of these findings is perhaps that while, on the average, men profit because women overproportionally occupy less advantageous jobs, this does not affect the relative inequality of opportunity—in the sense of social fluidity—between men and women. One must, however, ask what the findings on women's mobility (as measured through their own employment) mean for assessing class mobility of women. The central issue still is whether class location of women depends most on their own employment, on their husband's class, or on some kind of family class location. (For recent exchanges in this debate, see Haller 1981, Britten & Heath 1983, Goldthorpe 1983, Payne et al 1983, Heath & Britten 1984, Stanworth 1984, Goldthorpe 1984c.) While there are good arguments for the conventional thesis, defended by Goldthorpe (1983), that families are the units of the class system because they share resources, life-styles, social networks and values, it can also be held that the assignment of status varies between different situations and contexts.

A productive result of this longstanding debate has been the comparison of the empirical outcomes corresponding to the competing theoretical positions (Goldthorpe & Payne 1985). According to the most strict interpretation of the conventional view, the class position of women has to be equated with the class of the respective husbands, and class mobility has to be assessed in terms of marriage mobility. A less strict interpretation has been proposed by Erikson (1984) who equates the class position of a family with the position of that family member whose position may be considered as dominant according to a set of dominance rules. Finally, class position of women can be defined exclusively in terms of women's own employment. If now class mobility of women is assessed according to these different conceptions, class mobility patterns differ in absolute terms. In relative terms, however, the class mobility of women, however measured, corresponds very closely to the class mobility of men. Women experience slightly more mobility through marriage than men do through employment. The findings, however, are far from lending support to the notion that, through marriage, mobility between classes in modern societies is much less restricted than mobility through own employment (Handl 1982, Portocarero 1985, Goldthorpe & Payne 1985).

The commonality in social fluidity extends even further. Hout (1982: 397) reports a striking amount of similarity between the father-son association and the association found in a table crossing husband's and wife's occupation. The basic similarity is also replicated for ethnic or religious groups (Hout 1984a, 1986, Lewin-Epstein & Semyonov 1986).

Given this general result of an overwhelming commonality in social fluidity with minor, national, and group specific peculiarities, the question arises whether the common pattern of association between origin and destination—and possibly the deviations from the common pattern—can be accounted for by some general theoretically meaningful principles. On the one hand, researchers working with classifications of socioeconomic status have stressed the dominance of vertical effects in the mobility process. But attempts to model these effects have consistently shown that while they are indeed relevant, they are in no way sufficient to account for the whole range of the (im)mobility pattern. In particular, to explain specific inheritance features one must additionally refer to the resources governing the mobility process—such as capital, land, and cultural capital (or autonomy and special training with the resulting networks and practices of socialization; Hout 1984b). Similarly the barriers between farm and nonfarm positions can scarcely be captured in terms of hierarchical effects alone.

In an explicit class framework, though, considerations of this kind have been a matter of course. Characterizing the class structure as having at best only partial hierarchical orderings (e.g. Erikson et al 1979, Goldthorpe 1980), 'topological models' have been preferred. The theoretical interpretation of the distinguished levels of mobility propensities was, however, quite indeterminate. In order to overcome this problem Erikson & Goldthorpe (1985b, 1986), and similarly Jones & Davis (1986), explicitly introduce into their models four different effects, to capture the crucial factors that determine the pattern of relative mobility chances: first, hierarchy effects; second, inheritance effects, marking in particular those class positions with control of big amounts of economic and cultural capital; third, a sector effect between the agricultural and nonagricultural classes; and fourth, disaffinity and affinity effects to take into account effects that derive "from particular linkages or discontinuities between classes" (Erikson & Goldthorpe 1985b:22).

As Hauser (1984a:105) has argued, the relative merits of models of vertical distance and of class can only be appreciated by drawing evidence from sources outside the mobility process per se, and, one can add, from the plausibility of the results in a broader theoretical framework and their consistency in different populations (Grusky & Hauser 1984:26). Such criteria are the more needed because different models can produce the same fit or can be algebraically equivalent (Goodman 1979a, Hauser 1979, Macdonald 1981, Pöntinen 1982, Grusky & Hauser 1984). While the last few years have brought considerable insight through the intensive efforts to "mine for nuggets in the mobility table itself" (Hout 1984b:1380) it has been objected by many (most vigorously by Sørensen, 1987), that the standard social mobility table is an aggregated end-product of multiple processes intervening between a class position defined as origin and a class position somewhat misleadingly defined as destination. If the emergence of the particular association between origin and destination in a mobility table is to be understood, it is not through still more refined indexes and models of the table itself, but by disaggregating it into its constituent processes. In the next steps we therefore pursue this aim.

PROCESSES OF WORKLIFE MOBILITY AND THE EFFECT OF EDUCATIONAL SYSTEMS

If one of the main theoretical interests in social mobility is its consequences for class formation, then much depends on the stability of the class position, not only as it is revealed in a comparison with one's origin by a cross-sectional snapshot, but also in its stability in the course of a person's life. The more the class position of individuals changes in the course of their life, the less we can infer the demographic identity of classes from an intergenerational mobility table alone. In different societies, different patterns of mobility from origin to class position at the entry into employment, and from there through the working life, could in combination result in identical patterns of mobility in intergenerational perspective. (For respective results, see Erikson & Goldthorpe 1985c in their comparison of England and the United States.) Where there is an interest in class formation, the combination of both processes is thus of primordial importance.

Although our knowledge of the combined effects of both processes is still very limited, there is evidence on both similarity and difference among nations. As concerns similarity, four findings are perhaps most pervasive. First, there is generally less worklife mobility than intergenerational mobility, and its amount depends considerably on how first employment is defined (Coleman 1984). Worklife mobility greatly decreases with age (see e.g. König & Müller 1986:11; Sørensen et al 1986, table 4). This implies that beyond the point of occupational maturity, say about age 35, further worklife mobility does not alter strongly the patterns found in an intergenerational mobility table. Second, although working life is not without risks of downward moves, the larger number of moves are upward from lower level entry positions to higher level destinations, most clearly so in bureaucratic careers and with respect to entry into self-employment. Third, a considerable part of worklife mobility is mobility from an initial, generally lower, worklife entry position back to one's origin class. Thus, counter-mobility (Girod 1971; Goldthorpe 1980; Thelot 1980, 1982) contributes to a rather heterogeneous composition, particularly of the service class, in terms of the life-course experiences of its members. Even those who in intergenerational perspective appear to be immobile may have attained service class positions through very different channels; this is also true of those who attain this class from other class origins (Müller 1977, Goldthorpe 1980, Haller 1982a,b). Fourth, while retrospectively the service class is composed of individuals who attain it from heterogeneous backgrounds and through heterogeneous routes, prospectively it is the most stable and immobile class. It is repeatedly found in the nations studied that the security to stay is highest in the highest class.

Although the findings are not yet as thoroughly established as for intergenerational mobility, enough evidence exists to conclude that patterns of worklife mobility, even in terms of relative rates, are less stable, both over time (Featherman & Hauser 1978:115–38; Simkus 1981b; Thelot 1982: 95–115; Andorka 1983; Payne & Payne 1983) and across countries (Haller & Hodge 1981, Haller & Mach 1981, Erikson & Goldthorpe 1985c, Kappelhoff & Teckenberg 1986, König & Müller 1986) than are patterns of intergenerational mobility.

Variation across countries in patterns of worklife mobility can be expected mainly from differences in the institutional arrangements that bear on the employment of labor of different qualifications and experiences in different jobs. There is growing evidence that particularly the characteristics of a nation's educational system and correspondingly the structure and organization of a nation's labor market are closely linked with patterns of worklife mobility. These institutions appear to depend mutually on each other. The educational system, for example, develops in response to demands for qualifications from the labor market. But once the educational system has developed in a specific way, its structures strongly affect the opportunities of holders of different qualifications. Furthermore, worklife mobility directly depends on labor policy, labor legislation, and agreements between employers and unions. All these factors may substantially differ between countries.

The more an educational system provides training for specific jobs, the closer the association between education and class will be and the less mobility throughout worklife will occur. On the other side, the less that education provides qualifications of immediate use at work, the more firms will have to build up their own training programs. Qualifications attained this way will tend to be restricted in use to the needs of the training organization and will be less transferable between firms. Along these lines Maurice & Sellier (1979) and Maurice et al (1982) developed a typology of a 'qualificational mobility space,' which they see as characteristic for Germany, and an 'organizational mobility space,' which is more developed in France. With its apprenticeship system, they argue, Germany educates a labor force with quasi-professional qualifications for the overwhelming number of jobs, whereas France and most other countries have to rely more on firm-specific training solutions (see also Lutz 1976).

Recent studies on worklife mobility (Haller et al 1985, König & Müller 1986) show in fact a closer link between educational qualifications and jobs for countries relying on the apprenticeship system (e.g. Germany and Austria) than for countries with an organizational mobility space (France, United States). Accordingly, in Germany and Austria where credentials play a stronger role in allocating people to jobs, we find less worklife mobility. And furthermore, if mobility occurs, it is mobility of an 'orderly,' generally upwardly directed kind. France and the United States, on the other hand, show considerably more worklife mobility—but both more upward and more downward mobility. (For a discussion of further institutional effects see Haller 1982a,b, 1983a.)

Thus, while we begin to understand the institutional arrangements that contribute to cross-national differences in worklife mobility patterns, still far too little comparative research exists regarding these influences on intergenerational class mobility. In single country studies, some progress has been made in modeling the role played by education in mediating between origin and destination. They show that the significance of education varies considerably in mediating different types of mobility and immobility. As a generalized resource, education has high value for obtaining access to bureaucratic or professional occupations, but it cannot explain the inheritance in propertied classes, where specific resources are transmitted from one generation to the next (Yamaguchi 1982, Logan 1983). Robinson (1984a) and Robinson & Garnier (1985) additionally show that even the inheritance of positions of control is largely direct and not mediated through education.

Extensions of the mobility matrix approach to include education or occupational career steps seem to be promising for cross-national comparisons. The transition matrix approach should be particularly appropriate to grasp institutionalized links between specific educational attainments and specific jobs, which exist in some countries but not in others (such as e.g. the strong connection between apprenticeships and skilled manual jobs in countries with a widespread apprenticeship system). In addition, the transition matrix approach should also show the consequences of the fact that the distribution of educational levels varies cross-nationally as well as in the course of the national developments. Since the relative exclusiveness or generality of an educational credential can be assumed to be a major determinant of the potential of an educational level to secure access to specific positions (Boudon 1973), comparative research along these lines should clarify, on better grounds than have been possible so far, the extent to which different educational systems play a similar role in the intergenerational mobility process or can in fact be seen as responsible for part of the variation in social fluidity between different countries.

MOBILITY AND LABOR MARKET CONDITIONS

The inclusion of variables to capture labor market conditions has already some tradition in a branch of the study of social mobility: in status attainment research. As a reaction to the critique of its individualistic bias and lack of consideration of structural conditions and contexts, some researchers introduced a number of variables intended to measure labor market conditions that facilitate or impede the attainment process (for a review see Kalleberg & Sorensen 1979, and Sørensen 1983a). While it is true that the structural variables generally contributed to increase the variance explained and thus showed that structures matter, the studies share other drawbacks of the status attainment models in that they tend to neglect the time dependency of the attainment process—see Sørensen (1987) for an elaboration of this point. An appropriate answer to this criticism is now provided with the collection of complete life history data and its analysis with models of time-dependent transition rates (Tuma 1976, Tuma & Hannan 1984, Blossfeld et al 1986). Attainment is conceived as a series of job shifts. For any stage in an individual's working life, it is intended to explain the duration of stay in a job or class position, and the rate of transition between jobs or class positions, by individual attributes and resources as well as by the structural conditions of the labor market segment in which the individual is located.

In several papers from the German study Carroll & Mayer (1986), Mayer & Carroll (1986) draw insightful conclusions from this kind of analysis. Whereas previous research on structural effects of career developments has centered on either class, organizational, or industry factors (for the latter see e.g. Stinchcombe 1979, Tolbert 1982), Carroll and Mayer consider the complementarity of all of these factors. And while previous research on worklife mobility was never very clear about whether job shifts or class episodes should be the unit of analysis, these authors explicitly study the interdependence of both and find strong interactions between them.

Classes differ considerably in the extent to which they expose their members to job mobility or to which they retain members, given a job shift. The risk of job changes is largest in the working classes, particularly so in the unskilled and semiskilled working class. At the same time, this class has a strong holding power, in the sense that only a minority of job shifts involve moves to another class. The service class, on the other side, has a strong holding power without exposing its members to job shifts. A similar finding is replicated for gender differences. Women "experience greater job mobility than men but less class mobility, i.e. they are locked into the more disadvantaged positions." (Mayer & Carroll 1986:40; with respect to less favorable career prospects of women see also Felmlee 1982, Blossfeld (in 1987), Robinson & Garnier 1985, Hachen 1986).

Regarding the interdependence of different structural factors Carroll & Mayer find abundant evidence that the effects of class structure do not vanish if the size of the firm (indicating internal labor markets), industrial sector, and individual resources are controlled for (see also Jacobs 1983). In contrast, class membership in most cases rules out any vertical prestige effects in explaining job trajectories. However, class effects are modified by the labor market structures: "The less the firm or sector conforms to the market model, the less is the influence of the class structure on working lives" (Mayer & Carroll 1986:41). But if in internal labor markets, class effects are mitigated and replaced by bureaucratic promotion policies, it does not mean that in open market competition job trajectories are governed exclusively by attributes of the person and the job. Where the market rules, class structure matters most.

At any time, class, organizational, and industrial characteristics seem to make a difference in shaping worklife mobility patterns. However, job structures and opportunities change over time because of changing occupational structures and economic conditions. These macro-structural effects have traditionally been taken into account by controlling for marginal effects or by disaggregating data by cohorts or periods. However, this still leaves open the question, whether differences between cohorts or periods have to be attributed to different structures or to mechanisms transforming individual resources differently under different structural conditions. Although there are not yet undisputed solutions to this most intriguing problem, one can see progress along three lines of research.

One way is to include outside measures indicating macro-structural changes in the model to be tested. A lucid example of this approach is Blossfeld's paper (1986) on the career patterns of three German cohorts, born between 1920 and 1952. Because entry in the labor market as well as each successive job in the careers of these three cohorts took place under very different macro-structural conditions, the aggregate career lines of these cohorts visibly differ, indicating strong cohort and period effects. In order to index any single spell of each individual's worklife by the macro-level conditions present at the time, Blossfeld uses detailed time series data on the level of modernization of the job structure and on labor market conditions. Thus Blossfeld (1986) demonstrates a way to replace the uninterpretable cohort and period effects by the measured effects of specific variables operating at each point of the individual's career.

Against the direct control of macro-structural conditions it might be objected, however, that the measures are too global for characterizing the opportunity structure an individual is exposed to in terms of his or her resources and experiences, particularly if the individual is bound to an organization-specific internal labor market. A more micro-level approach thus limits itself to the study of organizations, the institutions in which careers take place. In the last few years, considerable interest has emerged to map explanations of worklife mobility patterns into the framework of organizational sociology (for a recent review of respective work see Baron 1984; for a recent case study Rosenbaum 1984). For instance, by analyzing personnel records over a long period of time, the path of individuals through the structure of an organization can be traced, as well as the trajectories of vacancies generated if a position holder leaves his or her position or if a new position is created (Stewman & Konda 1983; for ongoing work see particularly Petersen & Spilerman 1986 and Spilerman 1987). As a drawback of this approach, one has to note that the study of mobility patterns in a single organization will be affected by idiosyncratic particularities of the organization studied, its context, and its development in the time that the careers of individuals take place.

A third approach—mainly worked out by Sørensen & Kalleberg (1981), Sørensen & Tuma (1981), Sørensen (1983b), and Sørensen (1987) therefore starts from general theoretical derivations of the process of matching individuals to positions in different types of labor markets. Open position systems are governed by market competition. In closed position systems, the opportunity structure is mainly shaped by the structure of vacancies existing in a given internal labor market. Starting from this basic distinction, these authors attempt to model the opportunity structure and the mechanisms through which, under different labor market conditions, the supply of individuals with different characteristics and the demand of labor for different positions are mediated.

CONCLUDING REMARKS

When we now turn back to the main results of intergenerational class mobility, a very general conclusion is: In terms of the pattern of intergenerational social fluidity, industrial nations share a large amount of cross-national similarity, over-time constancy, and between group invariability. This is true once we account for the differences in the distributions of class positions, the differing rates of change in the course of time, and the global positive or negative discrimination against specific parts of the population like ethnic and religious groups or gender. Given this corpus of findings there appear to be three major tasks to be tackled in future research.

First, since the cross-national differences in absolute mobility rates are almost entirely dependent from the differences in the marginals, one of the most urgent tasks is to increase our knowledge of the forces responsible for the structural differences between countries. There is scattered research on a number of relevant issues, e.g. on the differential rates of the sectorial transformations of the economy and its effects on the decline of the working classes and the increase in the proportions of administrative and service occupations (Singelmann 1978, Payne & Payne 1983, Gagliani 1985, Rein 1985, Haller 1987, Kaelble, 1987); on the differential conditions of survival and coexistence if not complementarity of the traditional work organization of the petty bourgeoisie and the modern capitalist enterprise (Berger & Piore 1980, Goldthorpe 1984a, Müller 1987); on the effect of migrating labor both for the countries of emigration and the countries of immigration (Castles & Kosack 1985). Future research on the emergence of different class structures and the differential paths of their transformation will have to integrate these various aspects. It also will have to consider the division of labor between societies (Bornschier 1981) as well as the bearing of so-called societal effects, understood as relatively permanent features specific to particular societies (Maurice & Sellier 1979, Maurice et al 1982, and critically Rose 1985).

Second, even if it can be taken for granted that the pattern of relative mobility rates itself yields a large degree of constancy, the mechanisms and processes generating the large commonality have to be understood. Only if we have a better understanding of the forces and mechanisms producing the commonality can we expect appropriate explanations of the deviances. Any reader of the preceding sections reviewing the respective work, however, will certainly admit that the different approaches are far from being well integrated. Because different directions of research focus on particular parts of intervening mechanisms and processes, it is sometimes difficult to assess their contribution within the process at large, particularly so in cases where attention is directed exclusively to worklife moves, thereby neglecting the effect of origin resources in such moves.

Third, one of the major developments of the last few years is that the earlier preoccupation with questions of inequality of opportunity has been supplemented by a revitalized interest in the study of social mobility from the perspective of class formation. We now are quite well informed about the recruitment patterns to different classes and their risks and opportunities for maintaining class membership or being mobile to better or worse destinations. And we are also informed about national differences in these patterns. But the question is still nearly unsettled, as to which are in fact the consequences of the different degrees of demographic identity for the formation of classes in terms of the interpretation and organization of the interests resulting from their class position (Robinson 1983), in terms of class consciousness (Jackman & Jackman 1983, Hernes & Knudsen 1985) and of political action (Heath et al 1985, Herz 1986). It appears to be the order of the day that these questions are addressed directly now and that the step is taken from describing and explaining mobility to the study of its consequences.

Literature Cited

Andorka, R. 1983. Age, cohort and historical factors influencing inter- and intragenerational social mobility of men and women in Hungary. *Res. Soc. Strat. Mobility* 2:197–248

Andorka, R., Zagorski, K. 1978. Socioeconomic structure and socio-occupational mobility in Poland and Hungary. *Soc. Struc., Polish Sociol. 1977. Polish Sociol. Bull. (Supp)* pp. 139–74

Andorka, R., Zagorski, K. 1979. Structural factors of social mobility in Hungary and Poland. *Polish Sociol. Bull.* 46:127–40

Baron, N. J. 1984. Organizational perspectives on stratification. *Ann. Rev. Sociol.* 10:37–69

Berger, S., Piore, M. J. 1980. *Dualism and Discontinuity in Industrial Societies.* Cambridge: Cambridge Univ. Press

Bielby, W. T. 1981. Models of status attainment. *Res. Soc. Strat. Mobility* 1:3–26

Blau, P. M., Duncan, O. D. 1967. *The American Occupational Structure.* New York: Wiley

Blossfeld, H. P. 1986. Career opportunities in the Federal Republic of Germany. A dynamic approach to study life course, cohort, and period effects. *Eur. Sociol. Rev.* 2:208–25

Blossfeld, H. P. 1987. Labor market entry and the sexual segregation of careers in the Federal Republic of Germany. *Am. J. Sociol.* In press

Blossfeld, H. P., Hamerle, A., Mayer, K. U. 1986. *Ereignisanalyse. Statistische Theorie und ihre Anwendung in den Wirtschafts- und Sozialwissenschaften.* Frankfurt/New York: Campus

Bornschier, V. 1983. The division of labor, structural mobility and class formation: A theoretical note. *Res. Soc. Strat. Mobility* 2:249–68

Boudon, R. 1973. *Education, Opportunity, and Social Inequality: Changing Prospects in Western Societies.* New York: Wiley

Boyd, M., Goyder, J., Jones, F. E., McRoberts, H. A. et al. 1985. *Ascription and Achievement: Studies in Mobility and Status Attainment in Canada.* Ottawa: Carleton Univ. Press

Breen, R. 1984. Fitting non-hierarchical and association loglinear models using GLIM. *Sociol. Meth. Res.* 13:77–107

Breen, R. 1985a. A framework for comparative analyses of social mobility. *Sociology* 19:93–107

Breen, R. 1985b. Models for the comparative analysis of vertical mobility. *Qual. Quant.* 19:337–52

Breiger, R. L. 1981. The social class structure of occupational mobility. *Am. J. Sociol.* 87:578–611

Breiger, R. L. 1982a. *A relational hypothesis for the aggregation of categories in social mobility tables.* Presented at Ann. Meet. Am. Sociol. Assoc., San Francisco

Breiger, R. L. 1982b. A structural analysis of occupational mobility. In *Social Structure and Network Analysis,* ed. P. Marsden, N. Lin, pp. 17–32. Beverly Hills: Sage

Britten, N., Heath, A. 1983. Women, men and social class. See Gamarnikov et al 1983, pp. 46–60

Carchedi, G. 1975. Reproduction of social classes at the level of production relations. *Econ. Soc.* 4:359–417

Carchedi, G. 1977. *On the Economic Identification of Social Classes.* London: Routledge & Kegan

Carlsson, G. 1958. *Social Mobility and Class Structure.* Lund: Gleerup

Carroll, G. R., Mayer, K. U. 1986. Job-shift patterns in the Federal Republic of Germany: The effects of social class, industrial sector, and organizational size. *Am. Sociol. Rev.* 51:323–41

Castles, S., Kosack, G. 1985. *Immigrant Workers and Class Structure in Western Europe.* Oxford: Oxford Univ. Press

Clogg, C. C. 1981. Latent structure models of mobility. *Am. J. Sociol.* 86:836–868

Clogg, C. C. 1982. Some models for the analysis of association in multiway cross-classifications having ordered categories. *J. Am. Statist. Assoc.* 77:803–15

Clogg, C. C., Goodman, L. A. 1983. *Simultanous latent structure analysis in several groups.* Presented at Ann. Meet. Sociol. Assoc., Detroit

Coleman, J. S. 1984. The transition from school to work. *Res. Soc. Strat. Mobility* 3:27–60

Crompton, R. 1980. Class mobility in modern Britain. *Sociology* 14:117–19

Dahrendorf, R. 1964. Recent changes in the class structure of European societies. *Daedalus* 93:225–70

Dessens, J., Jansen, W., Verbeek, A. 1983. *Log-linear analysis of mobility tables using GLIM.* Presented at SMASBS-Conference, Amsterdam. Utrecht: Sociol. Inst.

Duncan, O. D. 1979. How destination depends on origin in the occupational mobility table. *Am. J. Sociol.* 84:793–804

Dunton, N. E., Featherman, D. L. 1983. Social mobility through marriage and through careers: Achievement over the life course. In *Achievement and Achievement Motives,* ed. J. T. Spence, pp. 285–320. San Francisco: Freeman

Erikson, R. 1983. Changes in social mobility in industrial nations: The case of Sweden. *Res. Soc. Strat. Mobility* 2:165–95

Erikson, R. 1984. Social class of men, women and families. *Sociology* 18:500–14

Erikson, R., Goldthorpe, J. H. 1985a. *Commonality and Variation in Social Fluidity in Industrial Nations; Some Preliminary Results.* Univ. Mannheim. CASMIN Project. Work. Pap. 4.1

Erikson, R., Goldthorpe, J. H. 1985b. *A Model of Core Social Fluidity in Industrial Nations.* Univ. Mannheim. CASMIN Project. Work. Pap. 5.1

Erikson, R., Goldthorpe, J. H. 1985c. Are American rates of social mobility exceptionally high? New evidence on an old issue. *Eur. Sociol. Rev.* 1:1–22

Erikson, R., Goldthorpe, J. H. 1986. *National variation in social fluidity.* Presented at Meet. Res. Comm. Soc. Strat., Rome

Erikson, R., Goldthorpe, J. H., Portocarero, L. 1979. Intergenerational class mobility in three Western societies: England, France and Sweden. *Br. J. Sociol.* 30:415–41

Erikson, R., Goldthorpe, J. H., Portocarero, L. 1982. Social fluidity in industrial nations: England, France and Sweden. *Br. J. Sociol.* 33:1–34

Erikson, R., Goldthorpe, J. H., Portocarero, L. 1983. Intergenerational class mobility and the convergence thesis: England,

France and Sweden. *Br. J. Sociol.* 34:303–43

Erikson, R., Pöntinen, S. 1985. Social mobility in Finland and Sweden: A comparison of men and women. In *Small States in Comparative Perspective*, ed. R. Alpuro, M. Alestato, E. Haavio-Mannila, R. Väyrynen, pp. 138–62. Oslo: Norwegian Univ. Press

Featherman, D. L. 1981. Social stratification and mobility. Two decades of cumulative social science. *Am. Behav. Sci.* 24:364–85

Featherman, D. L., Hauser, R. M. 1978. *Opportunity and Change*. New York: Academic Press

Featherman, D. L., Jones, L., Hauser, R. M. 1975. Assumptions of social mobility research in the US: The case of occupational status. *Soc. Sci. Res.* 4:329–60

Featherman, D. L., Selbee, L. K. 1986. *Class formation and class mobility. A new approach with counts from life history data*. Presented at Ann. Meet. Am. Sociol. Assoc., New York

Felmlee, D. H. 1982. Women's job mobility processes. *Am. Sociol. Rev.* 47:142–51

Flora, P. 1987. *Westeuropa im Wandel*. Frankfurt/New York: Campus. In press

Gagliani, G. 1985. Long-term changes in the occupational structure. *Eur. Sociol. Rev.* 1:183–210

Gamarnikov, E., Morgan, D., Purvis, J., Taylorson, D., eds. 1983. *Gender, Class and Work*. London: Heinemann

Ganzeboom, H. B. G., de Graaf, P. M. 1984. Intergenerational occupational mobility in the Netherlands in 1954 and 1977; A loglinear analysis. In *Social Stratification and Mobility in the Netherlands*, ed. B. F. M. Bakker, J. Dronkers, H. B. G. Ganzeboom, pp. 71–90. Amsterdam: SISWO

Giddens, A. 1973. *The Class Structure of the Advanced Societies*. London: Hutchinson

Girod, R. 1971. *Mobilité sociale: Faits établis et problémes ouverts*. Geneva: Droz

Goldthorpe, J. H. 1980. *Social Mobility and Class Structure in Modern Britain*. Oxford: Clarendon

Goldthorpe, J. H. 1982. On the service class, its formation and future. In *Social Class and the Division of Labour*, ed. A. Giddens, D. Mackenzie, pp. 162–85. Cambridge: Cambridge Univ. Press

Goldthorpe, J. H. 1983. Women and class analysis: In defence of a conventional view. *Sociology* 17:465–88

Goldthorpe, J. H. 1984a. The end of convergence: Corporatist and dualist tendencies in modern Western societies. In *Order and Conflict in Contemporary Capitalism*, ed. J. H. Goldthorpe., pp. 315–43. Oxford: Clarendon

Goldthorpe, J. H. 1984b. *Social Mobility and Class Formation: On the Renewal of a Tradition in Sociological Inquiry*. CASMIN Work. Pap. 1, Univ. Mannheim

Goldthorpe, J. H. 1984c. Women and class analysis: A reply to the replies. *Sociology* 18:491–99

Goldthorpe, J. H. 1985. On economic development and social mobility. *Br. J. Sociol.* 36:549–573

Goldthorpe, J. H. 1986. *Employment, class and mobility: A critique of liberal and Marxist theories of long-term change*. Presented at Conf. on Social Change and Development, Berkeley

Goldthorpe, J. H., Müller, W. 1982. *Social Mobility and Class Formation in Industrial Nations: A Proposal for a Comparative Research Project*. Nuffield College Oxford, Univ. Mannheim

Goldthorpe, J. H., Payne, C. 1985. *On the class mobility of women: Results from different approaches to the analysis of recent British data*. Mimeo, Oxford: Nuffield College

Goldthorpe, J. H., Payne, C. 1986. Trends in intergenerational class mobility in England and Wales, 1971–1983. *Sociology* 20:1–20

Goldthorpe, J. H., Portocarero, L. 1981. La mobilité sociale en France, 1953–1970: nouvel examen. *Revue francaise de sociologie* 22:151–66

Goodman, L. A. 1969. How to ransack social mobility tables and other kinds of cross-classification tables. *Am. J. Sociol.* 75:1–39

Goodman, L. A. 1972. Some models for the multiplicative analysis of categorical data. In *Proceedings of the Sixth Berkeley Symposium on Mathematical Statistics and Probability*, ed. L. LeCarr, J. Neyman, E. L. Scott, pp. 649–96. Berkeley: Univ. Calif. Press

Goodman, L. A. 1979a. Multiplicative models for the analysis of occupational mobility tables and other kinds of cross-classification tables. *Am. J. Sociol.* 84:804–19

Goodman, L. A. 1979b. Simple models for the analysis of association in cross-classifications having ordered categories. *J. Am. Statist. Assoc.* 74:537–52

Goodman, L. A. 1981. Criteria for determining whether certain categories in a cross-classification table should be combined with special reference to occupational categories in an occupational mobility table. *Am. J. Sociol.* 87:612–50

Goyder, J. C. 1985a. Comparisons over time. See Boyd et al 1985, pp. 163–200

Goyder, J. C. 1985b. Occupational mobility among women. See Boyd et al 1985, pp. 297–333

Grusky, D. B., Hauser, R. M. 1984. Comparative social mobility revisited: Models of convergence and divergence in 16 countries. *Am. Sociol. Rev.* 49:19–38

Hachen, D. S. 1986. *Gender differences in job mobility rates in the United States: A test of human capital and segmentation explanations.* Presented at Int. Conf. on Applications of Event History Analysis in Life Course Research. Berlin: Max-Planck-Inst. Human Dev. Educ.

Haller, M. 1981. Marriage, women, and social Stratification: A theoretical critique. *Am. J. Sociol.* 86:766–95

Haller, M. 1982a. *Klassenbildung und soziale Schichtung in Österreich.* Frankfurt/New York: Campus

Haller, M. 1982b. Klassenstrukturen und Beschäftigungssystem in Frankreich und in der Bundesrepublik Deutschland. Eine makrosoziologische Analyse der Beziehung zwischen Qualifikation Technik, und Arbeitsorganisation. In *Beschäftigungssystem im gesellschaftlichen Wandel,* ed. M. Haller, W. Müller. Frankfurt/New York: Campus

Haller, M. 1983a. *Klassenstrukturen und Mobilität in fortgeschrittenen Gesellschaften. Eine vergleichende Analyse der Bundesrepublik Deutschland, Österreichs, Frankreichs und der Vereinigten Staaten von Amerika.* Habilitationsschrift. Univ. Mannheim

Haller, M. 1983b. *Theorie der Klassenbildung und sozialen Schichtung.* Frankfurt/New York: Campus

Haller, M. 1987. Wandel der Berufsstruktur und Arbeitslosigkeit. See Flora. In press

Haller, M., Hodge, R. W. 1981. Class and status as dimensions of career mobility. Some insights from the Austrian case. *Zeitschr. Soziol.* 10:133–50

Haller, M., König, W., Krause, P., Kurz, K. 1985. Patterns of career mobility and structural positions in advanced capitalist societies: A comparison of men and women in Austria, France, and the United States. *Am. Sociol. Rev.* 50:579–603

Haller, M., Mach, B. W. 1981. Structural changes and mobility in capitalist and socialist society. A comparison of men in Austria and Poland. Univ. Mannheim. VASMA Project. Work Pap. 17

Handl, J. 1982. *Berufschancen und Heiratsmuster. Empirische Untersuchungen zu Prozessen sozialer Mobilität von Frauen in der Bundesrepublik Deutschland.* Habilitationsschrift. Univ. Mannheim

Hauser, R. M. 1978. A structural model of the mobility table. *Soc. Forc.* 56:919–53

Hauser, R. 1979. Some exploratory methods for modeling mobility tables and other cross-classified data. In *Sociological Methodology,* ed. D. R. Heise, pp. 141–458. San Francisco: Jossey-Bass

Hauser, R. M. 1984a. Vertical class mobility in England, France and Sweden. *Acta Sociol.* 27:87–110

Hauser, R. M. 1984b. Corrigenda "Vertical class mobility in England, France, and Sweden." *Acta Sociol.* 27:387–90

Hauser, R. M., Featherman, D. L. 1977. *The Process of Stratification.* New York: Academic Press

Hazelrigg, L. E., Garnier, M. A. 1976. Occupational mobility in industrial societies: A comparative analysis of differential access to occupational ranks in seventeen countries. *Am. Sociol. Rev.* 41:498–511

Heath, A. 1981. *Social Mobility.* London: Fontana

Heath, A., Britten, N. 1984. Women's jobs do make a difference. *Sociology* 18:475–90

Heath, A., Jowell, R., Curtice, J. 1985. *How Britain Votes.* Oxford: Pergamon

Hernes, G., Knudsen, K. 1985. *Gender and Class Identification in Norway.* Presented to ISA Res. Comm. Soc. Strat. Cambridge: Harvard Univ.

Herz, Th. 1987. The political effects of social mobility. In *People and their Politics,* ed. H. D. Klingemann. Beverley Hills: Sage. In press

Hope, K. 1981a. Trends in the openness of British society in the present century. *Res. Soc. Strat. Mobility* 1:127–70

Hope, K. 1981b. Vertical mobility in Britain: A structured analysis. *Sociology* 15:10–55

Hope, K. 1982. Vertical and nonvertical class mobility in three countries. *Am. Sociol. Rev.* 47:99–113

Hope, K. 1984. Comparative mobility: Can the structural model cope? *Comp. Soc. Res.* 7:427–41

Hout, M. 1982. The association between husbands' and wives' occupations in two-earner families. *Am. J. Sociol.* 88:397–409

Hout, M. 1983. *Mobility Tables.* Beverly Hills: Sage

Hout, M. 1984a. Occupational mobility of black men. *Am. Sociol. Rev.* 49:308–22

Hout, M. 1984b. Status, autonomy, and training in occupational mobility. *Am. J. Sociol.* 89:1379–1409

Hout, M. 1986. Opportunity and the minority middle class: A comparison of Blacks in the United States and Catholics in Northern Ireland. *Am. Sociol. Rev.* 51:214–33

Hout, M., Jackson, J. A. 1986. Dimensions of Occupational Mobility in the Republic of Ireland. *Eur. Sociol. Rev.* 2:114–37

Jacobs, J. 1983. Industrial sector and career mobility reconsidered. *Am. Sociol. Rev.* 48:415–21

Jackman, M. R., Jackman, R. W. 1983. *Class Awareness in the United States.* Berkeley: Univ. Calif. Press

Jones, F. L., Davis, P. 1986. *Models of Society: Class, Stratification and Gender in*

Australia and New Zealand. Sydney: Croom Helm

Kaelble, H. 1987. Was Prometheus most unbound in Europe? Labor force in Europe in the late 19th and 20th centuries. *J. European Econ. Hist.* In press

Kalleberg, A. L., Sorensen, A. B. 1979. The sociology of labor markets. *Ann. Rev. Sociol.* 5:351–79

Kappelhoff, P., Teckenberg, W. 1986. Career mobility in Germany and the U.S. In *Comparative Studies of Social Structure. Recent German Research on France, the United States, and the Federal Republic,* ed. W. Teckenberg. London: Eurospan

Kerckhoff, A. C., Campbell, R. T., Winfield-Laird, I. 1985. Social mobility in Great Britain and the United States. *Am. J. Sociol.* 91:281–308

König, W., Müller, W. 1986. Educational systems and labour markets as determinants of worklife mobility in France and West Germany: A comparison of men's career mobility, 1965–1970. *Eur. Sociol. Rev.* 2:73–96

Krauze, T., Slomczynski, K. M. 1986a. Matrix representation of structural and circulation mobility. *Sociol. Meth. Res.* 14:247–69

Krauze, T., Slomczynski, K. M. 1986b. Structural and circulation mobility in the linear programming framework. The critics in hot water—A rejoinder to the invited comment "Saving the bath water". *Sociol. Methods Res.* 14:285–300

Lewin-Epstein, N., Semyonov, M. 1986. Ethnic Group Mobility in the Israeli Labor Market. *Am. Sociol. R.* 51:342–52

Lipset, S. M., Zetterberg, H. L. 1959. Social mobility in industrial societies. In *Social Mobility in Industrial Society,* ed. S. M. Lipset, R. Bendix, pp. 11–75. Berkeley: Univ. Calif. Press

Logan, J. A. 1983. A multivariate model for mobility tables. *Am. J. Sociol.* 89:324–49

Lutz, B. 1976. Bildungssystem und Beschäftigungsstruktur in Deutschland und Frankreich. In *Betrieb—Arbeitsmarkt—Qualifikation,* ed. H. G. Mendius, W. Sengenberger, B. Lutz, N. Altmann, F. Böhle et al, pp. 83–151. Frankfurt: Aspekte

Macdonald, K. I. 1981. On the formulation of a structural model of the mobility table. *Soc. Forc.* 60:557–71

Mann, M. 1975. *Consciousness and Action Among the Western Working Class.* New York: Humanities

Marsden, P. V. 1985. Latent Structure Models for Relationally Defined Social Classes. *Am. J. Sociol.* 90:1002–21

Marx, K. 1958 (1852). *The Eighteenth Brumaire of Louis Bonaparte.* In *Selected Works,* K. Marx, F. Engels. Moscow: Foreign Lang. Publ.

Marx, K. 1959 (1894). *Capital Vol. III.* Moskow: Foreign Lang. Publ.

Matras, J. 1980. Comparative social mobility. *Ann. Rev. Sociol.* 6:401–31

Maurice, M., Sellier, F. 1979. A societal analysis of industrial relations: A comparison between France and West Germany. *Br. J. Ind. Relat.* 17:322–36

Maurice, M., Sellier, F., Silvestre, J. J. 1982. *Politique d'éducation et organisation industrielle en France et en Allemagne: Essai d'analyse sociétal.* Paris: Press Univ. France

Mayer, K. U. 1980. Berufsstruktur und Mobilitätsprozeß. Probleme des internationalen Vergleichs objektiver Indikatoren zwischen England/Wales und der Bundesrepublik Deutschland. In *Soziale Indikatoren im internationalen Vergleich,* ed. H. J. Nowotny, pp. 97–134. Frankfurt/New York: Campus

Mayer, K. U., Carroll, G. R. 1986. *Jobs and classes: Structural constraints on career mobility.* Presented at Meet. Am. Sociol. Assoc., New York

McClendon, M. J. 1980a. Occupational mobility and economic development: A cross-national analysis. *Sociol. Focus* 13:331–42

McClendon, M. J. 1980b. Structural and exchange components of occupational mobility: A cross-national analysis. *Sociol. Q.* 21:493–509

McRoberts, H., Selbee, A. K. 1981. Trends in occupational mobility in Canada and the United States: A comparison. *Am. Sociol. Rev.* 46:406–21

Müller, W. 1977. Klassenlagen und soziale Lagen in der Bundesrepublik. In *Klassenlagen und Sozialstruktur,* J. Handl, K. U. Mayer, W. Müller, pp. 21–100. Frankfurt/New York: Campus

Müller, W. 1986. Soziale Mobilität: Die Bundesrepublik im internationalen Vergleich. In *Politische Wissenschaft und politische Ordnung,* ed. M. Kaase, pp. 339–54. Opladen: Westdeutscher Verlag

Müller, W. 1987. Was bleibt von den Klassenstrukturen? See Flora. In press

Pareto, V. 1916. *Trattato di sociologia generale.* Florense: Barbera

Parkin, F. 1971. *Class Inequality and Political Order.* London: Paladin

Payne, G., Payne, J. 1983. Occupational and industrial transition in social mobility. *Br. J. Sociol.* 34:72–92

Payne, G., Payne, J., Chapman, T. 1986. Trends in female social mobility. See Gamarnikow 1986, pp.

Penn, R. 1981. The Nuffield class categorization. *Sociology* 15:265–71

Petersen, T., Spilerman, S. 1986. *Departures from an International Labor Market.* Presented at Int. Conf. on Applications of Event History Analysis in Life Course Research. Berlin: Max-Planck-Inst. Human Dev. Educ.

Pöntinen, S. 1982. Models of social mobility research: A comparison of some log-linear models of a social mobility matrix. *Qual. Quant.* 16:91–107

Pöntinen, S. 1983. *Social Mobility and Social Structure: A Comparison of Scandinavian Countries*. Helsinki: Finnish Soc. Sci. Letters

Portocarero, L. 1983a. Social fluidity in France and Sweden. *Acta Sociol.* 26:127–39

Portocarero, L. 1983b. Social Mobility in Industrial Nations: Women in France and Sweden. *Sociol. Rev.* 31:56–82

Portocarero, L. 1985. Social mobility in France and Sweden: Women, marriage and work. *Acta Sociol.* 28:151–70

Poulantzas, N. 1975. *Classes in Contemporary Capitalism*. London: New Left Books

Rein, M. 1985. *Women in the Social Welfare Labor Market. Discuss. Pap. IIM-LMP85-18*. Wissenschaftszentrum Berlin

Renner, K. 1953. *Wandlungen der modernen Gesellschaft*. Wien: Verlag der Wiener Volksbuchhandlung

Robinson, R. V. 1983. Explaining perceptions of class and racial inequality in England and the United States. *Br. J. Sociol.* 34:344–66

Robinson, R. V. 1984a. Reproducing class relations in industrial capitalism. *Am. Sociol. Rev.* 49:182–96

Robinson, R. V. 1984b. Structural change and class mobility in capitalist societies. *Soc. Forc.* 63:51–71

Robinson, R. V., Garnier, M. A. 1985. Class reproduction among men and women in France: Reproduction theory on its home ground. *Am. J. Sociol.* 91:250–80

Roemer, J. 1982. *A General Theory of Exploitation and Class*. Cambridge: Harvard Univ. Press

Rogoff-Ramsoy, N. 1977. *Sosial Mobilitet i Norge*. Oslo: Tiden

Roos, P. A. 1983. Marriage and women's occupational attainment in cross-cultural perspective. *Am. Sociol. Rev.* 48:852–64

Rose, D., Marshall, G. 1986. Review article: Constructing the (W)right classes. *Sociology* 20:440–55

Rose, M. 1985. Universalism, culturalism, and the Aix group: Promise and problems of a societal approach to economic institutions. *Eur. Sociol. Rev.* 1:65–83

Rosenbaum, J. E. 1984. Organizational career mobility: Promotion chances in a corporation during periods of growth and contractions. *Am. J. Sociol.* 85:21–48

Simkus, A. A. 1981a. Changes in occupational inheritance under socialism: Hungary

1930–1973. *Res. Soc. Strat. Mobility* 1:171–204

Simkus, A. A. 1981b. Comparative stratification and mobility. *Int. J. Comp. Sociol.* 22:213–36

Simkus, A. A. 1984. Structural transformation and social mobility: Hungary 1938–1973. *Am. Sociol. R.* 49:291–307

Simkus, A. A., Andorka, R. 1982. Inequalities in educational attainment in Hungary, 1923–1973. *Am. Sociol. Rev.* 47:740–751

Singelmann, J. 1978. *From Agriculture to Services*. Beverly Hills: Sage

Slomczynski, K. M., Krauze, T. 1983. Should the framework of structural vs. circulation mobility be abandoned? If so, not because of faulty logic. *Am. Sociol. Rev.* 48:850–52

Smith, R. 1983. Mobility in professional occupational internal labor markets: Stratification, segmentation and vacancy chains. *Am. Sociol. Rev.* 48:289–305

Snipp, M, C. 1985. Occupational mobility and social class: Insights from men's career mobility. *Am. Sociol. Rev.* 50:475–93

Sobel, M. E. 1983a. Structural mobility, circulation, mobility, and the analysis of occupational mobility: A conceptual mismatch. *Am. Sociol. Rev.* 48:721–27

Sobel, M. E. 1983b. "Frameworks" and Frameworks: Reply to Slomczynski and Krauze. *Am. Sociol. Rev.* 48:852–53

Sobel, M. E., Duncan, O. D., Hout, M. 1986. Saving the Bath Water. *Sociol. Meth. Research* 14:271–284

Sobel, M. E., Hout, M., Duncan, O. D. 1985. Exchange, structure, and symmetry in occupational mobility. *Am. J. Sociol.* 91:359–72

Sombart, W. 1906. *Warum gibt es in den Vereinigten Staaten keinen Sozialismus?* Tübingen: JCB Mohr

Sorensen, A. B. 1983a. Sociological research on the labor market. Conceptual and methodological issues. *Work Occup.* 10:261–287

Søorensen, A. B. 1983b. Processes of allocation to open and closed positions in social structure. *Zeitschr. Soziol.* 12:203–224

Sørensen, A. B. 1987. Theory and methodology in stratification research. In *Sociology: Aftermath of a Crisis*, ed. U. Himmelstrand. London: Sage. In press

Sørensen, A. B., Allmendinger, J., Sørensen, A. 1986. *Intergenerational Mobility as a Life Course Process*. Presented at Meet. Am. Sociol. Assoc., New York

Sørensen, A. B., Kalleberg, A. L. 1981. An outline of a theory of the matching of persons to jobs. In *Sociological Perspectives on the Labor Market*, ed. I. Berg, pp. 49–74. New York: Academic

Sørensen, A. B., Tuma, N. B. 1981. Labor market structures and job mobility. *Res. Soc. Strat. Mobility* 1:67–94

Sorokin, P. A. 1927. Social mobility. In *Cultural Mobility* (1959), ed. P. A. Sorokin, 1987. pp. 1–546. New York: Free Press

Spilerman, S. 1987. Organizational rules and features of work careers. *Res. Organ.* In press

Stanworth, M. 1984. Women and class analysis: A reply to John Goldthorpe. *Sociology* 18:159–70

Stewart, A., Prandy, K., Blackburn, R. M. 1980. *Social Stratification and Occupations.* London: Macmillan

Stewman, S., Konda, S. L. 1983. Careers and organizational labor markets: Demographic models of organizational behavior. *Am. J. Sociol.* 88:637–85

Stinchcombe, A. L. 1979. Social mobility in industrial labour markets. *Acta Sociol.* 22:217–45

Thélot, C. 1980. *Le poids d'Anchise.* Nantes: INSEE

Thélot, C. 1982. *Tel père, tel fils. Position sociale et origine familiale.* Paris: Dunond

Tolbert, C. M. 1982. Industrial segmentation and men's career mobility. *Am. Sociol. Rev.* 47:457–76

Treiman, D. J. 1970. Industrialization and social stratification. In *Social Stratification: Research and Theory for the 1970's,* ed. E. O. Laumann, pp. 207–34. New York: Bobbs-Merrill

Tuma, N. B. 1976. Rewards, resources and rates of mobility: A non-stationary multivariate stochastic model. *Am. Sociol. Rev.* 41:228–60

Tuma, N. B., Hannan, M. T. 1984. *Social Dynamics. Models and Methods.* Orlando: Academic Press

Tyree, A., Semyonov, M., Hodge, R. W. 1979. Gaps and glissandos: Inequality, economic development, and social mobility in 24 countries. 44:410–24

Weber, M. 1968. *Economy and Society.* New York: Bedminster

Wesolowski, W. 1979. Classes, Strata and Power. London: Routledge & Kegan Paul

Wesolowski, W., Slomczynski, K. M., Mach, B. W. 1979. Trends in social mobility studies and Marxist theory of class structure. *Polish Sociol. Bull.* 1(45):5–18

Westergaard, J., Resler, H. 1975. *Class in Capitalistic Society.* London: Heinemann

Whelan, C., Whelan, B. 1984. Social mobility in the Republic of Ireland. A Comparative Perspective. Dublin: Econ. Soc. Res. Inst.

Wright, E. O. 1978. *Class, Crisis and the State.* London: New Left Books

Wright, E. O. 1985. *Classes.* London: Verso

Yamaguchi, K. 1982. The structure of intergenerational occupational mobility: Generality and specificity in resource, channels, and barriers. *Am. J. Sociol.* 88:718–45

Zagorski, K. 1976. Changes of socio-occupational mobility in Poland. *Polish Sociol. Bull.* 34:17–30

ADDED IN PROOF

Mach, B., Wesolowski, W. 1986. *Social Mobility and Social Structure.* London: Routledge & Kegan Paul

Ann. Rev. Sociol. 1987. 13:443–64
Copyright © 1987 by Annual Reviews Inc. All rights reserved

INSTITUTIONAL THEORIES OF ORGANIZATION

Lynne G. Zucker

Department of Sociology, University of California at Los Angeles, Los Angeles, California 90024

INSTITUTIONAL THEORIES OF ORGANIZATION

Institutional theories of organizations provide a rich, complex view of organizations. In these theories, organizations are influenced by normative pressures, sometimes arising from external sources such as the state, other times arising from within the organization itself. Under some conditions, these pressures lead the organization to be guided by legitimated elements, from standard operating procedures to professional certification and state requirement, which often have the effect of directing attention away from task performance. Adoption of these legitimated elements, leading to isomorphism with the institutional environment, increases the probability of survival. Institutional theories of organization have spread rapidly, a testimony to the power of the imaginative ideas developed in theoretical and empirical work. As rigor increases, with better specification of indicators and models, it is likely to attract the attention of an even larger number of organizational researchers.

Institutional theory is inherently difficult to explicate, because it taps taken-for-granted assumptions at the core of social action. The main goal of this review, then, is to make institutional theory more accessible. The review begins with a brief summary of the two current theoretical approaches to institutionalization in organizations, moves to identification of indicators of central concepts, and then progresses to a review of empirical research. It concludes with two short sections, one on points of intersection with other theories of organization, the other on the "new institutionalism" in economics and political science.

443

0360-0572/87/0815-0443$02.00

CENTRAL CONCEPTS AND INDICATORS OF INSTITUTIONALIZATION

Defining Principles

What is the meaning of *institutional?* Two defining elements are shared by the theoretical approaches to institutionalization in organizations (most explicit in Zucker 1977:728): (*a*) a rule-like, social fact quality of an organized pattern of action (exterior), and (*b*) an embedding in formal structures, such as formal aspects of organizations that are not tied to particular actors or situations (nonpersonal/objective).

Contemporary institutional theories of organization attempt to avoid earlier conceptions that were tautological (e.g. persistence both defines and empirically indicates what is institutionized), purely descriptive (e.g. "family institution"), or untestable (e.g. internalization explanations). They do so in part by treating institutionalization as a variable, and by separating its causes from the major consequence: "establishment of relative permanence of a distinctly social sort" (Hughes 1936:180; see also Rose 1968).

Both approaches identify two defining processes (DiMaggio & Powell 1983:150): (*a*) imitative or mimetic, adopting others' successful elements when uncertain about alternatives, and (*b*) normative transmission of social facts, generally from external sources such as the professions. A third defining process, coercive, is central to state legitimation in the environment-as-institution approach, but it is explicitly considered deinstitutionalizing in the organization-as-institution approach, since any use of sanctions indicates that other attractive alternatives exist.

Four other defining principles diverge significantly: motif, source, locus, and outcome of institutionalization. As outlined in Table 1 and reflected in the discussion below, there are two distinct theoretical approaches: Environment as institution assumes that the basic process is *reproduction* or copying of system-wide (or sector-wide; see below) social facts on the organizational level, while organization as institution assumes that the central process is *generation* (meaning creation of new cultural elements) at the organization level. In this latter approach, reproduction is a consequence of institutionalization, not a cause.

ENVIRONMENT AS INSTITUTION   Institutional environments obtain their defining power from "rationalization" and from accompanying state elaboration. These environments are constructed as one consequence of a much wider "state project," related to expansion of state jurisdiction (Thomas & Meyer 1984:469). This "statist" view conceives of the collective normative order, including the professions and widespread agreements shared by members of organizational fields, as linked to a broad conception of the state (Thomas et

Table 1 Major points of theoretical divergence

Theoretical approach	Environment as institution	Organization as institution
Motif	Reproductive	Generative
Source	Growth of state	Small groups & imitation of other organizations
Locus	Outside organization State linked	Internal process Similar organizations
Outcomes	(1) Decoupling from technical core (2) Inefficiency	(1) Stability (2) Efficiency contingent on alternatives

al 1987, less clear in DiMaggio & Powell 1983). Conformity of organizations to the collective normative order increases the flow of societal resources and enhances "long-run survival prospects" (Meyer & Rowan 1977:252).

Institutional elements invariably come from outside the organization. These elements cause change in organizations, but the impetus for action is unclear because the organization is in an "iron cage" (but see DiMaggio 1987). When organizations respond to external institutional pressure (or possibly only to coercive pressure as in DiMaggio & Powell 1983), they protect their technical activities through decoupling elements of structure from other activities and from each other, thus reducing their efficiency (Meyer & Rowan 1977:357, Weick 1976, Selznick 1949). In contrast, in line with predictions from economic theory, firms that operate in the technical sector "succeed to the extent that they develop efficient production activities and effective coordination structures" (Scott & Meyer 1983:141). But efficiency and success do not necessarily covary in institutional theory:

> Organizational conformity to the institutional environment simultaneously increases positive evaluation, resource flows, and therefore survival chances, *and* reduces efficiency.

In this view, the social becomes mythical and implicitly dysfunctional in strict task performance terms, while the technical remains real and rational (Meyer & Rowan 1977:356–57). Institutionalized organizations serve many important legitimating functions, but the core tasks are not performed as well as they would be in a market-oriented organization, and basic organizational objectives are also often deflected (Selznick 1957, reviewed in Perrow 1986:159–64).

Three defining principles, then, are: (*a*) Institutional processes stem from overarching rationalization, a zeitgeist-like world-wide phenomenon, that fuels growth of the state; (*b*) institutions are commonly state-linked and invariably external to the organization; and (*c*) institutionalization produces task-related inefficiency, hence decoupling of internal structure. Refer to Table 1. Institutional processes are constrained and systematic.

ORGANIZATION AS INSTITUTION   *Implemented* institutional elements commonly arise from within the organization itself or from imitation of other similar organizations (Zucker 1977:728, 1983; Tolbert & Zucker 1983; Tolbert 1985), not from power or coercive processes located in the state or elsewhere. Use of sanctions implies availability of attractive alternatives, and it tends to deinstitutionalize.

Borrowing from ethnomethodology (Garfinkel 1967, Schutz 1962), the argument can be made that acts and structures embedded in organizations (where the "routines" and roles are highly formalized and have continuity over time) are more readily institutionalized than those embedded in alternative informal social coordination structures (Zucker 1977:728–29, 1983:16–18). Hence organizations are important sources of institutionalization of new action. Already institutionalized elements can "infect" other elements in a contagion of legitimacy. For example, universities can create new departments, simultaneously creating new structures, new knowledge that is defined as expert, and new sets of categories to which individuals are allocated. It is paradoxical that:

> Because institutional elements (structures, actions, roles) are authorized to legitimate other elements, institutionalized aspects are simultaneously highly stable *and* responsible for creating new institutional elements (Zucker 1987b).

Institutional elements are easily transmitted to newcomers, are maintained over long periods of time without further justification or elaboration, and are highly resistant to change (Zucker 1977, 1983, 1987b; also Nelson & Winter 1982: Ch. 5)[1]. The resulting stability increases effectiveness when it is linked to goals of the organization by creating "routines" that reduce search and evaluation costs. But stability decreases effectiveness if more efficient ways of organizing are ignored, often because they are literally not perceived (Zucker 1977:728; implicit in conceptual "blockbusting", Adams 1979:Ch. 4).

Three defining principles, then, are: (*a*) Institutional elements arise primarily from small group or organization-level processes; (*b*) formalized

---

[1]Not all elements of organizations, nor all types of organizations, are equally institutionalized. Habits must be distinguished from institutional elements, perhaps by resistance to change. Also, routines are static, while some institutional elements are always in the process of decreasing in institutionalization and others are simultaneously increasing.

organizational structure and process tend to be both highly institutionalized and a source of new institutionalization; and (c) institutionalization increases stability, creating routines that enhance organizational performance except when more efficient alternatives are ignored. Refer again to Table 1. Institutional order is negotiated and emergent, never systematically controlled.

Indicators of Institutionalization

Construction of indicators can be avoided by assuming institutional status and then studying institutional properties (Meyer 1977, Kamens 1977). This is a useful heuristic device when focus is on elaboration of structure within institutionalized systems, but differences in degree of institutionalization across the same system are obscured. For example, methods and content of instruction itself are not highly institutionalized (Rowan 1982), while use of a common grading system is.

Because of the "social fact" quality, indicators of institutionalization are more indirect than, say, measures of resource dependence. Table 2 groups the indicators under institutional environment, degree of institutionalization, and consequences or outcomes of the institutional process. Conceptually, the first two are independent variables, with consequences dependent. In fact, the empirical work examines the theory piecemeal, seldom testing the causal predictions (but see laboratory experiments by Zucker 1977 and Thomas et al 1987, and field studies by Zucker et al 1986, Dobbin et al 1987, and Meyer et al 1987).

Indicators of "institutional environment" in Table 2 reflect pressures generated external to the organization, such as those created by the state via law and regulation or by the professions, based on their widespread authority. Unaccredited hospitals are unlikely to attract top physicians and are barred from receiving state funds (Zucker & Taka 1986); industries that cannot use patents to protect innovations from imitation have lower financial returns (Hirsch 1975). There are two principal problems with indicators of the institutional environment. First, they are often global and thus invariant across organizations, requiring a comparative approach. Second, the power or authority is often translated into control over resource flow to the organization, making it difficult to distinguish institutional from resource dependence explanations (see Pfeffer 1982:Ch. 6 & 7, and discussion at the end of this chapter).

Changes in degree of institutionalization in the second section of Table 2 are often indicated by changes in language, shifting toward the more routine and positive. For example, justification of civil service reform changed from reforming city governments plagued by bossism and corruption to a required aspect of modern, efficient government structures (Tolbert & Zucker 1983:Tbl. 1). In a similar way, payoffs to prevent unfriendly takeovers of

Table 2 Indicators proposed for tests of institutional theory and competing interpretations

Indicator	Reference	Competing interpretation
Institutional Environment		
1. Outside elements subverting goals	Selznick 1949 Clark 1956 & 1960 Zald & Denton 1963	Relative power
2. Passage of law	Rowan 1982:Fig. 1, 2, 3 Tolbert & Zucker 1983:Fig. Zucker et al 1986:Tbl. 1	Resource dependence
3. Professionalism	Rowan 1982:Fig. 1, 2, 3 Powell 1985 & 1987	Authority & control
4. Regulation #; federal contracts in firms	Hirsch 1974 Scott & Meyer 1983 Dobbin et al 1987:Tbl. 2	Resource dependence
Degree of institutionalization		
1. Linguistic shorthand	Zucker 1983:Tbl. 12 Hirsch 1986:Tbl. 3	Frequency of use
2. Certainty of accuracy/ judgment	Zucker 1977:Tbl. 4	Information differential
3. Change in content or rationale	Tolbert & Zucker 1983:Tbl. 1 Armour & Teece 1978 M. Meyer et al 1985:Tbl. 5.2	Political shifts or competitive advantage
Consequences of institutionalization		
1. Maintenance; low failure rates	Zucker 1977:Tbl. 5 & 1983:Tbl. 5 Rowan 1982:Tbl. 2 Dobbin et al 1987:Fig 2 & 3	Power of organizations & elites
2. Resistance to change; reduce action	Zucker 1977:Tbl. 7 Zelditch & Walker 1984 Thomas et al 1986:Tbl. 1	Sanctioning; Information differential
3. Isomorphism	DiMaggio & Powell 1983 & 1984 Tolbert 1985 & 1987:Tbl. 3 J. Meyer et al 1987:Tbl. 3	Simple imitation; Population ecology
4. Centralization; evaluation in network	Kamens & Lunde 1987:Tbl. 4 Hinings & Greenwood 1987 Zucker 1986b & 1981:Tbl. 1	Resource dependence
5. Decoupling; loose coupling	Weick 1976 Meyer & Rowan 1977	Lack of commitment to element
6. Allocative power; Authorized to legitimate	J. Meyer 1977 Zucker 1983:Tbl. 10 Zucker 1987a	Value structure

corporations were shifted from illegal "blackmail" to "greenmail" (Hirsch 1986:Appendix).

Recently, research on causes of institutionalization has been eclipsed by study of its consequences or outcomes. The traditional concern with stability and resistance to change, reflected in Table 2, is often extended beyond the institutional element to the organization as a whole; this predicts: (*a*) low rates of organizational failure, i.e. probability of survival increases when the organization is embedded in the institutional environment (Meyer & Rowan 1977, Scott & Meyer 1983), and (*b*) an organizational structure closed to change from the environment except when first formed or during reorganization (Stinchcombe 1965:154–160; Meyer & Brown 1977:Table 1; Williamson & Swanson 1966:Table 4.3.A).

In institutionalized contexts, organizations are pressured to become increasingly similar, sometimes because of environmental constraint (Meyer & Rowan 1977, DiMaggio & Powell 1983), sometimes because of network ties with other organizations that make changing any one element difficult without altering other interconnected elements (Zucker 1986b). For example, if a college wishes to abandon grading practices and to give written comments instead, then graduate and professional schools have to agree to make admission decisions based on the written comments, without grades, for the change to be viable.[2]

Other consequences stem from the power that institutional elements have to create social categories that become redefined as fact. Allocation to them alters life chances and perceptions by actors, and it defines conceivable alternative lines of action (classic work on this problem in Durkheim & Mauss 1903:8, 66, 81; Sapir 1931:578). Educational systems expand the existing set of categories by, for example, creating the role "physician," and its reciprocal role, "patient" (Meyer 1977:73). These new categories may be more or less integrated with earlier categories, e.g. by giving families major roles in allocating personnel to firms (Zucker 1983:30–33, Udy 1962, Hall 1977).

Indicators similar to those listed in Table 2 are used to measure institutionalization in the empirical studies reviewed below.

REVIEW OF EMPIRICAL RESEARCH

Research is roughly categorized along three dimensions describing the *source* of institutionalization: the wider institutional environment, other organizations, and internal organizational structure.

Institutional Environment

What defines the institutional environment? Two somewhat different definitions have been proposed. In the first definition, "positions, policies,

[2]This example was drawn from lectures by Morris Zelditch, Jr., in an introductory sociology course in which he illustrated concepts developed by the impenetrable Nadel (1953).

programs, and procedures of modern organization . . . are manifestations of powerful institutional rules which function as highly rationalized myths" (Meyer & Rowan 1977:343), not explainable by direct task contingencies (Selznick 1957; Scott & Meyer 1983). Thus, organizations become a passive "audience" for institutional knowledge (Meyer 1983), because the rules are formed in the state or even world system, external and hierarchically superior to the organization (Thomas & Meyer 1984, Meyer & Hannan 1979). Hence, the institutional environment is *not* reducible to the "effects generated by the networks of social behavior and relationship which compose and surround a given organization" (Meyer & Rowan 1977:341).

It is just this network conception that is picked up in the second definition (DiMaggio & Powell 1983:148): "By organizational field, we mean those organizations that, in the aggregate, constitute a recognized area of institutional life . . .," defined in terms of increased density of interaction, information flows, and membership identification. This structuration of fields also generally includes domination and hierarchy (DiMaggio & Powell 1983; on analysis via block modeling, see DiMaggio 1986:347–58). The state is but one source among many, though an unusually powerful one (DiMaggio 1983).

Much as do "populations" in ecological approaches to organizations, fields or sectors also differ on a large number of factors, making it difficult to construct abstract divisions. Though the majority of ties may be with other organizations in the same "field," the most important institutionalization may occur along lines that crosscut fields. Objective personnel procedures and formation of personnel departments represent just two examples (Baron et al 1986). Also, even similar enterprises, such as professional, nonprofit organizations, can function in dramatically different fields. For example, in academic publishing, social networks and close exchange are critical to the on-going task activities, but editors are simultaneously shielded from undue outside influence (Powell 1985), while in public television exchange is formal, but the influence of external funders penetrates the internal operating structure (Powell 1987).

In one of the most systematic studies, art museums were shown to be more likely to share similar structures—in terms of allocation of staff and budgets among administrative and artistic functions—if they were subject to strong institutional pressures (DiMaggio & Powell 1984). These positions are part of the core technology, and hence DiMaggio & Powell (1984:24) conclude that not "all structural effects of institutional pressures can be easily decoupled from core activities." In a preliminary report of their research, based on a sample of 111 museums, they found: (*a*) size, age, and funding of museums reduced the variation among museums in allocation of staff and personnel, and (*b*) variation was greater in specialist museums (drawing intensively on different revenue sources) than among generalist museums (drawing from a wide range of revenue sources).

AGENCY AND INSTITUTIONAL INTERPENETRATION   The process leading particular actors, including the state, to exert pressure is underspecified (DiMaggio 1987). It may rest on relevance of interest and usable power (Selznick 1949), on the need for continual reproduction in the face of constant erosion of institutions (Zucker 1987b, DiMaggio 1987), or on the concerted efforts of "institutional entrepreneurs" who make use of personal resources to build or rebuild institutional structure (DiMaggio 1987).

When the institutional project is successful, why are some organizations interpenetrated by the institutional environment, while others are not? Three answers rest on differences between organizations: internal goals and values, legitimacy of external control, and relative control or power of the organization. First, organizations championing "precarious" values, those not widely shared, are more likely to have their goals subverted (Clark 1956:333, 1960:156). Such goal displacement is negatively evaluated when the original goals promoted the public welfare (Selznick 1949, Zald & Denton 1963, Zald & Ash 1966, Wamsley 1969, Nonet 1969). Subverting goals such as water or air pollution would probably be viewed more positively (e.g. Jaccoby & Steinbruner 1973, Ackerman & Hassler 1981).

Second, organizations may seek legitimation of their activities through active control or shaping of the institutional environment (Dowling & Pfeffer 1975, Pfeffer & Salancik 1978:Ch. 8) in order to gain access to societal resources, thus insuring their long-term survival (Scott & Meyer 1983). Public organizations, or firms with strong ties to the public sector via contracts, are likely to adopt innovations required or supported by government policy voluntarily and to reject those prohibited (Hinings & Greenwood 1987, Dobbin et al 1987).

Third, the relative power of the organization has an independent effect on compliance: The extent of an organization's continuing control over its own boundaries determines the amount of environmental penetration, institutional or otherwise (Meyer & Zucker 1986). Firms, with greater power than public organizations, use boundary units, contracting, or incorporating parts of the environment in internal hierarchies as means of reducing the effects on task performance of such environmental forces as suppliers and regulatory agencies (Thompson 1967:Ch. 3, Thompson & McEwen 1958, Williamson 1975). Owners generally exercise power to prevent other interested parties, including workers or community members, from influencing any internal decision-making, such as new products or investments. But owners typically have low nonpecuniary interests in the firm (except under special circumstances, as in the family firm), so their incentives to maintain boundaries decrease markedly if the firm becomes unprofitable, showing negative returns compared to alternative investments. For example, workers, community members, and even the state are often able to cancel or alter decisions about firm bankruptcy or liquidation (see Nelson 1981:69–71). Unlike public organizations, this seldom represents a willing embrace by the owners of the institutional environment for legitimating or survival purposes; rather, owners receiving low returns from firm operations are simply less interested in protecting it from outside interference (Meyer & Zucker 1986).

The concept "institutional environment" provides important insights concerning the organization/environment interface. Recent work has gone one step further and defined an institutional-technical continuum along which aspects of the environment can be arrayed.

INSTITUTIONAL VERSUS TECHNICAL   In Selznick's classic statement, to "institutionalize is to *infuse with value* beyond the technical requirements of the task at hand" (Selznick 1957:16–17), thus invariably impeding effective task performance and subverting the goals of the organization. This insight suggests a fundamental opposition between task and institutional elements, both internally and in the environment (Meyer et al 1981).

Organizations that function in institutional environments must "acquire types of personnel and . . . develop structural arrangements and production processes that *conform* to the *specifications of that sector*" (Scott & Meyer 1983:141, emphases added). Institutional environments are hierarchical (or "vertical"), with centralized decision-making, especially in funding as compared to programmatic decisions (Scott & Meyer 1983:143-44). While centralized funding may strengthen legitimate control over structure (inferred from the intersection of Propositions 4, 8, and 17, Scott & Meyer 1983:141–49), it is not necessary for sectoral effects. For example, substantial bureaucratic elaboration and convergence in education occurs *without* centralization of funding (Meyer et al 1987:Table 5).

Institutionalized fields limit the direction and content of change, causing "an inexorable push toward homogenization" (DiMaggio & Powell 1983:148). For example, when measured by coefficients of variation, educational structures in 48 states converge dramatically over a 40-year time span (Meyer et al 1987:Tables 3 and 5): the ratio of superintendents to districts decreased variability across states from 1.05 to .29 and state education agency staffs from 1.43 to .80.

While the institutional/technical dichotomy is an appealing one, both types of environments often impinge on a single organization (recognized in Scott & Meyer 1983, Scott 1987:125–34; see also Powell 1987, Hirsch 1975). Empirically, even private sector organizations are affected by institutional pressures (Tolbert 1985:2): "It is not the case that some organizations are constrained by their institutional environments, while others are not; rather there are different expectations for different types of organizations". Still, even those critical of the institutional perspective in general have noted the heuristic value of the technical-institutional distinction (Perrow 1985:152).

Other Organizations As Source

Moving away from the state as the primary source of institutional elements, other organizations—most not state-linked—diffuse both administrative and technological innovations, some of which become institutional elements. Also, interorganizational ties can produce institutional elements (reviewed in Turk 1985), but as in the case of institutional environments, it is difficult to separate the institutional and resource dependence arguments (Glasberg & Schwartz 1983, Pfeffer 1973). Some kinds of ties, such as those with regulatory bodies, professional associations, and financial and "business service" intermediaries, are more clearly independent of resource flows and institutionally define alternative structures, lines of action, and acceptable outcomes of transactions (e.g. Benson 1975, Zald 1978).

Two aspects of the basis for adoption of an innovation are related to institutionalization. One is the linkage between the innovation and organizational reputation (Zucker 1986b). If an innovation directly affects reputation, then it is more likely to diffuse rapidly, to be retained by the organization, and to increase the likelihood of continued organizational survival (Zucker 1987c). The other aspect is the replacement of independent evaluation of the innovation with uncritical acceptance based on its legitimacy (Tolbert & Zucker 1983).[3] Early adopters constitute a "template" for change (Hinings et al 1986). Initially, the adoption can be predicted on a "rational" basis as a needed change, related to specific organizational characteristics, but as diffusion continues the explanatory power of the variables decreases significantly: the percentage of foreign born population and the size of the city predict the adoption of civil service reform by city governments in the period from 1885 to 1914, but not from 1915 to 1934 (Tolbert & Zucker 1983:Table 2). In a similar way, task demands measured as budget complexity predict the growth of city finance agencies from 1907 to 1932, but not from 1933 to 1975 (Meyer et al 1985:Table 5.2). Also the size of a firm declines significantly as a predictor of adoption of specialized personnel units and job evaluation systems between 1935 and 1946 (Baron et al 1986:Table 8). Other supportive findings include patterns of adoption of new organizational management structure and corporate organization (Fligstein 1985, Armour & Teece 1978).

---

[3]For both technical and administrative innovations, evaluation is difficult and costly, increasing reliance on returns from innovation received by similar organizations. This is tricky, since many innovations are correlated, not causally related, to high performance. Other reasons for adoption, such as reputation, also need to be explicitly considered. Effects on organizational survival depend on such details of the adoption decision (Zucker 1986b).

While interorganizational ties in general can lead to institutionalization, intermediaries in particular both generate and institutionalize new "social facts" by reducing reliance on particular actors such as managers or boundary personnel; thus they increase the "objectivity" of interaction among organizations: Firms seldom borrow from each other; they borrow from banks that lend out funds deposited by other firms. Property is exchanged not on a literal handshake, but through an escrow account. A real estate agency rents excess office space of one firm to another firm, yet another agency arranges a merger, and so on. Intermediaries smooth transactions via a quasi-insurance of completion without opportunism or malfeasance by focusing on the transaction itself and remaining indifferent to the outcome (Zucker 1986a:60–65). This tends to reduce the importance of both dyadic trust relations (but see Macaulay 1963:63–64, Arrow 1974:23) and the "immediate social context" (but see Granovetter 1985:485, Baker 1984:783–4).[4] Since intermediaries "manufacture" trust as a commodity and market it, the actual transaction cost increases, since it often substitutes for "free" trust generated by kin ties or ethnic group membership (contrast Zucker 1986a:61–65, especially footnote 8, and Brewer 1981 with Williamson 1975, 1979, 1981).

Internal Organizational Structure As Source

In the research reviewed so far, institutional elements are uniformly generated *external* to the "target" organization. These elements operate independent of the individual—even if perceived as unfair and not supported by the person, the individual will still behave *as if* he/she supported them (Zelditch & Walker 1984, Thomas et al 1987, see also Kurke 1987).

But if within-group processes are a priori restricted from institutional creation, then institutional theory creates an "oversocialized" view of individual behavior that presents serious theoretical obstacles: (*a*) Creation of new social order is rendered problematic since the only elements that are institutional are external, in an infinite regression to God or, more commonly, the state; (*b*) the solution to individual choice problems between multiple

---

[4]Trust reflects information concerning the likelihood that the exchange will be completed in good faith. It requires repeated transactions, social similarities (e.g. ethnic identity) that are thought to indicate reliability, or formal structures, often using third parties or extensive socialization, that serve as quasi-insurance of the exchange (Zucker 1986a). Information at each level may be mutually supportive, or may actually undermine trust production (for a more extended discussion see Zucker 1987b). At the level of individual exchange, formal mechanisms may undermine trust (Arrow 1974:23): Trust is "not a commodity that can be bought very easily. If you have to buy it, you already have some doubts about what you've bought." At the level of formal rules, if an individual violates, for example, secrecy and impartiality in personel review processes, there is a simultaneous decrease in trust in the formal system (and increase in cynicism about its value), and increase in interpersonal trust of the violator, because he/she is seen as acting in the interest of the person informed.

social realities, containing context-specific rules, is not provided; and (c) on-going social relationships have little effect on behavior, creating social atomization and thus a widening gap between the institutional environment and the social world unfolding internally in the organization (Selznick 1949, 1957; Meyer & Rowan 1977). These obstacles have been acknowledged in a piecemeal way in institutional analysis, and partial solutions have been suggested. The role of the individual—atomistically creating social order as an "institutional entrepreneur"—has been asserted (DiMaggio 1987); the definition shifts that accompany changes in social contexts have been experimentally shown to alter relevance of rules (Zucker 1980, Alexander & Wiley 1981, see also Schutz 1970), and the importance of the embeddedness of individual action in social relations has been argued forcefully (Granovetter 1985:484).

However, the role of highly institutionalized elements *within* the group— formal positions coupled with continuity of position independent of occupant—in the creation of new social facts has been largely ignored.[5] Though the "Great Man" theory of historical change has been abandoned, the "Great Collective" theory has not yet fully emerged (but see Mann 1973 and Gamson 1975 for independent treatments of the importance of collective action). Recognition of organizations as the preeminent collective actor has been relegated to a footnote in most recent theorizing and research, despite empirical evidence of significant increase in the importance of organizational actors as compared to individual actors in modern social systems (Coleman 1974, Burt 1975, Zucker 1983). As part of this process, formal organizations, previously characterized as untrustworthy and ephemeral, come to be entrusted with central societal tasks such as regulation of investment markets (Davis 1965), organizing labor (McNeill 1887), or borrowing and lending money (Miller 1927, Southworth 1928, Cagan 1969).

Also, organizational categories now define societal position, so that, for example, occupation is used to measure social mobility (Featherman et al 1975). As early as the seventeenth century, occupations determined stratification in new, isolated communities (Diamond 1958). This reversed the traditional use of broad societal categories, such as family background, to determine organizational position in preindustrial societies (Udy 1962). Further organizational elaboration has created an intricate structure of interrelated

---

[5]Individuals are also interconnected via networks of relationships, both inside the organization and independent of organization boundaries. To the extent that these networks overlap (see Travers & Milgram 1969 for proof that they generally do), they tend to be stable to maintain their coherence, resisting change unless all interconnected elements can be changed simultaneously as in a hierarchical or power centralized system (Zucker 1986b, Marsden 1983). Both internal organization and network coherence and interconnectedness, then, act paradoxically to maintain the existing structure and related actions and simultaneously to encourage change in it.

supports: Educational organizations credential workers by assigning them to occupations (Collins 1971, Meyer & Rowan 1978); further refinement in these categories occurs at the level of individual firms by assigning job titles in internal labor markets (Doeringer & Piore 1971).

Within an organization, there may be many settings and many individual workers who perform tasks repetitively. Under these conditions, social defini-tion of tasks *within* the organization often transforms them from piecemeal performances into "routines" (Nelson & Winter 1982:Ch. 5)[6]. But some routines will be simple habits, easily changed when better techniques become known, while other will be taken-for-granted elements that resist change. In general, organizational routines increase institutionalization within a given organization as a function of (Zucker 1987b): (*a*) the degree of explicit codification in the form of work rules, formal promotion hierarchies, and other types of formalization of the specific routine; (*b*) the length of the history of the structure/task; and (*c*) the degree of embeddedness in a network of structures/tasks (see Nadel 1953), such that change in one part would make inevitable changes in other structures/tasks with which it is interdependent (e.g. long-linked technologies in serial interdependence, as described by Thompson 1967:15–16; and many professional tasks: Zucker 1986b, 1987a,d). These processes are more likely in the presence of some diffusion from the task or institutional environment; however, internal organizational processes predominate because of extensive buffering of outside effects (Thompson 1967) and because of an imperfect ability to imitate (Nelson & Winter 1982:123–25). Also, the role of managers in creating and maintaining the more institutionalized of these routines is substantial (Pfeffer 1981).

One empirical study provides some convincing evidence on the importance of internal organizational sources of structure, especially when the environ-ment is heterogeneous (Tolbert 1987). It examined socialization of new organizational members in law firms, critical to the ability of the firm to continue task routines largely unchanged. Internal socialization mechanisms included: the number of times associates were formally reviewed in their first year, the number of times they were reviewed per year after their first year, whether or not the firm reported the provision of special training programs for associates, and whether or not associates were given feedback on their progress toward partnership in the firm at specified times. As the proportion

---

[6]The process of creating routines is largely independent of skill level, much more directly related to the degree of institutionalization. As institutionalization increases, the extent to which all "competent" members of the system (e.g. social system, craft or professional subsystem) are expected to share the skill increases. The skill level is "low" only because almost everyone in the society can do it, such as drive a delivery car for a drug store. The actual skills are fairly complex, but in fact no one except the economist—and driver's training school—treats it that way (see Machlup 1946:534). Knowledge of routines is much more widespread than is suggested in revision of classic theories of skills and production sets (see Friedman 1953:22; Nelson & Winter 1982:Ch. 4).

of new members selected from the same law school as the older associates of the firm increased, the reliance on internal formal socialization mechanisms significantly decreased. Homogeneity of environment, then, decreased elaboration of internal organizational structure, contradicting the environment-as-institution approach, while heterogeneity—reflecting institutional dissensus—increased structure (contra Benson 1975, Rowan 1982). Internal task routines were thus maintained.

COMPETITIVE TESTS OF INSTITUTIONAL THEORY

In most of the research, institutional ideas are explicitly tested against global "rational" perspectives, but because of the definitional thicket that makes a clean test impossible, no further review is attempted here. Instead, two other areas of current competitive tests, resource dependence and population ecology, are examined.

Resource Dependence

Most studies use degree of control by the state, via law, regulation, or resource flow, as the measure of the degree of institutionalization. This makes it difficult to distinguish institutional from resource dependency explanations, since compliance with governmental edict depends on organizational dependence on the state in one form or another; noncompliance thus risks disruption in funding (Zald 1978, DiMaggio 1983). Passing new laws provides one such example (Tolbert & Zucker 1983:Figure, Zucker et al 1986). But even the use of subtle pressure is commonly associated with resource flows, as when schools are encouraged to apply for grants that provide special programs for disadvantaged pupils, or local governments are encouraged by central authorities who control funding to adopt a radically different mode of organizing, as they were in England and Wales (Hinings et al 1986).[7]

In a clever test between institutional and resource dependency explanations, Tolbert disentangled dependency and structure in a study of higher education by demonstrating that it is "only when dependency relations are not institutionalized that increasing dependence is strongly associated with the development of separate administrative offices to manage them" (1985:11). Moving from one institutional "niche" to another was found to affect heavily the creation of administrative offices (Tolbert 1985): (a) Public and private

---

[7]How can resource dependence be made a less plausible counter-explanation? One way is to construct separate measures of environmental pressure, often tied to resource dependence, and institutional status, for example, documenting that the same "fact" alters in social content over time: Content analysis of contemporaneous reports shows a shift from anticorruption to efficient government as the motive for civil service reform (see Tolbert & Zucker 1983, Table 1). Another way is to document the independent role of groups not directly influencing resource flow, such as professional associations (Hinings & Greenwood 1987). But when the effects of such associations cannot be fully separated from those of other organizations that do control resources, resource dependence is an equally compelling (and more parsimonious) explanation.

institutions had distinct administrative offices that reflected their relative dependence on public or private sources of funding; (*b*) increases in funding of the type "traditionally" associated with private or public institutions did not alter the pattern of administrative offices; however, (*c*) increases in funding of the type associated with nontraditional sources predicted creation of new administrative offices, strongest when resource flows came to public institutions from private sources. Hence, the strongest institutional response in this case was toward the private sector, not toward the state. Most important, since only changes in funding from nontraditional sources produced an institutional response, a straight resource dependence explanation is ruled out.

Population Ecology

Research in the population ecology framework has tended to atomize organizations, generally looking at the effects of a handful of variables on foundings and "deaths" of similar organizations grouped into industries by the economists (Mansfield 1962:Table 1) and into "populations" by the sociologists (Hannan & Freeman 1977, Freeman 1982). In most of the work, measures of the task environment that immediately affects the organization, both in time and in proximate location, predominate. Institutional variables, such as regulation, legislative change, and political turmoil have not been included until recently in population ecology models. At the same time, the institutional model can be faulted for not examining empirically the predictions of enhanced survival. Unlike the conflict with resource dependency predictions, it was expected that the population ecology and institutional models would supplement each other (Carroll & Huo 1986, Zucker & Taka 1986).

In a study of newspaper organizations from 1870 to 1980, a wide array of task-related variables and institutional (here, political and broad economic cycle) variables were assembled (Carroll & Huo 1986). There are two significant findings for the institutional/population ecology interface: (*a*) Institutional variables, principally political turmoil, affect founding and death rates of newspapers, while task variables for the most part do not (Tables 1–4); and (*b*) using data on performance of four newspapers, task variables appear to affect performance strongly, while institutional variables do not (compare Tables 5 and 6).

In a study of all general surgical hospitals in California over a much shorter time period (1959–1979) but with more complete information, no evidence of the sharp discontinuity between institutional (here, legislative change and accreditation), and task environmental effects were found (Zucker 1986c, Zucker & Taka 1986). While the most consistent effects on exits or "deaths" of hospital organizations were institutional (number of accreditations decreased the likelihood of exit; passage of MediCal reform legislation increased it), these effects differed dramatically by hospital type. County (public) showed strong institutional effects, and private, for-profit hospitals showed both institutional effects *and* task effects. County population density decreased the likelihood of exit, and personnel staffing costs increased it. Estimated separately, performance (occupancy rate) was about equally affected by institutional and task variables. With performance data for all hospitals in the sample, it was possible to enter the performance measure into the organizational survival analysis. The higher the performance, the lower was the exit rate, a finding strong and consistent across all types except county (public) hospitals. Thus, a tight coupling between performance and survival was found, heavily conditioned by institutional variables in all types of hospitals, especially county, and by task variables in private, for-profit hospitals.

THE NEW INSTITUTIONALISM IN ECONOMICS AND POLITICAL SCIENCE

Until recently, most work in economics and political science has treated organizations as black boxes that simply reflect aggregate interlocking individual choices (see especially Leibenstein 1966, Niskanen 1971). However, a new stream of work concerned with explaining action as the output of institutions rather than individuals has emerged. As in sociology, the initial focus has been on a rather diffuse set of processes, including law or rules (Levi 1981; North 1986b), contracts, government administration (Skrowronek 1982), regulation, hierarchies (Williamson 1975, Padgett 1981), professional codes, and social norms (Akerlof 1980). Even psychology, in recent work on social dilemmas, moves closer to an institutional perspective: It is rules, leadership, even trust that account for the individual willingness to forego self-interest and contribute to the common good (Brewer 1981, Kramer & Brewer 1984, Messick et al 1983, Yamagishi 1986).

Recent reviews in political science (March & Olsen 1984) and in economics (North 1986a) reflect emergence of explanations based on institutions "behaving" as actors in their own right. In economics, theorists grapple with the constraints that institutions place on the choices that individuals make, and little emphasis is placed on the character of the institutional structure. Instead, there is great interest in enforcement mechanisms that ensure individual compliance to institutional edicts (North 1986b; see also radically different solutions in Darby & Karni 1973 and Akerlof 1983). The current emphasis on social control has a natural but largely unexploited relation to psychological research on social dilemmas (see above). In political science, there seems to be more concern with the character of institutional structures, especially with how they are changed once formed, but this work is done primarily by political sociologists (e.g. Skocpol & Finegold 1982, Roy 1983). Political science is also examining unintentional effects on individual behavior, primarily through constraining the range of political alternatives. Political enforcement mechanisms are often not so valuable as a means of obtaining compliance (contrary to the economic assumption), but are used to signal seriousness of intention (Skocpol & Finegold 1982).

In political science and economics, and less surprisingly in psychology, there is very little interest in the problems of where institutions come from, the processes that produce institutionalization of one element but not another (or, conversely, the contagion of legitimacy), or the internal structure or coherence of institutions. Institutional production and legitimation processes are left to the sociologists; other means of producing stable and coordinated action have largely been dominated by the other disciplines. Clearly, a combination of insights would produce a more complete institutional theory, more testable, and significantly more explicit, since the hidden disciplinary assumptions would necessarily be questioned. We would all benefit from an institutional theory that is much more precise: (*a*) It must make explicit such starting assumptions as how stable and coherent the social system is net of institutional structure; (*b*) it must be definitionally tighter, and should limit the use of underspecified terms such as "norms" and "myths"; (*c*) the link between institutional elements and their consequences must be specified—and tested—in more detail; and (*d*) the line between what is institutional and what is not needs to be drawn much more clearly, so that institutional theory is falsifiable.

ACKNOWLEDGMENTS

I am indebted to Morris Zelditch, Jr., for helping me to explicate my own approach to institutional order. Special thanks go to Paul DiMaggio, John W. Meyer, Marshall Meyer, Woody Powell, and W. Richard Scott for useful comments on the penultimate draft, and especially to John and Paul for advice on the internal theoretical logic of the environment-as-institution approach. Pamela S. Tolbert and the OSS group at the Graduate School of Management, UCLA, provided useful comments on an early version.

Literature Cited

Ackerman, B., Hassler, W. 1981. *Clean Coal, Dirty Air*. New Haven: Yale Univ. Press

Adams, J. L. 1979. *Conceptual Blockbusting: A Guide to Better Ideas*. New York: Norton 2nd ed.

Akerlof, G. A. 1980. The economics of social customs, of which unemployment may be one consequence. *Q. J. Econ.* 95:749–75

Akerlof, G. A. 1983. Loyalty filters. *Am. Econ. Rev.* 73:54–63

Alexander, C. N. Jr., Wiley, M. G. 1981. Situated activity and identity formation. In *Social Psychology: Sociological Perspectives,* ed. M. Rosenberg, R. H. Turner, pp. 269–89. New York: Basic Books

Armour, H. O., Teece, D. J. 1978. Organization structure and economic performance: A test of the multidivisional hypothesis. *Bell J. Econ.* 9:106–22

Arrow, K. 1974. *The Limits of Organization*. New York: Norton

Baker, W. E. 1984. The social structure of a national securities market. *Am. J. Sociol.* 89:775–811

Baron, J. N., Dobbin, F. R., Jennings, P. D. 1986. War and peace: The evolution of modern personnel administration in U.S. industry. *Am. J. Sociol.* 92:1–23

Benson, J. K. 1975. The interorganizational network as a political economy. *Admin. Sci. Q.* 20:229–49

Brewer, M. B. 1981. Ethnocentrism and its role in interpersonal trust. In *Scientific Inquiry and the Social Sciences,* ed. M. B. Brewer, B. E. Collins, pp. 345–60. San Francisco: Jossey-Bass

Burt, R. S. 1975. Corporate society: A time series analysis of network structure. *Soc. Sci. Res.* 4:271–328

Cagan, P. 1969. The first fifty years of the national banking system—An historical appraisal. In *Essays in American Economic History,* ed. A. W. Coats, R. M. Robertson, pp. 247–67. New York: Edward Arnold

Carroll, G. R., Huo, Y. P. 1986. Organizational task and institutional environments in evolutionary perspective: Findings from the local newspaper industry. *Am. J. Sociol.* 91:838–73

Clark, B. R. 1956. *Adult Education in Transition.* Berkeley: Univ. Calif. Press

Clark, B. R. 1960. *The Open Door College: A Case Study.* New York: McGraw-Hill

Coleman, J. S. 1974. *Power and the Structure of Society.* New York: Norton

Collins, R. 1971. Functional and conflict theories of educational stratification. *Am. Sociol. Rev.* 36:1002–18

Darby, M. R., Karni, E. 1973. Free competition and the optimal amount of fraud. *J. Law Econ.* 16:67–88

Davis, L. E. 1965. The investment market, 1870–1914: The evolution of a national market. *J. Econ. History* 25:355–99

Diamond, S. 1958. From organization to society: Virginia in the seventeenth century. *Am. J. Sociol.* 63:457–75

DiMaggio, P. J. 1983. State expansion and the structuration of organizational fields. In *Organizational Theory and Public Policy,* ed. R. Hall, R. Quinn. Beverly Hills: Sage

DiMaggio, P. J. 1986. Structural analysis of organizational fields: A blockmodel approach. In *Research in Organizational Behavior,* ed. L. L. Cummings, B. Staw, pp. 335–370. Vol. 8. Greenwich, Conn: JAI

DiMaggio, P. J. 1987. Interest and agency in institutional theory. See Zucker (ed.), 1987a. In press

DiMaggio, P. J., Powell, W. W. 1983. The iron cage revisited: Institutional isomorphism and collective rationality in organizational fields. *Am. Sociol. Rev.* 35:147–60

DiMaggio, P. J., Powell, W. W. 1984. *Institutional isomorphism and structural conformity.* Paper presented at a special session on new developments in institutional theory, Am. Sociol. Assoc. Ann. meet., San Antonio, August

Dobbin, F. R., Edelman, L., Meyer, J. W., Scott, W. R., Swidler, A. 1987. The expansion of due process in organizations. See Zucker (ed.), 1987a. In press

Doeringer, P., Piore, M. 1971. *Internal Labor Markets and Manpower Analysis.* Boston: Heath

Dowling, J., Pfeffer, J. 1975. Organizational legitimacy. *Pacific Sociol. Rev.* 18:122–36

Durkheim, E., Mauss, M. 1903. *Primitive Classification.* Chicago, Ill: Univ. Chicago Press

Featherman, D. L., Jones, F. L., Hauser, R. M. 1975. Assumptions of social mobility research in the United States: The case of occupational status. *Soc. Sci. Res.* 4:329–60

Fligstein, N. 1985. The spread of the multidivisional form, 1919–79. *Am. Sociol. Rev.* 50:377–91

Freeman, J. 1982. Organizational life cycles and natural selection processes. In *Research in Organizational Behavior,* ed. L. L. Cummings, B. Staw, pp. 1–32. Vol. 2. Greenwich, Conn: JAI

Friedman, M. 1953. The methodology of positive economics. *Essays in Positive Economics,* pp. 1–29. Chicago: Univ. of Chicago Press

Gamson, W. A. 1975. *The Strategy of Social Protest.* Homewood, Ill: Dorsey

Garfinkel, H. 1967. *Studies in Ethnomethodology.* Englewood Cliffs, NJ: Prentice-Hall

Glasberg, D. S., Schwartz, M. 1983. Ownership and control of corporations. *Ann. Rev. Sociol.* 9:311–32

Gouldner, A. 1954. *Patterns of Industrial Bureaucracy.* New York: Free Press

Granovetter, M. 1985. Economic action and social structure: The problem of embeddedness. *Am. J. Sociol.* 91:481–510

Hall, P. D. 1977. Family structure and economic organization: Massachusetts merchants, 1700–1850. In *Family and Kin in Urban Communities, 1700–1930,* ed. T. K. Hareven, pp. 38–163. New York: New Viewpoints

Hannan, M., Freeman, J. 1977. The population ecology of organizations. *Am. J. Sociol.* 82:929–64

Hinings, C. R., Greenwood, R., Ranson, S., Walsh, K. 1986. *The Dynamics of Change.* San Francisco: Jossey-Bass. In press

Hinings, C. R., Greenwood, R. 1987. The normative prescription of organizations. See Zucker (ed.), 1987a. In press

Hirsch, P. M. 1975. Organizational effectiveness and the institutional environment. *Admin. Sci. Q.* 20:327–44

Hirsch, P. M. 1986. From ambushes to golden parachutes: Corporate takeovers as an instance of cultural framing and institutional integration. *Am. J. Sociol.* 91:800–37

Hughes, E. C. 1936. The ecological aspect of institutions. *Am. Sociol. Rev.* 1:180–89

Jacoby, H., Steinbruner, J. D. 1973. *Clearing the Air: Federal Policy on Automobile Emission Control.* Cambridge, Mass: Ballinger

Kamens, D. 1977. Legitimating myths and educational organization: The relationship between organizational ideology and formal structure. *Am. Sociol. Rev.* 42:208–19

Kamens, D., Lunde, T. K. 1987. Institutional theory and the expansion of central state organizations, 1960–1980. See Zucker (ed.), 1987a. In press

Kramer, R. M., Brewer, M. B. 1984. Effects of group identity on resource use in a simulated commons dilemma. *J. Pers. Soc. Psychol.* 46:1044–57

Kurke, L. B. 1987. Does adaptation preclude adaptability?: Strategy and performance. See Zucker (ed.), 1987a. In press

Leibenstein, H. 1966. Allocative efficiency versus 'X-efficiency.' *Am. Econ. Rev.* 56:392–415

Levi, M. 1981. The predatory theory of rule. *Polit. Soc.* 10:431–65

Macaulay, S. 1963. Noncontractual relations in business: A preliminary study. *Am. Sociol. Rev.* 28:55–67

Machlup, F. 1946. Marginal analysis and empirical research. *Am. Econ. Rev.* 36:519–54

Mann, M. 1973. *Consciousness and Action in the Western Working Class.* London: Macmillan

Mansfield, E. 1962. Entry, Gibrat's law, innovation, and the growth of firms. *Am. Econ. Rev.* 52:1023–51

March, J. G., Olsen, J. P. 1984. The new institutionalism: Organizational factors in political life. *Am. Polit. Sci. Rev.* 78:734–49

Marsden, P. 1983. Restricted access in networks and models of power. *Am. J. Sociol.* 86:1203–35

McNeill, G. E. 1887. *The Labor Movement: The Problem of Today.* Boston, Bridgman

Messick, D. M., Wilke, H., Brewer, M. B., et al. 1983. Individual adaptations and structural change as solutions to social dilemmas. *J. Pers. Soc. Psychol.* 44:294–309

Meyer, J. W. 1977. The effects of education as an institution. *Am. J. Sociol.* 83:55–75

Meyer, John W. 1983. "Organizational factors affecting legalization in education. See Meyer & Scott 1983, pp. 217–32

Meyer, J. W., Hannan, M. T., eds. 1979. *National Development and the World System.* Chicago: Univ. Chicago Press

Meyer, J. W., Rowan, B. 1977. In-

titutionalized organizations: Formal structure as myth and ceremony. *Am. J. Sociol.* 83:340–63

Meyer, J. W., Rowan, B. 1978. The structure of educational organizations. In *Environments and Organizations,* ed. M. W. Meyer, pp. 78–109. San Francisco: Jossey-Bass

Meyer, J. W., Scott, W. R. 1983. *Organizational Environments: Ritual and Rationality.* Beverly Hills, Calif: Sage

Meyer, J. W., Scott, W. R., Strang, D., Creighton, A. 1987. Bureaucratization without centralization: Changes in the organizational system of American public education, 1940–1980. See Zucker (ed.), 1987a. In press

Meyer, J. W., Scott, W. R., Deal, T. E. 1981. Institutional and technical sources of organizational structure. *Organization and the Human Services,* ed. H. D. Stein, pp. 151–78. Philadelphia: Temple Univ. Press

Meyer, M. W., Brown, M. C. 1977. The process of bureaucratization. *Am. J. Sociol.* 83:364–85

Meyer, M. W., Stevenson, W., Webster, S. 1985. *Limits to Bureaucratic Growth.* Berlin: Walter de Gruyter

Meyer, M. W., Zucker, L. G. 1986. *Permanently failing organizations.* Paper presented at the Yale Complex Organization Workshop, October

Miller, H. E. 1927. *Banking Theories in the United States Before 1860.* Cambridge, Mass.: Harvard Univ. Press

Nadel, S. F. 1953. Social control and self-regulation. *Soc. Forc.* 31:265–73

Nelson, P. B. 1981. *Corporations in Crisis: Behavioral Observations for Bankruptcy Policy.* New York: Praeger

Nelson, R. R., Winter, S. G. 1982. *An Evolutionary Theory of Economic Change.* Cambridge, Mass: Harvard Univ. Press

Niskanen, W. A. 1971. *Bureaucracy and Representative Government.* Chicago: Rand McNally

Nonet, P. 1969. *Administrative Justice: Advocacy and Change in Government Agencies.* New York: Russell Sage Found.

North, D. C. 1986a. The new institutional economics. *J. Instit. Theor. Econ.* 142:230

North, D. C. 1986b. *Institutions, economic growth and freedom: An historical introduction.* Presented at the Symposium on Econ., Polit., Civil Freedom sponsored by The Liberty Fund, October. *Political Economy Working Paper 110,* Ctr. Polit. Econ., Washington Univ., St. Louis

Padgett, J. F. 1981. Hierarchy and ecological control in federal budgetary decision making. *Am. J. Sociol.* 87:75–129

Parsons, T. 1956. Suggestions for a sociological approach to the theory of organizations, Parts I and II. *Admin. Sci. Q.* 1:63–85, 225–39

Pennings, J. 1973. Measures of organizational structure: A methodological note. *Am. J. Sociol.* 79:618–704

Perrow, C. 1985. Review essay: Overboard with myth and symbols. (Review of John W. Meyer and W. Richard Scott, Organizational Environments: Ritual and Rationality.) *Am. J. Sociol.* 91:151–55

Perrow, C. 1986. *Complex Organizations: A Critical Essay.* New York: Random. 3rd ed.

Pfeffer, J. 1973. Size, composition, and function of hospital boards of directors: A study of organization-environment linkage. *Admin. Sci. Q.* 18:349–64

Pfeffer, J. 1981. Management as symbolic action: The creation and maintenance of organizational paradigms. In *Research in Organizational Behavior,* ed. L. L. Cummings, B. Staw. Vol. 3. Greenwich, Conn: JAI

Pfeffer, J. 1982. *Organizations and Organization Theory.* Boston: Pitman

Pfeffer, J., Salancik, G. 1978. *The External Control of Organizations.* New York: Harper & Row

Powell, W. W. 1985. *Getting into Print: The Decision Making Process in Scholarly Publishing.* Chicago: Univ. Chicago Press

Powell, W. W. 1987. Institutional effects on organizational structure and performance. See Zucker (ed.), 1987a. In press

Rose, E. 1968. Uniformities in culture: Ideas with histories. In *Decisions, Values and Groups.* ed. N. F. Washburne, pp. 154–76. New York: Macmillan

Rowan, B. 1982. Organizational structure and the institutional environment: The case of public schools. *Admin. Sci. Q.* 27:259–79

Roy, W. G. 1983. The interlocking directorate structure of the United States. *Am. Sociol. Rev.* 48:248–57

Sapir, E. 1931. Conceptual categories in primitive languages. *Science* 74:578

Schutz, A. 1962. On multiple realities. In *Collected Papers I: The Problem of Social Reality,* ed. M. Natanson, pp. 207–59. The Hague: Martinus Nijhoff

Schutz, A. 1980. *Reflections on the Problem of Relevance.* Edited by R. M. Zaner. New Haven: Yale Univ. Press

Scott, W. R. 1981. *Organizations: Rational, Natural, and Open Systems.* Englewood Cliffs, NJ: Prentice-Hall

Scott, W. R. 1983. The organization of environments: Network, cultural, and historical elements. See Meyer & Scott 1983, pp. 155–78

Scott, W. R., Meyer, J. W. 1983. The organization of societal sectors. See Meyer & Scott 1983, pp. 129–53

Selznick, P. 1949. *TVA and the Grass Roots.* Berkeley: Univ. Calif. Press

Selznick, P. 1957. *Leadership in Administration: A Sociological Interpretation.* Evanston, Ill: Row, Peterson

Skocpol, T., Finegold, K. 1982. State capacity and economic intervention in the early New Deal. *Polit. Sci. Q.* 97:255–78

Skrowronek, S. 1982. *Building a New American State.* Cambridge: Cambridge Univ. Press

Southworth, S. D. 1928. *Branch Banking in the United States.* New York: McGraw-Hill

Stinchcombe, A. L. 1965. Social structure and organizations. In *Handbook of Organizations,* ed. J. G. March, pp. 142–93. Chicago: Rand McNally

Thomas, G. M., Meyer, J. W. 1984. The expansion of the state. *Ann. Rev. Sociol.* 10:461–82

Thomas, G. M., Meyer, J. W., Ramirez, F., Boli, J. 1987. *Institutional Structure: Constituting State, Society, and the Individual.* Newbury Park, Calif: Sage. In press.

Thomas, G. M., Walker, H. A., Zelditch, M. Jr. 1987. Legitimacy and collective action. *Soc. Forc.* 65. In press

Thompson, J. D. 1967. *Organizations in Action.* New York: McGraw-Hill

Thompson, J. D., McEwen, W. 1958. Organizational goals and environment: Goalsetting as an interactive process. *Am. Sociol. Rev.* 23:23–31

Tolbert, P. S. 1985. Resource dependence and institutional environments: Sources of administrative structure in institutions of higher education. *Admin. Sci. Q.* 30:1–13

Tolbert, P. S. 1987. Institutional sources of organizational culture in major law firms. See Zucker (ed.), 1987a. In press

Tolbert, P. S., Zucker, L. G. 1983. Institutional sources of change in organizational structure: The diffusion of civil service reform, 1880–1935. *Admin. Sci. Q.* 28:22–39

Travers, J., Milgram, S. 1969. An experimental study of the small world problem. *Sociometry* 32:425–43

Turk, H. 1985. Macrosociology and interorganizational relations: Theories, strategies and bibliography. *Sociol. Soc. Res.* 69:490–512

Udy, S. H. Jr. 1962. Administrative rationality, social setting, and organizational development. *Am. J. Sociol.* 68:299–308

Wamsley, G. L. 1969. *Selective Service and A Changing America.* Columbus, Ohio: Merrill

Weick, K. E. 1976. Educational organizations as loosely coupled systems. *Admin. Sci. Q.* 21:1–19

Williamson, J. G., Swanson, J. A. 1966. The growth of cities in the American Northeast, 1820–1870. *Explorations in Entrepreneurial History* 11 (Supplement):1–101

Williamson, O. E. 1975. *Markets and Hierarchies*. New York: Free Press

Williamson, O. E. 1979. Transaction cost economics: The governance of contractual relations. *J. Law Econ.* 22:233–61

Williamson, O. E. 1981. The economics of organization: The transaction cost approach. *Am. J. Sociol.* 87:548–77

Yamagishi, T. 1986. The structural goal/expectation theory of cooperation in social dilemmas. In *Advances in Group Processes: Theory and Research,* ed. E. Lawler. Vol. 3. Greenwich, Conn: JAI

Zald, M. N. 1978. The social control of industries. *Soc. Forc.* 57:79–102

Zald, M. N., Ash, R. 1966. Social movement organizations: Growth, decay, and change. *Soc. Forc.* 44:327–41

Zald, M. N., Denton, P. 1963. From evangelism to general service: The transformation of the YMCA. *Admin. Sci. Q.* 8:214–34

Zelditch, M. Jr., Walker, H. A. 1984. Legitimacy and the stability of authority. In *Advances in Group Processes: Theory and Research,* ed. E. Lawler, pp. 1–27. Vol. 1. Greenwich, Conn: JAI

Zucker, L. G. 1977. The role of institutionalization in cultural persistence. *Am. Sociol. Rev.* 42:726–43

Zucker, L. G. 1980. Altering demand characteristics: Cultural context and conformity in the laboratory. Paper presented at the Ann. meet. of the West Coast Conference for Small Group Research

Zucker, L. G. 1981. Institutional structure and organizational processes: The role of evaluation units in schools. In *Studies in Evaluation and Decision Making,* ed. A. Bank, R. C. Williams, pp. 69–89. CSE Monograph Series in Evaluation, No. 10. Los Angeles, Calif: Ctr. Stud. Eval.

Zucker, L. G. 1983. Organizations as institutions. In *Advances in Organizational Theory and Research,* ed. S. B. Bacharach,

pp. 1–43. Vol. 2. Greenwich, Conn: JAI

Zucker, L. G. 1986a. Production of trust: Institutional sources of economic structure: 1840 to 1920. In *Research in Organizational Behavior,* ed. L. L. Cummings, B. Staw, pp. 55–111. Vol. 8. Greenwich, Conn: JAI

Zucker, L. G. 1986b. *Networks for evaluation: Reputation in economic life.* Work. pap. presented at the COSI seminar, Yale Univ., April

Zucker, L. G. 1986c. *Institutional construction of public/private differences: Predicting organizational performance and survival.* Paper presented at the School of Organization and Management, Yale Univ., April

Zucker, L. G., (ed.) 1987a. *Institutional Patterns and Organizations: Culture and Environment.* Mass: Ballinger. In press

Zucker, L. G. 1987b. Where do institutional patterns come from?: Organizations as actors in social systems. See Zucker (ed.), 1987a. In press

Zucker, L. G. 1987c. Normal change or risky business: Effects of institutionalizing change on organizational survival. To appear in *J. Mgmt. Stud.*

Zucker, L. G. 1987d. *Overcoming corporate culture barriers.* Paper presented at the Human Resources Round Table (HARRT), sponsored by the Inst. Indust. Relat., UCLA

Zucker, L. G., Taka, P. L. 1986. *Survival of the adequate?: Institutional barriers to exit in organizational populations.* Paper presented at the OSS Organization Theory Seminar, Grad. School Mgmt., UCLA, December

Zucker, L. G., Taka, P. L., Turk, H. 1986. *The social construction of organizational populations: Institution building among non-profit California hospitals, 1959–1979.* Unpubl. Ms. UCLA

Ann. Rev. Sociol. 1987. 13:465–88

NEW DIRECTIONS IN ENVIRONMENTAL SOCIOLOGY

Frederick H. Buttel

Department of Rural Sociology, Warren Hall, Cornell University, Ithaca, New York 14853–7801

Abstract

Recent research in environmental sociology is reviewed. Following a brief overview of the development of environmental sociology over the past decade, five areas of environmental sociological scholarship are discussed: (*a*) the "new human ecology," (*b*) environmental attitudes, values, and behaviors, (*c*) the environmental movement, (*d*) technological risk and risk assessment, and (*e*) the political economy of the environment and environmental politics. It is argued that while the early environmental sociologists sought nothing less than the reorientation of sociology and social theory, environmental sociology's influence on the discipline has been modest. Instead, environmental sociology has steadily taken on characteristics of the discipline as a whole, especially its fragmentation and its dualism between theory and the pursuit of middle-range empirical puzzles. Encouraging examples of recent work that creatively integrates theory and empirical research in environmental sociology are discussed.

INTRODUCTION

When Catton & Dunlap published their pioneering papers in *The American Sociologist* and *Annual Review of Sociology* in the late 1970s (Catton & Dunlap 1978a, Dunlap & Catton 1979), relatively few Western sociologists had a clear idea of environmental sociology as a subdiscipline. Since that time, however, environmental sociology has made major strides and, by certain standards, has come of age. But while the field has done well for itself by conventional standards, environmental sociology hardly set out to be

465

0360-0572/87/0815-0465$02.00

conventional. During the early years of the ASA Section on Environmental Sociology, there was a vibrant *espirit de corps* that a new sociology was being nurtured—one that recognized the role of physical-biological factors in shaping social structures and behaviors, that was aware of the impacts of social organization and social change on the natural environment. Environmental sociologists sought nothing less than the reorientation of sociology toward a more holistic perspective that would conceptualize social processes within the context of the biosphere.

These lofty intentions, however, have largely failed to come to fruition. The discipline at large has handily withstood the challenges to its theoretical assumptions posed by environmental sociologists. Environmental sociology has become routinized and is now viewed—by both its practitioners and other sociologists—less as a scholarly "cause" or movement than as just another sociological specialization. More important for present purposes, environmental sociology has steadily taken on major characteristics of the larger discipline. It has become more specialized, fragmented, and dualistic. There is, on the one hand, a small core of largely theoretically oriented work, most of which is devoted to conceptualizing the human species and its constituent human societies as one species among many in the biosphere. On the other hand, the bulk of environmental sociological scholarship tends to consist of a "normal-science" working out of middle-range empirical puzzles.

The present paper is intended, in part, to update Dunlap & Catton's 1979 review paper. But whereas they sought to review the entirety of environmental-sociological scholarship, my effort is more circumscribed.[1] I focus on fewer areas of scholarship, ones that represent the major clusters of inquiry bearing on the dualism of environmental sociology. Five major areas of scholarship receive attention. First, I examine the theoretical core of environmental sociology, codified in the late 1970s. The next two sections of the paper deal with two areas—environmental attitudes and behavior, and the environmental movement—that were being actively researched before environmental sociology became recognized as a distinct subdiscipline and that continue to be major areas of research. The final substantive portions of the paper examine two relatively new foci of environmental-sociological scholarship—technological risk assessment and the political economy of the environment. Largely developed during environmental sociology's second half-decade, these draw relatively little on the core of environmental sociology.

Not only did Dunlap & Catton (1979) deal with a larger number of topics than does the present paper, but their framework for classifying environmen-

---

[1]In this review I thus neglect a number of substantive areas, such as social impact assessment and the built environment, that are of considerable importance in contemporary environmental sociology, in part because they have received admirable treatments in Freudenburg (1986) and Stokols & Altman (1986), respectively. I also deemphasize energy because it will receive extensive treatment in this *Review* at a later date.

tal sociological scholarship also reflects the higher degree of integration within the field in its first half-decade. Dunlap & Catton divided the literature into two major categories: "sociology of environmental issues" and "environmental sociology." By the "sociology of environmental issues," Dunlap and Catton referred to environmentally related phenomena (e.g. research on wildland recreation and resource management problems) that were of interest to sociologists before the rise of environmental sociology and that were explored through their traditional perspectives. By "environmental sociology" they meant inquiry that focused on "the physical environment as a factor that may influence (or be influenced by) social behavior" (1979:255). Much of this work is based on a recognition of the dilemma that "human societies necessarily exploit surrounding ecosystems in order to survive, but societies that flourish to the extent of overexploiting the ecosystem may destroy the basis of their own survival" (1979:250). Environmental attitudes and behavior and the environmental movement were among the major areas of work in Dunlap & Catton's framework. Had technological risk assessment and the political economy of the environment been major research foci at the time Dunlap & Catton were preparing their earlier review, these would probably have been included within the sociology-of-environmental-issues category as well. What Dunlap & Catton optimistically construed as the emergent, growing center of environmental sociology is here treated as a single category of scholarship, arguably in proportion to its representation at sociology meetings and in books and journals among contemporary environmental sociologists. In the final segment of the paper I comment on the implications of the relative decline of the core of environmental sociology for the future of this area of sociological specialization.

ENVIRONMENTAL SOCIOLOGY'S CORE: THE NEW HUMAN ECOLOGY

In their earlier review article Dunlap & Catton (1979) reserved the term "environmental sociology" for a specific category of inquiry focusing on the way in which factors in the physical environment shape and are shaped by social organization and social behavior. While the present review departs from such usage—basically by defining environmental sociology in terms of what self-identified environmental sociologists do—it is clearly the case that Dunlap & Catton's "environmental sociology" category comprises the core of the larger subdiscipline as I have construed it here.[2] To avoid confusion, I hereafter refer to the core of environmental sociology as the "new human ecology."

---

[2]It should be noted, however, that Dunlap & Catton's (1979) "environmental sociology" category is broader than that of the "new human ecology," since the former includes literature on social impact assessment, natural disasters, the built environment, and so on.

The core of environmental sociology is such not only because it has stimulated empirical research, but also because this theoretical work has been self-consciously fashioned as a critique of "mainstream" sociology. The common element within these otherwise diverse writings is a critique of the anthropocentrism of classical and contemporary sociological theory and of its limitations in understanding social change in a modern world that is increasingly constrained by ecology. Writers within the new human ecology often argue that Durkheim's social facts dictum has led sociology astray. Durkheim's *sui generis* conception of social facts has become widely accepted, and a virtual taboo has developed against explaining social phenomena by means of nonsocial factors. The new human ecology presents a variety of arguments to the effect that basic patterns of social organization are shaped by the imperative of human societies to derive their basic survival needs from the biosphere. Moreover, the new human ecology departs significantly from classical human ecology (e.g. Hawley 1981) by elaborating a distinctive argument: Instead of tending toward equilibrium with the natural environments from which they derive sustenance, modern societies tend to exhibit quite the opposite pattern—social dynamics that exacerbate environmental degradation and resource depletion. Analysts working from the new human ecology have generally asserted that a "genuine" environmental sociology (Dunlap & Catton 1983:119)—indeed, a sociology that is relevant to the pressing problems of the modern world—must shed its anthropocentrism and reject the notion that humans, because of their capacity for culture, technological innovation, and so on, are exempt from the ecological laws that govern the existence of lower species.

While the work of a good many environmental sociologists is typically seen to lie within the "new human ecology" (e.g. Burch & DeLuca 1984), the most influential work in this tradition has been by Catton & Dunlap (1978a, 1980; Dunlap & Catton 1979, 1983) and by Schnaiberg (1975, 1980). The tack taken here for examining the new-human-ecology core of environmental sociology is to compare and contrast the work of Catton & Dunlap with that of Schnaiberg.

The heart of Catton & Dunlap's formulation of a new human ecology is their analysis, at a broad "paradigmatic" or metatheoretical level, of the essential similarity of apparently diverse theories based on the classical tradition in terms of their "shared anthropocentrism" (1978a:41). They argue that "the numerous competing theoretical perspectives in contemporary sociology—e.g., functionalism, symbolic interactionism, ethnomethodology, conflict theory, Marxism, and so on—are prone to exaggerate their differences from one another." Instead of being "paradigms in their own right," these theories appear, to Catton & Dunlap, as minor variants on a larger "paradigm"; "we maintain that their apparent diversity is not as important as the fundamental anthropocentrism underlying *all* of them" (1978a:42, emphasis in original). The anthropocentric worldview underlying contemporary theories, based on ostensibly divergent views among the classical theorists, was labeled the "human exceptionalism paradigm" (HEP) by Catton & Dunlap. (It was relabeled in subsequent publications as the "human exemptionalism paradigm"; see Table 1). This anthropocentric paradigm is contrasted with a "new environmental paradigm" (NEP), which has been relabeled in subsequent versions as the "new ecological paradigm" (see Table 1).

Table 1 from Catton & Dunlap (1980:34) provides a summary of the authors' depiction of the fundamental assumptions of the HEP and the NEP. Table 1 also includes the major assumptions of the "dominant western worldview," which the authors consider to be the ensemble of values and ideologies that have predominated during the 500-plus-year boom of western expansion underwritten by finite supplies of fossil fuels and nonrenewable raw materials. Catton & Dunlap suggest that the dominant western worldview has been translated into the HEP in academic circles (see especially Dunlap & Catton 1983:115–16).

Clearly, the central issue involved in evaluating the new human ecology in general, and the work of Catton & Dunlap in particular, is whether the distinctions between HEP-NEP or traditional theoretical cleavages have the greater primacy (Buttel 1978; Catton & Dunlap 1978b, 1980; Dunlap & Catton 1983; Humphrey & Buttel 1982). Most environmental sociologists have accepted the validity of the HEP-NEP distinction, though many, including the authors themselves (Catton & Dunlap 1980), have come to argue that both cleavages are important.[3]

But because their theoretical work has been written at a highly abstract— essentially a metatheoretical—level, it has not been readily usable in empirical research. There have, however, been three areas of research stimulated by this theoretical work. The first, global-level research, has essentially been limited to one sociological study—Catton's own *Overshoot* (1980), an historical analysis of the increasing ecological impact of industrial societies. Catton's dire predictions are compatible with a good deal of nonsociological work, such as *The Limits to Growth* (Meadows et al 1972). Perhaps owing to its heavy use of bioecological concepts, however, it has stimulated only a modest level of sociological interest.

The second category of empirical research in the new human ecology has

---

[3]I have argued elsewhere (Buttel 1986a) that the major classical sociological theorists were concerned with natural and biological phenomena to a far greater degree than is typically acknowledged by environmental and nonenvironmental sociologists. That the contributions of the classical theorists to what is now referred to as environmental sociology have remained unrecognized can be largely explained by the fact that most sociologists have limited acquaintance with the full range of the classical theorists' primary writings and have learned the classical tradition through secondary treatments by sociologists with little or no interest in environmental and biological phenomena.

Table 1 A comparison of major assumptions in the dominant western worldview, sociology's human exemptionalism paradigm, and the proposed new ecological paradigm (Source: Catton & Dunlap 1980:34)

	Dominant Western Worldview (DWW)	Human Exemptionalism Paradigm (HEP)	New Ecological Paradigm (NEP)
Assumptions about the nature of human beings	DWW$_1$ People are fundamentally different from all other creatures on Earth, over which they have domination.	HEP$_1$ Humans have cultural heritage in addition to (and distinct from) their genetic inheritance, and thus are quite unlike all other animal species.	NEP$_1$ While humans have exceptional characteristics (culture, technology, etc.), they remain one among many species that are interdependently involved in the global ecosystem.
Assumptions about social causation	DWW$_2$ People are masters of their destiny; they can choose their goals and learn to do whatever is necessary	HEP$_2$ Social and cultural factors (including technology) are the major determinants of human affairs.	NEP$_2$ Human affairs are influenced not only by social and cultural factors, but also by intricate linkages of cause, effect, and feedback in the web of nature; thus purposive human actions have many unintended consequences.
Assumptions about the context of human society	DWW$_3$ The world is vast, and thus provides unlimited opportunities for humans.	HEP$_3$ Social and cultural environments are the crucial context for human affairs, and the biophysical environment is largely irrelevant.	NEP$_3$ Humans live in and are dependent upon a finite biophysical environment which imposes potent physical and biological restraints on human affairs.
Assumptions about constraints on human society	DWW$_4$ The history of humanity is one of progress; for every problem there is a solution, and thus progress need never cease.	HEP$_4$ Culture is cumulative; thus technological and social progress can continue indefinitely, making all social problems ultimately soluble.	NEP$_4$ Although the inventiveness of humans and the powers derived therefrom may seem for a while to extend carrying capacity limits, ecological laws cannot be repealed.

consisted of several subnational or sectoral macrosociological studies that followed Catton & Dunlap's arguments about the role of ecological factors in social change. Much of this literature, focused on agriculture, was stimulated by Dunlap & Martin (1983) and, to a lesser degree, by a commentary on that paper by Coughenour (1984). This work, for example, included ecological analyses of migration and the incidence of part-time farming (Albrecht & Murdock 1984), research on the social ecology of soil erosion (Ashby 1985), analyses of the role of climatic factors in shaping energy consumption in agriculture (Gilles 1980), studies of the impact of ecological factors on technological change and innovativeness (Albrecht & Murdock 1986), and research on socioeconomic aspects of degradation of agricultural environments (Heffernan & Green 1986).

The third area of empirical research related to Catton & Dunlap's paradigmatic analyses has been survey research devoted to exploring commitment to the "dominant social paradigm" (see Table 1) and the "new ecological paradigm" among mass publics and segments thereof, by Dunlap & Van Liere (1978, 1984). They found strong endorsement of NEP tenets such as limits to growth and antianthropocentrism among environmentalists and moderate endorsement by the general public, and they also found items reflecting the various tenets to comprise an internally consistent "NEP scale" (Dunlap & Van Liere 1978, but see Albrecht et al 1982). They subsequently found that commitment to the dominant social paradigm, which they measured in terms of eight dimensions, was inversely related to concern for environmental quality (Dunlap & Van Liere 1984). Dunlap & Van Liere's conceptualization of societal debate over environmental protection as reflecting paradigmatic conflict has been extended in subsequent empirical research in the US and abroad (see e.g. Cotgrove 1982, Milbrath 1984).

The other major figure at the center of environmental sociology has been Allan Schnaiberg. Schnaiberg's approach differs considerably from that of Catton & Dunlap, though, like them, Schnaiberg views social structure and social change as being reciprocally related to the biophysical environment. Schnaiberg, for example, draws unabashedly on many of the sources— Marxist political economy, neo-Marxist and neo-Weberian political sociology—that were essentially dismissed as irrelevant anthropocentrisms in Catton & Dunlap's (1978a, b) earliest work. Moreover, Schnaiberg begins his most influential work, *The Environment* (1980), with a clear expression of the point that ecological systems and human (especially capitalist-industrial) societies have qualitatively different dynamics and must be understood through different concepts. Schnaiberg (1980:19) notes that the fundamental difference in dynamics relates to the fact that "the ecosystem changes over time from a simpler, faster-growing one to a more complex, slower-growing entity," while "almost the reverse is true of human economies."

Schnaiberg has become most influential through his working out of the notions of the "societal-environmental dialectic" and the "treadmill of production," which have become two of the most central environmental-sociological concepts derived from "mainstream" political economy and sociology (Buttel 1986a). Thus, while Catton & Dunlap have probably been most influential within environmental sociology, Schnaiberg's influence has been greater in the discipline as a whole. Schnaiberg's work (especially 1980: Chap. 5–9), however, has been pivotal in stimulating research on the political economy of the environment.

ENVIRONMENTAL ATTITUDES, VALUES, AND BEHAVIORS

As noted earlier, research on environmental attitudes and values predated environmental sociology and has continued to be one of the most important areas of research in the subdiscipline. The literature on environmental orientations can be divided into three major categories. The first consists of studies, almost always involving sample survey methodology, in which environmental orientations are explored to examine a social-structural problematic such as whether there are differences in the environmental attitudes and beliefs of different segments of the public (e.g. according to social class, gender, or age groups). The second category is that of studies, often involving experimental but sometimes quasi-experimental survey methodology, in which the researcher seeks to test hypotheses deriving from social-psychological theory. Third, a number of applied studies have attempted to determine the social factors related to behavior associated with the environment (e.g. littering, participation in recycling programs, household energy conservation) and to specify what mix of media messages, appeals, and incentives will help to induce proenvironmental behavior. These categories do overlap, however, and particular investigators have done research in more than one of these categories. Nonetheless, most studies tend to fall in one or another category, and this schema provides the basis for the summary below.

Social-Structural Aspects of Environmental Attitudes

During the late 1960s public concern with environmental quality rose to a position of prominence on the national agenda (signified by the widespread "Earth Day" celebrations in April, 1970) so rapidly that it prompted Erskine (1971: 120), an editor of *Public Opinion Quarterly,* to refer to its rise as "a miracle of public opinion." But shortly thereafter, Downs (1972) published a widely cited analysis suggesting that environmental problems would likely proceed through the same "issue-attention cycle" experienced by most social problems, and that public concern about the quality of the environment was already showing signs of declining (also see Morrison 1973). Studies of trends in environmental concern in the early 1970s began to document the decline hypothesized by Downs (e.g. Dunlap & Dillman 1976). Other researchers, however, subsequently challenged this conclusion by calling into question the adequacy of the statewide samples often used as well as the manner in which environmental concern was measured (e.g. Lowe et al 1980). By providing new data they showed the continued strength of public support for environmental protection throughout the 1970s (e.g. Mitchell 1979). More recent research has consistently found a significant rise in public concern with environmental quality in the 1980s, apparently in response to the perceived anti-environmental posture of the Reagan Administration—especially the controversies sparked in the early years of the Administration by Interior Secretary James Watt and EPA Administrator Anne Gorsuch Burford (e.g. Dunlap 1986, Mitchell 1984).

In retrospect it appears that two methodological issues contributed to the controversy over trends in environmental concern in the 1970s. First, studies showing a decline in the early 1970s (e.g. Buttel & Flinn 1974) relied heavily on measures of the "salience" of environmental problems—i.e. volunteered responses to "most important problem" questions, which are particularly subject to rapid decline for most social problems. Second, studies showing the continued strength of environmental concern throughout the decade (e.g. Lowe et al 1980, Mitchell 1979) relied on cross-sectional data or trend data (such as the NORC General Surveys) beginning in 1973 or later—after public concern had already declined from the fervor of Earth Day. Taking these issues into account, a recent comprehensive review of available longitudinal data on public concern with environmental quality indicates that after rising rapidly in the last half of the 1960s, such concern peaked in 1970. It then declined fairly rapidly in the early 1970s and very gradually throughout the rest of the decade (though always staying above its mid-1960s level). It has again risen substantially in the first half of the 1980s (Dunlap 1986).

Research on the social bases of environmental concern initially focused on the socioeconomic variables that reflected differential interests in achieving environmental protection. Early studies reported fairly consistently that those most concerned with environmental protection were well-educated, affluent young urbanites (e.g. Buttel & Flinn 1974). As survey evidence mounted, however, education and especially age (Honnold 1981) turned out to be the only socioeconomic variables consistently and significantly related to environmental concern. A majority of studies found income and occupational prestige to be, at most, only weakly related to environmental concern (Van Liere & Dunlap 1980).

While age, education and, to a lesser extent, residence consistently predict environmental concern, these and other sociodemographic variables explain only modest levels of variance (seldom over 10%) in measures of environmental concern. Indicators of political ideology have frequently been better predictors, showing liberalism positively related to environmental concern (Buttel & Flinn 1978). Emphasizing these points, Mitchell (1980:5) has stressed that "support for the environmental movement is not limited to the affluent, the well-educated, or the young; it cuts across most demographic categories." Such findings suggest that support for environmental protection has "trickled down" the class and social structure of advanced industrial societies (see e.g. Cotgrove 1982, Morrison 1986).

The results from surveys of the general public thus provide little support for the widespread view that environmental concern is an "elitist" issue that may be inconsistent with the interests of the less affluent segments of society (e.g. Tucker 1982). The elitism charge (dealt with in more detail below) is often based on evidence of the above-average socioeconomic status of environmental *activists*—such as members of the Sierra Club—rather than on evidence of the correlates of environmental concern among the general public. Mitchell (1979) has shown that socioeconomic status is a much stronger predictor of membership in environmental organizations than of support for environmental protection, while Mohai (1985) has demonstrated that the link between socioeconomic status and environmental activism is primarily due to the link between socioeconomic status and general political activism.

Social-Psychological Research

Sociologists basing their environmental attitudes research on social-psychological theories have largely focused on issues relating to the cognitive structure of environmental orientations and to attitude-behavior congruence. Studies of the connections between environmental attitudes and behaviors have generally detected only modest associations. Heberlein in his own research and comprehensive review article on environmental attitudes (1981) noted, however, that the very general measures of environmental concern predominant in the literature tend to tap mere opinions (rather than attitudes). These environmental opinions are largely unembedded in cognitive structure and thus would not be expected to affect behavior significantly. Heberlein demonstrates that environmental attitudes, like most attitudes, show an internal cognitive consistency and are related to the number of accurate beliefs persons hold about attitude objects. Heberlein has suggested that environmental attitudes among the American public have become more differentiated since the early 1970s and that these more specific attitudes tend to be better predictors of environmental behaviors than are general environmental opinions (Heberlein & Black 1981).

Heberlein (1981) has noted that the vast bulk of research on environmental attitudes has been atheoretical and not rooted in attitude theory. Nonetheless, the most widely used attitude theory in environmental attitudes research has been norm-activation theory. Research in this theoretical genre was initiated by Heberlein (1972) and has been explored in both field (e.g. Van Liere &

Dunlap 1978) and experimental (e.g. Heberlein 1972) settings. The key argument within this perspective is that environmental behaviors or attitudes toward environmental protection reflect social-psychological processes involving the activation of moral norms against harming people (Stern et al 1986). Moral norms are activated when persons become aware of the negative interpersonal consequences of their actions and accept personal responsibility for the consequences of these actions. This theory has received substantial empirical support when applied to contexts such as littering, energy conservation, behavior in wildland recreation settings, and response to natural hazards (see the summary in Heberlein 1981). Social-structural-oriented researchers and practitioners of norm-activation theory have debated whether this theory is applicable to social changes associated with the environmental movement (see, for example, Dunlap & Van Liere 1977, Heberlein 1977).

Applied Research on Environmental Attitudes and Behaviors

The final major component of the environmental attitudes and behavior literature has been that devoted to improving or evaluating policy with respect to programs intended to influence environmentally related behaviors. The bulk of this literature concerns research on energy-related behaviors and how these behaviors are affected by attitudes, incentives, public programs, and related factors.

The most comprehensive program of research in this area has been by P. C. Stern and colleagues associated with the Committee on Behavioral and Social Aspects of Energy Consumption and Production of the National Research Council (Stern 1986, Stern & Aronson 1984), with other major contributions by Olsen & Cluett (1979), Cramer et al (1985), and Heberlein & Warriner (1983). Most of these studies attempt to determine whether energy conservation can be induced most readily through economic incentives or noneconomic motivations such as moral norms (Stern 1986). The predominant conclusion is that while economic motivations and incentives may have some impact, these factors tend to be less important than nonfinancial motives, effective communication and information, and the trustworthiness of information and sponsoring organizations (Stern 1986, Heberlein & Warriner 1983, Black et al 1985).

THE ENVIRONMENTAL MOVEMENT

The environmental movement also predated the institutionalization of environmental sociology and has remained important through the mid-1980s. Early studies of the environmental movement (e.g. Harry et al 1969) were primarily aimed at understanding the social base and composition of the major national environmental groups (e.g. the Sierra Club, the Izaac Walton League). Research over the past decade on major national environmental groups has built on the generalizations established in this early work and has shifted toward a more theoretical understanding of environmental movement mobilization. More recently, however, there has been an increased emphasis on local or specialized environmental groups such as the antinuclear and appropriate technology movements, as well as local movements generated by toxic waste and related environmental problems.

As noted above, the earliest studies of the major organizations of the nationwide environmental movement indicated that the members of these organizations tend to be predominantly upper-middle class. In particular, environmental movement members tend to be well-educated and to have professional and technical occupations. Shortly after the mobilization of the mass environmental movement in the late 1960s and early 1970s, criticisms of environmentalism argued it was elitist (see e.g. Neuhaus 1971 and the summary in Sills 1975). This criticism has continued (e.g. Tucker 1982) and has led to a long line of inquiry about the degree to which the movement is elitist (e.g. Gale 1983; Morrison 1973, 1986).

Morrison & Dunlap (1986) have provided a comprehensive overview and synthesis of this debate. They argue that the charge that the environmental movement is elitist logically has three components: (a) compositional elitism, the notion that environmentalists are drawn from privileged socioeconomic backgrounds; (b) ideological elitism, the notion that environmentalist activities serve to create an ideological rationale for distributing benefits to environmentalists and/or costs to other groups; and (c) impact elitism, the notion that environmental reforms, whether intentionally or not, have regressive social impacts. Morrison & Dunlap conclude that while environmentalists tend to be privileged, their class backgrounds do not differ from those of other sociopolitical activists, and the organized opposition to environmentalism, which draws heavily from the business community, is, if anything, more privileged than are the environmentalists. With regard to ideological elitism, Morrison & Dunlap suggest that some evidence supports the charge but argue that environmentalists tend not to act out of a consistent pursuit of self-interest. Impact elitism, in their view, "is clearly the bottom line" (p. 587), though Morrison & Dunlap see this aspect of elitism as the most complex and difficult to assess. They recognize that, on balance, environmental reforms tend to have modestly regressive impacts (see Buttel et al 1984 for a review of the evidence and a somewhat different conclusion). However, Morrison & Dunlap suggest that several environmental problems with disproportionate implications for the livelihood and well-being of the lower socioeconomic strata (e.g. workplace pollution) have received growing emphasis by environmental groups.

Prior to 1980 the bulk of the published research on the environmental movement treated the movement as a unique one—the "vanguard for a new society," to borrow from the title of Milbrath's (1984) recent book. Nonetheless, more recent research exhibits a major shift in emphasis, toward applying general theories of social movements and movement mobilization to the case of the environmental movement. Broadbent (1982) and Mohai (1985), for example, have applied variants of resource mobilization theory to, respectively, the differential patterns of environmental movement mobilization among the Western countries and to environmental movement participation in the United States. Both Broadbent and Mohai find resource mobilization theory helpful but incomplete. Broadbent argues that one must also consider center-periphery relations and the integration of the state to account for the low degree of environmental mobilization in Japan, while Mohai has argued for the need to integrate resource mobilization and social-psychological theory. Mitchell (1979), Godwin & Mitchell (1982), and Tillock & Morrison (1979) examined the US environmental movement in terms of the rational decision models of collective action developed by Mancur Olson (1965). Each of these studies found evidence of a "free-riding" phenomenon (as hypothesized by Olson), but Tillock & Morrison in particular argued that membership in and contributions to environmental groups cannot be fully accounted for by rational choice models of political behavior.

Environmental sociologists have also begun several lines of research into the political role of environmental organizations. Mitchell (1985) and Lowe & Goyde (1983) have done some of the major studies of environmental groups in national politics. Lowe & Goyde (1983) and Pepper (1984) found that British environmental groups tend to be internally divided—and often at odds with one another—because of very different orientations toward the environment, technology, and environmental reform. Buttel (1985) evaluated the recent US literature on environmental politics and found that it is dominated by pluralist approaches even though there was a major shift toward neo-Marxist and neo-Weberian theories of the state during the 1970s.

While a substantial amount of research by environmental sociologists focuses on the "mainline" national environmental groups, inquiry has increased into specialized environmental groups that are organizationally separate from—and, at times, at odds with—the large national organizations. Three types of specialized environmental movement groups have received the greatest attention: (a) the antinuclear movement and, in particular, the mobilization of protest in the aftermath of the Three Mile Island (TMI) accident in March 1979, (b) movements in response to toxic waste and other chemical disasters, and (c) the appropriate technology movement.

The US antinuclear movement began in the 1950s when an "elite quarrel" (Mitchell 1981) emerged over whether the Atomic Energy Commission's management of nuclear technology was excessively promotional. This elite quarrel became transformed into a mass movement in the 1960s when many local and national antinuclear groups engaged mainly in legal protest. In the middle and late 1970s the movement shifted to direct action, which was reinforced by the TMI accident in 1979.

Given that the antinuclear movement is, in part, organizationally distinct from the environmental movement, considerable research has sought to assess whether these two movements draw on the same sociopolitical bases. The weight of the evidence indicates that the enviromental and antinuclear movements have very similar bases of support in terms of social characteristics (Mazur 1981, Mitchell 1981, Dunlap & Olsen 1984, Scaminaci & Dunlap 1986) and political ideologies (Scaminaci & Dunlap 1986). But given the fact that the antinuclear movement has made a greater effort to attract a radical constituency (Mitchell 1981), its supporters may be somewhat more leftist or radical than those of the mainline environmental movement (Ladd et al 1983). However, the antinuclear movement has had an uneasy and ambivalent relationship with the traditional left in most Western countries (Nelkin & Pollack 1981).

The TMI accident has received a great deal of research attention, especially because it led to a demonstrable decline in public support for nuclear power (Sills et al 1981, Freudenburg & Baxter 1984, Freudenburg & Rosa 1984). The most longstanding research program in this area has been by Walsh and associates. Walsh has tested several hypotheses from resource mobilization and rational decision theories while documenting the massive local mobilization against the restart of TMI-1, spearheaded by existing and new antinuclear organizations. In contrast to one of the key premises of resource mobilization theory, Walsh (1981) has demonstrated that discontent should not be treated as a constant, since the TMI accident played a major role in generating grievances and mobilizing opposition to the restart of TMI-1. Walsh and Warland (1983) have found that "free-riding" among TMI-area residents opposed to restarting TMI-1 was pervasive, though the free-riding phenomenon was more complex than Olson (1965) has portrayed it.

A considerable literature on public mobilization against toxic wastes has recently converged on a number of generalizations. Lo (1986) has observed that the character of movement mobilization depends upon the class composition of the local community and the response of local government and business elites to initial protest actions. In working and lower-middle class communities where residents tend to lack the organizational resources to influence effectively the siting or operation of toxic waste facilities, unsatisfactory responses by local or extralocal elites tend to lead to feelings of powerlessness and ultimately to hostile outbursts and often to an expansion of the scope of the conflict to include larger issues such as democratic responsiveness (see also Levine 1982, Hamilton 1985, Finsterbusch & Humphrey 1986, Reich 1984). Lo (1986) has argued that the pattern of mobilization in upper-middle-class communities is quite different and depends upon the response of local elites. If the elite response is favorable, organizationally skilled community members become actively involved in influencing the political process, confining the protest to toxic wastes issues. Where initial protests fail to achieve the support of local elites, movement mobilization tends to follow the pattern of a combination of bureaucratic-political tactics and expansion of the scope of the conflict. Reich (1981) has investigated public and private responses to toxic chemical disasters in the United States, Italy, and Japan. He detected common patterns: Toxic chemical issues moved from private grievance to public concern and then to a political issue, and polluters attempted to resist grievances by "non-issue" strategies. He found that there were differences in mobilization and tactics among victims in the three national contexts, with victims in the United States utilizing state legislators as advocates, those in Italy utilizing parties and unions, and those in Japan using private groups and opposition parties.

The third type of specialized environmental group receiving significant research attention has been the appropriate technology movement. Several environmental sociologists have explored whether appropriate technology themes might redirect the course of the environmental movement or provide the basis for a broader mass movement that could more effectively link environmental and equity concerns (Schnaiberg 1983, Morrison 1980). Several researchers, however, have noted that the appeal of appropriate technology as a major environmental strategy must be tempered by a number of realities. Schnaiberg (1983), for example, has argued that the theoretical assumptions underlying appropriate technology strategy and appeals are naive because they fail to recognize the intensity of commitment from broad quarters of society to resource-intensive production and consumption systems. Frahm & Buttel (1982) have noted that the petty-bourgeois/anti-welfare-state ideology of the appropriate technology movement would ultimately lead to its being coopted by a rise in conservative sentiment such as occurred during the early years of the Reagan Administration. It is now widely acknowledged that the appropriate technology movement has declined greatly in its public visibility and appeal during the mid-1980s.

TECHNOLOGICAL RISK AND RISK ASSESSMENT

The environmental movement has played a major role in increasing public concern about technological risks (Nelkin 1974, Short 1984). The increased public recognition of technological risks and growing pressures to rationalize state regulation of risks have combined to lead to the creation of a "danger establishment," a major subset of which is an "environmental risk establishment" that conducts risk analyses, translates these analyses to policymakers, and weighs these analyses in the determination of policy (Dietz & Rycroft 1984). Until the 1980s sociologists had little interest in risk assessment (Short 1984), save for sociologists of science interested in technical controversies (e.g. Nelkin 1974, Mazur 1981) and social psychologists who studied risk perceptions (see Covello 1983). Since 1980, however, there has been an outpouring of research on technological risk phenomena.[4]

Attention by environmental sociologists to technological risk and risk assessment was greatly stimulated by TMI, Love Canal, and related instances of technological hazards and by the politicization of risk assessment. In the early 1980s several books and articles appeared that presented diametrically opposed arguments about the biases of and the nature of the public interest in technological risk assessment. Douglas & Wildavsky (1982) criticized the environmental risk establishment for exaggerating the magnitude of these risks and contended that the American public's risk perceptions have no basis in objective reality. Schnaiberg (1980), on the other hand, has stressed that biases exist in the assessment of technological risks in the direction of overestimating social benefits and ignoring major social costs (see also Clarke 1986, Jasper 1986).

Inquiry by environmental sociologists into technological risk has proceeded in several directions. Mazur (1981) has developed a research program on the dynamics of public protests against technological innovations and technical controversy. His studies provide support for the notion that mass movements against technology rise and fall according to the degree of public interest in a related larger issue. For example, nuclear power protests were high when the public was concerned about fallout (early 1960s), the environment (early 1970s), and the energy crisis (mid 1970s). Mazur shows that these movements follow a particular cycle in which media coverage of protests broadens the base of public opposition and leads to a mass movement. Dietz and colleagues (Dietz & Rycroft 1984, Dietz et al 1986) have researched the values and behavior of the "environmental risk establishment" and the role of risk assessment in the policymaking process. They have found that risk assessment professionals differ greatly in their support for the use of risk assessment and benefit–cost analysis—in particular, that persons employed by environmental groups are the least supportive. Nelkin and colleagues (Nelkin & Pollack 1981, Nelkin 1974, Nelkin & Brown 1984) have developed a longstanding research program on the origins of technical controversies and the politicization of public policymaking. Nelkin has emphasized the origins

[4]A related, rapidly growing area of environmental-sociological scholarship—one that links environmental sociology with the sociology of science and political sociology—is that of the political economy of technological innovation (see, for example, Perrolle 1986, Buttel et al 1985).

of technical controversies in disagreements within the scientific community and in the vague and shifting boundaries between competing technical and political aspects of risk assessment. Further, her studies have demonstrated that concerns about risk and declining trust in scientific judgments and in existing decision-making procedures often become transformed into more far-reaching scrutiny of the legitimacy of political systems, as in the context of the West German antinuclear movement (Nelkin & Pollack 1981).

The sociology of technological risk and risk assessment has been given particular impetus over the past few years by the work of Short (1984) and Perrow (1984, 1986). Short developed a comprehensive view of risk, risk perceptions, and risk assessment, and he set forth a research agenda for uniting these issues with contemporary sociological theory. Perrow has become widely known for his notion of "normal accidents," a concept that was developed during the course of his work on the TMI accident. By "normal" (or "system") accidents Perrow means inevitable failures in complex technical systems, such as nuclear power plants, petrochemical plants, and air traffic control systems, that result from the complex interactions of technical components and their tight coupling. Perrow has noted that while failures in such high-risk systems are inevitable and thus "normal," the political process in the aftermath of accidents such as that at TMI typically leads to diagnoses emphasizing human error. Such diagnoses are seen to result from the growth-oriented values and elite-biased political interests underlying risk assessment and evaluation procedures, and they serve to buttress continued use of the technology. Perrow (1984) has also developed a typology of technological systems based on the tightness of "coupling" and on the extent to which there are linear vs complex system interactions. He has argued that each type of technology and the risks it poses require a distinctive authority system consisting of different combinations of centralization and decentralization.

POLITICAL ECONOMY OF THE ENVIRONMENT AND ENVIRONMENTAL POLITICS

The political economy of the environment and environmental politics are not entirely new areas of inquiry in environmental sociology. From the early 1970s sociologists have devoted attention to the nature of environmental politics (see e.g. Morrison 1973, Schnaiberg 1975). Nonetheless, this area of inquiry has been considerably broadened during the 1980s. The 1970s can be seen in retrospect as an era of fundamental reorientation of political sociology, chiefly because of the scrutiny of pluralist theory and the increased prominence of neo-Marxist and neo-Weberian theories of the state (see e.g. Carnoy 1984). Save for the work of Schnaiberg (1980) and Humphrey & Buttel (1982), these new perspectives on political structures and processes had very little impact on US environmental sociology until the early and mid-1980s. Nonetheless, the 1980s have witnessed increased attention to the political economy of the environment and environmental conflict by US researchers, much of which appears to have resulted from collaboration with European colleagues (e.g. Schnaiberg et al 1986). The result has been a new literature that is rapidly growing.

The environmental–political economy literature in both the United States and Europe has largely drawn on a combination of neo-Marxist and neo-Weberian perspectives. Schnaiberg's (1980) *The Environment* is the best US example of this cross-fertilization, while Rudig & Lowe (1987) is a comparable European effort. Two major interrelated issues have been explored in this emergent literature: (*a*) distributional conflicts in and implications of environmental policy, and (*b*) the alignment of environmental and related movements and groups in national politics, particularly vis-a-vis labor and "new social movements." The major compilation of this research is the anthology by Schnaiberg et al (1986). Lehmbruch (1986) argues that while corporatism works well with regard to policy arenas such as economic stabilization, these arrangements are not conducive to environmental policymaking. Environmental organizations, characterized by a loose network structure rather than by dense interorganizational networks, find it difficult to function in corporatist arrangements. Also, environmental concerns, unlike wage bargaining, are more long-term and imprecise and do not have a developed exchange calculus vis-a-vis corporate interests. Meidinger (1986) notes, however, that there has been a trend toward market mechanisms ("emissions trading") in US air quality regulation and enforcement, despite environmentalist opposition to the notion of a "property right to pollute." This new pattern of regulation and enforcement has emerged because of corporate interests and the pervasiveness of a "new regulatory culture" that represents broad consensus on "interest group liberalism" (Lowi 1986). Meidinger argues that the key consequence of market mechanisms of regulation is that they render the regulation and enforcement processes largely invisible and depoliticized and tend to be biased toward the interests of wealthy groups with the greatest ability to purchase emissions permits.

Pollack (1986) and Buttel (1986b) have provided parallel insights into the nature of the "political opportunity structures" of environmental groups. Pollack has argued that these are shaped by the nature of political systems and activism. He has demonstrated that the breadth and intensity of antinuclear sentiment in the United States, France, and West Germany, along with variations in the degree of centralization of nuclear regulatory structures, have affected the political accomplishments of the antinuclear movement. Buttel (1986b) has argued that in addition to the degree of centralization, the degree of state autonomy vis-à-vis civil society, which is shaped by class structure and historical aspects of political development, is another important component of the political opportunity structure of environmental movements.

The second vital component of the political economy approach has been that directed at understanding environmentalism as a component of the broader phenomenon of "new social movements." Inglehart (1971) noted in the early 1970s that a "silent revolution" was emerging in the European countries. He postulated that a major transformation of social values was underway from an emphasis on materialism and physical security toward "post-materialism" (i.e. greater concern with the quality of life). Inglehart (1977) argued, following a Maslowian hypothesis of the hierarchy of needs, that this value shift was a product of adolescent socialization experiences in a milieu of 1960s affluence. Watts and colleagues (Handley & Watts 1978, Watts & Wandesfore-Smith 1981) were soon to stress that Inglehart's rendering of "post-materialist values" had major similarities with pro-environment attitudes (see also Cotgrove 1982).

During the late 1970s, however, a vigorous debate occurred as to the adequacy of Inglehart's conceptualization and empirical data (se Van Deth 1983, and references therein). In particular, theorists of "new social movements" (e.g. Burklin 1985, Kitschelt 1985) began to argue that conceptualization of this value change as "post-materialism" ignored the most fundamental aspect of the transformation: The emergence of a "post-industrial" occupational structure in advanced capitalism and the consequent undermining of the working-class base of social democratic and other left parties. Gorz (1982:69), for example, has argued that the industrial working class has ceased to be the principal motor of social change in advanced capitalism and that it has been replaced by new social movements—principally environmental, peace, and feminist movements—that reflect the interests of the "post-industrial neo-proletariat" (or "new middle class"). Many European researchers thus have moved toward understanding the environmental movement as a fundamental feature of the new political landscape rather than as an interest group or lobby, as has been the case in much US scholarship. These scholars have made major advances in making connections among the generation and persistence of environmental values, local and national mobilization of environmental groups, environmental degradition (especially episodic phenomena such as toxic waste incidents), the rise of "green parties," and the disintegration of traditional left parties (see especially Burklin 1985, Rudig & Lowe 1987, Papadakis 1984).

ENVIRONMENTAL SOCIOLOGY AFTER A DECADE AND A HALF: ITS STATUS AND PROSPECTS

Environmental sociology has exhibited both persistence and change since the time that the expression was coined in the early 1970s. These patterns of persistence and change have corresponded with several overall trends in environmental sociology. Environmental sociology has become less a scholarly cause or movement and more a conventional specialty area within sociology with relatively little influence in redirecting social theory as a whole. Less focused on its theoretical and metatheoretical core (the "new human ecology"), environmental sociology has become more diverse and fragmented, and afflicted with many of the same problems as sociology at large—innovative theoretical works tend to have a limited audience, and methodologically sophisticated quantitative research tends to be confined to problems that lend themselves to large data-sets and statistical precision. There has been uneven progress in environmental sociology toward bridging the dualisms—structure vs agency, nominalism vs realism, materialism vs idealism, methodological precision vs. substantive importance—that continue to pervade the discipline as a whole (Giddens 1979). In particular, the dominant feature of the theoretical core of environmental sociology and of the literature in several substantive areas of the field (e.g. some work in the political economy tradition) is that it is largely structural in nature and stands in need of modification in order to incorporate subjectivity and agency. Likewise, much of the empirical literature in environmental sociology receives theoretical guidance that is exclusively subjectivist and microsociological and that could benefit from a more macrostructural orientation.

There are several encouraging exemplars for bridging this gulf and reintegrating environmental sociology. Some of the more notable include Dietz's (1987) provocative insertion of the perspective of Jurgen Habermas into social impact assessment, Rudig & Lowe's (1987) methodological commentary on the literature on environmental values and politics, and Dunlap's continued efforts to flesh out his conception of the "new ecological paradigm" at both the micro and macro levels. But many of the more promising approaches to the reintegration of environmental sociology have, in my view, come from an unlikely origin: the sociology of development (see Buttel 1986c). Redclift (1984) and Bunker (1985) have developed powerful new approaches to the sociology of development by focusing on the interactions between the biophysical environment and third-world peasant economies. Each has sought to analyze the relations between development and ecological processes by focusing on both the subjectivity of actors and the objective or material aspect of agrarian structures in peripheral capitalism. These efforts, which have yet to be incorporated into the US environmental sociology literature, nonetheless indicate why environmental sociology stands to benefit considerably through cross-fertilization with other substantive areas within sociology.

ACKNOWLEDGMENTS

The author would like to extend his deepest gratitude to Riley E. Dunlap for his extraordinarily generous comments on an earlier draft of this paper. Stephen Bunker, Allan Schnaiberg, Denton Morrison, Marvin Olsen, Thomas

Dietz, and James Short, Jr., also provided helpful suggestions, as did Robin Williams, Jr., who commented extensively on a related paper (Buttel 1986a) in which some of the ideas presented here were originally developed. Finally, the author would like to thank Douglas Wilson for his bibliographic assistance.

LITERATURE CITED

Albrecht, D. E., Bultena, G., Hoiberg, E., Nowak, P. 1982. The new environmental paradigm scale. *J. Environ. Educ.* 13:39–42

Albrecht, D. E., Murdock, S. H. 1984. Toward a human ecological perspective on part-time farming. *Rural sociol.* 49:389–411

Albrecht, D. E., Murdock, S. H. 1986. Natural resource availability and social change. *Sociol Inq.* 56:In press

Ashby, J. A. 1985. The social ecology of soil erosion in a Colombian farming system. *Rural Sociol.* 50:377–96

Black, J. S., Stern, P. C., Elworth, J. T. 1985. Personal and contextual influences on household energy adaptations. *J. Appl. Psychol.* 70:3–21

Broadbent, J. 1982. *Environmental movements in Japan: Citizen versus state mobilization.* Presented at Ann. Meet. Am. Sociol. Assoc., Detroit

Bunker, S. G. 1985. *Underdeveloping the Amazon.* Urbana: Univ. Ill. Press

Burch, W. R., DeLuca, D. R. 1984. *Measuring the Social Impact of Natural Resource Policies.* Albuquerque: Univ. N. Mex. Press

Burklin, W. P. 1985. The greens: Ecology and the new left in West German politics. In *West German Politics in the Mid-Eighties: Crises and Continuity,* ed. H. G. P. Wallach, G. K. Romoser, pp. 187–218. New York: Praeger

Buttel, F. H. 1978. Environmental sociology: a new paradigm? *Am. Sociol.* 13:252–56

Buttel, F. H. 1985. Environmental quality and the state: Some political-sociological observations on environmental regulation. *Res. Polit. Sociol.* 1:167–88

Buttel, F. H. 1986a. Sociology and environment: the winding road toward human ecology. *Int. Soc. Sci. J.* 109:337–56

Buttel, F. H. 1986b. Discussion: Economic stagnation, scarcity, and changing commitments to distributional policies in environmental-resource issues. See Schnaiberg et al 1986, pp. 221–38

Buttel, F. H. 1986c. Toward a rural sociology of global resources: Social structure, ecology, and Latin American agricultural development. In *Resources and People,* ed.

K. A. Dahlberg, J. W. Bennett, pp. 129–64. Boulder, Colo: Westview

Buttel, F. H., Flinn, W. L. 1974. The structure of support for the environmental movement, 1968–1970. *Rural Sociol.* 39:56–69

Buttel, F. H., Flinn, W. L. 1978. The politics of environmental concern: The impacts of party identification and political ideology on environmental attitudes. *Environ. Behav.* 10:17–36

Buttel, F. H., Kenney, M., Kloppenburg, J. Jr. 1985. From green revolution to biorevolution: Some observations on the changing technological bases of economic transformation in the third world. *Econ. Dev. Cult. Change* 34:31–55

Buttel, F. H., Wiswall, I., Geisler, C. C., eds. 1984. *Labor and the Environment.* Westport, Conn: Greenwood

Carnoy, M. 1984. *The State and Political Theory.* Princeton: Princeton Univ. Press

Catton, W. R. Jr. 1980. *Overshoot.* Urbana: Univ. Ill. Press

Catton, W. R., Jr., Dunlap, R. E. 1978a. Environmental sociology: A new paradigm. *Am. Sociol.* 13:41–49

Catton, W. R. Jr., Dunlap, R. E. 1978b. Paradigms, theories, and the primacy of the HEP-NEP distinction. *Am. Sociol.* 13:256–59

Catton, W. R. Jr., Dunlap, R. E. 1980. A new ecological paradigm for post-exuberant sociology. *Am. Behav. Sci.* 24:15–47

Clarke, L. 1986. *The sociology of technological change: Toward middle range perspectives on acceptable risk.* Ms., Dept. Sociol, Univ. Calif., Los Angeles

Cotgrove, S. 1982. *Catastrophe or Cornucopia.* Chichester: Wiley

Coughenour, C. M. 1984. Social ecology and agriculture. *Rural Sociol.* 49:1–22

Covello, V. T. 1983. The perception of technological risks: A literature review. *Technol. Forecasting Soc. Change* 23:285–97

Cramer, J. C., Miller, N., Craig, P., Hackett, B. M., et al. 1985. Social and engineering determinants and their equity implications in residential electricity use. *Energy* 10:1283–91

Dietz, T. 1987. Theory and method in social impact assessment. *Sociol. Inq.* 77:In press

Dietz, T., Regens, J. L., Rycroft, R. W. 1986. *Sources of support for risk assessment and benefit-cost analysis in the environmental policy system.* Presented at Ann. Meet. Int. Assoc. Impact Assessment

Dietz, T., Rycroft, R. W. 1984. *The Washington danger establishment: A theoretical framework.* Presented at Ann. Meet. Am. Sociol. Assoc., San Antonio

Douglas, M., Wildavsky, A. 1982. *Risk and Culture.* Berkeley: Univ. Calif. Press

Downs, A. 1972. Up and down with ecology—the 'issue-attention' cycle. *Public Inter.* 28:38–50

Dunlap, R. E. 1986. *Two decades of public concern for environmental quality: Up, down and up again.* Presented at Ann. Meet. Am. Sociol. Assoc., New York

Dunlap, R. E., Catton, W. R. Jr. 1979. Environmental sociology. *Ann. Rev. Sociol.* 5:243–73

Dunlap, R. E., Catton, W. R. Jr. 1983. What environmental sociologists have in common (whether concerned with 'built' or 'natural' environments). *Sociol. Inq.* 53:113–35

Dunlap, R. E., Dillman, D. A. 1976. Decline in public support for environmental protection: Evidence from a 1970–1974 panel study. *Rural Sociol.* 41:382–90

Dunlap, R. E., Martin, K. E. 1983. Bringing environment into the study of agriculture: Observations and suggestions regarding the sociology of agriculture. *Rural Sociol.* 48:201–18

Dunlap, R. E., Olsen, M. E. 1984. Hard-path versus soft-path advocates: A study of energy activists. *Policy Stud. J.* 13:413–28

Dunlap, R. E., Van Liere, K. D. 1977. Land ethnic or golden rule? *J. Soc. Issues* 33:200–7

Dunlap, R. E., Van Liere, K. D. 1978. The 'new environmental paradigm': A proposed measuring instrument and preliminary results. *J. Environ. Educ.* 9:10–19

Dunlap, R. E., Van Liere, K. D. 1984. Commitment to the dominant social paradigm and concern for environmental quality. *Soc. Sci. Q.* 65:1013–28

Erskine, H. 1971. The polls: Pollution and its costs. *Publ. Opin. Q.* 35:120–35

Finsterbusch, K., Humphrey, C. R. 1986. *Community response to toxic wastes: Comparative case studies.* Presented at Ann. Meet. Soc. Stud. Soc. Probl., New York

Frahm, A. M., Buttel, F. H. 1982. Appropriate technology: Current debate and future possibilities. *Humboldt J. Soc. Relat.* 11:11–37

Freudenburg, W. R. 1986. Social impact assessment. *Ann. Rev. Sociol.* 12:451–78

Freudenburg, W. R., Baxter, R. K. 1984. Host community attitudes toward nuclear power: A reassessment. *Soc. Sci. Q.* 65:1129–36

Fruedenburg, W. R., Rosa, E. A., eds. 1984. *Public Reactions to Nuclear Power.* Boulder, Colo: Westview

Giddens, A. 1979. *Central Problems in Social Theory.* Berkeley: Univ. Calif. Press

Gale, R. P. 1983. The environmental movement and the left. *Sociol. Inq.* 53:179–99

Gilles, J. 1980. Farm size, farm structure, energy, and climate: an alternative ecological analysis of United States agriculture. *Rural Sociol.* 45:524–30

Godwin, R. K., Mitchell, R. C. 1982. Rational models, collective goods and nonelectoral political behavior. *West. Polit Q.* 35:161–81

Gorz, A. 1982. *Farewell to the Working Class.* Boston: South End

Hamilton, L. C. 1985. Concern about toxic wastes: Three demographic predictors. *Sociol. Perspect.* 28:463–86

Handley, D., Watts, N. 1978. Political psychology and environmental politics. *Zeitschr. Umweltpolit.* 4:295–320

Harry, J., Gale, R., Hendee, J. 1969. Conservation: An upper-middle class social movement. *J. Leisure Res.* 1:246–54

Hawley, A. H. 1981. Human ecology: Persistence and change. In *The State of Sociology*, ed. J. F. Short, Jr., pp. 119–40. Beverly Hills, Calif: Sage

Heberlein, T. A. 1972. The land ethic realized: Some social psychological explanations for changing environmental attitudes. *J. Soc. Issues* 28:79–87

Heberlein, T. A. 1977. Norm activation and environmental action: A rejoinder to R. E. Dunlap and K. D. Van Liere. *J. Soc. Issues* 33:207–11

Heberlein, T. A. 1981. Environmental attitudes. *Zeitschr. umweltpolit.* 4:241–70

Heberlein, T. A., Black, J. S. 1981. Cognitive consistency and environmental action. *Environ. Behav.* 13:717–34

Heberlein, T. A., Warriner, G. K. 1983. The influence of price and attitude on shifting residential electricity consumption from onto off-peak periods. *J. Econ. Psychol.* 4:107–30

Heffernan, W. D., Green, G. P. 1986. Farm size and soil loss: Prospects for a sustainable agriculture. *Rural Sociol.* 51:31–42

Honnold, J. A. 1981. Predictors of public environmental concern in the 1970s. In *Environmental Policy Formation,* ed. D. E. Mann, pp. 63–75. Lexington, Mass: Heath

Humphrey, C. R., Buttel, F. H. 1982. *Environment, Energy, and Society.* Belmont, Calif: Wadsworth

Inglehart, R. 1971. The silent revolution in Europe: Intergenerational change in post-industrial societies. *Am. Polit. Sci. Rev.* 65:991–1007

Inglehart, R. 1977. *The Silent Revolution.* Princeton: Princeton Univ. Press

Jasper, J. A. 1986. *From social organization to policy styles: Risk attitudes in the nuclear debate.* Ms. Dept. Soc., New York Univ.

Kitschelt, H. 1985. New social movements in West Germany and the United States. *Polit. Power Soc. Theory* 5:273–324

Ladd, A. E., Hood, T. C., Van Liere, K. D. 1983. Ideological themes in the antinuclear movement: Consensus and diversity. *Sociol. Inq.* 53:252–72

Lehmbruch, G. 1986. State roles in the articulation and mediation of distributional conflicts. See Schnaiberg et al 1983, pp. 337–47

Levine, A. G. 1982. *Love Canal.* Lexington, Mass: Heath

Lo, C. Y. H. 1986. Community based protests against toxic chemical pollution: preliminary report of research findings. Unpubl. ms. Dept. Sociol., Univ. Calif. Los Angeles

Lowe, G. D., Pinhey, T. K., Grimes, M. D. 1980. Public support for environmental protection: New evidence from national surveys. *Pacific Sociol. Rev.* 23:423–45

Lowe, P., Goyde, J. 1983. *Environmental Groups in Politics.* London: Allen & Unwin

Lowi, T. J. 1986. The welfare state, the new regulations and the rule of law. See Schnaiberg et al, 1986, pp. 109–49

Mazur, A. 1981. *The Dynamics of Technical Controversy.* Washington, DC: Communications

Meadows, D. H., Meadows, D. L., Randers, J., Behrens, W. III. 1972. *The Limits to Growth.* New York: Universe

Meidinger, E. 1986. Discussion: the politics of 'market mechanisms' in US air pollution policy, social structure and regulatory culture. See Schnaiberg et al 1986, pp. 150–75

Milbrath, L. W. 1984. *Environmentalists: Vanguard for a New Society.* Albany: State Univ. NY Press

Mitchell, R. C. 1979. Silent spring/solid majorities. *Publ. Opinion* 2:16–20, 55

Mitchell, R. C. 1980. *Public Opinion on Environmental Issues.* Washington, DC: Council Environ. Quality

Mitchell, R. C. 1981. From elite quarrel to mass movement. *Transaction/Society* 18:76–84

Mitchell, R. C. 1984. Public opinion and environmental politics in the 1970s and 1980s. In *Environmental Policy in the 1980s,* ed. V. J. Vig, M. E. Kraft, pp. 51–74. Washington, DC: Congr. Q. Press

Mitchell, R. C. 1985. *From conservation to environmental movement: The development of the modern environmental lobbies. Discuss Pap. AE85-12,* Resources for the Future, Washington, DC

Mohai, P. 1985. Public concern and elite involvement in environmental-conservation issues. *Soc. Sci. Q.* 66:820–38

Morrison, D. E. 1973. The environmental movement: Conflict dynamics. *J. Volun. Action Res.* 2:74–85

Morrison, D. E. 1980. The soft, cutting edge of environmentalism: Why and how the appropriate technology notion is changing the movement. *Natural Res. J.* 20:275–98

Morrison, D. E. 1986. How and why environmental consciousness has trickled down. See Schnaiberg et al 1986, pp. 187–220

Morrison, D. E., Dunlap, R. E. 1986. Environmentalism and elitism: a conceptual and empirical analysis. *Environ. Mgmt.* 10:581–89

Nelkin, D. 1974. The role of experts in a nuclear siting controversy. *Bull. Atomic Sci.* 30:29–36

Nelkin, D., Brown, M. S. 1984. *Workers at Risk.* Chicago: Univ. Chicago Press

Nelkin, D., Pollack, M. 1981. *The Atom Besieged.* Cambridge, Mass: MIT Press

Neuhaus, R. 1971. *In Defense of People.* New York: Macmillan

Olsen, M. E., Cluett, C. 1979. *Evaluation of the Seattle City Light Neighborhood Energy Conservation Program.* Seattle: Battelle Hum. Aff. Res. Ctr.

Olson, M. 1965. *The Logic of Collective Action.* Cambridge, Mass: Harvard Univ. Press

Papadakis, E. 1984. *The Green Movement in West Germany.* London: Croom Helm

Pepper, D. 1984. *The Roots of Modern Environmentalism.* London: Croom Helm

Perrolle, J. A. 1986. *Computers and Social Change.* Belmont, Calif: Wadsworth

Perrow, C. 1984. *Normal Accidents.* New York: Basic Books

Perrow, C. 1986. Risky systems: Inducing and avoiding errors. Presented at Ann. Meet. Am. Sociol. Assoc., New York

Pollack, M. 1986. Discussion: Patterns of interests in environmental policy conflicts. See Schnaiberg et al 1986, pp. 239–52

Redclift, M. 1984. *Development and the Environmental Crisis.* London: Methuen

Reich, M. R. 1981. *Toxic politics: a comparative study of public and private responses to chemical disasters in the United States, Italy and Japan.* PhD thesis. Yale Univ., New Haven

Reich, M. R. 1984. Mobilizing for environmental policy in Italy and Japan. *Comp. Polit.* 16 (4):379–402

Rudig, W., Lowe, P. D. 1987. Political ecology and the social sciences: The state of the art. *Br. J. Polit. Sci.* In press

Scaminaci, J. III, Dunlap, R. E. 1986. No nukes! a comparison of participants in two national antinuclear demonstrations. *Sociol. Inquiry* 56:272–82

Schnaiberg, A. 1975. Social Syntheses of the societal-environmental dialectic: The role of distributional impacts. *Soc. Sci. Q.* 56: 5–20

Schnaiberg, A. 1980. *The Environment.* New York: Oxford Univ. Press

Schnaiberg, A. 1983. Redistributive goals versus distributive politics: Social equity limits in environmental and appropriate technology movements. *Sociol. Inq.* 53:200–19

Schnaiberg, A., Watts, N., Zimmermann, K., eds. 1986. *Distributional Conflicts in Environmental-Resource Policy.* Aldershot, Hants: Gower

Short, J. F. Jr. 1984. The social fabric at risk: Toward the social transformation of risk analysis. *Am. Sociol. Rev.* 49:711–25

Sills, D. L. 1975. The environmental movement and its critics. *Human Ecol.* 3:1–41

Sills, D. L., Wolf, C. P., Shelanski, V., eds. 1981. *The Accident at Three Mile Island.* Boulder, Colo: Westview

Stern, P. C. 1986. Blind spots in policy analysis: what economics doesn't say about energy use. *J. Pol. Analysis Mgmt.* 5:200–27

Stern, P. C., Aronson, E. 1984. *Energy Use.* New York: Freeman

Stern, P. C., Dietz, T., Black, J. S. 1986. *Public support for environmental protection: The role of moral norms.* Ms. Nat.

Res. Council, Washington, DC

Stokols, D. Altman, I., eds. 1986. *Handbook of Environmental Psychology.* New York: Wiley

Tillock, H., Morrison, D. E. 1979. Group size and contributions to collective action: An examination of Olson's theory using data from Zero Population Growth research. *Res. Soc. Movements, Conflict, Change* 2:131–58

Tucker, W. 1982. *Progress and Privilege.* Garden City, NY: Anchor/Doubleday

Van Deth, J. W. 1983. The persistence of materialist and post-materialist value orientations. *Eur. J. Polit. Res.* 11:63–79

Van Liere, K. D., Dunlap, R. E. 1978. Moral norms and environmental behavior: An application of Schwartz's norm-activation model to yard burning. *J. Appl. Soc. Psychol.* 8:174–88

Van Liere, K. D., Dunlap, R. E. 1980. The social bases of environmental concern: a review of hypotheses, explanations, and empirical evidence. *Publ. Opinion Q.* 44:181–97

Walsh, E. J. 1981. Resource mobilization and citizen protest in communities around TMI. *Soc. Problems* 29:1–21

Walsh, E. J., Warland, R. H. 1983. Social movement involvement in the wake of a nuclear accident. *Am. Sociol. Rev.* 48:764–80

Watts, N., Wandesforde-Smith, G. 1981. Post-material values and environmental policy formation. In *Environmental Policy Formation,* ed. D. E. Mann, pp. 29–42. Lexington, Mass: Heath

SUBJECT INDEX

A

Administrative ratios
  retrenchment and, 344
Adolescence
  American family life and,
    204-7
Aid to Families with Dependent
  Children, 111, 399, 403
American family life, 193-212
  adolescence and, 204-7
  childbearing and, 197-201
  childrearing and, 201-4
  old age and, 207-11
Apprenticeship
  proletarian consciousness and,
    55
  worklife mobility and, 431
Asia
  rural poverty in, 329
Asian immigrants
  naturalization of, 379-80
Australia
  social mobility in, 427
Austria
  worklife mobility in, 431
Authority hierarchies
  Japanese industrial organiza-
    tions and, 298-99
Automation
  effects of, 43
  skills in the age of, 42-44
  skill degradation and, 29-30
Autonomy
  skill and, 31-32

B

Brazil
  income inequality in, 328
Bureacratic encounters
  evaluation of, 409-11
Bureaucracy
  welfare state
    social rights and, 397-401
Bureaucratic encounters
  power-dependence relations
    and, 403-7
Bureaucratization
  growing organizations and,
    342
Business administration
  management of decline and,
    343

C

California
  Hispanic minorities in, 360,
    372
Canada
  social mobility in, 427
Canadian immigrants
  naturalization of, 379
Capital
  gentrification and, 142-43
  protoindustrialization and, 99-
    100
Capitalism
  democracy vs., 114-17
Carrying capacity
  ecologic niches and, 348
Centralization
  organizational decline and,
    344-45
Childbearing
  American family life and,
    197-201
Childbirth
  quality of married life and,
    242
Childrearing
  American family life and,
    201-4
Children
  economic value of
    parenthood and, 239
  parental perceptions of, 249-
    51
  stressfulness of, 251-54
  time budget surveys and, 154
  working mothers and, 260
Citizenship
  Hispanic minorities and, 379-
    82
  welfare state and, 395-97
Civil rights
  citizenship and, 396
Class mobility
  See Social Mobility
Class struggle
  industrialization and, 100-2
Collective behavior
  mass persuasion and, 19-20
Colombia
  income inequality in, 329
Commodification
  citizenship in welfare states
    and, 397

Complacency
  organizational decline and,
    347
Conflict
  organizational decline and,
    344
Conflict theory
  crime control and, 77-84
  deviant behavior and, 9
Conservatism
  organizational decline and,
    344-45
Consumer behavior
  time budget surveys and, 153
Consumption
  employment and, 319
Contextuality
  everyday life sociology and,
    219
Control structures
  industrialization and, 102-3
Conversation analysis, 226-27
Corporate familism
  in Japan, 290-96
Corporatism
  environmental policymaking
    and, 482
Credentialism, 40
Crime control, 67-86
  conflict perspective and, 77-
    84
  economic perspective and, 68-
    71
  punishment and, 71-76
  structural functional perspec-
    tive and, 71-77
  See also Social control
Crime rates
  arrest rates and, 74
  punishment and, 69
Cuba
  out-migration in, 362-63
Cuban immigrants
  entrepreneurial orientation of,
    369-70
  historic sociology and, 362
  income of, 370-71
  knowledge of English and,
    376
  labor force participation of,
    367
  naturalization of, 379
  occupational attainment of,
    366

Florida
Hispanic minorities in, 360, 372
Food stamps, 403
Foreign direct investment
income inequality and, 318
Formalization
organizational decline and, 344
Fragmentation
industrial society and, 91-92
France
antinuclear movement in, 482
social mobility in, 427
welfare state formation in, 113
worklife mobility in, 431-32

G

Garbage-can model
strategic decision making and, 184-87
Gender relations
parenthood and, 254
Gentrification, 129-145
capital and, 142-43
culture and, 143-45
displacement and, 135-37
economic rationality and, 137-38
economic restructuring and, 138-40
historic preservation and, 134-35
Gini concentration ratio
income inequality and, 324-25
Government
welfare state bureacracies and, 398
Gratification
relative, 52-53
Great Britain
environmental movement in, 477
income maintenance programs in, 392
managerial capitalism in, 102
social mobility in, 427
welfare programs in, 111
welfare state formation in, 113

H

Habatsu, 297
Headstart Program, 202-3
Hermeneutics, 222
Hispanic minorities, 359-83
citizenship and, 379-82
complexity of, 360-61
demography of, 363

historic sociology and, 361-62
knowledge of English and, 372-76
labor market and, 364-72
out-migration and, 362-63
political behavior of, 376-79
Historic sociology
Hispanic minorities and, 361-62
Homemaker role
motherhood and, 246
Homicide
social control and, 78-79
Homo economicus, 218
Hong Kong
income inequality in, 328
Hospital administration
management of decline and, 343
Household economics
time budget surveys and, 155-57
Human exceptionalism paradigm, 469
Hungary
social mobility in, 426
time budget surveys in, 152, 156

I

Identity
role accumulation and, 251-52
Ideologic elitism
environmentalism and, 476
Imprisonment
unemployment and, 80
Income
Hispanic minorities and, 370-72
Income distribution
inflation and, 281-82
middle class and, 278-81
studies of, 261-65
limitations of, 271-75
unemployment and, 281-82
working women and, 259-85
Income inequality
economic development and, 313-30
measures of, 323-25
police force size and, 81
race and, 270-71
working wives and, 265-68
Income maintenance programs, 392
Income redistribution
effects of, 319
Incrementalism
strategic decision making and, 184-87

Industrialization, 89-107
control structures and, 102-3
epochs and processes in, 96-106
era of
crafts in, 32-38
proletarianization and, 103-4
skill degradation and, 29
social class and, 100-2
social differentiation and, 91-93
social mobility and, 424-27
uneven development and, 93-95
welfare state and, 112-13
Industrial organization
Japanese, 296-8
Industrial relations
Japanese, 290-96
Industrial societies
fragmentation and, 91-92
skill changes in, 38-42
Inflation
income distribution and, 281-82
unemployment and, 113
Innovation
organizational decline and, 345
organizational size and, 342
Innovation-decision process
social comparison and, 57-59
Innovativeness
organizational decline and, 344
Institutional environment, 444-46, 449-53
Institutionalization
indicators of, 447-49
principles of, 444-47
Institutional theory
competitive tests of, 457-59
organizations and, 443-60
Intermarriage
Hispanic minorities and, 363
Ireland
social mobility in, 426
Italy
welfare state formation in, 113
Ivory Coast
income inequality in, 329

J

Japan
environmental mobilization in, 477
income inequality in, 328
industrialization in, 103
industrial organization in, 296-308

CUMULATIVE INDEXES

CONTRIBUTING AUTHORS, VOLUMES 1–13

CHAPTER TITLES, VOLUMES 1–13

Sociology of Mental Health and Illness M. S. Goldstein 5:381–409
Sociology of Leisure J. Wilson 6:21–40
Sociology of Sport: Development, Present
  State, and Prospects G. Lüschen 6:315–47
Comparative Education: The Social
  Construction of the Modern World System F. O. Ramirez, J. W. Meyer 6:369–99
Black Students in Higher Education: A
  Review of Studies, 1965–1980 C. V. Willie, D. Cunnigen 7:177–98
Retirement as a Social Institution R. C. Atchley 8:263–87
The Sociology of Values J. L. Spates 9:27–49
Changing Family and Household:
  Contemporary Lessons from Historical
  Research A. Cherlin 9:51–66
Change in Military Organization D. R. Segal, M. W. Segal 9:151–70
Supply-Side Sociology of the Family: The
  Challenge of the New Home Economics R. A. Berk, S. F. Berk 9:375–95
The Changing Nature of Professional Control E. Freidson 10:1–20
Social Control Through Deterrence:
  Drinking-and-Driving Laws H. L. Ross 10:21–35
The Sociology of Tourism: Approaches,
  Issues, and Findings E. Cohen 10:373–92
Secular Symbolism: Studies of Ritual,
  Ceremony, and the Symbolic Order in
  Modern Life J. R. Gusfield, J. Michalowicz 10:417–35
Sociological Perspectives on the Mormon
  Subculture A. L. Mauss 10:437–60
The Impact of School Desegregation: A
  Situational Analysis D. Longshore, J. Prager 11:75–91
Popular Culture C. Mukerji, M. Schudson 12:47–66
A Sociology of Justice H. E. Pepinsky 12:93–108
Toward a Structural Criminology: Method and
  Theory in Criminological Research J. Hagan, A. Pallioni 12:431–50
Network Approaches to Social Evaluation C. D. Gartrell 13:49–66

FORMAL ORGANIZATIONS
Organizational Structure W. R. Scott 1:1–20
Environments of Organizations H. E. Aldrich, J. Pfeffer 2:79–105
Technology, Alienation, and Job Satisfaction J. M. Shepard 3:1–21
The Comparative Sociology of Organizations C. J. Lammers 4:485–510
Corporations and the Corporate Elite M. Useem 6:41–78
Continuities in the Study of Total and
  Nontotal Institutions C. A. McEwen 6:143–85
Recent Research on Multinational
  Corporations P. B. Evans 7:199–223
Organizational Performance: Recent
  Developments in Measurement R. M. Kanter, D. Brinkerhoff 7:321–49
Ownership and Control of Corporations D. S. Glasberg, M. Schwartz 9:311–32
Organizational Perspectives on Stratification J. N. Baron 10:37–69
Organizational Ecology G. R. Carroll 10:71–93
Negotiated Orders and Organizational Cultures G. A. Fine 10:239–62
White Collar Crime J. Braithwaite 11:1–25
The Organizational Structure of the School W. B. Tyler 11:49–73
Interorganizational Relations J. Galaskiewicz 11:281–304
Organizational Culture W. G. Ouchi, A. L. Wilkins 11:457–83
Associations and Interest Groups D. Knoke 12:1–22
Gender Differences in Role Differentiation
  and Organizational Task Performance H. A. Walker, M. L. Fennell 12:255–76
Alternatives to Bureaucracy: Democratic
  Participation in the Economy J. Rothschild, R. Russell 12:307–28
Decision-Making at the Top of Organizations D. J. Hickson 13:165–92
Japanese Industrial Organization in
  Comparative Perspective J. R. Lincoln, K. McBride 13:289–312
Organizational Growth and Decline Processes D. A. Whetten 13:335–58

Annual Reviews Inc.

A NONPROFIT SCIENTIFIC PUBLISHER

4139 El Camino Way
P.O. Box 10139
Palo Alto, CA 94303-0897 • USA

Annual Reviews Inc. publications may be ordered directly from our office by mail or use our Toll Free Telephone line (for orders paid by credit card or purchase order, and customer service calls only); through booksellers and subscription agents, worldwide; and through participating professional societies. Prices subject to change without notice. ARI Federal I.D. #94-1156476

- **Individuals:** Prepayment required on new accounts by check or money order (in U.S. dollars, check drawn on U.S. bank) or charge to credit card — American Express, VISA, MasterCard.
- **Institutional buyers:** Please include purchase order number.
- **Students:** $10.00 discount from retail price, per volume. Prepayment required. Proof of student status must be provided (photocopy of student I.D. or signature of department secretary is acceptable). Students must send orders direct to Annual Reviews. Orders received through bookstores and institutions requesting student rates will be returned.
- **Professional Society Members:** Members of professional societies that have a contractual arrangement with Annual Reviews may order books through their society at a reduced rate. Check with your society for information.
- **Toll Free Telephone orders:** Call 1-800-523-8635 (except from California) for orders paid by credit card or purchase order and customer service calls only. California customers and all other business calls use 415-493-4400 (not toll free). Hours: 8:00 AM to 4:00 PM, Monday-Friday, Pacific Time.

Regular orders: Please list the volumes you wish to order by volume number.
Standing orders: New volume in the series will be sent to you automatically each year upon publication. Cancellation may be made at any time. Please indicate volume number to begin standing order.
Prepublication orders: Volumes not yet published will be shipped in month and year indicated.
California orders: Add applicable sales tax.
Postage paid (4th class bookrate/surface mail) **by Annual Reviews Inc.** Airmail postage or UPS, extra.

ANNUAL REVIEWS SERIES		Prices Postpaid per volume USA/elsewhere	Regular Order Please send:	Standing Order Begin with:
			Vol. number	Vol. number
Annual Review of ANTHROPOLOGY				
Vols. 1-14	(1972-1985)	$27.00/$30.00		
Vol. 15	(1986)	$31.00/$34.00		
Vol. 16	(avail. Oct. 1987)	$31.00/$34.00	Vol(s). _____	Vol. _____
Annual Review of ASTRONOMY AND ASTROPHYSICS				
Vols. 1-2, 4-20	(1963-1964; 1966-1982)	$27.00/$30.00		
Vols. 21-24	(1983-1986)	$44.00/$47.00		
Vol. 25	(avail. Sept. 1987)	$44.00/$47.00	Vol(s). _____	Vol. _____
Annual Review of BIOCHEMISTRY				
Vols. 30-34, 36-54	(1961-1965; 1967-1985)	$29.00/$32.00		
Vol. 55	(1986)	$33.00/$36.00		
Vol. 56	(avail. July 1987)	$33.00/$36.00	Vol(s). _____	Vol. _____
Annual Review of BIOPHYSICS AND BIOPHYSICAL CHEMISTRY				
Vols. 1-11	(1972-1982)	$27.00/$30.00		
Vols. 12-15	(1983-1986)	$47.00/$50.00		
Vol. 16	(avail. June 1987)	$47.00/$50.00	Vol(s). _____	Vol. _____
Annual Review of CELL BIOLOGY				
Vol. 1	(1985)	$27.00/$30.00		
Vol. 2	(1986)	$31.00/$34.00		
Vol. 3	(avail. Nov. 1987)	$31.00/$34.00	Vol(s). _____	Vol. _____

ANNUAL REVIEWS SERIES	Prices Postpaid per volume USA/elsewhere	Regular Order Please send:	Standing Order Begin with:
		Vol. number	Vol. number

Annual Review of COMPUTER SCIENCE

Vol. 1	(1986) . . . . $39.00/$42.00		
Vol. 2	(avail. Nov. 1987) . . . . $39.00/$42.00	Vol(s). _____	Vol. _____

Annual Review of EARTH AND PLANETARY SCIENCES

Vols. 1-10	(1973-1982) . . . . $27.00/$30.00		
Vols. 11-14	(1983-1986) . . . . $44.00/$47.00		
Vol. 15	(avail. May 1987) . . . . $44.00/$47.00	Vol(s). _____	Vol. _____

Annual Review of ECOLOGY AND SYSTEMATICS

Vols. 1-16	(1970-1985) . . . . $27.00/$30.00		
Vol. 17	(1986) . . . . $31.00/$34.00		
Vol. 18	(avail. Nov. 1987) . . . . $31.00/$34.00	Vol(s). _____	Vol. _____

Annual Review of ENERGY

Vols. 1-7	(1976-1982) . . . . $27.00/$30.00		
Vols. 8-11	(1983-1986) . . . . $56.00/$59.00		
Vol. 12	(avail. Oct. 1987) . . . . $56.00/$59.00	Vol(s). _____	Vol. _____

Annual Review of ENTOMOLOGY

Vols. 10-16, 18-30	(1965-1971, 1973-1985) . . . . $27.00/$30.00		
Vol. 31	(1986) . . . . $31.00/$34.00		
Vol. 32	(avail. Jan. 1987) . . . . $31.00/$34.00	Vol(s). _____	Vol. _____

Annual Review of FLUID MECHANICS

Vols. 1-4, 7-17	(1969-1972, 1975-1985) . . . . $28.00/$31.00		
Vol. 18	(1986) . . . . $32.00/$35.00		
Vol. 19	(avail. Jan. 1987) . . . . $32.00/$35.00	Vol(s). _____	Vol. _____

Annual Review of GENETICS

Vols. 1-19	(1967-1985) . . . . $27.00/$30.00		
Vol. 20	(1986) . . . . $31.00/$34.00		
Vol. 21	(avail. Dec. 1987) . . . . $31.00/$34.00	Vol(s). _____	Vol. _____

Annual Review of IMMUNOLOGY

Vols. 1-3	(1983-1985) . . . . $27.00/$30.00		
Vol. 4	(1986) . . . . $31.00/$34.00		
Vol. 5	(avail. April 1987) . . . . $31.00/$34.00	Vol(s). _____	Vol. _____

Annual Review of MATERIALS SCIENCE

Vols. 1, 3-12	(1971, 1973-1982) . . . . $27.00/$30.00		
Vols. 13-16	(1983-1986) . . . . $64.00/$67.00		
Vol. 17	(avail. August 1987) . . . . $64.00/$67.00	Vol(s). _____	Vol. _____

Annual Review of MEDICINE

Vols. 1-3, 6, 8-9	(1950-1952, 1955, 1957-1958)		
11-15, 17-36	(1960-1964, 1966-1985) . . . . $27.00/$30.00		
Vol. 37	(1986) . . . . $31.00/$34.00		
Vol. 38	(avail. April 1987) . . . . $31.00/$34.00	Vol(s). _____	Vol. _____

Annual Review of MICROBIOLOGY

Vols. 18-39	(1964-1985) . . . . $27.00/$30.00		
Vol. 40	(1986) . . . . $31.00/$34.00		
Vol. 41	(avail. Oct. 1987) . . . . $31.00/$34.00	Vol(s). _____	Vol. _____